Aligning Human Resources and Business Strategy

What difference can the aspiring HR strategist really make to business value?

In the new and extensively updated edition of her ground-breaking book, Linda Holbeche answers this question and provides the tools and insights to help HR managers and directors add value to the organisation by implementing effective HR initiatives that are aligned to core business strategies.

This edition includes new chapters, fresh case questions, specific sector 'twists' like healthcare, the university sector, travel and tourism, alongside a greater mix of international case studies. Taking a more analytical approach than previous works, Holbeche discusses and explores a number of contemporary academic debates.

Learn how you can strengthen and prove the relationship between people strategy and business success through your approach to performance and development and impress at the highest levels with this new edition of an HR classic.

Linda Holbeche is an independent coach as well as developer, consultant, researcher and author in the fields of HR, strategy, organisation design and development and leadership. She works with UK and international clients in many sectors. A recognised thought and practice leader and voted one of the UK's *HR Most Influential*, Linda was previously CIPD's Director of Research and Policy. She is now Adjunct Professor at Imperial College London, Visiting Professor at four other UK universities, Honorary Fellow of the Institute for Employment Studies and of Roffey Park. She is also a Fellow of the Institute of Leadership and Management (ILM) and Fellow of the Chartered Institute for Personnel and Development (CIPD). Linda has written over 60 research reports, authored or co-edited 16 books, numerous book chapters and articles in the field.

"The recent turbulent years of change have emphasised even more the importance of people at the centre of business, and the need to align people strategy with business strategy. Linda draws on her extensive experience to provide a timely update to this theme, drawing on contemporary issues, academic research and salient case studies, to bring to life how HR and business leaders need to work together to build sustainable, responsible, and resilient organisations for the future."

Peter Cheese, Chief Executive, CIPD, the professional body for
HR and people development

Aligning Human Resources and Business Strategy

Third edition

Linda Holbeche

Routledge
Taylor & Francis Group

LONDON AND NEW YORK

Cover image: © Getty Images

Third edition published 2022
by Routledge
2 Park Square, Milton Park, Abingdon, Oxon, OX14 4RN

and by Routledge
605 Third Avenue, New York, NY 10158

Routledge is an imprint of the Taylor & Francis Group, an informa business

© 2022 Linda Holbeche

The right of Linda Holbeche to be identified as author of this work has been asserted in accordance with sections 77 and 78 of the Copyright, Designs and Patents Act 1988.

First edition published by Routledge 2002
Second edition published by Routledge 2009

British Library Cataloguing-in-Publication Data
A catalogue record for this book is available from the British Library

Library of Congress Cataloging-in-Publication Data
A catalog record has been requested for this book

ISBN: 978-1-032-11457-6 (hbk)
ISBN: 978-1-032-11458-3 (pbk)
ISBN: 978-1-003-21999-6 (ebk)

DOI: 10.4324/9781003219996

Typeset in Minion
by codeMantra

Contents

Preface to the Third Edition

So much has been written about the changing role of HR that the reader might wonder why I have sought to add to the debate. It seems that being an HR professional is a tough proposition these days. There are endless requirements to prove that value is being added by HR interventions and the HR function is frequently accused of being reactive. The pressures on the function are enormous and, in many cases, resources are thinly stretched. Yet I believe that the situation need not be so bleak, and that HR has potentially the most significant contribution to make of all the functions, if it manages to combine operational excellence with a really strategic approach.

In writing this book, I am not attempting to address all aspects of a strategic and operational HR agenda. I have focused on some of the performance, developmental and cultural issues which I consider key if business and HR strategies are to be aligned. I have tried to illustrate the theory with cases where time permitted. I hope that the ways in which the HR strategists featured in this book are approaching the challenges of aligning business and HR strategies in their organisations will provide evidence that outstanding value can be added by HR and offer encouragement to practitioners who are finding the quest to add value hard going.

Since the first edition of this book was published, so much has changed in terms of the employment landscape, HR theory and priorities, that simply updating the text has not been enough. Each edition of the book so far has coincided with pivotal moments in the business landscape. At the time of writing the first edition in 1999, businesses were concerned about the possible effect of the so-called 'Millennium bug' which highlighted business's growing dependence on, and the risks of, high technology. The revised edition published in 2002 followed the terrible events of 9/11, and the atmosphere of uncertainty, polarisation and risk aversion that ensued. The second edition, published in 2009, followed the financial crash that highlighted the need for better governance of de-regulated financial markets and marked the start of a period of financial turbulence and growing social and economic inequalities that continues to this day. This third edition has been written during 2020 and 2021, during what has been described as the ultimate game-changer, the coronavirus pandemic crisis, which has accelerated underlying trends with respect to technology and work, including the pursuit of organisational agility and resilience.

Against this volatile backdrop, the evolution of the HR function has perhaps been relatively slow, until recently. We have seen some amazing responses by business leaders and HR teams to some of the challenges posed by the health crisis, such as keeping workers safe and also connected after whole workforces became home-based overnight. Looking ahead and learning from their handling of the crisis, and to equip organisations to deal with the pressures they are likely to experience going forward, demands a truly strategic response from HR. And of all the business functions HR has potentially the most significant contribution to make to business success by building a context where humans can thrive, alongside technology. To do this HR must combine operational excellence with a really strategic approach, build talent pipelines, change organisational structures and cultures and themselves adopt employee-centric and agile ways of working. These are just some of the opportunities for HR to exercise leadership.

At the same time, much has stayed as it was ten years ago. Alongside the opportunities sit the pressures. Many of the capabilities HR is required to demonstrate remain as before. Credibility and influencing ability are central to HR's ability to work collaboratively with line managers to continually push up the standards and practice of people management and development. Such human capital standards provide a foundation of trust on which sustainable organisational effectiveness can be built. No HR professional can expect to be taken seriously if he or she is unable to understand and speak the language of business, or to translate the business strategy into relevant goals and practical people processes which are appropriate to the users and the context dynamics facing their organisation.

As the HR agenda moves on so the nature of HR interventions continues to expand, demanding new disciplines, skill sets and behaviours, even within HR's traditional heartland. Embracing technology and the use of analytics – for instance to automate transactional services or using AI and machine learning in recruitment and for succession planning purposes – is still not widespread and we are apparently some way off being able to use predictive analytics to help steer the ship. Strategic workforce planning can put organisations 'on the front foot' when it comes to optimising the changing labour market and demographic trends. Borrowing from other disciples like Marketing gives us techniques such as employer branding and employee segmentation while holistic approaches to reward enable organisations to attract and retain the talent they need for success. Organisational design and development is an essential aid to building flexible, agile cultures. Continuous professional development is key to raising the game.

The evolving HR role is moving ever more swiftly to becoming a core business leadership role, in which HR's own contribution is to ensure that the organisation is equipped for success, now and in the future. And in the wake of various corporate failures, particularly within the global financial services sector, there is increasingly a spotlight on HR's developing role in ethics and governance, raising questions about sensitive matters such as excessive executive pay deals and high bonuses that appear to lead to a culture of unfairness, excess and irresponsibility. Similarly, should HR professionals more obviously have a role to play as non-executives on boards, ensuring that good practice in appointments and reward at the most senior levels in organisations reflects the very best emerging practice and encourages high standards of executive behaviour?

So in writing this third edition of the book I have attempted to update my overview of the HR landscape, agenda, skill set and challenges in the light of the changing context, theory and practice. I have added new chapters on crafting HR strategy, workforce planning, employee engagement and well-being, designing and developing an agile organisation and learning across boundaries.

My motivation in researching and writing the book is to find out how excellent professionals are delivering value. This is not intended as a technical book, but one which highlights what practitioners are doing with respect to strategic recruitment, employee well-being, management and international leadership development, organisational development and change management. In some cases I have revisited and updated where possible case studies featured in the last edition of the book as well as adding other examples of what I consider interesting practice. That is not to say that I believe that the practitioners featured in this book have created a blueprint for success, but I hope that some of the approaches described here will provide food for thought for others.

OVERVIEW OF CONTENTS

In Part I, *The Need for Strategic Human Resources*, we consider why Strategic HRM (SHRM) is needed and what it entails. In Chapter 1, we consider a range of mainstream and critical theorist perspectives to examine what 'alignment' means both within the field of SHRM theory and within HR practice. Some critics argue for instance that putting business interests first means that HR loses what is distinctive about its contribution to business success – the focus on people. Much SHRM research takes the managerial/organisational perspective with an emphasis on the consequences for organisational performance. Few theorists, if any, question the impact of SHRM on individuals who are likely to suffer if they lack 'clout' in the employment relationship.

And indeed, in Chapter 2, I have looked again at HR transformation and the changing nature of business partnering in the wake of the influential 'Ulrich model.' Indeed, as we consider the evolution of the HR function from its Personnel antecedent, it is clear that many of the pressures on the function to provide value-added are concerned with HR's contributions to increased productivity, cost effectiveness and efficiency – against a backdrop of erosion of collective voice and its related protections for employees.

In Chapter 3, we consider context trends which are driving new practice in business. Longer term trends suggest that developments in advanced technology are irrevocably changing jobs and working patterns. Many workers suffer from work intensification while others have their jobs replaced by automation. Yet the longer-term impact of perhaps the most vivid example of a black swan event, the coronavirus pandemic of 2020–2021, has yet to be fully understood. What is apparent at this stage is that necessity has catapulted many organisations into seeking more agile ways of working, and there appears to be a growing recognition that organisations are after all human entities and should be led and managed as such.

In Chapter 4, we consider how the business context drives the HR agenda, especially as work becomes progressively more knowledge- and talent-intensive. I draw on a range of HRM theories to suggest that HR leadership should be the preferred direction of travel if the function is to really add value. HR leadership involves embracing an employee-centric, strategic culture-building agenda geared to creating healthy and sustainably high performing organisations. In Chapter 5, we look again at more recent developments in the transformation of the HR role in the digital age and consider what agility means for the HR function and skill sets. Delivering a value-adding agenda requires purpose, focus, a well-formulated strategy and effective methods, as well as effective measurement to ensure that the right kinds of impact on organisational performance are being achieved. In Chapter 6, we look at how such a well-formulated strategy can be crafted.

In Part II, *Strategies for Talent,* we consider a major aspect of HR's role – that of attracting, motivating and retaining talent. Talent management involves everything from recruitment to performance management, learning and development and succession planning, as distinct from the operational side of HR covering administration and so on. Traditionally, these practices have been geared to the interests of the organisation. We look at these various aspects of talent management and more besides through the lens of more agile practice and also from an employee experience angle.

The rapidly changing nature of work, demographics and the global labour market, together with changing talent requirements and various forms of talent shortfall are leading to great uncertainties about the workforce required for the future. A rumoured 'Great resignation' is underway. Hence the growing emphasis on workforce/talent planning, on developing enticing employer brands, on diversity and inclusion, on segmenting the talent base and personalising employee value propositions, on 'engaging' employees at an emotional level, on creating the organisational climate where people will give of their best.

In Chapter 7, we consider the start of the employee lifecycle by looking at the approaches to workforce planning and recruitment, including finding ways of sourcing talent other than through recruitment. In Chapter 8, we look at employee engagement and well-being, and at how building a context with line managers that is conducive to employee engagement is at the heart of the relationship between organisations and their workforces. We consider the challenges of maintaining and growing engagement and well-being in tough times. In Chapter 9, we look at changing approaches to performance management and reward, with today's fast-changing context in mind.

Historically, "talent" was seen as the high potentials – people coming up on a fast-track to the boardroom. But while this cohort is obviously important, it's only a small proportion of the talent in the business. In Chapters 10 and 11, we look at 'inclusive' approaches to learning and career development that should apply to anyone with talent. We then look at 'exclusive' talent development approaches in Chapter 12 where we consider high-flyer development and succession planning. In all of this, line managers are key partners, delivering the lived reality of the brand to employees. In Chapter 13, we consider some of the cultural and other complexities of Global HRM.

In Part III, *Building Strategic Change Capability,* we look at various ways in which HR teams are changing their organisations' cultures to meet business needs, for instance to become more customer focused or to enable greater knowledge-sharing. We consider the human dynamics of change and at what HR can do to support people through periods of change. We also consider how HR can contribute to successful integration, for instance in mergers and acquisitions, and build more change-ready cultures. In Chapter 14, we look at aspects of Organisation Design in the context of major transformation efforts. In Chapter 15, we consider Organisation Development in the context of culture change. We apply these OD&D theories in the context of designing and developing an agile organisation (Chapter 16) and in learning across boundaries (Chapter 17).

Finally, we consider the implications of the evolving HR role and structures for the skills, and behavioural competencies needed by professionals and for HR careers. These include a much greater emphasis than in the past on business acumen, consultancy skills, organisational design and development, as well as analytical approaches borrowed from other disciplines and the use of technology. We look at what the future might hold for HR, and at how HR's emerging purpose and role may well crystallise further into several key elements. For me, these include attracting and mobilising talent, building performance capability, creating healthy, inclusive and successful organisations, developing effective leadership, providing coherence and ensuring ethical practice and good governance. Above all, alignment is about ensuring that a 'win' for the business is also a 'win' for the workforce and other stakeholders. With an agenda such as this, I argue, the time has come for HR to get on the front foot and lead the way.

Acknowledgements

I am extremely grateful to all the people, too numerous to mention, who have contributed to this book, in particular all the people who have kindly shared their practice with me which has formed the basis of the case studies in the book.

I am extremely grateful for all the support I have received from Routledge. In particular, I would like to single out for special mention Senior Editor Rebecca Marsh who has waited patiently for this book.

Above all, I shall be always deeply indebted to my dear husband Barney, and my late parents Elsie and Bill, for their constant encouragement and faith in me.

Whilst every effort has been made to contact copyright holders, the author and publisher would like to hear from anyone whose copyright has been unwittingly infringed.

Part I
The need for strategic human resources

1

Strategic HRM theory

Since it emerged in the 1980s, Human Resource Management (HRM) theory and practice has been a pervasive theme in the mainstream literatures of organisational behaviour, strategic management, business policy, international and intercultural management. Indeed, HRM has become a recognised semiotic for 'modern people management' (Paauwe 2007: 9).

As an applied discipline, therefore, HRM is still relatively 'young' and the field continues to evolve. While still predominantly a US and UK theory phenomenon, in recent years, there has been a growing contribution to HRM theory development from various European and international centres of scholarship, especially in Australia and India.

DOI: 10.4324/9781003219996-2

Critical scholar Keenoy (2009: 466) argues that HRM, which began as a local US cultural artefact, has emerged as a global naturalised discourse which informs the social practice of international corporations.

CHAPTER OVERVIEW

In this chapter, I shall explore some of the debates regarding HRM, and Strategic Human Resource (SHRM) theory and practice. The intention is to respond to Janssens and Steyaert's plea for reflexivity in HRM, 'to make the plurality of HRM visible by pointing out various paradigmatic, theoretical and empirical communities of practice that partly are connected, partly overlap and partly avoid each other' (2009: 152). We shall cover:

- Defining HRM and SHRM
- From Personnel to Human Resource management
- People as resources or human capital assets
- Perspectives on alignment
- International and comparative IHRM

LEARNING OBJECTIVES

- Outline the evolution of HRM and SHRM theory
- Discuss human resource (HR) practices, HR outcomes and performance (the HR value chain)
- Identify the challenges in assessing the potential impact of human resource management (HRM) on performance
- Review the concept of competitive advantage and sustained competitive advantage of an organisation
- Identify how mainstream and critical theorist perspectives on HRM differ.

INTRODUCTION: DEFINING HRM

The notion that human beings are one of several 'resources' that are valuable, rare, inimitable and non-substitutable that an organisation can use to achieve competitive advantage stems from Resource-based theory (Barney 1997), now a major theme in strategic thinking. The term 'human resources' came to describe a specific type of strategic resource (increasingly referred to as 'human capital'); 'human resource management', as the way in which this could be acquired, developed and maintained; and the 'human resources function' (or 'HR') as the entity responsible for these activities.

As yet the nature and impact of HRM remain contested, with various traditions, multiple perspectives and no overall theory of HRM which has variously been defined as:

- All management decisions and action that affect the nature of the relationship between the organisation and its employees – 'its human resources' (Beer et al. 1984).
- HRM focuses on the exchange relationship between the organisation and the employee – both the legal contract of employment and the 'psychological contract' and the social contract which relates to the relationships and networks employees have within the company (Sonnenberg et al. 2011).
- The management of work and people towards desired ends (Boxall et al. 2007).

- Management decisions related to policies and practices that together shape the employment relationship and are aimed at achieving certain goals. These goals concern performance goals which have been defined and measured in multiple ways (Boselie 2014).
- A comprehensive and coherent approach to the employment and development of people (Armstrong and Taylor 2014).

There is, however, some consensus that HRM is a business concept reflecting a mainly managerial view of the employment relationship, with theory, policies and practices geared to enabling organisations to achieve flexibility, competitive advantage and high performance through people.

Moreover, almost since HRM first came to prominence as the preferred international discourse to frame employment management issues and as a field of practice within organisations, 'it is nearly unanimous that HR can and should add more value to corporations' (Lawler et al. 2005: 165); this adding value to be achieved by aligning people and organisational strategies to business strategies. Ulrich (1997), and Ulrich and Brockbank (2005, 2015), for instance, emphasise the role of the HR function in creating 'value' for business and its stakeholders, advocating an 'investor-literate' approach to HR strategy and practice.

Reflective activity

- What do you consider to be the primary role of the HR function?
- Think of an organisation with which you are familiar. To what extent is the HR function perceived as a strategic asset?

FROM PERSONNEL TO HUMAN RESOURCE MANAGEMENT

Though HRM emerged as a discipline in the 1980s, Kaufman (2001) argues that its intellectual roots can be traced back to the 1920s in the United States. Jacques (1999) suggests the origins of HRM can be found in ideas which emerged between 1900 and 1920 from the historical conjunction of scientific management, the employment managers' movement and industrial psychology.

Similarly, most theorists would agree that the field of human resource practice, and the HR function itself, came into prominence in the 1980s, replacing earlier conceptions of personnel management. Personnel had been seen mainly as a service deliverer to management, and as a bridge between management and the workforce, rather than as a strategic contributor. While managing people was 'line' management's responsibility, the work of Personnel centred around the administration of people and employee relations, providing specialist support on a range of issues such as pay and conditions, employee welfare, disciplinaries, recruitment and selection etc. The nature of Personnel roles and contribution often reflected the 'welfare' (after Tyson and Fell 1986) and 'clerk of works' models through which the status quo was enshrined in personnel policies and procedures. Personnel was also expected to act as 'company policeman', ensuring compliance with set procedures and employment regulations.

The emergence of HR at the expense of Personnel was due to a combination of economic and political context factors. The 1970s had been a prolonged period of industrial unrest, economic stagnation and crisis, and an era of adversarial industrial relations in the United States and the United Kingdom. Industrial Relations specialists played a key role in negotiating with (often militant) trade unions, especially in traditional industries, to break the perceived union stranglehold over production.

As the United Kingdom and the United States emerged from the prolonged period of industrial unrest, the Thatcher and Reagan governments were determined to advance economic growth by freeing up market competition through deregulation and reducing union power which was seen as a barrier to economic success. The new and invigorated neo-liberal form of global capitalism that was actively promoted (often referred to as 'Thatcherism' or 'Reaganomics') was underpinned by a political commitment to new forms of market, in particular to knowledge and service-based industries such as the financial services industry (Marquand 2008; Gamble 2009).

The acceleration of globalisation was reflected in the competitive restructurings of the 1980s and 1990s in which a new breed of 'hard' personnel disciplines came to the fore, such as organisation design, manpower planning and pay negotiations and the Personnel function started to attract men in large numbers for the first time. As 'fixers' of companies' 'difficult' people issues, such as major restructurings, redundancy programs and industrial disputes, some HR professionals claimed and won the right to be taken seriously as members of management. This period coincided with the relative decline of trade union power in the United Kingdom and the United States and in many workplaces the loss of collective workforce representation, especially in 'new' industries such as financial services. HR was to forge a new relationship with employees that would enable greater organisational flexibility.

As the power of the trade unions waned in the United Kingdom, and as new (deliberately non-unionised) sectors emerged, conversely, perhaps as a result of the significant part played by Personnel in employee relations during the period of industrial unrest, the power of the role grew beyond the original confines of the job. In large organisations specialist functions such as Compensation and Benefits were created. The more Personnel became the specialist repository of information about employees, including senior management, the more it needed to be consulted about any and every issue related to employees. Personnel began to be seen as a power in the land, even if, in most cases, the Personnel director was not a member of the board. Over time, in some cases, responsibility for managing people appeared to slip away from line managers who would refer to Personnel for everything from a minor disciplinary offence to recruitment.

By the mid-1990s some of the HR skills relating to collective bargaining and organisation design fell into decline. The skills void was filled to large extent by major consultancies who helped design and implement many of the large-scale reengineering projects and corporate downsizings of the 1990s. Industrial relations was superseded by the broader all-encompassing discipline of employee relations.

The Personnel function gradually came to be rebranded as 'Human Resources' and in large complex organisations came to be seen more as a specialist and quite powerful management function (Guest 1989). However, in other international contexts and in many Small- and Medium-sized Enterprises (SMEs) the earlier models of Personnel continued much as before. We shall return to these topics in later chapters.

Managerialism

Mainstream management theory since the 1980s has sought to advance business practice. The desire of the UK and US governments, and company owners for new forms of management and for less adversarial industrial relations, preferably on an individual rather than collective basis, led to the development of business schools and the emergence of managerialism as a philosophy and practice. This subsequently spread to all sectors, including charities, reflecting the perceived political need to expose all parts of the UK and US economies to the values of business.

By the 1990s company policies on employment, pensions, etc. became increasingly market-driven, reflecting neo-liberal economic policies. The emphasis in many organisations was on downsizing and change. The pursuit of competitive advantage on a global basis required strong international value chains and flexible workforces who could provide efficient services at a cost saving to business. Outsourcing and offshoring of 'non-core' activities to developing economies began, made possible by the development of call centre technology. Long-term employees, traditional career routes and pension obligations came to be viewed as expensive overheads – an obstacle to the flexibility and efficiency that many employers craved. The individualism implicit in HRM assisted the development of labour flexibility from the employer perspective by removing collective protections for employees.

The development and expansion of HRM since the late 1980s as an offshoot of managerialism, at the expense of personnel management and industrial relations, emphasised the requirement for the HR function to achieve a closer functional relationship ('alignment') between the needs of business and 'human resource' practices. HR's main purpose was conceived as alignment with business strategy – to realign people management to the new strategic realities of the organisation – in order to make cost-effective and efficient use of 'human resources' and ensure that the organisation was able to achieve success through people. Therefore HR functions were to secure and develop the flexible, compliant and productive workforces required by business.

HRM was supposed to be implemented via a division of responsibility between line managers who were responsible for the day-to-day utilisation, development and retention of people, while the HR function, representing the employer, was responsible for legal compliance and policies and delivering people-related administration and specialist services such as advising line managers, and designing and implementing development programmes.

Micro practice areas

To achieve such aims, the HR function's many specialist areas of practice, which Boxall et al. (2007) describe as 'micro' HRM (MHRM), typically sit alongside a generalist delivery medium. These MHRMs fall into two main categories: those concerned with managing individuals and small groups (e.g. recruitment, selection, induction, training and development, performance management, and remuneration) and others with managing work organisation and employee voice systems (including union-management relations).

Since the 1980s, there has been a gradual move to professionalise the HR/Personnel function and increase the perceived business value of its contribution. As the HR function aimed for professional status in both the United States and the United Kingdom in the late 1990s, Human Resource Development (HRD) was submerged within the general panoply of HRM, such as when the Institute of Personnel Management and the Institute of Training and Development merged to form the IPD and then the CIPD in the United Kingdom. Many major economies now have equivalent professional bodies such as the Society for Human Resource Management (SHRM) in the United States and AHRI in Australia.

More recently, the HR profession has expanded its scope and developed standards relating to HRM and HRD as well as other disciplines such as internal communications and organisation design and development (OD&D) and analytics, though quite where these disciplines sit remains contested. Many of the 'hard' HR disciplines, such as workforce planning are being revived and reclaimed by HR, after a period in the doldrums. The HR skills panoply is being continuously extended to include such 'new' skills to reflect the changing scope of the HR function.

People as resources or 'human capital' assets

Competitive advantage is an advantage that a firm has over its competitors that allows it to generate sales or margins and/or retain more customers than the competition. In contrast to the market-based view of organisational strategy, exemplified by Porter's (1986) early work, that suggests that organisations should base their strategy on the requirements of the market, in Strategic HRM (SHRM) the dominant resource-based view (RBV) of the firm, exemplified by Barney (1997) suggests that a firm's competitive advantage derives from the effective and efficient utilisation of organisation resources. These resources might include physical capital, for example, the company's finances, equipment, plant, etc; organisational capital resources, which include the firm's structure and systems for exercising control; and human capital resources, which include the skills, competencies, experience and intelligence of employees.

From the resource-based view (value, rareness, inimitability, non-substitutability and organisation), the HR function can create value by either decreasing costs and/or increasing revenues and it can acquire human resources with rare characteristics that are difficult to imitate. And, with the right organisational systems to get the most from its employees, a combination of factors can lead to competitive advantage. Therefore the organisation should look inside to identify its key unique capabilities and then find a market where these provide competitive advantage. Effectiveness is then understood in terms of how well human resource capabilities are built through innovations such as team-based job designs, flexible workforces, and employee empowerment.

'Our people are our greatest assets'

The relabelling of the function from 'Personnel' to 'Human Resources' should have indicated a real change in function, not just a rebranding exercise, moving away from 'looking after the people' through to 'building key resources' (Scott-Jackson and Mayo 2016). While describing human beings as a 'resource' is curious, to say the least, for all its limitations, the term 'human resources' does imply that people are assets, and while, as assets go, people may be a fragile and volatile resource, they have the potential to create greater value than other forms of asset. The resource-based perspective is reflected in HR terms such as 'Talent'. More specifically, people represent latent assets, whose value is unlikely to be realised if that latent contribution is left undeveloped.

Logically then, from an investment perspective, the human resource should be treated more as an asset, than as a cost. Indeed, in many sectors there is widespread recognition that the ability to attract and 'engage' talent to produce 'high performance' is key to business success. However, while we may all be familiar with espoused organisational values statements such as 'our people are our greatest assets', the reality on the ground is often different. Short-term business priorities, bottom-line considerations and the need to generate shareholder returns usually take precedence over employee considerations and 'people issues' are often way down the executive agenda. Where these do appear, they are often treated as short-term operational issues rather than as key areas for attention or investment.

Especially in today's information age, where knowledge-intensive work increasingly drives economic growth and when the value of intellectual capital is evident, the truth of organisational values-statements such as 'our people are our greatest asset' has arguably never been more obvious. For many organisations operating in a global marketplace, talent – the lifeblood of competitive advantage – is in short supply, impeding business growth. Even when global talent in some sectors may be abundant, local talent is not, and vice versa. In more recent times, the quest for improved productivity and for sustainable business performance has led to an increased understanding that even the right people, if they are poorly managed or are working in the wrong way, are unlikely to be productive. Getting the best out of 'resourceful humans' is perhaps a more appropriate way of thinking about the purpose of effective people management strategies. HR's potential contribution to attracting, managing, motivating and retaining the right people who are vital to business success, is all the more relevant.

Of course people are no passive 'human resource'. Increasingly companies are realising that if they want to be flexible to meet changing market requirements, they must also meet the needs, and improve the experience, of their staff, especially those with valuable 'knowledge skills'. Like customers, employees too have higher expectations of what they want from their working lives and 'knowledge workers' with transferable skills are able to make demands of employers. In industries as diverse as construction, IT and pharmaceuticals where skill-shortages exist, it would appear that the days of the 'War for Talent' are back with us.

STRATEGIC HUMAN RESOURCE MANAGEMENT THEORY

Early elements of strategic HRM theory emerged from the late 1980s on, in response to the volatile economic context at the time. Again, definitions vary widely and there is no overarching definition of 'strategic' HRM (SHRM) (see Chapter 3). It has been variously defined as:

- Human resource system that is tailored to the demands of the business strategy (Miles and Snow 1984: 36)
- Strategic HRM covers the overall HR strategies adopted by business units and companies and tries to measure their impacts on performance (Boxall et al. 2007)
- All those activities affecting the behaviour of individuals in their efforts to formulate and implement the strategic needs of business (Schuler 1992)
- The pattern of planned human resource deployments and activities intended to enable the forms to achieve its goals (Wright and McMahan 1992)
- The implementation of a set of policies and practices that will build an employee pool of skills, knowledge and abilities that are relevant to organisational goals (Jackson and Schuler 1995)
- A distinctive approach to employment management which seeks to achieve competitive advantage through the strategic deployment of a highly committed and capable workforce, using an integrated array of cultural, structural and personnel techniques' (Storey 1995)

- A strategic approach to managing employment relations which emphasises that leveraging people's capabilities is critical to achieving competitive advantage. This being achieved through a distinctive set of integrated employment policies, programmes and practices (Bratton and Gold 2017)
- A general approach to the strategic management of human resources in accordance with the intentions of the organisation and the future direction it wants to take (Boxall 1998)
- SHRM defines how the organisation's goals (such as organisational flexibility, labour productivity and social legitimacy) will be achieved by means of HR strategies and integrated HR policies and practices (Wright and McMahan 1992)

While there may be little consensus in defining strategic HRM, it might broadly be described as bridging business strategy and HRM, focusing on the integration of HR with the business and its environment to enable the organisation to compete effectively over time.

Since strategy is forward looking, for Stroh and Caligiuri (1998), SHRM requires practitioners to keep abreast of the times and develop organisational strategies that prepare organisations not only to respond to changing environmental pressures but proactively to seize the initiative in their various markets. Strategic HR departments are future-oriented and operate in a manner consistent with, and integrated in, the overall business plan in their organisations. The CIPD defines SHRM as supporting long-term business goals and outcomes within a strategic framework. It focuses on longer-term resourcing issues within the context of an organisation's goals and the evolving nature of work, and informs other HR strategies, such as reward or performance, determining how they are integrated into the overall business strategy.

SHRM is arguably a critical dimension affecting firm performance since it provides a strategic framework to support business goals and outcomes and is concerned with longer-term people issues and macro-concerns about structure, quality, culture, values, commitment and matching resources to future need. Thus, HRM becomes a strategic, integrated and coherent approach that develops in line with the concept of strategic management (Boxall 1998). According to Guest's (2002) typology, SHRM is distinguished by its emphases on:

- people as a source of competitive advantage
- the integration of people management plans, policies and practices with business strategy
- proactive line management
- action on organisational and people issues at the most senior levels.

The form and structure of organisational policies and practices that might produce a high performing work force, and in turn have an economically meaningful effect on firm performance, even if the causality is indirect, has been the focus of an emerging literature in strategic human resource management.

Perspectives on alignment

A plethora of early academic studies looked for links between particular HR and employment management practices and business performance (Huselid 1995; Becker and

Gerhart 1996; Delery and Doty 1996; Patterson et al. 1997). Theorists take different positions on how HR practices actually impact on organisational performance. Early US-based strategic HRM literature (e.g. Delery and Doty 1996; Huselid and Becker 1996; Wright and Snell 1998; Welbourne and Cyr 1999) examined the relationship between HR and business performance outcomes in large samples of firms, but they did not specifically study how HR practices directly affect the so-called 'intangibles' such as innovation.

Within that context, Huselid and Becker (1997) argued that strategic HRM created competitive advantage by building HR systems that cannot be imitated. They broadly defined High Performance Work Systems (HPWS) as a key strategic approach, both as a means to develop and sustain core competencies and as a necessary condition for strategy implementation. Such systems include rigorous recruiting and selection protocols, performance management and incentive compensation systems, and employee training and development activities that are designed to acquire, refine, and reinforce employee skills and behaviours necessary to implement the firm's competitive strategy (Huselid 1995).

However, there is a dearth of longitudinal studies to establish whether and how HR practices do lead to high-performance outcomes. There are relatively few such studies on the impact of HRM on SMEs or in international organisations.

Nevertheless, within the mainstream there is a strong ongoing focus on how to forge ever-tighter links between HR work and firm financial performance (Huselid 1995; Guest et al. 2003; Wright et al. 2005; Fleetwood and Hesketh 2006). Two schools of thought emerged early in SHRM research about how best to achieve the goals of SHRM. One group assumed that universal 'best practice' HRM would produce benefits for any organisation whatever its strategy, while others argued that what mattered was designing HR practices to match or 'best fit' the particular strategy and context of the organisation.

Best practice: 'bundles of HRM practice'

The universal perspective argues that some HR practices have a positive effect on organisational performance across all organisations and under all conditions. Various researchers (e.g. Delaney and Huselid 1996) claim to have found a statistically significant link between universal 'bundles' of HR policies and business performance. Guest (1989) incorporated the HR policy goals of strategic integration, commitment, quality and flexibility into a model with related HR practices. With respect to employee commitment for instance, Beer et al. (1984) found that, rather than a single system of employee involvement techniques, several approaches, such as employee briefings and work system design, may be used. Purcell (1999) suggested the following six elements as key to employee commitment:

- Careful recruitment and selection
- Extensive use of systems of communication
- Team working with flexible job design
- Emphasis on training and learning
- Involvement in decision making
- Performance appraisal with tight links to contingent pay.

From a resource-based viewpoint, Huselid (1995) and Pfeffer (1998) examined the impact of human resource development on firm performance, in particular exploring how utilising a system of management practices that gives employees skills, information, motivation and latitude results in a workforce that is a source of competitive advantage. Pfeffer (1998) identified seven integrated practices that should enable organisations to 'obtain profits through people'. These are:

- Employment security
- Selective hiring of new personnel
- Self-managed teams and decentralisation of decision-making as the basic principles of organisational design
- Comparatively high compensation contingent on organisational performance
- Extensive training
- Reduced status distinctions and barriers (including dress, language, office arrangements and wage differentials across levels)
- Extensive sharing of financial and performance information throughout the organisation.

Other lists have been produced by Appelbaum et al. (2000) and Thompson and Heron (2006).

Is there such a thing as universal best practice? What works well in one organisation may not necessarily work well in another because it may not fit with its strategy, culture, management style, technology or working practices. Boxall and Purcell (2008) argue that while universal 'best practices' provide a solid foundation of SHRM activities, to achieve a higher level of performance, contingent factors should be considered.

'Best fit'

'Best fit' theorists such as Schuler and Jackson (1987) argue that what firms do depends on their circumstances and that HR strategy (HRS) should therefore also be contingent. Early competing frameworks assessed fit between HR activities and desired strategic outcomes in different contexts as contingent factors. Fombrun et al.'s (1984) prescriptive and normative 'matching model' proposes that employees are a resource that should be treated as other business resources, to be managed in line with, and for the benefit of, the business. For any particular business strategy, there will be a matching HR strategy (Figure 1.1).

While this model emphasises the coherence of internal HR policies and the importance of 'matching' them to the (predominantly short-term) strategies of the business, it

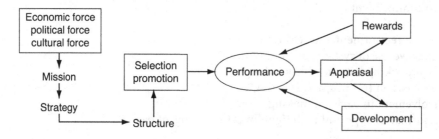

Figure 1.1 The human resource cycle and 'fit' with business strategy. Based on Fombrun et al. 1984.

ignores stakeholder interests, situational factors and the notion of strategic choice. Tichy et al. (1982) proposed that the HR department has a key role in driving organisational performance since human resource activities have a major influence on individual performance and therefore productivity and organisational performance. However, the matching model suggests that the management of human resources is a stand-alone function which should react to the needs of the business as opposed to taking a shaping role and planning growth. HR functions were to secure compliant and productive workforces, aligned to the needs of business. In particular, HR functions were to assist business in achieving labour flexibility and reducing workforce costs. In terms of employee relations, the matching model favours individual rather than pluralist perspectives.

In contrast, the Harvard model (Beer et al. 1985) recognises the need to address the concerns of various stakeholders. In practice, this has proved complex to operationalise and has perhaps been less influential on practice than the matching model or later theories.

The nature of the 'fit' required between the external business context, strategy, internal context and HRM would vary according to factors such as where the organisation is in its lifecycle: start-up, growth, maturity and decline, and also on the particular competitive strategy (Porter 1985) pursued by the organisation to achieve competitive advantage:

- Innovation – being the unique producer.
- Quality – delivering high-quality goods and services to customers.
- Cost leadership – the planned result of policies aimed at 'managing away expense'.

Schuler and Jackson (1987), representing the behavioural perspective of SHRM, argued that different strategy types (e.g. cost reduction, quality improvement and innovation) require different types of employee role behaviours. Therefore HR strategy should be geared to ensuring those behaviours are in place. For a differentiation strategy, where people carry out many complex tasks and need many skills, there would be little or no labour division, broad career paths, training for all employees, evaluation on long-term criteria and group incentives. In organisations following cost leadership strategies, where people carry out relatively simple tasks, with few skills required, the nature of HRM would be one of narrow career paths, training few employees, evaluation based on short-term criteria and individual incentives.

Two common forms of fit were described: strategic or vertical and internal or horizontal. Strategic or vertical fit is a necessary alignment between the overall business strategy and the HR strategy. Internal or horizontal fit is the link between individual HR practices, the argument being that a consistent and integrated set of HR practices would result in higher organisational performance. Delery and Doty (1996) argued that organisations will be more effective if they adopt a policy of strategic configuration i.e. where there is both a (vertical) fit between an organisation's HR strategy and its business strategy and also a (horizontal) fit of different HR practices with one another.

Many studies published from the late 1990s and early 2000s emphasised different types of fit and flexibility, suggesting that HR will only be effective if its own strategy is aligned with business strategy. Causal strategy mapping was introduced as a means for establishing the strategy to HR linkages (vertical fit). The best-fit model implies a causal chain that starts with the business strategy and leads, through HR strategy to HR processes such as hiring, training, appraisal and compensation, to delivering HR outcomes such as commitment, quality output, and engagement, and business outcomes such as (improved) financial performance such as profits, financial turnover, better margins, and Return on investment ('inside-out'). For instance Rucci et al. (1998) developed a case study of Sears' employee–customer profit chain that identified the causal sequence from mission, vision and strategy to operating level behaviours and customer satisfaction.

More recent models emphasise the importance of working 'outside-in', i.e. designing HR strategies back from the needs of the investor and customer to help the organisation deliver desired outcomes to meet these needs. Dave Ulrich, one of the most influential HR theorists on HR roles and practice, argues that value is what is generated by talent from which employers can derive profit or other forms of benefit. For Ulrich and Brockbank (2005), 'HR passes the wallet test when it creates human abilities and organisational capabilities that are substantially better than those of the firm's competitors—and thus move customers and shareholders to reach for their wallets'. For Ulrich and Smallwood (2005) HR must ensure that HR activities positively impact intangible value, as reflected in the premium the market is willing to pay above a firm's earnings and book value. They argue that a new, better human resource measure of return on investment (ROI) is return on intangibles.

However, there is as yet no overall agreed theory of performance, nor of how specifically HRM impacts on performance. Two interesting relationships are the unmediated HRM effect, which shows that some HR practices can directly lead to improved internal performance. For instance, a good sales training programme can directly result in better sales performance, without necessarily influencing broader HR outcomes. The reversed causality in a value chain model suggests that sometimes stronger financial performance leads to more investments in HR practices and better HR outcomes. When business performance is strong, employees are often more engaged (an HR outcome). Thus the relationships in such models are not always one-way.

Control or commitment

This brings us to another of the key discussions within contemporary HRM theory and practice (see Chapter 3): what is the best way to achieve high performance – through control or commitment approaches to HRM?

Control ('hard') approaches to HRM

HRM has evolved two distinct conceptions of the link between HR practice, employee motivation and behaviour and firm-level performance outcomes. Walton (1985) and other researchers drew a distinction between the 'hard' (control) and 'soft' (commitment) approaches to HRM. The control approach to HRM tends to focus on cost reduction and seeks to improve efficiency by enforcing employee compliance with organisational performance requirements (Arthur 1994). The control approach to HR systems is clearly represented in Fombrun et al.'s (1984) 'Michigan Model', which emphasised that superior firm performance is dependent on having in place systems for the regular assessment of individual employees. Associated with, and reinforcing these systems, are performance rewards based on measurable performance criteria and training whose performance-related outcomes are monitored.

High commitment HRM

In contrast, the 'soft' high-commitment–high-performance approach to the management of people aims to shape attitudes by forging psychological links between organisational and employee goals, or a 'hearts and minds' approach. Also known as the collaborative model of enhancing firm performance, Beer et al.'s 'Harvard Model' (1984) – aimed at promoting the goals of both employees and employer – illustrates the high commitment approach to HRM in emphasising the need for management to recognise employees as significant stakeholders in the enterprise. One of the key tenets of 'soft' HRM is the internal integration of HR policy goals with each other.

The notion that employee commitment is one of the outcomes of HR practices is also central to Guest's (1997) normative theory of HRM, which emphasises employee influence and the value of a common sense of purpose in engendering motivation, leading to firm performance. Employee influence is contingent on mutual influence between management and employees that enables management to understand employee interests. Without this, it is argued, employees' intrinsic motivation is undermined, thereby giving rise to employee resentment and distrust, which results in unwillingness to take responsibility for the performance of the firm.

There are tensions between the 'soft' and 'hard' approaches. In describing their human-resources approaches many organisations have embraced the language of the 'soft' approach in their recruitment literature, speaking of culture, training, development and commitment. However, an in-depth empirical study in Bailey et al. (1997) concluded that even if the rhetoric of HRM is 'soft', the reality is almost always 'hard', with the interests of the organisation prevailing over those of the individual since 'the underlying principle was invariably restricted to the improvements of bottom-line performance'.

Maximising the human asset

One contemporary debate concerns possible effects of HR work on 'employee engagement' and performance outcomes. From a resource-based view of the firm Boxall (1998) argued the HR function creates competitive advantage through what he calls 'Human Resource Advantage' – the strategic management of personnel using cultural, structural and personnel techniques. This comprises two components: human capital advantage (arising from having better people than competitors) and organisational processes advantage (arising from having better ways of working than competitors). Therefore HR practices must create commitment among an exceptionally talented supply of 'human resources' through the management of mutuality (or alignment of interests), while also developing employees and teams so as to create an organisation sustainably capable of learning across industry cycles. The aim is to generate strategic capability by ensuring that the organisation has the skilled, committed and well-motivated employees it needs to achieve sustained competitive advantage.

It is assumed that highly motivated employees – who are aligned with organisational goals, willing to 'go the extra mile' and act as advocates of their organisation – are most likely to perform well and are critical to business success. The argument goes that every organisation has a value chain to high performance which runs something like this: the right employees, with the right AMO – i.e. ability (A) and motivation (M) and the right opportunity (O) – will deliver the right performance to customers, who will produce the financial and other returns required by the organisation's stakeholders (Purcell 2002). Applebaum et al. (2000) identified links between the 'AMO tub' containing abilities, skills, motivation, incentives, opportunity to participate and the 'enabling tub' of effective discretionary effort which in turn leads to a 'tub' of firm performance outcomes.

Such arguments have focused attention on the management practices which drive employee performance, in particular those linked to employee 'engagement'. The state of employee engagement is characterised as a feeling of commitment, passion and energy, which translates into high levels of persistence, with even the most difficult tasks exceeding expectations and taking the initiative. In such a state, it is argued, people are more productive and more service- oriented, less wasteful and more inclined to come up with good ideas, take the initiative and generally help organisations achieve their goals than people who are disengaged.

Indeed, high-performance theory places employee engagement or 'the intellectual and emotional attachment that an employee has for his or her work' (Heger 2007: 121) at the heart of performance, especially among knowledge workers. Employee engagement has been linked in various studies with higher earnings per share, improved sickness absence, higher productivity and innovation – the potential business benefits go on and on.

Yet many scholars argue that engagement is a poorly defined concept which makes proving links with performance and business success difficult. Debates rage about whether engagement is intrinsic to the employee, with some people naturally inclined to feel more engaged than others, or whether it is extrinsic factors such as the job, pay and other factors which have the greater impact on engagement.

Moreover, the many available studies of engagement and its impact on organisational performance tend to be carried out by consultancies, some of whom provide employee engagement services to the business community. For instance, Gallup Consulting (Harter et al. 2020) found that, with regard to composite business/work unit performance, business/work units in the top half of a global scale on employee engagement have a 94% higher success rate in their own organisation and a 145% higher success rate across business/work units in all companies studied. In other words, business/work units with high employee engagement nearly double their odds of above-average composite performance in their own organisations and increase their odds for above-average success across business/work units in all organisations by 2.45 times. Similarly, a Corporate Leadership Council (CLC) study found that companies with highly engaged employees grow twice as fast as peer companies. A three-year study of 41 multinational organisations by (Willis) Towers Watson found that those with high engagement levels had a 2–4% improvement in operating margin and net profit margin, whereas those with low engagement showed a decline of about 1.5–2%.

Nevertheless, there is wide consensus that it is in the context of the employment relationship between the individual and the organisation that employee engagement is created or destroyed (see Chapter 8). At face value then, improving the context for employee engagement should be a key aspect of HR strategy. The challenge for managers and HR is to create, or avoid destroying, the AMO which leads to employee engagement and performance.

Focus on measurement

The desire to assess the effects of HR activity on business performance is reflected in an ongoing focus on measurement. Becker et al. (1997) estimated the impact of a HPWS, its effectiveness and alignment with firm competitive strategy, on shareholder wealth in 702 US firms. They found that a one standard deviation increase in these factors was associated with a $42,000 per employee increase in market value. What remains unclear from this perspective however is how organisations can consistently achieve superior performance via HR strategy.

Use of an expanded view of organisational performance and its emphasis on different stakeholder perspectives is evident within generic assessment and measurement frameworks such as those of ISO, the European Foundation for Quality Management (British Excellence Model), the Balanced Business Scorecard and Investors in People (IiP). These assume strong causal links between good people management practice, individual development and performance and business results. However, different types of business may have a different value chain. For instance in companies in retail and other service sectors models such as the service–profit chain (Sasser et al. 1997), a strong link between employee satisfaction, customer care and profitability, appears credible. These frameworks reflect some of the broader thrusts of strategic human resource management theory which associate 'hard' business results with 'soft' inputs such as learning, customer focus, processes, people management and leadership and where traditional financial measures of success are insufficient criteria.

Given the range of measures used in different organisations, the use of various 'value chain' or customer service impact models, such as the Business Excellence framework, tends to be inconsistent, making comparisons difficult. Moreover, proving HR's added value to business results has always been difficult since outcomes of HR interventions or practices are usually proximal, such as employee satisfaction, commitment, motivation, trust, loyalty, retention and turnover, absence due to illness and the social climate between employees and managers. After all, SHRM goals are mostly delivered by managers.

The Human Capital Movement (HCM) has attempted to define measures for valuing aspects of human performance and the various 'intangible' outputs associated with it, such as innovation, in order to be able to quantify in financial terms what this contributes to organisational performance and competitive advantage. Youndt and Snell (2004) proposed intellectual capital (human, social and organisational) as a mediating variable in the relationship between HR systems and organisational performance. They found that selection and training and development were related to human capital, the use of collaborative HR activities was related to social capital, and accessible information systems along with HR activities that encourage knowledge documentation were related to organisational capital. Human capital and social capital had strong relationships with organisational performance.

To some extent this should have strengthened the hand of those advocating effective people management, training and development and should have led to increased employer awareness that treating employees well is a key element of increasing performance and productivity. However, hopes that companies would be required to report on their human capital in annual reports have proved mostly ill-founded, suggesting that a causal link between people and organisational performance remains poorly understood in business circles. While the move to quantify human capital in company reporting largely failed, at least there is now greater awareness in risk registers of the various forms of people-related risk – including to company reputation.

The gradual consolidation of HRM (in organisations) into the general repertoire of managerialism is the outcome of a complex and paradoxical cultural process. On the one hand, HRM appears to have become less coherent, less centred, more dispersed and insubstantial when compared with other technical specialities of management such as strategy or marketing. In spite of this appearance, though, HRM has become a very strong cultural programme capable of extending its range to emerge as one of the most significant grounds of managerialism itself (Costea et al. 2007). Delbridge and Keenoy (2010) point out that since mainstream HRM became the dominant discourse relating to management practice from the mid-1980s on, what Keenoy (1997) terms 'HRMism' has enjoyed 'unparalleled success'.

CRITICAL HRM

Alongside mainstream theory, critical management (CMS), critical HRM (CHRM) and critical Human Resource Development (CHRD) studies offer a variety of different perspectives on the assertions of mainstream theory and on the role and purpose of the HR function. CMS is a disparate field encompassing critical versions of postmodernism (Alvesson and Deetz 2005) and radical humanist approaches (Burrell and Morgan 1979). Other critical scholarship derives from the industrial relations tradition within which HRM was seen as 'part of a system of employment regulation in which internal and external influences shape the management of the employment relationship' (Bach and Sisson 2000: 8).

Much critical management, HRM and HRD scholarship derives from a Marxist perspective. For instance, critics point out the different interests of employers/executives (representing 'owners' and shareholders) and those of employees, especially with respect to the way employers use technology to gain complete control of the labour process, increase flexibility and drive down costs, often at the expense of employees. In consequence, this 'structured antagonism' engenders a 'natural' conflict of interests within the employment relationship because the employers' interest in minimising labour costs constantly rubs up against the employees' interest in maximising rewards and/or reducing the duration and intensity of work (the effort-wage bargain). Labour process theorists argue that employers gain control over work, for instance by using technological substitutes to deskill workers, rendering them dispensable and without power in the employment relationship.

Unitarism and the 'HRM project'

This is in sharp contrast to the predominant unitarist view implicit within mainstream HRM, especially in American models of HRM i.e. it assumes that employees and employers are united in the common endeavour of achieving business success. The assumption is that management and employees have mutual interests and benefit equally from this interdependency. This may or may not always be the case of course.

Critics see HRM, an offshoot of managerialism, as a significant contributor to the deliberate shaping of a neo-liberal new work culture characterised by flexibility, work intensification and performativity. HRM prefers individual to collective employee relations, leaving workers quite exposed. From a critical perspective, HR acts solely to promote the employer's interests, despite HR rhetoric appearing supportive of employees.

Mueller and Carter (2005) argue that the discourse of HRM from the early 1980s onwards is closely intertwined with the shift in power relations between employers, managers, employees and trade unions. They propose the notion of an 'HRM project', which includes not only language but also HR practices, boundary-spanning linkages and external agents such as regulators and financial institutions. This overtly unitarist and managerialist framing of HRM represents a legitimising management point of view which has progressively edged out pluralist perspectives on the employment relationship, including what are described as 'traditional' personnel management or old-style industrial relations (Francis and Sinclair 2003; Wright and Snell 2005).

Mainstream HRM approaches are thus a managerial tool for controlling and managing the workforce in ways which are designed solely to meet business needs, but which appear less directive than the command-and-control structures of previous decades. Many critics highlight the contrast between HRM rhetoric and the reality as experienced by employees (Legge 1995, 2005). For example, Sennett (1998: 28) describes 'high performance work practices', such as teamworking, as 'the work ethic of a flexible political economy', since it relies on 'the fiction of harmony' and stresses mutual responsiveness at the expense of original thinking. Kochan (2013) argues that such gaps between espoused and actual practice lead to loss of trust.

For Watson (2010) the common core of what CMS offers to mainstream management theory is deep scepticism regarding the moral defensibility and the social and ecological sustainability of prevailing forms of management and organisation, which are considered manipulative – 'control by compliance' (Hugh Willmott 1993) – and hostile to the interests of employees. According to Watson (2010), CMS's motivating concern is the social injustice and environmental destructiveness of the broader social and economic systems that these managers and organisations serve and reproduce, rather than focusing simply on the practices of managers themselves.

Social and ethical dimensions of HR practice

Within mainstream HRM discourse, the dominant emphasis is generally placed on how to make HRM more effective in achieving managerial interests. The growing interest in the ethics of HRM is perhaps reflective of critics' concerns about the morality of certain aspects of HRM practice such as the use of contingent labour in the 'gig economy' which eliminates any employer responsibility towards workers who are treated as self-employed and lack any of the benefits of regular employment. Critical theorists therefore largely tend to critique mainstream theory and practice rather than advocating specific alternative forms of practice. Mainstream theorists in contrast are concerned with potentially developing and improving the field of practice.

Even within mainstream theory, in contrast to the notion that HR strategic alignment is all about developing the means to deliver a business strategy lies a more values-based way of thinking about the role of HR, which co-exists somewhat uneasily with the performance-based view. Syrett (2007) points out that HR's role should not treat employees as if they are mere instruments of organisational performance. The application of HRM requires the exercise of social responsibility – it must be concerned with the interests (well-being) of employees and act ethically with regard to the needs of people in the organisation and the community. The HR profession has taken a stance reflecting a responsibility to the wider society to defend the well-being and rights of people employed in the organisation, to safeguard the ethics of the organisation, to provide a moral compass and so on, and the HR function has built organisation and expertise to do this over the years. Arguably this is because organisations have an environmental, social and governance (ESG) duty to fulfil if only to protect their reputations.

HR has a key social role to play with respect to employees, due in part to the breakdown of the traditional social contract that exchanged employee loyalty for life-time job security, and the rise of individualism more generally in society. People have increased expectations about their quality of life, of which their workplace conditions and relationships form a very important part. Employees increasingly resist authoritarian management, require participation in decision-making and demand improved physical working conditions.

So HR has to address the issue of whether HR should be a business resource management function and/or an employee welfare facility. The latter brings with it responsibilities and commitments which may potentially bring HR into moral conflict with business and performance-driven objectives for example, when a factory is closed in a town with declining prospects of employment for workers whose skills base is limited.

HR is at the pivot point of debates about whether the rights and needs of employees to work–life balance and flexible working for instance, should be of greater priority than those of employers who may need staff to be available for business beyond conventional times, or vice versa. HR – to a far greater extent than other business disciplines like marketing and finance – has a role as 'guarantor' or 'guardian' of employee rights as well as representing the interests of the organisation. This has led to a continuing role for HR as arbiters between 'the business' and 'the workforce' (Ulrich et al. 2015). Not for nothing has Dave Ulrich's original conception of HR as 'employee champion' now become 'employee advocate' (see Chapter 2).

Reflective activity

- Keenoy (1997) referred to Storey's (1995) remark that HRM is a 'symbolic label' and suggested that it 'masked managerial opportunism'. Legge (2005) argued that HR language and practice represented rhetoric rather than reality. To what extent are these statements valid today?
- To what extent do you believe that should HR be the moral guardian of organisational practice?

INTEGRATION OF PEOPLE MANAGEMENT WITH BUSINESS STRATEGY AND CONTEXT

SHRM pays close attention to the changing organisational context and considers the potential alignment between the institutional context, business strategy, business systems and HRM, and the fit between HR practices (Boselie 2014). Jackson and Schuler (1995) identified internal and external components of organisational environments. Internal components include technology, structure, size, life cycle stages and business strategy. External components include legal, social and political environment; labour market conditions, including unionisation; industry characteristics; and national culture. Early theories in the HR field often emphasised HR's role as ensuring that employees had the ability and motivation to achieve established organisational goals and that there were enough workers with particular skills available to meet organisation needs. For instance, by the early 2000s, given the widespread shortages of 'talent' at the time, especially in many knowledge-based occupations, the concept of talent management became widespread as employers competed in what McKinsey dubbed the 'War for Talent' to attract highly skilled candidates by offering enticing 'employee value propositions'.

Organisational effectiveness (OE)

By the late 1990s, in the light of rapid technological innovation and economic turbulence, there was as shift to understanding HR's role as delivering organisational effectiveness: 'the capacity of the organisation to adapt rapidly to its external environment and to meet market and other external demands and with good resulting business performance'

(Grundy 1998). This means HR's role is to build not just the people capability to execute the business strategy but also involves creating the right organisation architecture to equip the organisation for the fast-changing global context.

Key to building organisational effectiveness (OE) is a skilful blend of HRM practices, organisational design and development (OD+D) to equip an organisation to succeed in its particular context. This includes HR systems such as human capital management (HCM), talent management, knowledge management, leadership development, learning and development, designing high performance work systems, rewarding high performance, employee development and culture management.

Challenges to the notion of 'fit'

The contrast between 'best practice' and 'best fit' approaches lies at the heart of conundrums about what HR's 'strategic alignment' means. For contingency theorists, the best personnel policy relates to the unique characteristics and circumstances of the organisation, while from a universalist or best practice perspective, alignment relates to the level of integration between HR practices that are understood to lead, for example, to employee engagement or high performance.

The belief that the closer the 'fit' between business strategy and organisational functions will result in organisational effectiveness has been challenged in recent times. The challenges relate to the lack of empirical evidence that this close strategic fit will automatically lead to improved effectiveness, and that such approaches do not take into account measures of organisational effectiveness (Truss and Gratton 1994; Huselid 1995).

There are also criticisms that such approaches can be too simplistic in their assumption that the creation of HR strategy inevitably follows the business strategy. There is danger of 'contingent determinism' (Paauwe 2004) – i.e. claiming that the context determines the strategy. There is also the risk of mechanistically matching HR policies and practices with strategy since it is not credible to claim that there are single contextual factors that determine HR strategy, and internal fit cannot therefore be complete.

While maintaining the importance of fit, Lengnick-Hall and Lengnick-Hall (2003), observed that fit is not always a desirable goal, especially during times of transition, and that a close fit can be considered the opposite end of the continuum from flexibility. So, a driver of high cost-effectiveness might inhibit flexibility because of its efficiency focus and would be negatively associated with social legitimacy because of its potential neglect of human issues (e.g. work-life balance practices). Conversely, from an efficiency point of view, focusing too much on flexibility might damage the firm's financial performance; focusing too much on social legitimacy might result in a loss of both flexibility and efficiency. Firms therefore should explicitly choose a position along the continuum to coincide with their assessment of upcoming competitive conditions.

Indeed, some theorists question whether too close an alignment with business strategy risks undermining HR's other main preoccupation: with people.

> "My worry is that HR is now too closely – and even solely – linked with organisational performance and it is in danger of becoming indistinguishable from other managerial functions if this develops much further".
>
> Marchington and Wilkinson (2008: 2)

In other words, HR seems to have lost its original principles of representing both management and employees.

Rediscovering mutuality

From the early 2000s social media started making an impact on society as well as on corporations worldwide. Along with the consumerisation of products, the behaviour and expectations of customers and employees were changing. Workers not only expect to connect through their social networks; they also expect to have more of a say over their destiny in the workplace. Arguably therefore, strategic HR goals and policies should aim for mutuality and produce the conditions for 'win-win' outcomes for both the business and the workforce, resulting for instance in employee engagement and well-being, sustainable performance and competitive advantage.

However, in discussing the importance of human resources in the creation of competitive advantage, Wright et al. (1994), point out that not all organisations have the ability to systematically develop human resources as a potential source of sustained competitive advantage through the use of HRM practices. Indeed, without structural support from the organisation (i.e. in how human resources are acquired, managed, developed, supported and rewarded), or in the organisational culture they must navigate, even the best people may be unable to achieve lasting success for themselves or their organisations.

Reflective activity

- Is alignment a desirable goal for HR these days?
- If yes, what should this entail?
- If not, what might a more desirable goal be?
- Why?

In an earlier edition of this book, I took the view that the best form of alignment was one that was relevant and 'best fit' i.e. contingent on the organisation's circumstances and strategic aims. Indeed, in many organisations, the notion of 'best fit' is attractive, especially if HR strategies are developed to meet the needs of the business in its context. Contingent HR strategies are more attractive to line managers since they can see the relevance to what the organisation is aiming to do in the short term and can enhance the credibility of the HR team who are seen to be business-focused.

However, I also considered that universal 'best practice' can inform local circumstances. Indeed, while Pfeffer's 'best practices' were criticised for their lack of context specificity, many measurement frameworks and competency-based standards, such as ISO, Investors in People frameworks or CMI Management competencies, assume a universal set of approaches that represent best practice on people management and development, regardless of context. Similarly, benchmarking processes derived from best practice can help organisations recognise choices in the way they address key issues. The danger of HR strategies built on 'best practice' is that they can seem 'ivory tower' and idealistic. Having an HR strategy that appears unrelated to the business strategy is far from useful.

While holding to my earlier view, several factors are causing me to modify it slightly. First, the body of thinking on what constitutes 'best practice' has expanded in recent times. With respect to high performance for instance, there does appear to be a growing evidence base and broad degree of consensus, which I share, about which key ingredients are almost always present in high performance contexts, e.g. high degrees of employee involvement. However, other less well-established factors are being added to the list of 'universalist' factors as time moves on and as research uncovers new 'drivers' of employee engagement and links with performance. For instance, work–life balance is coming to be viewed as a key factor in employee engagement, even though the link between that and high performance is not well proven. Similarly, the nature of the organisation's corporate reputation is thought to be an important factor in attracting and retaining talent. For instance, with environmental and climate change issues becoming more prominent, job candidates are increasingly reported to be taking into account an organisation's environmental policies on recycling, carbon offsetting, etc. when making their career choice.

To the extent that major social changes affect the daily work lives and expectations of employees, and help shape their attitudes and motivations, I would argue that the value and nature of 'universal' factors is also always contingent on external factors. Any bundles of HR practices need to be internally consistent and complementary, and depend on the organisational logic in that context. Thus, while individual aspects of 'best practice' are useful for benchmarking purposes, the approaches used must be congruent with the organisation's context and state of development if the real benefit is to be felt.

Other challenges to the nature of strategic alignment relate to the typical time-horizon within which business goals are planned and implemented. Usually, the business planning timeframe is three to five years at best. Now that there is growing recognition that HR has a key role to play in building culture – to support high performance – and the timeframe for developing the organisation is longer than the average business planning cycle.

Similarly, some HR strategies focus on building talent from within, growing leaders for tomorrow. The development of leaders with the behaviours and capabilities to lead tomorrow's business requires HR to look beyond today's practices and business strategies and work with line managers and executives to identify what will be required in the future workforce and leadership. Activities that involve growing talent and changing the 'way we do things around here' can take time, and an understanding of how to bring about change in complexity. These are issues on which HR needs to exercise leadership to produce real value for the organisation. However, gaining the license to focus on the longer term often depends on how effectively HR delivers in the short term.

Moreover, alignment is not always one-way since HR strategies can themselves influence business strategy and cannot be isolated from changes in the marketplace, most specifically trends relating to the labour market. New employment legislation, shortages in the labour market, demands for greater diversity and flexibility of service provision have to be taken into account. A business strategy that requires specific types of labour that are in very short supply will prove difficult to implement. Awareness of the talent challenges is one thing; knowing what can be done about them is another. This is where HR, as the key people specialist function in organisations, should be uniquely well placed to make a difference to the success of their business.

INTERNATIONAL AND COMPARATIVE HRM

The development of HRM and SHRM theory to date has largely been a UK and American/Australasian phenomenon. Even within the UK markets, there is debate about whether the principles of individualism endemic to the US culture apply equally to the wider British culture (Armstrong 2008: 16).

While Anglo-Saxon or US models mainly focus on creating shareholder value, often at the expense of other stakeholders, Germanic models acknowledge multiple stakeholders and explicitly take into account employee interests in terms of well-being and also societal interests. Brewster (1995) proposed a European model of HRM based on the assumption that European organisations operate with limited autonomy because the internal constraints on HRM include union influence and employee involvement in decision-making through various bodies such as workers' councils.

With respect to international HRM (IHRM) theory (see Chapter 12), various theoretical models have been developed (Scullion 2001; Brewster et al. 2005), which recognise the importance of linking international HRM strategy to the strategic evolution of the firm. Wood (1999) makes a distinction between four different 'fits': internal, organisational, strategic and environmental.

International HRM – defined as 'HRM issues, functions and policies and practices that result from the strategic activities of multinational enterprises and that impact the international concerns and goals of those enterprises' (Scullion and Linehan 2005: 356) is focused on issues associated with the management of employees across national borders in multinational (MNCs) and transnational corporations (TNCs). The core areas concern getting the right people with appropriate skills, knowledge, and experience in the right place at the right time on a global scale (Iles and Zhiang 2013), activities which are carried out by large multinational companies, small companies or public service organisations in a rapidly changing global context.

International HRM addresses a broader range of activities than domestic HRM. These include international taxation, coordinating foreign currencies and exchange rates, international relocation, international orientation for the employee posted abroad etc. There is heightened exposure to risks in international assignments, which include the health and safety of the employee and family. International HRM has to deal with more external factors than domestic HRM, for example, government regulations about staffing practices in foreign locations, local codes of conduct, influence of local religious groups etc. If a British organisation is sanctioned by license by the Indian government to set up its subsidiary in India, the British company is under legal obligations to provide employment to local residents.

One major aspect of risk relevant to IHRM today is possible terrorism. Another is safeguarding. Many international charities and NGOs for instance now have a much greater focus on safeguarding than in the past, following the scandal involving a major charity's director's sexual exploitation of women in receipt of aid after the 2010 earthquake in Haiti. UK charity staff now have background checks according to police guidelines. In other parts of the world where the charities operate, obtaining such background checks for local workers may not be possible due to different cultural practices, including the way police forces operate. As employers the charities are exposed to reputational risk if they are not able to prove that they have taken every care in ensuring that staff they employ are not a risk to the populations they are meant to serve.

More recently, intense competition among organisations at the national and international level, and the emergence of new markets have raised interest in comparative human resource management studies (Budhwar and Sparrow 2002), addressing the configuration of HRM in different national contexts (see Chapter 13). Comparative HRM (CHRM) considers the extent to which there are differences in HR practices across countries, with comparisons typically made of four different approaches: economic, environmental, behavioural and open systems (Nath 1988). Both IHRM and CHRM concur that a good working environment characterised by high levels of communication and teamwork could help employees gain high levels of autonomy, learning and excellence thereby improving their performance (Zheng et al. 2009).

An important strand of comparative HRM is the cultural perspective. Hall (1976) argues that a useful way of understanding cultural differences derives from the notion of high- and low-context societies. In high-context societies such as those in Japan and some Arab countries, the meaning of communication largely derives from facial expressions, setting and timings, while in low-context Northern European cultures, more explicit and clear forms of communication are preferred. In contrast, Hofstede (1980) argues that cultures can be categorised according to four distinct cultural value distinctions – power distance, uncertainty avoidance, individualism/collectivism and masculinity/femininity – which have become embedded in society over long periods.

Hofstede's work led to an explosion of investigations into cross-cultural differences, such as those by Fons Trompenaars and Charles Hampden-Turner. Although Hofstede's distinctions were criticised for their limited statistical derivation and for the assumption of the slow evolution of cultures, nevertheless these values are popularly used in understanding cultural differences in managerial intentions and behaviour.

Some national cultures could be said to be undergoing a more rapid transformation than Hofstede assumed, given the effects of globalisation and technological advances. For instance, Sarawagi (2010), discussing HRM issues at a number of Indian firms, found that managers are forced to think globally, which can be difficult for those who are used to operating in vast, sheltered markets with minimal competition from domestic or foreign firms. Sarawagi argues that, in the Indian context, to cope with the challenges of maintaining workforce diversity, motivating employees, communication, performance management, competence development and so on, firms will need to undergo a transformation from rigid hierarchies to flat, more flexible structures; from family-centric and secretive to dispersed ownership, open-mindedness and sharing; from caste-ridden and superstitious to rational thinking and a vibrant style for handling issues.

CONCLUSION

We have considered various theoretical elements of HRM and SHRM theory that impact on HR practice. We have discussed how the focus on performance and alignment to business strategy risks neglecting the 'human' in human resources. These varied approaches suggest a discipline which is evolving in complex ways as it reflects a wide range of issues in different contexts. Increasingly HRM researchers are paying greater attention to implementation issues experienced by practitioners. There is a growing recognition that intended SHRM practices may be different from actual SHRM practices. The mixed picture of perceptions about the role and value of the HR function may reflect legacy issues arising from HR's evolution. In the next chapter let us turn our attention to how the HR function was remodelled in the first few waves of HR transformation.

REFERENCES

Alvesson, M. and Deetz, S. (2005). Critical theory and post-modernism: Approaches to organisation studies. In H. Wilmott and C. Grey (eds), *Critical Management Studies: A Reader*. Oxford: Oxford University Press, pp. 60–106.

Appelbaum, E., Bailey, T., Berg, P. and Kalleberg, A. (2000). *Manufacturing Advantage: Why High-Performance Work Systems Pay Off*. Ithaca, NY: Cornell University Press.

Armstrong, M. (2008) *Handbook of Strategic Human Resource Management*, 4th Edition, Kogan Page.

Armstrong, M. and Taylor, S. (2014). *Armstrong's Handbook of Human Resource Management Practice*. London: Kogan Page.

Arthur, J.B. (1994). Effects of human resource systems on manufacturing performance and turnover. *Academy of Management Journal*, 37(3), 670–687.

Bach, S. and Sisson, K. (eds) (2000). *Personnel Management: A Comprehensive Guide to Theory and Practice*. Oxford: Blackwell Publishers.

Bailey, C., Gratton, L, Hope-Hailey, V. and Stiles, P. (1997). Soft and hard models of human resource management: A reappraisal. *Journal of Management Studies*, 34(1).

Barney, J.B. (1997). *Gaining and Sustaining Competitive Advantage*. Reading, MA: Addison-Wesley, pp. 53–73.

Becker, B. and Gerhart, B. (1996). The impact of human resource management on organizational performance progress and prospects. *Academy of Management Journal*, 39, 779–801.

Becker, B. E and Huselid, M.A. (1997). *HR as a Source of Shareholder Value*. Wiley.

Becker, B.E., Huselid, M.A. Pickus, P.S. and Spratt, M.F. (1997). HR as a source of shareholder value: Research and recommendations. *Human Resource Management*, 36(1), 39–47.

Beer, M., Spector, B., Lawrence, P.R., Mills, D.Q. and Walton, R.E. (1985). *Human Resource Management: A General Manager's Perspective*. New York: Free Press.

Beer, M., Spector, B., Lawrence, P.R., Mills, D.Q. and Walton, R. (1984). Managing Human Assets in a Conceptual Review of HRM. *Harvard Business Review*, 84, 15–38.

Boselie, P. (2014). *Strategic Human Resource Management: A Balanced Approach*. 2nd Edition, New York: Tata McGraw-Hill.

Boxall, P.F. (1998). Achieving competitive advantage through human resource strategy: Towards a theory of industry dynamics. *Human Resource Management Review*, 8(3), 265–288.

Boxall, P.F. and Purcell, J. (2008). *Strategy and Human Resource Management*. Hampshire: Palgrave MacMillan.

Boxall, P.F., Purcell, J. and Wright, P. (2007). The goals of HRM. In P. Boxall, J. Purcell and P. Wright (eds), *Oxford Handbook of Human Resource Management*. Oxford: Oxford University Press, pp. 48–68.

Bratton, J. and Gold, J. (2017). *Human Resource Management*, 6th Edition. New York: Red Globe Press.

Brewster, C. (1995). Towards a 'European' model of Human Resource Management. *Journal of International Business Studies*, 26, 1–21.

Brewster, C., Sparrow, P. and Harris, H. (2005). Towards a new model of globalising HRM. *Journal of Human Resource Management*, 16(6), 949–970.

Budhwar, P. and Sparrow, P. (2002). An integrative framework for determining cross national human resource management practices. *Human Resource Management Review*, 12(3), 377–403, Sept.

Burrell, G., and Morgan, G. (1979). *Sociological Paradigms and Organizational Analysis*. Heinemann.

Costea, B., Crump, N. and Holm J. (2007). The spectre of Dionysus: Play, work, and managerialism. *Society and Business Review*, 2(2), 153–165.

Delaney, J.T. and Huselid, M.A. (1996). The impact of human resource management practices on perceptions of organizational performance. *Academy of Management Journal*, 39(4), 949–969.

Delbridge, R. and Keenoy T. (2010). Beyond managerialism? *The International Journal of Human Resource Management*, 21(6), 799–817, May.

Delery, J.E. and Doty, D.H. (1996). Modes of theorizing in strategic human resource management: Tests of universalistic, contingency. *Academy of Management Journal*, 39(4), 802–835.

Fleetwood, S. and Hesketh, A. (2006). *The Performance of HR*. Cambridge: Cambridge University Press.

Fombrun, C., Tichy, N.M. and Devanna, M.A. (1984). *Strategic Human Resource Management*. New York: John Wiley.

Francis, H. and Sinclair, J. (2003). A processual analysis of HRM-based change. *Organization*, 10(4), 685–706.

Gamble, A. (2009). *The Spectre at the Feast: Capitalist Crisis and the Politics of Recession*. London: Palgrave Macmillan.

Grundy, A. (1998). How are corporate strategies and human resource strategy linked? *Journal of General Management*, 23(3), 49–72.

Guest, D.E. (2002). Human resource management, corporate performance and employee well-being: Building the worker into HRM. *The Journal of Industrial Relations*, 44(3), 335–358.

Guest, D.E. (1997). Human resource management and performance: A review and research agenda. *International Journal of Human Resource Management*, 8(3), 263–276.

Guest, D.E. (1989). Personnel and human resource management: Can you tell the difference? *Personnel Management*, January, 48–51.

Guest, D.E., Michie, J., Sheehan, M. and Conway, N. (2003). A UK study of the relationship between human resource management and corporate performance. *British Journal of Industrial Relations*, 41(2), 291–314.

Hall, E.T. (1976). *Beyond Culture*. New York, NY: Doubleday.

Harter, J.K., Schmidt, F.L., Agrawal, S., Blue, A., Plowman, S.K., Josh, P. and Asplund, J. (2020). *The Relationship between Engagement at Work and Organizational Outcomes 2020 Q12® Meta-Analysis*, 10th Edition, October, Gallup.

Heger, B.K. (2007). Linking the Employment Value Proposition (EVP) to employee engagement and business outcomes: Preliminary findings from a linkage research pilot study. *Organisation Development Journal*, 25(2), 121–131.

Hofstede, G. (1980). *Culture's Consequences: International Differences in Work-Related Values*. Beverly Hills, CA: Sage.

Huselid, M.A. (1995). The impact of human resource management practices on turnover, productivity and corporate financial performance. *Academy of Management Journal*, 38(3), 635–672.

Huselid, M.A. and Becker, B.E. (1996). Methodological issues in cross-sectional and panel estimates of the HR-firm performance link. *Industrial Relations*, 35, 400–422.

Iles, P. and Zhiang, C. L. (2013). *International Human Resource Management: A Cross-Cultural and Comparative Approach*. London: Kogan Page.

Janssens, M. and Steyaert, C. (2009). HRM and performance: A plea for reflexivity in HRM studies. *Journal of Management Studies*, 46(1), 143–155.

Kaufman, B. (2001). The theory and practice of strategic HRM and participative management. *Human Resource Management Review*, 11(4), 505–533.

Keenoy, T. (2009). 'Human resource management'. In M. Alvesson, T. Bridgman and H. Willmott (eds), *The Oxford Handbook of Critical Management Studies*. Oxford: Oxford University Press, pp. 454–472.

Keenoy, T. (1997). HRMism and the images of re-presentation. *Journal of Management Studies*, 4(5), 825–841.

Jackson, S.E. and Schuler, R.S. (1995). Understanding human resource management in the context of organizations and their environment. *Annual Review of Psychology*, 46, 237–264.

Jacques, R. (1999). Developing a tactical approach to engaging with 'strategic' HRM. *Organization*, 6(2), 199–222.

Kochan, T.A. (2013). Restoring trust in the human resource management profession. *Asia Pacific Journal of Human Resources*, 42(2), 132–146.

Lawler, E.E. III, Boudreau, J. W. and Mohrman, S.A. (2005). *Achieving Strategic Excellence: An Assessment of Human Resource Organizations*. Stanford, California: Stanford Press.

Legge, K. (1995) *Human Resource Management – Rhetorics and Realities*. Basingstoke: Macmillan Press.

Legge, K. (2005). *Human Resource Management: Rhetorics and Realities*. London: Palgrave Macmillan.

Lengnick-Hall, M.L. and Lengnick-Hall, C.A. (2003). *Human Resource Management in the Knowledge economy: New challenges, new roles, new capabilities*. San Francisco, CA: Berrett-Koehler.

Marquand, D. (2008). Never mind the role of the state. *The Guardian*, 11 December.

Marchington, M. and Wilkinson, A. (2008). *HRM at Work: People Management and Development*. 4th ed. London: Chartered Institute of Personnel & Development.

Miles, R.E. and Snow, C.C. (1984). Designing strategic human resource system. *Organizational Dynamics*, Summer, 16, 36–52.

Mueller, F and Carter, C. (2005). The "HRM Project" and managerialism: Or why some discourses are more equal than others. *Journal of Organizational Change Management*, 18(4), 369–382.

Nath, R. (ed) (1988). *Comparative Management: A Regional View*. Cambridge, Mass: Ballinger.

Paauwe, J. (2007). HRM and performance: In search of balance. *Inaugural Address as Professor of Human Resource Management at the Department of HR Studies at Tilburg University*.

Paauwe, J (2004). *HRM and Performance*. Oxford: Oxford University Press.

Patterson, P.G., Johnson, L.W., and Spreng, R.A. (1997). Modeling the determinants of customer satisfaction for business-to-business performance. *Academy of Marketing Science. Journal*, Winter, 25, 1.

Porter, M.E. (1985). *Competitive Advantage*. New York: Free Press.

Porter, M.E. (1986). *Competition in Global Industries*. Harvard Business Press

Pfeffer, J. (1998). Seven practices of successful organizations. *California Management Review*, 40(2), 96–124.

Purcell, J. (1999) The search for "best practice" and "best fit": chimera or cul-de-sac? *Human Resource Management Journal*, 9(3), 26–41.

Purcell, J. (2002). *Understanding the People and Performance Link: Unlocking the Black Box*. London: CIPD.

Rucci, A.J., Kirn, S.P. and Quinn, R.T. (1998). The employee–customer–profit chain at Sears. *Harvard Business Review*, 76(1), 82–98.

Sarawagi V.K. (2010). Challenges in Modern Human Resource Management, a Project Report by a Student of IMS, Ghaziabad, India.

Sasser, W.E. Jr, Heskett, J. and Schlesinger, L. (1997). *The Service Profit Chain: How Leading Companies Link Profit and Growth to Loyalty, Satisfaction and Value*. New York: Free Press.

Schuler, R.S. (1992). Strategic human resources management: Linking the people with the strategic needs of the business. *Organizational Dynamics*, 21(1), 18–32.

Schuler, R.S. and Jackson, S.E. (1987). Linking competitive strategies with human resource management practices. *Academy of Management Executive*, 1(3), 207–219.

Scott-Jackson, W. and Mayo, A. (2016). *HR with Purpose: Future Models of HR. Technical Report*. Henley Business School, University of Reading, Henley.

Scullion, H. (2001). 'International Human Resource Management', in J. Storey (ed), *Human Resource Management: A Critical Text*. International Thompson Business Press, pp. 288–313.

Scullion, H. and Linehan, M. (2005). *International Human Resource Management: A Critical Text*. Macmillan Education.

Sennett, R. (1998). *The Corrosion of Character, Personal Consequences of Work in the New Capitalism*. New York: W. W. Norton.

Sonnenberg, M., Koene, B. and Paauwe, J. (2011). Balancing HRM: The psychological contract of employees: A multi-level study. *Personnel Review*, September 20.

Storey, J. (1995). Human resource management: Still marching on or marching out? in J. Storey (ed.), *Human Resource Management: A Critical Text*. London: Routledge.

Stroh, L. and Caligiuri, P.M. (1998). Strategic Human Resources: A new source for competitive advantage in the global arena. *The International Journal of Human Resource Management*, 9(1).

Syrett, M. (2007). Commercial Acumen. Developing HR Strategy, Croner, Dec.

Thompson, M. and Heron, P. (2006). Nature of psychological contract in Knowledge-based firms: Relational quality and innovative performance in R&D based science and technology firms. *Human Resource Management Journal*, 16(1), 28–47.

Tichy, N., Fombrun, C. and Devanna, M. (1982). Strategic human resource management. *Sloan Management Review*, 23(2), 47–61.

Truss, C. and Gratton, L. (1994). Strategic Human Resource Management: a conceptual approach. *The International Journal of Human Resource Management*, 5(3), 663–686.

Tyson, S. and Fell, A. (1986). *Evaluating the Personnel Function*. London: Hutchison.

Ulrich, D. (1997). *Human Resource Champions: The Next Agenda for Adding Value and Delivering Results*. Cambridge, MA: Harvard Business School Press.

Ulrich, D. and Brockbank, W. (2015). Toward a synthesis of HR competency models: The common HR "Food Groups". *BYU Scholars Archive*, 38(4), 56–65.

Ulrich, D. and Brockbank, W. (2005). *The HR Value Proposition*. Cambridge, MA: Harvard Press.

Ulrich, D., Schiemann, W.A. and Sartain, L. (2020). *The Rise of HR: Wisdom from 73 Thought Leaders*, HR Certification Institute. https://hrpa.s3.amazonaws.com/uploads/2020/10/The-Rise-of-HR-ebook.pdf.

Ulrich, D. and Smallwood, N. (2005). HR's new ROI: Return on intangibles. *Human Resource Management*, 44(2), 137–142.

Walton, R.E. (1985). From control to commitment in the workplace. *Harvard Business Review*, 85, 77–84.

Watson, T.J. (2010). Critical social science, pragmatism and the realities of HRM. *The International Journal of Human Resource Management*, 26(6), 915–931.

Welbourne, T. and Cyr, L.A. (1999). The human resource executive effect in initial public offering firms. *Academy of Management Journal*, 42, 616–629, December.

Willmott, H. (1993). Strength is ignorance; Slavery is freedom: Managing culture in modern organizations. *Journal of Management Studies*, 30(4), 515–552.

Wood, S. (1999). Human resource management and performance. *International Journal of Management Reviews*, 1(4), 367–413.

Wright, P., Gardner, T., Moynihan, L. and Allen, M. (2005). The relationship between HR practices and firm performance: examining causal order. *Personnel Psychology*, 58(2), 409–446.

Wright, P.M. and Snell, S.A. (2005). Partner or guardian? *Human Resource Management*, 44, 177–182.

Wright, P.M., McMahon, G.C. and McWilliams, A. (1994). Human resources and sustained competitive advantage: A resource based perspective. *International Journal of Human Resource Management*, 5(2), 301–326.

Wright, P.W. and McMahan, G.C. (1992). Theoretical perspectives for strategic human resource management. *Journal of Management*, 18(2), 295–320.

Wright, P.W. and Snell, S.A. (1998). Toward a unifying framework for exploring fit and flexibility in strategic human resource management. *The Academy of Management Journal*, 23(4), 756–772.

Youndt, M.A. and Snell, S.A. (2004). Human resource configurations, intellectual capital, and organizational performance. *Journal of Managerial Issues*, 16(3), 337–360.

Zheng, C., O'Neill, G. and Morrison, M. (2009), Enhancing Chinese SME performance through innovative HR practices. *Personnel Review*, 38(2), 175–194.

2

The evolution of the HR function

A true HR transformation is an integrated, aligned, innovative, and business- focused approach to redefining how HR work is done within an organization so that it helps the organization deliver on promises made to customers, investors, and other stakeholders.

(Ulrich and Allen 2009)

DOI: 10.4324/9781003219996-3

In Chapter 1, we looked at some foundational elements of Human Resource theory. Broadly in line with such theory, HR functions have been transforming themselves since the late 1980s. The transformation journey has not been an easy one and HR still suffers from a bad press. An article about HR in *Fortune Magazine* asked: 'why not blow the sucker up?' Reinventing HR means looking at new ways to deliver services and answering the question 'What is the purpose of HR in this organization?'

CHAPTER OVERVIEW

In this chapter, we shall look at some of the ways in which the Human Resource function has been transforming itself in the first decades of the twenty-first century. Our principal focus will be on the dominant HR architecture adopted mainly by large organisations – the so-called 'Ulrich model'. We shall consider the process of reinventing HR which often involves reengineering the function to improve its effectiveness while reducing cost. We shall also look at the early evolution of the role of HR business partner to the era of 'the strategic business partner' and what this means in terms of HR competencies.

We shall look at:

- HR transformation
- The 'three-legged stool' HR structures
- The role of technology in HR transformation
- Approaches to restructuring HR functions
- Attributes of effective HR functions

LEARNING OBJECTIVES

- To consider options and challenges with respect to HR transformation
- To explore how HR might take on a more strategic role
- To consider the implications for HR skills

INTRODUCTION: THE TRANSFORMATION JOURNEY

The HR function, especially in large organisations, has evolved through a series of distinct yet overlapping phases. Back in the 1980s Personnel/HR typically offered a generalist service, with some training and development alongside the administrative work. Personnel was considered to be doing its job if the basics were consistently and cost-efficiently delivered – employees were paid, pensions where administered, attendance was monitored, and employees were recruited (e.g. cost per hire per employee would be a standard measure for HR) (Ulrich et al. 2015).

Bersin (in CIPD 2015) calls the first transformation phase 'moving from an operational role (the "personnel department") to HR'. The early stages involved improving core aspects of Personnel, for instance administrative work, such as terms and conditions of work, efficient delivery of HR services, and ensuring regulatory compliance. Indeed, for David Guest so little had changed by 1989 that he wrote an article asking – Personnel or HR – can you spot the difference?

The next phase of transformation, which Bersin (in CIPD 2015) calls 'HR as a service centre', began roughly in the early 1990s. HR functions continued to provide generalist service support to line managers but with a growing number of specialists the emphasis shifted to the design of innovative HR micro-practices – in sourcing, compensation or rewards, learning, communication and so on. The Personnel function gradually came to be rebranded as 'Human Resources' and in large complex organisations came to be seen more as a specialist and quite powerful management function (Guest 1989). HR effectiveness and credibility in this phase depended on innovating and the horizontal integration of HR best practices with each other to provide a consistent approach.

In large organisations, especially those with matrix structures, the strategic HR roles were typically concentrated in the corporate centre, with operational support to the line provided through divisional support units. Sometimes these devolved support units reported directly back to the head of HR, and so maintained a strong functional link, while other units reported to the divisional business director, maintaining only a dotted-line relationship with the head of HR.

The 'three-legged stool'

The third phase of HR evolution from the mid-1990s to this day has focused on the connection between integrated HR practices and business success through strategic HR. In this phase, Dave Ulrich's thinking about HR roles (1997) has been highly influential on the theory and practice of HRM especially in global companies. The assumption behind the Ulrich model is that, in order to free up HR to do higher value activities, different delivery models of 'transactional' administrative work should be found, leading to greater efficiency, higher quality and lower costs and responsibility for operational personnel issues should be devolved to line management.

Though the 'Ulrich model' is usually interpreted as a functional design, Ulrich himself insists that he was not describing a set of HR roles, in the sense of jobs, but a set of functions to be carried out. Nevertheless by 2008, of the 80% of organisations which had changed their HR function, 57% had introduced some form of 'Ulrich model' (Reilly 2008). The 'Ulrich model' led to the splitting out of previously integrated generalist HR teams that carried out the full range of HR activities, into what became known as the 'three-legged stool'. This comprises a (small) corporate centre, with service delivery via business partners, centres of expertise and shared services.

Corporate centre

Corporate HR, usually a small team, is responsible for the strategic direction and governance of the function as well as for executive recruitment and pay. The centre can come to be seen as peripheral since most strategic decision-making takes place in the business units. This can be particularly challenging when, for instance, HR attempts to take a corporate perspective on the development of high potential talent, yet business heads are reluctant to share information with the centre that might cause them to lose a 'star' employee to another region. One organisation's approach to resolving such tensions is described in the case study about Dr Candy Albertsson, formerly of BP Amoco in Chapter 12. Similarly, the market nature of relationships within which some HR teams operate can prove a barrier to a meaningful relationship with line managers. Some organisations overcome this difficulty by avoiding internal charging systems.

Business partner

The term 'business partner', already an outmoded term, is used to describe the business-facing roles through which relationships with key business unit stakeholders are built and maintained. Business partners act as internal consultants to business unit leaders and line managers, diagnose needs and commission solutions from former colleagues as suppliers. The aim is to ensure that the business can benefit from focused solutions, delivered in a timely and cost-effective way.

Early implementers of the Ulrich model typically experienced a number of challenges with working it through in practice, not least a lack of practitioner skill development for the changing role. Of course, effective consultancy is a highly skilled process and consultancy skills are now a vital part of an HR professional's toolkit. This set of skills includes relationship management, diagnostic and problem-solving skills as well an insight into organisation development, which enable consultants to take a systemic view to identify appropriate solutions. Yet success as an internal consultant in some ways can be harder to achieve than working as an external consultant since you have a longer-term set of relationships to maintain and also a set of client expectations of your function which can help or hinder what you can achieve.

To some extent, these consultancy-type relationships have left HR with less direct power since the line manager becomes the 'client' to HR's 'supplier'. Service level agreements can reinforce these respective expectations. Indeed, many HR teams resist the term 'business partner' as implying a role of lesser significance than other business roles. Some organisations have preferred to retain a 'rump' of the core Personnel function to provide generalist service delivery while other team members provide internal consultancy.

Centres of expertise/excellence

Specialists working in centres of expertise provide professional support to business partners in mission-critical HR disciplines such as change management, resourcing, learning and development, employee health and well-being, compensation and bonus arrangements. Ad hoc rapid response teams of different specialists are formed to deal with specific situations such as acquisitions or divestitures. In recent years, centres of expertise have generally been regarded as successful, though there can be problems with respect to how these centres interface with the rest of the HR organisation.

Getting HR transactional work 'done differently' – shared services

The third leg of the stool, HR administration, is the ongoing focus of HR transformation to improve the delivery of transactional work, including day to day operational guidance to managers and staff. CIPD research into the changing roles of HR (Reilly 2008) found that CEOs considered the quality of HR processes as HR's weakest area. The challenge is to ensure that transactional work is delivered accurately, efficiently and cost-effectively, or else it undermines HR's credibility and its ability to be seen to add value through more strategic work. Conversely, HR teams who concentrate mostly on administration tend to be criticised as being 'reactive' and are regarded as a cost. Since a key aim of HR teams must be to improve cost-effectiveness and efficiency, as well as business competitiveness and customer service (Ulrich et al. 1995) the paradox must be resolved.

In large organisations operational and administrative functions are often supplied through shared services, internal or through external, or outsourced provision enabled through technology (Reilly 2008). Administration service centres deliver low-cost, highly automated transaction processing and many provide operational support to employees and managers via call centres and help desks. Call centres may or may not be part of the shared services operation. Unisys for instance has established an international on-line service centre which provides HR solutions in a way which meets 'local' as well as corporate requirements.

The structure of HR shared services varies by organisation, especially in a global context and many are being expanded to provide an integrated service – a 'one stop shop' for queries relating to HR, Finance, IT and other service disciplines. However, in international contexts and in many Small- and Medium-sized Enterprises (SMEs) the earlier models of Personnel continued much as before. We shall return to these topics in later chapters.

The early challenges of HR transformation

Finding ways to get HR transactions done differently can be difficult. One of the key challenges to the successful functioning of the HR architecture described above is that it assumes that responsibility for routine aspects of HR delivery will be devolved to line managers.

Devolving to the line

HRM theory suggests that it is line managers who are responsible for implementing human resource management and development on a daily basis, while HR provides policies, processes and support to enable line managers to do this. However, what HR professionals are able to deliver in reality appears to depend on the way their role is perceived by stakeholders within their organisation. Line expectations about what HR is meant to deliver may well be rooted in the 'tea and sympathy' or the service delivery phase of Personnel evolution. As one line manager in a pharmaceutical company announced to his HR colleague when she came to tell him about her change of role; 'Don't tell me you're an internal consultant and here to solve my problems. Since you're leaving me to do my own recruitment, you are my problem'. It is understandable then that many HR teams choose to concentrate on delivering the core processes right without attempting to make a more strategic contribution.

Early adopters of the Ulrich approach often lacked the infrastructure for HR to deliver on its value-adding promise. While support for line managers via information technology could have made it easier for line managers to take on these devolved responsibilities, in practice devolution to the line was frequently hampered by poor or missing technology (e.g. self-service systems, HR information systems, help desks), limited HR technology skills, the extent to which line managers considered people management to be a key part of their role, and the skills and time available to them for people management tasks. Typically, little support was available to line managers to help them develop the skills needed to carry out the devolved HR activities now expected of them.

Moreover HR was often criticised for failing to deliver the basics accurately and quickly. A Personnel Today survey (Burden 2014) found that more than one-third (38%) of HR directors believed their teams spent too long dealing with straightforward requests from line managers which prevented them from playing a more strategic role within their companies. It has been easy over recent years, with the obsession with HR's strategic contribution, to overlook the value managers place on HR doing the bread and butter of people management work. Nearly two-thirds of HR directors said line managers wanted immediate responses to queries and 'are unforgiving if the process takes longer'. Half of line managers surveyed considered they did not have adequate support from HR to be good managers and were left feeling frustrated and their teams left in the dark. Somewhat alarmingly, four in ten said that Google is a better source of HR information than their own HR team (Burden 2014).

Even today, devolution to the line may not work if line managers are unwilling, unable or under-prepared for their personnel responsibilities. Some managers feel that they lack the skills required and prefer the idea that there is a function they can turn to, or blame, if problems occur. Occasionally, too, HR professionals are reluctant to devolve responsibilities to the line for fear of losing professional control and consistency in the way procedures are being implemented. They may lack trust in line managers, so do not give them enough discretion. As a result HR ends up focusing back more on administration than on strategic activity. The tension between HR and line managers can become an obstacle to the smooth implementation of people and business strategies.

To address this issue, HR and the line must find smarter ways of working together. If devolution to the line is to happen effectively, line managers must be equipped for their key roles and the process of devolution needs to be carefully thought through and planned. For instance, it may be better to phase the devolution of some activities to the line rather than simply making line managers responsible for all aspects of 'transactional' HR. It is reasonable to expect that all line managers have responsibility for some core 'people' processes – such as managing performance, communicating well with their teams and developing employees they manage. Preparing line managers well for these tasks may involve management development, providing user-friendly tools, learning groups and manager help – desks to ensure that managers reasonably can be expected to play their part.

The most successful organisations give managers better sight of strategy-aligned HR information, such as reward policies or grading procedures. This enables managers to be clearer with their teams and make decisions more efficiently. The facilitation role of HR is growing in importance and a key focus of this is encouraging and coaching managers to get the most from their staff. Similarly, technology, including applications, can provide managers access to guidance and development on a daily basis. While this allows line managers flexibility, if it is done within a framework of policies, HR remains in control and decides exactly what information their managers have access to.

In smaller organisations in particular, devolution to the line is less pronounced. HR still tends to directly manage or oversee the recruitment and retention of staff and ensures that they have the requisite competencies to do their work.

THE ROLE OF TECHNOLOGY IN HR TRANSFORMATION

Use of technology has the potential to transform HR's capability. For instance HR cloud technology is changing roles within HR, and, it is claimed, has improved operational efficiency and line managers' ability to perform people management activities. This provides the platform for HR business partners to perform a more strategic role. Mohrman, quoted in Weatherley (2005), predicted the contribution of technology could make to different HR roles:

- A personnel services role: transactional self-service processes
- A business support and execution role: HR systems administration; employee and manager tools
- A strategic partner role: business and HR data analysis, modelling and simulation capabilities.

As Bersin (in CIPD 2015) points out, as HR teams move from phase 2 to 3, they focus on driving the effectiveness of talent programmes, so 'quality of hire', 'time to fill', 'training utilisation' and 'leadership pipeline' are measures of success. In phase 3, technology can contribute to building world-class talent programmes and embracing social and network-based technologies that extend the company's brand, connect people, facilitate learning and collaboration, and build leadership.

HR outsourcing, off shoring and in-sourcing

Outsourcing is another potential means of freeing up HR to focus on more value-adding activities. Work that lends itself to being parcelled up as a process is typically a target for being delivered differently, for instance through outsourcing. Technology enables choice – to retain processes in-house or to use some form of external provision via outsourced or 'off-shored' solutions that need take no account of geographical location.

The potential benefits of outsourcing are wide-ranging and include:

- Cost reduction
- Increasing administrative efficiencies
- Access to updated technology
- Reducing risk
- Providing expertise not available internally
- Moving HR up the value chain.

As the use of technology generally, and HR information systems in particular, continues to accelerate, many organisations look to replace fixed costs associated with technology investments with variable costs associated with an outsourcing arrangement. Gaining access to up-to-date technology and the streamlined, simple, proven processes that the outsourcing provider has in place to deliver administrative efficiencies reduces the capital firms have tied up and can re-invest as technological advances dictate. Operational HR roles have been the most endangered as parts of the operation are outsourced. Indeed, some pundits predict that outsourcing most if not all the HR function's delivery is the future of the HR profession.

Outsourcing is not always plain sailing. The media hype surrounding the total business process outsourcing arrangements that various multi-nationals embarked upon a decade or more ago has subsided and outsourcing is often limited to specific elements of HR delivery – training, payroll and resourcing of temporary positions are most commonly outsourced. Many organisations have experienced problems with the quality of outsourced provision and have taken back in-house previously outsourced services such as recruitment that leave HR most exposed if they go wrong.

For those organisations that do decide that outsourcing is an appropriate way forward for them, the transition from in-house provision to outsourced solution requires careful consideration and strong vendor management. The chosen outsource provider should be a good cultural fit, there should be carefully articulated requirements, agreed performance measures and effective contract management to ensure that the arrangement delivers the maximum desired benefits. The typically long-term nature of outsourcing arrangements means that, as important as these contractual arrangements are, it is even more important to build good working relationships with the outsource provider.

SMEs might not consider that they have sufficient volume of activities to benefit from outsourcing arrangements, though some are linking together with other SMEs to pool their administrative activities into one shared service or outsourcing centre to gain the benefits of outsourced arrangements.

However, with respect to transactional HR, the cost of new supply arrangements, has often been greater than anticipated; line managers have frequently been under-prepared for what has been required of them, and the loss of what many HR professionals have considered their heartland has been a source of regret for some.

HR information systems (HRIS)

HRIS – also known as Human Resources Management Systems (HRMS), or Human Capital Management (HCM) software – are now commonplace in large organisations. With a strong technology platform, managers and employees can access help – desks and HR databases. Employee Self-service (ESS) typically enables staff to:

- View and download online payslips
- Add or amend contact details
- Start receiving email notification of payslip availability
- View absence data
- View changes made through the ESS system.

In the United Kingdom, the ESS at Nationwide allows employees to select their own benefits within the total value of the job. The National Health Service (NHS), the UK's largest employer, implemented the 'electronic staff record' (ESR), a national, fully integrated HR and payroll system that is used by all 600-plus NHS organisations. It is used to record and maintain employee information and has a number of 'self-service' modules which enable staff and managers to make changes to the information held. The IT contractors meet with NHS project staff working on the ESR on a daily basis.

Manager Self-service (MSS) can provide line managers with a variety of HR tools, access to information about their subordinates, and the opportunity to analyse information in order to improve their effectiveness. This drives responsibility and decision-making further down the organisation. MSS can ensure that transactional HR services are delivered consistently and that any change request approved by the line manager is within company guidelines. Some companies make available on-line self-sufficiency tools such as internal job posting systems, directories of all employees and their locations/contact details, training courses and other important information.

Human Resource information systems, some of which are Cloud-based, are usually built on People Soft and SAP packages or SaaS Workday platforms. Not surprisingly, companies in the advanced technology sector such as Apple Computers, Unisys and IBM have found innovative technology-based solutions to providing an effective administration service to the line while freeing up HR specialists for more strategic work, such as analysis, leadership development and so on. Hewlett–Packard Enterprises (HPE) have now implemented a Workday platform, which has made HR processes more efficient and includes support for its annual performance and compensation processes. The new platform has already delivered a range of tangible and intangible benefits.

Another driver for reengineering efforts is improving the quality and consistency of HR services. Yet in many companies, traditionally decentralised decision-making about IT systems has led to a plethora of legacy HR and business systems, which do not talk to each other, causing duplication and lost opportunities, especially when carrying out internal talent searches, for example. Reengineering itself can be costly, since the hardware, communications infrastructure and applications software need to be appropriate and require a heavy time commitment from staff involved (consultants, HR and IT staff). They can also feature poorly implemented software and spiralling costs.

Key to making the most of HRIS is appointing an intermediary to bridge the gap between HR and IT teams. Having a special HRIS team to manage the relationship between HR and IT helps close the communication gaps, which can lead to delays in developing and implementing the system.

Where they work well, HRIS do produce the intended benefits. The use of advanced information technology to transform the delivery of routine but important administrative activities is leading to greater efficiency and reduced HR-to-employee ratios. One company completely revamped its separate, people-related systems within a single shared system architecture. People management information was streamlined, automated and integrated. This means that continuous HR process improvements can be easily incorporated, ensuring that the systems continue to be relevant and supportive to managers.

US-based IT networking company Cisco Systems developed a sophisticated intranet system for its own staff which saved about £1.75 million in 'headcount avoidance', or about 30 HR jobs. Another company radically reduced the cycle time in salary planning while increasing accuracy. As we shall discuss in Chapter 7, technology is a vital part of the recruitment process from forecasting needs to identifying suitable candidates. HRIS can help to improve processes and empower line managers. Increasingly, companies are using online, telephone, e-mail and helpdesks to respond to routine enquiries about pay and benefits, medical and retirement plans and other issues where a 'human' response is required. This, of course, brings down the cost-of-service delivery and should allow professionals to concentrate on adding value through knowledge-based, problem-solving activities.

Technology is a key element of enabling change in HR architecture. In TfL the roles of business partners changed from 70:30 administration: strategy to 30:70 since the move to an HR service centre. Assuming that the new processes are correctly targeted, championed from the top and add value, this allows HR professionals to focus on areas where their contribution can significantly move the organisation forward.

APPROACHES TO RESTRUCTURING HR FUNCTIONS

Over the past 20 years, HR transformation has come to be seen for what it is: a means to an end, rather than an end in itself. It is crucially important that HR is set up to be able to address some of the people issues which will affect their organisation's success beyond the short-term. For instance today's global trends suggest that competition for scarce talent is going to increase, that competitive advantage can only be sustained through the skilful deployment and performance of highly talented and engaged employees; therefore, today more than ever should be the era in which HR can make its mark as a contributor to business success. The extent to which strategy has been implemented is a standard measure for HR.

Preparing for HR transformation

For organisations that are considering transforming their existing HR service provision, it is important to first consider existing provision in detail and consider whether you need to change the way you currently operate. If you decide that changes are appropriate, what is the extent of the changes that you need to make? Do you need to introduce wide-ranging transformational changes, or are you actually looking at minor tweaks? (Figure 2.1)

HR teams need the right kinds of 'architecture' to be able to deliver on strategic promises. Issues to consider when restructuring include:

- What do you believe are the strategic priorities?
- How can these be delivered, and by whom?
- What sort of service do clients need as opposed to want?
- What are the relative costs and benefits of different structures?
- If parts of the service are to be outsourced, how will service quality be maintained or improved?
- If the HR organisation is to be made up of separate elements, how can HR professionals develop the experience and skills to transition between different types of HR role?

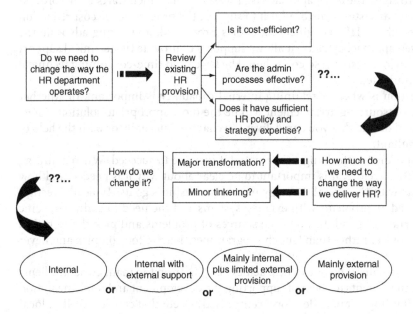

Figure 2.1 HR transformation process (after Reddington et al. 2006).

Arguably the most effective way of reorienting HR to make a more strategic contribution is when the HR team itself reviews what it could contribute as a function, and how it could structure itself, if HR operated in a 'greenfield site'.

Reengineering HR

Reengineering the HR function is a relatively radical option that often occurs as part of general restructure of central functions (see Chapter 4). Hammer and Champy (1993) define reengineering as 'utilizing the power of modern information systems to radically redesign processes in order to achieve dramatic improvement in critical performance measures'. Corporate centres are often thought to hold back individual businesses because of their desire for a common culture, or for system compatibility. Though these contributions are real, they are hard to quantify, and organisations periodically demerge or recentralise functions as a result.

Reengineering involves assessing how work is performed and how processes can be improved. A whole function or just a key HR process can be targeted. Customers' needs must be clearly defined and end-to-end processes, which have the greatest potential for improvement and cost savings identified. Typical process mapping questions include:

- Why is an activity done?
- Why is it done when it is done?
- Why is it done where it is done?
- Why is it done the way it is done?
- Who does it and why?

Yeung and Brockbank (1998) identified two main ways of reengineering HR. One is technology-driven, where an 'off-the-shelf' system package is used and HR processes are redesigned accordingly. The other approach is process driven, which starts with a process redesign and then has systems custom-built to support the process. Since cost reduction is a main driver behind HR reengineering efforts Brockbank and Yeung advocate the technology-driven approach because it allows suppliers to provide the technical support available from previous systems, so costs should be lower and time-consuming technical hitches can be eliminated.

The next question is whether retaining internal capability is important, or whether entering into an outsourcing arrangement will be the most appropriate solution. Alternatively, you might decide that you can deliver the changes internally or with the help of an external consultant.

Winning support for such changes is essential if they are to succeed. When planning to reengineer HR, therefore, it is important to be clear about why it is needed and how reengineering fits with the overall strategy to achieve business goals. Typically, reengineering is triggered by problems with existing systems and the need to address specific goals. It is important to think through the sources of problems and pick the right HR process from the outset rather than launch programmes that are too complex and never get completed.

Setting clear and realistic goals can help achieve buy-in from top management. Clients need to perceive the benefits to them of supporting the development and implementation of new systems. It is important to develop a centralised system that can flex to allow local autonomy and meet the varying needs of the business. Ideally, forming coalitions with internal clients who are champions of change can help create a culture supportive of change within the organisation.

A steering team, usually consisting of senior HR managers, line and MIS managers, is formed at an early stage. This team helps to find out the key concerns of users of the proposed process, works out the problems with the current process, sets new targets for the process and develops an implementation plan. Implementation teams are formed to provide solutions to each of the proposed processes and action plans and milestones are established. Implementation teams need to be held accountable to clear and measurable targets. Monitoring the processes and communicating results helps maintain support for the change.

Reflective activity

- Does your organisation have a clear business strategy?
- Do you have a clear HR strategy that is aligned with your organisation's strategy?
- Is your organisation structured to deliver this strategy?

Case example

A major international utilities company with an American parent, developed a new business strategy to become a global business and needed a global HR function to support this strategy. The existing HR service was mostly traditional Personnel, with local independence and a small mostly non-interventionist corporate centre. The goal was to create a more efficient HR service that could address local issues but also contribute to addressing global challenges, such as sourcing scarce skilled engineers.

A task force was formed comprising the HR team and managers from across the business to consider what might work most effectively and the CEO acted as sponsor. Recognising that HR touches all parts of the business, a systems model by Jay Galbraith's Star Model™ was used to map out some of the changes required and quantify the change impact of what was proposed on the organisation as a whole, particularly on people and culture, and on each of its parts, e.g. numbers of staff affected; how differently people would need to work. The team then identified the main change management issues that would need specific focus and effort during the change process. They did this by running a series of workshops with key stakeholders to share learning from previous changes, identify issues and risks, barriers and enablers as well as critical success factors. They also carried out focus group discussions across the business to gain input and insight into user views of potential improvements and hot spots. This output allowed the design team to identify how ready the organisation was to accept the proposed changes to HR and work out what was needed to both maintain business-as-usual and also to be 'change-ready' and build these actions into their transition plan (Figure 2.2).

Using the Star Model™, they compared how the existing HR function served the needs of the current system ('As Is'), then looked ahead at what would be needed under the global strategy ('To Be') (Figure 2.3).

The HR team's analysis and visioning process also allowed them to understand the size of the gap they needed to bridge and adjust timings and sequencing of activities in the change plan accordingly. They were also able to identify potential obstacles to enacting their vision and address these through their plan. They identified what needed to be done to maintain business-as-usual while moving to the new organisation. By creating

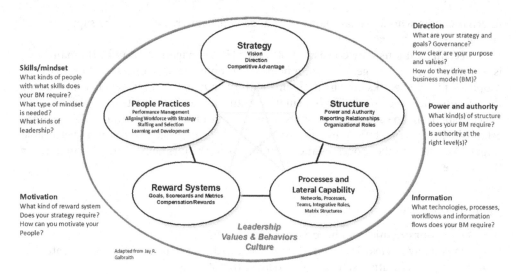

Direction
What are your strategy and goals? Governance?
How clear are your purpose and values?
How do they drive the business model (BM)?

Skills/mindset
What kinds of people with what skills does your BM require?
What type of mindset is needed?
What kinds of leadership?

Power and authority
What kind(s) of structure does your BM require?
Is authority at the right level(s)?

Motivation
What kind of reward system Does your strategy require?
How can you motivate your People?

Information
What technologies, processes, workflows and information flows does your BM require?

Figure 2.2 Assessing organisation effectiveness using Galbraith's Star Model™.

People

• Future HR capabilities have been defined and performance levels agreed • Capability assessment has been completed • A programme to develop HR capability has been agreed but not implemented • Still failing to deliver on HR basics • Managers still uncertain of impact of HR transformation on them	• HR Business and Specialists will have developed new capabilities in strategy & change management, consulting skills and project management • HR delivers to high standards on the HR Partners and Specialists influence at a strategic level HR professionals valued for their business skills as much as their technical skills

Structure

• Global Functions in place for business-facing and specialist areas – there is acceptance of this approach but it is too soon to say whether it is working well • HR is now organised around Partners, Specialists and Shared Services – although the Partner roles aren't fully operational • Opportunities to outsource have been initiated	• HR aligned to the new business structure • Specialists have a global role • Hand-offs within HR resolved • A smaller HR Function of less than 200 people (from 450) • Outsourcing options agreed and early outsourcing opportunities taken • HR operates effectively as one global team

Processes & Policies

• We still need to be clearer about which processes and policies need to be global • Global employment principles have been developed but are not yet embedded – where they are reflected in HR practices it is more through default than intent. More work needed • Function moving towards fit for purpose global processes	• Boundary between global and local has been agreed • A clearly articulated global reward philosophy is in place • A global employment framework is in place and being used • HR processes are fit for purpose – transparent, simple and consistent and understood by HR and Line users • HR processes aligned to new HR information systems

Technology

• SAP chosen as global back-office system – blueprint for development still being defined/outsourcing options being considered • Areas for workflow have been defined but not yet implemented • Web-enabled HR route-map defined • Integration with non-HR systems defined • Common data standards/definitions agreed	• Global HR back office system fully implemented • Web-enabled tools implemented for all areas in business case • E-learning embedded throughout the organisation • HR systems integrated with non-HR systems • Common HR reporting and decision-support capability implemented • Employee and Manager self service phase 1 delivered

Figure 2.3 Worked example – Assessing progress of global HR transformation.

a shared vision for the proposed change with some urgency they were able to align key stakeholders around the proposal.

They tracked progress toward the new design at regular intervals by using this emerging blueprint to assess progress towards the 'To be' and understand the benefits of what was being achieved. Though it was expected that the transformation would take two years in fact the bullet points above show what was achieved within a year.

Reflective activity

- Looking at what was achieved in the first year of transformation ('To Be'), what do you think should follow next to successfully implement the new HR service?

Making the most of HRIS

As in the case above, once the processes have been reengineered, additional training is generally required to help staff, line managers and HR professionals use the new processes effectively. Training can overcome one of the commonest pitfalls, which is that users do not understand the new system. Some resistance can be anticipated since reengineering can also present risks to existing systems and threats to jobs. The level of psychological resistance should not be underestimated. In the NHS, training for ESR users was designed in consultation with staff whose preferred method of training was classroom based. Training was designed on that basis, but a blended approach was also adopted, including an element of e-learning, to overcome travel difficulties for some staff. E-learning is also evolving with training packages moving away from long videos to shorter clips, viewable via mobile technology.

Various organisations evaluate the impact of technology on HR processes using customer satisfaction ratings as a measure of success. Aviva examines the accuracy of data entry in order to assess improvements and at Transport for London (TfL), HR services have set service level agreement targets (such as response time for answering calls, and the time it takes to close a case), which are measured daily using the new technology.

The ongoing challenges of HR transformation

CIPD research suggests that the very process of HR transformation itself runs the risk of creating something of an 'own goal' for HR effectiveness. So much time, effort and expenditure are typically put into transformation that HR can become too internally or overly focused on 'ideal' HR processes and roles with the effect that practitioners become 'cleverer at being HR'; as a result they run the risk of losing sight of client needs and business relevance. Pragmatic and gradual shifts of role may be more effective than leaping into complete restructuring in pursuit of an 'ideal' delivery model. As one respondent advises: 'do not worry about the theory, worry instead about what the business needs and what you currently have'.

What happens to HR careers?

Another question for HR functions that have separated out into different roles is what an HR career looks like. Segmenting HR into business partners, service centres and areas of expertise can create silos and for HR specialists who may find themselves in only one 'leg' of the 'three-legged stool', for instance managing an outsourced call centre/help-desk, career development may be very different from that of a business partner for whom progression may be more obviously towards HR director roles. Some will choose to specialise in service management. Others may want to move into specialist areas and focus on OD, L&D or Reward. For others this will be a route to becoming an HR Director. The structure should not become an inhibitor to lateral movement of transferable talent. Projects and secondments provide a good opportunity for HR talent to work on business improvement ideas and so expand their skillset and reputations.

Lack of teamwork

Similarly, the move to transform HR by creating business partner roles and using various 'arm's length' solutions, such as outsourcing, shared service centres and help desks can result in complicated and overwhelming structures with duplications of effort throughout (Ekhtiari 2018) and may restrict the amount of real teamwork across the function as a whole. In the early days, debates raged between HR colleagues about who 'owned' the 'client' – business partners acting as internal consultants, or those who supplied the service.

If excellence is being developed in each of the channels, the challenge for a fragmented HR function is to act as organisational role model on cross-functional learning and sharing of good practice.

And yet ... there are benefits

Despite the 'growing pains' of HR transformation, the benefits of change are more evident and much learning has taken place about what works in real contexts. For instance, there is growing recognition that higher-level skills are required for HR roles today than in the past. These days, implementers of the 'three-legged stool' approach have tended to put in place training and development to help business partners understand their role and equip them for it. Typically, the number of business partners has been trimmed down to focus on key internal business relationships and challenges. 'Strategic business partners', usually HR directors, manage the most senior relationships and take an overview role about where value needs to be added. Some HR functions have retained or reinstated a rump of HR generalist support provided directly to business units in the traditional way, or via shared services. Better preparation of line managers for their role is helping free up business partners to add value.

In many organisations, shared services have developed so effectively that they are now able to operate, as in the case of Fujitsu Services, as a profit centre, providing outsourced HR solutions to other companies.

Case: HR transformation at Fujitsu Services

I featured the case of HR transformation in Fujitsu Services (formerly ICL) in the last edition of this book. At the time HR was emerging from a period of major transformation which has resulted in HR being at the top table. In the years since Fujitsu ceased to be a manufacturer of computer mainframes and moved to being a professional services company there was a clear recognition that the company's only real asset is people and that margin is to be gained through the intellectual property they represent. Therefore being able to identify, develop and retain talent was right at the top of the CEO's priorities and at the heart of business strategy. Resourcing and talent management were therefore central to HR strategy.

During those years of transformation, the company was almost completely reengineered, roles were changed and the skillsets required for success changed too. Role distinctions between technical and programme management were broken down and a key requisite therefore for anyone working in Fujitsu Services was the ability to adapt and potentially be mobile. At the same time the organisation had a strong task culture which could sometimes cause teamwork and relationship tensions and could potentially lead to employee relations problems. In such circumstances, HR had a key role to play in coaching senior managers, building effective relationships and leveraging expertise. In particular, HR had to 'walk the talk' through facilitating and acting as beacons of expertise within the business.

In common with many organisations, the HR team at Fujitsu Services concluded that HR's contribution to business was hard to quantify and assess, but that did not stop HR paying attention to what appeared to matter most. Typical measures of HR contribution included:

- Attrition
- Failed recruitment
- Benchmarking, e.g. costs of recruitment, rewards, ratios HR: line
- IIP accreditation – which was seen as key to access to government bids.

In transforming HR, Fujitsu's business partner model was based on demand-pull. So HR operated principally as an internal consultant. This meant having to deal with ambiguity in order to find the right solution for the client. This required viewing the business as a customer rather than a partner and translating the business strategy into the HR agenda. It also required HR professionals to move away from HR jargon to 'business speak', underpinned by a deep understanding of what the business is about and where it is going.

HR transactions were user-friendly and there was a deliberate simplification of processes following a major review of all services from the user perspective. Employees could access Internet-based forms for calculating their pensions, for example. They could also update their own personal information so that employees can guarantee its integrity.

To achieve this transformation required training for all HR practitioners, resulting in customer-friendly teams. The HR Academy training programme included a series of modules covering the whole employment cycle. The role of business partner was understood by all as being about distilling best practice in HR and 'finessing' it in the way the organisation could understand and use it. The business partner role was seen as making sure that HR delivered to tough service level agreements, as well as delivering on internal projects. The focus was on identifying problems, aligning initiatives, focusing on the benefits to be delivered to the organisation as well as on direct interventions, in the client's language and focused on their problem.

Given the ongoing growth of Fujitsu Services through acquisition, change management was a key responsibility of business partners and a range of tools and methods were applied to achieve effective integration. Use of a change network map helped clarify key roles and responsibilities for sponsors and change agents. Force field analysis and behavioural profiling were just two of a range of other tools in regular use which helped focus effort appropriately. These helped all concerned take a strategic approach to organisational design and development. Behavioural profiling, for instance, was a means of creating culture audits. It was then possible to decide the target profile of the new organisation and the initiatives required to achieve that. So great was the accumulated skill in the HR team regarding workforce transfers and change management that HR itself was able to offer valued services as a part of client bids and became a profit centre.

In switching from a product-based economy to a people-based economy, Fujitsu Services was at the forefront of knowledge-intensive organisations in coming to grips with a new business model fit for the twenty-first century. The people-based economy greatly enhanced the importance of HR to the business. HR's ability to effectively manage change and to build talent strategies that work puts it rightly at the top table.

In more recent times Fujitsu has deliberately fostered a rewarding workplace culture that encourages learning, with a major focus on helping employees acquire digital skills. Design thinking is positioned as a component of digital literacy and is used to establish skills and behaviours to provide support for Fujitsu customers' businesses and to innovate within the company.

A learning platform supports the growth of all employees at all times, no matter where they are. The content is constantly updated with a wide variety of internal and external information and courses. For example, 'Edge Talk' videos feature stories of practical knowledge shared by personnel who are experts in specific fields at Fujitsu and domestic group companies, and promote internal company learning which transcends organisational boundaries, so employees can learn from each other.

Fujitsu also values careers. Each employee's autonomous career development is supported through the Career Ownership Program and career counselling that are attuned to employees' aspirations. The firm is increasing opportunities for career choices, including significantly expanding the internal posting system from 2020 to make open positions available to the entire Fujitsu Group, enabling all employees to take up the challenge and apply for these positions. Through one-on-one dialogue, supervisors provide specific advice and support to their subordinates, based on their career aspirations and characteristics. Fujitsu is also providing specific career support for senior-level personnel. Through these efforts, Fujitsu aims to increase the mobility and diversity of its human resources and ensure that the right people are in the right places.

Reflective activity

- Bersin (in CIPD 2015) describes the third phase of transformation as transition to HR focused on 'driving talent outcomes'. With reference to Bersin's 3 phases of HR transformation described earlier, where does this case study sit?

MORE RECENT PERSPECTIVES ON TRANSFORMING HR OPERATING MODELS

HR structures continue to occupy column inches in the HR press. While the Ulrich model has been refined and remains current in many large organisations, the challenge is to work out what form of HR organisation is right for your business. The shape and content of HR organisation and practice, including strategy, will need to reflect the changing trends for technology in the workplace. With the advent of digital, the next phase of HR transformation is becoming ever more urgent. HR will need to prepare for the short- and long-term effects of technology on culture, and the design of work. To enable this focus, the aim should be to strike the right balance between strategic and operational, ensuring both effective delivery in the short-term and also longer-term organisational capability building.

Digital

The latest wave of transformation is technology driven, with cloud computing and new providers generating a major investment in HR technology. This is driving the requirement for HR to become a more data-driven function so that HR data can be used to influence business decisions and ultimately fulfil the long aspired to role of a strategic partner. However, Sage research (Burrin 2020) finds that technology adoption is slow, with just 46% of HR teams having adopted modern HR technologies in recent years. Only just over a third of HR leaders have adopted new ways of working such as flexible working, data-driven decision-making and continuous performance management.

Moreover, the new systems bring their own risks with respect to HR delivering value. They are end-user focused (employee and manager), not specifically designed for experts (HR professionals) – and with new generations of computer users at work, these end-users have higher technology expectations than ever. In other words, this transformation wave will only succeed when it meets the requirements of employees and managers. We shall return to the topic of digital HR in Chapter 4.

Despite the transformation journey, in many cases HR still experiences ongoing internal and external stakeholder pressures to add value. Even where HR manages to free itself up to carry out a more strategic role, the HR function still struggles to focus on strategic matters beyond immediate business planning cycles, even though many of today's challenges in the competition for talent require longer-term solutions, as research by Lawler and Mohrman (2003) and Lawler (2015) concluded. There are many possible reasons for this, not least the politics and power relationships as well as the skills and credibility of the HR team itself. We shall consider these issues in later chapters.

While the internal consultancy of business partners does provide value at local level it alone is not enough to enable HR professionals to really add value to the organisation. Part of the problem is that the more highly client-focused you are, the more likely it is that you will be delivering solutions that fix that particular client's immediate problem, perhaps at the expense of corporate needs. Typically, internal clients of HR are interested in solving problems that affect them in the short term; they are less interested in what they fear will be the over-engineered corporate solution, which is delivered too late to be of real use. There is also the human tendency to reject solutions that are 'not invented here'.

Consequently, internal consultants can often find themselves chasing local issues where the business head has seen a 'people problem' and tried to fix it. It can be hard to challenge a powerful player who perceives you to add value only if you do what they say. The focus on short-term issues then gets in the way of being able to produce the bigger wins for the organisation in equipping it for its future challenges because you are too busy focusing on, or repairing damage in, the short term.

The vicious cycle of lots of activity without clear strategic goals can lead to ineffectiveness. Many commentators argue that the business partner model has failed to deliver its promise, and some have advocated separating HR's transactional/operational roles from the strategic roles. The real value that can be added through HR, including the development of effective workforce planning, talent management and succession strategies, and strategic recruitment for the organisation as a whole, can get dissipated at business group level, and make it difficult to create breakthroughs on significant issues. Indeed, Dave Ulrich (1997) challenged HR professionals to distinguish between the 'doables' that represent day-to-day activity without reference to more strategic goals and the 'deliverables', or activities with a real purpose, which will make a real difference to the business and organisation.

Organising HR for a potential strategic contribution

Various pundits in recent years have suggested that a more radical functional redesign may be necessary to exploit HR's potential critical strategic contribution to improving organisational effectiveness. This involves continually improving the context in which people work – culture, processes, leadership, capability and so on – and not just focusing on individuals and teams. Lawler (2005) for instance recommends creating a new, separate unit that focuses on organisational effectiveness. Similarly, Lambert and Newall (2016) argue that HR should become a slimmer, higher calibre, organisational effectiveness function working with the leadership team and managers on the full range of their strategic and tactical responsibilities for people policies, practices and performance.

Henley Business School (Scott-Jackson and Mayo 2016) propose that the HR function in large organisations could in future comprise three distinct entities – delivery, expert and strategy – each of which would require different skills. The leader of the delivery function would require many of the skills needed to manage any delivery/process management function such as capabilities in people-related process design, technology, business understanding, account management/customer service, digital expertise, data analytics, process management, project management, communications, effective procurement and supplier management.

The leader of an expert function would have capabilities in people-related issues, such as engagement, well-being and retention. The leader of the strategy function would have expertise in developing strategy and designing capabilities from organisational strategy. Such leaders would typically have developed these skills by rotating in and out of HR and other business roles throughout their career.

People operations

Farrer (2019) suggests that a People Ops function could be set up alongside HR or as part of a unified HR and Operations function which would be responsible for the engagement and development of employees. Farrer argues that People Ops aims to understand employees holistically as individual contributors and is about designing work so that they want to be there – present, engaged and proud of what they do – while the traditional HR mindset views people more as a resource to be calculated and managed for efficiency. People Ops, it is argued, would benefit first the employee, then, and as a result, the company as a whole. A People Ops director would be responsible for:

- Project Management – Tracking the deadlines, bandwidth and production pace of their workforce.

- Rituals – From slackbots to stand-ups, facilitating check-ins without interrupting productivity.
- Culture Development – Strengthening interpersonal relationships of the team is crucial.
- Employee Loyalty – Keeping staff happy and healthy by preventing isolation with employee appreciation strategies will drastically improve profit margins.
- Change Management – Ensuring new practice implementation goes smoothly in both the people and the processes.
- Goal Setting – Setting and managing the Objectives and Key Results (OKRs) and KPIs of individuals, two of the most crucial elements of the business.

Ram Charam (2014) argues that since people create value, not organisations, a powerful triumvirate of the CHRO, CFO and CEO should work closely together on strategic people issues, with the CHRO in particular becoming a close adviser to the CEO and the Board. This would require the CHRO to release time-consuming activities such as the transactional and administrative work of HR, including managing benefits, which could be reassigned to the Finance function. Eventually, process management across functional areas may become centralised and integrated to include, for example, financial and people processes. HR administrative functions would then be better placed in a combined Operations or Corporate Services function along with Finance – leaving strategic HR to concentrate on adding value via change management expertise.

'High impact' HR

Phase 4 of Bersin's (2015) model of HR evolution is that of high impact HR. This is where HR supports the business directly and locally and the operating model is less centralised and more 'co-ordinated but distributed' into the business. HR teams able to operate this way have built credibility through a strong track record of HR service delivery capability and have spent three to five years optimising their talent programmes. And these programmes don't sit still; they are continuously improved.

Reflective activity

- Which of these and other HR architectures/operating models do you consider would be most appropriate in your organisation?
- What are the implications for the roles and responsibilities of HR professionals?
- To what extent do you think it would be a good idea to set up a People Ops organisation, separate from HR, to focus specifically on employee needs?
- In what ways can managers and HR specialists work more closely to link strategy and HR practice?

Of course, creating an HR organisation that can add strategic value does not happen overnight or in a vacuum. In the last edition of this book, I described the HR transformation process in Microsoft UK led by Dave Gartenberg, previously HR Director of Microsoft's UK organisation. I feature it again, slightly updated, as an example of how structures can be adapted and improved to enhance service delivery and also make it possible for HR professionals to develop their careers.

Case: building HR strategic capability at Microsoft UK

Dave Gartenberg had a clear vision for HR. He believed that HR should be a driving force in the business, helping it hit its potential through its employees and leaders. For Dave, HR's critical success factors included:

- Exploiting (getting the best from) talent
- Reducing the need for external hires
- People being able to grow and have work–life balance
- People feeling they have made a difference.

Dave valued the Ulrich model but recognised when he arrived at Microsoft UK in 2005 that even the transactional work was not being done well. Drawing on his previous experience in the chemicals industry, Dave introduced a deep process orientation, using principles from Total Quality Management and Six Sigma. Having mapped key transactional HR processes, the team improved them and thereby managed to reduce some of the dissatisfaction with HR. This was a stepping-stone to higher value-added contributions. An HR shared service centre was formed which pulled much of the administrative work off the generalists' plate so it could be redeployed to higher value-added spaces (as well as improving the cycle times for employee requests for the administrative support).

The next stage was to find out how HR could help the business to grow. Dave introduced the role of Organizational Development Director to the team and created roles for Business Partners whose roles were to understand the business drivers and goals, identify the barriers to success and use HR levers to help the business achieve success. At the same time, Dave introduced an ongoing programme of formal and informal on-the-job development for the HR team, helping them to develop business acumen and consultancy skills.

Even so, Dave recognised that as the team developed, the organisational design for HR was still not right. For business partners, being an end-to-end generalist for the client groups meant that the ability to focus on any one part of the HR agenda was seemingly random. Too much effort was still being put into transactional and generalist HR, with the effect that more strategic initiatives were being starved of time and attention.

Dave recognised that demand for the work of the HR consultants could at times be a bit unpredictable. Similarly, there was no easy way for resources to flow across businesses when there were seemingly random (but consistent) spikes in HR issues in the businesses since in the 'intact' team design it was very difficult to move resources from one business to others. As a result, there was not always consistent alignment between what the client's needs were and the Career Stage Profile (level) of the generalist in that business. For HR professionals, the levelling and career path within HR was seemingly random. Nor was HR consistently challenging managers and business leaders to establish and help drive a strategic HR plan that is aligned and supports the business.

Accordingly, Dave's new design took into account both the needs of the business and the career development needs of HR professionals. He and his team came to the conclusion that they needed to divide the HR work into two areas. In terms of responsibilities, a simple way to describe the split is that the 'consultants' will drive front line manager capability and resolve employee issues, and the 'business partners' will work with the leadership teams on the overall HR agenda and strategy. Responsibilities look like this.

The second change was how the team was organised. The consultants were formed into one team, which allowed for many benefits but the most significant were (1) giving

Table 2.1 HR team member responsibilities

HR consultants	HR business partners
The focus of the role is to work with employees and front line managers – the kind of activities that tend to be more immediate in nature, and very problematic if not done exceptionally well	The focus of the role is to work with managers and their leadership teams – the kind of activities that tend not to be as urgent in nature, but critically important to the longer-term health and capability of the organisation
Front line manager induction and onboarding	Leadership team (LT) induction and onboarding
Manager coaching	Leadership coaching
Employee relations and performance issues	Leadership team effectiveness
Trends and statistics in employee relations	People review
Initiating the recruitment process for information technology positions	Talent management
Redundancy situations	Work with leadership teams to define HR priorities/agenda
Shared responsibilities	
• On interview loops for all people manager openings. Providing feedback on manager competencies	
• Review model implementation	

one team line of sight to the manager capability issues which could help the team identify root causes, and (2) allowing for a critical mass under one manager who could easily see where the peaks and troughs in demand were and flow the resources accordingly. So the consultants had a primary alignment to organisations but knew they would receive back-up when peaks hit their business, and conversely, they would back up their peers when they were lacking 'bandwidth'. As a result, HR and line managers had the benefit of deep understanding of given business areas but the capacity was available in the design to ensure a high degree of flexibility and responsiveness.

The generalists who were switching client groups and/or roles met with the people taking over the responsibilities. During these handovers they covered issues like:

- Key business issues facing business units (BU)
- A walk-through BU organisation chart
- Key people in the organisation
- Any employee relations issues in the works
- Which managers are either new and/or not (yet) strong.

Business partners were a ring-fenced resource to help drive BU HR plans and constructively challenge BU leadership teams with respect to discussions about people, organisation and culture. This allowed for a more strategic approach to a variety of key talent and organisational issues. For Microsoft this model proved very useful and has been applied elsewhere.

In more recent times, service delivery in Microsoft is via an AI-based HR support platform, where employees will be able to self-service HR questions 24/7 without call centre support. This 'Modern HR' will help employees to complete tasks as quickly and seamlessly as possible so they can get back to their jobs with an enhanced employee experience. From seemingly simple efforts like automating travel letters to more complex solutions like helping employees find answers to specific HR issues, PowerApps, such as AskHR, LUIS-based bots and Microsoft SharePoint are critical to creating a Modern HR experience. With each employee interaction, the AI gets smarter.

For HR teams in companies like Microsoft going through a digital transformation and as the world of work evolves, culture is a hot topic and an important focus area. The cultural change is towards a 'Growth Mindset', shifting from a company that 'knows it all', to one focused on curiosity and learning, which, it is believed, will drive insight and innovation. Technology can help accelerate culture change through collaboration tools like Yammer and Teams where leaders and employees can share and nurture company culture. Real-time telemetry surveys track employee sentiment and enable employees wherever they are located to connect with monthly Q&A sessions led by the Microsoft CEO. At the same time, analytics tools like Workplace Analytics and PowerBI help leaders track progress and gain insights into their culture change so that it is easier to know where to focus next.

Reflective activity

- What examples did you find in this case study of HR delivering strategic value?
- What were the key enablers of this happening?

ATTRIBUTES OF AN EFFECTIVE HR FUNCTION

HR practitioners can and do adopt a range of roles, variously described as strategist, mentor, talent scout, architect, builder, facilitator, coordinator and champion of change. The art is to have awareness of, and flexibility for what is needed in different situations. Many an HR strategist takes up a new role in an organisation that is apparently ripe for change but meets with deeply embedded practices that are difficult to shift. The strategist usually experiences great frustration as he or she sees their attempts to bring about change wither away. The pragmatist works within this context to make change happen at the pace which is likely to lead to the embedding of new approaches, rather than seeking to bring about widespread initiatives in order to make their mark.

A CIPD (2019) inquiry into the *Future of HR* highlighted the following attributes of effective HR functions:

- Specialist and expert: uses deep insight and expertise across the business and employee life cycle, to target positive outcomes and get the best from people.
- Informed by data: has high standards and good principles when collecting and analysing data and uses it in an insightful and evidence-based way, to inform people and business decisions.
- Focused on solutions: operates in an internal consultant/change agent capacity, asking pertinent questions and diagnosing issues and solutions to bring about the most appropriate results. Sees opportunities and helps the business to unlock these.

- Agile: highly flexible and dynamic in response to any situation and able to act at speed where necessary. Builds agility and resilience into the workforce and the design of the organisation.
- Aligned to the business: works closely with the business, understanding commercial and operational realities and being financial astute. Has the ability to see issues from every angle and apply great business judgement.

The CIPD study concluded that, while there is no single future HR operating model that will apply in organisations of different sizes and contexts, good HR functions will need the following:

- Principled function leader: ensuring ethical ways of working with, for example, technology and employment models. Upholds organisational values.
- Partnership with CEO and functions: aligned to the business and uses strategic and influencing skills. Asks insightful and challenging questions.
- Consistent compliance: consistency and professionalism in compliance and administrative tasks, providing a strong platform for more strategic work.
- Deep understanding of people (employees, customers, partners) and the culture that is required to support motivation, well-being and business success.
- On-demand access to specialists: on-demand access across the business to highly focused and selective centres of expertise.
- Innovation in areas of opportunity: highly context driven and organised, to operate in and capitalise on, the areas of biggest opportunity for the organisation, such as compliance, technology, data and skill development.
- Empowered line: partnering, coaching and facilitating operational and front-line management to deliver the people strategy. Developing great people managers through a distributed model.

How these components are delivered (through internal and external partnerships) and what is appropriate will depend on the specific focus of the business and on having an enabling context.

HR competencies

The skills of HR practitioners are key to the effective development and implementation of people strategies. And there is no shortage of HR competency models. SHRM for instance carried out research with HR professionals in 33 countries and identified nine competency categories: Communication; Relationship management; Ethical practice; HR expertise (HR knowledge); Business acumen; Critical evaluation; Global and cultural effectiveness; Leadership and navigation; Consultation. A SHRM/Ulrich survey concluded that strategic contribution accounted for 43% of HR's total impact on business performance. Specifically, successful HR professionals focus on culture management, facilitate rapid change while simultaneously eliminating 'low-value work and information clutter', and identify problems central to business strategy while suggesting alternative solutions.

The CIPD identified 9 professional areas and four bands for HR's professional map: Organisational design; Organisational development; Resourcing and talent planning; Learning and talent development; Performance and rewards; Employee engagement; Employee relations; Service delivery; Information.

Certain competency areas stand out from all these maps:

Business acumen

If HR is to truly act as a business partner, specialists need to really understand the business and be able to reflect that understanding in their actions. This of course requires business knowledge, organisational analysis and what the CIPD describes as 'business acumen'. This goes beyond knowing the nature of a particular business and its sector, markets, operations, processes, finance and technology. It also entails 'the ability to apply that knowledge—contributing to strategic decision making, developing competitive cultures, making change happen fast, and creating market-driven connectivity'.

Consultancy skills

Basic consultancy skills, such as gaining entry and diagnosis, should be part of the professional toolkit. This requires client servicing and relationship skills, influencing ability of a high order – to be a good listener, effective persuader and negotiator – and facilitation skills. Consultants need good 'human' attributes and skills such as empathy, compassion, emotional intelligence, knowledge of diversity and inclusion issues, coaching and more.

Bringing about change

Perhaps the core expertise lies in managing ongoing change and working with managers to develop a robust and resilient workforce able to thrive on change. HR professionals also need to be able to understand and manage culture, recognising what needs to be maintained, strengthened or changed, as well as manage the change process. The skills of bringing about change extend beyond being able to take a longer-term view. Organisational design and development, project management skills and the ability to work successfully in cross-boundary teams are essential to effective delivery of outcomes. HR teams need to be able to cope well with change and help others to do so.

Bringing about change requires HR specialists to be able to influence key players and to have the confidence to challenge. This means being politically aware and being prepared to use various forms of influence, including power, to get the job done. Of course, the most easily available form of power is personal power, which stems largely from an individual's personality. This kind of power is reflected in being respected as a professional, being a team player and being the kind of person who is trusted and to whom people at all levels can turn.

Micro-practice specialist expertise

Today's HR managers are expected to deliver in HR's micro-practice areas such as staffing, career planning services and internal communications, so a broad skillset is vital. For this they need a sound grounding in the classic and emerging HR functional knowledge areas – underpinned by an understanding of related theory. While HR generalists do not need to be experts, they should be able to use creative approaches to designing HR processes that really meet needs.

Able users of technology

MIT research (in Jacobs 2016) suggests that technology is dissolving boundaries between HR and Marketing, for instance being able to articulate their organisation's value propositions and brand as an employer through compelling stories, what Bersin calls the 'consumerisation of HR'. HR professionals are expected to use technology to deliver HR services and to shift from 'transaction processing to strategic functioning'. In this regard, technology's impact is more in time savings than cost savings.

This is emerging as a very important HR competency as HR professionals get involved in the broad field of information management. Three levels of such involvement may be differentiated. At the most basic level, HR professionals should be able to leverage the human resource information system to track talent, enable employees to manage their benefits, enable supervisors to access real-time employee performance and other related data, and to provide on-line basic training programmes. Increasingly, they must also be able to apply predictive analytics to answer important HR questions such as: What factors predict the likelihood of key talent leaving? What factors predict the kind of leaders who are most likely to optimise key talent? (Ulrich and Brockbank 2015)

Credibility

Which traits might be more critical than others may depend on the leader, the company, its culture and context. However, above all, professionals need to be personally credible. They need courage – to stand up for what is right, and prove it – and resilience – patience, calmness and persistence. For SHRM, credibility is based on HR managers establishing a successful track record with HR counterparts and business line managers whom they serve. It can be argued that personal credibility and delivering the HR basics are the foundation stone for HR professionals to be allowed to contribute at the strategy table, but if they stop there, they waste their potential strategic contribution.

HR leadership

For Ulrich and Brockbank (2005), an HR perspective that is both unique and powerful is one that establishes the linkages between employee commitment, customer attitudes and investor returns. Part of the art of the HR business partner is knowing when to take the lead in initiating a new people-related process and when to begin by building line ownership; how to build the corporate from the local and vice versa. This means that HR must be proactive - on the look-out for useful initiatives that have begun elsewhere in the organisation which can be built on in order create greater coherence and avoid 'death by a thousand initiatives'. Also, HR should be willing to take the initiative to identify opportunities and solutions, suggest ideas and draw up business cases to support them. Good data analytical skills are important and ability to use relevant metrics, understand the implications of trend data and to make a convincing case are all part of the HR toolkit.

While such a list may seem daunting, Bersin (2015) argues that the HR team itself does need to have all of these competencies. For what he calls 'high-impact' HR, specialist skills should be brought into the business where they can drive the most value. Bersin talks about these as 'networks of expertise' because of how highly connected the specialists are despite being aligned with and embedded in different parts of the business.

Reflective activity

Where are you now in terms of your HR function?

- How much does IT play a part in your overall HR strategy?

- Who will champion reengineering efforts?
- In what ways could reengineered processes be superior to existing ones?
- In moving from operational to strategic, how should the gap be filled, and by whom?
- If you devolve aspects of HR to the line, how do you maintain consistency?
- How should line managers be prepared for their role?

CONCLUSION

We have discussed how HR functions need to systematically assess and improve all basic HR processes in order to increase efficiency and effectiveness. HR Operations should be managed, monitored and measured in the same way any other business process would be. Transforming HR and prioritising the HR agenda requires stepping out of the vicious cycle of constant delivery in order to choose the key areas of focus if value is really to be added. Winning the right to contribute strategically comes from credibility earned by delivering results.

While line management is responsible for the growth and operation of the business, HR has a key role to play in partnering with the line to prepare the organisation and its employees for future challenges. So while day-to-day people management is mainly the responsibility of line managers, the HR function's unique selling point (USP) should be its ability to develop healthy and effective organisations, with the right people, with the right skills, working in the right ways to achieve the right results. This is where HR operational effectiveness has to be reinforced by a strategic perspective. This requires strategic thinking, a tolerance of ambiguity and a willingness to take risks. This strategic yet practical orientation should be reflected in HR's working practices, mindsets and skillsets.

As we have discussed, HR value and the merits of HR transformation continue to be called into question. Critics have seen the function as overly process-oriented, fad-prone, insufficiently business-focused, poor at customer service and timid in the face of challenges (Lambert and Newall 2017). Whether HR transformation is producing the right results, or advancing as quickly as it might, is up for debate. According to Jacobs (2016), less than 20% of all HR transformation programs produce the aspired to results. Moreover, the process of HR transformation often tends to be expensive and poorly executed.

Certainly the more strategic contribution expected of HR has been slow to materialise. This has led many commentators to question whether HR's future is essentially transactional, or whether HR is capable of a more strategic contribution and what value this would bring. After all, according to Scott-Jackson and Mayo (2016: 16), HR currently falls between two stools: 'What has happened, in the urge to be strategic, and in the development of distributed technology, is that the original "employee champion" role, the "human face" of HR, has diminished. What has developed are call centres for queries, and "business partners" preoccupied with management or process issues. No longer would anyone join HR because they "liked working with people"'.

Similarly, Marchington (2008: 4) argues that this has led to a neglect of what is distinctive about people management: its understanding of a range of stakeholder needs, its attempt to balance the competing demands of different constituents and its ability as a profession to solve problems rather than merely provide answers others want to hear. So will the next phase of HR evolution feature both strategy and tactics, people and technology? The question is, should HR evolve, or transform itself further to meet the challenges of the ever-changing context. We shall consider more recent developments in HR transformation in Chapter 5.

At this point, the HR function has the potential to develop further, moving beyond HR management to more of a leadership role, given that HR's core contribution relates to culture, processes and that most precious asset of all, people. HR's primary functions include finding tailored ways to attract and retain much-needed talent, to design systems, structures, roles and processes that allow talent to be well deployed and utilised, to develop management and leadership capability and capacity and to build organisational climates and cultures that can be a source of sustainable competitive advantage. This USP should form the basis of a proactive leadership contribution from HR – if HR is ready to take the opportunity.

Adding to already complex HR agendas, the latest challenge involves defining what lies within the scope of the HR role. So should CSR, ethics, environmental policies, organisational development, work–life balance, internal communications, employer branding all be part of the HR agenda? Arguably yes. It could also be argued that all HR functions will need to demonstrate a degree of agility, a theme we shall discuss in Chapter 4, if they are to help their organisations adapt to the changing landscape which is the focus of the next chapter.

As always, making the right choice on where to focus is a leadership task. This is where HR leadership is needed that is both proactive and responsive to business needs, underpinned by humanistic values and capable of shaping thinking and practice with respect to the management and development of people. With respect to value-added 'deliverables', it is increasingly clear that when HR professionals understand the context, they can create tailored HR practices that will serve external investors, customers and communities as well as internal employees and organisational cultures. These contextual factors set criteria that guide actions and increase HR value. This, I believe, is the next step on the evolutionary ladder for HR, a function on the high road towards delivering value for today's and tomorrow's organisations. The changing context is the focus of the next chapter.

REFERENCES

Bersin, J. (2015). HR's Role in the Digital Workplace, in D. Ulrich, B. Schiemann and L. Sartain (eds), *A Time for Reinvention: The Rise of HR: Wisdom from 73 Thought Leaders*. London: CIPD, pp. 19–25.

Burden, A. (2014). HR vs the line manager: How to make strategy a reality. *Personnel Today*, 20 August. https://www.personneltoday.com/hr/hr-vs-line-manager-make-strategy-reality/

Burrin, P. (2020). From HR to people: Addressing new technologies and the digital skills gap in the workplace. *trainingmag.com*, June. https://laptrinhx.com/tag/trainingmag-com/

Charam, R. (2014, July–August). It's time to split HR. *Harvard Business Review*.

CIPD (2019). *The Future of HR, A Review*. London: CIPD.

CIPD (2015, February). *Changing HR Operating Models: A Collection of Thought Pieces*. London: CIPD.

Ekhtiari, H. (2018). Future of HR: Avoiding misguided transformation strategies. *HR Professional*, 35(2), 47–48.

Farrer, L. (2019). Human resources 2.0: How people operations is powering higher productivity. *Forbes*, 28 March. https://www.forbes.com/sites/laurelfarrer/2019/03/28/human-resources-2-0-how-people-operations-is-powering-higher-productivity/

Guest, D. (1989). Personnel and human resource management: Can you tell the difference? *Personnel Management*, January, 48–51.

Hammer, M. and Champy, J. (1993). *Reengineering the Corporation: A Manifesto for Business Revolution*. New York: Harper Business.

Jacobs, V. (2016). How to reverse the HR transformation death spiral. *MIT*, April. https://www.ti-people.com/reversing-the-transformation-death-spiral.

Lambert, A. and Newall, A. (2017). A new HR blueprint: Organisational effectiveness. *HR Magazine*, 23 January. https://www.hrmagazine.co.uk/article-details/a-new-hr-blueprint-organisational-effectiveness.

Lawler, E. E. III (2015). HR: From criticism to destruction. *Forbes*, 25 August. https://www.forbes.com/sites/edwardlawler/2015/08/25/hr-from-criticism-to-destruction/

Lawler, E. (2005). From human resources management to organizational effectiveness, in M. Losey, S. Meisinger and D. Ulrich (eds), *The Future of Human Resource Management*. Hoboken, NJ: Wiley.

Lawler, E. and Mohrman, S. (2003). HR as strategic partner. *Human Resource Planning*, 26(3), 15–29.

Marchington, M. and Wilkinson, A. (2008). *HRM at Work: People Management and Development*. London: CIPD.

Reddington, M., Williamson, M. and Withers, M. (2006). *Transforming HR: Creating Value through People*. Oxford: Elsevier Butterworth-Heinemann.

Reilly, P. (2008). *HR Roles in Transition*. London: Chartered Institute of Personnel and Development.

Scott-Jackson, W. and Mayo, A. (2016). *HR with Purpose: Future Models of HR*. Technical Report. Henley Business School, University of Reading, Henley.

Ulrich, D. (1997). *Human Resource Champions: The Next Agenda for Adding Value and Delivering Results*. Cambridge, MA: Harvard Business School Press.

Ulrich, D. and Allen, J. (2009). *HR Transformation*. New Delhi: Tata McGraw Hill Education Private Ltd.

Ulrich, D. and Brockbank, W. (2015). Toward a synthesis of HR competency models: The common HR "Food Groups". *BYU Scholars Archive*, 38(4), 54–66. https://hrpa.s3.amazonaws.com/uploads/2020/10/The-Rise-of-HR-ebook.pdf.

Ulrich, D., Brockbank, W., Yeung, A. K. and Lake, D. G. (1995). Human resource competences: An empirical assessment. *Human Resource Management*, 34(4), 473–495.

Ulrich, D., Schiemann, W.A. and Sartain, L. (2015). *The Rise of HR: Wisdom from 73 Thought Leaders*. HR Certification Institute.

Weatherley, L. (2005). *HR Technology: Leveraging the Shift to Self-service: It's Time to Go Strategic*. Alexandria VA: Society for Human Resource Management.

Yeung, A. K. and Brockbank, W. (1998). Reengineering HR through information technology. *Human Resource Planning*, 18(2): 24–37.

3
The changing context for SHRM

It is not the strongest of the species that survives, nor the most intelligent that survives. It is the one that is most adaptable to change.

(After Charles Darwin)

DOI: 10.4324/9781003219996-4

No organisation is immune from the changing tides of global economic, social, political and technological trends. Context matters and in the volatile, uncertain, complex and ambiguous (VUCA) twenty-first century executing business strategies becomes very challenging. In developed economies, currently the world of work is undergoing profound change, as wider context shifts such as political and economic instability, climate change, demographics, social changes, the consumer revolution and new technologies drive new business models and the growing demand for agility and innovation at work. And of course the Covid-19 global pandemic has acted as the 'great accelerator' of many underlying trends, potentially heralding the start of a new era.

While the Darwinian notion of adaptation to changing contexts originally applied to the evolution of species, arguably it now applies just as much to organisations, albeit at a faster pace. Context is key to business success and to management in general. We have seen whole industries founder in the wake of changing consumer habits and 'black swan' events such as the pandemic. We are seeing rapid changes in the world of work enabled by technology, so context is also key to strategic HR management. To develop organisational strategies that prepare organisations to not only successfully respond to environmental pressures and opportunities but also to proactively develop the future workforce of the future, HR must keep abreast of the changing times. The HR function must be able to manage the tensions between the 'looking-in' agenda, i.e., aligning people management to the organisation's strategy, business model and the performance challenges this creates; and the 'looking out' agenda, where the HR function helps the organisation adjust its people management to institutional, social and technological change (Sparrow 2017). It is this latter agenda we look at in this chapter.

CHAPTER OVERVIEW

In this chapter, I shall compare some of the previous trends with current events and also make some predictions about how context elements arguably detectable today (CBRE 2014), may influence the future of work. So, at the risk of faulty foresight, looking to the near future, what Sharpe (2013) calls the 'Second Horizon', this is an attempt to deduce some of the likely human implications for work as we have known it. We shall cover:

- The changing business environment
- Impact of technology
- Workforce of the future
- The quest for organisational agility

LEARNING OBJECTIVES

- To provide an overview of context themes that will be picked up throughout the book.
- To consider some of the context changes underway which will have an impact on the implementation of strategic HRM.

INTRODUCTION: THE CHANGING BUSINESS ENVIRONMENT

Change is not new, but arguably the velocity and scope of change today is very different from in the past. The accelerating pace of global events, the flow of goods, information and capital around the world, and the explosion of new technologies, are disrupting every industry, making previous formulae for business success largely redundant. In 2005, Hiltrop predicted: 'As we move deeper into the twenty-first century, we can realistically expect that pressures to change the culture, purpose and shape of organisations will intensify as the needs for flexibility, competitiveness, innovation, speed and punctuality improvements become even greater'. In today's context we can expect more disruptions and turbulence to come, as Hiltrop's predictions prove correct.

GLOBALISATION

Globalisation continues to drive growth and wealth creation. Underpinned by neo-liberal free market principles, Anglo-American style globalisation was made possible through deregulation of markets, availability of technology and other factors from the mid-1980s. Much manufacturing capability migrated from the developed to parts of the developing world. With rapid growth in new and emerging markets, economic power is shifting from developed countries to developing countries. China and India are developing rapidly and differently as global economic superpowers, as they make use of industrialisation, internet technology and increasingly skilled labour forces to build a potentially dominant position in the economic hegemony. The West, with its ageing population, is becoming predominantly a service economy, with the United Kingdom in particular seeing the development of high technology, financial services and, until recently, travel and tourism as major growth areas.

Corporations now face a myriad of markets and products where once there were stable brands spreading across the globe. As a result, they need to balance global scale with local responsiveness and local brand identification. For Kenichi Ohmae, author of *Triad Power* (1985), the route to global competitiveness is to use each of the three Cs of commitment, creativity and competitiveness. As Ohmae points out, 'The essence of business strategy is offering better value to customers than the competition in the most cost-effective and sustainable way. But today, thousands of competitors from every corner of the world are able to serve customers well'. Ohmae (1985) signals the importance of taking account of context:

> To develop effective strategy, we as leaders have to understand what's happening in the rest of the world and reshape our organization to respond accordingly. No leader can hope to guide an enterprise into the future without understanding the commercial, political and social impact of the global economy.

As competition in the service economy becomes more intense – and the financial services industry is a prime example of this – markets tend to consolidate through restructurings and acquisitions. Similarly, the ability to innovate, at speed, is required to keep ahead of the game since customers always want something new – and with increased competition, customer loyalty to brands is far from guaranteed.

With respect to labour markets, the United Kingdom prior to Brexit, with its open capital markets and flexible labour markets, had fewer constraints on growth than many other countries. Indeed, neo-liberal operating principles and employment practices were adopted in all sectors of the economy, including in charities and the public sector. Even in the post-Brexit era, the UK labour market is predicted to become ever more mobile, more diverse and, as a result, more complex. Van Barneveld et al. (2020) argue that in countries with neoliberal regimes of labour market regulation, such as the United Kingdom, these policies have privileged private markets, corporate wealth and 'flexible' labour markets while widening inequalities, weakening long-term community voice and enabling the growth of precarious work.

Push-back

While economic growth through globalisation is expected to continue, at the same time it is subject to the '…highest level of risk in years' (EIU 2018) thanks to growing threats from protectionism, trade wars and terrorism including cyber. Add to that social, economic and political trends such as the fluctuating price of energy, the personal and national consequences of global politics and extremism which are driving perceptions of a less secure and stable world.

The after-effects of the financial crisis of 2008–2009 are still being felt, and capitalism's excesses, such as the extreme rewards for success – or failure – awarded to some 'winners' have led to globalisation being blamed for growing socio-economic inequalities globally and for the rise of populism and nationalism in several countries, such as former US President Trump's America First, Brexit and other examples illustrate. So with populism on the march across much of the world, the liberal 'centre ground' appears to be eroding in the face of more extreme political voices. US President Biden faces a Herculean task to achieve consensus on a more moderate way forward. For despite political, religious and cultural differences, collaboration can abound, especially in times of crisis, as some responses to the coronavirus crisis illustrate, with pharmaceutical companies sharing their breakthroughs with others so that vaccinations and treatments can be developed apace. Similarly, despite the nationalist vogue of the day, our increasing awareness of global interdependence is also driving concerns about some of the environmental challenges, which can appear beyond ready control, such as climate change and pandemics. In earlier editions of this book, I wrote about the SARs and Avian Flu epidemics. This edition must reference an even greater game-changer – the Covid-19 pandemic.

Covid-19 pandemic

Dealing with the pandemic has been a test for individuals and governments worldwide and laid bare the values and competence of those in charge. Van Barneveld et al. (2020) argue that the pandemic's disastrous worldwide health impacts, devastating as they are, have been exacerbated by, and have compounded, the unsustainability of economic globalisation based on the neoliberal dismantling of state capabilities in favour of markets. Lack of global leadership and narrow nationalistic approaches such as 'America or Europe first' have compounded the crisis. For van Barneveld et al. (2020) a change of policy is needed:

> COVID-19 demonstrates that societies need to prioritise a range of social objectives including public health and wellbeing. If they are to safeguard their citizens, they must acknowledge that economic systems promoting inequality are not compatible with this. As governments resurrect their economies, retraining and finding suitable employment for displaced workers loom as critical labour market policy challenges.

In many parts of the world, the pandemic has led to lockdowns and the suspension of economic and social life. Governments are loaded with seemingly unsustainable levels of debt for years to come. While technology has enabled some social connection to continue and some work to be carried out remotely, whether remote working will remain mainstream after the crisis remains to be seen. For many young people hoping to enter the job market, the immediate prospects look bleak while for those laid off in their middle years, future job opportunities may look very different from the work they had been doing prior to the crisis. The need for ongoing learning and retraining is apparent.

Trust, values and ethics

In this context, the role of business is increasingly under the spotlight. The debate centres around the relationships between business, society and the public good. So will the pandemic crisis accelerate underlying trends and calls for a more responsible form of capitalism? Opinion polls carried out in various Western countries suggest that many people have lost trust in their institutions, politicians and conventional democratic procedures, with younger people often said to be particularly disaffected and alienated. We live in an era of protest and people from all walks of life have risen up in recent times in grassroots movements for change (including #MeToo, #TimesUp, Black Lives Matter, Extinction Rebellion, and, arguably, Brexit).

High-profile cases of corporate corruption and scandal in a number of large global organisations (Enron, Arthur Anderson, Parmalat, WorldCom, Fifa, Adelphia, Global Crossing, ImClone) have shaken consumer and investor confidence leading to the erosion of trust in business. These events have led to new corporate governance regulations and compliance requirements increasing the workload of boards. The World Economic Council argues that corporate scandals have led to public cynicism and account for the rise of populism. Tyson and Mendonca (2020) call for the death of 'shareholder-only capitalism' in today's political economy 'which currently resembles a dangerous mix of 1920s capitalism and 1930s politics'. Indeed, rebuilding trust in global business is one the strongest motives behind the growing corporate support for stakeholder capitalism by the World Economic Council.

Sustainable business

In the fiercely competitive global environment of the first few decades of the twenty-first century, the struggle for business survival is being superseded by the search for sustainable business performance. Two decades ago, Charles Handy (1997) argued that firms must see their roles as contributing to society over the long term, rather than simply increasing shareholder dividends in the short term. Compare this with the views of the 1970s US economist and free-market advocate Milton Friedman, who described the then-growing demands for business to have a social conscience as 'pure and unadulterated socialism'. He argued that business has a duty to make a profit first – anything else will create confusion.

Today, there are signs that some businesses at least are espousing attempts to find better balance between profit and purpose, across a wide range of environmental, social and governance (ESG) priorities, thanks largely to increased pressure from customers, employees and other stakeholders. More than 90% of 2000 CEO respondents in Deloitte's (2020) annual global survey say their companies have sustainability initiatives in place or on the drawing board. Indeed, Deloitte (Volini et al. 2020a) propose that a new form of capitalism may be emerging, one that considers a broader group of stakeholders and measures societal impact alongside financial performance. Many business leaders are asking themselves how to deliver a sense of purpose. Will this mean losing focus on bottom-line results? Will transparency expose painful tensions better left unexamined? Will our boards, management teams, employees, and stakeholders want to follow us, or will they think we have 'lost the plot'? There are no easy answers to these questions; corporate engagement is messy and full of pitfalls, including criticism from sceptical stakeholders.

Yet when companies fully leverage their scale to benefit society, the impact can be extraordinary (Deloitte 2017). The power of purpose is evident as the world fights the urgent threat of the COVID-19 pandemic, with a number of companies renewing their purpose, and collaborating across their ecosystems to produce high value outcomes at the very time stakeholders need it most (McKinsey 2019). For Deloitte (2020), it is not a question of either/or, but both/and:

> a social enterprise is an organization whose mission combines revenue growth and profitmaking with the need to respect and support its environment and stakeholder network. This includes listening to, investing in, and actively managing the trends that are shaping today's world. It is an organization that shoulders its responsibility to be a good citizen (both inside and outside the organization), serving as a role model for its peers and promoting a high degree of collaboration at every level of the organization.

Reputational risk

But beyond debates about the purpose of business, there are strong brand drivers for addressing ethical issues since corporate reputations are at stake. In this age of relative transparency, how a company operates has become as important as what it produces. Many of the corporate scandals of recent years have fundamentally undermined the 'licence to operate' of the organisations in question.

Through social media, bad 'news' travels fast, shaping customer and societal opinions. For instance, in the early 1990s Nike executives began to see reports of abusive labour conditions in their supplier factories as a risk to their brand image. Nike was criticised for sourcing its products in factories and countries where low wages, poor working conditions and human rights problems were rampant. At first, Nike managers took a defensive position vis-à-vis labour, environmental and occupational health problems found at their suppliers' plants. Workers at these factories were not Nike employees, so Nike felt no responsibility toward them. However, Nike leaders realised they were facing a supply chain crisis. They needed a new strategy to deflect the growing criticism and improve their suppliers' performance. By 1992, this hands-off approach changed as the company formulated a code of conduct for its suppliers that required them to observe some basic labour, environmental and health and safety standards (Locke and Romis 2007).

Corporate reputations can also be put at risk by the behaviours and decisions of those who work for or represent an organisation. Disgruntled employees have used various media platforms to broadcast perceived poor employment practice such as bullying, inequality or being vindictive towards whistle-blowers. In the United Kingdom, the lack of collective employment protections and the growth of a litigation culture, echoing US practice, is reflected in the plethora of employment tribunals brought by employees alleging that their employment rights or, in some cases, their human rights have been infringed. These are just some of the defensive reasons why addressing ethical considerations with regard to the workforce, such as addressing perceived inequality and unfairness at work, and improving employee engagement, have risen up the business (and therefore HR) agenda.

As a more positive driver for responsible business practice, organisations are also more attractive to potential recruits if they are seen to be active in supporting their community, and in other ways practising corporate values. According to Emma Schmitt of Standard Chartered Bank:

> Doing business in an ethical way is increasingly important for international companies like Standard Chartered. Half of our graduates cite our ethical approach as a reason for joining the bank. We give our employees two days additional leave each year to volunteer for community initiatives and we find it really enhances employee engagement.
>
> (quoted by Davidson 2007)

One such project involved 12 staff members helping to teach blind students interview and career development techniques.

Whereas a decade ago many firms adopted corporate social responsibility (CSR) policies mainly as tick-box exercises to minimise risk, now there is a growing emphasis on embedding responsible business practice as a positive source of competitive advantage. Management teams are being encouraged to take their corporate citizenship roles seriously. For instance, sustainability and corporate citizenship are an integral part of the Marks and Spencer (M&S) brand as well as a key part of its commercial recovery. In the past decade, levels of ethical consumerism have grown steadily, with no signs of slowing down. Consumers are no longer making decisions based solely on product selection or price; they're assessing what a brand says, what it does and what it stands for. They support companies whose brand purpose aligns with their beliefs and reject those that don't.

Other non-financial benefits of responsible business practice include building trust in the brand, increasing customer satisfaction, improving staff morale, reducing absentee rates, strengthening community relations in addition to reducing the organisation's carbon footprint. Arguably, the best leaders – in business and elsewhere – are those who are prepared to hold themselves and their companies to account and, in some cases, executives are now rewarded partly on the basis of how they demonstrate corporate values, including 'community involvement'.

Climate change

Environmental concerns about climate change and global warming are a particular focus for activism, and the geo-political move towards a carbon-free world is rapidly gaining ground, amid rising demands for businesses to avoid damaging the environment. The use of fossil fuels is increasing blamed for resource scarcity, extreme weather, rising sea levels and water shortages are becoming. While low-cost air travel opened up the prospect of increasing global mobility, the cost in terms of carbon emissions is increasingly being calculated down to the level of an individual's 'carbon footprint'. Even before Greta Thunberg's galvanising campaign to limit potentially irreversible damage to the world's climate and eco-system, social behaviour was heading towards more responsible individual practice for instance with respect to recycling and limiting unnecessary travel.

Major businesses are responding to the spirit of the times, with some making bold pledges to speedily become carbon neutral and rolling out programmes to address resource scarcity and environmental sustainability. For corporations, addressing public concerns about climate change, despite powerful political vested interests, has become a test of trust. Accenture (2018) has found that when trust is put at risk, companies suffer financially. Trust in the traditional competitive model of oil and gas companies is diminishing amid declining returns and growing demand for cleaner energy and sustainable products. For large or integrated oil companies, a material drop in trust could translate into a loss of US$9 billion in future revenue. Investors are scrutinising the industry as never before. They are making it clear that it is not only morally preferable to be socially responsible but is also a sign that a company is managing risk. Energy suppliers are making a determined drive to find alternative energy sources of cheap, clean and renewable energy. Bernard Looney, CEO of BP seized the initiative in 2020, pledging to speedily eliminate almost all carbon emissions from the firm's operations and from the fuel it sells to customers.

Airlines are under particular pressure as passengers increasingly look to find alternatives to plane travel in order to reduce carbon emissions. United Airlines invested more than $16 billion to replace all of its airplanes with more fuel-efficient models and looks to continually lower its carbon emissions. The slowdown of air travel during the pandemic may cause a structural reset of the industry as large jet aircraft are mothballed years ahead of their time. The automotive industry is under similar pressure, with many Western cities banning diesel-fuelled vehicles. The UK Government in 2020 set ambitious climate change targets, with other governments likely to follow suit, for instance proposing banning sales of vehicles with internal combustion engines by 2032. The rush is on to find means to power 'green' vehicles that do no harm to the environment. 'Green energy' targets set in 2020 may see the phasing out of central heating and domestic appliances using fossil fuels to be replaced by green alternatives.

Consequently, to protect their reputations, many organisations are now paying serious attention to the ethics of how they treat their employees and communities, how they reduce their carbon footprint, how they deal with corruption in their midst and how they source from suppliers who are known not to exploit their workers.

Reflective activity

- What are the main risks facing your organisation in the current context?
- How can HR help mitigate those risks?

THE IMPACT OF TECHNOLOGY

Rapid advances in technology are facilitating the rise of the virtual world. In particular, technological advances associated with the so-called 4th Industrial Revolution (4IR) – such as digitisation, block chain, Big Data, robotics, automation, artificial intelligence, machine learning, 3D printing and nanotechnology – are disrupting traditional business models and transforming working environments, blurring the boundary between the work tasks performed by humans and those performed by global machines and algorithms. The World Economic Forum (WEF 2018) suggests that four specific technological advances – ubiquitous high-speed mobile Internet; artificial intelligence (AI); widespread adoption of Big Data analytics; and Cloud technology – will dominate the next few years and beyond as drivers positively affecting business growth.

Knowledge economy

In this global marketplace and thanks to technology, new services and channels abound, niche players can take on the big conglomerates and national boundaries become irrelevant. In this 'New Economy' also known as the 'Collaborative Economy', the twin thrusts of competition and collaboration are evident. Thanks to the Internet, information is no longer the privileged preserve of professions or specialist groups but has been democratised. Commercial service providers such as Google and Yahoo! vie for share of market with 'volunteer'-led services such as Wikipedia, whose data are provided by contributors who are also users of the service. Social media use – such as 'Myspace', 'Facebook', 'YouTube', Twitter, LinkedIn, WhatsApp etc – has led to the growth of personalised messaging and online communities comprising thousands of new 'friends'.

Yet social media has also become a multiplier of the so-called 'echo chamber' effect when people identified as having similar views connect with each other, reinforce these views and become impervious to other viewpoints. Moreover, there is now greater awareness of the potential use of such data freely provided by individuals for political advantage by hostile forces. There were lively debates about free speech after Twitter and Facebook suspended the accounts of the then US President Trump in 2020. This has also led to questions about whether such media companies are simply platform providers, as they claim, or publishers with the right and responsibility to edit material they judge to be harmful.

In the pharmaceutical industry, research and development (R&D) historically has been predominantly an in-house activity. To fuel their pipelines, some pioneers started to complement their internal R&D efforts through external collaborations as early as the 1990s. In recent years, multiple extrinsic and intrinsic factors created an opening for multiple external collaborations that have resulted in new models for open innovation, such as open sourcing, crowdsourcing, public–private partnerships, innovation centres and the virtualisation of R&D. What may previously have seemed improbable alliances, such as those between former competitors, are becoming commonplace. Networks of small-scale companies increasingly find common interest in pursuing business opportunities. Adopting a fail-early paradigm through the implementation of clinical proof-of-concept trials enables investments for game changing late-stage assets (Schumacher et al. 2018).

Changing customer demands

Many pundits suggest that digital technologies are driving patterns of consumer behaviour that are profoundly changing how companies relate to their customers and increased consumer choice. Customers expect personalised services and ever-higher service standards while companies seek to reduce their costs. Public and private sector services are increasingly provided online, via call-centre-based helplines telephone or the Internet, including access to round the clock health advice. Selling or buying via the internet has become the 'normal' way to do business. Thanks to technology, companies can operate 24/7, for instance by running on a 'sun-time' basis from different parts of the world, automating, outsourcing, 'off-shoring' or 'right-shoring' key parts of their operations which can be done more cheaply and effectively elsewhere.

As the 24-hour shopping and service culture takes root, changing working patterns are an inevitable consequence. For instance, supermarkets have responded to changing consumer demands, and also saved costs, with new services made possible by technology – such as 'click and collect', home deliveries, self-service checkouts – thus significantly changing the nature of the shopping experience and the work of those who provide it.

Indeed, whether human beings will be needed at all in future increasingly becomes questionable. In 2020, Amazon opened supermarkets without human staff or check-outs, offering an entirely technology-driven service. Trials carried out in Iceland, parts of the United Kingdom and the United States suggest that home deliveries might before long be carried out by drones or robots, replacing the need for delivery van drivers.

Technology and employment

Of course, new technology, jobs and skills are closely interlinked and as business models change so too does the nature of work (McKinsey Global Institute 2017). However, in future job growth may be increasingly decoupled from economic growth due to more automation within various industries.

Debates rage as to whether technology will displace more jobs than it creates by 2025. Contemporary commentary on the potential impact of the fourth industrial revolution (4IR) on employment tends to divide into either an optimistic vision or pessimistic, dystopian predictions (Tegmark 2017). Optimists argue that new technology itself creates new jobs, not just in the development and use of the technology but also by enabling new ways of working and new services to be created. Developments such as Artificial Intelligence and robotics are more likely to alter jobs than eliminate them as many of the more apocalyptic commentaries suggest.

On the other hand, pessimists point to the likely impact of the rising tide of technologies on the workforce, with AI and automation potentially accentuating existing labour market inequalities, widening the opportunity gaps between the digital haves and have nots, displacing tasks and potentially whole occupations (Frey and Osborne 2013; The Economist 2016; Ernst et al. 2019). Brynjolfsson and McAfee (2014) sum up the potential risks and the benefits for workers as follows:

> Technological progress is going to leave behind some people, perhaps even a lot of people, as it races ahead… there's never been a better time to be a worker with special skills or the right education because these people can use technology to create and capture value. However, there's never been a worse time to be a worker with only 'ordinary' skills and abilities to offer, because computers, robots, and other digital technologies are acquiring these skills and abilities at an extraordinary rate.

The OECD (2019) estimates that, looking ahead, new technologies will eliminate 14% of jobs held by humans over the next 15–20 years and has also predicted that a million UK workers could lose their jobs to robots by 2030. Other predictions (McKinsey Global Institute 2017) suggest that robot automation will 'take over 800 million jobs' globally by 2030. The Financial Services sector is most likely to signal the planned adoption of humanoid robots in the period up to and beyond 2022 (WEF 2016). Thus customer service is increasingly likely to be delivered by robot representatives with a human touch.

The 'hourglass' labour market

Already we are seeing an increasingly 'hourglass' shaped labour market emerging along the so-called 'digital divide' which has significant social and economic consequences for individuals. At the top is knowledge work requiring higher-level skills – and ongoing development, especially updating in new technologies. Local or specialised knowledge makes workers more attractive to (many) employers and it is predicted that complex jobs will multiply. Such work will be augmented by technology. The OECD (2019) concludes that jobs involving creativity, complex reasoning and adaptation to variable contexts are least under threat. Nine in ten of such employees will work under full-time contracts. Organisations that provide effective development are more likely to attract and retain such employees than those that do not. It is for those workers at the top whose valuable, transferable skills give them power and choice in the job market that employers develop enticing value propositions.

In the 'squeezed middle' are many of the traditional middle manager positions and white-collar professions which over recent years have been the most affected by technological advances – for example as core financial and legal processes are automated. The OECD estimates that 32% of full-time middle skilled jobs are likely to be fragmented as tasks are automated. Poor job quality is likely to be a growing problem as many jobs are 'hollowed out' by technology and there will be rising wage inequality (Graeber 2018). For such workers the standard contract of full-time ongoing employment is likely to be replaced by insecure work arrangements.

At the bottom of the hourglass are routine jobs where people with the fewest skills and least training are most at risk of being replaced by automation. The periodic WERS survey in 2004, reported that 11% of UK workplaces with 100 or more employees used zero hours contracts. This had increased to 21% in 2011 and will rise considerably in coming years. Factories now often have a tiny human workforce managing the entire production process – machines do the rest. For low-skilled workers there is an employers' market of low paid, precarious 'gig' work, where workers lack employee status and carry all the risks in the work relationship without the collective protections of union membership. Amazon reportedly sacked employees who had attempted to organise in warehouses (O'Donovan 2020). Some delivery workers on minimum wage rates found themselves financially unable to take time off during the pandemic, even if it meant putting themselves and others at risk.

Whether gig economy workers are self-employed or not is often unclear, with cases being settled in employment tribunals. Deliveroo's decision to class riders as self-employed was upheld because they could pass on jobs to other people (Ghosh 2017), whereas Uber lost its case on the same issue and was told by a court that since it works like a traditional cab firm it must classify its drivers as workers (Shead 2017). As the driverless car/taxi/lorry revolution gradually takes place, in future even such non-jobs may be looked back on with nostalgia.

Those lucky enough to have ongoing employment contracts may find themselves treated as mere cogs in a machine. Some companies are using modern Pavlovian methods to motivate people who carry out repetitive routine tasks in today's growth industries such as packing. In one home-delivery company's warehouse, the company is seeking to improve efficiency and performance by 'gamifying' its packing workers:

> The games are displayed on small screens at employees' workstation. As robots wheel giant shelves up to each workstation, lights or screens indicate which item the worker needs to pluck to put into a bin. The games simultaneously register the completion of the task, which is tracked by scanning devices, and can pit individuals, teams or entire floors against one another to be fastest. Game-playing employees are rewarded with points, virtual badges and other goodies throughout a shift.
>
> (The Washington Post, 21.5.19)

As a result, productivity improves.

Technology then is making possible choice, personalisation, free and constant access to information, networking, collaboration as well as competition but it also has a powerful shadow side with potentially damaging effects. Just some of the challenging questions raised by these technologies concern issues such as widespread unemployment, workplace privacy and surveillance, skill development, acquisition and utilisation, manipulation, bias, conflict and resistance, work/life balance, human rights and dignity, the need for human-centred job design, corporate social responsibility and democracy itself.

The 4IR therefore highlights the strong need for ethics and AI governance frameworks to be considered in the context of labour regulation. The European Parliament (2020) has reviewed the potential impacts of AI on the labour market – on economic growth and productivity, on the workforce, on different demographics, including a worsening of the digital divide, and the consequences of deployment of AI on the workplace. In Singapore, the authorities have developed a governance framework to assess and manage the probability of harm to individuals as a result of automated systems and AI. The governance framework proposes a matrix to classify the probability and potential harm to an individual that could arise from organisations using AI in the management of individuals. If both the probability and degree of harm to an individual are considered low, then it is appropriate for automated decision-making in which a human being is out of the loop. On the other hand, if both the probability of harm and the degree of harm are considered high, the matrix recommends active intervention in which human beings are involved in decision-making (Waring et al. 2020).

Reflective activity

- Which of these 'new realities' are true for you?
- (How) should organisations be responding to these and other trends?
- How should firms think about their strategic choices and their allocation of resources when faced with high levels of uncertainty?

WORKFORCE OF THE FUTURE

One of the key challenges facing HR is ensuring that organisations have the right people in the right places with the right skills. At a time when, despite short-term recessions, many developed economies are experiencing underlying growth, there is a risk that talent shortages will become a key factor affecting organisations' ability to achieve their goals. This raises questions about the nature and shape of the future workforce.

Global demographic realities

Globally, we're in a period of declining population growth which between 1980 and 2014 averaged 1.3% but is expected to drop to 0.5% between 2015 and 2050, with the European labour force suffering a decline of over 20% (EIU 2016: 6). In Europe and the United States declining birth rates generate future shortages of both employees and consumers. The so-called 'demographic timebomb' in Europe and the United States is paralleled by other social trends reflected in the phrase 'the Age of Individualism'. In the West more men and women than ever before live in single-person households, leading to increasing numbers of small occupancy housing being built. Single women are said to be healthier and fitter than single men living alone, and though people are living longer than in the past, they are not necessarily leading healthier lives.

Economic growth and population growth are understood to be powerfully linked since they produce labour market and talent shortages and increase the competition for scarce talent. So managed migration and technology have become significant elements of some countries' business and economic strategies. Germany for instance boosted its labour market by accepting large numbers of technically well qualified refugees and asylum seekers. In parallel with the rise of nationalism globally, new arrivals were not universally welcomed, creating a different headache for the German government. Without the workforce, another avenue to pursue is the use of technology and AI to replace people in specific roles. In the United Kingdom with nationalist polices such as Brexit and immigration controls, shortages loom of human labour not easily replaced by technology in sectors as diverse as agriculture, hospitality, healthcare and the care industry.

The multi-generational workforce

Throughout Western Europe the workforce is ageing, and fewer young people are entering the workforce. In 2020, there were 2.7 workers to every non-worker, compared with 4:1 in 1990. With respect to pensions, people of the 'baby boomer' generations (born 1944–1964) will be among the last to be able to enjoy a comfortable retirement from the age of 60. The extension of the right to work beyond the age of 60 means that many older people will remain in the workforce. Many organisations now have a multi-generational workforce and there are predictions of intergenerational tensions in the workforce particularly among the low-skilled who will face ferocious competition for jobs, as young people compete with older workers staying in employment longer, to supplement inadequate pensions and ongoing living costs.

Gen X (born between 1965 and 1980) is numerically the smallest generation. By 2025, Millennials or Gen Y (born 1981–1996) will account for 75% of the global workforce. With a growing proportion of the workforce being Generation Y, employee values are changing, bringing a focus on corporate social responsibility including climate change and democratised organisational cultures and 'flexibility' as a priority. Gen Z (born 1997–2012) are entering the workplace. Various reports suggest that Gen Z employees, especially young high-flyers, not only want to make a good living, but also want to make a difference. Compared with their predecessors, Gen Z are reported to be:

- more mobile and connected. They expect workplace flexibility. In turn, they are comfortable and proficient at working anywhere and everywhere.
- more tech-driven
- ore educated but likely less skilled
- ore discerning
- ore social but less trusting
- oth great content creators and content consumers
- ore diverse and yet share more global cultural norms

Each workforce group needs to be managed with an understanding of their specific needs and motivations, including providing opportunities for younger workers. However, the different generations may have more in common than differences. Today's workforce is increasingly tech-driven and expects greater choice and control over its physical space. Organisational values are seen as most important to attracting candidates, followed jointly by career development opportunities and pay and benefits (CIPD 2017).

Since people know that traditional careers and related benefits such as job security are mostly a thing of the past, work appears to hold a less central part in many people's lives than in the past, especially for those employees who lead an entrepreneurial lifestyle. A CIPD report in 2014 reported that work was central to the lives of only 28% of respondents, compared with 50% of respondents in the same survey in 2005. With the demise of traditional careers and conventional career paths, portfolio and multiple careers in one working lifetime are becoming more common. Entrepreneurial lifestyles are predicted to become increasingly the norm, especially portfolio careers in which people combine a range of paid and unpaid activities at one time.

Retention will be key

Retention will be key to avoiding talent shortages and costly turnover. However, this may not be straightforward when a strong labour market returns post-pandemic. As users of technology, employees in the top part of the 'hourglass' increasingly view their employer through the lens of the discerning and demanding consumer and many have growing expectations about what work can do for them, as much as what they bring to their work. If their needs are not met, they are likely to move elsewhere as opportunities permit. Moreover, what motivates and retains employees may reflect perceived opportunities, expectations about pay and benefits, and attitudes towards work that may differ according to class, age, gender and occupation. Turnover is usually highest amongst young workers, who may be attracted by better salaries, more security and better career progression and challenges elsewhere. According to Rene Schuster, Adecco Group country manager:

> The labour market is changing, and self-starting employees are demanding more from companies and it is up to businesses to realize this and close the gaps in employee management. If businesses don't start engaging with their employees on the issues central to them, they will ultimately vote with their feet and leave.

Peter Reilly of IES argues that

> a strong labour market creates choice and freedom for employees. This leaves employers vulnerable, if people management falls through the management cracks, to increased turnover and labour costs, unproductive workers and the risk of not quickly replacing highly valued employees.
>
> (quoted by Peacock 2007)

According to the Work Institute's 2020 Retention report an estimated one in four employees voluntarily left jobs in 2018 but the report suggests that 75% of that turnover could be prevented by employers.

The pandemic crisis may have led to significant restructuring and job losses in some sectors, such as retail, and staff shortages in others, such as healthcare, hamper performance. Employees are most at risk when they become disengaged so much current HR practice is geared towards improving the employee experience in order to increase employee engagement and retention – and improve business performance. While many organisations focus their branding campaigns and budgets externally on prospects and customers, some may fail to invest in internal communications that align and engage their workforce. Defining and communicating their Employee Value Proposition(s) could potentially improve both recruitment and retention.

THE GROWING QUEST FOR AGILITY

The main challenge faced by all organisations is to build company performance in an increasingly difficult market. Changes of the digital era mean disruptions to a company's existing business models, which may not have substantially evolved since the start of the internet age. Even against a general backdrop of slow economic growth and unpredictable and disruptive political and economic events, such as Brexit for the United Kingdom, the question is not whether business models will have to change but when and how.

Digital is expanding customer expectations – for personalisation, value and low-cost delivery - leading to accelerating global competition, shrinking product life cycles and disruption of industries worldwide. Customers, enabled and empowered through their digital devices, expect greater choice and a voice in co-creating the products and services they consume. To compete, products and services must be innovated continuously to meet the changing demands of customers and markets. Given the pace of change across the board, and the increasing role technology plays in our lives, the demand is high for speed, innovation, flexibility and efficiency. Consequently, the need to develop business agility increasingly drives strategic agendas. A global survey of 998 executives by Workday (2020) shows the majority recognise the importance to their business's long-term success of driving digital growth and the strong relationship between digital revenue growth and organisational agility.

Organisational agility

Organisational agility, or 'an organization's capacity to respond, adapt quickly and thrive in the changing environment' (Holbeche 2018), has become a strategic imperative for many CEOs, as organisations struggle to keep up with, and adapt to, the rapidly shifting business context (Timmermans and Schulman 2017). The concept of 'organisational agility' encompasses both flexibility and adaptability. For the Agile Alliance, agility is 'the ability to create and respond to change in order to succeed in an uncertain and turbulent environment'. An agile organisation is not only 'flexible' to cater for predictable changes but also is able to respond and adapt to unpredictable changes quickly and efficiently (Oosterhout et al. 2006). Rapidity is an essential quality of agility in order to operate in a dynamic environment (Sherehiy et al. 2007).

For Workday (2020), organisational agility is a set of capabilities that are critical to reacting quickly and effectively to opportunities created by new digital technologies and evolving customer behaviours. Agile approaches emphasise 'continuous design, flexible scope, freezing design features as late as possible, embracing uncertainty and customer interaction, and a modified project team organization' (Serrador and Pinto 2015: 1041). Typically, agile organisations are structured around teamwork to enable fast experimentation and innovation. Everyone needs to be externally aware and savvy – willing to voice and act on such knowledge.

From shareholder to customer value

A central facet of organisational agility is customer-centricity (Galbraith 2011). Competitive advantage increasingly depends on the quality of the experiences that a company provides for its customers (Rebours and Pauly 2016). After all, technology creates and stimulates new and empowered consumer behaviours, and social media provide accessible platforms for consumers to exercise their collective voice, and in so doing to demand innovative products, directly affect organisational reputations and stimulate change. Consequently, in many sectors business models are undergoing a metamorphosis from strategy based on product or service to a business model built on cultivating customer relationships while transforming back-end operations at the same time:

> ... Yes, we do have a customer-centric movement going on - among customers.... (they) are acting more empowered and emboldened and are continually upping their expectations of companies. More than just a "movement," this is a large rock rumbling downhill at increasing speed that imperils anything in its way.
>
> (Marsh et al. 2010: 14)

This focus is challenging traditional ways of doing business in the globalised Anglo-American economy where, since the latter part of the twentieth century, the dominant goal of business has been to generate shareholder value through delivering on short-term priorities, driving both volume and margin growth, often achieved by cost-cutting. In the past, business models were based on predictable commercial patterns that company leaders believed they could plan for. They would respond with distinctive value propositions to meet the needs of their chosen sets of customers, mobilise resources and then gain competitive advantage by reconfiguring their value chain to best support the creation, delivery and selling of their products or services. While most traditional hierarchies were designed for efficiency and effectiveness, this often led to complicated and siloed organisations.

Today the organisational metaphor of modern era management thinking, typical of bureaucracies, that of a (well-oiled) machine (Morgan 1986), that leaders could direct, control and re-engineer, is being called into question. The dynamic pace and wide-ranging nature of change in the business landscape make such models, and related organisation designs, unsuited to an era of unpredictability and disruption.

New competitors entering markets are using web technology and global connectivity without the need for high capital (Kickstarter) or assets (the platform economy). Digitally-enabled, so-called 'disruptive' companies can swiftly leverage innovative business models to uncover new growth drivers and produce break-through services and products; for instance in retailing, customer preference for online shopping and home delivery services is leaving traditional shops standing empty. While conventional businesses such as hotels and taxi firms carry significant overheads, costs to disrupters can be kept low and customer choice increased – Airbnb owns no hotels; Uber owns no taxis, and both have used a 'self-employed' workforce model. Other new entrants are shifting market demand, so they can capture the marginal value that has been overlooked by the established players.

Implementing customer-centric strategies and delivering innovation are therefore key to organisational agility and enduring business success. The values of agility and Agile are generally on adding value for customers, as reflected in the IT sector's 'Agile Manifesto'. These include favouring individuals and interactions over processes and tools, working software over comprehensive documentation, customer collaboration over contract negotiation, responding to change over following a plan. The Agile development process familiar to software engineers institutes a set of customer-focused management values achieved through iterative and incremental development, in which requirements and solutions evolve through collaboration between self-organising, cross functional teams and their customers (Denning 2013).

Barriers to agility

Yet more than a decade after Galbraith approached the question of customer-centric organisation design, agility was failing to take hold more generally beyond software development. A major Economist Intelligence Unit (EIU 2009) report found that the vast majority of organisations struggle to upscale agility. As Denning (2013) points out, US manufacturing took a different path, with some manufacturers continuing to pursue mass-production methods with increased emphasis on saving through economies of scale while other firms pursued 'Lean' manufacturing that continued to focus on enhanced efficiency and cutting costs. More recent research confirms this continues to be the case. According to McKinsey (Aghina et al. 2020), only 4% of organisations reach enterprise level agility. Traditional ways of running businesses and related mindsets take time to shift.

So while the rhetoric of agile is everywhere, making the shift to a digitally driven agile customer-centric growth model can be difficult for many established businesses and represents a significant challenge to conventional bureaucracy. Weber (1978) proposed that bureaucracy is the most efficient form of organisation and superior to any other organisational forms. He defined the five features of bureaucracy as hierarchy, division of labour, rules and procedures, impersonality and technical qualifications. However, for some subsequent authors, bureaucracy may not be as ideal as Weber claimed (Gajduschek 2003); indeed, some have argued that, for creating more innovative and dynamic organisations, bureaucratic structures should be avoided altogether (Adler 1999; Kotnis 2004).

As with any transformation process, there are winners and losers, and some level of resistance can be expected if agile is implemented inappropriately. It is no use simply adopting agile techniques, such as Scrum and lean methodologies, without embracing the underlying agile principles of empowerment, client-centricity, experimentation, teamworking, co-creation and win-win outcomes for people and business. In such mechanistic scenarios, 'lean' tends to be 'mean' – hardly the basis for collaboration, empowerment, innovation and other desired outcomes. Similarly, in a period when time- and location-based work is increasingly eroded, and flexibility and collaboration are essential, many organisations seek flexibility by engaging with staff through a variety of transactional contractual relationships rather than offering permanent roles. Hardly a sign of employer commitment!

McKinsey (2018) found that the biggest leadership challenge in transforming the culture and ways of working towards Agile was 'resistance' to change. Workday (2020) found that a lack of motivation to move away from inflexible legacy processes was the top barrier to process change. Other impediments to adaptability identified by Workday (2020) included a lack of relevant digital skills, and, from a cultural perspective, heavy bureaucracy and risk-averse mindsets within the business. Only a quarter of respondents had made significant progress in establishing performance metrics to measure digital revenue growth and 55% of organisations lacked KPIs that are reflective of the digital era in which they now operate. How can organisations operate with agility and flexibility when technology, people and processes live in different systems with little or no integration?

Failure to address these barriers to agility can be costly. Lack of integration and mobility remains a threat to businesses as they shift toward digital innovation. Business leaders risk developing innovation silos unless their organisation is fully aligned. Only one-fifth of Workday (2020) respondents were confident in their ability to quickly reallocate people to where their skills are needed in order to take advantage of new opportunities. Often, internal mobility is hampered by hiring managers considering only the existing skills of internal hires rather than recognising their capacity to learn and become more capable, given the opportunity for development or a new role.

Understanding the barriers to change can not only inform leaders and HR about where to focus but also help them decide where to invest, what initiatives are most feasible, how to communicate with the workforce, what training should be offered, what incentives may be necessary and more.

Reflective activity

- What do you consider the biggest barriers to agility in your organisation?
- What might need to shift to enable greater agility?

SHIFTS REQUIRED FOR AGILITY

Leading an agile organisation is very different from traditional models of running organisations – it requires shifting mindsets and also focusing on culture (Heifetz et al. 2009). A Bain and Co. study (Dale and Miles 2013) reported that executives are recognising the importance of 'soft issues', with nine out of ten executives agreeing that they are also looking beyond cost-cutting to be successful, and that 'culture is as important as strategy for business success'. It's about putting the client/customer at the heart of culture and strategy and being flexible, learning from experience.

McKinsey research (2019) found that organisations that reach enterprise level agility are able to make decisions three times faster than others. Achieving the holy grail of democratised decision-making is not only about giving functional leaders access to timely, relevant and non-siloed data; it's also about ensuring that teams have full access to such data, without bottlenecks within the business, and empowering them to make decisions. This requires structural, process and behavioural shifts to happen. 'Leader organisations' in the Workday (2020) study have found ways to break down the data silos that constrain many established organisations and that exist for example, in the separate domains of finance, HR, marketing and IT. A clear customer purpose needs to underpin the shift.

Collaboration is another key feature of organisational agility. A CIPD (2014) report considers how organisations might build 'environments geared for collaboration, innovation and ongoing – rather than intermittent – adaptation'. Organisations attempting to introduce more agile ways of working typically adopt new routines and organisational forms that are team based and less hierarchically structured to enable a fluid multiplicity of collaborations (McKinsey 2019). Thanks to the convergence of a complex technologies virtual project teams can be based almost anywhere. These come together around specific business issues and disband when their task is finished. Virtual enterprises tend to relocate to areas where there is least regulation or most profit.

Technology can help foster a culture of collaboration by streamlining processes and creating online spaces for employees to share ideas, track performance with colleagues around the world and create new projects. American Express GBT aims to build a collaborative culture by offering regular online interactive chats with executives, holding virtual roundtables, conducting all management development programmes virtually and featuring a combination of online learning, work and learning circles that bring people together in a virtual classroom. For employees and managers, the ability to work effectively across and between organisational, geographical and time boundaries to achieve common purpose is likely to become a key capability in years to come. For Gratton (2007), the four key elements that must be mastered are a cooperative mindset, an ability to span boundaries, productive capacity and a shared purpose.

The changing roles of managers

A few years ago, managers seemed an endangered species; managing a departmental team of full-time workers was becoming a thing of the past and in an empowerment context it was argued, were 'checkers checking checkers' necessary? Perhaps the reality is that managers are needed more than ever, but that their role is changing. No longer are they expected to be the 'first among equals' or the technical expert but managers are increasingly required to act as organisational 'glue' between workers of all kinds, including employees and contractors. Given the increasing trend towards virtual working, managers must develop new work methods and ways of communicating appropriate to remote working – those which counter isolation and increase mutual trust and high performance.

The current trend in management thinking is to see the manager as helper rather than as problem-solving hero. In agile organisations line managers, including professionals and technical managers, are expected to become coaches/facilitators/supporters of mainly self-directed teams, whether or not they have appropriate skills for this. The emphasis is on building team capability, enabling diversity and employee well-being, providing focus during times of change, managing more age-diverse workforces and improving performance at the same time!

Highly skilled knowledge workers whose technical skills are likely to be superior to those of the manager generally can be critical of management if their needs are not met. Managers then have the tricky task of managing performance, raising standards and gaining commitment from people on whom business results depend. They also have to act as a 'shield' to protect employees from bureaucratic and other barriers to innovation. No wonder that increasing management capacity and capability is considered key to building and sustaining high performance.

HR can help managers understand the new management practices and how to practise them and communicate them to others. Helping managers to develop coaching skills will be worthwhile:

> With productivity being such an important measure of business potential and success, employers need to invest in recruiting and training up managers to be a real asset to their teams through facilitating, not hindering, productivity. The difference this can make is transformational.
>
> (ADP 2019)

Changing notions of work and jobs

Digital is transforming the nature of work and job quality. Robotic Process Automation (RPA) can take away from employees the mundane and repetitive work, allowing them to concentrate on the more value-added work where the human abilities of relationships, assessing and interpreting data are crucial. AI and automation can assist job holders to quickly access relevant data and standardise time-consuming tasks. At the same time, automation may be hollowing out many jobs, or making them redundant. *Automation and 'thinking machines' are replacing human tasks and jobs and changing the skills that organisations are looking for in their people. These momentous changes raise huge organisational, talent and HR challenges – at a time when business leaders are already wrestling with unprecedented risks, disruption and political and societal upheaval.* (PwC Workforce of the Future 2017). On a positive note, it is thought that for the foreseeable future, technology is more likely to augment work as humans and machines collaborate on decision-making.

Technology is changing our understanding of what constitutes a 'job'. For Boudreau (2018), 'work' and 'a job' should be considered separately and work should be disaggregated from individual job holders. Work, he argues, is better understood as a series of tasks, combining automation with human activity. Jobs can be put together in different ways and work reinvented, with organisational and power structures and responsibilities following suit. So increasingly people are likely to find themselves working in networks of teams that include both people and machines. Organisational structures will be flatter and more adaptable to drive greater agility.

Technology is also transforming the notion of 'workplace'. The extent of home working and the exponential use of communications networks such as Zoom and Microsoft Teams, etc. during the pandemic lockdowns has led many pundits to predict that virtual working, or hybrid working patterns, will become the norm. This in turn will reduce the numbers of workers who need to travel to the workplace and could increase the pool of potential job candidates exponentially, if geographical location is no longer a key criterion for appointments. Similarly, people with disabilities who previously might have found office work difficult could become part of the potential labour pool. Sourcing and enabling talent to thrive in remote contexts will involve technology and also require deep HR and psychological expertise, as some of the downsides of remote working, such as mental health challenges, become better understood.

Demanding work environments

To be agile, organisations need key staff to be highly engaged, able and willing to give of their best, and to continuously develop themselves to keep pace with the human/ technology interface. Yet in the dash to adopt new technologies many organisations have not considered what other changes may be needed to unlock the potential of new technologies and also create a context for human growth. Work environments are becoming ever-more demanding with various studies over a decade reporting unreasonable workloads that result in quality being compromised and a significant deterioration in worker satisfaction.

The challenges for many workers are reported to include the 'always on' 'long hours' culture, harassment, politics, overload through having to deal with too much information, burnout, discrimination, bullying, stress and ineffectiveness. It's as if working harder, not smarter is expected. Indeed, there is an increasing call for organisations to protect their workers from the trap of making sacrifices for the 'privilege' of having a job. For many workers caught in this trap this means enduring long hours and poor treatment in the name of 'being part of the family', when as Jaffe (2021) points out, 'work won't love you back'.

Mental health issues are reported to be on the increase. Deloitte (Volini et al. 2020b) describe as the 'overwhelmed employee' workers who are unable to escape from work, given the widespread use of multiple sources of contact, and the growing perception that accessing messages and e-mails at any time, even on holidays, is expected. Many employees experience a lack of work–life balance, whereas for others this is a price they are prepared to pay for career advancement. While some employees find remote working liberating, with its ready access to information and the ability to work at times to suit themselves, others experience a worsening work–life imbalance when working from home.

Work-related stress not only affects individuals' health but also productivity. Stress is a commonly reported explanation for growing levels of sickness absence in the United Kingdom that costs employers £13bn each year with £3.9bn directly attributable to mental ill-health (HSE, 2016). The average employer spends 10% of its annual pay bill managing the consequences of absence and there is compelling evidence that higher employee absence is correlated both to declining employee commitment and to declining customer satisfaction with service, and customer intention to spend more with the company (Bevan et al. 2007).

The unprecedented pressures placed on many parts of the workforce by the ongoing demands for improved speed, quality and productivity has given rise to a new 'stress-busting' industry. A whole range of counselling and stress mitigation consultancies has sprung up. City workers can now enjoy gym memberships, holistic therapy treatment during lunch periods and some firms are hiring specialists in Indian head massage to provide relief to employees at their desks. A more systemic approach may be needed to address the long hours culture, the unremittingly demanding roles and also to build resilience.

HR can offer workshops to support managers and workers going through change, provide tools to help them support their teams when the pressure is high, teaching them how to spot signs of stress and/or manage uncertainty with their teams. HR can provide or arrange for counselling to help people deal with stress. They can help managers review their own and others' ever-expanding workloads and design work tasks that are meaningful. They can co-design flexible working policies that work for both the organisation and for individuals without incurring career penalties.

A new deal?

As businesses seek flexibility and collaboration as core skills, and seek to retain core staff, how should HR and talent strategies respond? HR must be at the forefront of building a new psychological contract with employees and should aim for their organisations to become employers of choice for employees – current and potential. Like customers, the needs and expectations of employees are also changing. Many don't just want interesting work, but the emotional experiences it provides. Many young people are looking less for a job or even a career, and more for an experience that will increase their personal identity and well-being. For young people, sustainability has become a recruitment issue. Companies with strong CSR and diversity policies are generally seen as more attractive to potential candidates than those without. Most also have increasing expectations about flexible working – this includes opportunities to work from home and to have hours that suit domestic circumstances as well as building the job around 'me' rather than the other way around. Consequently, in sectors where the employee has the power to choose, employees can specify when and how they work, and whether the role is permanent or fluid, so employers are expected to offer a lot more flexibility.

Will a mutually beneficial 'new deal' or psychological contract emerge for all workers? For individuals in the top of the labour market hourglass it's an employees' labour market, and the talent strategy challenge will be to attempt to 'woo' and retain them through development, providing opportunities to explore how society works and get engaged in the wider world and more obviously create fulfilling and flexible roles. Arguably, for these highly skilled workers it is in the interests of employers to forge a new psychological contract with employees. Employers who fail to recognise this are more likely to lose the talent they need to build competitive advantage.

Workers in the squeezed middle and the bottom of the hourglass are usually engaged on a variety of contractual arrangements such as non-employed 'freelancers', contract workers, non-standard, temporary, part-time and 'zero hours' (CIPD 2013). Few HR teams have been used to incorporating this 'non-employed' group into the workforce, or their people strategy. Studies show that many organisations aren't providing training, appraisal, or even including them in internal communications. This comes from an outdated mind-set and concept of the 'organisation' and who's in and who's out.

Taking such a differentiated approach also raises issues of fairness, and social and organisational justice in how a business treats those at the bottom. Arguably it is in the interests of employers to 'walk' and the 'talk' on values with respect to these groups since these matter to the highly skilled Gen Ys at the top and becomes part of their calculation as to whether you're an attractive place to work, or not. So if you are aspiring to retain your key talent, taking a crude transactional approach to the pay and conditions of those at the bottom can scupper your talent strategy for those at the top.

In a full employment market, employees have more choice about who they work for, and employees everywhere are challenging their organisations to uphold fairness and respect for all in the workplace. To maintain and improve trust among the workforce HR must ensure there is regular and honest communication and a culture that encourages behaviour in line with corporate values and holds senior leaders to account as much as people on the shop floor. This means employers listening to what workers want too and tackling some of the big issues that matter to people.

Reflective activity

- If which areas should HR best focus to build organisational capability and adaptability?
- To what extent is a 'new deal' needed? What are the implications of having different 'deals'?

LOOKING TO THE FUTURE

So if organisational change is here to stay, it becomes the norm. Therefore creating agile, productive, empowered and dynamic organisations characterised by continuous improvement, learning and innovation makes sense. For transformative innovation, nothing short of culture change may be required (Leicester 2016). The strategic HRM contribution is essential in helping organisations become more agile, capable of change and high performance (Beer 2009). This means HR embracing the role of change agent, working closely with other change leaders as part of an integrated team to implement new structures and more agile ways of working without demotivating and losing staff. Building a responsive, agile twenty-first-century workforce is not just about the skills of the workforce; it's about improving the employee experience.

HR has a potentially major role to play in effectively managing restructuring processes, ensuring structures, systems, processes and, most importantly, people have sufficient flexibility to allow them to adapt. As change agent, HR needs a vision of the future, and a mindset that views change as opportunity rather than threat. Any and every aspect of change should be used as to build a more 'change-able' and agile culture where people are empowered and enabled to do a good job. Improving staff communications, developing a culture of participation and empowerment and building constructive employee relations become urgent priorities. HR must ensure fairness by implementing inclusive voice mechanisms and effective well-being and diversity policies.

HR professionals should keep a finger on the pulse of the workforce, monitoring the effects of change from the employee angle and anticipating some of the priorities that will need to be addressed if organisations are to attract and retain a knowledgeable and committed workforce. Managers may need help in managing complex change and understanding how to adapt both the formal and informal aspects of organisation in a rapidly shifting environment. After all, people 'cannot adapt to changes they cannot see' (Joiner 2019: 143).

In later chapters we shall explore how HR can become an agile role model, applying agility to its own work practices, demonstrating visible leadership and new values, anticipating and acting on key areas for improvement, especially with respect to employee engagement. As agile role model, HR should follow through on employee surveys, addressing the most frustrating 'pain' points. HR should ensure HR processes and systems are simple, fit-for-purpose and enable people in the organisation, and the HR team, to move faster, for instance using relevant, comparable people data for greater transparency, open discussions, intelligent risk taking and data-driven decision-making, so that hiring, training communications and performance management can be done at pace to match the new organisational model.

CONCLUSION

We have discussed some of the major context changes affecting organisations of all types and the growing need for organisational agility. The burgeoning of customer demands, availability of new products and service, increasing competition and the need for speed, innovative solutions and cost reduction mean that change has become the norm in organisations of every kind. Even though the robot revolution may not have fully arrived yet, many traditional full-time jobs may soon become a thing of the past. Rapid adaptation to the changing context and new labour market is possible but this requires creating a strong, unique workplace culture that puts people at its centre.

As we shall discuss in the next and later chapters, HR's agenda becomes ever more strategic and vital to future success. HR must lead on ensuring that the future of the workplace is human by balancing people and costs, transforming the organisation to ensure it meets its full potential and has the right people in the right place at the right time, including the right forms of leadership capable of enabling and empowering employees and the right kinds of growth and development opportunities. So HR must lead on helping the organisation develop more agile ways of working and also transform its own service delivery accordingly. Above all, concerted effort is needed by all stakeholders to ensure that workplace practice is fair and ethical.

The challenges organisations face in making this transition are significant, but those who act with determination on the trends they see happening today will be better positioned to develop a future workforce that can thrive in the Fourth Industrial Revolution. After all, the stakes are high:

> These transformations, if managed wisely, could lead to a new age of good work, good jobs and improved quality of life for all, but if managed poorly, pose the risk of widening skills gaps, greater inequality and broader polarization. In many ways, the time to shape the future of work is now.
>
> (WEF 2018)

REFERENCES

Accenture (2018). *The Bottom Line on Trust*, November 15. https://www.accenture.com/gb-en/insights/strategy/trust-in-business.

Adler, P. S. (1999). Building better bureaucracies. *The Academy of Management Executive*, 13(4), 36–47.

ADP (2019). *The Workforce View in Europe 2019*. https://www.adp.co.uk/hr-insights-topics-trends/employee-engagement-talent-management/workforce-view-2019/.

Aghina, W., Handscomb, C., Ludolph, J., Rona, D., West, D. (2020). *Enterprise Agility: Buzz or Business Impact?* McKinsey & Company, March 20. https://www.mckinsey.com/business-functions/organization/our-insights/enterprise-agility-buzz-or-business-impact.

Agile Alliance. (2020). *What Is Agile?* https://www.agilealliance.org/agile101/.

Beer, M. (2009). *High Commitment, High Performance: How to Build a Resilient Organization for Sustained Advantage*. San Francisco: Jossey-Bass.

Bevan, S., Passmore, E. and Mahdon, M. (2007). *Fit for Work: Musculoskeletal Disorders and Labour Market Participation*. London: The Work Foundation.

Boudreau, J. (2018). The impact of automation on jobs: A conversation with John Boudreau. *Workday*. Jan 22. https://medium.com/workday-summit/the-impact-of-automation-on-jobs-a-conversation-with-john-boudreau-fc98a3d8361f.

Brynjolfsson, E. and McAfee, A. (2014). *The Second Machine Age: Work, Progress, and Prosperity in a Time of Brilliant Technologies*. New York: W. W. Norton & Company.

CBRE (2014). *Fast Forward 2030: The Future of Work and the Workplace*. http://www.cbre.co.jp/AssetLibrary/CBRE_Genesis_FAST_FORWARD_Workplace_2030_Exec_Summary_E.PDF.

CIPD (2017). *Resourcing and Talent Planning Report*. London: CIPD. https://www.cipd.co.uk/Images/resourcing-talent-planning_2017_tcm18- 23747.pdf.

CIPD (2014). *HR getting smart about Agile Working*, London: CIPD. https://www.cipd.co.uk/knowledge/strategy/change/agile-working-report.

CIPD (2013). *Megatrends*. https://www.cipd.co.uk/Images/megatrends_2013-trends-shaping-work_tcm18-11401.pdf.

Dale, S. and Miles, L. (2013). *Integrating Cultures after a Merger*. Washington D.C.: Bain and Company.

Davidson, A. (2007). Doing the right-on thing. *Sunday Times Magazine*, 1 April.

Deloitte(2017).2030Purpose:Goodbusinessandabetterfutureconnectingsustainabledevelopment with enduring commercial success. *Deloitte*. https://www2.deloitte.com/content/dam/Deloitte/my/Documents/risk/my-risk-sdg12-2030-purpose-good-business-and-a-better-future.pdf.

Denning, S. (2013). Why agile can be a game changer for managing continuous innovation in many industries. *Strategy & Leadership*, 41(2), 5–11.

Economist Intelligence Unit (2016). *Data Tool*. Economist Intelligence Unit. Available from www.eiu.com.

Economist Intelligence Unit (EIU) (2009). *Organizational Agility: How Business Can Survive and Thrive in Turbulent Times.* sponsored by EMC, EIU.

Economist Intelligence Unit Report (2018). *Risk 2018: Planning for an Unpredictable Decade.* Economist Intelligence Unit. http://graphics.eiu.com/upload/BT_RISK.pdf.

Economist Intelligence Unit Report (2009). *Organisational Agility: How Business Can Survive and Thrive in Turbulent Times.* https://www.emc.com/collateral/leadership/organisational-agility-230309.pdf.

Ernst, E, Merola, R, Samaan, D. (2019). Economics of artificial intelligence: implications for the future of work. *IZA Journal of Labor Policy*, 9(1), 20190004.

European Parliament (2020). The Ethics of Artificial Intelligence: Issues and Initiatives. Scientific Foresight Unit (STOA) PE 634.452RS | European Parliamentary Research Service (EPRS), March 2020. https://www.europarl.europa.eu/RegData/etudes/STUD/2020/634452/EPRS_STU(2020)634452_EN.pdf.

Frey, C. and Osborne, M. (2013). The future of employment: How susceptible are jobs to computerisation? Working Paper, Oxford Martin School, Oxford University, Oxford. https://www.oxfordmartin.ox.ac.uk/downloads/academic/future-of-employment.pdf.

Gajduschek, G. (2003). Bureaucracy: Is it efficient? Is it not? Is that the question?: Uncertainty reduction: An ignored element of bureaucratic rationality. *Administration & Society*, 34(6), 700–723.

Galbraith, J.R. (2011). *Designing the Customer-Centric Organization: A Guide to Strategy, Structure, and Process.* San Francisco: John Wiley & Sons.

Ghosh, S. (2017). Deliveroo riders are self-employed, not workers, according to a UK ruling. *Business Insider.* Available at: http://uk.businessinsider.com/deliveroo-self- employed-workers-rights-tribunal.

Graeber, D. (2018). *Bullshit Jobs: A Theory.* New York: Simon and Schuster.

Gratton, L. (2007). *Hot Spots: Why Some Teams, Workplaces, and Organizations Buzz with Energy – and Others Don't.* Harlow: FT Prentice Hall.

Handy, C. (1997). *The Empty Raincoat.* London: Hutchinson.

Health and Safety Executive (HSE). (2016). *Work Related Stress, Anxiety and Depression Statistics in Great Britain 2016.* http://www.hse.gov.uk/statistics/causdis/ stress/stress.pdf?pdf=stress.

Heifetz, R.A., Grashow, A. and Linsky, M. (2009). *The Practice of Adaptive Leadership: Tools and Tactics For Changing Your Organization and the World.* Boston: Harvard Business Press.

Hiltrop, J-M. (2005). Creating HR capability in high performance organizations. *Strategic Change*, 14(3), 121–131.

Holbeche, L.S. (2018). *Organizational Agility*, 2nd Edition, London: Kogan Page.

Jaffe, S. (2021). *Work Won't Love You Back: How Devotion to Our Jobs Keeps Us Exploited, Exhausted and Alone.* London: C. Hurst & Co, Publishers.

Joiner, B. (2019). Leadership agility for organizational agility. *Journal of Creating Value*, 5(2), 139–149.

Kotnis, B. (2004). Enabling bureaucracies in education: A case study of formalization in an urban district and schools. Thesis for the degree of Doctor of Philosophy (PhD). The Faculty of the Graduate School of the State University of New York at Buffalo.

Leicester, G. A. (2020). *Guide to Transformative Innovation: A Guide to Practice and Policy*, 2nd edition. Charmouth, Dorset, UK: Triarchy Press. https://amzn.to/2JAICyn.

Locke, R. and Romis, M. (2007). Improving work conditions in a global supply chain. *MIT Sloan Management Review*, 48(2), 54–62.

Marsh, C., Sparrow P., Hird, M., (2010). *Is Customer Centricity A Movement or Myth? Opening the Debate for HR.* Lancaster University Management School White Paper 10/02.

McKinsey (2019). *How the Best Companies Create Value from their Ecosystems*, McKinsey & Co, Nov 19. https://www.mckinsey.com/~/media/mckinsey/industries/financial%20services/our%20insights/how%20the%20best%20companies%20create.

McKinsey and Company (De Smet, A.) (2018). *Scaling up Agility*, Feb. 23. https://www.mckinsey.com/business-functions/organization/our-insights/the-organization-blog/scaling-up-organizational-agility.

McKinsey Global Institute (Nov 2017). *Jobs Lost, Jobs Gained: What the Future of Work Will Mean for Jobs, Skills, and Wages*. https://www.mckinsey.com/featured-insights/future-of-work/jobs-lost-jobs-gained-what-the-future-of-work-will-mean-for-jobs-skills-and-wages.

Morgan, G. (1986). *Images of Organization*. Newbury Park, CA: Sage Publications Inc.

O'Donovan, Caroline (April 12, 2020). Amazon fired and employee involved in workplace organizing in Minnesota. *Buzzfeed*. Retrieved April 14, 2020.

OECD (2019). *Employment Outlook 2019: The Future of Work*. DOI: https://doi.org/10.1787/9ee00155-en.

Ohmae, K. (1985). *Triad Power*. New York: Free Press.

Oosterhout, M.V., Waarts, E., and van Hillegersberg, J. (2006). Change factors requiring agility and implications for it. *European Journal of Information Systems*, 15(2), 132–145.

Peacock, L. (2007). *Personnel Today*, 24 April.

PwC (2017). Workforce of the future: The competing forces shaping 2030, pwc.com. https://www.pwc.com/gx/en/services/people-organisation/publications/workforce-of-the-future.html.

Rebours, C. and Pauly, I (2016). *L'expérience: le nouveau moteur de l'entreprise*, Diateino, October.

Schumacher, A., Gassmann, O., McCracken, N. and Hinder, M. (2018). Open innovation and external sources of innovation. An opportunity to fuel the R&D pipeline and enhance decision making? *Journal of Translational Medicine*, 16, 119. https://doi.org/10.1186/s12967-018-1499-2.

Serrador, P. and Pinto, J.K. (2015). Does agile work?—A quantitative analysis of agile project success. *International Journal of Project Management*, 33(5), March.

Sharpe, B. (2013). *Three Horizons: The Patterning of Hope*. Axminster, Devon, UK: Triarchy Press. https://amzn.to/2JCc9rq.

Shead, S. (2017). Uber loses appeal in landmark UK case over its drivers' employment rights. *Business Insider*. http://uk.businessinsider.com/uk-judge-rejects-uber-appeal-over-driver-employment-rights-2017-11.

Sherehiy, B., Karwowski, W. and Layer, J.K. (2007). A review of enterprise agility: Concepts, frameworks, and attributes. *International Journal of Industrial Ergonomics*, 37(5), 445–460.

Sparrow, P. (2017). HR and tsunamis: time for a new model? *HR Insight*, Winter, IES.

Tegmark, M (2017). *Life 3.0: Being Human in the Age of Artificial Intelligence*. New York: Alfred A. Knopf.

The Economist. (2016). *Automation and anxiety: Will smarter machines cause mass unemployment?* http://www.economist.com/news/special-report/21700758-will-smarter-machines-cause-mass-unemployment-automation-and-anxiety.

Timmermans, K. and Schulman, D. (2017). *Increasing agility to fuel growth and competitiveness*, Accenture Strategy. https://www.accenture.com/t20170331T025702Z__w__/us-en/_acnmedia/PDF-4/Accenture-Strategy-Increasing-Agility-to-Fuel-Growth-and-Competitiveness-Research-v2.pdf.

Tyson, L. and Mendonca, L. (2020). *Making stakeholder capitalism a reality*. Project Syndicate, Jan 6. https://www.project-syndicate.org/commentary/making-stakeholder-capitalism-reality-by-laura-tyson-and-lenny-mendonca-2020-01?barrier=accesspaylog.

Van Barneveld, K., Quinlan, M., Kriesler, P. et al. (2020). The COVID-19 pandemic: Lessons on building more equal and sustainable societies. *The Economic and Labour Relations Review*, 31(2), 133–157.

Volini, E., Schwartz, J. and Denny, B. (2020a). 2021 Global human capital trends. *Deloitte*, 18 May.

Volini, E., Schwartz, J. and Denny, B. (2020b). Designing work for well-being, living and performing at your best. *Deloitte Insights*, 15 May. https://www2.deloitte.com/us/en/insights/focus/human-capital-trends/2020/designing-work-employee-well-being.html.

Waring, P., Bali, A. and Vas, C. (2020). The fourth industrial revolution and labour market regulation in Singapore. *Economic and Labour Relations Review*, 31(3). https://journals.sagepub.com/toc/elra/31/3.

Weber, M. (1978). *Economy and Society: An Outline of Interpretive Sociology.* Oakland, California: University of California Press.

World Economic Forum (2018). *The Future of Jobs Report 2018.* http://www3.weforum.org/docs/WEF_Future_of_Jobs_2018.pdf.

World Economic Forum (2016). *The Future of Jobs - Employment, Skills and Workforce Strategy for the Fourth Industrial Revolution.* http://www3.weforum.org/docs/WEF_FOJ_Executive_Summary_Jobs.pdf.

Work Institute (2020). *2020 Retention Report.* https://info.workinstitute.com/hubfs/2020%20Retention%20Report/Work%20Institutes%202020%20Retention%20Report.pdf.

Workday (2020). *Organisational Agility at Scale: The Key to Driving Digital Growth.* workday.com.

4

A strategic agenda for HR

The context of a business setting captures the "why" of HR transformation. This means linking HR efforts directly to the business strategy and to the environmental factors that frame the strategy.

(Ulrich and Allen 2009)

DOI: 10.4324/9781003219996-5

As we have discussed, business and the world of work are being shaped by the rapid adoption of new technologies, which are challenging conventional business models and placing customer experience at the heart of business efforts to survive and thrive. Economic and societal upheavals add to the disruptive context mix. Alongside these existing trends, the coronavirus pandemic crisis has seemingly catapulted us into a new era, shining a spotlight on many potential changes in store for business, ways of working and for society as a whole. In the Digital Age, successful organisations are customer-centric and must be designed for speed, agility and adaptability to enable them to innovate and compete effectively.

CHAPTER OVERVIEW

In this chapter, we shall consider how HR's strategic agenda might respond to the context trends and help organisations achieve sustainable success in such a fast-changing environment by:

- Adding strategic value
- Ensuring availability of competent human capital
- Building and maintaining key organisational capabilities
- Shaping an agile, high-performance culture

In the next chapter, we shall consider how HR might organise to deliver this agenda, but in this chapter, we explore ways in which HR can create a bigger win for the organisation by driving through a longer-term agenda underpinned by agility and customer-centricity.

LEARNING OBJECTIVES

- To consider some of the implications of context trends for HR strategy
- To explore some of the key areas where HR can add strategic value

INTRODUCTION: ADDING STRATEGIC VALUE

HR exists to deliver value to key stakeholders, including investors and customers in particular, according to Ulrich et al. (2017). For Ulrich, the answer to the questions 'what's the purpose of HR'? or 'what's the most important thing HR can give an employee?' should still always be 'a company that wins in the marketplace'.

Conventionally this is achieved by a tight 'fit' between business strategy and HR strategy, but today alignment also involves taking context into account. In HR's latest stage of evolution, Ulrich argues, HR must shift focus away from mainly inside the organisation (to business leader stakeholders) to align its work with changes in external business contexts and also address the needs of stakeholders, especially customers and investors. 'HR from the outside-in' requires understanding how value is created for customers and investors and how HR can contribute to this agenda. This means taking account of key current and future trends, understanding what is going to drive business results, identifying and addressing the key people and culture issues which will affect their organisation's success beyond the short-term and building specific goals with stakeholders towards these. It's about creating innovative and aligned HR practices that will increase organisational capability.

Similarly, Lawler and Boudreau (2015) argue that to operate 'outside-in' HR must span the boundaries between the function, the organisation as a whole, and the dynamic environment within which it operates. This requires external sensing capability, with HR actively engaging with customers, looking at market opportunities, the business and its products and services, from the perspectives of customers and investors, and working out what needs to change/improve to better meet changing customer needs. For investors and executives, it seems the main differentiator for business success is talent – over 80% of HBR articles are about people. Ulrich now argues that it is not just the workforce that drives business results, but the workplace; not just the people but the process – organisational systems and culture – that create a great place to work and help it succeed in the marketplace.

Following or leading?

What HR can actually deliver and how much strategic value can be added may depend on where HR sits on an adapted Wyatt-Haines (2007) functional value ladder as follows.

Following

This is the first and lowest level, where HR follows the business and reacts to its needs, but is capable of delivering consistently and reliably, as well as managing costs, effectiveness and efficiency of HR systems. Regrettably, some HR functions fail to deliver even at this basic level. When responses are late or inconsistent, and practitioners find themselves leaping from one crisis to another, such HR functions are perceived as ineffective.

Enabling

With better organisation and delivery standards, and a deeper understanding of the business strategy, the HR function is able to facilitate business units in delivering current business priorities. For instance, globalisation is driving the need for effective and efficient cross-cultural collaboration. HR can play a significant role in ensuring that employees working in such complex alliances have the skills they need for success, including influencing, political and strategic thinking skills.

Leading

'Leading' requires the ability to both 'enable' and 'follow' business needs but goes beyond this to proactively create value. This means HR must look ahead at industry trends and predict likely needs, resource priorities and strategic issues that could affect the business and target HR delivery to maximise the performance of the business (Wyatt-Haines 2007). For instance, in companies with a global strategy, with broader spans of control and global teams, HR must analyse the implications of global business models and align its people systems and structures to fulfil the strategy, keeping pace with the realities of a global customer base and looking at innovative ways to deliver service while reducing costs. This will involve building a global identity and a communication strategy underpinned by values and ethics; it will require cultural awareness, sensitivity to partners' concerns and regional issues and regulations. So while HR can add some value through following and enabling, a more strategic and impactful contribution requires leadership.

The typical business decision taken at senior level focuses on projected costs, risks and revenues, and the people implications tend to be an afterthought. Any really strategic HR director recognises that alignment with business strategy is not about simply obeying bottom-line imperatives, such as designing the most cost-effective structure, or integrating cultures as fast as possible following a merger but is also about looking ahead, building an organisation that people want to work in, give of their best to, and produce the enhanced revenues that so frequently do not materialise when change processes are badly handled. These different goals may be in tension and the HR director's role will inevitably be challenging to some extent. The effective HR leader is in there when the business decisions are taken, influencing and shaping thinking with reasoned and data-based arguments so that the people implications become integral to the business decision-making process.

The whole HR team, regardless of their roles and responsibilities, need to see how what they are doing contributes to the whole. The focus should be on what Ulrich terms the 'deliverables' or strategic outcomes, rather than just the 'do-ables' or tasks. Together, the vision and short-term needs should drive decisions about how HR should be structured, about the calibre and experience needed in the team, and the implications for line managers of any shift in HR roles. The short-term agenda should be prioritised, costed and delivered in a way that transfers skills to line managers.

Relationships

Any HR leader will set great store by developing a wide range of working relationships across the business, especially with key decision-makers and staff representatives. These relationships, and those developed by the HR team, will form the basis of business partnerships and will be key to preventing time being wasted on back-biting and political games.

The 'leading' HR team itself will be modelling agile, high performance work practices, especially learning from each other and developing expertise in key specialist areas such as mergers and acquisitions, organisation design, employee relations, analytics and so on. The team will import and export staff members with other functional and business backgrounds so that HR's language and modes of delivery are seen as integral to the way the business operates at its best, rather than ivory tower.

Since very few of the issues that HR need to engage with are likely to be one-dimensional or HR's sole responsibility – such as CSR, health and safety, employee communication, diversity, ethics, innovation, supply chain, productivity – Ulrich and Yeung (2019) suggest that HR should create multi-functional teams and work in partnership with other functional specialists such as IT and Finance. Indeed, HR functions aiming to deliver innovation value in the digital context should work with digital experts to encourage a culture of digital competence and gain a clear understanding of how and when digital can enhance human potential.

DELIVERING STRATEGIC OUTCOMES

In a changing context the strategic HRM focus should be on delivering the HR outcomes, which improve the probability of achieving the business strategy, for instance:

- Ensuring availability of competent human capital
- Building and maintaining key organisational capabilities
- Shaping a high-performance, agile culture and
- Managing risk.

What do CEOs want?

As key stakeholders, CEOs typically want HR to deliver a high-performance agile culture, flexible management of teams and transparent availability of information – all facets of organisational agility. HR has two important roles to play in agile transformation. One is to transform the function's own operating models and itself adopt agile ways of working. This is the focus of the next chapter. HR's second key role is supporting and enabling organisations moving through digital transformation, delivering much needed talent and new ways of working that enable adaptability, innovation, collaboration and speed. Deloitte's 'Agile Model of HR' (Mazor et al. 2015) states that human resources' job is not just to implement controls and standards and drive execution, but rather to facilitate and improve organisational agility. McKinsey research (Aghina et al. 2020) identified three main outcomes of agile transformations: improved customer satisfaction, employee engagement, and operational performance which make up what they call the 'agile impact engine'.

Vision of a high performing organisation

How does HR achieve these outcomes? This is where a clear, shared vision about how the organisation can be built over time to achieve agility and sustainable high performance can be helpful. Ever since Peters and Waterman (1982) published their work on 'excellence', many high-performance organisation frameworks have been developed and described in the literature. These all offer a 'best practice' perspective. A typical vision of a high performing organisation is one that attracts and retains the best people, is a great place to work and has high commitment work practices and strong corporate values which people are attuned to. Such an organisation has excellent leadership and a culture supportive of innovation, flexibility, knowledge-creation and sharing, where people are involved and able to work well across and beyond organisational boundaries.

This vision defines some of the key areas of longer-term focus, while the short-term immediate priorities should be filtered and delivered with the vision in mind. It's crucial to get the operational fundamentals right, since credibility will be based on high quality short-term delivery. Ulrich argues that HR should focus on achieving organisational outcomes in three generic areas of capability – Talent, Leadership and Organisation – that enable strategy to happen, that ensure customer share over time and increase investor confidence. By taking responsibility for the creation of the strategic capabilities – whether human or technological – that an organisation requires to win in the marketplace, HR demonstrates value since these provide intangibles such as innovation for investors (Scott-Jackson and Mayo 2016; Ulrich et al. 2017). In a merger scenario, for instance, how the change process is handled fundamentally affects the strategic potential of the new organisation. The emerging culture can become win-lose and undermine the whole point of the merger since people do not warm to cultural integration initiatives months after the event.

Whichever outcomes HR strategy sets out to achieve, agility should be a 'red thread' running through them. Focusing on outcomes that help organisations become more agile, enabling them to faster serve the market and seize opportunities, shows the added value of HR to the business. And by engaging proactively and leveraging technology HR can reimagine the organisation, create the conditions for expanded levels of creativity, exploration and problem-solving (Dignan 2019).

Encouragingly, the rapid response shown by many management teams and HR professionals to the challenges presented by the 2020–2021 pandemic suggests that, in the face of extreme pressure, organisations and HR teams can act with agility. Also, that people are front and centre of business recovery.

TALENT AND TALENT MANAGEMENT

As we discussed in Chapter 3, the experience economy is one of the more active trends deriving from the digital economy which is shaping personal lifestyles and being woven into architecture choices and organisation processes. Customer-centricity is key to business success in the digital age but how can HR impact on customer needs? Arguably by an intense focus on talent. Talent drives business results because the skilful deployment and performance of talented and engaged employees is widely recognised as key to achieving customer satisfaction and gaining and sustaining competitive advantage (Porter 1985). Similarly, Ulrich's *Leadership Capital Index* (2015), indicates that quality of leadership may affect 25% to 30% of a firm's market value.

Employee experience

Customers expect personalised products and services. So too do employees. In any 'war for talent', prospective employees are key stakeholders, and the 'digital native' generation of young people have their own demands and expectations that are making their way onto HR's agenda. In today's digital world, where technology plays an increasingly important role in the day-to-day lives of employees and smartphone use is ubiquitous, today's 'mobile native' workforce expects their employer to provide them with the same level of technology as they use in their personal lives as consumers. Organisations are being forced to rethink the way they work, recruit and communicate with their workforce to enable a better 'customer' experience for current and potential employees who want HR tools to be as intuitive and mobile as consumer apps.

Ensuring availability of competent human capital

Global trends suggest that competition for scarce talent is going to increase. As the digital revolution fundamentally transforms the ways we work, for workers there is a seemingly constant flow of new capabilities to acquire. Today, chief executives expect their strategic HR business partners to help them understand what must be done with regard to attracting and upskilling people to ensure the business strategies can be successfully implemented. HR can help their organisation secure the best available talent in a candidate-driven market, for instance by developing an attractive employer brand fit for the digital age that distinguishes the company from its competitors and makes it harder for other organisations to compete.

NB Since the 1998 publication of McKinsey's 'War for Talent' study, many managers have considered talent management to be synonymous with human capital management.

Expanding scope of talent management

Conventional work and talent models tend to be company focused, one-size-fits-all, rules-based, internally consistent and bureaucratic. In the past, early talent offerings were often transactional, antiquated and uninspiring. Having a joined-up approach was difficult since many HR functions were quite siloed and disconnected, for example with specialists in talent acquisition not talking much with the chief learning officer about the links between talent and learning organisation practices. Success was typically measured in terms of getting ROI, e.g., from training investment and the integration of HR strategy with business planning processes, as one HR director describes here:

> We have integrated our talent management processes with the business planning process. As each major business area discusses and sets their three-year business goals, they will also be setting their three-year human capital goals and embedding those human capital goals within their business plan. Achievement of these goals will be tracked through our management processes.

The scope of talent management has gradually expanded over the last two decades to include such processes as:

- Workforce/talent planning
- Recruitment and onboarding
- High potential development
- Succession planning
- Leadership development
- Motivation and Retention
- Career pathing and development

Today, in order to source and retain the workforce needed for success and to use HR activities such as workforce planning, and so on, to best effect, systemic, rather than siloed, thinking is needed. As an Accenture report (2017) highlights, taking a one-dimensional approach is unlikely to pay off: *Whilst many have made recent investments in workforce reform, change is needed to develop a workforce that is sufficiently flexible, specialised and self-renewing to be properly responsive to changing stakeholder expectations.*

As businesses adopt new work models and agile practices, such as rapid prototyping, iterative feedback, team-based decisions, and task-centred 'sprints', which are better suited for adapting in the short term, they are looking for more agile talent practices that can ensure a good supply of the right kinds of talent, available when they need them. They want an Agile HR function that becomes a fluid broker of people, able to secure the people with the right skills for the organisation at the right time and on the right employment contract. To be credible, HR must act as role models of agility and agile values and work with top management to ensure sign up and clarity about purpose, fairness and ambition.

The talent broker role is very challenging given that, in their search for flexibility, many organisations have adopted more fragmented employment models comprising variations on the use of contract workers alongside employees who often have little job security. As more individual tasks become automatable through AI and sophisticated algorithms, jobs are being redefined and re-categorised. A PwC (2018) study reports that a third of people worldwide are now worried about losing their job to automation. And this risk is real in many cases. For people lacking ability to add value in new ways, obsolescence beckons unless they can upskill (Manyika et al. 2017; Pew Research Center 2017): Should HR be leading the argument for investing in people, reskilling them for more value-adding roles? Building and maintaining trust with employees and wider society is essential for corporate reputation, especially when it comes to the use of automation and job losses.

There is also an ethical dimension to this – how to use technologies to get a better grip on productivity without electronic surveillance that covertly controls workers; how to deploy technologies without infringing employees' privacy and breaching compliance rules and regulations such as GDPR, especially in a remote working situation? Trust is at the heart of productivity. Showing faith in employees and transitioning to output based metrics helps establish rules that avoid micro-management, such as demanding more frequent check-ins, and also demonstrates respect for boundaries so that people can have work-life balance.

As companies seek their employees' commitment, company values and fairness increasingly matter, and HR must lead the charge on rebuilding trust. Trust is the bedrock of a healthy employment relationship between employer and employee, where a 'win' for the organisation should be matched by a 'win' for the employee. Being clear about accountabilities – who will do what when – is more important than ever.

A humanising influence

In an increasingly virtual digital work world, HR should be a humanising influence, acting to personalise service and connect people to one another. For instance, HR can promote remote working rituals such as end-of-day 'stand downs' that both track progress and alignment and allow some social interaction. They can encourage community collaboration through hackathons and social get-togethers via virtual coffee meetings. Similarly, HR must provide a strong voice externally and internally on embedding company values within a multigenerational and diverse workforce.

Arguably, the primary beneficiaries of an HR strategy are the employees themselves, in terms of what they have, feel and do. With digital and other forms of talent in short supply, talent strategies must adjust to meet the changing needs of the workforce. So rather than applying a solely top-down planning approach, now it's more about achieving employee outcomes and enhancing the employee experience. To bring this new lens to talent management requires a mindset of agile learning on the part of HR, company leaders and workers.

Since today's workforce is more diverse than ever before, workforce strategies must be designed to meet different needs and expectations. Accenture (2017) argues that for real agility, human-centric workforce strategies are needed:

> The key to workforce agility lies in a strategy that puts people first, enabled by technology. With an eye on business outcomes, leaders will develop talent strategies that liberate human potential and help shape an agile workforce – one able to confidently face the challenges ahead.

Yet Accenture concludes that, despite the scale of change, relatively few organisations so far appear to have formulated comprehensive workforce strategies for the Fourth Industrial Revolution.

De Waal's High Performance Organisation (HPO) framework (2018) suggests that Employee Quality is a key factor in high performance. HPOs deliberately improve employee quality by continuously working on the development of the workforce, training them to be flexible, resilient and creative. HPOs inspire people to improve their skills for extraordinary accomplishment, making them responsible for their performance at the same time. This suggests that HR must proactively facilitate rapid learning, embrace the dynamic career demands of their people and also redesign their talent practices to help employees to own their own development. The result of talent planning should be that organisations have the talent they need to succeed, and that employees feel their needs and aspirations have been heard and taken into account.

A win-win psychological contract

Since behaviour is induced, not compelled, this means that the employment relationship underpinning conventional talent strategies must shift too. Coyle-Shapiro and colleagues (2019) argue that the implications for employment relations of globalisation, organisational restructuring and downsizing have led to renewed interest in the concept of psychological contract. This has become a framework for understanding the shifting exchange relationship between employers and employees. This can be examined at the individual level – discretionary effort etc; organisational level – the different HR micropractices (like attracting, recruiting, rewarding, training, developing and appraisal) and topics like diversity, flexibility, work systems etc; and societal level – industrial relations, employee relationships, future of work and so on.

In contrast to the old relational 'psychological contract' of mutual commitment and paternalistic career processes, based on managerialist approaches to people management, a new psychological contract is emerging that tends to be more transactional and less long-term in focus (Sonnenberg et al. 2011). Employees expect an adult-adult and more value-laden, ethical and fair relationship with their employers, and at the same time they want to be involved in decisions that affect them and supported during change. Essentially, this means co-creating a new partnership with employees, aiming for a win–win relationship, a product of which is employee engagement (Holbeche and Matthews 2012).

For a win–win employment relationship, employers should listen to what workers want too. Today's workforce is more tech-driven than its forebears and expects greater choice about when, where and how they work and control over their physical space. The idea that employees can have choice should be embedded in the culture, even something as simple as having the ability to change the temperature in an office space can help people feel appreciated, engaged and happy in their day-to-day work. This also means tackling some of the big issues that matter to people:

- How can we build workplaces where diversity is celebrated and ensure good work practices for all, with fair pay and opportunities for progression and an organisational culture where people are free to be themselves?
- How can we address the growing demand to address some of the more damaging aspects of contemporary work-life – the long hours, work intensification, pressure and 'always on' elements which are reported to be contributing to growing mental health issues in the workplace?
- How do we prepare people for flexible careers of the future as part of an agile workforce? Since career impatience is a driving factor, does the organisation have lateral or cross-functional moves available, or could employees even move into a new role with less responsibility to learn a new area, without risking future promotion opportunities within the organisation?
- How can HR develop engaging managers and values-based leaders? Are there opportunities to increase employee voice by actively involving people in change? How can we build a strong focus on employee well-being?

Agile HR should create employee experiences that add value at every stage of the employee life cycle, for instance by developing authentic employer brands that attract candidates, enabling employees to experience work–life balance and well-being and advance their career while also addressing organisational needs for flexibility. As demand from employees grows for greater flexibility, will demand for flexible working continue and become an essential part of a mutually beneficial 'new deal'? By offering employees work/life programmes that they actually want – with flexible hours and more benefits, such as on-site wellness programmes, aerobics and yoga classes, and educational advancement opportunities – HR can help organisations achieve reduced turnover, more highly motivated employees and improved productivity.

Enabling remote working and virtual management

Technology and telecommuting enable employees to work across geographies in virtual teams on a variety of tasks. During global lockdowns due to the coronavirus crisis, many workers and managers found working from home to be effective. The United Kingdom research by ADP (2019) suggests that the idea of a four-day week is becoming popular, especially for those workers in the top part of the labour market hourglass. However, telecommuting does not suit everyone, and for some people, the constant focus required in meetings conducted via Zoom and Slack etc is exhausting. HR should therefore review how well they currently manage their flexible workforce and identify new ways to increase mutual commitment and benefits.

Looking ahead to more hybrid ways of working, recruiters and employment specialists should work with managers to identify specific positions and staff best suited for telecommuting. HR practitioners must address the health and safety, legal and tax ramifications connected with telecommuting work arrangements, as well as put in place resources to deal with the ergonomics, mental health and provision of equipment issues.

Grant Thornton's HR team created a trusted platform 'Where's your head at?' for sharing resources and information about mental illness. Mental health training is at the heart of the site. Using the company intranet, employees can open discussions and share their own stories of mental illness – efforts that should help to counter the many stigmas attached to mental health. The first week alone drew more than 7,500 views. The CEO, a very supportive advocate of mental health, personally replied to some submissions. It has made the business feel like more of a community (People Management, Sept 2016).

Enabling employees to feel connected to the organisation remotely goes beyond leveraging tech resources. Developing protocols around virtual check-ins, such as weekly 'stand ups' helps people keep in touch with developments in the team. Communication platforms that go beyond email can help ensure that all employees, regardless of function, level or location, feel included. Providing high quality online training and development modules such as robust virtual onboarding programmes, and training managers in remote coaching, can equip people with the tools they need to succeed.

Careers

Retention of talent is a key outcome of any HR strategy. Gallup's State of the Global Workplace report (2021) suggests that the primary reason people leave their jobs is for career growth opportunities. After all, with the prospect of longer working lives, people will naturally think more strategically about their jobs. Similarly, Glassdoor research suggests that articulating a prosperous career path and maintaining a positive culture appear to be important ways to ensure worker satisfaction. More personalised approaches to development, training, recognition and rewards need to co-exist alongside the collective – being able to balance both will be a key measure of effective HR approaches.

Employee engagement

Employee engagement and retention are a primary focus for agile HR and L&D teams. Every organisation needs employees who not only possess the skills and knowledge required for the job but are also motivated and committed to using those skills on behalf of the employer. Yet employee 'engagement' has become a major challenge for HR teams in every sector because the changing work environment has resulted in a loosening of the conventional emotional ties by which employees remained attached to their employer. According to Gallup's State of the Global Workplace report (2021), only 15% of employees are engaged.

'Engagement' describes an employee's emotional attachment to and/or identification with the organisation and is what most employers would like to see in their workforce. Some argue that engagement reflects an individual's intrinsic motivation, and that work itself, access to resources and the success of the organisation are important motivators. Others argue that it is very easy to demotivate otherwise productively motivated staff by managing them poorly. So HR needs to consider which factors may increase the potential for increased engagement, especially of key groups, and also must act on areas that undermine engagement.

How employee engagement is achieved remains a source of much debate, though there is some consensus on the categories of ability, motivation and opportunity that make up commitment-type HR strategies, as we shall discuss in Chapter 9. Other people, especially senior leadership, line managers and co-workers directly impact on engagement. Opportunities for learning, career growth and recognition, quality of work/life balance, the physical work environment and safety are typical important factors, as are fair pay and benefits.

However, which specific practices should be assessed within each category is less clear since each organisation tailors its people strategy to its own needs. For instance, in a business with a clear people-centred value chain, such as the UK's National Health Service, it is recognised that

> High-quality, patient-centred care depends on …managing staff well, allowing staff to exercise control over their work, listening to what they have to say, involving them in decisions, training and developing them and paying attention to the physical and emotional consequences of caring for patients.
>
> (Dr Jocelyn Cornwell, Chair of the advisory group; Director, The Point of Care Foundation 2014)

There are strong correlations in the literature between how much an employee personally identifies with the organisation and wants to see it succeed and a commitment-based HR strategy. Commitment-based HR strategies are assumed to have a positive effect on employee satisfaction and organisational commitment; they generally produce better performance on core tasks, with more people going beyond the call of duty, greater willingness to share knowledge and generally lower turnover rates (Sun et al. 2007).

Nowadays, Ulrich places some emphasis on HR's role in employee advocacy, safeguarding employee well-being and enabling people to have meaningful working lives. However, critics argue that a commitment HR strategy can also be used to exploit workers by making them (willingly) work harder, yet without genuine commitment from their employer in return (Francis et al. 2011).

Purpose

Feeling emotionally aligned to the organisation's purpose and values makes it more likely that people will 'go the extra mile'. Research by Richard Boyatzis (in McKinsey 2020) suggests how, especially in fast-changing times, a shared vision or shared sense of purpose is the strongest predictor of organisational-leadership effectiveness, engagement, organisational citizenship and even product innovation.

> That's because people get into that physiological and neurological state where they are more open to ideas, more connected, and more engaged when the sense of purpose, not the goals, is clear and when people know that you care about each other.

Edmondson (in McKinsey 2020) agrees that purpose and vision are critical today, but only to the extent that both are recognised as updatable, and reflective of a continuous learning process. She points out that what makes management-by-wandering-around so successful is the ability to make a genuine link between a person's task or job and a larger overarching purpose. That link, which might not be immediately obvious, can become very clear if leaders help people look for, and then make, those connections, and if these are genuine. And now, with tools like Zoom, communications have become more explicit and structured; so leaders must ask direct questions about what's working and what isn't and engage in thoughtful discussions on how – in a rapidly evolving context – implementing the vision is shifting accordingly. *'Although not as spontaneous as walking around, these Zoom chats, when kept to relatively small sizes, can still develop the connective tissue linking actions to a shared vision for the future'.*

'Voice' is another significant element in many engagement definitions – the chance for employees to be consulted and have a say about what happens at work. The specific practices of direct participation in decision-making, challenging jobs and extensive and open access to information are associated with both work and life satisfaction. These are also key ingredients of organisational agility which favours flat structures that enable people to contribute their ideas.

Edmondson (in McKinsey 2020) argues that if people are to speak up with work-relevant content, they need to feel psychologically safe, with an absence of interpersonal fear. Ironically, for many people during the pandemic, the explicitness of the physical lack of safety has been experienced as a shared fear, which has allowed leaders and workers to be more open and better able to voice their thoughts and concerns with colleagues. This collective fear thus becomes a potential driver of collaboration and innovation, further contributing to an open environment for producing and sharing ideas that under normal conditions may have remained unshared. Beyond crisis situations, HR must strive to create the context for psychological safety and employee engagement by working with leadership, line managers and trade unions to create policies and encourage inclusive communication practices that build effective employee relations.

So at a time of radical transformations like this, when there are choices to be made about how 'human' they want their organisations to be, employers, in particular HR, must stand up and argue that genuine commitment-type strategies are preferable.

Integrating a contingent workforce

The scope of HR strategies must take account of the changing nature of the workforce. It is predicted that location and time-based employment will be increasingly eroded and permanent, full-time jobs will dwindle. Contingent workers are noncompany employees who work in jobs structured to last a specified period of time. Today organisations use a variety of contractual arrangements to secure the human resource they require. For instance, non-employed 'freelancers' & contract workers make up 11% of the Singapore resident workforce (HRM, Asia 2017). In the United Kingdom, 40% of jobs are non-standard; temporary, self-employed, part-time (CIPD 2013). Most contingent workers hold from one to two assignments within a six-month period, although assignments can last as long as five years. Contingent assignments are available in virtually every field and profession.

The challenge for some HR functions is that they have not been used to incorporating this 'non-employed' group into the workforce, or their people strategy. Companies have traditionally kept contract workers or part-time workers on the fringes of their organisation. Studies show that many organisations do not provide training, appraisal, or even include them in internal communications.

Given that such workers increasingly make core contributions, and as work arrangements become ever more fragmented, there is a need to rapidly update mind-sets and concepts of the 'organisation' and who's in and who's out. HR specialists dealing with legal issues, employment, reward, benefits, employee relations and employee services should award proper contingent worker status in accordance with, or ahead of, employment legislation and ensure the fair and productive integration of contingent workers into the organisation's workforce. There needs to be a consistent employee experience for all.

LEADERSHIP

If there is one priority that CEOs and HR leaders agree on, it is the ongoing need for the best people and the best leaders. Leadership, Ulrich argues, accounts for between 30 and 40% of what investors look for in a company. Dysfunctional leadership teams act as brakes on organisational agility and effectiveness. The 'turn-off' factor of inappropriate management styles is a major risk factor for organisations since it is a major reason for people wishing to leave their organisations. Neubauer et al. (2017) found that one of the main blockers of agility is leaders not embracing new ways of working (35%), leaving people feeling unempowered. That is perhaps not so surprising given that, many management-driven strategies appear built around cost-saving and compliance rather than commitment or innovation. Senge et al. (1999) argue that this is sub-optimal since deep changes – in how people think, what they believe, how they see the world – are difficult, if not impossible, to achieve through compliance. Once we know our purpose and direction and performance requirement, to translate 'strategic intention' into 'reality'(performance output), the challenge is to mobilise people, which is hard to do if people are required to simply obey company edicts, or if people expect to be replaced by machines.

In an agile organisation, the task of senior leaders becomes creating a broad sense of direction and empowering the organisation to make the changes required. To build organisational resilience, senior leadership must more actively anticipate competitive changes and move from reacting to proacting. This means 'getting on the balcony' (Heifetz and Laurie 1997), anticipating change, moving from reacting to proacting and providing sponsorship of initiatives. Leaders need to lead from the front by setting the tone, role modelling the ability to cope with ambiguity and change themselves and living the values. Transformational leadership, as exercised by senior management, will be a key ingredient in leading people through change, engaging employees and harnessing their initiative to achieve innovative solutions to business problems.

Leadership is vital to establishing learning environments where innovation can flourish and people can better connect and decide to work, learn and change together (Edmondson 2018). For this, people need to believe that they, and their team, are 'safe' to experiment without fear of blame. If there is defensive siloed thinking, innovation and agility are undermined. Leading organisations in a Workday (2020) study have a culture and climate where learning from failure is well-established so people can try things out, take risks and embrace a more agile way of working.

Senior leaders can create a climate of 'psychological safety' by encouraging people to exchange ideas and demonstrating respect, sharing their own challenges and fallibilities, and taking the long-term view, tolerating failure in the spirit of learning (De Smet 2020; Edmondson 2020). Thus they reduce the 'fight or flight' response so typical of when people feel at risk. HR's task is to develop emotionally intelligent leaders who can create that psychological safety so that employees can experience the autonomy, mastery and purpose that make work fulfilling (Boyatsis, 2020; Pink 2018).

Leadership at all levels

Reflecting the move to agility and worker empowerment, many organisations are flattening structures and adopting results-based work models underpinned by worker autonomy. The trend is away from classic authoritarian leadership to new forms of distributed decision making, where decisions get pushed to the peripheries of the organisation to meet the demands of faster business cycles that have been accelerated during the coronavirus crisis.

Developing leadership and accountability at all levels will be key to agility. To create greater empowerment at all levels, HR should coach senior leaders to build a cascade of accountability through the middle and front-line management spine and establish the principle of taking decisions as close to the action as possible (Anand et al. 2019; Carney and Getz 2009). Senior leaders should be encouraged to practise 'tight-loose' leadership (Weick 1976) which they can both generally encourage decision-making at the right level but can also impose 'tight' leadership if circumstances dictate. Leaders may need help to make this transition. HR can also develop leadership at all levels directly, for instance by involving people in reviewing and revitalising the values, strategising around key challenges, sharing ideas about how to make HR processes simpler, more effective and user-friendly.

Developing leaders

Developing top management to embrace and enact their changing leadership roles, and building pools of talent for future leadership roles, should be a key HR contribution to business success. HR can expose leaders to fresh thinking and help them look beyond their current horizons for instance through scenario planning, by arranging visits to other organisations that leaders can learn from and other strategic activities (Luthans and Avolio 2003). Action learning–type interventions and formal mentoring, lateral movements, 'stretch assignments', and opportunities with higher responsibilities help managers develop awareness of the multiple roles of a leader as peer, follower and stakeholder (Hirst et al. 2004).

Although training and development is important, it can be difficult to influence individuals who are unintelligent, dogmatic, narcissistic, unethical or impassive toward others (Eva et al. 2019). OD approaches like story-telling can reach managers at a deeper emotional level to persuade them to stop acting like the traditional boss in order to become a more agile and humane leader. As Margaret Wheatley says, 'We need leaders who put service over self, who can be steadfast through crises and failures, who want to stay present and make a difference to the people, situations and causes they care about' (Wheatley 2017).

Who should be developed as future leaders? In line with other talent processes, succession planning is moving into a more consensual mode, with both individual and organisational interests equally taken into account. Therefore, as Joiner (2019) points out, along with extensive leadership development, HR should actively recruit individuals who show moral traits and have attributes such as cognitive agility and emotional intelligence, perseverance, humility and empathy that further contribute to and facilitate responsible leadership behaviours. HR can also build a pipeline of future leaders who 'get it' and who are capable of delivering a successful business by making the most of the potential of both technology and humans.

HR should also actively monitor how leadership is enacted, working to improve the calibre of current and future leaders, and ensuring that an ethical approach underpins business practices, leadership behaviour and decision-making. Current metrics used to assess leaders' performance such as balance sheets, market shares and quarterly reports based on short-term evaluation are focused mostly or exclusively on shareholder value and profitability (Svensson and Wood 2008). However, given the present context, performance metrics should be adopted that are associated with responsible leadership behaviours and take a longer-term perspective on achieving performance as well as a broader definition of stakeholder network value (Svensson and Wood 2008). This will be a means of holding leaders to account for adherence to ethical standards in their behaviours with stakeholders, as well as a means of defining success. This means HR must be prepared to challenge poor management practice – a potentially risky endeavour – but also a powerful contribution to enable better top team functioning and build more effective organisations.

ORGANISATION

Ulrich has always argued that the added value of HR is essentially about its impact on the business. Ulrich's third generic capability is **Organisation.** In a 2016 paper, (Ingham and Ulrich 2016) Ulrich argued that since the 'war for talent' of the late 1990s, talent management has promoted the cult of the individual. In today's context of ongoing change individual talent is not enough. It is groups of people working as an organisation that can be far more effective than the same number of individuals, even if those individuals are highly talented. In other words, the whole organisation should be greater than the sum of its parts. Under *Organisation* Ulrich includes three dimensions:

- Capabilities – What is the organisation good at doing and what should it be known for? Competitive differentiators.

- Management action – Create a clear message about the desired culture to share inside and outside; turn culture identity into employee actions; and create, shape and reinforce culture through management practices.
- Culture – How do we shape the right patterns and routines that will enable us to win? How the organisation works: event, pattern and identity.

Competitive differentiator capabilities

The resource-based view of the firm (Barney et al. 2011), suggests that for sustainable competitive advantage resources are needed which are rare, valuable, inimitable and owned by the organisation. The dynamic capabilities perspective (Teece and Pisano 1994) on the other hand, considers capabilities such as 'change-ability' – that allows organisations to integrate cultures, build and reconfigure resources and capabilities to address rapidly changing environments – as a stronger source of sustainable advantage. Others include sensing, seizing and reconfiguring capabilities, knowledge creation, product development, change management and strategic planning routines. These capabilities evolve over time in response to the organisation's environment. In today's parlance, these are agile capabilities.

Building and maintaining key capabilities

Some of the capabilities that have become increasingly important to competitive advantage and strategic success include innovation (in product, market, services, business models), agility (speed of change or flexibility), collaboration (teamwork, cross-functional teams, merger or acquisition integration), customer service, efficiency, managing risk and changing culture. None of these capabilities is developed in a vacuum or silo but requires a systemic approach. Consequently, organisational development has risen in importance and should be a key part of HR professionals' toolkit.

Take business agility for instance: since the dimensions of strategy, people, task, structure, skills and systems are closely interlinked, agility does not just happen – we need to plan it into our thinking and our decisions – including our workforce and employment decisions. To embed agility at enterprise level requires a virtuous circle in which HR works with leaders to define what agility looks like in business and strategy, socialises new thinking, creates a dynamic learning environment, reinforces and rewards agility in action and builds stakeholder coalitions for success. This will require sustained attention to building flexibility and skills through deployment, careers and establishing a culture that expects and supports learning so HR should be in the forefront of facilitating organisational learning.

Linking capability

Organisations also need the ability to operate effectively across boundaries since it is a given that many of the challenges facing organisations cannot be addressed independently but require broader interagency approaches across sectors. Many organisations are now less hierarchically structured than in the past and operate through a fluid multiplicity of collaborations, so businesses seek flexibility, and collaboration as core skills. A CIPD (2014) report on agile working described organisations increasingly operating as 'network orchestrators' (P11). The report cites the example of Proctor and

Gamble which in 2010 sourced over 50% of its innovations externally through a pro-gramme called 'Connect + Develop', in contrast to less than 10% in 2001.

HR can help strengthen an organisation's linking capability – enabling the organ-isation to achieve synergies through collaboration – for instance by upskilling people for different ways of working when in partnership with other organisations. HR can help managers ensure that cross-boundary team roles are appropriately designed and structured; good communication processes established; and cross-organisational inter-dependencies identified, with teams able to share learning across boundaries. HR should be able to identify where broader system improvements can be made in the light of what the business is aiming to do since, from its cross-organisational perspective, HR can see how all the internal processes and systems within the business interlink, including where there are areas of duplication and unnecessary activities that add little to business effectiveness.

Management action

HR strategies are delivered mainly through management action which affects employee capabilities and attitudes. Line managers are the primary players in shaping a high-performance work environment. It is managers who create, shape and reinforce culture through day-to-day management practices. The way employees perceive their experience with management is strongly related to employee and customer satisfaction results.

Since workers in agile organisations supervise their own results, the role of operations managers changes away from controlling resources and work distribution towards be-coming coach/facilitator/supporter of mainly self-managing teams. The task of manag-ers is to build individual and team capability, enable diversity and employee well-being. Some managers may need help in developing the skills they need for this role because breaking habits and acting differently can be demanding (Gustafsson et al. 2012). HR can help managers understand the new management practices and how to practise them and communicate them to others. HR can support line managers to diagnose needs, design-effective structures, embed agility into roles, find ways to incorporate new skills into daily work and identify ways of managing accountabilities – as seen most clearly with multiskilling in some manufacturing roles. As a result, managers can deliberately develop individual, team and organisational learning.

In particular, HR can help managers to develop coaching skills, locate learning op-portunities for their teams and help them reflect and make sense of new experiences. Providing support will be worthwhile:

> With productivity being such an important measure of business potential and suc-cess, employers need to invest in recruiting and training up managers to be a real asset to their teams through facilitating, not hindering, productivity. The difference this can make is transformational.
>
> (ADP 2019)

In addition, HR can provide workshops and other resources to support managers and workers going through change, equipping them with tools to manage uncertainty and deal with the situation as well as possible, such as how to spot signs of stress and access coun-selling/support for team members experiencing stress. They can help managers review their own and others' ever-expanding workloads and design roles that are meaningful.

HR can also provide advice and development to help managers guide their increasingly complex teams, many of whom will comprise 'non-employees' or contract workers, or teams working virtually, often across organisational or geographical boundaries. HR can provide robust and straightforward policies, tools and management processes which improve the ways managers and leaders manage performance. They can also create a range of communication vehicles through which employees can become involved in decision-making and feel a sense of community and belonging.

CULTURE

Developing strategy can be challenging enough; implementing it can be more demanding since it requires others to change their behaviour. As Ulrich (1998) suggests, '…the successful organizations will be those that are able to quickly turn strategy into action: to manage processes intelligently and efficiently: to maximize employee contribution and commitment; and to create the conditions for seamless change'.

However, the challenge that many strategic leaders face is that it is NOT enough to change strategies, structures and systems, unless the thinking that produced those strategies, also changes. In this respect, strategy and culture are twins. The culture itself, and therefore the environment at the organisational level has the potential to 'trump' strategic ambitions: *'Good people, for example, in corrosive or toxic environments have been known to collude in undesirable behaviour. It is the collective set of systems, processes, practices and disciplines that establish the boundaries of action'* (*Leading with Compassion*, NHS England, Nov 2014).

Organisational culture is therefore increasingly recognised as central to organisations' ability to achieve sustainable high performance and productivity. On top of robust planning, development of resources, and so forth, successful strategy implementation also requires adjusting beliefs, values, and assumptions which will ensure the appropriate patterns of behaviour to implement the strategy. Agile, for instance, starts with a mindset and culture, before being translated into strategies, structures, HR processes and business performance. It is the right mix of mindsets, plans, assets, leadership and culture that lead to superior performance.

Shifting culture and mindsets takes some doing. To close the strategic implementation gap leaders need to put more emphasis on making congruent the inner and outer changes required to get to the heart of the delivery issues. At organisational level, this means listening to the first-hand experiences of staff and customers together; engaging the leadership; connecting the organisational strategy with individual goals and objectives, while also holding people to account on both performance and values; signalling what is valued and working to retain your best people. It also means defining and clearly articulating or revisiting and re-affirming organisational values in behavioural terms and incorporating them into organisational life.

Organisations will need creativity, innovation and continuous renewal if they are to sustain success HR can play a key role in designing structures, roles, processes and practices that facilitate creativity and enable knowledge to be captured and disseminated, so that wheels do not have to be continuously reinvented. Companies most likely to succeed will be those that find ways of maximising the knowledge present in today's ever-more fluid organisation structures and of applying that knowledge to continuously produce new products and services, achieving competitive advantage. A customer-centric learning culture is needed where continuous innovation is prized, and an organisational climate that attracts key workers – where transformation is ongoing, not something that is 'completed'. The question of whether and how this can be achieved will be explored in Chapters 14–17.

To create 'just, learning cultures where improvement methods can engage colleagues, patients and carers, deliver cumulative performance improvements, and make health and care organisations great places to work' the UK's National Health Service has found that compassionate, inclusive leadership is required to enable teams to deliver better patient care and value for money while also delivering continuous improvements to population health *(National Improvement and Leadership Development Board 2016)*. For leaders, this means paying close attention to all the people they lead, understanding the situations they face, responding empathetically and taking thoughtful and appropriate action to help. Inclusive leadership means progressing equality, valuing diversity and challenging power imbalances.

Since Agile is primarily a team-based approach, scaling up agility can be challenging. HR practitioners will need at least some knowledge of organisation development and design if they are to contribute effectively. Large organisations are typically far from nimble, though they may have the ability to buy in necessary insight and adopt various models, for example Spotify, the SAFe model or Scrum at Scale, whereas a small organisation has to innovate step by step. While HR does not need to be an expert in each of these models, it's important to be aware of them and be ready to ask the right questions and help leaders make the decisions about what's right for the organisation, right for your culture and what you're trying to achieve.

And, as Aghina et al. (2015) point out, not everything has to change. The ability to be both stable and dynamic is the essence of true organisational agility. Organisations need a firm yet flexible 'backbone' that binds together structural stability (standard operating procedures; governance which dictates how decisions are made; and processes which determine how things get done) and cultural stability (shared purpose, direction and values). This stability acts as a balancing platform for dynamic capabilities (for instance, fluid changes to strategy and team setup). The challenge is to manage the tensions between them and find the right balance of agility and stability.

HR needs to take stock of the current culture (including within the HR function itself), identify the critical few behaviours that could make a difference, and be willing to break established patterns, including challenging 'sacred cows'. They need to develop change leaders at all levels since new practice modelled by change leaders is a powerful means of demonstrating the way ahead. They must also work with managers to identify and remove barriers to performance and engagement.

ETHICS AND TRUST

The HR system should be based not only on added value, but also on moral values. Corporate culture, reputation and ethics are often synonymous and also represent risks. It is in the organisation's interest to establish sustainable and trustworthy relationships with both internal and external stakeholders based on criteria of fairness and legitimacy (Paauwe 2004). Taking a value-laden or 'ethical' HR approach will bring major benefits to all stakeholders. Organisations with an effective risk culture address risk quickly and effectively by acknowledging it, encouraging transparency and enforcing respect for controls.

Fairness and legitimacy are synonymous with 'treating people well'. Deloitte research (2017) states that 'topics such as "mission", "values" and "contribution to society" are driving engagement more than ever. Culture and work environment have become the new drivers of employment brand and employee passion'. Similarly, the CIPD (2017) found that organisational values, including authentic CSR policies, and company culture are most important factors in attracting candidates, followed jointly by career development opportunities and pay and benefits (CIPD 2017). Indeed, when selecting an employer candidates value 'culture' and 'career growth' almost twice as much as they value 'compensation and benefits'. Organisational practices with respect to climate change for example can attract or deter both customers and potential employees. Similarly, how fairly or otherwise an organisation treats its contingent workforce, especially those in the gig economy, will affect how an employer is perceived, not just by the people on zero hours contracts but also by many employees in the top part of the labour market hourglass who view dimly any poor treatment by their employer of people in the bottom part of the hourglass. Some are choosing to walk away.

So as companies seek their employees' commitment, HR must lead the charge on rebuilding trust. Trust is at the heart of productivity, the bedrock of a healthy employment relationship between employer and employee, where a 'win' for the organisation should be matched by a 'win' for the employee. Employees everywhere are challenging their organisations to uphold fairness and respect for all in the workplace. Precisely how employers maintain and improve trust among the workforce will depend on the organisation and the context in which it operates. However, typical actions that build trust include regular and honest communication and holding to account senior leaders as much as people on the shop floor for their behaviour in line with corporate values.

HR should take stock of its practices from the ethical and fairness perspectives. Do HR processes reinforce the desired cultural direction? For example, do training, evaluations and promotions emphasise collaboration? Are rotations required for moving up? Are there fair performance and reward processes? Do people get promoted despite not behaving in line with the values? As always, policies count for little since action speaks louder than words.

Diversity, inclusion and equality

In recent times, public awareness of inherent injustices and various forms of discrimination suffered by different groups has been raised through protest movements such as #Me Too, Black Lives Matter and the Transgender Rights Movement. Yet achieving diversity, and ensuring fair treatment for all, remains a major challenge for many organisations and is becoming a corporate reputation and also a recruitment and retention issue. Many HR practitioners recognise that the organisation's composition should reflect its diverse customer base and should also be responsive to the needs and demands of an increasingly diverse workforce.

Organisations view diversity differently. For some, diversity is about an organisation's effectiveness at using the talents of people of different backgrounds, experiences and perspective; for others diversity includes group differences along the lines of 'protected characteristics' such as age, race, gender, sexual orientation and disabilities, as well as individual differences, such as communication style and career experience. For yet others, diversity is about paying special attention to improving the representation of women and minorities in key positions and respecting people's different religious beliefs and practices. And in global organisations a person's nationality can also be viewed as an advantage or disadvantage.

Some organisations approach diversity solely from a compliance perspective. HR has the challenge of protecting the organisation from infringement of the increasingly copious amounts of employment law. Take age discrimination for example which is outlawed across Europe. Not only can people work into older age; in many cases they will have to. Equally many older workers have the prospect of drawing generous final salary scheme pensions while younger workers will have a much less advantageous pensions deal. The growing pensions burden on companies has resulted in virtually closed access to final salary schemes or their equivalent.

Others go further, developing inclusive policies that support the recruitment, management, motivation, welfare and retention of a more diverse workforce as a key part of the evolving HR agenda. For instance, the Royal Mail Group's long-standing culture meant making gender diversity a priority. Within two months of starting with the company, women are given an opportunity to take part in an 'onboarding interview' aimed at identifying any reasons they might want to leave the business. All senior managers have taken unconscious bias training and hiring managers are required to complete an unconscious bias e-learning module as part of wider interview training. Assessor panels are required to be 'balanced' in diversity terms. All senior succession pipelines have diversity targets across gender and ethnicity and all cohorts of graduates must meet those targets. Senior men are actively encouraged to champion diversity. Female successors have now been identified for half of all critical roles and the culture has shifted significantly, though it is recognised that the transformation will have taken five years to achieve (People Management, Sept 2016).

Reflective activity

- In implementing your organisation's strategy, which features of your current organisational culture are an asset and which are a liability?
- What would it take to build a more agile, 'compassionate' and engaging culture? (Assuming this was desirable.)
- How can we build workplaces where diversity is celebrated and ensure good work practices for all, with fair pay and opportunities for progression and an organisational culture where people are free to be themselves?

CONCLUSION

In this chapter, we have taken account of some of the context trends discussed in Chapter 3 and considered several areas where HR could contribute strategic value, many of which we shall explore in more detail in later chapters. To gain traction requires HR to build social capital inside and outside the organisation, fostering trust and breaking down silos.

As we have discussed here, HR can help build an agile and diverse workforce and attract potential recruits with attractive and authentic employee value propositions. They can develop agile management and leadership. They can stimulate culture change to focus on improving the quality of customer experience. They can create awareness of the need for change, mobilising and engaging staff to support the organisation's vision and mission. They can devise policies which are completely in line with, and provide line of sight to, the organisation's purpose and values.

They can help build more agile organisational forms and equip people for new ways of working. They can design the organisation into small, high-performance teams that set their own targets, and also help transcend barriers between functions and geographies, allowing the organisation to solve problems or approach new opportunities collaboratively. They can encourage and teach people to give each other direct feedback, create programmes for recognition and peer-to-peer rewards and develop policies to foster diversity in teams. They can also help managers to support front-line staff with coaching and by creating simple and effective performance management processes (Anand, 2019). They can enable people in the organisation to act quickly, providing skill-building tools and resources so that people can help themselves, rather than doing it for them. Thus, HR's agenda becomes ever more strategic and vital to future success.

As a cautionary note, when aspiring to create a receptive culture for change it's important to be realistic about the time and capacity needed to support change, however agile the intention. It's important to choose what's right for your organisation and what it is trying to achieve in its circumstances. No single HR strategy will be the same as another. HR must look ahead, plan for the future workforce and target effort where it is most needed, preparing for all eventualities, while also keeping employees onside. As we shall explore in more detail in later chapters, almost all aspects of HR's role have the potential to transform cultures.

In the next chapter, we shall again turn our attention to the HR function – looking at how to ensure its people operations are fit for purpose in the digital age and also enable the HR team to deliver their strategic outcomes more swiftly.

REFERENCES

Accenture (2017). *Shaping the agile workforce.* https://www.accenture.com/_acnmedia/PDF-60/Accenture-Strategy-Shaping-Agile-Workforce-POV.pdf

ADP (2019). *The workforce view in Europe 2019.* https://www.adp.co.uk/hr-insights-topics-trends/employee-engagement-talent-management/workforce-view-2019/

Aghina, W., De Smet, A. and Weerda, K. (2015). Agility: It rhymes with stability. *McKinsey Quarterly,* 51, 2–9.

Aghina, W., Handscomb, C., Ludolph, J., Rona, D. and West, D. (2020). *Enterprise agility: Buzz or business impact?* New York: McKinsey & Company, March 15. https://www.mckinsey.com/business-functions/organization/our-insights/enterprise-agility-buzz-or-business-impact

Anand, A., Merchant, S., Sunderraj, A. and Vasquez-McCall, B. (2019). *Growing your own agility coaches to adopt new ways of working.* Available online: https://www.mckinsey.com/business-functions/digital-mckinsey/our-insights/growing-your-own-agility-coaches-to-adopt-new-ways-of-working# (accessed on 23 April 2020).

Barney, J.B., Ketchen, D.J., Jr. and Wright, M. (2011). The future of resource-based theory: Revitalization or decline. *Journal of Management,* 37, 1299.

Boyatsis, R. (2020). *Psychological safety, emotional intelligence and leadership in a time of flux.* New York: McKinsey &Company. https://www.mckinsey.com/featured-insights/leadership/psychological-safety-emotional-intelligence-and-leadership-in-a-time-of-flux

Carney, B.M. and Getz, I. (2009). *Freedom, Inc.: Free Your Employees and Let Them Lead Your Business to Higher Productivity, Profits, and Growth,* Crown Business

CIPD (2017). *Resourcing and Talent Planning Report.* https://www.cipd.co.uk/Images/resourcing-talent-planning_2017_tcm18- 23747.pdf

CIPD (2014). *HR Getting Smart about Agile Working.* https://www.cipd.co.uk/knowledge/strategy/change/agile-working-report

Cornwell, J. (2014). *Introduction to the Point of Care Foundation Report on NHS Performance.* London: Point of Care Foundation. https://engageforsuccess.org/the-point-of-care-foundation-report-on-nhs-performance

Coyle-Shapiro, JAM., Pereira Costa, S., Doden, W. and Chang, C. (2019). Psychological contracts: Past, present, and future. *Annual Review of Organizational Psychology and Organizational Behavior,* 6, 145–169.

Deloitte (2017). 2030 *Purpose: Good business and a better future: Connecting sustainable development with enduring commercial success.* https://www2.deloitte.com/content/dam/Deloitte/my/Documents/risk/my-risk-sdg12–2030-purpose-good-business-and-a-better-future.pdf

De Smet, A. (2020). *Psychological safety, emotional intelligence, and leadership in a time of flux.* McKinsey & Company. https://www.mckinsey.com/featured-insights/leadership/psychological-safety-emotional-intelligence-and-leadership-in-a-time-of-flux?cid=other-eml-alt-mcq-mck&hlkid=47412f67796a49349afd4c4e30f80eb7&hctky=2592654&hdpid=56858a2a-c937-40c6-acf5-6a225laea78e

De Waal. (2018). Success factors of high performance organization transformations. *Measuring Business Excellence, 22*(4), 375–390.

Dignan, A. (2019). *Brave New Work: Are You Ready to Reinvent Your Organization?* Portfolio.

Edmondson, A. C. (2020). *Psychological safety, emotional intelligence and leadership in a time of flux.* McKinsey & Company, https://www.mckinsey.com/featured-insights/leadership/psychological-safety-emotional-intelligence-and-leadership-in-a-time-of-flux

Edmondson, A. C. (2018). *The Fearless Organization: Creating Psychological Safety in the Workplace for Learning, Innovation, and Growth*, 1st Edition, Hoboken, New Jersey: Wiley.

Eva, N., Robin, M., Sendjaya, S., van Dierendonck, D. and Liden, R. C. (2019). Servant leadership: A systemic review and call for future research. *The Leadership Quarterly, 30*(1), 111–132.

Francis, H., Holbeche, L.S. and Reddington, M. (eds) (2011). *People and Organisation Development: A New Agenda for Organisational Effectiveness.* London: CIPD.

Gallup (2021). *State of the Global Workplace 2021*, gallup.com. https://www.google.com/url?sa=t&rct=j&q=&esrc=s&source=web&cd=&cad=rja&uact=8&ved=2ahUKEwiw-fHDq7DvAhWMOcAKHRP2BEcQFjACegQIFhAD&url=https%3A%2F%2Fwww.gallup.com%2Fworkplace%2F238079%2F-state-global-workplace-2017.aspx&usg=AOvVaw0UYAA_w4lEvz3eGyQuumgp

Gustafsson, A., Kristensson, P. and Witell, L. (2012). Customer co-creation in service innovation: A matter of communication? *Journal of Service Management, 23*(3), 311–327, June.

Heifetz, R. and Laurie, D. (1997). The work of leadership. *Best of HRBR.* http://www.kwli.org/wp-content/uploads/2015/01/Heifetz-Laurie-2001.pdf

Hirst, G., Mann, L., Bain, P., Pirola-Merlo, A. and Richver, A. (2004). Learning to lead: The development and testing of a model of leadership learning. *The Leadership Quarterly,* 15(3), 311–327.

Holbeche, L.S. and Matthews, G. (2012). *Engaged; Unleashing the Potential of Your Organisation through Employee Engagement.* Chichester, UK: Jossey Bass.

Ingham, J. and Ulrich, D. (2016). Building better HR departments. *Strategic HR Review,* 15(3), 129–136.

Joiner, B. (2019). Leadership Agility for Organizational Agility. *Journal of Creating Value,* 5(2), 139–149.

Lawler, EE. III and Boudreau, J. (2015). *A Strategic HR Function, in Changing Operating Models Thought Pieces*, London: CIPD https://www.cipd.co.uk/knowledge/strategy/hr/operating-models#

Luthans, F. and Avolio, B. J. (2003). Authentic leadership development. In K. S. Cameron, J. E. Dutton and R. E. Quinn (Eds.), *Positive Organizational Scholarship.* San Francisco: Berrett-Koehler, pp. 241–258.

Manyika, J., Lund, S., Chui, M. Bughin, J., Woetzel, J., Batra, P., Ko, R. and Sanghi, S. (2017). *Jobs Lost, Jobs Gained: What the Future of Work will Mean for Jobs, Skills, and Wages.* New York: McKinsey Global Institute. https://www.mckinsey.com/featured-insights/future-of-work/jobs-lost-jobs-gained-what-the-future-of-work-will-mean-for-jobs-skills-and-wages

Mazor, A. et al. (2015). Reinventing HR: An extreme makeover, in Global Human capital Trends 2015. *Leading in the New World of Work.* Westlake, Texas: Deloitte University Press. https://www2.deloitte.com/content/dam/Deloitte/tr/Documents/human-capital/GlobalHumanCapitalTrends2015.pdf

National Improvement and Leadership Development Board (2016). *Developing People – Improving Care: A national framework for action on improvement and leadership development in NHS-funded services.*

Neubauer, R. Tarling, A. and Wade, M. (2017). *Redefining Leadership for a Digital Age*. Lausanne, Switzerland: IMD, Global Center for Digital Business transformation.

NHS England (2014). *Building and Strengthening Leadership. Leading with Compassion*. https://www.england.nhs.uk/wp-content/uploads/2014/12/london-nursing-accessible.pdf

Paauwe, J. (2004). *HRM and Performance: Achieving Long-Term Viability*. Oxford: Oxford University Press.

Peters, T.J. and Waterman, R.H. Jr. (1982). *In Search of Excellence: Lessons from America's Best-Run Companies*. New York: Harper.

Pew Research Center (2017). *The Future of Jobs and Jobs Training*. http://www.pewinternet.org/2017/05/03/the-future-of-jobs-and-jobs-training/

Pink, D. H. (2018). *Drive: The Surprising Truth About What Motivates Us*. Edinburgh: Canongate Books.

Porter, M. E. (1985). *Competitive Advantage*. New York: The Free Press.

PwC (2018). Will robots really steal our jobs? An international analysis of the potential long term impact of automation, *PwC*. https://www.pwc.co.uk/economic-services/assets/international-impact-of-automation-feb-2018.pdf

Scott-Jackson, W. and Mayo, A. (2016). *HR with Purpose: Future Models of HR*. Henley: Henley Management School, henley.ac.uk/hrc

Senge, P.M. et al. (1999). *The Dance of Change: The Challenges to Sustaining Momentum in Learning Organizations*. New York, NY: NY Doubleday.

Sonnenberg, M., Koene, B. and Paauwe, J. (2011). Balancing HRM: The psychological contract of employees. *Personnel Review*, 40(6), 664–683.

Sun L., Aryee, S. and Law, K.S. (2007). High performance human resource practices, citizenship behavior, and organisational performance: A relational perspective. *Academy of Management Journal*, 50(3), 558–577.

Svensson, G. and Wood, G. (2008). Model of business ethics. *Journal of Business Ethics*, 77(3), 303–322.

Teece, D. and Pisano, G. (1994). Dynamic capabilities of firms: An introduction. *Industrial and Corporate Change*, 3(3), 537–556.

Ulrich, D. (2015). *The Leadership Capital Index: Realizing the Market Value of Leadership*. Oakland, CA: Berrett-Koehler Publishers.

Ulrich, D. (1998). HR with attitude. *People Management*, 13 Aug. https://www.peoplemanagement.co.uk/long-reads/articles/hr-with-attitude#grefUlrich, D. and Allen, J. (2009). *HR Transformation*. New Delhi. Tata McGraw Hill Education Private Ltd.

Ulrich, D. and Yeung, A. (2019). *Reinventing the Organization*. Boston: Harvard Buisness Review Press.

Ulrich, D., Kryscynski, D., Ulrich, M. and Brockbank, W. (2017). *Victory through Organization: Why the War for Talent Is Failing Your Company and What You Can Do About It*. New York: McGraw-Hill Education.

Weick, K. E. (1976). Educational organizations as loosely coupled systems. *Administrative Science Quarterly*, 21(1), 1–19

Wheatley, M. (2017). *Who Do We Choose to Be? Facing Reality | Claiming Leadership | Restoring Sanity*. Oakland, California: Berrett-Koehler.

Wyatt-Haines, R. (2007). *Align IT: Business Impact Through IT*. Hoboken, New Jersey: Wiley.

Workday (2020). *Organisational agility at scale: The key to driving digital growth*. workday.com

5

HR in the digital age

> HR has always been more than a back-office function, but rather a core piece of the organi-
> zational fabric, one with the ability to influence the most powerful asset of any organisation:
> its people.
>
> Volini et al. (2020)

In Chapter 2, we looked at trends in HR transformation since the 1980s. Typically, these included the implementation of HR operating models that separated HR strategy and business partnering from expert HR functions and transactional administration. We discussed whether HR still has some way to travel before it can be considered effective both operationally and as a strategic function. In the last chapter, we considered some of the strategic agenda items arising from the changing context.

DOI: 10.4324/9781003219996-6

CHAPTER OVERVIEW

In this chapter, we shall consider a range of perspectives on how HR functions should develop their operating models to be fit for the digital age, looking in particular at how technology, particularly digital technologies, has become both a driver and enabler of HR becoming more agile in its transactional and strategic endeavours. Indeed, Deloitte (Volini et al. 2020) argue that rather than 'transformation', 'reinvention' or even 'revolution' are more appropriate words to describe what HR needs to do to its own service. We shall also consider the implications of these shifts for HR skills and capabilities and how these might be developed. We shall cover:

- Adapting to a changing context
- Implications of context trends for HR organisation
- Embracing technology
- Towards HR agility
- Putting the foundations in place

LEARNING OBJECTIVES

- To consider whether HR does need to radically transform, or merely evolve, to be effective in the changing context
- To explore some of the implications of technology for HR
- To consider what Agile HR might involve, and ways to become agile.

INTRODUCTION: ADAPTING TO CHANGING CONTEXT

When HR transformation connects to the context of the business, it is more likely to be sustained because it responds to real needs. As we discussed in the last chapter, this means linking HR efforts directly to the business strategy and to the environmental factors that frame the strategy (Ulrich and Allen 2009). Forty years on from the introduction of strategic human resource management, there is much debate about how HR should organise itself to best address the major changes in the business context that are likely to grow in significance. If HR's traditional function was to implement controls, systems and standards to drive alignment and efficient execution, what should HR's purpose and function be in the digital age?

As we discussed in the last chapter, HR's purpose is increasingly conceived as building the capabilities needed by organisations to achieve agility, effectiveness and sustainable strategic success. From this purpose should stem HR's priorities, activities, skills and operating systems required to deliver desired outcomes. As Lucy Adams (2019), who describes herself as 'recovering HR Director' puts it, 'we in HR can only make a lasting difference if we're willing to take a fresh look at how we work too'.

Ulrich (2017) maintains his 'investor-literate' approach to HR's value added, arguing that some of the principles that will help HR deliver victory in the marketplace in 2025 will be the same as those in his earlier books. The earlier measures of HR success are still important. To help an organisation 'win', HR administration must be flawless; HR practices must be innovative and integrated; and HR must turn strategic aspirations into HR actions that produce business outcomes (e.g., increased investor, customer and community value). But the skillset around Organisation must be developed apace.

Evolution or radical transformation?

When determining how HR should operate to deliver its purpose, HR leaders may have to choose between a more gradual evolution or a radical transformation of their function. This involves taking account of the broader context trends, the appetite for change within organisations and the capabilities of HR teams themselves. In many large organisations, evolution is about continuously improving existing provision which may be a variation on the widely adopted 'three-legged stool' operating model based on Ulrich's thinking. Evolution could involve utilising advances in process technology to create a more efficient delivery function; developing an expert function which offers reliable specialist expertise; and a high-powered strategic function where the greatest value contribution is likely to be made. Arguably the things that will determine the effectiveness of HR's contribution are:

- Strategy. Do you have the ambition, objectives and processes that are going to make a difference to your business through your people?
- Technology. Are your processes supported by good and effective HR systems that enable you to implement the processes you've designed?
- Capability. Do your business partners understand what partnering really means, and do they have the skills to achieve this?
- Measurement. Do you know how well you're doing – in partnering and in delivering enhanced business results?

Ulrich (with Ingham 2016) himself has continuously advocated looking at HR roles more as mindsets and areas of responsibility deriving from the strategic needs of the business, rather than as a single structural solution. Indeed, his model suggests that HR structure should match the way the business is structured. So if your business is centralised and functional, your HR function should be organised around HR specialisms such as recruitment, training and reward. In a diversified matrix, multi-divisional organisation, HR should be organised as a professional services firm with centres of expertise (specialists that could be external as well as internal) and embedded HR (generalists) plus project teams, networks and communities. It's about designing a best fit solution that meets your organisation's specific needs and building the capability of the team to deliver.

Maturity levels – linking context to delivery

Another factor affecting what HR can achieve is the function's state of maturity and organisational readiness. Deloitte (Fineman 2016) suggests that in maturity levels one (Personnel Department) and two (Operational HR), the main focus is on efficiency, so HR's focus is on containing costs and improving service quality. In level three (Integrated Talent Management), the focus is on effectiveness. HR is expected to develop leaders at all levels, both globally and locally. There is typically a younger workforce than ever before with new and different demands, often low levels of engagement and heavy competition for top talent, so CEOs demand that HR 'solve talent problems'. Performance management and succession planning in this phase are often weak, technology is still not integrated and there is an imperative to become evidence-based – informed, rather than overwhelmed by data.

At level four (High Impact HR) – which is where Fineman argues HR needs to be – the organisation is gearing up to agility – so HR's focus is on enabling organisational responsiveness.

Since innovation demands collaboration and engagement, HR itself must demonstrate agility, reorganise its structure and delivery mechanisms to create new ways of working within HR teams, use data skilfully and support higher levels of autonomy, accountability and performance across the business. This is for many the 'revolutionary' option. Whichever approach is taken, the fundamentals for Ulrich et al. (2017) are that HR must:

- Become the acknowledged experts in people management and people issues
- Become a close advisor to the CEO and board
- Become an expert in future work and how this can impact the organisation
- Become 'business savvy'
- Manage extremely effective people processes
- Identify and take on critical 'orphan functions', e.g. ethics, CSR, well-being
- Carry out effective account management (through business partners) to maximise 'client' satisfaction.

So with a focus on 'Organisation', HR should draw on systems thinking in organisation development and design, change management and emerging tools such as people/talent analytics, to help achieve business outcomes. This requires an ongoing dialogue with the line business organisation to win commitment. Therefore HR need to be experts in process skills, both to plan change and also bring others effectively through change. In their regular surveys of HR competencies, Ulrich and colleagues (2017) define the primary capabilities required of HR to drive forward the mission as:

- Strategic positioner: Able to position a business to win in its market
- Credible activist: Able to build relationships of trust by having a proactive point of view
- Paradox navigator: Able to manage tensions inherent in businesses (e.g. attend to both long and short term; both top down and bottom up)

They also identify three domains of HR competence as organisation enablers, helping position HR to deliver strategic value:

- Culture and change champion: Able to make change happen and manage organisational culture
- Human capital curator: Able to manage the flow of talent by developing people and leaders, driving individual performance and building technical talent
- Total reward steward: Able to manage employee well-being through financial and non-financial rewards

The three other delivery enablers for managing the tactical or foundational elements of HR are:

- Technology and media integrator: Able to use technology and social media to drive create high-performing organisations
- Analytics designer and interpreter: Able to use analytics to improve decision making
- Compliance manager: Able to manage the processes related to compliance by following regulatory guidelines.

Each of these HR competencies, Ulrich et al. (2017) argue, is important for the performance of HR professionals. While some of the 'deliverables' that HR uniquely delivers remain much as before, such as using HR's traditional body of expertise in staffing, development, employee relations and reward to win the 'war for talent', an agile HR function must adapt and evolve people processes at pace with unpredictable and ever faster changes – to support individual, strategic and organisational goals. Approaches to achieving this will be examined in Chapter 16.

Reflective activity

- Is it unrealistic to expect HR to be able to develop such competencies?
- If so, which should be the primary areas HR should focus on developing?

IMPLICATIONS OF CONTEXT TRENDS FOR HR ORGANISATION

Alongside the technological and other trends that were already changing the nature of business and of work, the coronavirus crisis has seemingly catapulted us into a new era, shining a spotlight on many potential changes in store for business, ways of working and for society as a whole. Three trends in particular, that were already starting to impact on HR operations before the crisis, have been given greater urgency post-crisis:

- The experience economy – and the need to become employee-centric
- An imperative to become evidence-based – informed, rather than overwhelmed by data.
- The Digital Age – and the need to embrace technology and agility

Arguably these trends are likely to grow in significance. Let us consider first some of the implications of the experience economy for the HR function and what employees may now expect from employers.

Employee-centric HR

Jacobs (2016) describes the next HR transformation phase as focused on the employee, what Accenture calls 'the workforce of one', with HR developing more personalised employee-focused propositions and practices. Increasingly HR is being rebadged as 'People and Culture', 'Human Capital', 'Employee Experience', People and OD or simply the 'People' function. Sage research (McIntosh 2020) reports that 94% of HR leaders anticipate this transition in the next few years. Indeed, some argue that HR should retain just two areas of focus – OE/OD and Talent Management, as the most important determinant of the impact of the function.

With 80% of global workers not stationed behind a desk every day, providing employees with a mobile experience is imperative. By using tools that allow employees to work seamlessly on mobile devices, HR can be at the leading edge. To be employee-centric businesses must be ready to support the ways people want to work and meet their expectations, not just with smart technology but with an employment relationship that is less paternalistic and more like a contract between equals. Will such flexibility and employee centricity be maintained post-coronavirus crisis with the economic downturns and huge increases in unemployment predicted to follow? This will put employers in the driving seat as to how they treat their employees; how they choose to respond will reflect their priorities and put their values to the test.

Becoming evidence-based HR – informed, rather than overwhelmed by data

Many commentators have joined the call for HR to become 'evidence-based'. With respect to people, CEOs want rapid decision-making and are impatient with HR teams that can't deliver actionable information and insights. For Rousseau and Barends (2011), this means making decisions, promoting practices and advising the organisation's leadership by conscientiously combining four sources of information:

- The best available scientific evidence
- Reliable and valid organisational facts, metrics and assessments
- Practitioner reflection and judgement
- Concerns of affected stakeholders.

John Boudreau (2016) has long advocated that HR should become a 'decision science' capable of making evidence-based decisions informed by meaningful data. Fineman (2016) too argues that, as companies move from maturity level three to four, they will need an established, efficient and effective HR function that is capable of generating and integrating reliable, quality data. The essence of evidence-based HR is making choices – have we chosen the right issue and the right approach to the right issue? The important thing is to start with a business problem and try to identify and quantify the people drivers of a desired business outcome. So to make a business case for a professionally administered employee engagement survey, for example, it would be helpful to include employee statistics showing the cost of sickness absence to the business, the opportunity cost of high attrition rates and the cost of hiring new colleagues.

To develop evidence-based practice requires an inquiring mindset, to question your assumptions, ask more probing questions and take a logical and systemic view of both issues and solutions. It's also important to concentrate on just a few key priorities to achieve realistic results, with prioritisation taking place through a constant cycle of value and risk. However efficient an HR process, it has to be necessary – does it fit the strategy, vision and values, and is it a priority? Then at least two possible alternative solutions should be considered which can be tested against the best available evidence. In addition to practitioner experience and judgement, this will include different kinds of evidence – both external (competitor, scientific and practice-oriented information) and internal (hard and soft data). Techniques such as experimentation, prototyping and user research can help HR work in a more evidence-based way. Visualisation techniques using artificial intelligence can make decision-making transparent and in real time.

Analytics – the interpretation of data patterns – can help HR professionals turn data into insights, identify the issues that count and enable better decisions. Getting some grounding in data analytics can help so that you can back up what your argument. Using analytics should also help challenge unconscious bias and strengthen HR's confidence to relay some potentially tough messages to management about what needs to be done. This is the quality described by Dave Ulrich as 'HR with attitude' while Unilever's CHRO suggests that HR needs more swagger (in Harrington 2019). We shall return to the topic of Analytics later in this chapter.

Embracing technology

As the benefits of a plethora of new technologies become more widely understood it is vital to harness their potential for the business, the workforce and for HR itself. Technology can help people engage differently with organisations and put organisations on the front foot, enabling them to detect patterns, anticipate and proactively respond to changes in their environment. For instance, the UK's National Housing Federation ('Creating our Futures') is using machine learning to help housing associations detect patterns of anti-social behaviour by tenants. This has enabled them to put preventative measures in place, rather than punishing tenants. Technology is transforming how people communicate with colleagues, absorb information and expectations around the timeliness and quality of data.

While take-up of new technologies in HR is generally proceeding slowly, in remodelling its own service delivery, HR needs to be a champion and should lead by example, building trust and confidence in the use of digital technology. Use of Cloud, Agile and AI are set to transform HR operations and transactions. In the first half of 2018 in the United States, $1.33 billion was invested in HR Technology, surpassing the total spending of 2017. And that's just for new technologies, not upgrades to existing systems.

The move toward Cloud-based self-service software, which was happening anyway, potentially reduces the need for large numbers of people to be assigned to working on 'transactional' HR processes. One of the main criticisms of conventional HRIS was that the data provided tended to be backward-looking and stand-alone, so did not lend itself to insightful analysis or predictive forecasting. Cloud-based HR technology enables transparency and sharing of information, facilitates connections and collaborations across silos, and can get more people involved in decision-making. Cloud has made it easier to improve the design and efficiency of HR tasks and processes and gain greater transparency around key HR functions.

Many traditional approaches to recruitment, onboarding and programme coordination are likely to be replaced by new approaches underpinned by technology, such as using secure Cloud-based collaboration tools; re-checking on remote access daily; creating transparency via virtual team environments and benchmarking leading-edge practice, such as what can we learn about how to bring on board 'digital natives'?

App-based tools can allow supervisors, colleagues and clients to give one another immediate feedback from wherever they are. Because team feedback flows in all directions, many companies use technology to manage its sheer volume. Cisco for instance uses technology to collect raw data from employees about their peers' performance which allows managers to note fluctuations in individual performance over time, even within teams. Peer-led feedback should be encouraged and rewarded formally.

Some organisations are giving employees access to their own personalised employee portal where they can view and manage matters concerning their employment, including their online benefits anywhere, anytime through mobile apps. This more personalised form of self-service enhances the employee experience since the user is shown relevant content and recommendations specific only to him or her. Employers can communicate with their employees wherever they are through push notifications, SMS messages or in-portal messages.

In a context of transparent access to talent information which empowers employees to take ownership of their own development, talent management is facilitated rather than 'owned' by HR. Employees can become active participants in talent acquisition, evaluation and development processes. For example, every job description and competency profile might be made accessible via a centralised platform, so that anyone can see the requirements for any job in the organisation. Employees could evaluate their own competency profile against those required for various jobs, see where there are gaps, and access a range of self-managed development options, including direct portals to web-based training options on a variety of platforms. HR success is measured in terms of retention, employee satisfaction levels, innovation levels and organisational goodwill and trust.

Gamification can help facilitate HR innovation in staffing, development, rewards and involvement since it's about engaging candidates and employees, enhancing their self-motivation and encouraging collaboration. HR platforms can track performance and reward high performers with recognition and better pay and allow responsiveness to changing demands. GE, for instance, long considered a leading exponent of management through control systems, switched to FastWorks, a lean approach that cuts back on top-down financial controls and empowers teams to manage projects as needs evolve. Their HR practices, such as performance management, followed suit as we shall discuss in Chapter 10.

TOWARDS HR AGILITY

In many organisations, more radical approaches are being adopted by HR teams as agile methods have gradually spread across from IT to other business disciplines like HR, marketing and finance. Central tenets of organisational agility are essentially principles deriving from the concept's software development origins:

- Collaborative teamwork
- Worker empowerment
- Delivering value through incremental delivery
- Short iterations of one to two weeks
- Experimentation
- Feedback loops
- Continuous improvement.

Before aiming for agility, it's important to gauge the risk appetite within organisations – do leaders want their organisation to be leading edge or 'wait and see'? Especially in organisations pursuing a digital growth strategy the move to agile HR has been fast and deliberate since HR must become agile to stay current and aligned with the realities of business and talent requirements. Agile HR is characterised by greater transparency and a commitment to ongoing and continuous engagement. Jacobs (2016) argues that in future there will be three big clusters of so-called 'Alpha tasks' for HR:

(a) HR will own and manage employee data and influence business decisions with data.
(b) HR will create and grow the company culture towards agility.
(c) HR will act as a project manager in cross-functional, one-off people related projects with business and IT.

This requires HR to be a strategic data manager, business influencer and corporate culture builder. Building and implementing an HR function that is agile and excellent at HR data, company culture and projects is very different from today's HR function – a truly transformative change. Some writers suggest that these specialist and expert roles should be carried out by centres of excellence (or as Josh Bersin suggests, 'networks of excellence') which for Bersin (2016) form the most important part of the HR model since specialist skills in learning and so on can contribute greatly to creating both culture and competence.

Barriers to HR agility

However, as we have discussed previously, implementing an agile approach generally can be difficult, especially so in HR. In many cases the HR service is out of date, with lots of heavy, compliance-driven processes and static best practice systems that reflect a traditional, hierarchical top-down pyramid structure. A Workday (2020) study found that HR's own structural blockers included legacy perceptions of the function in the business, lack of capacity to dedicate time and budget to innovation, lack of links with other functions within the business or externally to create synergies, as well as high dependency on business priorities and values which prevents those working within the HR function from acting on their own ideas and values (CIPD 2013). HR is generally at the back of the queue when it comes to IT investments. Legacy IT – older-generation software and hardware that are not readily compatible with a modern, Cloud-based environment can impede progress toward agility. Similarly, crossing bureaucratic silo barriers to achieve integrated solutions can be difficult. In addition, a common reported barrier was the lack of individual practitioner knowledge of the external context and lack of horizon scanning to help set direction for innovation.

Agile HR ways of working

However, these barriers are not insuperable. In HR, 'adding value' is a common goal, but this is often poorly defined and quantified. Since Agile is about customer value it can help HR to modernise, digitalise and deliver value to its 'customers' at speed, constantly enriching the HR users' experience of work. It's about redesigning HR and people practices to literally co-create the future of work with employees through a test and learn approach. Of course, this is not a one-way street since employees too must be willing to take the initiative and become involved with the HR function, whether that takes the form of self-directed learning and development, referral-based recruiting, or embodying and promoting organisational values internally and to the outside world.

There is no single blueprint for an agile HR style of working and it is important to find the right framework that fits an organisation's industry, culture, team structure and size. There are however some similarities between frameworks which are common to all agile HR teams. Agile changes the cadence of work, moving HR away from the more traditional annual cycle, e.g. for performance management or reward into a weekly, to a monthly cycle with feedback loops. It's a shift away from a rules – and planning-based approach toward a simpler and faster model driven by feedback from participants. It's about building a culture and mindset for doing things differently, looking at how other organisations are implementing projects and improving services.

For Cappelli and Tavis (2018) HR is going 'agile lite', applying the general principles, such as quick cycles of development, working in 'Sprints', understanding what the client wants and acting as 'bridge' between the technical team and the business, without adopting all the tools and protocols from the tech world. Some teams have embraced the

Scrum framework and sprint back-to-back, because they want to innovate and deliver at speed. Other HR teams use more of a Kanban approach to manage a more continuous flow of work. Some use a combination, discovered through a test and learn approach. What is key is to co-create a contextual design and way of working that's right for your culture and your industry.

Embracing the agile mindset

Remodelling HR's own service delivery to be nimble, responsive and provide a personalised employee experience may require a cultural paradigm shift in service design. Agile methodology is more than a set of processes, tools and techniques to be learned; it is first and foremost a team-based working model. Agile requires a mindset that recognises the importance of team dynamics and individual responsibility. HR must adopt the agile mindset to revolutionise its own ways of working and increase organisational effectiveness. HR will require cognitive flexibility, insight into learning, an understanding of organisation development and design and a holistic perspective on how to deliver to meet customer needs.

Delivering value through iterations

The traditional 'waterfall' way of running a project or multi-year change programme – with everything decided upfront, handovers, inflexible plans and hierarchies that can slow things down, block innovation, waste time and prevent organisations from taking advantage of new opportunities – was just too rigid and did not allow for a change in scope, customer needs or budget in a rapidly changing business environment. How can HR deliver refined customer value in more agile ways?

An agile operating model starts from a small nucleus and involves learning new behaviours. For Bersin (2012), Agile principles, that date back to the origins of Agile in software development in the late 1990s, must underpin the design of continuous learning and talent acquisition processes that enable organisations to attract, develop, and engage talent in the twenty-first century. Agile breaks down major challenges into smaller chunks of work and starts to deliver slices of value to HR's customer at a faster pace. Small-scale initiatives are piloted on the basis of inclusion, within a specific team, job family or business unit. If something fails, a new direction can be taken. Working iteratively means decisions are taken continuously and validated by feedback gathered early and often from service users to determine whether the initiative should be expanded or scrapped.

You still have the same vision and goal, and you still write down all the things you think, or assume, you might have to do at the start, but then it's important to focus on the most important thing, or perhaps the highest risk thing, deliver that to the customer quickly, get feedback from the customer to find out 'does this work, does this not, are we on the right track?' and then use that feedback to guide the next increment of work. By keeping this agile feedback loop going – a cycle of plan, do, check, act- you get to solutions more quickly. Value is delivered incrementally as projects improve and become new working practice.

You need all the relevant skills within the same team – such as specialists in reward, recruitment, talent, learning – along with people from the line, solving complex problems together. Similarly, to bring together the digital and the human factor to produce integrated solutions HR must also work cohesively with other support services such as digital experts as teams of 'joined up' expertise (Aghina et al. 2020). It's about moving away from silo mentality and asking peers to contribute their expertise to produce a 'minimum viable product' which showcases the art of the possible and gets early buy-in.

Interestingly, in the wake of Coronavirus crisis lockdowns, where dealing swiftly and effectively with the very real people issues has been paramount for business survival, HR's strategic, tactical and agile contribution has been widely recognised. The challenge will be to avoid 'snap-back', i.e. being sucked back into conventional priorities and ways of working once the 'new normal' is under way. For many organisations the challenge post-pandemic is the addressing the question of where people will work. For many home, working will continue to be the norm, while for others a more hybrid pattern will be adopted. This has implications for the layout, size and nature of buildings – will people need to have their own desks or will more collaborative spaces be required for when people are in the office? It also has implications for management styles, forms of communication, employee well-being and so on. Such a strategic challenge will lend itself well to co-created iterative solution-seeking.

Co-creating the employee experience

The key to reinventing HR and people practices in order to enhance the employee experience and ensure that services are designed to meet employee and manager needs is involving the service user/customer in service design and testing sessions because the customer is the ultimate owner. At the very least HR must attempt to step into the shoes of the service user to understand how the service is perceived and what might be better.

Co-creation is very powerful, transforms the notion of change management and highlights the importance of discovery work in HR in which people experiment with you and discover together what works and what does not. So, for example you might invite employees in to map out a whole HR service and start to redesign it together in order to improve their experience of work. Or it can be as simple as walking down the corridor and asking five people what they think about a piece of communication before you send it out. It's about using feedback from the customer to guide the next piece of work. So instead of managing people through change, people are in the change with you, co-creating the outcome.

NB Experimentation is very different from running an HR pilot. An HR pilot is usually a 'done deal', i.e. investments have already been made and even if the pilot does not go that well, it often gets rolled out after a few tweaks or improvements. In contrast, if an experiment fails it can be left behind once the data from that failure have been used to validate a wholly different direction, or to run a very different kind of experiment.

This built-in ability to adapt to change makes it possible to pivot and re-plan as customer needs evolve or as the business environment shifts and builds an environment of continuous learning. Not only does this approach decrease project risk, it also decreases the risk of committing time, money and people to a flawed idea.

Design thinking

HR teams are increasingly using design thinking to redesign people practices for the future of work and to help people adapt – leaders and organisations to technology; employees to new models of work and careers; and the company as a whole to changes in society, regulation and public policy. Using tools and techniques from Design Thinking, like personas, experience mapping and prototyping, can help to gain insights that can guide the design. Design thinking is a human centred approach to innovation that draws from the designer's toolkit to integrate the needs of people, the possibilities of technology and the requirements for business success (after Tim Browne, Executive Chair of IDEO). Depending on the model used, design thinking typically involves working with key stakeholders to generate new approaches through a series of (non-sequential) phases in short sprints (often lasting a week):

- Discovery – I have a challenge; how do I approach it? (Understand the challenge, prepare research, gather inspiration, what data can I gather that might help?)
- Interpretation – I learned something; how do I interpret it? (Tell stories; search for meaning, frame opportunities)
- Ideation – I see an opportunity; what do I create? (Brainstorm to generate ideas, refine ideas).
- Experimentation – I have an idea; how to build on it? (Make prototypes, get feedback)
- Evolution – I tried something new; how do I evolve? (Track learning; move forward).

Design thinking empowers HR to reimagine every aspect of work: the physical environment; how people meet and interact; how managers spend their time; and how companies select, train, engage and evaluate people. According to Josh Bersin (2020), 'Design Thinking casts HR in a new role. It transforms HR from a "process developer" into an "experience architect"'. Zappos for instance used design thinking to reimagine the job application process resulting in a higher candidate experience with a 97% satisfaction score. Airbnb has used design thinking to change the role of the Chief HR Officer into the Chief Employee Experience Officer to emphasise the shift in focus. Qualcomm used Design Thinking to develop experiential learning programmes that are helping build a culture of entrepreneurship, creativity and risk taking. Cisco ran a 24-hour HR 'Breakathon' in which they reimagined their HR solutions for their 71,000 global employees. Using design thinking, they came up with hundreds of innovative solutions to people challenges, many of which were implemented. They also used design thinking to reimagine the employee experience specifically in new hire onboarding, recruitment and career development.

The key to emergent transformation is to co-create with staff a contextual design that's right for your culture and your industry and what you are trying to achieve. With greater flexibility and mobility, service delivery should result in improved productivity and enhanced employee satisfaction.

Case example: re-designing people processes at W.S. Atkins UK and Europe

In 2016–2017, the HR team in W.S. Atkins UK & Europe business, formerly led by HR Director Sharron Pamplin, gradually redesigned itself by working back from the end-user experience, in true agile, customer-centric manner. This shift in HR's role put a premium on effective communication and role modelling to raise people's awareness of the need for change. In HR, as with other parts of the Atkins UK & Europe business, on-going dialogue amongst all HR team members was made possible via the HR function's own regular global cadence calls – video conference calls which brought the whole HR community together virtually to help people understand the bigger picture and discuss their part of it. Similarly, the One HR Forum helped HR to develop shared understanding and purpose and build trust. It provided an environment where people were genuinely empowered and willing to change.

In redesigning the people processes in the W.S. Atkins UK & Europe business, staff involvement was crucial. For example, an Employee Journey Mapping workshop took place involving staff from across the business to explore the key HR experience touchpoints along the employee journey from 'hire' to 'retire'. For example, when and how did people first know about Atkins? Was Atkins attractive as an employer? How did they know what is available in terms of career opportunities? What did they experience in their first week? Were HR sufficiently focused on them?

By drawing on employees' actual experience it was possible to identify how HR practices could be improved to create stronger links between employees and the company. For example, based on employee feedback about people's experience of Atkins at the hiring stage, managers were then encouraged to interact with potential and newly appointed employees before they join via LinkedIn Yammer to make them feel welcome and well informed.

This also fed into the development of a new employee value proposition that provided a bold and relevant voice on how the company aspired to be as an employer. Some practices that were previously considered counter-cultural, such as rehiring former employees, were then embraced – people were actively sought out, rehired and welcomed back as alumni with enhanced experience. By thinking about processes differently and asking, 'what value is this adding?', things changed for the better. The Indian and UK HR teams worked together virtually to simplify the rather convoluted procedures required at the end of probation. Managers were then required to take action and report to HR only if there was a problem.

Work also got underway to develop a more long-term yet agile approach to succession planning and talent management. A job families' approach was adopted, together with a strategic workforce planning initiative over a 12-year horizon called Workforce Futures 2030, with much of the initial focus on critical value generators. This strategic initiative, led by HR, was another example of staff involvement. The leadership team had framed the challenge (the problem to solve). They wanted to get to grips with what the future Atkins workforce might look like. Instead of HR taking the usual short-term reactive approach to resource planning, looking just a few months ahead, HR worked with leaders to think about what kinds of skills and capabilities would be required ten years out. In particular the leadership team wanted to understand what would be required to attract people in the early stages of their careers – why would they join Atkins? How would they work with Atkins – as employees or be connected to the firm in some other way? How would Atkins face up to the challenges identified?

Two different employee groups from diverse business areas came together for separate one day workshops to address this challenge. Participants ranged from senior and experienced staff members to graduates and apprentices. The workshops allowed people to explore the challenge imaginatively, using story-telling. The teams then worked on the challenge for six weeks and made various proposals to the leadership team, of which three were selected. These were sponsored by different senior leaders, with resources made available within the business.

One innovative proposal was the concept of The Atkins Campus, created by apprentices and graduates during a strategic workforce planning workshop. They suggested that the Campus should exist in 50 locations across the globe, from Silicon Valley to Japan, as a physical place for innovation, shared learning and development. Alongside this was the concept of the Atkins 'Workery', a live/work option for staff to live close to the Atkins Campus in 50 cities worldwide. This would offer staff reduced living costs without commutes in a neighbourhood of colleagues and would be co-created and designed by the early careers team.

Sharron takes up the story: 'We've come a long way. The HR function is better able to change now. Team members are coming forward saying "I've identified this problem – we need to change it"'. Sharron's response is 'Great – you all know this really well – What do you propose?' The team uses agile methodologies such as 100-day sprints, pop-up projects, hackathons and lock downs, and involves their customers in the process.

The results started to speak for themselves. In the Atkins UK and Europe business, different business groups are saying that HR is now working better, and they have brought on board colleagues who were not involved in the change process. As Sharron notes, 'We've seen an improvement in employee engagement and involvement at all levels. The Young Professional Awards for graduates and apprentices was introduced in 2017 as a means of giving high profile recognition to people making a difference. One of the shortlisted apprentices is actively disseminating learning, using One Note to track workplace and college learning. More widely, interesting practice is now shared via stories on Yammer and the company's website so is accessible to all'.

Reflective activity

- What do you consider the benefits and risks of involving employees in co-creating HR services?

Putting the foundations in place

Transitioning from traditional to Agile HR methodology and approach is a behavioural and cultural change that requires change management, communication and transparency to really 'stick', both within the HR function and within the wider organisation. Many cultural practices have to change, including a move away from a conventional planning-based, operating model (which is linear) towards a more flexible and adaptive model. The fundamental shift toward teams has resulted in organisations pushing decision rights down to the front lines. For many this is a huge behavioural change, and may meet resistance – especially within HR. Such resistance may be cultural – vested interests can be hardwired into budgets, information systems, job titles and so on – and people issues are often a sticking point.

Before putting a shift to Agile in motion, it's important to have some underlying supports in place:

An amenable organisational culture

An amenable culture is one that prioritises engagement and empowerment and trusts its employees. This means developing teams to have true autonomy at team level and who can make data-driven decisions. The example is set by leaders who demonstrate alignment in purpose, vision and behaviour so that everyone knows where they are going and why. Such leaders are also willing and able to let teams make decisions since they are the closest to the customer. HR policies are clear and simple and provide the guidance people need to make good decisions.

Getting people on board for change in most cases is about appealing to people's self-interest, showing how the new methods can benefit them and their customers, referencing tangible outcomes elsewhere. Much will depend on the perceived relative power levels in the employment relationship. If people are desperate to hold on to their jobs, they may feel they have no choice but to grudgingly accept the new ways of working.

When one large supermarket chain wanted to get its employees behind its digital strategy, management described the threat that digital retailers posed and presented it as a 'do or die' imperative. In sharing their vision, the company's leaders put a spotlight on workers who had piloted a new AI tool that helped them optimise stores' product assortments and increase revenue. They argued that AI could help fend off the competition by improving the firm's operational efficiency and responsiveness. In rousing employees around a fight for survival, management emphasised the critical role that employees had to play. This inspired workers to imagine how AI could augment and improve their performance.

More generally, people may need support to embrace new ways of working, so equipping and empowering employees with the skills they need to operate more independently helps get them on board. HR team members with OD and OE capabilities can provide relevant advice and support groups on the change journey. L&D can provide training in relevant digital skills, as well as coaching and facilitation to support performance improvement and capability development. Rather than taking a worker utilisation, 'click and collect' approach to development it will be important to approach this task as part of developing a learning culture.

A high performing HR team

Embracing a more agile approach is not about hollowing out HR expertise – indeed, intelligent application of professional knowledge about people and organisations will be needed more than ever, but HR's skillset must evolve. HR's emerging skills in analytics, organisation development and design, combined with understanding of finance and systems, provide a unified organisational effectiveness capability, according to Ulrich. Finance and HR teams therefore should work more closely together to build a greater mutual understanding of their respective cultures and perspectives, including of the significance of HR to the business model and how its performance can be best measured.

The HR Director should be a catalyst for change and support the HR team in making the transition to new roles by clarifying what they look like in practice and actively coaching the team in the early stages of transition, rather than letting the team muddle through. So when recruiting for new roles in Agile, HR must update and modernise its current understanding, for example, of how do you hire a Product owner or Scrum master? How do you develop them and make sure you capture their contribution to the business?

A really high performing HR director has a high calibre team to match. The team's roles will have been carefully chosen and staged in over time so that line managers are ready for their devolved responsibilities and have the human resource information systems, helpdesks and training to prepare them to take on these responsibilities. HR roles – typically expert, business partner and shared services – will have been worked through so that colleagues do not end up competing with each other for the 'client' but see greater credibility in ensuring that the client receives exactly what is needed, from the best people to deliver the service.

The HR team itself will be modelling high-performance work practices, especially learning from each other. Foundational elements include the basic consultancy, facilitation, project management and change management skills, and the business acumen practitioners need to equip them for their roles. HR professionals should also be developing key specialist expertise in areas such as merger and acquisition experience, organisation design and employee relations, to name but a few. The team will import and export staff members with other functional and business backgrounds so that collectively the language and service delivery modes are seen to be integral to the way the business operates at its best, rather than ivory tower.

Managers who are willing and able to support teams

Many managers have no problem coaching individuals, yet struggle to coach teams, or to navigate team dynamics when teams are mainly self-organising. Some managers may lack the skills for this, and some may consider that acting as coach undercuts their status and formal authority. As Cappelli and Tavis (2018) point out, the companies that most effectively adopt agile talent practices invest in sharpening managers' coaching skills. By providing support tools and development HR can make all the difference to manager effectiveness in coaching teams.

One company helped managers with a technical background to develop coaching skills by using virtual reality 'embodiment' to help managers experience what the 'coachee' might feel when being coached by them. This provided a safe and personalised space for managers to practise and grow in confidence and competence until they were ready to coach people for real. Supervisors at Cigna go through 'coach' training designed for busy managers. This is broken into weekly 90-minute videos that can be viewed on demand. The supervisors also engage in learning sessions, which are brief and spread out, like 'learning sprints' in agile project management, to allow individuals to reflect and test-drive new skills on the job. Peer-to-peer feedback is incorporated in Cigna's manager training too: colleagues form learning cohorts to share ideas and tactics.

Another company in the healthcare sector uses findings from its annual Employee Experience survey to help develop manager awareness and skills. In healthcare, the close link between employee satisfaction and patient satisfaction has been extensively researched. In follow up to the survey, managers receive an aggregated report of their respective team responses and the information is also captured in the organisation's talent platform. Through cutting-edge analytics, employee survey results are linked to patient satisfaction data, allowing managers to prioritise employee experience improvements that positively impact patient outcomes.

Making resources such as self-guided development programmes widely accessible

Learning and Development will be key to upskilling people. Technology broadens access to experiences and magnifies the learning through sharing them. Technology-enabled training allows insights to be shared from training platform to application and can also create active networks of learning among the individuals that are trained. New applications which help learners to do things in real time and in real situations (rather than learning and remembering) and which provide accessible curated knowledge, have been given a boost by the coronavirus emergency lockdowns. Some universities for instance are now offering students online courses that go beyond e-learning to also provide a rich learner experience.

Thus potentially, technology can lead to an improved employee experience because a less submerged HR has the means to improve its service levels by being both relationship-led and also through the use of next-generation automation and artificial intelligence. This could enable HR to more actively play a strategic role and act as innovation hub – collaborating with other disciplines to share knowledge, working on change programmes, designing spaces and facilitating connections. HR teams should therefore consider which core elements of HR process can be standardised, to free up space for needed innovation and shared learning.

Analytics

Today, the discipline of people (or workforce) analytics, that in large organisations typically began as a small separate technical group who analysed employee engagement and retention, and used digital tools and data to measure, report and understand employee performance, has now gone mainstream. Cloud computing and Big Data should revolutionise the HR function's potential for fact-based decision-making and provide new value for the bottom line (KPMG annual 'HR transformation study', 2016). Analytics and AI have come together, along with machine learning, in companies like Ford that have expanded the people analytics function to work across all segments of the business, including finance, HR and operations with analytics embedded into their entire workforce management process and operations. Analytics are being applied to recruitment, performance measurement, reward, workforce planning and retention. Recruitment, especially high-performance hiring, is the primary area of HR practice being revolutionised by analytics and artificial intelligence (Collins et al. 2017).

What Josh Bersin (2013) once called the 'datafication of HR' is not about building an HR data warehouse but delivering actionable business information. This can be used for the systematic identification and quantification of the human drivers of business performance – such as what are people doing, how engaged they are, how much absenteeism is there, how competent are they – and to understand how these drivers influence business outcomes.

However, take up of analytics by many HR teams remains slow. In the CIPD 'HR Outlook' survey (2016) only a third of HR respondents reported a 'managed' and robust approach to analytics. Similarly while most HR respondents in Deloitte's 'Global human capital trends' (2015) rated analytics as 'important' or 'very important', only a few reported improvement in analytics capabilities.

Things are changing however and in some global companies digitally powered enterprise analytics give companies a much more detailed 'real-time' view of management and operational issues that can produce actionable insights for the business. This is usually only possible when HR data is integrated with financial and other business data and when systems give more flexible access to information, so a multi-disciplinary approach to data is required. HR must therefore become comfortable in creating and using data differently and take steps to ensure its accuracy. This is not just a question of software, but data function, data quality and also requires a range of skills – business knowledge, problem solving, data visualisation, statistics and consulting – within the HR team or which the HR team can access.

Using data skilfully can transform how HR influences business decision-making. While management teams may sometimes accept at face value that investment in recommended activities is a good idea – proposals for leadership training, for example – evidence of value added makes the case more powerfully, focusing on outcomes not just processes. Analytics can help HR tell the story about the potential business benefits of HR processes and initiatives, such as return on investment. For instance, the HR team at Unilever has quantified that for every $1 invested in health and well-being initiatives, they get a return of $2.50, thus demonstrating both the business and the employee value of people analytics. Using analytical methods to understand links between people and results can help diagnose problems more clearly and evaluate the impact of interventions. In future, predictive analytics tools and Deep Learning, as yet in their infancy, should make it possible to gain insights from data regarding future engagement, recruitment, performance, employee mobility, retention and other issues.

Monitoring employee interactions

The increasing efficacy of big data and data analytics is helping businesses make better informed decisions about talent management, succession planning and health and well-being. Qualitative data can be as, or more, important than quantitative. There has been significant growth in the use of organisational network analysis (ONA) and of 'interaction analytics' (studying employee behaviour) to better understand opportunities for business improvement, according to Bersin by Deloitte (2017). It is also used to monitor worker collaboration patterns with external and internal stakeholders. GM for instance used ONA to stimulate innovation by analysing the connections between employees to determine how to bring together the people most likely to have the highest impact on innovation and product design to work together on projects and teams. People who are intrinsically motivated for innovation usually have more interest and curiosity, which in turn enhances performance, persistence and creativity (Ryan and Deci 2000). GM also used a variety of methods to help create the environment most conducive for creating and sharing ideas, which is known as the 'Adaptive Space'. This HR-initiated process has enabled GM to launch many innovative products, as well as initiate a new process to improve buyer–supplier relationships.

Understanding the employee experience

Data analytics can be used to constantly track and assess the employee experience. It can reveal different patterns of workplace behaviour, demographics and workplace absence that can inform well-being interventions and improve workplace culture, work-life balance and employee engagement. Sentiment analysis using social media makes it easier to keep in touch with employee concerns and mood. It helps identify workforce feelings about particular topics and provides a granular look at employee engagement without the need for a major survey. Many companies now actively use social network analysis and external data to understand attrition, retention, and other performance metrics and identify local candidates who may be 'likely to look for new jobs'. At Microsoft people and network data has provided critical insights about work-life balance in a high-performing team.

Unilever has infused AI and analytics throughout the employee journey. Unilever has also invested in listening to employees through natural language processing tools such as Unabot, the chatbot built in partnership with Microsoft. This continually learning bot is the first port of call for all Unilever employee questions and is able to filter and apply information and respond appropriately based on whom it is speaking to, recognising factors such as geographical location and level of seniority in the company.

However, due to the sensitive nature of people analytics programmes, organisations must treat very seriously questions of data confidentiality, local regulations regarding the use of employee data, and the risk of public disclosure of private information on the organisation and its employees. Advanced people analytics programmes increasingly rely on the intersection of data from HR, operations and external sources. Data quality must be part of every analytics discussion and it is t important to educate HR's stakeholders and implement data governance programmes to clean and maintain data accuracy and consistency across HR and operational data stores. Moreover, training for both HR and other business functions – for instance on the application of standard tools, and standardisation of reports and dashboards – will be critical to operating at scale.

Therefore, it is becoming important for HR to have specialist analytical expertise within the function, or at least readily available, to improve the function's ability to collect and manipulate internal data. AI has the biggest impact when it is developed by cross-functional teams with a mix of skills and perspectives. Having diverse teams of business and operational people working side by side with analytics experts should ensure that initiatives address broad organisational priorities, not just isolated business issues. This will improve HR skills, not just in data analysis and research methods, but also in relating HR data to business – and taking a wider, systemic view of evidence and how different HR policies or interventions work together. Becoming evidence based helps HR to move away from silos, make accurate and timely decisions with committed outcomes and be seen as a more credible business partner.

Making the transition

Though transition to a more agile and strategic role can be difficult, it is certainly not impossible. Several of the case studies in this book, featuring the activities of HR practitioners who are making a strategic contribution to their organisations, should offer hope and practical insights into how others have made the shift. I am very grateful to Frances Hewison, Director of Human Resources and Organisational Development and her colleagues at the UK's Manchester Metropolitan University (MMU), for the following case study which illustrates elements of co-creation in the digital transformation of HR.

Case: transforming HR into a strategic partnership at MMU

With a workforce of 5000, MMU is one of the UK's top ten universities for knowledge transfer partnerships. Back in 2016, the University's HR&OD Directorate was facing a few challenges. It was operating as a high-volume transactional service provider, yet the service team involved were mostly not engaged, there was high staff turnover, a pressurised working environment and a good deal of firefighting. Systems and processes were mostly paper based and complicated; there was no standardisation and unclear 'hand offs'. From the customer perspective, the HR function was inaccessible and provided inconsistent service with poor response times. Other professional service units were viewed in similar light by their users.

'One PS'

In early 2018, a new vision was established for Professional Services. The purpose was clear: to enable students and colleagues to achieve their best and to set the bar for Professional Services in Higher Education. The aim was to bring together over 2,000 staff into one integrated Professional Services function, with structures, processes and systems united under the brand 'One PS' (One Professional Services).

It was recognised from the start that shared values and ethos would be critical to success. HR led in shaping the values and a shared identity for 'One PS' whilst delivering a university-wide structural change programme. The four 'One PS' Values are:

- We Are One Team
- We Understand Our Contribution
- We Are Proud of our University
- We Are Future Focused

The process of co-creating the values, and the conversations and connections generated, was fundamental in the establishment of 'One PS', since it empowered and enabled colleagues to think beyond the boundaries of their immediate teams. Through workshops, stories and real-life examples, the supporting behaviours for the values were identified and exemplified through a range of examples. This creative and authentic approach was well received and provided an opportunity to explore what the Professional Services Values mean within different functional contexts.

A 'One Team' Service Delivery Group was created to support the University's ambitions and the 'One PS' vision by identifying opportunities to improve the end-to-end customer experience across PS functions. As part of One Team, the HR team took a strategic approach to their programme of work, both developing new ways of working for the University and also exemplifying these behaviours through their own work and interactions.

Transforming HR and OD

'One HR' was established to improve and integrate the core HR service delivery offer. 'Big HR Conversations' brought together staff in workshops and focus groups to identify challenges and co-create solutions that would shape future HR services. The HR team defined what they wanted to be known for: 'A supportive team who respond to queries efficiently and offer constructive advice and guidance'.

The People Strategy (2020–2025) vision statement is as follows:

'Our people's collective talents will deliver the University's driving ambition to discover and disseminate knowledge and make higher education accessible and beneficial to all those with a passion and ability to succeed. The People Strategy provides a framework for how we recruit, engage, manage, develop, reward and retain people to deliver this mission'. The strategy would be supported by the following enablers:

- A mainstreamed approach to equality and diversity
- A governance structure that enables delivery and embedding of the strategy

- A HR & OD Service that is sufficiently flexible to support the delivery of the University's objectives; is data informed, digitally enabled and human at heart
- A framework of co-created values and behaviours that supports an environment of engagement and achievement

Having reviewed resources, the HR&OD team partnered with Accenture to process re-engineer the function to better support University priorities and produce customer focused service improvements. A new team structure and training approach were introduced. This work also included:

- Establishing the HR Service Centre, strengthening professional expertise in service delivery, and moving towards more generic roles and secondments to broaden and enhance skill sets.
- Realigning similar services and connected disciplines (service centre, resourcing, reward and systems) to remove silo working and develop consistent approaches.
- Moving the University Teaching Academy (UTA) into HR, to ensure a coherent approach to organisational development for all staff.
- Implementing HR Service Management in partnership with IT (ISDS) and External Relations, streamlining and automating HR services for quick, efficient case management and data.
- Introducing a new HR&OD intranet, co-created via informative feedback, enabling 'employee relevant' first line support.

Processes were simplified and digitally enhanced through Robotics Process Automation (RPA). Colloquially known as 'HRbert' RPA was applied to the top five processes that impact on many people:

- New Starters
- Contract Changes
- Family Leave
- Sessional Contracts for Associate/Hourly Paid Lecturers
- Leavers

The automation of such fundamental, high-volume processes has resulted in many benefits such as reduced transaction volume, improved speed of process, greater visibility of information and accessibility of data. The team can now use data to inform service improvements, manage and measure performance, flex the service to meet business needs and introduce innovative ways of working. The team has also collaborated with other services to share best practice in streamlining processes through Robotics Process Automation.

Recruitment was an early target for process improvement. Research confirmed that the University faced a number of candidate attraction challenges. There was an uninspiring careers site, an Applicant tracking system (ATS) that was not fit for purpose and a poor mobile experience for candidates that failed to fully showcase the University's brand or promote its proposition as an employer. There was a lack of social media presence for a 'candidate audience' and not surprisingly low numbers or quality of applications. In addressing the challenge, the team looked at the candidate experience, benchmarked the old careers site, then built a new recruitment website, created more people focused content, developed recruitment collateral such as electronic magazines and brochures and a LinkedIn presence to elevate the university's digital brand awareness and replaced the ATS. These measures have produced a digitally simplified and enhanced process that has increased the attractiveness of the university's offer to candidates and significantly improved results and appointments.

The team's collaborative approach to reviewing and co-creating key HR processes with a range of stakeholders resulted in an improved customer experience. Communication about actions being progressed by HR&OD, with results shared in a 'you said, we did' style, has been key to building confidence in the service. Other major projects, already in development, include a revitalised leadership and management development programme and a new PDR scheme, underpinned by the principles and behaviours set out in the Professional Services Values.

The 'One PS' values were also used to inform and shape a number of targeted joint development activities with teams across Professional Services. A Professional Services conference, themed around the values, led to a number of projects and priorities being identified where respective Professional Services Directorates can collaborate together, combining resources to strengthen capacity and desired outcomes. For instance, teams across HR, Careers and Employability and External Relations work together to support priority initiatives connected with student and graduate employability, a key business target. This has created impetus for further engagement with other Directorates to participate in joint working on projects and initiatives.

The HR&OD team also guided the wider transformation of Professional Services. Relocating into a new building with 650 other Professional Services colleagues, HR&OD led on developing a shared way of working that was a critical success factor in aligning Directorate teams beyond mere organisational structures. In a pioneering move for the higher education sector benchmarking took place both internally and externally across Professional Services utilising the Professional Service Quality Survey (PSQS). Survey results were the focus of senior executive level scrutiny and were shared with the Professional Services leadership group as well as the wider staff community. Actions for improvement were identified by each Directorate. The results provided the team with excellent insights and benchmark data which have enabled them to identify trends and make significant improvements, strategically and collaboratively.

The University continues to reap longer-term benefits from this work as well as measurable short-term improvements including a positive impact on customer service and reductions in work volume. Previously siloed and competitive approaches have been replaced by a shared focus on Professional Services improvement, driven by the Professional Services Leadership Team, and a strongly collaborative culture. By increasing engagement and breaking boundaries down between teams there has been greater sharing of ideas, greater efficiency and added value. Thus, through the core themes of collaboration, shared working and learning underpinned by the 'One PS' values and measuring performance and impact, HR&OD have embedded a strong customer service ethos throughout the HR and OD Directorate as well as 'One PS'. As leaders and partners in cultural change HR&OD are making a measurably positive difference to this university.

Reflective activity

- Where on the HR maturity scale below would you place the case study described above?

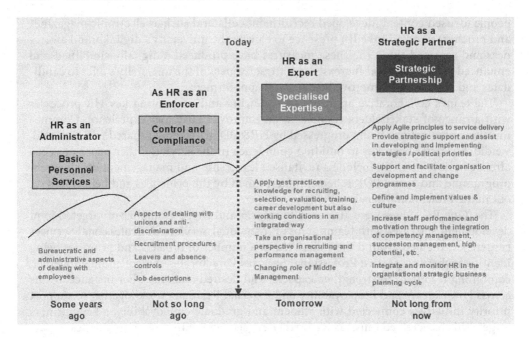

Figure 5.1 A typical HR maturity scale.

CONCLUSION

We have discussed the need for HR to become agile and employee-centric. Digital tools can help HR (continue to) provide a relevant and effective service in a fast-changing landscape. We have looked at agile working practices such as co-creation and working iteratively and explored the necessity of embracing technology, analytics and becoming evidence-based. We have discussed some of the barriers to HR becoming agile. Because HR touches every part of an organisation – and every employee – its own agile transformation may be even more extensive (and more difficult) than the changes in other functions. The shift entails moving from a 'supply-led' agenda to delivering a 'demand-led' outward-focused strategic agenda, focused on stakeholder outcomes.

To become an agile function that can exploit its potential critical strategic contribution, the shift required is perhaps less about structures and more about mindset. HR teams must understand and reflect the business context and direction in their own priorities. The HR function's own work practices must become agile and provide end-to-end employee/customer value at speed, which may require upskilling HR itself. By turning analytics/data into insight, HR can become a thought-leader and identify where best to channel its energies to support the workforce, organisation culture and values. HR should also build relationships with key stakeholders and work collaboratively with IT, finance, marketing and other functional departments to deliver greater value. In the next chapter, we shall explore what crafting an agile HR strategy might entail.

REFERENCES

Adams, L. (2019). *The HR Change Toolkit: Your Complete Guide to Making It Happen*. London: Practical Inspiration Publishing.

Aghina, W., Handscomb, C., Ludolph, J., Rona, D. and West, D. (March 2020). *Enterprise Agility: Buzz or Business Impact?*, McKinsey & Co. https://www.mckinsey.com/business-functions/organization/our-insights/enterprise-agility-buzz-or-business-impact

Bersin, J. (2016). *HR Technology for 2016: 10 Big Disruptions on the Horizon.* Deloitte.

Bersin, J. (2013). The datafication of human resources. *Forbes,* 19 July. https://www.forbes.com/sites/joshbersin/2013/07/19/the-datafication-of-human-resources/

Bersin by Deloitte (2017). *Rewriting the Rules for the Digital Age. 2017 Deloitte Global Human Capital Trends,* https://www2.deloitte.com/content/dam/Deloitte/global/Documents/About-Deloitte/central-europe/ce-global-human-capital-trends.pdf

Boudreau, J. (2016). Why HR must evolve to address the 'future of work'. *The Water Cooler, LinkedIn,* 10 August, https://www.linkedin.com/pulse/why-hr-must-evolve-address-future-work-john-boudreau/

Cappelli, P. and Tavis, A. (2018). HR goes agile, *Harvard Business Review,* March–April, https://hbr.org/2018/03/hr-goes-agile

CIPD (2016). *The Employee Outlook.* London: CIPD.

CIPD (2013). *The Innovation Imperative: The Challenge for HR,* London: CIPD, https://www.cipd.co.uk/Images/hr-and-its-role-in-innovation_2013-part-4-challenge-for-hr_tcm18-9960.pdf

Collins, L., Fineman, D. R. and Tsuchida, A. (2017). *People Analytics: Recalculating the Route,* Bersin by Deloitte, https://www2.deloitte.com/us/en/insights/focus/human-capital-trends/2017/people-analytics-in-hr.html

Deloitte (2015). *Global Human Capital Trends: Leading in the New World of Work.* Westlake, Texas: Deloitte University Press.

Fineman, D. (2016). *Enabling business results with HR measures that matter.* (Deloitte). https://www2.deloitte.com/content/dam/Deloitte/us/Documents/human-capital/us-hc-enabling-business-results-with-hr-measures-that-matter.pdf

Harrington, S. (2019). HR needs more swagger says Unilever CHRO. I couldn't agree more. *LinkedIn,* June 13, https://www.linkedin.com/pulse/hr-needs-more-swagger-says-unilever-chro-i-couldnt-agree-harrington/

Ingham, J. and Ulrich, D. (2016). Building better HR departments. *Strategic HR Review,* 15 (3), 129–36.

Jacobs, V. (2016). How to reverse the HR transformation death spiral. *MIT,* April, https://www.ti-people.com/reversing-the-transformation-death-spiral.

Bersin, J. The eight key areas HR should focus on right now (Aug. 7, 2020). *The Bersin Company,* https://enboarder.com/2020/08/07/josh-bersin-employee-experience-is-more-important-than-ever/

KPMG (2016) *HR transformation study 2016. The future belongs to the bold.* KPMG.

McIntosh, S. (2020). *The Changing Face of HR: A Research Report for HR and People Leaders.* Sage, 18 Jan. https://www.sage.com/en-gb/blog/the-changing-face-of-hr/.

Rousseau, D. M. and Barends, E. G. R. (2011). Becoming an evidence-based HR practitioner. *Human Resources Management Journal,* 21(3), 221–235.

Ryan, R. M. and Deci, E. L. (2000). Self-determination theory and the facilitation of intrinsic motivation, social development, and well-being. *American Psychologist,* 55(1), 68.

Ulrich, D. and Allen, J. (2009). *HR Transformation.* New Delhi: Tata McGraw Hill Education Private Ltd.

Ulrich, D., Kryscynski, D., Ulrich, M. and Brockbank, W. (2017). *Victory through Organization: Why the War for Talent Is Failing Your Company and What You Can Do About It,* New York: McGraw-Hill Education.

Volini, E., Schwartz, J. and Denny, B. (2020). *2021 Global Human Capital Trends,* Deloitte, http://response.deloitte.com/HCTrends 2021.

Workday (2020). *Organisational Agility at Scale: The Key to Driving Digital Growth,* workday.com.

6
Crafting HR strategy

As discussed in the last chapter, the outcomes of a strategy (variously called an HR, or Human Capital, or People, or Talent, or Workforce, or Organisational strategy) have become the specific people capabilities – including talent, leadership and culture – that an organisation needs to succeed in its marketplace. While the outcomes of these activities will vary according to the nature of the business strategy, the HR strategy itself should be integral to business strategy and adapt to meet the evolving needs of the business.

DOI: 10.4324/9781003219996-7

CHAPTER OVERVIEW

HR strategy defines the strategic and operational HR contribution to shaping a high-performance culture and work environment and ensuring availability of competent people. In this chapter, we consider how such a strategy (referred to here as 'HR strategy') can be developed, especially for an organisation pursuing agility. There is no one 'right way' to develop an HR strategy. What is proposed here is intended as a set of thought starters rather than a methodology. We shall cover:

- About HR strategy
- Developing HR strategy
- A process for developing HR strategy
- HR strategy as culture change

LEARNING OBJECTIVES

- To explore a process for developing HR strategy
- To identify some of the factors that must be considered in crafting a strategy

INTRODUCTION: ABOUT HR STRATEGY

A well-crafted HR strategy provides the route map for HR to add value and be seen to do so. HR strategy connects the efforts of the HR team to business strategy, helping to secure, develop and retain the people the organisation needs for success. It sets out the desired outcomes, priorities and ways of achieving these. Alongside the strategy, detailed plans specify who is responsible for doing what by when. The outcomes of successful HR strategies should improve the probability of achieving the business strategy, providing an answer to Ulrich's challenges:

- How can we build an organisation that adds value to customers, investors and employees?
- How can HR do something that makes a difference in business results?

Any HR strategy should set out a clear vision for how HR can help the organisation achieve sustainable high performance when confronting today's volatile and complex business landscape. Wayne Brockbank (1997) suggests that HR teams must define how they are going to contribute unique value to their organisations: 'if HR as a whole is unclear about its purpose, what can be expected from the rest of the company about the purpose of HR'? Brockbank's criteria for developing a departmental point of view include:

- Is it formally stated or is it ad hoc and assumed?
- Does it comprehensively cover the whole organisation thereby encouraging the corporate whole to be greater than the sum of the parts?
- Is it linked to issues that are critical to long-term corporate success?
- Does it create explicit and measurable results?

To these criteria I would add, does it promote good outcomes for both the business and its workforce?

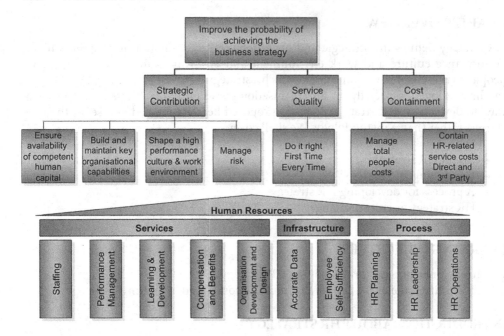

Figure 6.1 Business-centred value chain and strategic HR outcomes.

So what kind of organisation would you wish to see? As we discussed in the last chapter, this vision defines some of the key areas of HR's longer-term focus, as well as the immediate priorities within that. A typical vision of a high performing organisation is one that attracts and retains the best people, is a great place to work and has high commitment work practices and strong corporate values which people are attuned to. Such an organisation has excellent leadership and a healthy culture and structure supportive of innovation, teamworking, flexibility, knowledge-creation and sharing, where people are able to work well across and beyond organisational boundaries.

Delivering such a vision in a fast-moving context can be challenging since little stays the same for long. As organisations seek greater flexibility by adopting the techniques and methodologies of agility, business leaders increasingly expect the Human Resource function to manage the planning and transition to new organisational forms and ways of working and to ensure their organisation is prepared for all eventualities, while also keeping employees onside (World Economic Forum 2018).

Agility will mean reimagining the routines and limits of today's jobs to embrace agile principles and philosophy, for instance empowerment, customer-centricity experimentation and iteration. In today's competitive marketplace products and services must be innovated continuously to meet the changing demands of the marketplace and customers. Desired outcomes might be specified in terms of behaviours. For innovation, everyone needs to be externally aware and savvy, allowed to act on such knowledge and willing to share ideas. What will be required to achieve such behaviour change?

A systemic view of how behavioural change can happen is needed. So for an agile business strategy which calls for human flexibility, joint working and responsiveness, it's about building flexibility and adaptability into roles, responsibilities and structures to enable people to act quickly and effectively. It's about developing agile leadership, for example through the integration of leadership development, high potential development, career and succession planning. It's about building dynamic, two-way communications across the organisation.

Since sustainable high performance and innovation depend on high levels of employee engagement and well-being, HR strategy must also focus on activities, such as training, well-being and career programmes, that enhance the employee experience and lead to outcomes such as increased staff motivation, competence and performance and build a better, more effective organisation culture that is conducive to innovation and in which employees can thrive.

Being future-focused, HR strategies should be transformational and set clear objectives for HR in the areas of workforce planning, talent development, succession planning, and organisation development and change programmes to ensure the future of the organisation. HR strategies define the values, culture and the key principles which will underpin organisation design and reward and differentiate the organisation in the employment market. HR strategy identifies key gaps with respect to desired ('to be') and current ('as is') culture and people management and how these gaps can be closed. In a very real sense, an HR strategy becomes a culture change tool.

HR strategy should also outline HR's proposed service quality and cost containment contributions to business success. It should clarify the underlying philosophy behind how the HR function delivers to the business and the nature of service that it wraps around the core products and role, as we have discussed in previous chapters. It should acknowledge that, to be sustainably high performing, HR itself must be agile. An agile HR function keeps HR processes and systems simple and fit-for-purpose to enable workforce empowerment and the HR team to move faster. The function continues to provide recruitment, development, performance management and other HR services – but using an agile approach that is less bureaucratic, customer-centric, embraces technology and open to co-creation.

In short, an HR strategy should:

- Create a people and organisational mission for the business, not an HR agenda
- Identify and build the people and organisational capabilities required for sustainable success e.g. agility, innovation, speed, customer focus, flexibility and employee engagement
- Ensure the organisation has the right talent and leadership in the right place at the right time focused on the right things
- Transform the business to ensure it meets its full potential
- Create an agile and high performing HR team.

DEVELOPING AN HR STRATEGY

Developing such strategies requires an understanding of the business, its business model, market strategy, value chain, core business processes, industry dynamics and the competitive landscape, and how all these elements impact human capital requirements and HR activities. HR leaders must use these insights and the vast amounts of data they can now access on recruitment, retention, performance, employee engagement and so on, to work out the implications for human capital and the employee experience throughout the HR lifecycle – everything from hiring and performance to well-being, diversity and inclusion. It is how HR gathers, evaluates and interprets that data to drive their strategy that really matters.

Crafting an HR strategy provides an opportunity for the HR Director and team to influence thinking and practice at senior levels and more widely. HR is responsible for agreeing with senior executives which HR goals and practices to introduce and for their quality. Business decision-making at senior level typically focuses on projected costs, risks and revenues, with the people implications often an afterthought.

While costs need to kept low on all fronts – not least within HR itself – alignment with business strategy is not just about obeying bottom-line operational imperatives, such as designing the most cost-effective structure, or integrating cultures as fast as possible following a merger. Since a company's workforce is its most precious asset, it is also crucial to work out how to build an organisation that people want to work in and give of their best to, and therefore what deserves attention. After all, people implement strategies, people envision the future, people get engaged and excited about their organisation, people lead others, people undermine efforts, people require re-skilling, people follow processes, people connect to customers, people generate business results and so on. For instance, staff well-being, previously often considered an expensive 'nice-to-have', is now recognised as intricately linked to talent retention and business success. So HR strategy must spell out respective responsibilities: if HR teams are responsible for designing and implementing well-being policies, the C-suite must be involved in the planning and championing of robust initiatives and line managers in their implementation.

To influence the conversation, given the significant shifts in culture and people capabilities required in the digital age, the effective HR director is in there when the business decisions are taken, shaping thinking with reasoned and data-based arguments so that the people implications become integral to the business decision-making process. A critical success factor is to think and talk like a business leader – making sure you know all the business issues your firm is facing as well as understanding the concerns and level of strategy experience of the management team. This can help you position the people implications as strategic risks or opportunities and avoid potential pitfalls.

Planning is vital

Business agility does not just happen – we need to plan it into our thinking and decisions – including our workforce and employment decisions – to pave the way for dealing with increasingly complex systems and problems in new ways. Of course, when crafting a people strategy, it is much easier to plan if there is a clear business strategy on which to focus. However in fast changing times, when business strategy has to dynamically adapt to new circumstances, and a large organisation may have several business models running concurrently, such clarity is often lacking. Similarly, business strategy may be out of date before it is implemented if rigid thinking causes executives to ignore the changing demands of the market. Take the demise of the clothes retailer The Arcadia Group in 2020 which had failed to move with the times, had not developed an active online presence and whose leadership approach was described as 'analogue thinking in a digital age'.

I would argue that there is no inherent contradiction between agility and longer-term planning, as long as planning is underpinned by resilience competencies – such as anticipation, cognitive agility and learning from experience – that enable the organisation to change tack and adapt to changing needs. In previous editions of this book, I drew distinctions between planned and emergent approaches to strategy and change. I would argue that the ability to 'strategise' encompasses both. In times like these, it's not a case of working either on the short-term issues or the long-term goals; it's important to do both/and, even if that means adjusting priorities from time to time as conditions change.

Capacity to act is essential

Planning alone does not result in action. Purcell (2006) and Becker and Huselid (2006) emphasize the importance of strategy implementation. Strategising helps close gaps between awareness-raising, planning and implementation since when people are involved in the formulation of the strategy, they 'own what they help to create'. This is not necessarily strategy in the sense of analysis and planning, systems and processes. It's more about strategy operating as a way of thinking and of acting – as communication, mindset, flexibility of thought and awareness. That change-ability develops when more people are involved in the strategy-making process and can co-create elements of strategy, therefore stakeholder involvement is a vital ingredient in the development of any strategy, especially HR strategy.

Since HR strategies are mostly implemented by line managers, involving these key stakeholders whose combined knowledge of the business is wide-ranging can help determine the priorities and ensure relevance and ownership. Strategising also applies to the workforce who are closest to the customer. If staff are given opportunities to understand the business challenges and feed insights into management decisions, they are more likely to understand and be open to change if adjustments to new situations are necessary.

A speaker at a business conference likened strategy in turbulent times to steering a canoe through fast moving water. If you paddle at the same speed as the water, the current will take you where it chooses. If you paddle fast to get ahead of the stream, you have more chance to progress in the way you desire. Therefore people strategies must be adaptable and evolve with the needs of the business. In other words, the HR team and executive leaders must be able to think and act in a strategically aligned way, identify the broad direction of travel, act on issues that must be addressed swiftly and ensure that short-term demands can be met in a way that delivers longer-term value.

Implementation is likely to be more effective if the strategies formulated are practical and can be put into effect without too much difficulty. The aims should be to (1) keep it simple; (2) spell out how the strategy is to be implemented as well as what is to be implemented and (3) ensure that support is given to line managers in the shape of advice, guidance and training (Guest and Bos-Nehles 2013: 80–81).

Considerations in developing an HR strategy

Where to focus?

The key question is – where should HR strategy focus? Even when an organisation is in steady state there are so many areas where an HR team potentially could add value that there is a risk that effort is spread too thin. Conversely, in times of change, the danger is to focus only on the highest priority short-term items. The challenge is to strike the right balance. The choice of where to focus will depend on the type of organisation, its situation, what it is trying to achieve, whether the organisation is downsizing, growing – through acquisition or organically – going international and a host of other variables. It will also depend on labour market conditions, employee relations and other issues which affect the organisation's ability to deliver its business goals.

The HR value chain, based on the work of Paauwe and Richardson (1997), and one of the best-known models in HR can help provide some focus. According to this, everything we do (and measure) in HR can be divided into two categories: HRM *activities* and HRM *outcomes*, which are supported by HR *enablers* such as HR's own organisation design, budget, technology, processes, functional organisation, budget, capable professionals and other key elements. If HR lacks well-trained professionals, if the budget is low, or if the systems are outdated and hamper innovation, HR will be less efficient in delivering its services, or reaching its HR outcomes and business outcomes.

HRM outcomes are the goals we try to achieve with the HRM activities. These are the outcomes that are traditionally seen as important HR Key Performance Indicators (KPIs). Typical HR outcomes might include employee engagement, retention, workforce competence and performance, workforce costs and talent metrics. Wright et al. (2003: 324) argue that we should move away from standard measures of performance such as productivity, sales and profits, to a wider definition that takes into account performance in terms of flexibility, agility and legitimacy (Boxall and Purcell 2003), as well as aspects of employee well-being such as satisfactions, stress, job security and so on (Peccei and Van De Voorde 2019).

A coherent HR strategy will prioritise those issues which have the biggest potential impact on the organisation's ability to deliver its strategy. To deliver these outcomes, various HR activities need to take place – such as workforce planning, recruitment and selection, performance management, development, compensation and benefits, training, and succession planning. As we discussed in Chapter 1, exactly how HR practices impact on individual and organisational performance is unclear, often referred to as the 'black box' (Purcell 2002) and remains a source of debate. Yet there is broad consensus that three categories of HR activity, often referred to as 'bundles', act on intermediaries to performance – such as employee retention, engagement and commitment – since they affect employee ability, motivation and opportunity (AMO). In the ability bundle, HR activities that enhance people's skills include recruitment, onboarding, training and rotations. For motivation, HR activities that enhance employee energy levels include appropriate goal setting, feedback, career growth and compensation, employee well-being. Opportunity bundles contain activities that empower employees such as voice, interesting jobs, working in cross-functional teams, diversity and flexible job descriptions. Although the basic commitment strategy principles may be the same everywhere, how they are put into operation may differ across business strategies and across jobs.

PROCESS FOR DEVELOPING AN HR STRATEGY

A typical flow of activities in developing strategy is as follows:

- Understanding the business and its people
- Horizon scans internally and externally
- Establish the top five priorities
- Involve others and share widely to gain maximum input at all stages
- Benchmark across both industry-specific and non-specific companies
- Monitor and measure progress
- Produce a user-friendly working document in a simple language

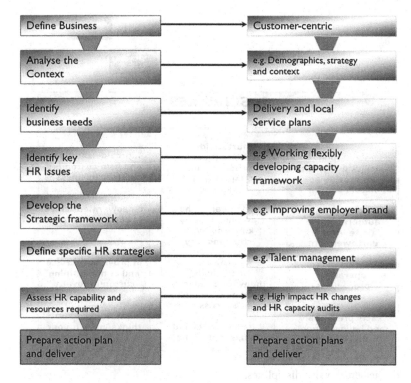

Figure 6.2 Process flowchart for developing HR strategy.

Another process flow maps out the following key stages. As with any strategic planning process, the first stage usually involves conducting a rigorous initial analysis – to cover business needs, corporate culture and internal and external environmental factors. Diagnosis is required to get to the root cause of problem areas, or where there are large gaps between the 'as is' and 'to be'. For Ulrich et al. (2017), organisational diagnosis should be at the heart of strategic partnership – analysing what factors make for effectiveness and generating ways to assess and improve those.

Define the business – what is it aiming to achieve?

Business strategy types

Of course, business strategies come in many forms. Michael Porter (1985) defines three generic strategy types that can attain competitive advantage: cost leadership (achieving scale economies and utilising them to produce high volume at a low cost); differentiation (creating uniquely desirable products and services) and market segmentation (or focus – offering a specialized service in a niche market). Porter then subdivided the Focus strategy into two parts: 'Cost Focus' and 'Differentiation Focus'. A company also chooses one of two types of scope, either offering its products to selected segments of the market or industry-wide, offering its product across many market segments.

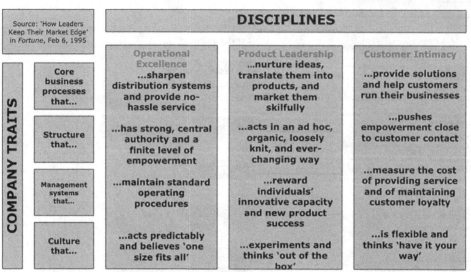

Figure 6.3 Treacy and Wiersema's value disciplines.

Employee role/behaviour

- creativity: seeking new solutions
- risk-taking behaviour
- medium-term focus
- collaborative & co-operative behaviour
- concern for quality & continuous improvement
- equal concern for process & outcomes
- high tolerance of ambiguity & unpredictability
- encouragement for learning & environmental scanning

Reward policy thrust

- mix of individual & collective rewards
- use of 'soft' performance measures, periodically monitored
- emphasis on medium-term performance
- use of learning & personal growth opportunities as a 'soft' reward
- broad-banded & flexible pay structure
- high relative market pay

Other HR policies

- broadly defined job roles
- cross functional career paths to encourage the development of a broad range of skills
- appraisal focusing on medium-term and collective achievement
- high investment in learning & development
- frequent use of team-working

Figure 6.4 Matching strategy to HR policies. Example: innovation-led strategy.
Source Professor Stephen Bevan, IES.

Another of the many models for categorising business strategy types, similar to the Porter categories, is Treacy and Wiersema's Value Disciplines (1995).

To align with each business strategy type (Operational Excellence, Product Leadership and Customer Intimacy) different practices and capabilities are required so HR strategies will vary accordingly in terms of the work arrangements, staffing, skills, style of management, reward policy required and so on. So, for a product leadership/innovation strategy, talent with high levels of mental agility is required.

Paauwe (2004) argues that HRM should be an enabler of a whole range of strategy options and be organised to do so. Organisations may have a number of business strategies running concurrently in different parts of the business so different HR plans may be required for each distinct subset of the main business according to the market conditions of the time, and whether appropriate talent is plentiful or scarce.

Business processes

Businesses often use value chain models to identify opportunities for cost savings and differentiations in the production cycle. Value chains track the elements and streamline the processes that take a product from concept to market. External factors also affect company value chains, including HR's own value chain to the business, such as talent shortages. Value chain analysis is a tool (first introduced by Michael Porter in 1985) for understanding where a company creates superior value to that of its competitors. So HR practitioners must understand the company's value chain, how value is created, how well key process are working and how their people elements can be improved.

Reflective activity

- Where is your company/institution going? What are its key strategies and business goals (Cost? Quality? Innovative products?)
- What is its competitive advantage? Is the product innovative? Will customers pay for it?
- How well are the key business processes working? What are the barriers?
- What is changing to address these barriers, e.g. new technology?
- What do these strategies imply for the nature of people, skills and ways of working required to deliver the business?

Analyse the context

To develop 'outside-in' strategies a thorough study of external factors affecting the business and its customers is required: competition, economic conditions, political/legislative atmosphere, competitive climate, market conditions, industry outlook, labour market and trends in technology. Within any industry, many of the dynamics change over time in ways that alter the nature of competition. Key factors are momentum, windows of opportunity and the social/organisational climate as well as the phases and cycles of change. HR must fully understand the strategic drivers for the business and implications of the competitive environment, including the political and cultural context of the organisation. For instance, with a Product Leadership strategy, how technology can help worldwide project teams to bring new concepts to market faster and respond more quickly to customer needs, while at the same time reducing costs, including workforce costs.

A Pesteli analysis looks at some of the external context factors bearing on the business that potentially influence demand for company services, such as the changing customer base and customer needs that affect the resources and level of funding required:

- **Political** factors – both big and small 'p' political forces and influences that may affect the performance of, or the options open to, the organisation
- **Economic influences** – the nature of the competition faced by the organisation or its services, and financial resources available within the economy
  - What customer categories within the industry are changing and in what ways? How are their demands changing? Are different customer segments growing at different rates?
  - How many new competitors are entering and on what basis are they able to enter?
- **Sociological trends** – demographic changes, trends in the way people live, work and think
- **Technological innovations** – new approaches to doing new and old things and tackling new and old problems; these do not necessarily involve technical equipment – they can be novel ways of thinking or of organising. Automation and 'robots' are replacing human tasks and jobs and changing the skills that organisations are looking for in their people.
- **Ecological factors** – definition of the wider ecological system of which the organisation is a part and consideration of how the organisation interacts with it.
- **Legislative requirements** – originally included under 'political', relevant legislation now requires a heading of its own.
- **Industry analysis** – a review of the attractiveness of the industry of which the organisation forms a part, e.g. Is it in a growth market or is the market plateauing or declining?

This environmental scan identifies potential threats the organisation faces and opportunities to exploit. The changing labour market, with shortages of skilled workers in particular areas is often a key element of risk. Elements of the company's value chain might be another, especially in times of political uncertainty. Other aspects of risk you might consider in this kind of analysis include those relating to corporate reputation:

- Ethics
- Stakeholder values
- Media impact
- Supplier work practices

Of course, the future is not likely to be the same as the past. So how can organisations prepare for a future that is likely to contain both predictable and highly uncertain elements? How will your talent requirements change? How can you attract, keep and motivate the people you need? And what does all this mean for HR?

Scenario planning

This is where another method – scenario planning – can be useful. Various large consultancies such as PwC and McKinsey have written extensively about scenario planning as key to broadening minds in the context of planning for the future. While it is often assumed that in a fast-changing environment the future is so unknowable, and therefore makes planning for the future challenging, scenario planning can be used to reduce the uncertainty to a manageable set of plausible scenarios. The method previews potential environments in which an organisation might operate and helps participants to explore potential risks and opportunities to the business model. Taking part in scenario planning is also a valuable spur to strategic thinking and can involve large groups of staff at all levels, in addition to management.

The process starts with a central question to be answered: e.g. whether to invest in new plant, what to do about new products, how to address the future market for oil, etc. A structured brainstorm of PESTELI factors identifies trends which are likely to affect your business, especially interconnections between issues and markets: What do we know will change in the next one to five years? What key things do we not know at the moment? Some users of this technique seek to introduce the idea of probabilities, but there is a good deal of debate about this approach in scenarios where the number of variables is high, and the situation or scenario is chaotic hence not capable of cause–effect analysis.

The next step is to identify and prioritise those drivers for the business which have high impact and are very uncertain. A range of scenarios is then developed based on the selected drivers. Scenarios can help you consider:

- What external/internal events might influence you or force you to change?
- Under what circumstances might you become incredibly successful?
- Under what circumstances might you be at greatest risk?
- Are the current business plans and goals realistic?

One example might be a scenario where new technology emerges from competition in a market where demand is slack, or supply exceeds demand in relation to decisions about new product development. What are the implications? Will there be a need for new or better skills, services or relationships? How can we prepare for any potential future scenario? The analysis is used to engage executives, stress test current and proposed strategies as well as to generate strategic options. Scenarios can usefully help combat over-confidence and encourage free and open debate.

Assess the internal environment

The internal analysis centres on the degree of alignment between your strategy, its changing context and various aspects of organisation. Incorporating analytics and design thinking to predict where there are gaps and where to best target programmes increases the chance that they will be successful and speeds up the time it takes to develop and then implement a response. For instance, Galbraith's Star model™ analysis considers internal alignment between strategy, technology, structure, reward and key work processes – those that are most critical to the successful implementation of each component of the company's value chain – and must be executed almost flawlessly to truly set you apart from your competitors. These processes also include management processes, such as communication and decision-making.

To explore the internal context, create questions, starting with some that seem obvious from what you know about the business and people, then review these against your chosen model, e.g. the Star model™, Burke-Litwin framework (1992, later in this chapter), Nadler-Tushman (1988) and other models, to make sure you're not missing a vital factor. The focus should be on identifying where action may be needed that will make a measurable difference to the whole.

Identify your key people

Taking stock of the human capital currently employed provides a foundation for determining future staffing needs. Many firms have more than one HR strategy, with different kinds of people who bring different value to the organisation. Firms can distinguish the skill sets of particular jobs in terms of their value to the firm and their uniqueness in the labour market. In this value/uniqueness matrix, known as the human capital architecture, each quadrant includes descriptions of the appropriate HR strategy. Lepak and Snell (1999), suggest that a firm can implement four possible HR strategy types (commitment, performance, compliance and partnership) tied to four distinct job groupings representing different types of workers (strategic, core, support or collaborative).

- If your value chain is relatively stable, who are the people (either job groups or subgroups in a particular job) who are most critical to effectively executing each portion of the value chain?
- If your industry is changing and this is influencing your value chain, who are the key people (again, either job groups or subgroups of unique employees in a particular job) in the parts of the value chain that need to change?

Chances are that the people identified as most valuable and unique are those who are critical to the execution of the most important parts of your value chain. And if your industry is changing, the key people will be in those areas of the value chain that are becoming increasingly important.

What are the key people issues?

For each of those groups identified above, what are the key HR issues? How unique are their skills? Can these skills be easily developed? Do you have enough of these people? Where are they located? Can they be easily found in the open labour market or are they hard to find? What do these key people expect and want from the employer, e.g. to work flexibly? What are the demographics? Are they people who need to be brought into the organisation as employees or can you contract with them as 'alliance/partners', to gain access to their skills? As the nature of work changes, some skills and capabilities become redundant while new skills are needed. Which parts of the workforce are at risk? As we shall explore in coming chapters, by anticipating how work will change, HR can help build development paths to equip people, including managers and leaders, with the skills they need to meet changing business needs.

Reflective activity

Have the competencies that are required in your industry changed? If so,

- Is there a good process for developing needed competencies and making sure people have meaningful and developmental job experiences and meaningful career paths?

- Have your people practices kept pace?
- Where do established HR practices facilitate and/or impede performance, collaboration and integration?
- Is your firm developing the needed leadership capability at all levels and the lateral leadership capabilities required for success in its complex matrix?

How does the culture need to change?

Identifying the key HR issues is not limited to the workforce, and changing ways of working, but also to culture. Peter Drucker is often quoted as saying 'culture eats strategy for breakfast'. In the light of your intended strategy, how well does 'the way we do things around here' support, or act as a barrier to, the strategic intent, especially in fast change?

There are many frameworks for assessing organisational culture. The Burke-Litwin open systems model suggests that the strategic elements of organisation – how mission and strategy, external environment, organisational culture and leadership interrelate – have a knock-on effect on individual and organisational performance. For instance, if the leadership is disunited and if the organisation is too inwardly focused, the chances are that it will miss vital opportunities to innovate and fail to adapt to the changing environment. The most direct link between these strategic elements and individual performance is via the vertical 'spinal column'. So management practices will directly impact on work unit climate and affect people's motivation. In a healthy organisation the strategic and transactional elements are all aligned.

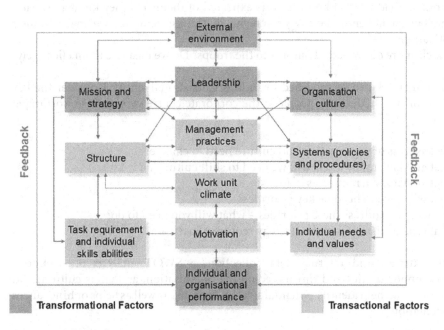

Figure 6.5 The Burke-Litwin framework.

An audit based on the Burke-Litwin framework can assess overall organisational health:

- How externally focused is our organisation?
- How effective are leaders in taking the lead on:
  - external scanning (regular assessment of the environment)?
  - setting strategy to achieve our vision/mission?
  - aligning culture to deliver strategy?
- Are we sufficiently externally sensitive – so that we can stay ahead of the environmental challenges? How can we get better at building and using our external antenna?
- What is our knowledge of clients and partners like? How can we do better?
- Do we have a united vision and mission – that appeals to ourselves and our staff at a deep level (and unites us for action and change)?
- How aligned are our culture and vision/strategy? Do they support each other or cancel out each other?
- How effective are our strategies – do we have annual, bi-annual planning cycles? Do our strategic intentions match our vision? Do we measure our outputs?
- What kind of culture bearers are our leaders? Holding on to the old or championing the new? Do our leadership qualities and styles bring out the best in us? What do we do to build future leaders?
- How effective are our middle management population in managing the work unit climate?
- What do our employee engagement survey results tell us?
- Is our structure 'fit for purpose' – does it help to organise tasks to deliver our strategy?
- How do our systems and processes support our culture?
- Do our individual staff know what is expected of them? Do they know how their contribution fits into the bigger scheme of things? How do we manage their motivation?
- How clear are our required outputs to the troops? Do we measure them effectively?

The same framework can be modified to audit organisational agility. Consider the key implications of this analysis for people at the corporate centre versus those working at local levels:

- What aspects of organisation and culture need to change?
- What and how many levels will we need to shift culturally?
- What are your current areas of focus?
- What will need to become key priorities?
- How will you address these priorities – what will you need to do?
- What type of change will the strategy require of us?

From this external and internal data collection, a SWOT analysis of strengths, weaknesses, opportunities and threats facing the organisation, as well as cultural and people factors – can help identify potential strategic options as well as helps or hindrances to implementation.

Reflective activity

- What data would you want to gather to examine how to improve the health of the organisation?
- What would you look at when considering an organisation redesign? What else would need to change beyond structure?
- Which of the models mentioned in this chapter works best as a guide? Which others do you find work well, and why?

Prioritise strategic options against the business need and the vision

Working back from the desired business results, and checking against the external and internal analyses and the vision, what are the people outcomes that are vital to support broader business goals, objectives and decisions? Which HR activities are most likely to impact on these? To create the rich mix of talent, engagement and performance that will drive culture change towards the more participative, collaborative and innovative aspects of business, new approaches to managing talent may be needed. The following non-exhaustive list culled from many HR strategies suggests some of the typical strategic priorities and related HR activities aimed at helping organisations to achieve high performance.

Source, develop, engage and retain the right talent through HR activities such as:

- Improving workforce planning for the future workforce – working out what kinds of employees and skills the organisation really needs, as well as what it already has
- Earlier action with talent pools, i.e. links to schools, universities, etc.
- Recruiting for diversity, resilience and underlying aptitudes and values
- Recruiting large pools of applicants that enable you to be more selective
- Using valid selection tests to assess the skills of the applicants.
- Retention of high performers, e.g. tying monetary incentives (merit increases, bonuses, etc.) to high performance.
- Offering competitive pay packages.
- *Build agility into the organisations, its work practices and its workforce by:*
  - Working with the line to design teamwork processes which enable speed and quality while reducing cost
  - Training line managers in their devolved responsibilities
  - Developing managers as coaches
  - Helping managers to deal with poor performance and raise standards
  - Helping managers to effectively manage workloads
  - Developing appropriate performance management processes to distinguish levels of performance and provide regular formal and informal feedback.
  - Providing simple and effective self-help HR processes through help desks, mobile, etc.
  - Keeping bureaucracy to the minimum
  - Facilitating team working
  - Proactively developing collaborative consultative arrangements with staff representatives and unions
  - Preparing people for new roles, e.g. providing substantial training to upgrade or maintain skill levels.

- *Design the elements of a high-performance structure and a learning culture through:*
- Giving sustained attention to flexibility and skills through deployment and careers
- Developing a culture that expects and supports learning
- Flexible resourcing models
- Organisation and work design – flexibility, productivity, costs, using scarce resources better, designing in engagement
- Embedding the identification of learning agility within your succession planning efforts
- Interviewing for learning agility during the selection process
- Better engaging the high potentials in your organisation
- Developing and modelling the values
- Working with managers to ensure that roles are stretching and provide growth for the post-holder
- Upskilling the workforce in new job skills such as digital
- Creating high quality learning processes for teams and individuals
- Providing employees with the tools and training to manage their own development
- Creating reward systems which reflect business goals and are also employee-centric
- Encouraging knowledge-sharing processes, such as team reviews and learning sets
- Making sure that internal communications are working effectively (genuinely two-way)
- Supporting the transition to virtual working
- Working with managers and integrated project groups to bring about change
- Consciously building in diversity and flexibility into company policies and practices
- *Create a great place to work by:*
- Building an authentic employer brand and attractive employee value proposition
- Focusing on improving employee engagement, addressing the most frustrating 'pain' points in employee surveys to resolve issues, e.g. allowing employees to participate in decisions.
- Building policies and benefits which reflect what these people actually value, such as work-life balance, flexible working options and benefits
- Developing clear and manageable career tracks so that people can move laterally and continue to grow
- Developing tailored induction and onboarding processes for new starts which reflect what the organisation is becoming
- Encouraging cultural practices which are important to people – such as having fun, being part of a community, a member of a successful team, etc.
- *Develop leadership by:*
- Selecting leaders who have high levels of mental agility and who actively model shared purpose, values and behaviours through symbolic/substantive actions
- Leaders who can cope with ambiguity, uncertainty and complexity and also lead others through change

- Creating effective succession planning processes, not just for the top jobs
- Clarifying organisational values with managers and making sure that people who get promoted actually practise them
- Challenging managers who are not practising the values
- Linking leadership development to organisational values and business results
- Developing leadership at all levels

Narrowing down the focus

The question is, what is right for your organisation? Carrying out a SWOT analysis followed by a SWOT strategy generator can help you narrow down the focus of the HR strategy.

Some of the priorities you may wish to address are those with potential opportunities for the business, in which your organisation can play to its strengths (SO strategies). Others may be competitive or other threats where your organisation's strengths can be used to advantage (ST). For instance, in a tight labour market for key talent, strengthening your reputation as an employer of choice can enable you to continue to attract the talent you need. In areas of threat where the organisation is weak (WT), you may need to do damage limitation, develop robust contingency plans, or over-compensate in your efforts to secure advantage. Where there are opportunities, but the organisation is currently weak (WO), you may decide that focusing energy and other resources on these may be worthwhile but harder to achieve.

HR should lead in proposing the key priorities. The group HR director of a large Danish company explicitly linked activities to sources of added value. He began by encouraging the top team to identify three major sources of corporate added value:

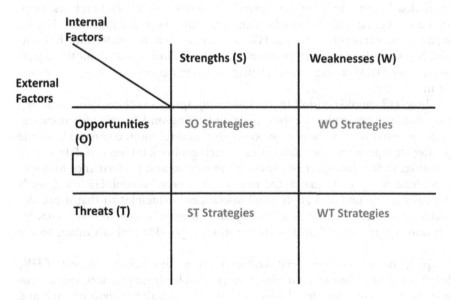

Figure 6.6 SWOT strategy generator.

driving costs down, even in good times; getting the timing right on asset decisions; and building the industry's best management cadre. He then assessed all HR initiatives to determine whether they enhanced the company's competencies in those three areas. For example, leadership development training was aligned more closely with all three, and the assessment of corporate managers was adjusted to recognise contributions to them. The director also stopped certain activities altogether, assigning some talent management and organisational development to the business divisions (Kunisch et al. 2014).

However, to ensure relevance and ownership, it is essential to involve key stakeholders in agreeing the top priorities. In selecting strategic options to be pursued through the HR strategy, it's important to understand the extent of change required to move toward the vision, with a view to selecting those actions which help close the gap from how things work currently 'As is' to how they need to work in future 'To be'.

Having narrowed down your list of priority items, the next stage is working out the 'how':

- How will you address these priorities – what will you need to do?
- How will this affect your current areas of focus?
- How will you need to organise yourselves to deliver this? This includes choosing the HR systems and infrastructure best suited to deliver these strategic goals.

Assess HR function capability and effectiveness

In developing the HR strategy, it is also important to assess the effectiveness of the HR function itself – its processes, structure and competencies – and its potential for high impact HR changes. If HR lacks well-trained professionals, if the budget is low, or if the systems are outdated and hamper innovation, HR will be less efficient in reaching its HR and business outcomes.

Gaining feedback from other business units and monitoring satisfaction levels helps the function stay aligned with the needs of internal customers and gets more buy-in. Some companies use surveys to carry out HR capacity audits and to determine how satisfied the business divisions are with corporate functions. Finding out about the organisational structures, HRM strategies and challenges of your company's key competitors can also be instructive.

To be credible, HR should commit to role modelling agility to others, demonstrating visible leadership and new values, anticipating and acting on key areas for improvement. As agile role model, HR should use technology and relevant, comparable people data for greater transparency, open discussions, intelligent risk taking and data-driven decision-making, so that hiring, training communications and performance management can be done at a pace to match the new organisational model. HR itself needs to be technically competent and apply good operational principles so that it can deliver consistently and reliably as well as strategically. It must be able to take a concept and turn it into reality faster than the competition to provide real advantage to the organisation.

In developing and implementing HR strategy what might executives expect of HR? The whole HR community has a part to play. Strategic HR business partners with a focus on future strategy and organisational effectiveness will typically analyse internal and external intelligence, develop scenarios with the Strategy Unit, undertake organisational reviews, plan and facilitate M&As and other restructurings, provide project management expertise, design change processes, support innovation and stimulate breakthrough thinking. HR services can help leaders and managers and employees to manage the current business for instance by analysing employee data and customer feedback, feeding data and ideas for improvement to BPs and specialists, initiating or getting involved in improvement groups. HR(D) specialists such as L&D and Reward can work with BPs on planning, carrying out research and policy development, facilitating practice and process improvements, as well as providing learning programmes.

Reflective activity

Thinking of the HR function:

- What is its purpose (Why does it exist?)
- What are its key priorities and why? What makes it distinctive?
- What do your customers think of your service?
- What, if anything, is constraining progress and sustainable success?
- Given the trends, opportunities and threats, how well does your current HR plan take these into consideration?
- What HR activities could add maximum value?
- What does the Function/Unit need from you as a HR leader to sustain its success?

Drawing conclusions from this stock-taking, consider why some aspects of the service may need to change. Are you clear about what you are trying to achieve? Can you complete the statement 'I want to [..........] so that [benefits]?'
On a scale of 1 to 10 (1 = low, 10 = high) .... Rate

- How dissatisfied key stakeholders are with the way things are
- Is there a shared vision of what different will look like – including the benefits?
- Your team's capability for new ways of working
- Whether you know the next steps to get you moving towards the vision
- Do your key stakeholders have the will to see your idea through to a successful conclusion?

Where you have score less than 10,

- Are you clear about the actions you need to take to get you nearer to 10?
- Are you clear about the perceived costs of delivering this change and making it stick?
- Can you describe what the current situation is and what different will look like once you have implemented?

Thinking about the Galbraith model we discussed – which of the areas are you most clear about and which are you least clear about? (People, Structure, Process, Technology, Behaviours, Culture and Performance).

- What do you need to do to close gaps?
- How big a change are you proposing? Where will the biggest impacts be?
- How ready is the organisation for the change you want to implement?

Discussion on key emergent themes and issues can help identify potential priorities with respect to improving HR's own service and building distinctiveness.

Develop the strategic framework

The strategy document should explain the rationale for the strategy and spell out its aims, costs and benefits. The strategic framework sets out the key themes of the strategy within which goals are set for priority activities to deliver high value outcomes.

In terms of format, the following is suggested:

* **Company vision and mission statement – our ultimate aim, why we exist**
* **Company strategic imperatives/goals – how we intend to reach towards our vision**
* **HR vision and mission statement**

The following framework sets out the proposed HR outcomes and the impact HR's contribution should make on business success through people outcomes, HR impact and HR function effectiveness.

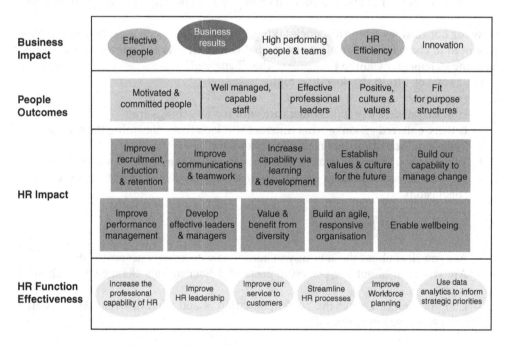

Figure 6.7 Example of a strategy framework for HR.
Based on source PPMA.

Case example: professional services firm (PSF)

The vision of one PSF's People strategy is to lead the organisation in creating a culture that inspires excellence.

The People Strategy has three strategic themes:

- *An open and transparent culture* that empowers people to perform at the highest possible levels
  - Commitment to professional growth
  - Aspiration for excellence in all that we do
  - Developing excellence in professional skills, leadership and management
- *An agile organisation*
- Commitment to an outstanding customer and employee experience
  - Structures that adapt to internal and external change and challenges
  - Effective information sharing and evidence-based decision-making protocols
  - Talent management and succession planning
  - Focus on innovation and appropriate risk-taking
- *An inspiring place to work*
  - Strong employer reputation
  - Competitive employee benefit package
  - Values and behaviour-led organisation
  - Helping people manage work and home priorities

People priorities

The Strategy will be enabled by five people priorities which form the basis of strategic imperatives/goals/outcomes:

- A high engagement with professional growth, talent management and leadership excellence
- A diverse, respectful and inclusive culture
- Enabling talent and high performance
- An engaging and sustainable reward and recognition programme
- Sustainable workloads, well-being and resilience
- Outstanding recruitment practices leading to a high-quality candidate and new employee experience.

Each of the people priorities has measurable anticipated outcomes (i.e. what does good look like?), principles, aims and the priorities for the year that allow the goals to be converted into plans. The activities involved in delivering on these priorities should be underpinned by the organisation's values and delivered by a professional and innovative Human Resources and Organisational Development team.

Action planning

Converting these intentions into action requires planning and the allocation of responsibilities and resources including budget.

Strategic plans

These detail the overall steps and priorities by which the goals and mission will be achieved. Many goals might be achieved simultaneously while others may need to be staged over time. Some goals might be dependent on one another. For example, developing managers to play their part in delivering these priorities might be necessary. The budget and allocation of funds reflects the priorities.

Tactical/operational business plans

Convert these goals into actionable areas, with clarity of responsibility about who does what.

Measuring HR activities and outcomes

Metrics allow progress to be monitored and results evaluated. Traditional HR metrics are based on customer satisfaction, added value and cost efficiency. Metrics including value for money tell us whether the money we spend in delivering our services is what our stakeholders want and need. The question is, what are the most meaningful things to measure? An effective HR measurement framework distinguishes between three types of measurement: efficiency, effectiveness and impact.

Efficiency

Efficiency metrics reflect the value for money argument – that the cheaper we hire and the faster we train, the better. They ask, 'What is the level and quality of HR practices we produce from the resources that we spend?' Typical efficiency measures of HRM Operations include cost-per-hire, time-to-fill, training time in days, learning and development budget/ training costs, time since last promotion, ratio of HR staff to total employees. All these metrics measure HR processes and give information about how efficient the HR function is. However, if we just focus on measuring HRM activities, we will automatically focus on reducing costs (i.e. maximising efficiency). This doesn't say anything about how well HR is delivering greater value, or HR effectiveness. Operationally effective HR teams focus less on cost savings and more on how they can reach their HR outcomes in a cost-efficient way.

Effectiveness

All HR activities should be carried out for a reason – they should lead to certain HR outcomes, such as those in the Standard Causal Model of HR (Paauwe and Richardson 1997) which shows a causal chain that starts with the business strategy and ends, through the HR processes, with (improved) financial performance. So, we engage in well-being programmes in order to lower absence; we are training our people to help them perform better and retain them. Outcomes include employee satisfaction, motivation, retention and presence.

Effectiveness metrics focus on the relationship between HR practices and the quality of talent pools and measure how HR programmes affect employee *capability* (are employees skilled enough to contribute?), *opportunity* (do employees get the chance to contribute?) and *motivation* (do employees want to contribute?). Effectiveness measures include individual and team performance and quality of hire measured against 'Best Practice' or Human Capital Indexes and Human Capital Benchmarks. However, HR effectiveness also depends on how well the intended HR practices are executed by managers. HR can provide great policies and opportunities but with bad managers, employees will be more absent, less engaged and much more likely to leave.

Impact

Impact measures focus on the business contribution HR makes with all of their people policies. HR outcomes lead to critical HR goals (i.e. cost-effectiveness, flexibility, legitimacy and so on), which in turn lead to ultimate business goals (i.e. profit, market share, market capitalisation – all related to the viability of the organisation, and other factors that help to build a competitive advantage). Impact measures examine for example the relationship between the changes in the quality of the talent pools and competitive success. 'Impact' asks questions such as, 'What difference does it make to have top performers versus simply average performers in this role?' Impact metrics measure the HR outcomes that are traditionally seen as important HR KPIs such as employee engagement, retention/turnover and so on and the link with important business goals such as productivity, customer satisfaction. This focus on HRM outcomes helps to align our processes with our goals.

All these metrics provide information about how well the workforce is doing. This involves **both HR** *and* **line management**. For example, when engagement is high, HR is perceived to be more effective than when engagement is low. The same holds true for retention and (inversely) for employee absence. However, organisations often have too many initiatives, targets and KPIs. Given the risk of widespread information overload, executives have long wanted meaningful metrics, including with respect to people, to help them understand what drives results, but in the past HR did not always have the data to form a view and successfully contribute to the business discussion (Sasser et al. 1978).

In a previous edition of this book, I discussed the example of Sears, Roebuck & Co, a large U.S. retailer, whose Causal Chain Model linked employee attitudes to service behaviour to customer responses to profit. The company used data to connect the attitudes of store associates, their on-the-job behaviours, the responses of store customers and the revenue performance of the stores (Rucci et al. 1998). The drawback is that all causal chains simplify reality.

HR analytics

The Board needs to know what you're measuring and why. How will gathering this data help the organisation meet its obligations to its shareholders? As Boudreau and Ramstad (2002) point out, there are many variations on HR measurement, 'So, the key consideration in any human capital measurement system is its ability to enhance decisions by articulating the logical connection between talent and organization outcomes'. Boudreau and Ramstad (2002) argue that true strategy integration requires identifying the 'pivotal talent pools' that have the largest strategic effect, and then measuring the changes in their actions that 'move the needle' on key processes. HR should focus on data – and measures – that truly inform management decisions and help address questions executives need answered, i.e.:

- Do we have the talent needed to succeed?
- Are we losing our best talent? How many have we left?
- Are we improving month after month?
- How many of our top performers have we promoted from within?
- What openings have been filled from within?
- How do we understand from the data what drives employee productivity? How can we create bonus structures that reflect this?

Using people analytics can help. HR analytics is the process of measuring the impact of HR metrics, such as time to hire and retention rate, on business performance. HR analytics is coming on apace, and increasingly enables a clearer picture of how HR outcomes impact on business performance. Blockchain for instance is expected to become a trusted source of information.

Whereas a metric often uses a single data point – such as the number of applications received to understand what is happening for instance with female candidates for jobs – analytics uses multiple data points to reach an answer. New sources of data and forms of analytics can provide metrics that will help HR to manage the intangibles that result in better overall business performance. By adding different kinds of data – especially employee attitudes, financial and business measures – it has become possible to gain granularity in understanding people costs and also to examine the links between employee experience, customer or operational measures and bottom-line outcomes. Analytics helps HR to move from an ad hoc set of workforce metrics to more refined and business-aligned scorecards or sets of human capital measures that can be embedded in operational processes. This helps keep HR measurements aligned to overall business objectives and assists HR in providing actionable information to leadership.

About the balanced business scorecard

Deloitte (Fineman 2016) argues that as HR moves from transactional and administrative to operational and strategic, many organisations are adopting a 'top down' approach to determining where to focus HR activity. With the 'top down' approach, organisations first identify the 'Measures that Matter' – those HR measurements that are crucial to support broader business goals, objectives and decisions.

Traditionally business success was assessed mainly on financial performance. The balanced scorecard approach to strategic management, developed in the 1990s by Robert Kaplan and David Norton at Harvard, is a management system (more than a measurement system) that suggests that financial results are a consequence of other activity undertaken by the business, which therefore need to be actively managed. So in a balanced scorecard, key performance indicators (KPIs) are identified from four perspectives – financial, customer, process and learning.

Traditional financial KPIs are considered 'lag' measures, inadequate for guiding and evaluating the journey of information age companies, while 'lead' measures link to investment in customers, suppliers, employees, leadership, processes, technology and innovation, which produce the financial results. So KPIs can be set, monitored and evaluated in the light of the nature of strategic goals - Customer Intimacy, Operational excellence, Product Leadership and so on. By defining key performance indicators in all result areas, a balanced scorecard can provide feedback on salient measures so that performance can be improved along a number of complementary tracks. Organisations are thus able to understand their operating marketplace more fully and balance conflicting stakeholder expectations.

Typical KPIs using the Balanced Scorecard might include:

- Financial
  - Turnover
  - Profit margins
  - Market share
  - Market capitalisation

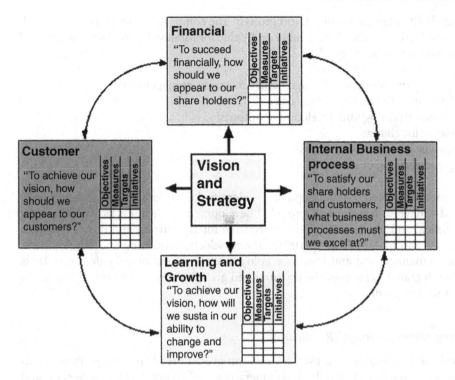

Figure 6.8 The Balanced Scorecard, after Kaplan and Norton, 1992.

- Customer
  - Customer satisfaction
  - Net promoter score
- Process
  - Accuracy of delivery
  - Throughput time
  - Product quality
- For Learning and Growth, KPIs are based on HR outcomes:
  - Engagement
  - Retention
  - Presence
  - Workforce competence and performance
- Workforce cost
- Talent metrics

In an HR scorecard, the desired organisational performance outcomes are defined in terms of the balanced scorecard. This helps clarify the HR vision, strategy and actions and evaluate the added value of HR's contribution to the business. By way of example, the HR team of one organisation, which supplies a UK-wide repair service to individual and corporate customers, analysed the links between business strategy and HR actions. The business mission and strategy is to meet customer needs – provide best service possible – unequalled value for money; build on strengths of brand, customer database and IT capability; manage for profit and growth. The company's core values are: Brand, Courtesy and Care, Stakeholders, Quality and Value for Money. The *People/Learning and growth* measures were set around:

- Capability (performance management, succession management)
- Culture and climate (survey measures)
- Skills mix (training and development outputs)
- Capacity for change
- Employee profile (statistics, costs)
- Organisation structure

This HR team segmented the staff population, identified the relevant development needs, established behavioural standards, provided development in business skills and the areas of technical and professional mastery required for the current and future business. HR processes and tools such as recruitment and selection, training and development, performance management and reward, employee relations and management standards were fully integrated to support the learning and growth goals to help the organisation achieve its strategic aims.

Monitoring and evaluating HR measures

Dashboards and milestones are used to track progress towards outcomes Typical categories of measurement include Impact, Operational efficiency, Customer Service and Strategic alignment. HR Dashboards or scorecards are designed to be dynamic and visual, including charts and graphs that illustrate key trends and insights and enable stakeholders to filter information according to their needs. Strategically focused one-page HR Dashboards or HR Scorecards allow real-time interactive updates and provide a snapshot of overall HR performance against strategic goals at a particular point in time. They are used to monitor and drive performance improvements across HR processes in support of broader leadership and organisational objectives.

Truly strategic HR functions focus on the business contribution they make with all of their people policies. Alongside the financial and other strategic goals, the organisation is trying to reach there are also cultural goals, such as fairness, moral values, legitimacy, that are harder to measure. Nevertheless, setting targets and measures can both guide and drive performance improvements. For example, one Financial Services company was keen to improve its gender representation at senior levels. It set targets and measures which allowed success or otherwise to be measured using a dashboard. Targets were set around hiring – % of women management hires; promotions; vacancies for which women were shortlisted; representation of women on vacancy panels. Targets were also set for Retention: % men vs women on voluntary turnover; compa-ratio and salary analysis; exit interview data; EVP analysis; policy and process implementation. Business units were given targets to achieve 31% female leadership with a year. Gender Pay Equity Gap was benchmarked against cross-sectoral data. Dashboards and scorecards helped validate progress – did we achieve the agreed goal? and evaluate its success – what value was generated, was it the right thing to do, and what can we learn for the future? Setting clear KPIs and actively monitoring progress helped the firm close its gender representation gap.

But what of metrics for agility?

Agile firms tend to be more resilient to environmental shocks and upheavals than other firms and may remain largely unaffected in terms of reliability, production cycle time and inventory turn. McKinsey (Aghina et al. 2020) tracked a broad set of outcome metrics during agile transformations that fell into four categories, similar to the balanced scorecard, that compose the structure of what they call the 'agile impact engine':

- customer satisfaction
- employee engagement
- operational performance
- financial performance

Clearly, organisations undergoing agile transformations will differ in the emphasis they place on outcome categories. In the McKinsey sample (Aghina et al. 2020), firms who needed to recruit talent focused more on employee engagement, whereas those in financial distress concentrated on financial gains. Those facing competitive pressure valued customer satisfaction.

Employee engagement

Thanks to the flatter structures and cross-functional nature of teams in agile organisations, three motivating factors of employee engagement tend to be present – a strong sense of autonomy, mastery and purpose – which have a positive influence on employee satisfaction and engagement (Pink 2009). Autonomy and mastery are enhanced because employees in Agile units have greater visibility of their tasks since strategy is expressed in terms of objectives and key results (OKRs), team-level milestones and deliverables. These act as a common language between distributed and autonomous teams. Teams are also clear about their current performance since real-time key-performance-indicator dashboards allow for feedback and rapid adjustments if needed. Of course, it is important to track changes over time to confirm a measurable impact of employee engagement on successful agile transformations.

A study into the effect of HR metrics on organisational agility at Kenya Airways (Opwaka 2018) argued that while the use of efficiency metrics in the areas of staff productivity, cost management and the provision of quality HR services is important, the use of impact metrics relating to employee engagement is essential. These include metrics relating to communication, decision making, talent management, employee relations, turnover, recruitment and ensuring good management of these at functional level. Presenting the metrics using HR dashboards helps the leadership team understand and apply them.

Aghina et al. (2020) note that, in service operations, speed arising from agile transformations of customer-service and back-office activities can drive significant gains in productivity and customer satisfaction as well as many other organisational outcomes. With agility, organisations can increase the speed of decision-making and shorten the time-gap between the conception and release of a product (known as time to market), as happened with the unusually rapid development cycle from concept through to licensing for use of several anti-Covid vaccines in 2020.

Aghina et al. (2020) suggest that if the business impact of improvements in customer satisfaction, employee engagement and operational metrics (such as speed) arising from agile transformation is to be understood, it would be better to measure increased revenue or margin uplift rather than simply tracking productivity gains and cost savings. McKinsey's research found that implementing an agile transformation can improve operational-performance metrics – such as speed, target-achievement rates (TARs) and other industry-specific metrics – by 30–50%; with enhanced team visibility and understanding of objectives, as well as improved team dedication, making a difference.

HR STRATEGY AS CULTURE CHANGE

Developing and implementing an HR strategy is the opportunity for teams that can seize it to spur on culture change and model new practice. I am very grateful to Rachel Adams, Director of Human Resources at the UK's Keele University, for the following case study.

Case: HR transformation at Keele University

The global university sector is undergoing significant change as a result of multiple challenges in the competitive marketplace, not least dealing with the consequences of the Covid crisis on student demand and the health of staff and stakeholders. Keele University is no exception. In the United Kingdom in 2019, many universities experienced industrial action led by the University and College Union (UCU) over changes to academic pensions (the Universities Superannuation Scheme).

Rachel Adams was appointed as Keele University's HR Director in 2018 having previously developed her career in the private sector, including at JCB and Fujitsu. During this turbulent time for the sector, Keele's Human Resources directorate was transformed from a well-respected, effective and trusted if traditional function into a high performing, strategically aligned and progressive team who have made an immediate and sustained impact on business effectiveness and organisational performance. Here Rachel describes the transformation of the HR team over a two-year period.

'Keele has developed a strong reputation as a broad-based research-led institution offering a high-quality education and student experience. Our vision which describes our ambitions to firmly establish Keele as a world class institution and to accelerate further improvements in the quality of research is articulated in the "Our Future" strategic vision document which was developed through a comprehensive consultation over many months with staff, students, alumni and wider stakeholders and partners.

In simple terms, the "Our Future" vision presents five key themes (P's): Purpose, People, Place, Partnerships and Performance, the People theme being of particular relevance to the work of the HR Directorate and providing the strategic direction of travel which guides our priorities and annual planning. Underpinning the "Our Future" vision is a number of enabling strategies, including a People strategy, EDI strategy and Health and Well-being strategy, each of which, whilst being owned by University leaders and managers, have a key role for HR in their delivery'.

Rachel wanted to deliver an ambitious HR agenda for Keele, in a more collaborative and innovative way than had been seen previously. The Human Resources directorate is a relatively small team of HR generalists (21 FTE HR professionals and administrators supporting a diverse staffing base of around 2000) who, until the recent past, had a relatively low profile in the institution and the sector. Rachel's vision for the directorate placed new expectations on colleagues which, whilst exciting for some, would be challenging for others.

Open, honest communication was a critical starting point. Through a number of workshops '**better and bolder HR**' became a shared mantra for the directorate and this was well received by key stakeholders, including the Executive team and governing body, who approved a small-scale restructure resulting in internal promotions and a number of mutually agreed departures. Two new 'Head of HR' posts (focusing on operations and on strategy and policy respectively) replaced the previous Deputy role, delivering an overall payroll saving and clearly signalling the dual focus of the directorate on operational excellence and delivery of the People strategy.

Rachel led the programme of change for the team, coaching the senior members of the directorate to move them to a position of increased confidence in their own leadership and decision making. New ways of operating were co-created with the wider team in sessions based on shared values to explore enablers and barriers to delivering **better and bolder HR**.

Financial sustainability

Given the turbulent context the 'Our Future' vision was underpinned by a three-year Financial Sustainability Plan (FSP), announced in February 2019, which focused on cost reduction, efficiency and growth and required major savings in workforce costs through pay restraint, voluntary severance and so on. The HR Director was invited to be a member of the small leadership team (VC, DVC, COO) responsible for overseeing delivery of the FSP. A specific HR strategy was developed and delivered by the HR team, bringing together a range of interventions and developments resulting in recurrent pay savings of over £6.8 million at the end of Year 1, against a target of £8million at the end of Year 3.

How was this achieved? As Rachel recounts: 'Throughout the period of cost savings, fortnightly meetings were held with the campus trade unions and, as far as possible, we operated an open book approach where they were free to scrutinise the University's finances and recovery plans. We were open and honest with staff from the outset that delivery of the strategic ambitions would require a significant improvement in the University's operating performance, and this is where the FSP with its initial focus on achieving recurrent cost savings came into play. The progress against this plan, facilitated by HR, to realise the required savings links directly to the organisation's strategy of delivering financial surpluses that can be re-invested to support our teaching and research priorities and enhance the student experience.

Traditionally Keele has had a fairly militant University and College Union (UCU), and inevitably there were disagreements along the way. For example, UCU objected strongly to the proactive manner in which HR and line managers brought the voluntary severance scheme to the attention of staff in areas where there was significant financial under-performance against budget.

The transparency and openness of senior management, including the HRD and Heads of HR, along with the volume and quality of staff engagement was appreciated by staff and their representatives and is therefore likely to have played a part, we believe, in UCU's failure to secure a mandate for industrial action with respect to the 2019/20 pay award. The more moderate response from UCU in 2019 contrasts strongly with our experience in 2018, and points to the positive impact of our work to engage staff on the Keele's financial situation (i.e. the need to address rising staff costs as a percentage of income) by communicating effectively to staff in a series of understandable "explainers" posted to our staff intranet and reinforced with management briefings'.

Thinking and acting 'Better and bolder'

The innovative approach taken by the newly formed HR senior team was underpinned by encouragement to think differently and creatively about the financial challenges facing Keele and to frame initiatives in the wider context of the People Strategy. Hence, the introduction of recruitment controls which meant that all professional services roles could only be filled internally, was used positively to support career development planning (highlighted as an issue in the staff survey) and showcased during our Professional Services conference which saw record attendance in 2019. Similarly, the fast-track application process that was introduced to consider flexible working requests and the new scheme to enable the purchase of additional annual leave were linked clearly to our EDI objectives in creating a working environment in which flexibility is embedded.

For Rachel, 'What was outstanding was the "**better and bolder**" approach that members of the HR team adopted consistently. Everyone in the team stepped up to new situations that they had not encountered previously. For example, HR managers were involved in negotiating settlement terms for staff leaving under the voluntary severance scheme – an activity that had been the responsibility of the Deputy Director in the previous structure. Colleagues operated outside of previous comfort zones in the knowledge that they were supported and trusted at all times. The open, honest team working ethos meant that problems and learning were shared and, consequently, despite the pressure placed on HR colleagues, motivation and satisfaction in the team remained high (89% employee engagement score for HR in 2019 staff survey).

Importantly, by the end of year one, having made very significant progress against the three-year target, we were able to announce that the university was no longer in a position where compulsory redundancies needed to be considered as a means of affecting campus wide delivery of cost reduction targets. This had been a particular concern for staff and trade unions and the reassurance offered meant that we could move our collective attention to the efficiency and growth aspects of the FSP'.

A strategic agenda

The dual focus on operational excellence and strategic developments, delivered through strong HR leadership and guided by the People Strategy has positively affected the performance of individual business units as well as the whole institution.

Committed to making social progress and founded on a vision to make a positive difference to the communities it serves, at University level there is an increased focus on Equality, Diversity and Inclusion (EDI), through a refreshed EDI strategy and new governance structure. These have led to tangible results over a two-year period: Keele is one of just 14 UK institutions to have secured the Race Equality Charter award and has been commended for advancing race equality through a comprehensive programme focusing on culture and communications in the institution. Keele has also been identified as an exemplar institution with regard to action planning for the Gender Pay Gap, has maintained its Disability Confident recognition and was commended by Stonewall for not just focusing on any one initiative to score points but for embedding LGBT equality throughout the institution. Keele aims to build on these firm foundations to become a truly anti-racist institution.

The institutional staff engagement survey managed and coordinated by HR in February 2019, was the first of its kind at Keele and solicited an 81% response rate which exceeded expectations. In order to 'get underneath' the responses and to ensure actions address the core issues, a new Staff Voice Group was introduced which is proving a very effective forum to listen directly to the views of staff, in parallel to established fora and channels, such as trade union meetings, management groups, etc.

Key themes from the staff survey have informed a high-level action plan for the institution, which in turn is being driven through our People strategy. These themes are:

- Supporting health and well-being
- Improving positive performance management
- Creating an environment where all colleagues feel it is safe to speak up
- Enhancing opportunities for career development for professional services staff

Drilling down to specific business units, HR colleagues have worked closely with Heads of School/Service to develop local action plans to address concerns raised in the staff survey. Twenty-seven plans are in place and progress is monitored on a six-monthly basis, to ensure this programme of work is kept alive. This is challenging in an environment where cost reduction has been at the forefront of people's minds. However, HR colleagues have skilfully and persistently worked with a dual focus, delivering savings through voluntary severance, for example whilst driving improvements to the staff experience.

A refreshed strategy People Strategy drafted in 2020 sets out how the University will support the future vision and invites all members of the community to work together to co-create a strong future for Keele. Safeguarding the positive aspects of the Keele culture, what we call 'the Keele difference', is woven throughout the strategy which relies on colleagues adopting behaviours and values that we see as being critical: collegiality, ambition, accountability, respect, fairness and consistency.

Through their dual focus on operational excellence and strategic delivery, adopting a 'better and bolder' approach to service delivery, the team have demonstrated excellence across a range of objectives including reduction of recurrent pay costs, advancement of the EDI agenda and improvements to the staff experience through a new and exciting approach to staff engagements. The transformed HR team and its achievements have been recognised internally and externally in multiple awards and commendations.

Lessons learned

Rachel reflects on key lessons learned as a new team, while supporting delivery of a significant change programme (FSP) and maintaining focus on the People Strategy as follows:

The incredible results that can be achieved by people when they are supported to raise their aspirations!

Creating a new team does not necessarily require external appointments: Providing opportunity and support to existing HR staff who are talented and enthusiastic about new ways of working was, and continues to be, a highly successful approach.

The importance of a shared vision: As a lean team with an ambitious agenda, we all needed to be bought into the same goals. The time invested in the developing a collective understanding of how HR could make a **bolder and better** contribution to the University was time well spent.

The power of the team: A simple model we use in our HR team is to liken ourselves to a flock of geese: all flying in same direction to create extra velocity, leaders at the front who from time to time rotate to cover each other, all members 'honking' encouragement for each other. The simple but powerful analogy is effective for us.

Communication and engagement are vital: A key factor of the successful transformation of the HR team and the results we have delivered over the past two years has been our enhanced approach to communicating and engaging with managers and staff. This has involved a carefully planned internal comms plan (over 90 communications on the FSP in a 12-month period), blogs from senior HR staff (including one on racial harassment which was picked up nationally) and the establishment of the new Staff Voice Group bringing together a cross section of around 50 staff to explore themes from our institutional staff survey.

HR as role models: Keele's 'Our Future' vision and new People Strategy highlight the following values as being crucial: collegiality, ambition, accountability, respect, fairness and consistency. The HR team live by these values and this is evidenced by feedback that members of the team frequently receive from their internal client groups.

Feel the fear and do it anyway! In the past, the HR team at Keele have had a lower profile internally and externally, due, in part, to a lack of ambition and confidence. Over the past two years colleagues have 'found their wings' (to go back to our geese analogy), have moved out of their comfort zones and have demonstrated that a small team can punch its weight, to really good effect for the institution.

Reflective activity

- What does this case study illustrate with respect to how this HR team responded to context drivers?
- How has this HR team been able to pursue both financial and ethical/cultural goals?
- What are the implications for stakeholder management?
- How was the HR team equipped for new ways of working?

CONCLUSION

Developing and implementing an effective HR strategy is a challenging process and can be a highly political one at that. We have considered some elements of a strategy development process and discussed considerations regarding stakeholder involvement and the kinds of measures that might be used to track progress. We have also explored an example of how HR strategy can help stimulate and steer culture change.

In the next section, Strategies for Talent, we move on to consider various aspects of HR strategy implementation that relate to talent. We shall start by looking at workforce planning and recruitment in the next chapter.

REFERENCES

Aghina, W., Handscomb, C., Ludolph, J., Rona, D. and West, D. (2020). Enterprise agility: Buzz or business impact? McKinsey & Company, March 15. https://www.mckinsey.com/business-functions/organization/our-insights/enterprise-agility-buzz-or-business-impact.

Becker, B. and Huselid, M.A. (2006). Strategic human resources management: Where do we go from here? *Academy of Management Journal (Special Issue: Human Resources and Organizational Performance)*, 39(4), 779–801.

Boudreau, J.W. and Ramstad, P.M. (2002). *Strategic HRM Measurement in the 21st Century: From Justifying HR to Strategic Talent Leadership, CAHRS Working Paper Series*, Personnel Decisions International, Cornell University ILR School. https://digitalcommons.ilr.cornell.edu/cgi/viewcontent.cgi?article=1055&context=cahrswp

Boxall, P. and Purcell, J. (2003). *Strategy and Human Resource Management*. New York: Palgrave.

Brockbank, W. (1997). HR's future on the way to a presence. *Human Resource Management*, 36(1), 65–69.

Burke, W.W. and Litwin, G. H. (1992). A causal model of organisational performance and change. *Journal of Management*, 8(3), 523–546.

Fineman, D. (2016). *Enabling business results with HR measures that matter*. (Deloitte). https://www2.deloitte.com/content/dam/Deloitte/us/Documents/human-capital/us-hc-enabling-business-results-with-hr-measures-that-matter.pdf.

Galbraith, J. https://www.jaygalbraith.com/images/pdfs/StarModel.pdf.

Guest, D. and Bos-Nehles, A. (2013). HRM and performance: The role of effective implementation, in Jaap Paauwe, David E. Guest, Patrick M. Wright (eds), *HRM and Performance: Achievements and Challenges*. Wiley.

Kaplan, R.S. and Norton, D.P. (1992). The balanced scorecard—measures that drive performance. *Harvard Business Review*, January–February.

Kunisch, S., Müller-Stewens, G. and Campbell, A. (2014). Why corporate functions stumble. *Harvard Business Review*, 92(12), 110–117.

Lepak, D.P. and Snell, S.A. (1999). The human resource architecture: Toward a theory of human capital allocation and development. *The Academy of Management Review*, 24(1), 31–48.

Nadler, D. and Tushman, M. (1988). *Strategic Organization Design: Concepts, Tools & Processes*. Northbrook, Illinois: Scott Foresman & Co.

Opwaka, I.B. (2018). *Critical Human Resource Metrics Which Support Organizational Agility to Emerging Challenges, To Sustain Industry Competitiveness: A Case Study of Kenya Airways PLC, Thesis*, United States International University-Africa.

Paauwe, J. (2004). *HRM and Performance: Achieving Long-term Viability*. Oxford: Oxford University Press.

Paauwe, J. and Richardson, R. (1997). Introduction special issue on HRM and Performance. *International Journal of Human Resource Management*, 8(3), 257–262.

Peccei, R. and Van De Voorde, K. (2019). Human resource management–well-being–performance research revisited: Past, present, and future. *Human Resource Management Journal*, 29(4), 539–563.

Pink, D. H. (2009). *Drive: The Surprising Truth About What Motivates Us*. Edinburgh: Riverhead Books.

Porter, M. E. (1985). *Competitive Advantage*. New York: Free Press.

Purcell, J. (2006). Foreword. *Human Resource Management Journal*, 14(3), 3–5.

Purcell, J. (2002). *Understanding the People and Performance Link: Unlocking the Black Box*, London: CIPD.

Rucci, A.J., Quinn, R.T. and Kim, S.P. (1998). The employee-customer-profit chain at Sears. *Harvard Business Review*, 76(1), 82–97.

Sasser, W. E., Olsen, R. P. and Wyckoff, D. D. (1978). *Management of Service Operations*. Boston: Allyn & Bacon.

Treacy M. and Wiersema F. (1995). *The Discipline of Market Leaders: Choose Your Customers, Narrow Your Focus, Dominate Your Market*. New York: Perseus Books Group.

Ulrich, D., Kryscynski, D., Ulrich, M. and Brockbank, W. (2017). *Victory through Organization: Why the War for Talent is Failing Your Company and What You Can Do About It*. New York: McGraw-Hill Education.

World Economic Forum (2018). *The Future of Jobs Report 2018*. http://www3.weforum.org/docs/WEF_Future_of_Jobs_2018.pdf.

Wright, P., Gardner, T. and Moynihan, L.M. (2003). The impact of HR practices on the performance of business units. *Human Resource Management Journal*, 13(3), 21–36.

Part II
Strategies for talent

7

Workforce planning and recruitment strategies

DOI: 10.4324/9781003219996-9

The two decades since the first edition of this book was written have witnessed surges, ebbs and flows in demand for key talent. The first edition in 1999 coincided with what McKinsey dubbed 'The War for Talent'. Fears of shortages of the talent required to fuel the burgeoning knowledge and service economy led to a growing focus on how to source, recruit and retain high potential workers who could fuel business success. The second edition of this book in 2009 coincided with the immediate aftermath of the financial crisis, which brought the practices of many global firms into disrepute and led to large-scale lay-offs, whose repercussions are being felt to this day. The current edition (2021) written during the global pandemic raises questions about the future of work and the kinds of workforce required going forward.

Identifying, sourcing and retaining those people who breathe life into an organisation in this changing landscape is essential if businesses are to thrive and make the most of a return to positive market conditions. Consequently, talent management and workforce analytics are once again integral elements of companies' future-readiness plans. To secure the workforce an organisation needs, recruitment is only part of the talent picture. In later chapters, we shall consider approaches relating to motivation, retention and performance such as development, engagement, performance management and reward. We focus specifically on the inter-related strategies of developing people and the creation of effective career paths in Chapter 9.

CHAPTER OVERVIEW

In this chapter we shall explore elements of a strategic approach to addressing some of the talent challenges facing organisations, focusing in particular on workforce planning and recruitment. We shall cover:

- Talent shortages: an ongoing War for Talent
- Defining talent and talent management
- Workforce planning process
- Recruitment and selection process
- Use of technology

LEARNING OBJECTIVES

- Provide overview of talent management
- Outline an approach to workforce planning
- Consider recent developments in recruitment

INTRODUCTION: AN ONGOING WAR FOR TALENT

With ongoing uncertainty at the time of writing about the continued impact of COVID-19, many organisations will need to reduce workforce costs while also ensuring they have the people required to keep business-critical operations running and recover from any recessionary downturn. Aside from the pandemic, the implications of the political, demographic and technology trends shaping businesses and the workforce are profound. What is unclear is whether the acceleration of business closures and job losses during 2020, and the technology-driven transformation of many large corporations, will result in a new structural status quo and a very different workforce from what went before.

As organisations look to embrace agility and new ways of working and, with the prospect of resurgent economic activity after the pandemic, shortages of key talent risk setting back business recovery and growth across the globe, with the greatest year-on-year talent shortage increases in the United States, Sweden, Finland, Hungary and Slovenia in what has been dubbed 'The Great Resignation'. As talent and skills gaps grow, as many as 40% of companies in Accenture research experience shortages that drastically impact their ability to adapt and innovate. Various studies confirm similar messages for the UK. In their 2019–2020 survey *Closing the Skills Gap: What UK Workers Want in 2020* the Manpower Group found that 23% of UK employers were unable to find the talent they needed. UK organisations also have to respond to the continuing impact on their resourcing and talent planning activities of leaving the EU, especially the ending of free labour movement and related shortages of certain types of labour.

As a result, many leadership groups worry that their organisation might be facing an existential crisis and competition has increased to attract and retain individuals who demonstrate the most potential and who have sought-after skills. The 'War for Talent' has not gone away, merely changed shape.

DEFINING 'TALENT' AND 'TALENT MANAGEMENT'

To address such challenges, the need for new approaches to talent management has rarely been greater. Yet while many organisations are investing heavily in IT strategies to support their increasingly complex and dynamic operations, most have been slow to respond when it comes to the workforce. They still rely on a single inflexible talent strategy for a work world that soon will look nothing like it did a few years ago.

The terms 'talent' and 'talent management' became commonplace following the coining of the 'War for Talent' by McKinsey at the end of the last century. A CIPD sponsored research project (Tansley et al. 2007) found several variations on how organisations understood these terms. Where there was some coalescence was in the following definition of 'talent':

> Talent consists of those individuals who can make a difference to organizational performance, either through their immediate contribution or in the longer term by demonstrating the highest levels of potential.

With respect to talent management, various theorists argue that this is simply a relabelling of old processes. It is defined as:

> The systematic attraction, identification, development, engagement/retention and deployment of those individuals with high potential who are of particular value to an organization.

In recent times the definition of 'talent' has broadened beyond those people deemed to have high potential (the 'exclusive' view), to a much wider definition of talent that embraces people at different levels on whose skills business success depends, even though they may not be future leaders. Increasingly therefore talent management involves looking at the 'talents' of the whole workforce and finding ways to develop their strengths (the 'inclusive' view).

Early talent management theories emphasised the importance of recruitment as a means of filling talent gaps, yet in more recent times the focus has expanded to include areas such as building organisational capability, workforce and succession planning, individual performance and policies aimed at talent development, management and retention. Talent management activities today typically include:

- Workforce planning
- Recruitment (talent acquisition)
- Building talent 'pools' – internal and external
- Succession planning
- Leadership development
- Career management
- Deployment
- Performance management
- Employee engagement
- Employee retention
- Life-long learning.

Conventional talent management practices tended to assume that employers have the upper hand in the employment relationship. In recent times, with rapid innovation a strategic imperative for most companies, top-down planning models are giving way to nimbler, more customer focused, user-driven methods. In similar vein, employees increasingly want the same kind of personalised attention and experience that customers receive, and skilled workers can and do exercise their options if they are not happy with their lot. Employers have to come up with innovative, more responsive, employee-focused and personalised approaches to talent management if they are to attract and retain the people, they need to fuel their business success.

Though recruitment and retention are often spoken of in the same breath, as here, the factors driving them are not necessarily the same. Companies typically develop 'employer brands' to attract potential employees, yet if the lived reality of the brand is different from the promise, the customer–employee goes elsewhere. This potentially broadens the scope of talent management to include factors such as management development, employee communications and organisational culture – which reflect how the employer brand is lived and have a bearing on retention.

This means, according to Chris Gray, director of the Manpower Group UK, 'Organisations need to be agile, and willing to stretch their candidate offering; increasing salaries isn't enough of a differentiator anymore'. These solutions must reflect an understanding of employee motivation and be closely linked to trends in the changing labour market, as well as to the organisation's needs.

The need for a talent management strategy

Given the changing world of work, organisations must take a strategic approach to talent management and regularly evaluate their practices. As Guthridge et al. argue (2008), talent management is very much a business issue: 'demographics, globalization and the characteristics of knowledge work present long-term challenges that reinforce the argument for putting workforce planning and talent management at the heart of the business strategy and for giving those issues a bigger share of senior management's time'.

Senior leaders need to be actively involved in the talent management process and should make involvement in the recruitment, succession planning, leadership development and retention of key employees their high priorities. Unilever, for example believes in recruiting only the very best people and requires top-level managers to make time for interviews, alongside their other responsibilities. Since the way people are managed can make a difference to collaboration and retention, the question arises: do we have the right kinds of managers with good emotional intelligence? In Unilever line managers play an active role in the recruitment and development of talent. They are expected to act as coaches or mentors, provide job-shadowing opportunities and encourage talented employees to move around within the organisation for career development.

Managing talent means being clear about which of the different elements of the talent process are more important at any given time, including being aware of where the pressure points are. There is no point in recruiting people satisfactorily on the one hand but failing to retain them on the other hand or losing people further down the pipeline at the same time (Taylor 2018). A more comprehensive, agile and holistic approach to predicting, sourcing, reskilling and deploying talent is needed, that is owned by leaders who want to purposefully design their workforce to keep pace with technological and other changes and to get the best from people and technology.

WORKFORCE PLANNING

As we discussed in the last chapter, an integrated talent management strategy starts with the organisational strategy and business plan. It brings together the operational and the strategic planning processes. Many businesses are thinking hard about their future skills requirements. There is a growing realisation that, with an increased emphasis on agility and responsiveness, good quality management information set within a planning framework is the key to identifying and maximising the drivers of performance before circumstances force managers to act to close workforce gaps. Creating a talent management strategy therefore requires workforce planning.

The organisation-wide workforce plan should be driven by the business strategy and be 'future-focused', to equip the organisation with the workforce of the right size, shape and nature, comprising permanent and contingent staff, that enables the organisation to deliver the business strategy while at the same time remaining flexible enough to deal with constant change. It will clarify both demand (i.e. what the organisation needs) and supply (i.e. the people you will have). The workforce/talent plan will help to focus and prioritise talent goals, especially with respect to critical roles and where investment should be made. Getting the right focus and blend of approaches for capability-building is important.

This is a dynamic, ongoing process that aligns the needs and priorities of the organisation with those of its workforce to ensure it can meet its legislative, regulatory, service and production requirements and organisational objectives. A strategic workforce plan informs good business decisions and vice versa, especially when skilled people are in short supply and finding, hiring and retaining employees with the right skills is a key challenge (Aon 2019).

Deloitte (2004), suggested six questions CEOs should ask their HR Leaders:

1   Which segments of the workforce create the value for which we are most rewarded in the marketplace?
2   Which areas of our business will be most impacted by impending waves of retirement? What are we doing to prepare successors? What impact will the anticipated retirements have on the skills and productivity necessary to meet future demand?
3   In what areas is the talent market heating up (i.e. demand will outpace supply)? Which segments of our workforce will be most impacted? What are the potential top-line and bottom-line implications?
4   What skills will we need over the next five years that we don't currently possess? How will we create that capacity? What happens to our business if we don't?
5   What is our turnover within critical areas? How much is it costing us? In customers? In productivity? In innovation? In quality? What are we doing to resolve the root causes?
6   Are we actively developing talent portfolios or workforce plans that will help us to understand and communicate the financial consequences of talent decisions on our business?

In today's fast-moving context, with the conventional business planning horizon becoming ever more short-term, workforce planning is increasingly difficult. A greater focus is needed on how to prepare organisations and people for the future of work (WEF 2018).

Demand for new roles

Technology is changing the future of work since it changes the types of work – and jobs – required and the skills needed to do them. A major transformation of the jobs market is underway thanks to the 'fourth industrial revolution' (4IR), with the emergence of machine learning, the integration of Big Data, Cloud computing, robotics, artificial-intelligence and additive manufacturing. Many jobs have been automated out of existence and some of the most in-demand roles are completely new. Many organisations are finding that a growing share of their revenue is directly linked to digital skills areas and jobs that did not exist ten years previously. Just some of today's emerging occupations include: –data analyst, data scientist, user experience designer, AI and Machine Learning Specialists, Big Data Specialists, Robotics Specialists and Engineers and Digital Transformation Specialists, User Experience and Human-Machine Interaction Designers Information Security Analysts, Ecommerce, Social Media Specialists, Innovation Professionals and Algorithm trainer. People to fill such roles are in short supply.

In a 2018 Deloitte survey over 75% of executives reported challenges in recruiting individuals with the relevant digital skills, with data scientists and analysts among the most difficult roles to fill and retain. Consequently, there is likely to be fierce competition between employers to attract the best.

Changing job skills

Even though some roles may look similar to those in the past, the skills required to do them continue to evolve rapidly. In this fast-moving context even conventional roles that are still needed - such as General and Operations Managers, Sales and Marketing

Professionals, Organizational Development Specialists, Training and Development Specialists, People and Culture Specialists – are being given a new twist by technology. Can people be developed to meet the new demands of their roles or must new 'ready-made' talent be brought in?

PwC observe that the 'low carbon workforce' will treble by 2030 and that demand for digital skills and transferable skills such as creativity, critical thinking, interpersonal communication skills and leadership skills will also become more important as technology advances and virtual working becomes commonplace.

Kruse (2020) reports on research into the skills required by employers.

The top 'soft' skills identified were:

- Creativity: how to generate original ideas and solutions.
- Persuasion: convincing others to support your ideas, buy your solutions or to take action.
- Collaboration: able to work on a team and unlock synergies towards a common goal.
- Adaptability: thriving in change and uncertainty.
- Emotional intelligence: able to perceive and understand the emotions of yourself and others and to modulate your own natural emotions.

The top 'hard' skills were:

1. Blockchain: a novel way to securely store, validate, authorise and move digital assets across the Internet.
2. Cloud computing: design, delivery and maintenance of cloud architecture on platforms like AWS and Azure.
3. Analytical reasoning: able to understand data and generate conclusions based on analysis.
4. Artificial intelligence: embodying AI, machine learning and natural language processing.
5. UX design: conducting research and designing software and other products to maximise the 'user experience'
6. Business analysis: able to work with data for analysis, problem-solving and presentations.
7. Affiliate marketing: the hottest new hard skill is about marketing through others' trusted channels.
8. Sales: perhaps both a hard skill and a soft skill as sales involves persuasion, but for a specific commercial end in mind.
9. Scientific computing: able to apply statistical and analytical approaches to large data sets using programs like Python, and MATLAB.
10. Video production: mobile video is quickly becoming the dominant form of all communication and companies are fighting to create effective digital video assets.

Given that workers with sought-after skills appear to have many employment choices available to them, employers are increasingly having to compete hard for the best candidates.

Conventional 'hard' workforce planning is about numbers: effective and timely workforce planning goes beyond forecasting headcount and workforce supply and demand to also focus on skills, potential and how these are deployed and organised. Executives must ask the difficult questions: Do we have the right capabilities across the organisation? Are they available at the right time and the right cost?

Data need to be analysed and understood in context, for instance current demographics, predictions for skill shortages or surpluses, the labour market and other workplace trends. Workforce planning should yield important data such as ease or difficulty of hiring, time to hire, time to productivity, attrition rates and so on, which can help identify risks and contingency actions. The advent of Big Data and predictive analytics has made it possible to establish a comprehensive workforce plan which can feed into recruitment, development, succession planning, career planning, talent planning, organisation design and a number of other HR practices.

'Soft' (or strategic) workforce planning is about defining a strategic framework within which such information can be considered in order to provide agile people solutions to complement the future direction of the business. This is particularly important for attracting, developing and retaining those sought-after people who ultimately determine the organisation's success in the marketplace. In developing the strategy, it's important to think in terms of well targeted practical outcomes that can be carried out as effectively as possible by key stakeholders such as line managers. Since it encompasses the whole organisation the planning process requires buy-in at all levels and should seek to enable co-operation between managers to minimise any competition for people resources between departments.

Elements of a typical workforce planning process

As we discussed in the last chapter, the process requires understanding the organisation and its environment, analysing the current and potential workforce, determining future workforce needs, identifying the gap between the workforce you will have available and your future needs, and implementing solutions to address shortages, surpluses or skill mismatches so that an organisation can accomplish its mission, goals and strategic plan.

Understand the organisation/business strategy and the operating environment

Working with stakeholders is key, especially the Executive team, to answer questions such as: Where is the organisation going? How are needs changing? What are the plans to increase productivity, including changes to organisation structure and processes? What does the organisational structure look like now and what's likely in future? How will you deliver your next product or service? Do you have the workforce you need to deliver your growth agenda in a way that beats the competition? Are there intentions to introduce or update technology? Are you becoming international/global? How much change and innovation do you wish to inject into the system? What costs are you expecting? How much flexibility will be needed in servicing customer needs (e.g. 24-hour retailing)?

Predict future needs

Preparation benefits from anticipating future work demands earlier in the cycle. Scenario planning, for instance, can be used to show different possible futures and their different people requirements. Technology is likely to feature in all future scenarios so HR should assess the expected impact on current roles within their organisation and identify the key future critical skills required for future business success at all levels – from corporate to functional/individual – and predicting the timeframes involved.

Many companies will have three to five key capability areas which reflect the way their business wants to go. One organisation decided that it needed just one distinctive skill area – data science – for its future success. Another concentrated on building the capability of creating a powerful brand. This is about understanding:

- What capabilities do we do very well?
- Within those capabilities, what positions do we need?
- Who do we have in those roles? What is their delivery value?
- How do we leverage these positions to make a difference?

Though not yet widely adopted, predictive intelligence can aid in assessing current workforce needs and can also guide workforce requirements up to 18 months out, including the traits of future leaders, according to Accenture. Predictive intelligence must be continuous, iterative, and remain a closed-loop process that involves all parts of the organisation to remain effective. Such an exercise can help to formulate Contingency and Adaptive plans to mitigate potential risks to achieving future goals.

Determine current workforce to deliver the strategy

Collecting and analysing workforce data can help identify the knowledge, skills, abilities, demographics, talent profiles, attrition rates and other factors such as employees' views on job security, satisfaction and intention to leave. With respect to the current workforce, it provides answers to questions such as:

- How many people do we have?
- What are their skills, knowledge, experience, attitudes to change?
- What do our current staff want in terms of career development? Are these expectations realistic?
- Who has particular talents which we wish to nurture?
- Who do we especially want to retain?
- Who is at risk of leaving?

Other parameters can provide a fine-tuned analysis, such as people by geographical location or business division (some functions stretch across divisions); demographic differences within the workforce, or contractual differences as to how work is resourced.

However the CIPD (2020) report that only 14% of organisations collect and use good-quality data to forecast hiring demands, and just 8% assess the availability/supply of talent in the market. Only 19% currently measure the return on investment of their recruitment processes.

Identify gaps in the skills and knowledge required to deliver future business plans

Roles should be built on a detailed understanding of the work, staff skills and customer needs. Bear in mind that future roles will often involve a greater use of technology and require a greater digital awareness. Identifying gaps involves three distinct phases including Supply Analysis, Demand (or Needs) Analysis and Gap Analysis.

- What key skills areas are we likely to be short of?
- Where do we have too many of the 'wrong' skills?
- How much will people be willing to retrain?

Develop an action plan

This should allow for functional, numerical and adaptational flexibility:

- External – develop hiring plans or alternative sources of relevant talent
- Internal – identify internal talent; create development plans; develop retention strategies; removal plans

Options for closing skills gaps will depend on the situation. Where recruitment, retention, or both, present a resourcing challenge, greater focus will be needed on building required skills via staff upskilling or reskilling, though this may take some time. To address their urgent skills gaps employers must decide whether to hire new permanent staff with the relevant skills; seek to automate the tasks concerned partially or completely; use contractors, temporary staff and freelancers and/or retrain existing employees. Since doing things differently can require behaviour change as much as a skill change, a mix of up-skilling, reskilling and unlearning may be required. Sources: CIPD 2018; OECD 2019.

Generate consensus on the plan

A collaborative approach is vital and will involve wide-ranging consultation with stakeholders to enable all parties to agree and understand the rationale for the actions being taken.

Ensure clear allocation and understanding of responsibilities

It's essential that all those involved are clear about what they are responsible for and what actions they need to take.

Provide support for managers

Line managers will need support and information from HR and others to fulfil their responsibilities. For example, the skills to interpret data, to input good quality information and perform analysis are essential to ensure managers can fully participate in the planning process and act on the outcomes.

Establish and embed clear evaluation processes into all stages of the process

The evaluation criteria and measures – such as effectiveness and cost – will depend on the objectives. Essentially, workforce planning is about trying to predict the future to inform decision making so evaluation needs to relate to the outcomes of those decisions and their consequences, i.e. an agile, skilled workforce who can adapt to change. Evaluation should be iterative – the more proficient organisations become at planning the more likely they are to be able to identify relevant evaluation criteria to demonstrate their ability to make more accurate future predictions.

Review and capture learning

The process needs to incorporate clear and robust mechanisms to review and capture learning and feed this back into the process. These insights provide a valuable map to guide future significant enterprise transformations.

Create an infrastructure for development

The Chief Human Resources Officer (CHRO) must oversee an integrated effort to keep all teams moving in the same direction and:

- Develop HR policies that support development, upskilling and learning
- Ensure that organisational values, feedback processes, senior management behaviour, reward mechanisms and development all align
- Create mechanisms for self-development such as 360-degree feedback, development reviews, development centres, learning resources, career workshops etc.
- Ensure that line managers are trained to help others with their development.

Though a workforce planning process is often described as a series of steps, it is important to recognise this as an iterative process, not a rigidly linear one. It is also important to join up talent management practices in a strategic way from recruitment through to development, progression and retention, which play a part in building the organisation's capability in a changing marketplace. If the plan is to remain relevant in a rapidly changing environment, it should be subject to constant feedback and review. Creating a useful workforce plan is as much art as science. No single formula exists that will produce a 'correct' workforce plan. However, with a wealth of data available, the art is to bring this together and interpret it in a meaningful way.

RECRUITMENT

One likely outcome of workforce planning is a decision to recruit. Recruitment should rarely be about straightforward replacement or gap filling but should ideally be part of your recruitment strategy that should align with your wider approach to talent and people management. For example, what should be the right balance between developing current staff and external recruitment? Every recruitment process is a strategic opportunity to bring into the organisation the kinds of skills and experience that cannot easily be built from within. If recruitment from outside becomes the only means by which senior positions are filled, internal candidates soon realise that they must leave the organisation if they want to be promoted. Moreover, due to talent shortages, recruiting people with the skills you need may not be an option. Conversely, with too little external recruitment an organisation's processes and staff can start to stagnate. Every decision not to recruit externally is an opportunity deliberately to grow internal talent.

Campbell and Hirsh (2014) recommend a systematic approach to talent management. However, strategic approaches to recruitment are rare; most are tactical and short-term. CIPD research (2020) found that few organisations take a comprehensive data-based approach to improving their resourcing decisions. Few organisations currently collect and use good-quality data to forecast hiring demands or assess the availability/supply of talent in the market.

The most obvious alternative to sourcing the right skills is growing the skills of your own workforce, which is the focus of Chapter 10. Making the right choices requires a long-term intent and focus on capability-building, allied with pragmatism to take into account specific short-term business needs and the state of the labour market at the time (Turner and Kalman 2014).

SOURCING TALENT

So if recruiting employees to permanent roles is not always the right answer, sourcing talent in other ways requires some experimentation to find what works for your organisation in its circumstances. Some of the talent acquisition options for expanding workforce models in the short-term follow here.

Redesign jobs

Cheese (2007) argued that closing talent gaps requires innovation in thinking through the design of working processes and jobs themselves:

- Jobs or tasks can be redesigned to reduce the level of skills proficiency (i.e. down-skilling)
- Jobs can be moved or relocated to access different talent pools (i.e. near-shoring or off-shoring)
- Jobs can be moved to another organisation better equipped to find the right talent (i.e. outsourcing or partnering)
- Technology can reduce the need for some jobs completely and provide many opportunities to change job and skill requirements (i.e. automation)
- Jobs can be structured to be carried out virtually to allow people to do the work from anywhere (i.e. restructuring)
- Particular tasks may be thrown open to the free networks and talent now available on the Internet (i.e. the 'wiki' economy).

Another option is to augment the human workforce with machine capital. Accenture (2017) research proposes that, in the countries it studied, AI has the potential to boost labour productivity by up to 40% in 2035. This rise will be driven not by longer hours but by innovative technologies enabling people to make more efficient use of their time.

As technology becomes more embedded into work, its design and use must be monitored for fairness and equity. A Deloitte Insights survey (2020) found that, while only a small percentage of respondents are currently using robots and AI to replace workers, organisations that are implementing technologies to drive efficiencies can expect to make decisions sooner or later about whether and how to redeploy people to add strategic value elsewhere, or, if they decide to eliminate jobs, what they will do to support the workers thus displaced.

Redefine concept of 'workforce'

Accenture (2017) argue that to source the talent they need for competitive agility must redefine and expand the concept of 'workforce'. They point out that, as the 'one role, one worker' approach gives way to more fluid and task-based ways of approaching work, the term 'employee'will increasingly encompass a broad spectrum spanning internal to external, human to machine, and short-term gig working to full-time work.

Matching skill to business need is where digital comes in. By exploring digital talent platforms such as Upwork employers can expand their talent ecosystem to include networks of freelancers to find the temporary talent they need to complement employee teams and create access to potential opportunities. These new talent platforms draw on data from multiple sources, including HRIS systems or cloud-based productivity and collaboration software. Procter and Gamble (P&G) used Upwork for new product development R&D needs, supplementing their internal teams. Once teams are set up, and feedback collection is automated, just-in-time feedback can confirm if the match is working.

To reduce costs and improve speed other companies are creating their own talent networks to access diverse skillsets for just-in-time staffing. This allows companies to tap into specialised talent pools in an agile manner when they are needed and on terms that deliver value to both parties (Jesuthasan et al. 2018). For example, a company may occasionally need to access a group of world-class software engineers who prefer to work as free agents to develop a unique portfolio of skills and accomplishments.

Engage contingent workers

Bringing in freelancers offers the flexibility to meet business goals, with the added advantage of scalability to meet fluctuating demand. With talent moving in and out of the organisation, even though these workers are not employed on a full-time basis, companies must understand what drives their engagement because of the value they deliver to the organisation. How organisations treat contingent workers becomes known. After all, workers from diverse organisations share their knowledge about companies via peer-to-peer networks, online blogs, Facebook communities etc and bad experiences soon become known. And, as Uber and other 'gig economy' firms are finding, this does not absolve companies of responsibility for treating such workers well.

This means that organisations need a detailed approach for integrating all types of diverse talent across the workforce, expanding collaboration and creating a consistent experience inside and outside the traditional boundaries of the organisation. To engage talent on a deeper level requires organisations to connect workers to the culture and develop relationships with all talent – regardless of work arrangement – so that people choose to work for the organisation when needed and are committed to its purpose.

This also means moving beyond the traditional employee value proposition aimed exclusively at permanent employees to develop a differentiated talent value proposition that considers the needs and preferences of all workers – both employees and non-employees. This should ensure that all workers are treated fairly in how they connect to each other and the organisation, and in how they experience an organisation's culture. Consequently, many organisations that rely on contingent talent are tailoring their talent value propositions to address the pain points of these workers (Jesuthasan et al. 2018).

Careers matter to most people. Today people expect to work for a number of employers during their careers and workers value being able to design their own careers. So a more individualised definition of work is emerging which, in turn, requires more agile organisational approaches to the 'work deal'. Given the significant shifts in the demographics of the workforce, namely an increased proportion of women, greater ethnic diversity, more educated employees and an ageing workforce, there is increasing demand from workers for work–life balance. This means that people seek choice in their assignments, flexible schedules and the opportunity to develop new skills and engage with a variety of organisations that will enhance their CVs.

Reskilling is important for all workers – and for non-FTEs in particular. Mercer's 2018 *Future of Work Survey* reveals that almost half of organisations (47%) offer learning and development opportunities to contingents. About 45% of employers are considering offering recognition programs to free-agent workers and 41% expect to provide benefits including access to health and wellness programs such as gym memberships and fitness consultations.

Unlike full-time employees, contingent workers face considerable instability in the following key areas: financial risk due to variable cash flow; increased tax burdens; inadequate saving for retirement without adequate guidance and support. So some organisations are also supporting contingent workers for instance by offering specialist workshops on financial and pensions planning.

Recruit older workers

With Age Discrimination legislation in force throughout Europe and organisations experiencing key skills shortages, employing older workers is increasingly common, even though in practice there appears to be a continuation of subtle age discrimination in many organisations, with older workers often missing out on promotion or development opportunities. However, legislation has made it illegal to exclude candidates on the basis of their age and recruitment advertising, job specifications and the recruitment process as a whole have to be 'age-proofed'.

Create a talent 'stream' not just a 'pool'

Many organisations seek to create an internal talent pool from which to select future candidates for senior roles. Graduate recruitment, a traditional way of doing this, was badly hit during the pandemic. Today, reinvesting in graduate schemes, apprenticeships and internships can help employers gain access to a steady stream of entry-level talent. Online recruitment can speed up and streamline the process of recruitment as well as expand company graduate outreach programmes.

Employers want to be able to target specific groups of candidates and candidates want to work for employers who share their values, and who are interested in investing in them to help them reach their goals. So communications should be personalised. Online recruitment networks feature portals, with databases of students and graduates from across a spectrum of UK universities. Graduate recruitment websites offer diversity zones, where candidates can look for jobs that encourage applications from specific groups of people such as women and ethnic minorities.

These portals are designed to help employers and graduates to find each other. Employers can tap into online these pools of talent, hosting online chat rooms or e-mailing targeted candidates. Once the graduate applies to the employer online, the portal service may provide the online application form (under the employers' own identity), screen it to ensure the candidate is suitable for the role, and be further involved in seeing the application progress online. However, such tools cannot replace a company's presence on campuses; they mainly serve to increase the size of the talent pool available to the company.

Develop a 'passive' external talent pool

Filling jobs requiring specialist skills and knowledge can often be a costly and lengthy process, yet in the past, only professionals who were on head-hunters' books actively looking for a new job were considered part of the available talent pool. Often suitable candidates slipped through the organisation's net because there wasn't a vacancy at that particular time. Nowadays, 94% of professionals would be open to being approached about a role even if they weren't actively looking for a new job, providing they were approached in the right way. Passive candidates value direct and personalised communication that makes it clear that their skills and experience are particularly valuable rather than general approaches via social media or email. Nearly a quarter of organisations recognising this have included direct targeting of passive jobseekers among their most effective attraction methods over the last 12 months (CIPD 2020). Despite this, two-thirds of employers do not have a plan in place to reach this potentially huge latent source of talent.

Ideally, employers should build long term relationships with potential employees, creating relevant and meaningful engagement and building a positive employer brand and reputation. Philips TA has been moving from a 'Business-driven structure' to a more 'Candidate Centric Organization'. Philips Healthcare has a systematic approach to proactively building talent pipelines in certain key areas. They: (a) Have a target set of companies, (b) research their employee base and (c) actively reach out to the ones they are interested. They do not pitch a job; the idea is just to get to know people, talk to them about what Philips are all about and if they are interested include them in their candidate CRM. (d) Have regular interactions with their potential talent pool through a good mix of engagement forms including emails, newsletters, meetups or 1-1 interactions. The essence is to get to know your talent pool and build a long-term relationship with them. The starting point is a CRM from where you think about: how and who cultivates your talent pool? How often? What should you include in your communication? The second important aspect is systems and tracking. If not tracked appropriately, such engagement withers away and would not create long-term value.

At Nestle, the large global food and beverage manufacturer, the recruitment services team is one of several HR centres of expertise, the others being learning and development, the information and administration centre, and policy, remuneration and reward. The recruitment services team have worked with a number of functions to develop a multi-channel approach to filling their recruitment needs. Supported by the HR business partners, the function identifies its talent shortfalls then recruitment services devise an attraction strategy to fill the specific talent gap.

One initiative to help overcome the shortage of skilled applicants is Nestlé's 'talent puddles' approach. This is a targeted pool of talent that acts as a talent bank in areas of the business where there is a shortage of skilled applicants for specific jobs and difficult-to fill roles. Creating a small puddle of talent that can be readily brought into the business, thus reducing the costs and speeding up the recruitment process, is easier to manage than a broad generic talent database, which over time can grow too unwieldy to identify the most appropriate candidates.

Increasing the diversity of talent pools

Many organisations are placing greater emphasis on ensuring diversity throughout their organisations and are improving the inclusivity of their recruitment processes by taking a comprehensive approach that includes measures to eliminate bias. Equality, Diversity and Inclusion (EDI) is a complex area with multiple strands of issues, legal frameworks and frequent legal minefields. The systemic nature of prejudiced practice requires systemic action to overcome many of the business, structural and other obstacles that get in the way of recruiting and developing a productive, diverse workforce. Yet CIPD (2020) research found that only half of organisations have a formal diversity strategy. While progress is being made in pockets, it is only by fully aligning brand, attraction, selection, hiring manager training, onboarding, retention and ongoing career progression that organisations will gain full visibility of what is and isn't working so they can make informed changes.

Building an inclusive work environment doesn't just happen; it requires sustained effort (Frost and Kalman, 2016). The first step is reviewing current practice. For instance, how can you ensure that your recruitment practices eliminate bias and discrimination – what channels are you using to recruit talent? How can you de-bias job postings and the recruitment process? Are you varying how and where you are doing your outreach? Are the images and language you are using inclusive and not putting people off from applying to your organisation? If you have a recruiter acting on your behalf, are they aware of your values and commitment to diversity? Are you confident that your line managers are recruiting fairly?

The next step is actively improving recruitment practice to reach a wider range of candidates. Many organisations now adopt gender, age and racially neutral recruitment practices and 'blind' or 'neutral' job posting to ensure that the right candidates are not overlooked. By garnering and assessing information from a variety of sources and providing deep-dive reports for senior management, HR can highlight areas where action is most likely to produce positive movement on difficult issues.

The CIPD (2020) suggest the following actions to increase the diversity of your candidate pool:

1. Broaden your pool of potential candidates by varying your recruitment outreach and placing more rigour, consistency and challenge in your recruitment and selection approaches.
2. Ask questions about what is critical to the role. People from different industries or backgrounds may have transferable skills and knowledge and can bring fresh insight.
3. Build a strategic approach to attracting and developing diverse candidates to fill senior positions. Consider targeting attraction strategies for people with characteristics that are under-represented in particular roles.
4. Critically evaluate your organisation brand to see how attractive it is to diverse candidates. What changes can you make to your brand and your culture to help attract, select, develop and retain more diverse employees?
5. Evaluate your recruitment activities to assess which are most effective in broadening your talent pools.
6. Develop programmes like career returners and mid-career change to help broaden your talent pool and diversify people's skills.

Living up to business values and offering a fair employee value proposition will be critical to building trust and creating an inclusive workplace during these challenging times. So if you held a mirror up to the policies and practices in your company, would you win a national diversity award? Are you inclusive? Are you leading diversity best practice or trailing a long way behind, doing just enough to meet the legal requirements?

RECRUITMENT STRATEGIES

Technology, globalisation and evolving demographics are all driving changes in the ways workers shape their careers, engage with potential employers and make decisions about the roles they apply for. Recruitment approaches must keep pace.

Attracting potential recruits

Thanks to technology the recruitment process is being radically transformed. At a time when competition for certain jobs is growing increasingly fierce, traditional job adverts and recruiting tactics just aren't going to work. Organisations that manage all aspects of recruitment themselves must expand the ways they reach out to potential recruits. It is now no longer enough for employers to consider their online talent acquisition strategies; they must also consider mobile accessibility. Additionally, video content is becoming more important. It is vital to ensure technology is adopted carefully and complements an organisation's brand and values and is optimised with the end-user experience in mind.

Use of search agencies

Similarly, search agencies are themselves undergoing something of a transformation. They increasingly provide website-based recruitment services, where the consultancy's added value is in the quality of candidate assessment and in their systematic closing procedures. Candidates, typically mid-level professionals, are encouraged to complete a set of questionnaires and instruments, including psychometrics, which produce a profile. They can place their CV on the web which means that their details become available through the search consultant's website to potential employers around the world. Private sector organisations are more likely than their public or not-for profit counterparts to include recruitment/search consultants, professional networking sites, direct targeting of passive jobseekers and professional referral schemes among their most effective attraction methods, and less likely to include specialist journals/trade press and newspapers. The public sector is more likely to take traditional routes to find the candidates they seek, including via apprenticeships, job fairs and secondments, and less likely to include professional networking sites and commercial job boards (CIPD 2017).

Employer branding

In conventional marketing, developing a successful company brand is part of the distinctiveness of the product and is used to gain customer awareness and loyalty. The brand implies a 'promise' and creates customer expectation; the consumer 'buys' that promise and is satisfied or otherwise. As a result the customer continues to buy the product, or not; speaks well or badly of the product and, if disappointed, goes elsewhere. When a brand is closely identified with its 'product', for example as a prestige item, every element of the design, production, quality of finished goods and after-care service need to be aligned with the brand promise.

Similarly, employer branding is how an organisation markets what it has to offer to make itself attractive both to potential and existing employees:

> An employer brand is a set of attributes and qualities – often intangible – that make an organization distinctive, promise a particular kind of employment experience, and appeal to those people who will thrive and perform to their best in its culture.
>
> (Walker 2007)

An organisation's ability to attract external talent depends upon how potential applicants view the organisation, the industry or sector in which it operates and whether they share the organisation's values, and what applicants learn about the reality of the brand from various sources.

Understand expectations of your target groups

It is therefore important to understand the likely expectations of potential candidates and work out how these might be met, or not, by your employment offer and employer brand. This is all the more important when talent is in short supply. Looking back to the 1980s many employers were concerned at what was seen as the impending demographic 'timebomb' – that there would not be enough 18-year-olds and graduates entering the workplace in the 1990s. As things have turned out, the nature of the problem was not so much the shortage of individuals as the mismatch between what young employees expected and what organisations delivered. This may be because a broader shift in social values and expectations of work was also be occurring, and the old certainties of work and family life had been crumbling. By the 1980s, stereotypical time-honoured values such as security, authority, tradition and a rigid moral code had been eroded and replaced by more outward directed values of status, image and consumption. In the 1990s, these were replaced by more inward directed values of empathy, connectedness, emotion, autonomy and ease and in more recent times a desire for flexibility and autonomy.

There is growing evidence that the criteria used by today's younger workers to select their future employer include the chance for learning and growth and respect for them as individuals. Many employers use their employer brand to promote their career and development opportunities as well as flexible working (CIPD and British Chambers of Commerce, 2007). Employer brands that promote this kind of employee value proposition are likely to be attractive to potential recruits as in this example from a job advertisement for a commercial manager. There is tacit acknowledgement that employees are attracted by more than pay and the work itself:

> What does success mean to you? It could mean having a major say in a FTSE 100 company, a truly global organization where you enjoy real influence. That is what you will get here without question. But you will also gain so much more. You will find an atmosphere of change, growth and innovation; where the IS department is recognized and rewarded as a key driver in our business development; and your ideas will be heard throughout the entire organization...

The rise of employee review sites and the increase in professionals using social media channels to find out about the culture, values and reputation of an employer – i.e. the reality of the brand – means that employers must focus on building a positive employer brand reputation. This means making the most of digital media and using your current staff as ambassadors for your brand. Second only to searching online, jobseekers regard referrals from friends or colleagues and testimony from people currently employed by the company as important when deciding whether to apply for a role. Yet relatively few employers use a referral scheme as part of their recruitment strategy. Employers should therefore take a proactive approach to incorporating testimony from their current staff into their recruitment strategy.

Employee segmentation

Just as companies segment their customer base to be better able to target their products and services, so organisations increasingly attempt to understand the motivations of current and potential staff by segmenting their employee base into various categories, such as by age, professional groupings etc. Employee segmentation approaches are driving a more 'scientific' approach to the use of organisational data in order to devise and deliver more tailored and specific forms of employment offer and employer brand.

Large HR functions now often employ analysts to identify from employee data what seems to drive employee engagement in different segments of the workforce, so as to better target initiatives that meet both current and potential employee needs. These human capital data are also being used to understand in detail the causal links between employee engagement, performance and business success. HR professionals at Southwest Airlines treat front-line staff as internal customers. They use employee segmentation approaches to research employee needs and preferences as energetically as the company's marketing team investigate those of its external customers.

Employee segmentation can therefore help both develop a better understanding of who, or which groups of employees, are considered 'key' to the organisation's success, and also help devise specific employee value propositions for these groups which are tailored to their needs. For instance, with respect to reward, companies that previously introduced broad banding are increasingly superimposing 'job family' or 'professional community' approaches to ensure that reward matches the market for particular types of talent. So professionals who have taken a career break may have accumulated new skills during the break and may be keen to return to work as long as flexible working options are open to them.

With respect to recruitment, UK retailers are leading the field in the use of employee segmentation to better tailor employee value propositions to attract old and young employee candidates alike, according to Guthridge et al. (2008). Tesco explicitly divides its potential front-line recruits into those joining the workforce straight from school, students looking for part-time work, and graduates. The company devotes a separate section of its career website to address each of these groups with specific recruiting materials designed for that group.

The importance of values

When it comes to attracting candidates the company's mission, ethics and values are the main elements of the employer brand to be communicated (Volini et al., 2020). For example, GlaxoSmithKline (GSK), the pharmaceutical giant, promotes its employment brand and reputation through regular news releases and media events at key recruitment locations, stressing in particular its corporate social responsibility activities. IKEA, the Sweden-based furniture retailer, selects applicants using tools that focus on values and cultural fit, with the job applicants' values and beliefs becoming the basis for screening, interviewing, and training and development. CIPD (2020) research found that after values, candidates also place great store on pay and benefits which had moved up the rankings from third to second place (2020: 44%; 2017: 37%), in response to candidates' demands.

Networking and recruitment in knowledge-intensive firms

According to a CIPD study (Swart and Kinnie 2003), the process of attracting human capital in knowledge-intensive firms (KIFs) has distinctive characteristics. There recruitment is seen as a continuous process, one in which knowledge is exchanged through 'talent networks' characterised by continuous interaction and conversation about cutting-edge skills. Many KIFs forge relationships with universities, competitors and professional bodies in order to have access to a pool of relevant talent, or knowledge workers. A formalised way of developing networks for recruitment is via the placement system – graduates and postgraduates are given the opportunity to work for the KIF for a fixed period and can 'try each out'. During their placement, the student is encouraged to develop organisation-specific skills and knowledge while other employees learn cutting-edge skills from the placement employee through shared practice.

Jørgensen et al (2011) found that KIFs emphasise a desire for challenging work and the ability to work collaboratively as key selection criteria. KIFs are also more likely to provide a breadth of training and development opportunities for teams and individuals, to make extensive use of performance management systems, and to utilise a range of strategies to encourage and reward innovation.

THE SELECTION PROCESS

A well-designed recruitment and selection process can impress good candidates and give the employer useful indications of future performance. Flexibility is also important in ensuring that excellent candidates can be seen at times which are possible for them, rather than to a fixed interview schedule. This conveys the message to candidates that they are considered an important part of the organisation's future.

The interview process should help candidates to understand the brand, culture and, with respect to graduates, the company's commitment to graduate recruitment. Candidates are usually more positive about the organisation if they can see a clear link between the recruitment process and the job. Structured interviews, using behavioural and critical incident interviewing, can be helpful as they allow specific job-related areas such as team leadership and customer service to be explored. Psychometrics that are relevant to the work content and realistic simulations can also be useful. Simulations in particular allow managers to see a candidate's performance at first hand. They also provide the candidate with a chance to assess the role and to gather information about the company's approach to doing business.

Decisions should be conveyed early, and feedback offered so that even an unsuccessful application becomes a development opportunity. Disappointed candidates can still become advocates of the company if they feel that they have had a useful experience and been treated with respect. The professional image created by the recruitment process can therefore be an important part of attracting quality candidates in the future.

For senior management and other key positions, search agencies are often used, though it is thought that 40–50% of top appointments are filled by contacts. Increasingly, search agencies are adding a suite of activities to their portfolio which should ensure that the successful candidate becomes effective in their new role. Typically, these include follow-up counselling sessions with the search consultant, one-to-one coaching and specific accelerated skills training.

There will inevitably be a process of negotiation around those respective needs, usually over pay, or the type and level of work on offer. Increasingly, individuals wish to ensure that the organisations they are thinking of joining can offer some form of ongoing development and CV enhancement. Organisations that recognise this and put concrete plans in place to enable development are more likely not only to attract but also to retain good candidates.

Getting the right 'fit'

In essence, success in attracting and recruiting new talent means that the needs and offers of both the organisation and the individual marry up. Especially in large global companies there is usually a strong emphasis on cultural fit and values. Many companies assess applicants' personalities, attitudes and values to determine whether they will be compatible with the corporate culture; the assumption is that formal qualifications are not always the best predictors of performance and compatibility with the culture.

For instance, in evaluating entry-level job applications, Infosys considers a good cultural fit, the right attitude and what it refers to as 'learnability' are more important than some immediate skill requirements. Infosys puts applicants through an analytical and aptitude test, followed by an extensive interview to assess cultural fit and compatibility with the company's values. At American shoe chain Zappos, all colleagues are involved in selecting candidates to join them. If the fit does not work out after a month or so, the firm offers recently appointed staff a generous departure payment. So important is getting the 'fit' right at the supermarket chain Asda that all colleagues, including checkout staff, are selected according to a rigorous procedure, which includes a half-day assessment process to ensure that the candidate's attitudes will match the company culture of customer service. Every new recruit is carefully inducted so that there is commonality of purpose and a level of generic skills development.

However, rather than selecting employees for attitude and cultural fit, many companies opt instead to promote the organisation's core values and behavioural standards through induction, 'onboarding' and training, often accompanied by individualised coaching or mentoring activities. Moreover, to match talent to opportunity the skills and experience 'fit' also has to be right. For instance, if the position is new; in a quickly changing field; or in an area of business where the future is undefined or emerging; and if it requires political savvy, fresh ideas, strategic thinking and/or strategy development; and is supported by strong technical help, this would be a good fit for a candidate with high levels of learning agility. If the position requires considerable in-field experience or depth of knowledge, is relatively stable, involves the development and/or mentoring of others, is relationship driven or depends on continuity and requires understanding of the past in order to address future situations and strong and decisive tactical skills, this would be a good fit for a highly professional candidate.

ROLE OF TECHNOLOGY IN RECRUITMENT

Technology is now playing a major role in all aspects of the recruitment process. Well-designed career websites and mobile internet sites boost firms' profile with high-calibre graduates. Internet-based recruitment is a major trend for junior/middle management posts. Online recruitment opens up the potential field of candidates for any given job to those with access to a computer. Corporate websites and professional networking sites, such as LinkedIn (CIPD 2020) are used to attract candidates and track applications. Social networking sites, such as My Space and Facebook, are now recruitment tools for employers and candidates. Employee blogs on company websites are designed to explain what it is like to work at a particular company. However, it is thought that there are cultural differences in the way these are accepted, with UK candidates being less likely to believe them than candidates in the United States.

Artificial intelligence (AI)

Dynamic talent strategies, by their very nature, require experimentation. To keep up with the ever-changing recruitment landscape recruiting strategies are being continuously developed as organisations increasingly use Artificial intelligence (AI) and machine learning to streamline and automate parts of the recruitment process. Some companies are using artificial intelligence and social media (such as Glassdoor) to give a rich picture of the company to potential recruits and also to screen out candidates who may not be suitable.

AI can predict potential challenges before a requisition is opened such as how long did it take to fill this role previously? Which job boards are most effective? AI can offer suggestions for optimising your job descriptions to align more closely to similar roles in the industry. Software tools can harness and apply the power of data and predictive analytics to online job postings to come up with the most effective language patterns proven to appeal to the specific audience you're looking for. Tools are available to enable self-selection, such as pre-application assessments and tests online, as well as sophisticated automated screening to identify the best matched candidates automatically, grading them based on their relevance to the information provided about the role. AI can personalise content to candidates, analyse CVs, automate assessments and provide candidate rankings. Although there are potential privacy issues at stake, when employees' skills are in the public domain, Big data can enable recruiting companies to proactively target and approach potential candidates.

Technology can be used to manage the expectations of candidates at recruitment stage so that they have a realistic expectation of what opportunities they may have open to them. For instance, some firms use virtual reality to give potential employees an opportunity to 'experience' a job before applying. Chatbots can actively interact with applicants while creating candidate profiles, potentially reducing the number of unsuitable candidates for roles, shortlisting some of them, as well as scheduling interviews. For instance, RPM Pizza, the largest Domino's franchisee in the United States, uses AI to communicate with job seekers through text and live chat. The AI-powered chatbot – nicknamed 'Dottie' – answers job seeker questions and even initiates the screening process. Just like the restaurant's beloved 'pizza tracker', Dottie offers candidates an application tracker to boost engagement and free up time from the hiring team.

AI is increasingly used in recruitment to screen potential candidates for instance using facial recognition and other software. Video interviews are also becoming an integral part of the recruiting and selection process. Artificial intelligence software can analyse video interviews and help assess candidate honesty and personality in simulations. Some AI-driven platforms can help detect inconsistencies during video interviews and thus check whether a candidate is being genuine. Advances in facial recognition technology can provide insights into an applicant's confidence levels when answering questions. For example, if the applicant regularly looks away from the screen a few times, it may indicate the use of cue cards (Craig 2020).

Unilever has invested in artificial intelligence to help the company process the applications of the 2 million people who apply to Unilever every year. Candidates play neuroscience-based games on a Pymetrics platform and, if they match the requirements of a position, they move to an interview using a HireVue video platform that analyses keywords and body language. Successful candidates are then invited to a discovery day at Unilever. This recruitment process, which is transparent on the Unilever career site has saved 100,000 senior leadership hours, as well as general recruiter hours and also reduced bias in the recruitment process (Harrington 2019).

These technologies work by analysing data and making informed decisions out of it, in addition to saving recruiter time in reaching the best matched individuals and making real-time assessments more quickly. They are also supposed to offer the added advantage of removing conscious or subconscious discriminatory human bias from the first phase of screening such as interviews and can potentially give companies access to a more diverse talent pool. However, employers should recognise that biases are often embedded within AI and as a result many women and people of colour may be rendered invisible.

These biases may stem from the lack of diversity in the field of Artificial Intelligence itself. WEF (2018) found that in 2018 only 22% of AI professionals globally were female, while Black workers represent only 2.5% of Google's entire workforce and 4% of Facebook's and Microsoft's. Considering the growing role that AI plays in organisations' business processes, in the development of their products, and in the products themselves, the lack of diversity in AI and the invisibility of women and people of colour could result in a multitude of crises, if these biases are not addressed soon. So employers should be alert to potentially discriminatory biases in their recruitment processes and weed them out.

DELIVERING THE BRAND PROMISE

Once the successful candidate joins the organisation, both employee and employer will be monitoring the situation to ensure that the other party is living up to their promises. Whatever the implied brand promise, it is vital that this is delivered in reality. After all, recruitment is an expensive business. With up to 30% of jobs vacated again within months of recruitment due to disappointment on either side, ineffective recruitment is a major source of wasteful expense. There is plenty of anecdotal evidence to suggest that the more that new recruits receive help and support in the first few months, the more likely it is that they will quickly be able to perform satisfactorily and will feel more inclined to stay in their new organisation.

'Onboarding' has become a key means of helping new recruits to successfully 'bed in' to the organisation. Far more than traditional induction training, onboarding bonds people to the organisation by building relationships with new recruits before they join, with designated 'buddies' and potential sponsors keeping in close contact with recruits for a few months, aiding their transition into the organisation and ensuring that they have the information and any support needed to make a successful start in their new organisation.

Voyages-sncf.com, as an e-tourism business, has always aimed to develop an innovative employer brand that attracts younger workers. Gaming is among the offers it promotes to potential recruits and this promise is delivered in practice. To engage its millennial (and older) workforce, Voyages-sncf launched an initiative offering off-duty 'gaming time'. A specialised team known as Team Loco takes part in e-sport competitions during downtime in its Paris office. There is a state-of-the-art gaming room, equipped with all the necessary equipment for training and play, and the firm covers any competition expenses. This helps develop skills that are vital to the firm's future, such as coding and 'soft' skills such as collaboration and teamwork. Voyages-sncf has also invested heavily in employee well-being, with a 'I Feel Good' programme that encompasses everything from teleworking, job exchanges, courses to help employees enhance the skills required for hobbies such as photography and 'kids at work' days (Source: peoplemanagement.co.uk, June 2017).

Especially in today's working environment, building trust and an enduring culture as connective tissue when so many teams are working virtually is a real challenge for both hiring managers and employees. KPMG, who provide audit, tax and advisory services across the United Kingdom, has an ethical employer brand. The company believes it differentiates itself from its competitors for potential recruits by its culture. This is reflected in strong working and social relationships among teams and with managers, together with opportunities for career development, stimulating work and the flexibility to enjoy a rewarding home life. Departments have a strong social identity and the company values have been formalised into the 'KPMG way'. A 'management for excellence' scheme has embedded the KPMG values through personal development. Progress is supported with mentoring and training.

'Out of the box' assignments are given to those who have been at the firm a number of years and are moving up to partner level. These usually involve working for a client company or for KPMG abroad. And the company's profit share pool is divided among employees. A flexible benefits package includes the chance to buy up to 35 days' additional holiday per year, on top of the regular 25. Unpaid leave of between three months and three years is available to those with at least two years' service, making it possible to realise personal ambitions without compromising on professional ones.

Putting in place a range of robust measures to assess the return on investment of your recruitment activity (such as cost per hire, performance and turnover rates of new hires as well as overall effectiveness of attraction methods) is important. With recruitment budgets increasingly squeezed, it is more important than ever to ensure this is being spent in the most effective way. Taking a comprehensive data-based approach to understand how effectively your talent acquisition and retention strategies work is vital. Learning from this evaluation can inform your resourcing decisions going forward and strengthen your approaches based on the insights gained.

CONCLUSION

In a fast-changing context, organisations need to develop a thorough understanding of their current talent profile and gauge their future requirements. In this chapter, we have considered how, by looking ahead, taking a proactive, anticipatory, methodical approach to workforce planning, HR practitioners can help leaders recognise where the workforce risks and opportunities are going to come from and how they can ensure they have the resources they need to respond successfully, to whatever future scenario emerges. Thus, they equip the organisation for change.

We have discussed how recruitment is not the only means of accessing required skills and talent and have looked at a range of options to sourcing the talent you need. Any recruitment exercise should ideally be in line with a strategic plan and bring wider benefits. We have considered how HR can devise recruitment processes, using employer brands, candidate-centric approaches and technology to secure best-fit candidates for the organisation.

While attracting and recruiting talent presents one set of challenges, managing and retaining talent presents others. After all, recruitment is of little use if an organisation cannot retain key employees. We have discussed the importance of understanding the aspirations of your people and delivering the employer brand promise in practice. Since human motivation is extremely fragile and capable of being damaged by a range of factors, over the next few chapters we turn our attention to the theme of retention, looking next at employee engagement.

Reflective activity

- Looking ahead, how are the roles, skills and structures in your organisation likely to change?
- Where do you have gaps? What might be the most effective ways of filling these, e.g. through permanent, temporary or flexible employment, use of freelancers, technology, building skills of existing workforce?
- How can you create a more diverse workforce?

REFERENCES

Accenture. (2017). *Shaping the Agile Workforce,* https://www.accenture.com/_acnmedia/PDF-60/Accenture-Strategy-Shaping-Agile-Workforce-POV.pdf.

Aon. (2019). *Unlocking the Power in Your People,* https://insights.humancapital.aon.com/talent-rewards-and-performance/unlocking-the-power-in-your-people-why-data-and-empathy-are-both-needed-to-drive-digital-transformation.

Campbell, V. and Hirsh, W. (2014). *Talent Management: A Four-Step Approach.* Brighton: Institute for Employment Studies.

Cheese, P. (2007). Strategic Talent Management. *Strategy Magazine.* Issue 14. December.

CIPD. (2020). *Resourcing and Talent Planning Survey 2020.* London: Chartered Institute of Personnel and Development.

CIPD. (2018). *UK Working Lives: The CIPD Job Quality Index.* https://www.cipd.co.uk/Images/UK-working-lives-2_tcm18-40225.pdf.

CIPD. (2017); *Resourcing and Talent Planning Report.* London: CIPD. https://www.cipd.co.uk/Images/resourcing-talent-planning_2017_tcm18- 23747.pdf.

CIPD and the British Chamber of Commerce. (2007). *Flexible Working, Good Business, How Small Firms Are Doing It.* http://www.cipd.co.uk/research/rsrchplcvpubs/guides.litm?vanitv=http://www.cipd.co.u k/guides.

Craig, J. (2020). *Improving Recruitment Strategies with AI in 2020,* 19 November, Smartrecruitonline. com. https://www.smartrecruitonline.com/recruiting-with-ai-in-2020/.

Deloitte (2020). *Deloitte Global Human Capital Trends,* Deloitte Insights. https://www2.deloitte.com/content/dam/Deloitte/cn/Documents/human-capital/deloitte-cn-hc-trend-2020-en-200519.pdf.

Deloitte (2018). *Deloitte Global Human Capital Trends,* Deloitte Insights. https://www2.deloitte.com/content/dam/Deloitte/at/Documents/human-capital/at-2018-deloitte-human-capital-trends.pdf.

Deloitte (2004). *It's 2008: Do you know where your talent is? A Deloitte Research Study.*

Frost, S. and Kalman, D. (2016). *Inclusive Talent Management: How Business Can Thrive in an Age of Diversity.* London: Kogan Page.

Guthridge, M., Komm, A.B. and Lawson, E. (2008). Making talent a strategic priority. *McKinsey Quarterly,* January.

Harrington, S. (2019). HR needs more swagger says Unilever CHRO. I couldn't agree more, *LinkedIn,* June 13. https://www.linkedin.com/pulse/hr-needs-more-swagger-says-unilever-chro-i-couldnt-agree-harrington/.

Jesuthasan, R., Jilek, L. and Poonja, J. (2018). Agile rewards in a modern work ecosystem. *Workspan,* November/December.

Jørgensen, F., Becker, K. and Matthews, J.H. (2011). The HRM practices of innovative knowledge-intensive firms. *International Journal of Technology Management,* 56(2/3/4), 123–137.

Kruse, K. (2020). Skill Gap 2020: 5 Soft skills and 10 hard skills companies need now. *Forbes.* https://www.forbes.com/sites/kevinkruse/2020/04/17/skill-gap-2020-5-soft-skills-and-10-hard-skills-companies-need-now/.

Manpower Group (2020). *Closing the Skills Gap: What UK Workers Want in 2020.* https://www.manpowergroup.co.uk/wp-content/uploads/2020/01/MPG_WhatWorkersWant_2020_UK_V3.pdf.

OECD (2019). *Employment Outlook 2019: The Future of Work.* DOI:https://doi.org/10.1787/9ee00155-en.

Swart, J. and Kinnie, N. (2003). *Managing People in Professional Services Firms.* London: CIPD.

Tansley, C., Turner, P. and Foster, C. (2007). *Talent: Strategy, Management, Measurement.* London: CIPD.

Taylor, S. (2018). *Resourcing and Talent Management.* 7th ed. London: Chartered Institute of Personnel and Development and Kogan Page.

Turner, P. and Kalman, D. (2014). *Make Your People Before you Make Your Products: Using Talent Management to Achieve Competitive Advantage in Global Organizations.* Chichester: Wiley.

Volini, E. et al. (2020). Ethics and the future of work. *Deloitte Insights*, 15 May, https://www2.deloitte.com/us/en/insights/focus/human-capital-trends/2020/ethical-implications-of-ai.html.

Walker, P. (2007). *Employer Branding: A No-nonsense Approach.* London: CIPD

World Economic Forum (2018). *The Future of Jobs Report 2018.* http://www3.weforum.org/docs/WEF_Future_of_Jobs_2018.pdf.

Employee engagement and well-being

Employee engagement has been something of a holy grail for employers in recent years. That's because high performance theory places employee engagement or 'the intellectual and emotional attachment that an employee has for his or her work' (Heger 2007) at the heart of performance, especially among knowledge workers. Employee engagement is a reflection of the quality of employee experience. Arguably in today's context of more for less and ongoing change, employee engagement is at significant risk.

CHAPTER OVERVIEW

In this chapter, we look at some of the underlying context challenges which may make employee engagement something of a chimera in contemporary organisations. I shall argue that if leaders want their organisations to survive and thrive in today's challenging economy, they must become intensely focused on improving employee engagement and well-being.

DOI: 10.4324/9781003219996-10

- What is employee engagement?
- Engagement deficit
- The contested role of HR
- Stimulating growth through employee engagement
- Employee well-being

LEARNING OBJECTIVES

- To consider how a culture conducive to engagement can be built
- To explore the links between employee engagement and employee well-being.

INTRODUCTION: WHAT IS 'EMPLOYEE ENGAGEMENT'?

Engagement has risen up the HR agenda because in today's knowledge and service-intensive economies, people are the main source of innovation, production and service excellence. How people feel about their work makes a difference to their performance and innovation.

Definitions of engagement vary and are somewhat contested. Engagement is thought to be a barometer of the health of the employment relationship between employees and employers. The concept is also linked with notions of workplace happiness, citizenship behaviour, employee voice and individual well-being – all good things to which employees themselves no doubt aspire (Christian et al. 2011; Hakanen and Schaufeli 2012; Soane et al. 2013).

Most definitions agree that the state of employee engagement is characterised as a feeling of commitment, passion and energy that translates into high levels of persistence with even the most difficult tasks, exceeding expectations and taking the initiative, which Pink (2009) refers to as 'Drive'. At its best, it is what Csikszentmihalyi describes as 'flow' – that focused and happy psychological state when people are so pleasurably immersed in their work that they freely release their 'discretionary effort' and don't notice time passing. In such a state, it is argued, people are more productive, more service-oriented, less wasteful, more inclined to come up with good ideas, take the initiative and generally do more to help organisations achieve their goals than people who are disengaged.

Employee engagement is conflated with two types of commitment – emotional and rational – with emotional commitment thought to be four times more valuable in driving employee effort than rational commitment. Employees stay with their organisations when they believe it is in their self-interest (rational commitment). But they exert discretionary effort when they believe in the value of their job, their team and their organisation (emotional commitment).

The organisation provides the context in which engagement is created. Kahn (1990: 702) proposed that personal engagement occurs when individuals can satisfy through their work some important needs:

- Social – is this an organisation where I feel involved, part of a good team; is my organisation serving the community?
- Intellectual – am I able to grow; is my job stretching and interesting; do I know what's happening; do my opinions count?
- Emotional – do I care about the organisation and feel I belong; am I valued?

Schaufeli and colleagues (2013) refer to this as 'work engagement' rather than 'personal engagement' and propose that engaged workers are likely to perform better than their disengaged peers.

If what employees want from work is matched by what employers want and provide, a positive psychological contract (Guest 2004) is thought to exist in the minds of employees who are then more likely to be positively engaged with the organisation and willing to 'go the extra mile'.

What's the evidence?

Employee engagement has been linked in various studies with improved key business indicators such as higher earnings per share, improved sickness absence, higher productivity and innovation – the potential business benefits go on and on. For instance, a Corporate Leadership Council (CLC) study found that companies with highly engaged employees grow twice as fast as peer companies. A three-year study of 41 multinational organisations by Willis Towers Watson found those with high engagement levels had 2–4% improvement in operating margin and net profit margin, whereas those with low engagement showed a decline of about 1.5–2%. Many studies also suggest that highly engaged employees tend to support organisational change initiatives and are more resilient in the face of change. Some pundits argue that this may be due to reverse causality: that successful organisations are more likely to have employees who feel proud to work for them and such organisations may provide employees with a more meaningful and enjoyable work experience than less successful organisations.

Engagement deficit

Gallup found that in 2019, 35% of US employees were engaged, one of the highest levels of engagement since their annual surveys began in 2000 (Harter 2020). However, they found that the remaining 52% of workers were in the 'not engaged' category – those who are psychologically unattached to their work and company and who put time, but not energy or passion, into their work. Not engaged employees will usually show up to work and contribute the minimum required. They're also on the lookout for better employment opportunities and will quickly leave their company for a slightly better offer. Moreover, an exhaustive report by The Engagement Institute – a joint study by The Conference Board, Sirota-Mercer, Deloitte, ROI, The Culture Works and Consulting LLPD (2019) estimated that disengaged employees cost US companies up to $550 billion a year – underlining the importance of engagement to the bottom line. Therefore, rather than a 'nice to have' to be addressed only in good times, growing employee engagement may be key to business survival and growth.

For years the United Kingdom has been reported to suffer from a growing 'engagement deficit' relative to many other countries, including the United States. Indeed, so concerned was a previous UK Government about the national 'engagement deficit' that the Department for Business, Innovation and Skills (BIS) sponsored *Engaging for success* (aka the 'MacLeod report' 2009) to explore the assumed links between employee engagement, performance and productivity. The report's conclusion – that the business case for employee engagement is overwhelming – has been strongly reinforced since then, as more research is published. Therefore building a context of engagement is likely to produce multiple dividends.

While post-pandemic engagement levels appear to be improving slightly, many surveys still report people feeling under intense work pressure and experiencing a level of insecurity both about their job and the future generally. Underlying structural shifts, as many organisations continue to downsize or implement other cost-reduction measures, suggest that engagement cannot be disassociated from the fragmentation of the employment relationship and work intensification. In all sectors, against a backdrop of ongoing change and stringent business targets, workers are under ongoing pressure, leading to exhaustion and poor morale. Indeed, it could be argued that the balance of power and benefit in the employment relationship has shifted to employers at the expense of employees. In such a context, many employees have found that their individual psychological contract – or what they expect from their employment relationship with their employer – has been breached in recent years. Given that implicit in psychological contract theory is the notion of reciprocity, how likely is it then that employees will remain engaged with their organisations?

Similarly remote working brings new challenges for managers seeking to engage their teams via Zoom, Teams and so on. As location and time-based employment is increasingly eroded, the modern workforce no longer comprises just full-time 'employees' but typically a mix of workers on non-standard contracts; temporary, self-employed, part-time and non-employed 'freelancers'. The challenge for some HR functions is that they have not been used to incorporating this 'non-employed' group into the workforce, or their people strategy. Studies show that many organisations aren't providing training, appraisal, or even including them in internal comms. Thus a large sub-section of workers is unlikely to be in focus when engagement strategies are developed. This comes from an outdated mind-set and concept of the 'organisation' and who's in and who's out.

THE CONTESTED ROLE OF HR AND ENGAGEMENT

As the professional people function in organisations, responsibility for employee engagement strategies typically falls to HR and/or Internal Communications functions. Engagement has become a central plank in the high commitment, high performance aspirations of HRM. HR functions organise employee surveys and follow-up on key findings.

Yet HR's position with respect to engagement is somewhat ambiguous. While most HR professionals typically embrace the engagement agenda with enthusiasm, critics argue that engagement has been appropriated to managerialist agendas and extended beyond its meaning of being an individual state of mind to encompass workforce strategies designed to persuade people to willingly work harder without regard to worker well-being. Peccei (2004) questioned whether the set of HR practices that are good for management, from the point of view of enhancing productivity, are equally good for employees in terms for instance of enhancing their well-being. In her book *Work won't love you back*, Jaffe (2021) points out the danger that people can become unwitting hostages to their desire to perform well, encouraged by management, often resulting in burnout and disillusion.

As discussed in earlier chapters, HR has previously played an active role in increasing organisational flexibility by transforming employee relations away from the collective, based on union representation, towards individualised HR-based 'employee engagement' approaches, which offer employees fewer protections and make individual employees vulnerable to replacement.

Thus, HRM has arguably played a key part in installing what Sennett (2006) calls a 'new work culture of capitalism' which supports business ambitions to achieve 'more for less'.

For instance, performance management systems expose individual performances to scrutiny and remind people that they are only as secure as their last performance (and as long as their skills are needed). The emphasis on performance rather than length of service, has afforded employers greater discrimination in how employees are recruited, managed and rewarded, with increasing polarisation of treatment between those deemed to be 'talent' – who receive significantly greater opportunities – and those who are viewed as of lesser potential or value. Market forces arguments have been used to justify extremes of pay for individuals in some sectors while workers in other sectors struggle to achieve a living wage. There is growing protest about unilateral changes to pensions, job cuts, work intensification ('more for less'). Jenkins and Delbridge (2013) argue that the conflation of engagement with performance management reflects a 'hard' approach to HRM, despite the 'softer' language of meaning and commitment.

Technology has led not only to work intensification, it has also enabled closer monitoring of the work of employees (Gunsel and Yamen 2020). Critics argue that technology enables the widespread application of scientific management practices (or 'Taylorism') that originally applied to 'blue-collar' work has been extended to apply to skilled professional and managerial work in a similar way. By separating the conception of work from its execution, work can be broken down into manageable routine 'chunks', which require less skill to execute and allow only management to control both the work process and the workforce. Brown et al. (2010) describe 'Digital Taylorism' as enabling employers to convert not only clerical work into outsourceable chunks but also to hollow out roles and transform the professional and technical know-how of individuals into easily accessible 'working knowledge' that can be readily accessed by others and renders anyone expendable.

In today's uncertain context, all the risk in the employment relationship is with employees. The dismantling of the 'old' psychological contract has been used by managements in ways that F.W. Taylor, a significant early proponent of 'scientific management' practices, might have dreamed of to secure control over – and produce greater output from – what is arguably an insecure, over-worked, over-managed and alienated workforce. So to paraphrase David Guest (2013) and Stephen Overall (2008), are notions of 'employee engagement' and 'meaningful work' a fashionable fad, simply fey issues, a luxury residue of the times of growth?

Meaningful work

Central to engagement is the notion of meaningful work that Sennett (2008) argues managers have not paid enough attention to in recent decades. Pink (2009) argues that most employers use traditional 'carrot and stick' approaches to motivation (i.e. using rewards external to work to motivate people), particularly among older employees who are accustomed to such tools. These, Pink suggests, are becoming outdated, and do not adequately address the needs of the creative and innovative workplaces of the twenty-first century. However, intrinsic motivation, (when people are self-motivated because they are given the freedom to do the work they enjoy), is not fully understood. A Ceridian study (2020) confirms that engaging work is the most important factor that keeps workers with their employer.

Meaningful work has concrete characteristics: people must feel there is procedural justice in work: i.e. when they do something right, they are rewarded and if they are maltreated there is some way in which they can find redress. Other vital elements for

Sennett (2008) include not being treated as just a commodity but being recognised for doing something distinctive; and craftsmanship – when people feel they can build a skill that can help them take real satisfaction out of their work. For Pink (2009), intrinsic motivation is based on three key factors: Autonomy, Mastery and Purpose. So, if people are allowed to thrive by doing work that they are truly passionate about, innovation and creativity are more likely.

However, in *The Corrosion of Character* Sennett (1998) argues that, owing to the pressure to do more for less, the seemingly never-ending flow of work and reduced individual autonomy, loss of job security and job satisfaction, work is degraded, undignified and damaging to worker well-being. As a result, pride among workers has dissipated and people don't look 'long term'. In today's workplace he proposes, one must be very flexible, therefore loyalty and commitment are not part of a fast-paced, 'short-term' society. Workers know that they are simply a tool that can be replaced with the twist of a wrench. In such a context, Sennett argues, people's interests are with themselves – they don't look at what they can offer, but instead at what they want to receive. Consequently, Sennett argues, people struggle to sustain a meaningful life narrative that comes out of their work and as a result, personal character is corroded. Indeed, various recent studies have highlighted the desire of many highly skilled workers for greater fulfilment from work, since it now occupies so much space in their lives, and for better work-life balance.

Mutual trust is especially important in tough times, yet when jobs, or job quality, are at risk, employee trust will soon dissipate. If people feel badly treated by employers, employee relations deteriorate. Even if they keep their jobs, 'survivors' may experience loss of status, role ambiguity and chronic work pressure. Typical reactions include people coming to believe worst-case scenarios, responding to change with inertia, risk aversion, a sense of paralysis, change-weariness and cynicism. Now people are more inclined to distrust first rather than trust and are less willing to give discretionary effort. There may be lack of follow-through on key projects and increased political behaviour as people protect their backs. These reactions are symptomatic of damaged psychological contracts. When these are violated (such as by not being honest about the challenges faced by the business, or by being uneven in sharing out cutbacks), employees tend to withdraw their goodwill, discretionary effort is suspended, and trust undermined. The employment relationship then typically becomes more transactional. As Hamel points out, 'Mistrust demoralises and fear paralyses, so they must be wrung out of tomorrow's management systems' (*Hamel* 2009).

For employers, the business consequences of loss of employee engagement could be severe. First there is the challenge of retaining of key people. Recruitment firms are aware of wide-scale, pent-up career frustration and, as employment opportunities grow again, significant employee turnover can be anticipated. With high levels of unemployment, it's easy to dismiss the retention risk in the short-term but employees who remain may no longer give their discretionary effort, with potentially damaging consequences for performance.

For employees, what might be the consequences of ever greater demands? Will employees be induced to comply even more, to become 'willing slaves' (Bunting 2004) who continuously 'go the extra mile' in order to survive and thrive – until they 'burn out' (Maslach 2019)? Will people then game the situation, profess to be 'engaged' in order to keep their jobs? If people don't trust their employer, how likely is it that they will admit their stress and diminishing ability to cope? Will employees continue to seek identity and self-actualisation (in Maslowian terms) through work or will more basic concerns such as safety and job security take precedence? In such a context, notions of social justice, fair treatment and employee engagement are compromised and mutuality of interest in the employment relationship exposed as a myth.

Leaders and managers

The longer economic instability goes on, and the tougher the measures taken to keep organisations viable, the greater the risk of strained employee relations and 'survivor' employees simply doing the minimum necessary to get by. Given that tough times are when organisations most need people to be willing to go the extra mile, this really would be the worst of all worlds.

So should business leaders be worried? Arguably, yes.

The MacLeod report (2009) considered that 'engaging managers' and 'engaging leadership' are pivotal to creating work contexts conducive to engagement. Yet, instead of seeking to understand how to maintain or enhance employee engagement, many UK top leaders appear to ignore it, possibly because they are simply unaware of employee engagement or do not understand its importance:

> The issue seems to lie in their unwillingness to 'talk the talk' and truly relinquish command and control styles of leadership in favour of a relationship based on mutuality.
> (MacLeod and Clarke 2009)

As Professor Cary Cooper (2012) noted, post the financial crisis of 2008 onwards: '... we now have a much more abrasive, bureaucratic and autocratic management style as a result of this recession, which is disappointing given this is supposed to be the HR era of engagement!'[1] Similarly Gapper (2013) argues that 'a combination of high unemployment and technology hands managers a lot of power. Some will abuse it'.

A report by the American Psychological Association comments that many executives lack skill in culture building: 'A lot of senior leaders may have all the outward-facing skills but they might not know how to build an organisation, or how to tell a genuine story to share and create together an emerging new future'. They also note that in organisations where employees do not view leadership as committed to their well-being, only 17% of employees would recommend the company as a good place to work.

Is it up to employees to adjust their expectations about work or should employers be taking a lead in developing a more sustainable approach to employing and managing people? I would argue that both are necessary. Engagement is not a one-way street. There are multiple stakeholders involved, not least employees themselves, who need to collaborate to produce the benefits of engagement and reduce the barriers. As Budd (2004) points out, organisations cannot be run with efficiency as the only goal, and it is also incumbent upon individuals to look further than their own direct personal interests.

Reflective activity: in your organisation

- How important is employee engagement considered to be?
- What are the key engagement issues?
- What do you consider to be the main barriers to employee engagement?

STIMULATING GROWTH THROUGH EMPLOYEE ENGAGEMENT

What can employers do to engage employees? Work is central to engagement and the 'workplace' – physical or remote – is where engagement is enacted. In this new era the employment relationship needs to be genuine and based on adult–adult rather than parent–child relationships. There need to mutual benefits (as well as risks) for both organisations and employees in becoming more flexible and sustaining high performance.

Surveys

Understanding what turns people on or off in the workplace is key to engagement, retention and performance. Carrying out a survey is only one aspect of employee voice and companies typically seek their employees' opinions when times are good but not when times are bad, even though this is when feedback tends to be most valuable. HR must keep a finger on the pulse of how people are feeling and ensure that executives respond promptly to the most important issues. Whether large-scale or pulse surveys, focus groups, exit interviews, or qualitative research are used, the risk is that feedback is collected but not fully understood. Analytics can help synthesise and pinpoint key themes and issues.

Geoff Matthews's (2012) '5 Cs' checklist can help: *Check* for understanding of the initial review of results; *Calibrate* the findings with further interviews or focus groups to better understand specific issues flagged up by the initial findings, drawing key lessons; then *Commit* to taking action on some key issues; *Conclude,* measure and improve; and *Communicate* throughout the process. Of course, savvy employees do not necessarily expect all their concerns to be fixed overnight, but they do want to be consulted and asked for their point of view.

Implementing meaningful engagement actions will involve leaders, managers and employees themselves as well as HR. Each has their role to play. Some of the issues flagged up by the survey will be matters that employees can deal with themselves. Others require management action and progress shared of the 'You said… we did' variety. It's important for people to understand what's been achieved so by measuring progress on these actions it is possible conclude by drawing key learning from the process. Closing the loop and communicating back therefore matters. It's not one of these things which happen overnight. It's a dynamic; people change, strategies change, engagement is something to keep working at. Survey findings can provide valuable clues as to what employees want and need if they are become and remain engaged, especially in challenging times.

What do employees want?

Changing workforce demographics, a more educated workforce and different motivators by generational group mean that many organisations have a diverse workforce, not least by age. There are said to be five generations in the workforce currently – Traditionalists, Baby Boomers, Gen Xers, Gen Y/Millennials and Gen Z. Gen X is numerically the smallest generation. There is no 'one size fits all' in terms of what engages and motivates individuals. Each cohort needs to be managed with an understanding of their specific needs and motivations, recognising also that individuals within cohorts will differ in their needs.

As employee values change, there is a growing focus on flexibility, corporate social responsibility and the need to change organisational cultures, for instance to become more inclusive. Portfolio careers are increasingly common, in which people combine a range of paid and non-paid activities at any one time and also people progress between a number of careers in one working lifetime.

So a new and personalised psychological contract may be emerging at the heart of the employment relationship based on flexibility – desired by both employees and employers – but whether the deal on offer appears equitable and is mutually beneficial to both parties is another matter.

Is it possible then to generalise about what employees want from work? In researching our book, Geoff Matthews and I examined a wide variety of studies about what employees appear to want and need from work. We concluded that most employees want work with meaning and purpose that offers a degree of autonomy, control and task discretion and strong workplace relationships – and this is closely associated with motivation and ultimately the commitment and effort workers are prepared to put in. Employees want to be valued for their contribution, and to be dealt with in a fair and consistent manner. While pay remains important, other reward issues such as flexibility are also important. They also want to be able to influence matters which affect their working lives, and therefore want to be able to participate in decisions that affect them. And while acknowledging the risk of generalisation, from our research Geoff Matthews and I (2012) categorised these as employee desires for *connection, support, voice* and *scope:*

Connection

Most employees want to work for organisations whose purposes and values they can embrace – we found this to be closely associated with motivation, commitment and ultimately the energy and effort workers are prepared to put in. Employees want job security, strong relationships and to be valued for their contribution, and to be dealt with in a fair and consistent manner. So do you identify, do you connect, are you accepted?

Support

Valuing employees is crucial. While pay remains important, development and other forms of recognition and reward – such as flexibility – are also important. So do you feel you are set up for success, do you have the right tools to do your job?

Voice

Employees want to be able to influence matters which affect their working lives and therefore need to be informed and able to participate in decision-making. So do you know what's going on and have a say, or do things just happen?

Scope

They also want opportunities for personal and career growth and high-quality work that offers a degree of meaning, stretch, control and task discretion. So do you have clear role boundaries, no role confusion; are you in a situation where you can achieve mastery and flow or are you working below your capabilities?

Underpinning these elements are the key principles of trust and fairness. If people don't trust or don't believe they are treated fairly they can't predict outcomes and are less likely to be engaged or give of their best.

The blend and intensity of these different desires will differ according to individual preferences, career needs and most particularly, organisational context and what is happening that affects individuals. In challenging times for instance people may need more support and voice. They may (temporarily) prefer job security to career growth. Keeping alert to what people need is the essence of managing engagement.

What does this look like in practice?

To respond to the engagement challenge in this new era, we looked at examples of management practice in organisations where employee engagement levels remain high despite the challenging context. Here are some examples of what we found.

Creating connection through purpose

Engaging leaders look beyond the current challenges, anticipate the big business issues and plot a way through to recovery taking short-term decisions with the longer-term in mind. Such leaders are strategic, anticipatory, proactive and people – focused. They reshape the work environment and culture to enhance performance and match their unique basis of competitive advantage. They understand that for real empowerment, leadership styles must evolve beyond command and control towards more collaborative, participative approaches as the basis of mutual trust and respect.

For MacLeod (2009) such leadership 'ensures a strong, transparent and explicit organisational culture which gives employees a line of sight between their job and the vision and aims of the organisation'. Engaging leaders provide a clear strategic narrative about where the organisation is going and why, and where it has come from, in a way that honours the past and gives employees information and insight for their own job. They set a clear direction and priorities so that employees know what is required and feel empowered to deliver the right outputs without the need for micro-management. Engaging leaders focus people and structure the organisation and its tasks so that people can get on with what matters. Bureaucracy, inconsistent behaviours, policies and practices act as barriers and lead to cynicism and disengagement.

A common cause is essential, with an aligned strategy that people can sign up to. Engaging leaders actively lead culture change, working to create shared purpose and a positive sense of the future: something to aim for that people can connect with. The nature of the organisation's purpose may have a differentiating effect on levels of engagement. Research by Holbeche and Springett (2005) into how people experience meaning at work found that an organisational purpose, which focuses intensely on customers is more likely to engage staff than purposes focused on shareholders, profits or a mix of stakeholder needs. In recent times, many employees, inspired by investors, are increasingly calling for companies to embrace purposes that have environmental, social and governance (ESG) aspirations. Professor Colin Mayer, academic lead for 'The Future of the Corporation' research (2020) proposes that profits do not equate to purpose. Instead, purpose is about:

> *Profitably solving the problems of people and planet, and not profiting from creating problems.*

However, it is essential that there is a clear line of sight to this purpose in people's day jobs if the motivational effect is to be achieved. Deloitte has a 'Chief People and Purpose' officer to ensure this happens. Brand values must be well communicated but the most powerfully engaging visions and values are not developed as a top-down exercise since two-way approaches are more likely to lead to effective engagement. Values that are truly 'lived' and translated into meaningful experiences for customers and employees alike provide parameters for people's actions since values and behaviours are aligned, creating trust. Any gap between these creates distrust and cynicism.

So engaging leaders deliberately adopt a collaborative decision-making style and set key principles and parameters that empower others: 'Managers/leaders must leverage the power of shared values and aspirations while loosening the straight - jacket of rules and strictures' (Hamel 2009). They strive to role model the values; they use and act on 360 degree and other feedback to show commitment. They grow tomorrow's leaders and nurture leadership at every level, using language that is less about 'I' and more about 'we'. Thus people can confidently use their initiative to deliver what is required without the need for micro-management.

Technology can help with the challenge of engaging people working remotely, with software services enabling asynchronous online meetings that allow people working in different time zones to join in. People can be engaged before, during and after the event itself. 'Campfires' and 'lunch-rooms' that people can go to if they choose allow deeper conversations to happen. For instance, Selina Millstam, who heads up talent management and culture change at the Swedish communications technology company Ericsson, wanted to have a companywide conversation that would encourage people to share and coordinate their beliefs about which values and behaviours would be crucial to the long-term success of the business. The moderated conversation took place over 72 hours, with more than 95,000 employees across 180 counties invited to participate. The shared time allowed people in different time zones to connect, with each participant encouraged to reengage with the exchange in an asynchronous way over the three days, thus building a strong sense of community across the global workforce (in Gratton, November 9, 2020).

So HR teams should re-evaluate communications tools for how well they serve community building – for instance using two consistent channels such as Teams Chat – and encourage more frequent, regular check-ins. A question could be posed before the Chat to encourage discussion. Meetings should ideally start with space to discuss how people are feeling that day, at that moment, so that people can open up about their concerns. HR should encourage managers to apply a growth mindset and show empathy: put themselves in other people's shoes and humanise communication at every point.

In tough times

The global pandemic, a divisive political environment and protests against racial and gender injustice are reflected in organisations as concerns for employee safety and well-being and a desire to build a diverse and inclusive workplace. The Qualtrics 2021 Employee Experience Trends Report found that, during the pandemic, having a sense of belonging to an organisation was emerging as the most important driver of engagement. Staff want employers to stand for certain values and will agitate when necessary, with many younger employees valuing purpose above pay (Alvarez-Williams 2020).

To respond to the engagement challenge in this new era, the importance of values-based leadership cannot be overstated. Leadership styles must evolve beyond command and control towards building a firmer foundation for mutual trust and respect. Executives need to show visible leadership, build trust – 'walk the talk' – and create energy around mission and vision. They must take the long view, keep faith with employees and make sure employees know they are trying hard to keep them. Leaders should balance current reality and optimism – provide a longer-term perspective, give people confidence about the future and create a climate for change.

And the good news is that many staff in various sectors say their leaders have responded well to the coronavirus pandemic and to resolving problems of social justice, according to a 2020 poll by Weber Shandwick. This both underlines the level of trust placed in employers and serves as a potential source of criticism if companies fall short. We shall consider how leadership can be developed in later chapters.

Supporting people

So as well as feeling connected to the organisation and their team, people need to feel they are listened to, supported in the workplace and have a degree of autonomy and the opportunity to stretch and grow. Line managers shoulder the day-to-day challenge of supporting people and maintaining or boosting employee morale, even though they may themselves be under pressure from every angle, juggling both business-as-usual and managing change. Their own roles are being transformed as the principles of agility and team work gradually filter through organisations. They too may need support from top management and should be developed as coaches, giving them access to new tools, techniques and ideas.

- Manager's job is shifting to:
  - support the team and focus on capability building
  - enable diversity and employee well-being
  - deliberately develop organisational learning capability
- Managers must:
  - keep sight of the importance of teamwork, flexibility, agility and broad vision
  - work actively to achieve local optimisation and prevent siloes.

The defining contribution of great managers is that they make engagement part of their daily work and boost the engagement levels of the people who work for them (Michelman 2004). Engaging managers engage their staff on the three levels identified by Kahn (1990): intelligence - making sure they know what the organisation does and their part in it; society – being part of a team with a manager that supports them, and lastly, emotion – do they care about what they are doing and do they feel cared for? In Standard Chartered Retail Bank, the task of managers in engaging employees is summarised as 'Know me, focus me, value me'.

Engaging managers are approachable and able to create an open and fulfilling working environment. They build, facilitate and empower teams and also treat people as individuals, with fairness and respect and a concern for employees' well-being. MacLeod (2009) reports that engaging managers '... offer clarity about what is expected from individual members of staff, which involves some stretch, and much appreciation and feedback/coaching and training. They also ensure work is designed efficiently and effectively'. HR can contribute to a positive work climate by helping managers understand what motivates their employees and supporting them in designing challenging jobs through which people can experience meaning, purpose and enjoyment.

Engaging managers strive to deliver on the employer brand promise and ensure employees get a fair deal. Effective managers are versatile, able to judge when to involve employees, and when to direct them. Engaging line managers manage for performance and execute tasks in an enabling way, aiming to keep staff motivated and develop people's performance potential. They involve staff in setting clear objectives so that people know what is required but allow staff to work out how to deliver them. They design interesting and worthwhile tasks that often involve collaborative work and have clear end goals. This helps to promote a sense of purpose. They ensure employees have the skills, authority and resources they need to deliver results that matter.

HR can coach managers who are struggling to navigate their own change journey or who find managing the 'people side' of change daunting. The best organisations focus their training and development programmes on building local managers' and teams' capability to solve issues on their own. Training should be strengths-based so that managers learn how to identify, use and build the strengths of team members to achieve better outcomes.

HR can also co-create, and help line managers implement, simple and effective performance management processes, which are relationship-based rather than system-led. Some managers may need coaching around their own leadership style or help with standard setting, providing clarity of goals and targets, managing team dynamics and developing team members. HR can build effective reward and recognition systems which differentiate and reinforce good performance and also offer a degree of individual choice in how performance is rewarded. Instead of focusing on where individuals need to be more productive, HR can openly ask people for their input and gather anecdotal evidence on how to boost productivity and present this data back to leaders. HR can develop competent employees through relevant training, job rotation, and developmental assignments. After all, when people are valued and have opportunities to grow, they are likely to perform well.

However, as a point of caution, a Yale University study (Moeller et al. 2018) found that some hard working, highly engaged academics gradually were becoming exhausted and burnt out, even with all the resources and support they needed to do the job. These workers felt that the demands made of them were too high. In contrast, the optimally engaged colleagues reported having high resources, such as supervisor support, rewards and recognition, and self-efficacy at work, but lower demands such as low workload, low cumbersome bureaucracy, and low to moderate demands on concentration and attention. Similarly, a report for the UK NHS's Point of Care Foundation (2014) found that 'Far too many healthcare professionals feel overworked, disempowered and unappreciated. Healthcare professionals generally suffer higher rates of stress, depression and burnout than their counterparts in other areas of the public sector' (Staff Care, Point of Care Foundation 2014). So even when people have a strong sense of purpose, overloading people with too many demands can lead to serious harm.

HR can help managers and leaders reduce the demands they're placing on people – ensuring that employee goals are realistic and 'de-cluttering' jobs of unnecessary bureaucracy so that people have a clear line of sight through their day job to the purpose, mission and goals of the organisation and letting employees disengage from work when they're not working. Effective managers are willing to address difficult situations. This involves carrying out regular workload reviews and rebalancing who does what: ensuring that engaged employees do not end up having to pick up the workload of those who are less engaged. Managers can also try to increase the resources available to employees, not only material resources such as time and money, but intangible resources such as empathy and friendship in the workplace.

Effective managers create a climate for development: they coach their teams and ensure people have the chance to develop new skills and capabilities and then put those new skills into practice, for instance by moving between functions to achieve what Pink calls 'mastery'. Effective managers promote cross-skilling or up-skilling by encouraging people to share their skills and collaborate with others using practices such as peer feedback and check-ins as aids to successful performance. Since people grow through variety, effective managers also encourage staff to spend 10% of their time on other projects that fall outside of their day-to-day work but offer benefits to the business.

To stay motivated and in control people also want to know that their work has purpose and meaning and want feedback that their contribution and progress has been recognised. Rather than simply relying on feeding back via an annual performance appraisal process, effective managers provide clear and regular feedback and recognition that is values-based and ties back to the company's core values and mission. Effective managers encourage learning from failure as well as sharing good ideas and practice as part of a wider learning culture. They also celebrate successes with their teams.

In tough times

Engaging managers are especially vigilant about the risk of burgeoning workloads and make clear what should be de-prioritised so that people can put their energies into what matters most. While no organisation can guarantee job security, engaging managers help employees adapt to change and cope with stress and anxiety. Since some of the human reactions to change can be anticipated, simply giving people opportunities to talk – in one to ones and in groups – can be enough. Keeping a positive outlook, encouraging people and maintaining active team communication is all the more important when the team is dispersed and working remotely to help people feel connected and able to make sense of what is happening. Managers should encourage teams working at home to build in some 'buffer' time between activities so they can take a break. HR should rethink its processes to make sure they optimise the user experience in the virtual world, including shifting from output-based metrics to employee engagement/experience.

Providing meaningful support not only shows employees that they are valued, even though their job may be at risk, but it can also help survivor employees (those whose jobs remain after downsizing) remain productively focused on their work. To prepare people for new roles, managers need more of a coaching style, to be willing and able to involve staff in implementing change. When making change becomes part of every employee's job, it can become the spur to innovation and improvement.

Being a manager is incredibly demanding, yet effective managers make a huge difference to the success of the organisation. Even if the organisation as a whole is a rather hostile environment to work in, having a great relationship with a good manager can keep people happy and motivated and helps create a more dynamic culture. Their team will be the one everyone wants to work for.

Voice

Employee voice, which is about employees being informed, heard and involved is a key driver of engagement. It is the means by which people communicate their views to their employer and influence matters that affect them at work. This not just about formal consultation and participation but also when 'employees feel able to voice their ideas and be listened to, both about how to do their job and in decision-making in their own department, with joint sharing of problems and challenges and a commitment to arrive at joint solutions' (MacLeod 2009).

Today's multi-generational workforces may have different needs one from another, yet many employees share some common expectations – for self-management of data, fair pay, opportunities for development and more accessible styles of management and leadership. These expectations are ill-matched by traditional long-term employee value propositions and command and control styles of leadership. With smartphones being more powerful than the supercomputers of the past, people now have access to information and knowledge that would have been impossible to access before. Just as today's customers expect more choice, better communication from firms and the opportunity for co-creation, so too do workers – and today's increasingly multi-generational work-forces/workers expect a say, elite workers in particular. Consequently, there is a growing demand for democratisation of access to information, increased and meaningful communication, participation and involvement in decision-making at all levels.

Engaging leaders take a participative approach, building consensus between different groups and individuals within the business. Useful communications translate high level business information to the local level and make it relevant to individuals. Effective communicators use a mix of metaphor, stories, jokes, pictures as well as business-speak to engage their audience. Whether dealing with business problems or developing new ideas for growth, leaders make sure that people can see clear signs of progress by marking milestones, celebrating successes, stabilising what works and sharing the benefits of change.

However, communication should not be just top-down but should involve genuine dialogue at team level. Voice can be formally expressed, for example through suggestion schemes and attitude surveys, as well as informally such as in team meetings or 'huddles', rapid cascades, Q&As – face to face and via social media. Employees can use individual and collective channels to speak directly to management or indirectly through representatives. In companies that do this well there is a constant free flow of ideas up and down and across the organisation.

A study by Forbes Insights (2017), found that employees who felt their voices were being heard were 4.6× more likely to do their best work. Knowing your manager is willing to listen to any problems you're experiencing makes it much easier to get behind their vision for the company. So managers must be willing to listen to people, be open to new ideas and not afraid of relinquishing control. In high performance workplaces a joint approach to solving business problems is usual. This involves establishing dialogue between different groups and individuals within the business, building mutual understanding and respect, and committing to work together constructively to achieve business success.

When employees are genuinely involved in decision-making, they are usually motivated to implement what has been decided. Conventional ways of informing or consulting with staff – via bulletins, newsletters, briefing packs, e-mail and electronic newsletters, intranet, video/TV, large-scale (Town Hall) gatherings, roadshows, helplines, focus groups and line managers briefing individuals and groups – can be complemented by employee surveys for upward feedback. More effective in terms of really engaging people are OD methods such as Real-Time Strategic Change where people have a real chance to understand the issues and together work out potential solutions.

The Forbes Insights report (2017) claims that companies with greater gender and ethnic diversity consistently outperform the competition since they more accurately reflect the diversity of society and reach more potential customers. They also incorporate a broader range of perspectives into their decision-making. Inviting more people to the table, and ensuring their voices are heard, is a win-win for everyone.

Teamwork and team building are key elements of Voice. To break down unhelpful silos, one major hospital set up 23 self-managing teams, each under trained team coordinators. The teams receive on-going HR, clinical and budgetary support from three senior managers. Weekly support meetings promote inter-team communication and collaboration. Evaluation of the team working initiative revealed various benefits such as:

- Greater ownership of issues.
- People are happier in their jobs.
- A climate of cooperation has facilitated better inter-departmental and multi-agency communication and practices. Communication with agencies such as social services has improved.
- Patients are receiving more integrated care, and quicker discharge times, so hospital beds are available more quickly.
- Better quality of working life. Individuals reported that they felt involved in decision-making processes, they benefited from the professional and emotional support they gained as part of a team, and they experienced greater job satisfaction.
- Reduced sickness absence rates.

In tough times

Especially in tough times, frequent and honest communication is vital for (re)building employee trust, resilience and engagement. Every meeting or contact sends a message too - for good or ill. Engaging leaders and managers are visible, accessible and approachable; they communicate authentically and consistently about the bigger picture, strategy and direction. They are also willing to listen and act on what they hear. Engagement and empathy are inextricably linked, and showing empathy is an important way to connect with and retain employees. Empathy is also key to trust determination theory: 'When people are upset, they want to know that you care before they care what you know'.

During the pandemic there were numerous examples of CEOs communicating with their remote workforces in empathetic and informal ways that kept people connected in challenging circumstances. A vital component of the best communication was honesty and speed – leaders telling staff what was really happening, being open to dialogue and exploration which builds trust, as well as creating energy around organisation's mission and values. Concentrating on the positives achieved during the first wave of change, can influence and motivate people for the next wave of change. This is about creating a climate for change. When tough decisions have to be taken, people need to feel confident that the right decisions have been taken and that all concerned have been treated fairly. Transparency is the basis of trust.

The benefits of Voice are multiple. For employers, effective voice contributes to innovation, productivity and organisational improvement as well as keeping the organisation honest, assuming whistleblowing is not discouraged. For employees, it often results in increased job satisfaction, greater influence and better opportunities for development. CIPD research (McCartney and Willmott 2010) suggests that employees' satisfaction with their involvement in decision-making is significantly and positively linked to their overall job satisfaction. This suggests that voice is an important part of employee well-being.

Scope

Scope is where individual motivation is at its highest. It's where people feel they have the opportunity to pursue their own sense of purpose through the work they do, and to have the possibility of growth and fulfilment. This is what Isles (2010) describes as 'Good Work'. Career development matters to most people. For all its challenges, change can also open up opportunities for autonomy, development, better work-life balance and growth as people gain new skills, new networks and new responsibilities. And as we shall discuss over the next few chapters, engaging managers design rich and rewarding roles and help people develop the skills and competencies they really need, focusing in particular on people in new roles. They spot opportunities for employee development and actively coach their teams, involving them in working on real business issues, providing job shadowing and mentoring and championing employee interests. They deliberately encourage people to change roles/re-energise themselves by moving between domestic and international divisions or from one country to another. This allows people to gain new experiences and helps develop different parts of the business – and is also a great motivator. After all, when people feel valued and have opportunities to grow, they are likely to perform well and grow.

Scope is also about people taking the initiative, managing their own contribution and development and embracing the philosophy of lifelong learning. In a context where the organisation values the individual and the feeling is mutual, there is the possibility of a grown-up employment relationship. We shall explore various aspects of Scope in more detail in the next three chapters such as how HR/L&D can help develop people, create meaningful jobs and craft career paths that keep people moving forward.

EMPLOYEE WELL-BEING

The most successful businesses empower their employees to do their best work by encouraging learning, reskilling, and growth, keeping people connected and informed. But that is only part of the engagement picture. Well-being is another important part. MacLeod (2009) define well-being as '... a state ...in which every individual realises his or her potential, can cope with the normal stresses of life, can work productively and fruitfully, and is able to make a contribution to his or her community'.

Research suggests the picture today is far from rosy. The CIPD Good Work Index (Gifford 2020) shows a significant level of work-related poor health among UK workers. About one in four workers report that their job has a negative impact on their mental or physical health. One in five say that they always or often feel 'exhausted' at work, a similar proportion say they are under 'excessive pressure' and one in ten say they are 'miserable'. The CIPD reports that the UK ranks 24th out of 25 for work/life balance compared with other 'comparator economies'. Three in five UK employees are working longer hours than they would like, even when considering their need to make a living. 32% also report being given excessive workloads. Similarly, Gartner's 2019 Modern Employee Experience survey found that only 21% of highly engaged respondents reported having a 'high-quality work-life experience'.

According to Deloitte's (2020) report, poor mental health costs UK employers up to £45 billion per year, a rise of 6% since 2016. In CareerBuilder's survey on stress in the workplace 31% of respondents reported extremely high levels of stress at work and 61% of employees reported being burned out on the job. Those high-stress levels were manifested in poor physical health (fatigue, aches and pains, weight gain) and compromised mental health (depression, anxiety, anger). These findings emphasise the links between wellness and engagement, and how stress undermines both. Where a combination of lack of recognition, increased workloads, poor management and lack of career opportunities exists, some people opt to voluntarily 'downshift', i.e. stepping off the career ladder in order to 'get a life'. Where the pressures on employees undermine their performance, the real impact of such stresses will be felt on business results.

A Glassdoor survey reports that employees are also looking for help and support in achieving balance and being able to attend to the non-work areas of their life. Extra work pressures call on employees to make sacrifices, particularly with respect to their home life and spending time with their children though many people work long hours in order to make career progress. In many surveys, employees report that truly flexible working is the main enabler of work–life balance as we shall explore in Chapter 11.

So HR has the challenge of reconciling organisation demands for agility with individual employee well-being. Well-being includes physical, emotional, moral and financial factors so it is important to take a multi-faceted approach to employee engagement that embraces employee well-being and leads to enthusiasm, motivation and productivity, without the burnout. Companies should promote well-being and ensure psychological safety so that employees are balanced, healthy, can do their job well, feel good about their work, and feel equipped to do their best work.

Research by Willis Towers Watson suggests that a growing number of employers are defining workplace health as a central part of company culture and strategy. Indeed, the focus appears to be shifting away from a piecemeal approach to stress issues, towards a holistic approach to employee well-being which means that wellness must permeate every aspect of an organisation. Robertson Cooper (2014) argue that high psychological well-being leads to positive individual outcomes, such as commitment, morale and health, which in turn lead to improvements in organisational performance in areas such as productivity, customer satisfaction, attractiveness to recruits and lower turnover and sickness absence. Offering people the chance to balance work and personal life therefore makes good business sense.

HR has a significant role to play in ensuring that their organisations enable employees to have some form of balance. Many HR teams, knowing employees are feeling stressed, offer wellness programmes on improving work-life balance and stress management – usually through healthy eating, exercise, or mindfulness. Some of the more interesting practice on this front comes from the United States. For instance, years ago stressed-out employees of Boston City Council had an automated phone system which screened calls for depression. Callers listened to recorded descriptions of how they feel ranging from 'I get tired for no reason' to 'I feel others would be better off if I were dead'. They punched the appropriate number and could hear a recorded diagnosis that urged severe cases to seek counselling (London Evening Standard, May 1999).

Mental health tools have become more common, such as virtual yoga sessions, mental health support websites or expanded options for counselling through the company employee assistance programs (EAP). Many organisations implement initiatives/standards to reduce stress, develop health and well-being strategies, run Occupational Health roadshows and offer staff access to personal financial advice. Some employers have reshaped the physical environment to encourage healthy behaviour for instance by adding healthy foods to breakrooms and restaurant delivery menus, ergonomic workstations, appropriate lighting and subsidising gym membership. Some offer specialist workshops offering menopause support. Developing employee-friendly policies is part of the solution, but such policies need to be owned by employees and senior managers if they are to become a reality.

Employee well-being should be championed from the top. The need for inclusive leadership and an authentic focus on employee experience and well-being has never been more pressing. One group of NHS hospitals has a 'Wellbeing Guardian' at board level who provides active sponsorship of the staff well-being work. One trust set up small-scale 'think tanks' involving over 250 staff, each tasked with solving problems in specific areas, including sickness, use of data, retention and well-being. Since NHS many front-line staff are worn out caring for the pandemic's victims, HR teams are training mental health first-aiders, offering rest rooms and 'oasis spaces', setting up Well-being Hubs, offering virtual well-being sessions and 'sleep hygiene' resources, and introducing psychological services for staff that provide one-to-one and team support on dealing with grief, stress, anxiety and depression.

The Saint-Gobain company believes there are clear links between staff engagement, well-being and business performance. The firm developed a programme 'Fit to Lead' that was aimed at senior leaders, some of whom were becoming burnt-out. The programme integrates leadership development with mental and physical well-being, the idea being that to inculcate a culture of well-being across the organisation it was important to start at the top. As well as improving their well-being, the programme has also made the participants more effective at their jobs (People Management, April 2018).

A holistic approach to combatting stress is needed, with well-being acting as a golden thread throughout the support on offer. For instance, with respect to bullying, harassment or other form of 'moral injury' people should feel free to speak up and have a formal mechanism to do so. Companies need to signpost people where to report and reassure people via communications that if they do raise a complaint, it will be taken seriously. When an incident is reported, HR teams or senior leaders must ensure they have a clear plan in place for what happens next. Some organisations are offering staff access to a mediation service for relationship issues including domestic abuse. So while workshops on stress management and resilience can contribute to a workforce that is healthier, more engaged, and more productive, if the workplace remains a largely stressful environment, standalone wellness programmes tend to produce limited returns.

Management style and the chance for personal development appear to be two factors that relate closely to whether people perceive the work pressures they experience to be positive or negative. The extent to which people feel able to grow and 'empowered' to do their jobs appears to be closely linked to job satisfaction and resilience to extra pressure. Since the main stressors tend to be the work itself, HR should work with front-line managers to monitor the level of demands they're placing on people and encourage a better balance between demands and resources, particularly during high pressure periods, so that people can recover from the demands they experience through work. They can encourage managers to increase the resources available to employees by building in some 'slack' in the form of time, as well as introducing protocols such as avoiding emailing people after hours, setting a norm that evenings, weekends and holidays are work-free.

L&D has a strong role to play in addressing well-being. The NHS provides mental health training for managers as part of their onboarding process. They are also offering trauma-informed leadership training to help teams going through tough times. Some organisations are teaming up to provide peer-to-peer reciprocal mentoring at all levels with a special focus on well-being, D&I and minimising the negative impact of change on people.

So rather than addressing employee well-being as a silo initiative it must instead be accepted as everyone's responsibility. A well-crafted employee well-being strategy offers immediate support for employees while simultaneously delivering long term preventative approaches that deliver stability and well-being over time.

Reflective activity

- As remote working becomes increasingly the norm, what are the implications for employee engagement, work-life balance and well-being?

I am grateful to Claire Stone, formerly Senior Consultant in the Employee Engagement team, and Tracey Tennet, Head of Health and Wellbeing at EDF Energy for the following case study.

Case: Agile working in EDF Energy

EDF Energy is the UK's largest producer of low-carbon energy, meeting around one-fifth of the country's demand and supplying millions of customers and businesses with electricity and gas. The company operates 8 nuclear power stations, more than 30 wind farms and has more than 5 million customer accounts in the United Kingdom. It employs around 13,000 employees across England and Scotland. With a new CEO and recent changes to office locations, and the introduction of 'modern ways of working', e.g. hot-desking, the new culture emerging is one that moves away from everyone working in a set space to people moving around.

Accordingly, the firm has a fast-growing number of agile and remote workers. EDF Energy's own definition for Agile working is as follows: 'Agile working provides a framework for modernising the way we work. It's about working flexibly, securely and appropriately from an EDF Energy site, from home or other location. Agile working encourages teams and individuals, where appropriate, to take a fresh look at where, how and when work is carried out'. On the whole agile working is popular with employees and in the 2017 employee engagement survey, 35% of respondents (3,528 people) reported having an agile working arrangement in place, whether formally or informally.

Why research agile working?

EDF Group uses Ipsos to carry out annual employee engagement surveys. With agile working a growing trend, Claire Stone, formerly Senior Consultant in the Employee Engagement team, noted that the engagement survey in 2017 showed some differences between the views of agile workers and those of others. There was some good news, for instance, 'All employees who spend at least some (but not all) of their time working remotely have higher engagement than those who don't ever work remotely'. This mirrored research findings published by Gallup.

Yet the survey revealed other areas of concern with respect to employee well-being that echoed observations by Tracey Tennet, Head of Health and Wellbeing, who was aware that there was a growing number of work-related ill-health cases affecting agile workers that were shown to be work aggravated and where feelings of loneliness and isolation were impacting on employees. A similar theme was reflected in wider publications in the management press and academic journals.

EDF Energy takes health and safety very seriously indeed and has a mandatory policy with respect to not causing harm. The Agile Working policy is based on advice from Employee Relations teams and helps people to 'self-select' for agile working by asking questions that test its appropriateness for individuals such as 'Have you considered these factors...?' and 'Would it suit you...?' At the same time, agile working is agreed locally at managers' discretion. How well people feel able to manage their own well-being tends to reflect the way their own line managers react, show trust in the employee and role model new ways of working themselves.

So the team decided to investigate the issues further to better understand what was happening with the agile and remote working population, including field staff, many of whom had been with the company for over 20 years. Working in partnership with researchers at City University of London, they used an on-line survey to explore the following questions:

- What are the benefits of agile working for this growing population – at work and at home?
- What are people doing themselves to adapt and make new ways of working 'work'?
- Is the EDF Energy agile and remote population more engaged – in line with external research?
- Are people more committed as a result and are they more likely to stay with the organisation?
- Are any adverse impacts evident? (e.g. loneliness or workplace isolation) How is everyday well-being (e.g. happiness and anxiety) affected?

The survey was designed to produce quantitative and qualitative responses so that specific comments could shed light on key issues. Various aspects of organisational engagement were explored: the impact of agile working (both positive and negative) on organisational engagement, work engagement, organisational commitment and intention to quit. Aspects of well-being explored included: workplace isolation (support), loneliness and affective well-being (e.g. happiness and anxiety).

All responses were anonymous and confidential. Participants were actively recruited via networks and key channels for field staff:

- News stories and reminders on the company intranet
- E-mails to target employees
- Postings on internal social media

People were keen to participate in the survey and a diverse population took part.

Response rates were monitored daily and 741 responses were received over three weeks.

Key findings

The EDF Energy agile and remote population with 'formal' agile arrangements demonstrated higher organisational and work engagement than others – in line with external research. With respect to organisational commitment, there was no significant difference between agile workers and the mainstream population; for Intention to Quit, though there were more men than women in the agile population considering quitting. Similarly with respect to everyday well-being, e.g. happiness and anxiety, there was no significant difference on well-being measures. However, when looking at adverse impacts, e.g. loneliness or workplace isolation, the people experiencing the highest levels of workplace isolation and loneliness were those working remotely 80–100% of the time. And these people had the lowest Intention to Quit.

This might be explained by the qualitative responses, especially with respect to the wide range of benefits for this growing population – both at work and at home. People considered the top work-life benefits as follows:

- More time to get work done (51%)
- Having essential equipment nearby (45%)
- Reduced travel (33%)
- Increased productivity (32%)
- Fewer distractions (26%).

The top home-life benefits included:

- More time to get work done (44%)
- More time to spend with family (37%)
- Reduced travel (26%)
- Increased flexibility (23%)
- Better able to meet personal commitments (20%).

In particular it seems that people were more committed to the company because agile working allowed them to both work and meet their wider responsibilities, including caring, thus achieving a better work-life balance. There were over 150 suggestions on the theme of setting up an agile or remote working arrangement and 'making it work'. Regular communications and feedback were felt to be key, though the preferred frequency varied. The importance of building honest, trusting and supportive relationships between agile and remote workers and their line managers was a key theme.

What are the practical implications of the research?

EDF's Stress Risk Assessments have been updated and enhanced based on the findings, including new insights on mitigating risk. The results have also been fed into informing guidance on optimum arrangements for agile working, e.g. working remotely 40–60% of the time seems to bring about the greatest benefits.

The results have also helped equip agile workers to better help themselves. The 'Top Tips' for agile and remote working that were provided by respondents were shared within a newly created Yammer community. The tips relate to what people themselves are doing to adapt and make new ways of working 'work' for instance:

Assessing readiness for agile working

Respondents suggested ways of thinking about whether this way of working is right for you, e.g. 'does it fit with your character/working style?' 'only do it if you are (i) independent (ii) organised (iii) disciplined'; 'will you go crazy alone all day?' 'be sure you are the kind of person who is happy in their own company and can work with minimal supervision'. 'Be honest with yourself about whether you are someone who enjoys being alone and will be able to get down and work if alone'.

They also suggested considering the suitability of the work you do – 'only go down this route if you are in a role which enables communication via telephone/Skype, or where specific tasks can be completed in blocks away from the office' – as well as considering the impact on both colleagues and family. One recommendation is 'Do a 3-month trial before fully committing to this style of working – it doesn't suit everyone'.

Setting up an agile or remote working arrangement

Many 'Top Tips' referred to agreeing flexible working arrangements with line managers, setting expectations and contracting, agreeing 'ground rules' (and exactly what they mean in practice) then making a formal application. 'Have an honest conversation with your line manager to set expectations'. 'Fully explain what "agile" means to you so expectations are set at the outset'. Discussing the level of autonomy needed plus how and when support might be required (and how it could be provided) was felt to be a very useful area to address in advance too.

Agreeing ground-rules on communication was felt to be especially important – when and how best to check in so that managers and team-mates know where people are and how to contact them. This also means that people are kept in the loop. EDF Energy's work on Inclusion is taken seriously so making sure that agile workers can take part in team events, even remotely, at times that work for all, is important. All concerned are encouraged to become competent at stakeholder management, proactively updating people, being more transparent in communications.

There were lots of useful pieces of advice on 'starting out' and the transition process – e.g. 'the first few weeks are the hardest', 'expect to take a few weeks/months for it to feel "normal"!'; 'gradually transition to working remotely: I would not recommend starting full-time' and 'do not underestimate that this will be a change and give yourself time to adjust/adapt'. Trying out a number of different options was suggested too.

Respondents often observed their managers as role models for working arrangements, e.g. 'look at what your manager does to guide what you can do'. Respondents were keen that people considering agile and remote working should be familiar with the relevant EDF Energy policies and getting to know their rights – but at the same time could 'rest assured in the knowledge the company will do their very best to support you'.

Managing your time and organising your week

There were plenty of suggestions about planning your approach and setting boundaries so that people don't feel obliged to be at 'work' 24 hours a day and can protect their personal life. These included tracking hours worked and keeping a record of progress on projects/tasks. 'Best practice' included, e.g. 'find a good way to record your working time that works for you. Whether it's in a different diary or on an excel spreadsheet, just set a rule then do it!' 'Ensure you record how many hours you're doing a day/week as it's easy to work much longer days'. 'Keeping a personal log of any incidents or issues was also recommended'. 'Keep track of the number of hours you work. It's easy to do so many more when not in the office. There is less chit-chat, less coffee runs, less time taken for lunch'.

Looking after your Health and Well-being and combatting isolation

Raising any concerns 'sooner rather than later' was another important message; along with 'if something doesn't work straight away don't be afraid to change it, keep tweaking it' and 'it's not for everyone – don't be afraid to say if it isn't working for you'. 'If something isn't working, talk about it with your manager… to find a solution to make this a working arrangement which truly works for you'.

'Agile working is such a great thing to have, there is a risk that if you overwork you will lose it'. 'If you find that "agile working" is becoming "fragile working" and affecting your performance or health and well-being, be brave and flag it to your manager'. 'Be open to other suggestions. Be prepared to compromise'. 'Don't take advantage (you'll spoil it for others as well as yourself'.

Raising management ability to manage people working remotely

The research findings have also been fed into the leadership and management development curriculum which has been enhanced with programmes on 'Managing Remote Workers'. These are helping equip managers for managing an agile workforce for instance by promoting the 'business case' for new ways of working, using different types of survey data to raise awareness of agile workers' needs. As a result the management culture has become looser as managers actively make agile working work.

With case studies of agile workers appearing in EDF Energy company newsletters, there is growing awareness of how to make the most of agile working – for the company and its employees. EDF Energy is already building a lively on-line community amongst its remote workers, with the likely outcome of reducing feelings of isolation. With a joint company and employee effort such as this, the greater sense of connection and well-being across this growing population is starting to pay dividends.

As this case study illustrates, embracing employee wellness and engagement as strategic imperatives is a significant paradigm shift in the business world, one that will only grow stronger as agile, remote and hybrid forms of working become the norm. Determined effort will be needed to heighten energy, engagement, focus, coordination and cooperation to make hybrid work productive and healthy work.

Looking ahead, taking a holistic approach to health and well-being will involve good use of technology. Managers and HR must consider how digital well-being can be enhanced through training and managing expectations around being 'visible' online as well as providing informal spaces for team members to check in with one another. Leaders must make sure they're sending a consistent message that balance matters and bring the same energy, care and attention to employee wellness and engagement as to their core products and services. Organisations that ensure their employees flourish and thrive will always be ahead of the curve.

CONCLUSION

So, as organisations plot their way to recovery, today's challenges could prove a blessing in disguise since they highlight that employers who focus on engagement and well-being can motivate and retain valued employees. Sustained agility requires us to proactively plan for how we will continually assess employee needs, engagement and wellness from the beginning, and test, learn and adapt our plans accordingly. Rather than attempting to *force* engagement, it is healthier to encourage it by managing change with a human touch. After all, employees will welcome change if, as a result, they work in a positive environment, are part of a winning team, are more capable and empowered, have learned from their experiences and have the tools to be self-managing. We have discussed how, if a workforce believes in the organisation's purpose, it will probably buy into change. Ensuring that employees' voices are heard should be part of a larger push for equality and inclusiveness in the workplace.

To build a culture conducive to engagement may require a mindset shift and a willingness to try something new – for employees as well as employers. While organisations have become more flexible about where and when employees work, now they need to be more intentional about their choices and trade-offs. This is the time above all where the 'values on the wall' need to work in practice. So even if business leaders cannot provide job security, they can keep people informed and listen to what employees are telling them. While they cannot provide meaning for their employees, as this is individual and subjective, they can offer a clear purpose for their organisations. They can ensure that values-based behaviours are reflected in appraisals and promotion criteria, and that line managers are recognised for their efforts in engaging employees. They can demand that good intent, in the form of work-life balance, well-being or diversity policies, is translated into practice, and make every effort to close any 'say-do' gap of their own.

Employers who are forward-looking, who sustain their investment in people, who build a climate of trust, and continue to develop the abilities of their workforce, are likely to maintain their competitiveness and be well-positioned for growth when the economy picks up. The engagement-performance potential is there – delivering the results is a shared effort. Leaders, managers, HR and employees themselves have key roles to play since employee engagement flows up, down and across the organisation. Ensuring mutual benefits (as well as risks) for both organisations and employees is potentially the most sustainable and honest basis for an employment relationship better suited to the demands of today's volatile global economy.

As we shall consider in the next chapter changes in jobs and job design, performance management and reward systems have major implications for employee engagement, performance and retention We shall consider how both organisations and employees can benefit from these changes. In the next chapter we shall consider how jobs, performance management and reward systems are changing.

Reflective activity

- Paauwe (2004) highlighted the tension between added value and moral values in shaping the employment relationship and related HR practices. What are the paradoxes and dualities you note with respect to the pursuit of Employee Engagement?
- Are productivity and employee well-being competing goals? Can they be optimised jointly?

REFERENCES

Alvarez-Williams, J. (2020). BLM movement adds pressure on start-ups to diversify. *Financial Times*, Nov 9. https://www.ft.com/content/aa5e1536-992a-4bb6-a3b3-cd9daefcd0dd

Beatson, M. (2019). *Megatrends: Flexible Working*. London: Chartered Institute of Personnel and Development. www.cipd.co.uk/Images/megatrends-report-flexible-working-1_tcm18-52769.pdf

Brown, P., Ashton, D. and Lauder, H. (2010), *Skills Are Not Enough: The Globalisation of Knowledge and the Future UK Economy*, Praxis, No. 4, March, UK Commission for Employment and Skills.

Brown. P., Lauder, H. and Ashton, D. (2010). *The Global Auction: The Broken Promises of Education, Jobs and Rewards*. New York: Oxford University Press.

Budd, J.W. (2004). *Employment with a Human Face: Balancing Efficiency, Equity, and Voice*. Ithaca, NY: Cornell University Press.

Bunting, M. (2004). *Willing Slaves: How the Overwork Culture is Ruling Our Lives*. London: HarperCollins.

Ceridian. (2020). *Rethinking Employee Engagement: how to engage your modern workforce*. https://www.ceridian.com/uk/resources/uk-rethinking-employee-engagement-to-engage-modern-workforce

Chartered Institute of Personnel and Development and the British Chamber of Commerce. (2007). *Flexible working, good business, how small firms are doing it*. Guide. http://www.cipd.co.uk/research/rsrchplcvpubs/guides.litm?vanitv=http://www.cipd.co.u k/guides

Christian, M. S., Garza, A. S. and Slaughter, J. E. (2011). Work engagement: A quantitative review and test of its relations with task and contextual performance. *Personnel Psychology*, 64(1):89–136

Cooper, C. and Worrall, L. (2012). *Improving the quality of working life: Positive steps for senior management teams*, CMI Article of the year 2012

Engage for Success (2014). Sustaining employee engagement & performance – Why wellbeing matters. *Engage for Success Website*.

Forbes Insights in association with Salesforce (2017).*The experience equation; how happy employees and customers accelerate growth*. https://www.salesforce.com/content/dam/web/en_us/www/documents/reports/forbes-insight%20experience-equation%20final-report.pdf

Gallup (2020). *The State of the Global Workplace*. Washington, DC: Gallup.

Gapper, J. (2013). Bosses are reigning in staff because they can. *Financial Times*, Feb 28.

Gartner (2020). Why employee experience initiatives fall short. *Harvard Business Review*, July–August.

Gifford, J. (2020). *CIPD Good Work Index 2020 UK Working Lives Survey*. London: CIPD. https://www.cipd.co.uk/Images/good-work-index-summary-report-2020-1_tcm18-79211.pdf

Gratton, L. (2020). Four principles to ensure hybrid work is productive work. *MIT Sloan Review*, November 09, 2020 https://sloanreview.mit.edu/article/four-principles-to-ensure-hybrid-work-is-productive-work/?og=Home+Editors+Picks

Guest, D.E. (2004). The psychology of the employment relationship: An analysis based on the psychological contract. *Applied Psychology*, 53(4), 541–555.

Guest, D. (2013). Employee engagement: Fashionable fad or long-term fixture?, in Truss, C., Alfes, K., Delbridge, R., Shantz, A., Soane, E.C. (eds.), *Employee Engagement in Theory and Practice*. London: Routledge.

Günsel, A. and Yamen, M. (2020), Digital Taylorism as an answer to the requirements of the new era, in Akkaya, B. (ed.), *Agile Business Leadership Methods for Industry 4.0*. Bingley, UK: Emerald Publishing Limited, 103–119.

Hakanen, J.J. and Schaufeli, W.B. (2012). Do burnout and work engagement predict depressive symptoms and life satisfaction? A three-wave seven-year prospective study. *Journal of Affective Disorders*, 141, 415–424.

Hamel, G. (2009). Moon shots for management. *Harvard Business Review*, February.

Harter, J.K. et al. (2020). *The Relationship between Engagement at Work and Organizational Outcomes 2020 Q12® Meta-Analysis: 10th Edition*. Washington DC: Gallup.

Heger, B.K. (2007). Linking the Employment Value Proposition (EVP) to employee engagement and business outcomes: Preliminary findings from a linkage research pilot study. *Organisation Development Journal*, 25(2), 121–131.

Herriot, P. and Pemberton, C. (1995a). *New Deals: The Revolution in Managerial Careers*. Chichester: Wiley.

Holbeche, L.S. and Matthews, G. (2012). *Engaged: Unleashing the Potential of your Organisation through Employee Engagement*. Chichester, UK: John Wiley/Jossey Bass.

Holbeche, L.S. and Springett, N. (2005). *In Search of Meaning in the Workplace*. Horsham: Roffey Park.

Isles, N. (2010). *The Good Work Guide: How to Make Organisations Fairer and More Effective*. London: Earthscan.

Jaffe, S. (2021). *Work Won't Love You Back. How Devotion to Our Jobs Keeps Us Exploited, Exhausted, and Alone*. London: Bold Type Books.

Jenkins, S. and Delbridge, R. (2013). Context matters: Examining 'Soft' and 'Hard' approaches to employee engagement in two workplaces. *International Journal of Human Resource Management*, 24(14), 2670–2691.

Kahn, W.A. (1990). Psychological conditions of personal engagement and disengagement at work. *Academy of Management Journal*, 33, 692–724.

Macleod, D. and Clarke, N. (2009). *Engaging for Success: Enhancing Performance through Employee Engagement*. London: Department of Business, Innovation and Skills.

Maslach, C. (2019). *Understanding Job Burnout*, DevOps Enterprise Summit, Feb 18. https://itrevolution.com/understanding-job-burnout-christina-maslach/

Mayer, C. (2020). *The Future of the Corporation*. London: The British Academy. https://www.thebritishacademy.ac.uk/programmes/future-of-the-corporation/

McCartney, C. and Willmott, B. (2010). *The Employee Outlook*. London: CIPD

Michelman, P. (2014). Methodology: How great managers manage people. *Harvard Management Update*, 1 August. http://blogs.hbr.org/hmu/2008/02/how-great-managers-manage-peop-1.html

Moeller, J., Ivcevic, Z., White, A.E., Menges, J. and Brackett, M.A. (2018, January 25). *Highly engaged but burned out: Intra-individual profiles in the US workforce*. Yale Center for Emotional Intelligence and Yale Child Study Center, Yale University, https://osf.io/h6qnf/

Overall, S. (2008). *Inwardness: The Rise of Meaningful Work*. London: The Work Foundation.

Paauwe, J. (2004). *HRM and Performance*. Oxford: Oxford University Press.

Pink, D. (2009). *Drive: The Surprising Truth about What Motivates Us*. Edinburgh: Riverhead.

Point of Care Foundation (2014). *Staff care: How to engage staff in the NHS and why it matters*. https://s16682.pcdn.co/wp-content/uploads/2014/01/ POCF_FINAL-inc-references.pdf (archived at https://perma.cc/72KL-34VT)

Robertson Cooper (2014). *Good day at work - Annual Report 2014/15*. Robertson Cooper Website. Manchester.

Sennett, R. (2008). *The Craftsman*. New Haven, CT: Yale University Press.

Sennett, R. (2006). *The Culture of the New Capitalism*. New Haven: Yale University Press

Sennett, R. (1998). *The Corrosion of Character, Personal Consequences of Work in the New Capitalism*. New York: WW Norton.

Soane, E., Shantz, A., Alfes, K., Truss, C., Rees, G. and Gatenby, M. (2013). The association of meaningfulness, well-being, and engagement with absenteeism: A moderated mediation model. *Human Resource Management*, 52(3), 441–456.

Sparrow, P.R. and Cooper, C.L. (2003). *The Employment Relationship: Key Challenges for HR*. Oxford: Butterworth- Heinemann.

The Conference Board and The Engagement Institute (2019). *Engagement and culture*. The Conference Board, December 21, https://www.conference-board.org/topics/engagement-and-culture.

UKCES and ESRC 2012 Skills and employment survey (May 2013). UK Commission for Employment and Skills and the Economic and Social Research Council.

Zuboff, S. (2010). Creating value in the age of distributed capitalism. *McKinsey Quarterly*, http://www.mckinseyquarterly.com/ Creating_value_in_the_age_of_distributed_capitalism_2666.

NOTE

1 Professor Cary Cooper (January 2013) commenting at a CIPD meeting on findings from the Worrell and Cooper report (2012).

9

Managing and rewarding for high performance

DOI: 10.4324/9781003219996-11

As we considered in earlier chapters, businesses need to be innovative and nimble to respond to customer needs and succeed in the dynamic competitive environment. The pandemic and its consequences have accelerated underlying trends. Organisations and work therefore must be designed for agility and high performance. A new operating system for work is needed — one that better supports the high degree of organisational agility required to thrive amid increasingly rapid change and disruption, and that better reflects the fluidity of modern work and working arrangements (Jesuthasan and Boudreau 2018, 2021).

CHAPTER OVERVIEW

In this chapter we shall consider how HR can drive '…programs that create adaptability, innovation, collaboration, and speed' (Rigby et al. 2016). Such programs include designing roles, performance management and reward systems which foster expertise, collaboration, decision-making, employee engagement and high performance.

We shall consider:

- The changing workplace and jobs
- High-performance work practices
- How does performance management work in this environment? Is it needed at all?
- Reward and recognition

LEARNING OBJECTIVES

- To consider the challenges arising from the trend to deconstruct jobs
- To explore how conventional approaches to performance management and reward may be changing

INTRODUCTION: THE CHANGING WORKPLACE

Workplaces are changing and the forms, structures and work practices which were familiar a few years ago are undergoing a serious, longer-term appraisal. The cultural shift to Agile means embracing a range of methodologies, work practices and values that originally arose from software development and were described in the Agile Manifesto (see Chapter 3).

Rather than a particular methodology, 'Agile' is more a set of customer focused principles and values based on achieving innovations through iterative and incremental development, where requirements and solutions evolve through collaboration between self-organising, cross-functional teams and their customers. Incorporating lean practices and agile principles enables people to solve problems in adaptive ways, within a systemic framework. In an agile organisational culture, experimentation is considered the norm and continuous learning is valued. Thus empowerment, continuous improvement, radical transparency, knowledge-sharing and different communications (horizontal conversations) become key cultural features.

To succeed in the digital age, the organisation will become a more flexible, customer-centric, task-oriented organic structure. The challenge will be to create organisations, however decentralised, which are completely unified and coordinated, with aligned goals, and where employees experience high levels of participation and commitment.

Operating models must allow for the creation and maintenance of new organisational capabilities through nimble or 'agile' production, knowledge-intensive work, high labour flexibility and the idea of devolving decision-making down the organisational hierarchy. The workforce will typically be a mix of permanent staff and workers on different types of fixed-term contracts.

Agile teams and work practices

Agile, high performing teams are part of this new vision of work. An agile team, or squad, is a temporary, self-organising group of people from different disciplines with different experiences. Agile teams set up, move and disband fast and are empowered to make their own decisions within boundaries. Agile uses many principles of Lean (such as continuous improvement) but applies these to the process and overall way of working, rather than just to the product. For example, in the popular Agile framework Scrum, product development cycles are called sprints. A sprint is a short (typically two-week) period in which the team focuses on building a tightly scoped set of deliverables chosen on a rolling basis.

Phase 1 – Sprint planning. The team, which includes experts as well as other key stakeholders, such as customers, determines what new features are highest priority for the next sprint to deliver.

Phase 2 – Sprint. Each team member works on their part of the delivery, checking in regularly – usually daily – to update each other on progress and request help as needed.

Phase 3 – Retrospective. At the end of the sprint, team members present their progress and reflect on their experience in the sprint. New needs are surfaced, and changes are made to roadmap and strategy.

This way of working requires teams with high levels of trust, and an openness to experimentation, so team members must establish connections rapidly. Research by Deloitte demonstrates that high-performing teams are diverse and inclusive. Such teams are more innovative, engaged, and creative in their work since when people feel included, they are more likely to speak up and fully contribute.

Today, as companies increasingly operate as networks of teams, agile organisational designs are typically characterised by a small core centre and alliances with suppliers and customers.

Building customer-centricity

HR can play a key role in supporting agile working and enabling the integration needed to optimise the business model. Tyson (1995) described the HR department itself as an integrating device since its remit usually operates across organisational boundaries and often carries responsibility for the internalisation of corporate values. HR can help embed customer-centricity into the organisational culture as a whole, by taking a systemic approach:

- Combining a number of HR practices such as individual training and development to communicate the what and why of customer-centric values, and to teach positive behaviours and practices such as coaching for performance, providing feedback that is real-time, continuous and multidirectional.
- Building (or acquiring) new capabilities and embedding new cultural norms to create a workforce which recognises the importance of the customer and feels both capable and empowered to support them and to innovate.

- Developing more flexible organisational structures, taking into account new approaches to work enabled by the technological advances, such as the rise of virtual working, and of 'non-standard' work (*e.g.* flexible working and zero-hour contracts), and the idea of devolving decision-making down the organisational hierarchy (Deloitte 2017).

Formal and informal integration mechanisms

For agility, too much rigidity leads to stagnation; too much flexibility can lead to duplication and potentially chaos. The challenge is to strike the right balance. Therefore the flexible and the informal must co-exist with formal, integration mechanisms. Structures, systems, processes, standards and rules are all integrating devices within an organisation's bureaucracy. Matrix structures are formal integration devices, and these are increasingly being simplified to make them less complex and more effective. In sectors where there is intense competition, such as the pharmaceutical, the financial services or the hospitality industries, integration often occurs through formal amalgamation via mergers and acquisitions.

One way agility can be increased is by simplifying unnecessary 'red tape'. GE, a company long been admired for the way its approach to strategy, portfolio and talent interconnect in a strong HR culture, has been making breakthroughs in this area. Today, in line with an increasingly VUCA environment, GE's broader business strategy shift is towards growth through innovation and culturally GE aims to become an agile, customer-centric organisation. To deliver the strategy, employees need to collaborate, make quick and effective business decisions, and provide customers with superior products and services. Simplification is a key operating principle which means reducing bureaucracy and 'siloes', introducing new ways of working, getting close to the customer, producing better, faster outcomes for customers and a new performance-development approach.

CHANGING NATURE OF JOBS

As AI systems, robotics, and cognitive tools become more sophisticated, organisations are redesigning jobs to take advantage of technology's potential. This has implications for the skills required from employees. For instance, thanks to automation and robotics there is a significant decline in requirement for workers to perform physical and manual tasks or basic cognitive chores. So what is the role of people as more and more work is automated? Could such workers be retrained to add value in new ways? Multiskilling and rapid reskilling strategies can help fill temporary skill gaps and aid staff redeployment if jobs become obsolete.

Simultaneously, there is a significant rise in demand for higher cerebral skills and advanced technological capabilities for knowledge-intensive work. There is also a new focus on the 'people aspects' of work and an increase in customer-facing roles involving some form of 'emotional labour' – with the requirement for employees to express positive emotions when interacting with customers. Organisations should focus heavily on retraining people to use cognitive tools and rethink work around what Deloitte (2017) call 'essential human skills'.

In today's and tomorrow's organisations, sustainable business performance is going to require ever-greater discretionary effort from people. Job design, and the way people are managed, must enable knowledge workers and those involved in 'emotional labour' to give of their best. And with demographic shifts, growing skills gaps and the need to meet the aspirations of the 'new workforce', organisations may suffer shortages of the key talent they need unless they can offer potential candidates the careers, learning and flexibility they crave.

Several pieces of research illustrate how organisations benefit from providing people with flexibility and increased opportunity to learn from their jobs. Wall and Wood (2005) for instance looked at the impact of job design on knowledge and skill acquisition. They concluded that the organisation of work and the ability of the individuals to manage this is a significant driver of discretionary performance and is strongly correlated with an individual's ability to learn. The idea of the connection between work organisation and learning is also explored by Leach et al. (2005). They focused on the effect of autonomy and teamwork on Knowledge, Skills and Abilities (KSA), concluding that KSA mediates the relationship between autonomy and performance and between autonomy and job strain.

Smart work

So how can firms respond to this constantly evolving landscape, and design roles that meet changing business needs and also attract, motivate and retain the best employees? The CIPD and CapGemini (2008) drew on high performance theory and early examples of organisational agility to explore how work and organisational design can evolve to create a win–win situation for both employers and employees. They defined as 'smart work' the dynamic interplay between organisational elements such as role design, leadership and management, and employee elements such as an individual's motivation and willingness to deploy his or her discretionary effort to the benefit of the organisation and its customers. This suggests that a job system that will meet both employer and employee needs will be characterised by:

- A higher degree of **freedom to act** than traditional roles, frequently characterised by **self-management, a high degree of autonomy** and a **philosophy of empowerment**
- Management interventions that focus on **outcome-based indicators of achievement** (role descriptions, performance management processes, strong processes to cascade corporate objectives to individual level)
- Work location that is (to a greater or lesser degree) **flexible** (working hours/location)
- **Physical work environment** conditions; hot-desking, working from home, mobile communications technology (*e.g.* laptops with ability to remotely connect to network, iphones, online application and portals, teleconference facilities

Cultural enablers of smart working included:

- Training leaders at all levels of the company to act as hands-on coaches, not 'managers'
- Creating systems with lots of transparent information, i.e. what are our goals, who is working on what project, who are our experts?
- Building a focus on continuous learning and learning culture at all levels
- Encouraging and teaching people to give each other direct feedback
- Creating programs for peer-to-peer rewards and recognition

- Developing programs to foster diversity in teams
- Creating customer interactions within all groups and functions in the company
- Implementing 'systems of engagement' not just 'systems of record', i.e. collaboration, information-sharing, project management (Deloitte 2015)

Berson et al (2008) found clear links between CEO values, organizational culture and firm outcomes. Similarly, according to CIPD/CapGemini research (CIPD 2008), High Performance Workplaces tend to manifest the following:

- igh Trust' management culture and organisational beliefs – a belief that people will generally strive to perform
- A philosophy of collaboration between employer and employee: participative decision-making and open communication
- A high degree of individual freedom to act, discretion and autonomy in work practices
- Employees managed by outcome

Importantly a strong, focused mission and values and clear business objectives are needed to keep everyone aligned and to create a 'triple win' for the organisation, its employees and its customers.

Job fit and job design – what role can HR play?

Conventional job design has approached the challenge of reconciling employer and employee needs by considering both required job characteristics and psychological drivers of employee performance. Hackman and Oldham (1975) identified the following 'core job characteristics' which should be taken into account in job design:

- Skill variety
- Task identity
- Task significance: the degree to which the job outcome has a substantial impact on others. The meaning of 'task significance' in the context of many roles involves –
  - Autonomy: the degree to which the job gives an employee freedom and discretion in scheduling work and determining how it is performed
  - Feedback: the degree to which an employee gets information about the effectiveness of their efforts – with particular emphasis on feedback directly from the work itself rather than from a third party (e.g. manager).

What is needed for effective job design is a broad role description, with some 'fuzzy' boundaries to allow for growth, yet not so loose that needless confusion and duplication occur. Such roles are more likely to lead to 'smart work'. Taken together, the core job characteristics are said to produce three 'critical psychological states':

- Meaningfulness – the employee perceiving the work as worthwhile or important
- Responsibility – the belief that the employee is accountable for the outcome of his or her efforts
- Knowledge – of whether or not the outcome of the employee's work is satisfactory

Designing jobs in a way that maximises the probability of all three of these 'critical states' being present is, in turn, believed to drive four positive outcomes:

- High internal work motivation
- High-quality work performance
- High job satisfaction
- Low absenteeism and voluntary staff turnover

There is a large volume of literature on the 'job characteristics' theory alone, some of it disputing the link between employee satisfaction and performance. However, it would seem that these factors remain broadly relevant, even though the nature of work is changing for many.

HR can help managers design roles in the light of business drivers, so that there is a clear 'line of sight' between the business strategy, the deliverables required and the end-user or other 'customer', regardless of sector. Key performance indicators for each role should derive from the business drivers and strategy, making each job role more responsive to the changing business environment. Customer focus is key to stimulating higher levels of performance, especially when there is a regular feedback loop built in such that employees understand their impact on the customer experience. Empowerment and accountability should be characteristic criteria for role design, with employees given the right levels of freedom and autonomy with respect to decision-making, and appropriate training and information to ensure that they can be trusted to deliver to the standards required. Information and processes should be synchronised to the line of sight so that people receive the data they need to do their job well, rather than being bombarded with unnecessary bureaucracy.

Similarly, HR can help line managers identify the capabilities required to do the job and design roles that provide employees with 'stretch' yet contain enough 'slack' to be achievable and not compromise the employee's ability to achieve work–life balance. Ideally roles should be designed in a way that reflects employees' different life stage needs, for instance for flexible working. Role design should also take into account the social environment in which work needs to take place. If the employee works from home, thought should be given to how relationships can be maintained, how communication needs can be met, as well as the health and safety aspects of the physical environment.

Line managers should also be encouraged to review workloads to ensure that people are not overloaded, especially if workload distribution across a work unit is uneven. Performance management should recognise contribution and achievement, not simply effort expended. HR should encourage managers to assume that most employees are motivated to do a good job and to measure performance based on the actual outputs of work instead of focusing on the visibility of an individual in the office.

When Ulster Bank attempted to introduce a cultural shift towards more flexible working it initially hit resistance with its nine flexible work options under-utilised. HR set up Project Choice and carried out a survey to find out why. While 80% of staff wanted to work more flexibly, 60% said that the bank's culture did not go far enough to support this in practice. Regular listening groups were set up to explore the issues and identify possible solutions. It seemed that line managers were the main obstacle since many considered flexible working should be the exception rather than the rule. Senior leaders however were convinced by the staff feedback that flexible working would have a positive impact on recruitment and retention, efficiency, engagement and well-being, so leaders were driven to break down the cultural barriers holding the business back. The Choice team set up e-learning modules on what flexible working looks like and how to manage more remotely. The positive benefits of employee voice and flexible working are now coming through (People Management, May 2016).

Job sculpting

'Job sculpting' is an approach that combines individual employee and organisational needs into roles (Butler and Waldroop 1999). The basic idea is that if a job allows an individual to pursue their deeply embedded life interests, i.e. long-held, emotionally driven passions, they are more likely to be happy, experience job and career satisfaction, and stay with the organisation. Job sculpting is the art of matching people to jobs that allow their deeply held life interests to be expressed. This can be challenging because many employees are only dimly aware of their own deeper motivations and also because the approach requires a degree of psychological insight from both a person's line manager and HR.

Job sculpting begins when managers identify individual employees' deeply embedded life interests, ideally by bringing the process directly into the performance review process. Butler and Waldroop found eight deeply embedded typical life interests for people drawn to business careers which they call the 'Big 8':

1 Application of technology – some people are intrigued by the inner working of things and are curious to find better ways to use technology to solve business problems.
2 Quantitative analysis – some people excel at numbers and see mathematical work as the only way to figure out business solutions.
3 Theory development and conceptual thinking – some people enjoy thinking and talking about abstract ideas and may be more interested in the 'why' of strategy than the 'how'.
4 Creative production – some people thrive on newness and are most engaged when they are inventing something original – be it product, service or process.
5 Counselling and mentoring – some people enjoy guiding peers, subordinates and even clients to better performance, and many may be drawn to community service.
6 Managing people and relationships – some people enjoy dealing with people on a day-to-day basis and derive satisfaction from workplace relationships and focus on outcomes.
7 Enterprise control – some people love running things and feel happiest when they have the ultimate decision-making authority.
8 Influence through language and ideas – some people love expressing ideas for the enjoyment that comes from story-telling, negotiating or persuading.

The techniques of job sculpting are as follows:

- Both employees and managers should prepare their thoughts in advance of the conversation. Employees might be asked to write up a couple of paragraphs about their personal views of career satisfaction, what kind of work they love, favourite activities on the job etc. These will form a starting point for the conversation.
- Managers listen carefully when employees describe what they like and dislike about their jobs and ask probing questions to ensure mutual understanding.

- The next work assignments are customised accordingly to begin the process of moving the individual to a role that is more satisfying.

Job sculpting may require initially more sacrifice on the part of the employer, and some parts of the employee's role which have been left behind may need back-filling, which may be a challenge if staffing levels are tight. Nevertheless, in a knowledge economy, talented people tend to stay in jobs they are enjoying and are fundamentally interested in, and even in challenging economic times, that is a prize worth going for.

Reinventing jobs

However, is even the notion of a 'job' out of date? The pace of change is so fast that job descriptions, which create tight boundaries, and where responsibilities can fall between the gaps are not current for more than a few months. In earlier work on this theme, Boudreau and Ramstad (1997) cited Disney as one organisation that had understood the need to look past traditional static job descriptions to think intelligently about which roles were pivotal to delivering business strategy:

> We suspect that … some minority of jobs (perhaps 20%) will require significant changes in the traditional job system to capture and exploit their pivotalness … one implication of effectiveness is that the organization must become more adept at identifying how to conceive and manage these new roles, which will be constantly changing and not easily captured in traditional job descriptions … a maturing talent decision science will undoubtedly mean more pressure for flexibility in traditional job descriptions.

More recently, Jesuthasan and Boudreau (2021) have found that most organisational work systems still remain built upon work as a 'job' and workers as 'jobholders', despite long-standing systems (such as O*Net) that can help combine job elements. Such thinking, they argue, prevents organisations from adequately responding to challenges such as digitalisation, work automation, alternative work arrangements, global economic and social equity, and the future of education and learning.

As technological change gathers speed, almost every job is being reinvented, creating what Deloitte (2017) call the 'augmented workforce'. Schwartz et al. (2017) suggest that one of the new rules for the digital age is to expand our vision of the workforce; think about jobs in the context of tasks that can be automated (or outsourced) and the new role of human skills; and focus even more heavily on the customer experience, employee experience and employment value proposition for people. They recommend using design thinking and the development of journey maps that outline and document the actual work taking place, and the tools, people and information involved in a job.

As organisations reconsider how they design jobs, organise work, and plan for future growth, the question of how each job will change, adapt or disappear has become both a design and a moral decision. What aspects of work do you replace with automated machines? Do you want to 'augment' workers with machines that make work easier and more scalable? What will be the impact of AI and robotics on the customer experience, service quality, and brand? How can humans benefit from robots? Will the 'human-centric' aspects of work be centre-stage? This kind of analysis helps designers understand where tasks can be outsourced and human empathy and skills optimised.

Looking ahead, various studies predict that jobs as we have known them will disappear or be deconstructed into more granular units such as tasks. For example, 79% of executives surveyed by Accenture Technology (2019) agreed the future of work will be based more on specific projects than roles. So as the 'one job, one worker' approach gives way to more fluid and task-based ways of approaching work, the term 'employee' will encompass a broad spectrum spanning internal to external, human to machine, and short-term gigs to full-time work. The 2018 Willis Towers Watson 'Future of Work Survey' reflects this shift and reveals that, while organisations expect to reduce the percentage of full-time employees (FTEs), they also anticipate using more non-FTE talent. These shifts from 'jobs to work' in their company operations have been accelerated by responses to the COVID-19 pandemic, which has underlined the critical importance of enabling agility and flexibility.

Jesuthasan and Boudreau (2021) propose that organisations must understand and anticipate how automation might replace, augment, or reinvent human work and develop a new operating system built on deconstructed jobs and organisational agility. This would assimilate new knowledge flows into the working environment, facilitated by the free flow of information and feedback that are the hallmarks of an agile organisation. As work is deconstructed, new options must be found for sourcing, rewarding, and engaging workers. Such a system must enable leaders to increasingly — and continually — identify and deploy workers based on their skills and capabilities, not their job descriptions. New questions arise about how human well-being is affected when meaningful jobs disappear; conversely, how humans can thrive when demeaning and dangerous jobs are taken over by robots.

Matching skill supply with work demand

New approaches to work, enabled by the technological advances, are transcending the traditional axes of location and time, such as the rise of virtual working, and of 'non-standard' work (e.g. flexible working and zero-hour contracts). During coronavirus lockdowns, for many people, work is now located in their personal spaces — their homes – and there is now flexibility around *time* — the periods when people are actively engaged in work.

How can HR creatively enable dynamic teams to connect in real time? Gratton (2020) argues that to ensure that a hybrid work arrangement works, leaders must understand the upsides and downsides of the axes of hybrid work — where and when people work — and align them so that they feed the energy, focus, coordination and cooperation required to be productive. This means building a context of place and time that accentuates rather than depletes productivity and considering key elements of productivity that are particularly sensitive to these features, such as energy, the need for coordination and cooperation with others. When the contexts of place and time create barriers to cooperation, productivity can suffer.

With respect to time various aspects are in play: *chronological time* (based on a specific schedule, such as nine to five); *synchronous vs. asynchronous time* (the extent to which colleagues' schedules coincide); and *control of time* (the degree of autonomy that can be exercised about work hours). Choices about place and time present trade-offs. When some people are in the office and others are not, there is a risk of a two-tier workforce developing. Working from home can boost energy but may also reduce cooperation. Challenges may arise around communication, inclusion, engagement and collaboration.

In designing new ways of working, Gratton argues, be prepared for the downsides of each model.

Within organisations that are embracing a more flexible future, HR teams have a critical role to play. Every aspect of the employee lifecycle is challenged by hybrid: induction, learning and development, reward and recognition, performance management, well-being, employee engagement, recruitment, communication and voice. Successful implementation of hybrid working will require planning, training, the right technology and communication practices – and the deliberate creation of a supportive culture, lived and breathed by senior managers.

PERFORMANCE MANAGEMENT

Talent management has clear links with performance management. For Jim Collins author of *From Good to Great* (2001), the secret of high performance is getting the 'right people on the bus'. The best companies to work for have a great culture (O'Malley, 2019). So after recruitment, the question is how to manage talent and ensure that talented individuals stay with the organisation? Managing performance is perhaps the *key* responsibility of line managers who must ensure that employees are appropriately focused into roles and developed.

The four key outcomes of performance management are:

- A common understanding of the organisation's goals
- Shared expectations of how individuals can contribute
- Employees with the skill and ability to meet expectations
- Individuals who are fully committed to the aims of the organisation.

To achieve these outcomes, a partnership between line and HR is crucial.

Reflective activity

- What are the main features of a Performance Management system?
- How can HR ensure that such systems fulfil strategically useful outcomes?

Designing effective appraisal and development processes

Arguably the top-down cascading annual appraisal process designed and managed by HR has had its day. Traditional performance appraisals are based on the assumption that people give their best performance as a result of competition. They are an annual event consisting of a backward-looking conversation between manager and employee comparing achievement against objectives. They involve form filling, comparative ratings and forced ranking; and tight links to reward and bonuses that discourage people from being honest about areas where they are struggling. In many organisations, appraisal is viewed as an administrative chore, and the link between personal development and performance is weak, so many employees fail to take personal development seriously.

SHRM (2018) argue that the control orientation approach, in which the organisation decides the goals, targets, objectives and rewards for the employees to achieve, are based on faulty assumptions about human behaviour and motivation, such as the belief that candid performance ratings will motivate employees to improve their performance.

Appraisals, and ratings in particular, are thought to demotivate employees since they trigger a neurological 'fight or flight' response in employees that can stifle engagement, learning and creativity (Mercer 2015) and leave employees feeling insecure as they believe that they are being constantly monitored.

A neuroscience-based framework called the SCARF model (Rock 2008) suggests that five organisational factors have an immense, but often unnoticed, effect on negative human reactions. These factors are:

- Status – Am I considered better or worse than others?
- Certainty – Am I certain my hard work will get me a better rating?
- Autonomy – Do I have any control over what will happen?
- Relatedness – How do I make myself look better than others?
- Fairness – Am I being treated fairly?

When an organisation's perceived level of any SCARF factors is low, people feel threatened and perturbed, which impairs their productivity and willingness to show commitment. Performance reviews arguably perturb feelings in all five ways.

Various studies confirm that a growing number of organisations are looking at alternative approaches to performance management because traditional approaches are no longer seen as effective in achieving the outcomes described above. For example, 95% of managers were dissatisfied with their performance management systems (CEB); 48% were evaluating or planning to review their performance management (Mercer Snapshot Survey 2015); 48% reported the performance management system needs further work to be effective (Mercer 2013); just 3% reported the performance management system delivered exceptional value (Mercer 2013).

The emerging practices in new performance management systems are based on a philosophy of coaching and supporting people to give of their best. They are typified by more frequent, forward-looking and development-focused feedback, with adjustments to, or elimination of traditional ratings. Microsoft had previously used a stack-ranking system to rank employees directly against their peers. The company found that this practice resulted in unhealthy competition; so to drive greater collaboration, they moved to a system of ongoing feedback (in Warren 2013). Another pioneer of new approaches, Deloitte, decided to get better value from the process having concluded that their review-time added up to 2 million hours per year: 'We wondered if we could somehow shift our investment of time from talking to ourselves about ratings to talking to our people about their performance and careers' (in Buckingham and Goodall 2015).

Goal setting

It is still important to agree performance expectations. SMART goals (specific, measurable, achievable, relevant and time-bound) are about both results and behaviours, with competencies defining desired behaviours by level. Expectations at individual level should be aligned with the overall organisation's strategic goals and vision through an appropriate goal cascade. In Agile, alignment to organisational goals is achieving by linking up instead of cascading down.

Goals should have shorter rather than longer timelines; it is difficult for long-term goals to be specific enough. Team-centric goals should be aligned but also localised. In agile settings, flexible goal setting (often called Real-Time Performance Measurement and

Feedback) allows for goal format and timing to be tailored to the work and arises from ongoing feedback conversations. 'Objectives and Key Results' (OKRs) is a collaborative goal-setting tool used by agile teams and individuals to set challenging, ambitious goals with measurable results. Measures should be part of the goal as indicators of quality, quantity and/or timeliness.

To make goal setting a collaborative process, employees and managers should discuss why goals are important, how they relate to higher-level organisational priorities and how they connect to the employee's interests and personal values. Goals work best when they are personally meaningful to the individual, regardless of whether they are set by the employee or manager (SHRM 2018). Goals should be limited to three to five so that each goal receives attention and focus and also moderately challenging so accomplishing the goal should take effort but not feel impossible. Employees should believe that it is within their power to achieve the goal and that their efforts, not external factors, will determine success or failure, so managers must ensure employees have the knowledge, tools and resources necessary to meet their goals. When goals are aspirational, yet attainable, and employees know specifically what they will be held accountable for, they are more likely to succeed.

Measuring and evaluating performance

The old management dictum 'if you can't measure it, you can't manage it' is starting to be turned on its head. While measures undoubtedly send strong symbolic messages about what is valued, the question of what is being measured and therefore considered important is increasingly being called into question. Success criteria should be those that make a (positive) difference to the organisation. Targets need to be set for the deliverables that are required as well as for how the deliverables are to be achieved.

Balance is needed. If measures are set around 'soft' targets such as behaviours, these need to be taken seriously or employees will soon understand that only performance with direct impact on the bottom-line counts. Many organizations use 360-degree feedback processes as part of performance management, culture change initiatives and senior management development. While some organisations claim that the feedback is incorporated into decisions about pay, more often pay relates entirely to bottom line performance with the achievement of other 'soft' behavioural targets ignored. Dorsey and Mueller-Hanson (2018) advocate an evidence-based approach in order to avoid neglecting important contributions.

Towards a coaching model

Companies such as Motorola, Medtronic, Spotify, Netflix, Deloitte, Accenture and Adobe have now adopted such approaches, using regular check-ins rather than the annual review. The new approaches may not work everywhere so it is helpful to take an iterative approach to change, piloting new processes with small groups and making improvements based on lessons learned. A 'half-way house' between traditional and new approaches involves retaining ratings but putting the emphasis on streamlining administrative requirements and eliminating unnecessary documentation. So rather than requiring extensive narrative documentation to justify ratings, instead provide checklists and other simple tools to make documentation easier for every employee.

One 'half-way house' approach is the competency-based performance management system at Bayer Pharma's R & D division. The competencies on which the scheme is based were derived from the overall company vision and the strategy for R & D. The performance management scheme is very future-oriented, rather than being simply a review of past performance. The R & D system puts individuals in control of their own performance and development since the individual is expected to take the lead when meeting with their boss to review performance. The Annual Performance Review assesses performance against last year's objectives and a competency assessment identifies areas of development which may have had an impact on performance. The individual prepares examples of work to refer to and is responsible for documenting the discussion. The manager acts as facilitator. Several weeks later a Development Review assesses possible development priorities from the organisation's perspective. The individual identifies their own personal development priorities in the light of their aspirations and a detailed development plan addresses both sets of needs.

A financial services organisation, on the way to developing a coaching culture, translated its strategic imperative to achieve loyal and satisfied customers into key performance indicators in which all business units and managers are expected to deliver results. These include leadership, management of process quality, operational results and customer focus and satisfaction. Each of these is supported by behavioural dimensions, together with resources to help people develop effectiveness in these results areas. The HR team created a list of ways of developing these behaviours, based on the work of the Center for Creative Leadership. They include suggestions such as:

- Take part in a task force on a pressing business problem
- Plan an off-site meeting, conference, convention
- Integrate systems across units
- Business trip to a foreign country

Appraisal discussions take place annually, while objective-setting and development planning are separate processes which are carried out more frequently.

Adobe was an early adopter of a coaching-based approach in 2011 when Adobe's HR team crowdsourced internal feedback and scrapped their rating system after consistent engagement survey results identified it as an area in need of change. Employees wanted more regular feedback – not just once a year. Members of the senior team were asked to set an example by engaging in regular feedback and holding managers accountable for engaging in feedback with their employees.

Instead of filling out endless forms, employees and managers engage in regular 'Check-in' discussions to set expectations and commit to them in writing – using a sheet of paper, cloud-based document, or any other tool with which they were comfortable. 'Check-ins' are about goals, careers and development. Targeted sessions equipped managers and employees for the new Check-in approach. Managers for instance explored how to set expectations more effectively and provide more impactful feedback, shifting from being critical judges to helpful coaches (Mercer 2016).

To be successful in the coaching model, managers need to establish trust, believe in employees' growth potential, create a flexible, humane work climate where there is investment in people and stay committed to the process over time in order to create a sustained culture of high performance. For the process to be motivating for those involved, managers and employees need a relationship in which discussing performance is not seen as a burden or a threat. To ensure managers make time to appraise people's performance well, team supervisors should receive basic training on providing a minimum of continuous feedback that is honest, specific, strengths-oriented and focused on behaviours rather than on personal characteristics. Feedback is best delivered in a timely manner and as part of a two-way dialogue. It comes from a credible source who knows the recipient's work and can provide useful insights to help the individual improve and identify strengths.

To broaden the dialogue beyond manager and employee and gain a more holistic view into areas of progress and/or development, some companies crowdsource feedback, with HR adding value by automating feedback collection, or making performance reviews portable via block chain. Employees and managers can identify people to provide feedback from all directions (e.g. peers, managers, direct reports) and employees can self-select to provide feedback to a colleague (anonymously, privately or publicly). This is especially appropriate with project-based teams, where management changes from project to project. To encourage more teamwork, some companies utilise a social approach to gathering feedback via online and/or mobile platforms. The continual integration of peer-sourced feedback can allow for more frequent recognition and rewards, leading to increased morale and retention. It is also applicable for all levels of the workforce (i.e. does not need to be reserved for higher-level employees) so can result in increased personal accountability and broader distribution of performance management ownership (Mercer 2015).

In the case of a total system redesign, a clear statement of purpose and guiding principles (starting with the end in mind) are needed that can be used to evaluate proposed interventions or processes. In the agile world, rather than designing a system in its entirety, components of the system are launched as early as possible, and through ongoing testing, evaluation and customer feedback the offering is shaped and reshaped. So a performance management system rollout should include the bare minimum of rules and processes needed to achieve the desired result, with training plans reshaped as user expectations and needs change. Only new rules or processes that have a demonstrable positive return on investment should be added.

Whichever approach is adopted, by designing user-friendly performance development approaches which focus both on the current position and are also future focused, HR gives employees a strong message about the value they bring to the organisation and prepares them for changing work demands.

I am very grateful to Janice Semper, GE Culture Leader and Crotonville Executive Learning Leader for the following case study.

Case: performance development (PD) in GE

GE aims to be an agile organisation and uses its FastWorks platform for creating products and bringing them to market. This is a successor in many ways to Six Sigma and borrows from agile techniques to a large extent. GE's cultural focus on simplification is helping employees to focus as well as helping the company to operate faster, compete more vigorously, reduce costs and improve quality (Semper 2017). At the heart of the cultural shift are GE's Beliefs which were articulated through a crowdsourcing process and reflect the nature of the changes taking place within this huge company. These are expressed in five simple statements focused on reducing complexity, delivering fast, better solutions to customers:

- Customers determine our success
- Stay lean to go fast
- Learn and adapt to win

- Empower and inspire each other
- Deliver results in an uncertain world

Essentially, the GE Beliefs help leaders and employees operationalise the strategy since they bring simplification to life. When everything is changing all round, these act as a central reference point (the 'North Star'), and hub for new behaviours and mindsets while other aspects of the company's ecosystem – all the things that influence culture – are gradually rewired for agility. They play a large role in leadership development and are also used to change how GE recruits, manages and leads, and how its people are evaluated, developed and rewarded.

The philosophy of continuous improvement is reflected in the new approach to performance management. While the performance review process for which GE has long been well known (often referred to as 'rank and yank') worked well for GE in times gone by, by 2015 it was no longer deemed to deliver for the business in the twenty-first century, or for GE's younger workforce who wanted more real-time feedback. There was real institutional will from the top to see through a new approach which embeds the philosophy of continuous improvement and depends on continuous dialogue and shared accountability. The performance review process was redesigned to support FastWorks and help people to live the GE Beliefs.

In true agile manner, GE launched a two-year pilot in 2015, with about 87,000 employees in different groups, of different sizes and industries. The HR group was one of the first to adopt it, including the experiment with no numerical ratings. Today, rather than targeting annual goals, managers emphasise shorter-term 'priorities'. The emphasis is on agility, continuous discussions and customer outcomes, on helping employees continuously adapt and channel their efforts to the most important customer needs.

Essentially, the approach depends on continuous dialogue and shared accountability. The goal is to promote frequent, informal and meaningful conversations (GE calls them 'touchpoints') between managers, individuals and teams about performance and development where priorities based on customer needs are set or updated. Touchpoints allow managers and employees to discuss progress toward those priorities and note what was discussed, committed to, and resolved. Two basic questions are revisited: What am I doing that I should keep doing? and What am I doing that I should change? The focus is on continuous improvement and on building the workforce the organisation needs to be competitive both today and in the future.

Of course, few managers find the process of giving constructive, critical feedback easy, and done badly, such feedback can damage both employee morale and relationships. To socialise in a more effective approach to giving and receiving feedback so that it becomes more acceptable, useful and actionable by the recipient, the language of feedback has been more intentionally connected to continuous improvement. For instance, rather than talking of 'strengths and weaknesses' which can follow an individual long past the point of applicability, managers are encouraged to use more 'free form' constructive feedback. The focus is on contributions and impact within the context of current priorities; the behaviours employees may want to 'continue' doing and forward-looking actions, as well as on changes they may want to 'consider' making and for which they may require coaching. With this new positive vocabulary, the emphasis is on development and coaching.

Since GE aims to work more horizontally, peers too are encouraged to give each other feedback on an ongoing basis, especially those working in self-directed teams. Employees can give or request feedback at any point through a feature called 'insights', which is not limited to their immediate manager, or even their division, but can come from anyone in an employee's network. The focus is on contributions and impact within the context of current priorities.

To support the new approach, a smartphone app, called 'PD@GE' for 'performance development at GE', developed internally, accepts voice and text inputs, attached documents, even handwritten notes. The app can provide summaries on command, through typed notes, photographs of a notepad or even voice recordings. The immediacy of the feedback makes it relevant and potentially actionable.

Rethinking the role of the manager

Managers still have an annual year-end summary conversation with employees where they look back at the year and set goals, but these are more meaningful and future-focused – and less over-loaded with expectations than the formal review the company is replacing because they are simply part of an ongoing dialogue. Thanks to the new performance development approach, the manager and employee can now draw upon a much richer set of data regarding an employee's unique contributions and impact throughout the year. A summary document, which both parties finalize and submit together, reflects on the impact achieved and provides a look ahead.

The learning and development (L&D) contribution

Of course, the new performance development approach makes it incumbent on managers to act as coach to their team members. Consequently, one of the change work streams explored how to upskill and build coaching competency within the population 38,000 people leaders, many of whom have long-service histories within GE.

GE recognises that some managers may find shifting to a more coaching and empowering style of management difficult. Some people leaders will have to unlearn certain behaviours so that they can become coaches who can effectively engage in dialogue with their teams. A global training programme, piloted in 2017, was rolled out to all 38,000 people managers in GE. This training is deliberately geared towards reinforcing the behavioural shifts reflected in the new Personal Development (PD) approach. This helps managers develop new skills needed to have dialogues with team members, set a vision for the team and go forward together; run empowering team meetings and one-to-one sessions; coach people and help teams take accountability for their work; and also know how to report up to their own managers; and break some old habits.

Of course, not all managers will be able to make the shift from managing task to becoming an empowering leader. The intention is to help such managers move to roles where they can become instead great individual contributors. With the fluidity possible in GE, there are many opportunities for talented people to find their niche, work on things they feel passionate about and thrive in the right roles. The new approach at GE encourages flexibility and agility. It's about building a culture of a better tomorrow, in keeping with the legacy of continuous improvement.

Helping managers deal with poor performance

In some organisations, poor performance is handled by simply passing on the underperformer to another department. Sometimes, managers find difficulty in confronting aspects of poor performance because they lack confidence in their ability to handle the conflict which might arise. Similarly, some managers find it hard to delegate, and others are so thinly stretched that there is no one to whom they can delegate. Some managers are managing teams of contractors rather than full-time or permanent employees. HR needs to be able to support managers in understanding how they can achieve high standards with slim resources. They can help establish networks of peer coaches amongst line managers, coach managers directly and provide 'rehearsal' opportunities for difficult conversations, help managers think through the options available to them, as well as advise on disciplinary procedure as appropriate.

Reflective activity

In your organisation, how effectively is individual and team performance managed??

- Are business goals and individual objectives aligned?
- How honest is communication about performance?
- How are poor performers dealt with?

REWARD

When companies must compete for talent and expertise, rewards play an important role in both the recruitment of new talent and retention of long serving employees who have difficult-to-source tacit knowledge in their field of expertise. Unless reward is taken into account, increasing investment in talent management does little to retain key individuals.

The need to revise reward strategies

In times gone by, when organisations had relatively stable hierarchical structures, jobs were defined and allocated according to a clear set of job grades, each of which had a salary range. Job evaluation was used to decide how much each job was worth in terms of its contribution to the organisation. The majority of staff would be on a fixed pay arrangement and pay was usually linked with seniority and subject to almost automatic increases regardless of performance. Of course, this made managing the salary pot relatively straightforward.

However, as organisations' needs changed, a system that reinforced the status quo was increasingly out of step with the need for greater and more flexible performance outputs from employees. In attempting to move towards a performance culture, many organisations introduced performance-related pay schemes which are intended to reflect performance in the job more than the job grade itself. Yet a large proportion of UK companies have still not developed reward schemes that link pay and benefits to a team's performance or their contribution to corporate values. Instead, paying market rates remains the preferred model for many organisations alongside schemes that recognise individual short-term performance but not long-term development.

In these changing times, reward schemes quickly become sources of employee discontent. In organisations that have delayered significantly, traditional job evaluation-based pay structures seem outdated and inappropriate. Reward systems should help people feel a real sense of progression, or at least not demotivate employees when promotion opportunities are fewer. Yet with flatter structures, the reduced number of management levels usually means that people's job responsibilities have grown way beyond the original job description. Instead of vertical promotion, organisations actively promote the idea of lateral careers. However, fixed grading schemes often deter people from making 'sideways' moves since they may actually lose pay in the bargain.

While many HR professionals are keenly aware of the need to reshape reward strategies, according to Jeffrey Pfeffer (1998), 'The successful investment in new reward practices involves a great deal of effort, commitment and expertise. And it is probably the most difficult task facing HR managers'. Pfeffer suggests that there is no such thing as a perfect pay system, but that good systems are about customisation and tailoring, rather than off-the-shelf solutions.

Broadly speaking, any reward system should reinforce the behaviours needed to drive skilled performance and organisational success in the short and medium term. Rewards can motivate employees to grow and develop their potential, thereby increasing the quality of efforts contributed towards the company. Reward systems are integral to aligning the efforts of the employees with the culture, objectives and philosophies of the company. Feeling fairly rewarded allows employees to identify themselves with the company and strengthens their loyalty and commitment towards the company and its objectives (Sheppard and Sherman 1998).

Line of sight

Aspirational corporate values statements tend to have little impact on employee behaviour without reinforcement. What is really valued in an organisation is most evident in management behaviour and HR practices, especially reward systems. Of course, there should be a direct line of sight for employees between the organisation's goals and strategy, the individual's role, how well they perform in their role and reward. Reward is perhaps the HR practice that most clearly represents this line of sight to employees, both symbolically and practically, teaching what is really required of them and how much they are valued.

In developing reward strategies that respond to business drivers some basic questions need to be answered. What, for instance, are the critical roles, tasks, skills which should be rewarded? What are the new working practices that the organisation wishes to encourage? Will teamworking be more critical to achieving business goals than individual performance? Is having one system the only way of thinking about a revised system?

For example, if the business is following an innovation-led strategy, the thrust of reward policy should be a mix of individual and collective rewards; the use of 'soft' performance measures, periodically monitored; emphasis on medium-term performance; use of learning and personal growth as 'soft' rewards'; broad-banded and flexible pay structure. For a cost-reduction strategy the reward thrust should be on individual rewards; short-term performance; with a high proportion of earnings at risk and use of 'hard' measures, frequently monitored. (Source: Professor Stephen Bevan, Institute for Employment Studies).

The symbolic power of reward systems

Reward schemes are a powerful symbolic means of teaching employees what is actually valued in the organisation, as well as what is not. Typically, this is achieved by incentivising particular types of performance, such as increased sales, or by penalising employees deemed to be underperforming. Rewards therefore have a greater impact on employee attitudes and behaviour than corporate rhetoric or values statements which encourage teamworking, for example. So if the organisation encourages teamwork but continues to award significant bonuses for individual achievement alone, teamwork is less likely to be taken seriously.

The financial package and various benefits increasingly act as 'lure' factors to attract new recruits or 'golden handcuffs' for existing employees. Equity participation can be helpful in this respect, with various forms of gainsharing and broad-based stock plans being formulated to increase employees' sense of ownership of what they do. While this works fine when the value of shares is increasing, the depressing effect of a drop in share prices reduces the retention value of such schemes, especially as they are often matched or exceeded by other companies' offers. Sometimes too the value of even highly expensive benefits is not recognised by employees if they compare packages on the basis of salary alone.

In theory, reward schemes should be motivating, offering appropriate incentives for, and recognition of, desired performance. Whether schemes that focus exclusively on the financial aspects of reward achieve this aim is debatable. While money is often thought to be a motivator, and it certainly appears to be for some people, at least at some stages of their career, Herzberg's (1966) well-known motivation theory suggests that money is just as likely to demotivate. Take the example of someone who is told by their manager that they are going to get a 10% pay rise in recognition of superb performance. The employee will no doubt be very pleased unless he or she finds that other members of the team are going to get a 15% pay rise. This is where the principle of equity – or at least what feels fair – becomes paramount to employees. Similarly, once the employee has grown used to a level of pay, no matter how large the initial rise, money in itself ceases to be motivating, according to Herzberg. Losing money, on the other hand, continues to be universally demotivating.

Many people's jobs have been effectively downgraded thanks to automation, as have their pay and benefits. Many final salary pension schemes have been replaced by salary-based schemes, money purchase schemes. However, some employers differentiate themselves by maintaining their commitment to final salary pensions. At the Royal Bank of Scotland (RBS), for example, benefits include flexible working hours, a final salary pension, share options and profit-related pay.

The 'running sore' effect of such organisational decisions can cause people to see themselves as victims. Almost inevitably, loyalty to the organisation suffers as a result. Changing reward arrangements therefore is likely to be as much a source of concern for the organisation as it is for employees.

Reward and employee segmentation

Reward schemes should meet the organisation's needs both for managing its pay bill and ensuring that it is getting good performance from its employees. They must also be designed to meet employees' needs to be appropriately recompensed for their efforts. The dynamic link between performance and reward has been much debated and if employees are to feel fairly treated, pay needs to be competitive, and benefits should reflect what matters to different segments of the employee population (Heneman 2002). There should be incentives for higher performance, and the opportunity for share ownership. Recognition awards are also important in ensuring that employees feel their work is being noticed and valued.

When it comes to designing reward systems from the employee perspective, it is clear that 'one size' does not 'fit all'. Employee segmentation is useful in understanding the relative importance of certain employee segments, as defined by the nature and criticality of their work to the organisation's success and the relative scarcity of their skills. Those key employees should also be defined by their needs, life cycle stages, aspirations and expectations. Reward and other HR processes should then be designed to meet the needs as far as possible of key segments of the workforce, without unduly disfavouring others.

Reward options and processes

Since it is recognised that both employee inputs and outputs are different from in the past, rewards must adapt to meet both employee and business needs.

Broad banding

To make job enrichment and lateral moves easier many organisations use broad banding, where a small number of wide salary bands encompasses many varied roles. However, the process of introducing broad bands can be difficult. Increasingly, 'job families', or 'professional communities', are being added to broad bands to ensure market fit and relevance to employees. These approaches allow different professional and business groups to be rewarded differently according to market conditions.

For the job family system to work, the required capabilities are established and combined into roles. The key performance measures are then directly cascaded from the measures of business performance. The focus is on 'total pay', which includes both benefits and pay as well as taking into account employees' perception of the package. The notion of individual value and capability is crucial, with increased value reflected in earnings.

Competence-based pay

Some organisations are experimenting with competence-based pay (CBP), also known as knowledge- or skills-based pay that reflects the need to acquire new skills and knowledge so as to enable organisations to meet the new market challenges. CBP works on the basis of rewarding the skills an individual possesses, acquires and actually uses. Typically, completion of a training unit relating to a particular competency or skills unit results in a pay increase. The downside of such schemes is that they can be very complex. The emphasis on individual competence can be at odds with sought-after cross-organisational business goals such as teamworking and quality.

Equal pay

Pay is an ongoing source of inequality. Since 2017, UK employers who have a headcount of 250 or more must comply with regulations on gender pay gap reporting. In 2020, the gender pay gap among all employees was 15.5%. Ethnicity pay gap reporting is not yet a legal requirement. PwC's 2021 voluntary disclosure of ethnicity pay gap statistics shows that their black staff are paid an average of 40.9% less than their white colleagues. PwC also published targets to increase the number of women and people from ethnic minorities in senior roles by 2025. The firm wants 15% of partners to be from ethnic minorities and 30% to be women by 2025. PwC's gender pay gap decreased from 14.7% in 2019 to 11.6% for 2020 (O' Dwyer 2021).

Public vs private sector pay

It used to be thought that since public sector pay lags behind the private sector, the index-linked pensions representing financial security in old age were a compensation for lower lifetime earnings. Perhaps for that reason, pensions reform is progressing slowly in the public sector and final salary pension schemes for existing employees have largely survived the reform process to date. In turbulent economic times, public sector pay may exceed much comparable private sector pay. A key challenge is the question of pay parity across sectors when public, private and not-for-profit organisations work in partnership to deliver performance outcomes. The question will be how to develop cross-sector reward strategies to avoid significant anomalies.

Performance-related pay

Incentive schemes and performance-related pay continue to provoke debate. While some believe fixed pay schemes to be archaic, others find variable pay schemes problematic. Performance-related pay is now commonplace in private and public sectors and not-for-profit organisations, even for junior roles whose jobholders may have only small, indirect effects on overall organisational performance. Such schemes need to be responsive to the business drivers, the changing technology, the new skills required and the fact that to be successful in a new environment, people need to do different things.

Ironically, at a time when performance-related pay has become 'the norm', it is being called into question – is it the panacea for encouraging excellence that the theorists thought would be the case? The effectiveness of performance-based pay remains hotly contested. Research by Scholtes (1995) and SHRM (2018) lists various reasons why performance-based reward, recognition and incentive systems generally do not work well:

- The links between extrinsic rewards and employee motivation are not always direct. External rewards can sometimes decrease internal motivation, creativity and performance and set up internal competition and can undermine teamwork and cooperation.
- Annual raises are typically on the scale of 2–5%, thus providing little opportunity to differentiate performance or to increase what extrinsic motivation is present. They create cynics and losers.
- Due to ratings inflation and idiosyncratic rating patterns, most real-world rating systems have insufficient variance to support decision-making. They often reward those who are lucky and miss out those who are unlucky. Even when they are used, ratings are often an intermediary in actual decision-making. Managers are often better off using rank-order priorities against job-relevant criteria and a set budget.
- In many pay-for-performance schemes, linkages to organisational, unit or employee goals are hazy at best. There are no data to show long-term benefits. Thus, demonstrating bottom-line value for such systems often falls short.

This highlights the danger that with today's increased spans of control, variable pay risks becoming a proxy for performance management. The more performance is rewarded through variable pay, or if the bonus is small, the greater the disappointment of the individual who feels that his or her talents have not been recognised. For example, the managing director of a small consultancy decided to introduce a new form of performance-related pay which singled out the achievement of a number of business goals for special reward. Junior staff had relatively less access to the resources needed to achieve these targets. Nevertheless, one junior consultant put in a major effort to achieve the targets and succeeded in achieving the performance threshold required for a bonus. Her reward turned out to be £10, accompanied by a letter from her boss encouraging her to try harder next year! Not surprisingly, the consultant decided to test her fortunes elsewhere.

Pay for performance works best when organisations can isolate, measure and clearly link employee effort to outcomes (e.g. individualised sales or production roles). When substantial monetary rewards are used, they are frequently tied to concrete outcomes/accomplishments (e.g. profit sharing). To create conditions that promote pay-for-performance success, SHRM (2018) recommends that organisations should focus on the following:

- Reward contributions that truly add value to the organisation's mission or bottom line;
- Ensure that employees have line of sight between their inputs and rewards and sufficient personal control over rewarded outcomes;
- Communicate aspects of the reward system clearly and consistently, in line with effective implementation strategies;
- Evaluate pay-for-performance systems over time, assessing both intended and possible unintended consequences.

More flexible approaches to reward

This makes responding to the question of how modern performance management systems can be linked to pay or 'pay for performance', even more difficult, particularly in cases in which simplified or 'ratingless' systems are used (in Deloitte 2015, 90–91). As CIPD Pay and Benefits surveys have reported, many employers are revising pay mechanisms to reflect the broad shifts in the competitive marketplace. So as organisations increasingly focus their business strategies on customer needs, many are reorganising around teamwork, broader roles and non-traditional work arrangements in order to develop more flexible, innovative products and services.

Reward systems need to be flexible as well as integrated, with job grading, performance assessment, reward and development systems linked up with future opportunities. At the same time, no system can allow its costs to escalate out of control. The challenge therefore is to find a flexible and tailored alternative, or set of alternatives, which allows for a better match between organisational needs and constraints and employee needs and aspirations.

Many organisations are experimenting with more flexible packages, which include elements of variable pay, linked to job performance, competence, skills development and desired team and leadership behaviours. The new systems include a greater element of discretion for the line manager, feedback processes and a degree of individual choice in benefits. The area of voluntary benefits presents many opportunities for this type of personalisation and can help to meet the unmet needs of a diverse, multigenerational and multicultural workforce (CIPD, 2014).

What do employees want?

Thanks to HR analytics, organisations are increasingly able to personalise and enhance their value proposition to workers. For many employees, permanent employment and career progression are being replaced by various forms of flexible work arrangement including fixed-term contract working, part-time and temporary arrangements. In a period of unprecedented wage stagnation (OECD 2018), pay may have replaced promotion as representing career progress for many employees. Increasingly employees want portable benefits that they can take with them if their role disappears. The past few years has seen the introduction of a range of extrinsic rewards such as:

- Profit (gain) sharing
- Flexible benefits
- Bonuses payable in terms of extra leave rather than pay
- Bonuses payable towards prestigious qualifications
- Long-term incentives (LTIs)
- Deferred incentives
- Extending private health schemes to all employees and their families
- Longer holidays
- Sponsored holidays
- 'Free' family holidays in company-owned cottages
- Enhanced early retirement

Conversely, there seems to be a growing use of long-term incentives (LTIs) and share ownership. The practice of retaining key people through the use of incentives has long been popular in the United States. In the United Kingdom and other parts of Europe where the incidence of such schemes is much lower, various multinational companies such as Shell and Total are extending these incentive schemes to European senior employees. Employee share ownership appears to be also on the increase. Companies such as Procter and Gamble are giving all employees share options to encourage continued commitment to the organisation.

What is becoming more apparent is that money is not everything when it comes to attracting and retaining people. Research suggests that intrinsic motivators such as the chance to do something worthwhile, to have a development stretch, to increase job satisfaction are all as important as the financial package and represent 'psychological' rewards. Many people want to feel that their skills and contribution have been recognised by others, especially their boss.

Rewards such as having opportunities for learning and growth, being part of a successful, winning team, having a valuable role and working in a feel-good climate seem to be the sort of factors which influence people's decisions about staying or leaving. People will often put up with relatively poor pay for a time as long as these other factors are right. Similarly, in a buyer's market, the 'triple bottom-line' factors, i.e. how the business is performing, its ethical and environmental stance and its commitment to being socially responsible are increasingly becoming key factors in attracting potential recruits. However if these non-financial rewards are not working, employees typically negotiate hard about pay and benefits, which can be costlier in the long run. And Glassdoor research (Chamberlain, 2018) suggests that wage growth is far from even across many sectors and job types, creating both 'winners' and 'losers' even within the same company.

That's not to say that financial reward packages are unimportant – quite the contrary. Nor am I implying that non-financial rewards have no costs attached to them. Investment may be needed to apply policies such as work/life balance or ethical trading more rigorously, training managers, offering employees development and a greater chance of participation. If reward packages are to help organisation's win the competition for talent, they need to be strategic, closely linked to business objectives and also be customised. The most effective reward packages meet both individual and organisational needs as closely as possible, have flexibility built into them and have obvious benefits for all concerned.

Revising reward schemes for agility

Revising a compensation system to reflect agile working performance raises fundamental questions for HR: What should be rewarded? Should agile working be rewarded differently? As Cappelli and Tavis (2018) point out, a simple adaptation to agile work, seen in retail companies such as Macy's, is to use spot bonuses to recognise contributions when they happen rather than rely solely on end-of-year salary increases. Instant rewards reinforce instant feedback in a powerful way. Annual merit-based raises are less effective, because too much time goes by.

Current reward practice tends to focus on the individual – their qualifications, experience and unique performance – while agile principles emphasise different attributes, such as collaboration, learning and collective intelligence, and performance achieved by the team above the individual. Typically, problems can occur when work processes are supposed to be underpinned by teamwork, yet only individual bottom-line performance is taken into account when determining pay. It is difficult to foster team spirit if individuals are concentrating on promotion. Johnson et al. (2019) report on three shifts underway in reward policy. These are: agile working having its own aligned reward arrangements; team reward; and a re-examination of differentiated individual rewards.

Team reward

How can reward be used to motivate the behaviour change required of agile teams? Team-based schemes link pay to team performance or the achievement of agreed team objectives. The CIPD found that team pay works best for stand-alone teams that have agreed targets and standards, autonomy, are composed of people whose work is interdependent, are stable, well established and make good use of complementary skills.

One of the drawbacks of the wider spread of team pay is that every scheme is unique, so it is not possible to simply adopt practice from other organisations. Nor are such schemes easy to design or manage. In practical terms, who makes reward decisions for the individual? The team? What happens when colleagues leave agile teams and return to their previous divisions? Do they revert to the prior reward policy? What other elements of the value proposition may be appropriate, such as opportunities for advancement?

Nevertheless, three basic elements of a team-based reward package (in the form of cash or shares assuming that the base pay is right) are:

- Individual, i.e. the basic salary but varied in relation to performance or skills/ competence
- Team – related to the achievement of team targets
- Organisational – related to business performance measured as profit or added value.

Some incentive schemes couple team and individual bonuses while others flatten pay differentials and put little emphasis on incentives. Johnson et al. (2019) describe a client who is testing a dual approach, where the team's achievement is rewarded by assigning part of the reward equally to all members of the squad, while the other part is assigned according to the individual's role in a tribe (business unit) or chapter (function) using a peer recognition system.

Transparency

The question of what constitutes performance continues to be debated. Since reward is one of the most visible signs of the value proposition or 'contract' between employers and employees, it is important that every aspect of the pay system should be transparent, including what is being rewarded.

Many organisations want people to be willing to take on broader responsibilities, learn new skills and develop wider competencies. Organisations are demanding more from their staff, not only in terms of 'output', in other words, performance against agreed targets, but also in terms of 'input' or how targets have been accomplished. Inputs include the new skills which people are required to use in their jobs and the cultural targets in terms of attitudes and behaviours which the organisation wants to encourage. In addition, technology is bringing about a more fundamental change to the way work is carried out, shifting from directive tasks to process-driven activities. Typically, new areas of incentivisation include behavioural areas such as making creative suggestions, receiving positive feedback from customers, teamworking and demonstrating leadership. To support this approach there is usually an emphasis on competencies and various feedback mechanisms are used.

This raises tricky questions such as: how clear is 'transparent'? Should the pay system reward only the outputs of individual performance, or how these are achieved as well? In some organisations only outputs are assessed for bonus purposes while in others, inputs are also taken into account. Should individual 'stars' who have shone thanks to help from their team be singled out? Should higher levels of skill be reflected in performance, or should developing and applying new skills, albeit at a more basic level, be incentivised? Simply unpacking the diverse aspects of behaviour, skills and experience which lead to the sorts of performance organisations require can be complex.

Flexible benefits

Benefits are a vital part of the package for employers who are looking to recruit and retain the best people. For 60% of respondents in Glassdoor's 2015 Employment Confidence

Survey, benefits and 'perks' are important in considering whether to accept a job offer. Indeed, 80% of employees would choose additional benefits over a pay raise. Another survey found that 89% of people in the US value additional benefits as much as pay (Jones 2017).

Companies are more likely to attract and retain the best talent if they offer people choice and add attractive financial incentives and goodwill gestures that reward loyalty, learning and development, like tuition reimbursement and student loan repayments (Friedman 2018). The important thing is to find out what people want, how they perceive their benefits and whether these are valued. This is a growing trend towards benefits personalisation such as offering autonomous working and flexibility, parental leave and unlimited time-off/unplug policies to cultivate well-being and improved lifestyle.

Introducing and operating a flexible benefits scheme requires sophisticated software. However, it should allow for a closer matching of individual needs as they change over time with the organisation's goals. Some pundits advise adjusting one or two benefits, rather than a complete scheme. Some US companies, such as Lotus Development and Apple Computers, are now extending benefits to domestic partners as well as spouses. In the United Kingdom, Cable and Wireless has developed a cafeteria-style benefits system that includes pensions, healthcare, childcare vouchers, annual leave, life cover and dental insurance for employees and their partners. Their HR team emphasises the importance of good communication about the nature of the scheme. At Cancer Research UK, employees have online access to self-service benefits from which they can choose options to the value of their entitlement.

Total rewards

The notion of total rewards brings a holistic, people-centric perspective to the value exchange between workers and the organisation. Zingheim and Schuster (2007) argue that by understanding how extrinsic rewards such as pay sit alongside sources of deeper motivation, such as the opportunity for growth, and by adopting a total reward philosophy, designers of reward processes can more obviously meet employee needs to be treated fairly, and organisational needs for a manageable pay bill. They suggest that six key principles should underpin the approach:

1 Create a positive and natural reward experience
2 Align rewards with business goals to create a win–win partnership
3 Extend people's line of sight
4 Integrate rewards
5 Reward ongoing value (i.e. skills, consistent performance and value relative to the market) with base pay
6 Reward results with variable pay

They describe four categories of tangible and intangible reward which make up Total Rewards:

1. *Individual growth* – workers must understand and enjoy their work and have the opportunity to contribute to a thriving organisation. Reflected in:
   • A challenging role
   • Investment in people
   • Development and training

- Performance management
- Career enhancement

Employees should feel challenged in their day-to-day role, with a support network such as mentors and teammates to fall back on if they require further help. The opportunity to develop and progress makes a position much more rewarding. Giving employees access to qualifications, working on PDPs, and showing routes for progression makes for a more satisfying role.

2. *A compelling future* – workers seek a strong sense of purpose. They need to understand and support the direction of the organisation even if their relationship is occasional and more irregular than that of a full-time employee. Reflected in:
   - Vision and values
   - Company growth and success
   - Company image and reputation
   - Stakeholdership
   - Win – win over time
3. *Positive workplace* – an organisation must have an inclusive culture that supports diverse talent across the spectrum of relationships as well as leaders who inspire workers to make a difference. Reflected in:
   - People focus
   - Leadership
   - Colleagues
   - Work itself
   - Involvement
   - Trust and commitment
   - Open communication

The employee experience can be greatly improved by a positive working environment (CLC, 2012). Enhancing the workspace with coffee machines, artwork, greenery, snacks, standing desks and other improvements can seem rewarding for employees.

Strategies to build an open culture are part of HR a long-term strategy. Employees must feel comfortable raising issues of concern and should be involved in decisions about the way work is done. The best places to work have a few things in common: they put people first, help workers pursue their passions, empower people to own their projects, encourage authenticity, and create opportunities for worker to connect on a personal level. Autonomy and accountability are important to employees and should be instilled within company values. Measuring the results, rather than the means to getting there, gives employees chance to manage their own work processes and improve their performance.

4. *Total pay*
   - Base pay
   - Variable pay, including stock
   - Flexible benefits and indirect pay
   - Recognition and celebration

Not every member of staff will wish to take advantage of every reward that you could offer, so rewards should be designed in such a way that they're flexible and give each member of staff choice. To ensure that these benefits are accessed fairly, some employers give employees credits and members of staff can combine these to access benefits that are useful to them. Others place a cap on the number of benefits that can be accessed through the year, ensuring that all employees get equal financial value from these benefits.

These four dimensions, which comprise the reward/talent experience, are a means of engaging an organisation's entire network of talent. Total reward strategies are people-centric and not every policy will work in every workplace, as they should be tailored to the individuals. Organisations contemplating introducing some form of Total Reward system usually focus their attention first on the employees they most want to re-cruit and retain, which is where employee segmentation is a vital tool for understanding what different employee groups want and need. The question frequently asked is: 'Do we need to make our different offerings meet the needs of our current and future key staff?' and the answer has to be 'Yes'.

Unilever, the consumer goods multinational employing 300,000 people in more than 60 countries, has been an exponent of performance-related pay for almost three decades. Nowadays Unilever has been piloting a 'flexible pay' scheme that allows junior staff to join its executive share scheme, a privilege usually reserved for senior employees, and choose the percentage of their pay they take as a bonus. The trial was carried out on 200 staff across the United Kingdom, the United States, and the Netherlands. The scheme allowed employees to personalise their benefits. Some 20% of staff chose to pay their entire bonus into the share scheme, while 20% opted to alter the balance between their fixed and variable pay. Those on a higher wage invariably decided in favour of a higher bonus and were twice as likely to shift the balance of their pay while, among lower paid staff who moved their salary, the percentage of those who opted for a greater proportion of fixed pay was significantly higher (90%). Unilever believes that not only does this make the firm a more attractive employer, but also saves valuable cash on recruitment by up-ping retention and attracting the best talent. Another advantage is that those who choose in favour of a performance-related bonus will always be more invested in the overall success of the company (Caldwell 2019).

RECOGNITION

Especially in organisations where the scope for modifying the reward system may appear limited, high performing employees can easily become disengaged if there's no culture of recognition in place. Recognition schemes are a symbolic way of reinforcing the 'new' behaviours and performance needed in the organisation. Yet research suggests that for-mal recognition schemes rarely motivate people in the long term and can be laborious to administer.

Despite this, there are many examples of recognition schemes which are perceived to be successful since they link to the business strategy, are imaginative and regularly modified and offer individuals a degree of choice in how they wish to be recognised. So in devising recognition schemes it's important to think about how individual employees would like to be recognised; not everyone wants to stand up and be applauded during a meeting. Consider additional incentives for high performing employees, such as extra holidays, gift cards and travel vouchers.

Recognition is increasingly being given for the practice of organisational values, espe-cially those relating to community service. At Cadbury–Schweppes, for instance, an infor-mal award scheme recognises outstanding employee contributions in community-based activities. The firm also recognises staff efforts as volunteers through its Big Heart award. Winners receive a certificate and a cash donation to charity.

Research suggests that specific recognition by line managers and peers has a greater impact than any company scheme and can be very reinforcing, supportive and confidence inspiring. Just taking time to thank employees keeps them motivated. As such it can form part of an individual's 'psychological' income or what makes coming to work really worthwhile.

Reflective activity

- How well does your reward strategy build commitment to teamwork and performance?
- Is it flexible enough to cope with change?
- What innovative approaches to reward and recognition might add value?

CONCLUSION

We have discussed various ways through which HR can help build a high-performance organisation. HR can advise line managers on how to devise roles, structures and work processes that both enable the organisation to achieve its goals and also meet employee needs. Performance management and reward systems must be integrated with other management practices in supporting the business strategy. Performance management should be feedback-rich and geared to development. According to Jeffrey Pfeffer (1998), it is important to recognise that 'pay is just one element in a set of management practices that can either build or reduce commitment, teamwork and performance'.

With reward systems, it seems that the more impersonal and corporate the scheme, the less employees find financial reward motivating. If excellent performance is required, people need to see the link between what they have achieved and what they are paid. Producing excellent performance then becomes a matter of individual pride and motivation. Of course, the more 'individual' the package, the more difficult the reward system becomes to administer, but this in itself should not deter the HR strategist who wishes to develop reward systems which are more likely to meet current and future needs.

And reward strategies should not focus solely on pay and tangible benefits. No matter how rigid the pay system appears to be, the importance of recognising the unique contribution of each individual is obvious. This is where HR, line managers and peers have such an important role to play. If an organisation is considering revising its reward systems, it is vital to ask employees what matters most to them among possible 'Total Rewards'. The more employees feel a sense of involvement and ownership of the scheme, the more likely they will find it motivating. The more choice, flexibility but transparency that can be built in, the better.

The main criterion for a successful reward scheme is that it motivates, rather than 'turns off'. When people feel valued and confident, they are likely to release their potential to the benefit of the organisation. Reward strategies which take a holistic perspective of what people consider to be rewarding and offer choice in the design of any new system are more likely to motivate and retain skilled employees who are keen to help the organisation achieve its short- and longer-term aims. When this happens, the virtuous cycle of motivation is under way.

REFERENCES

Accenture Technology (2019). *Empower the human+ worker*, Accenture, Feb. 7. https://www.accenture.com/gb-en/insights/technology/future-of-work

Berson, Y., Oreg, S. and Dvir, T. (2008). CEO values, organizational culture and firm outcomes. *Journal of Organizational Behavior*, 29(5), 615–633.

Boudreau, J. and Ramstad, P. (1997). *Beyond HR: the New Science of Human Capital.* Boston: Harvard Business School Press.

Buckingham, M. and Goodall, A. (2015, April). Reinventing performance management. *Harvard Business Review.* https://hbr.org/2015/04/reinventing-performance-management

Butler, T. and Waldroop, J. (1999). Job sculpting: the art of retaining your best people. *Harvard Business Review*, 77(5), 144–152, 186.

Caldwell, G. (2019). One size fits all? Unilever pilots personalised pay. *Global Cosmetics News*, Nov 6, https://www.globalcosmeticsnews.com/unilever-pilots-personalised-pay/

Cappelli, P. and Tavis, A. (2018). HR goes agile. *Harvard Business Review*, March–April. hbr.org › 2018/03 › hr-goes-agile

CEB study cited on fairness and goal setting in *Deloitte, Global Human Capital Trends 2015*

CIPD (2014). *Managing an Age-diverse Workforce: Employer and Employee Views.* London: Chartered Institute of Personnel and Development.

CIPD/Cap Gemini (2008). *Smart Work. Discussion Paper.* London: Chartered Institute of Personnel and Development.

Collins, J. (2001). *From Good to Great.* New York: Harper Collins.

Corporate Leadership Council (2012). *Driving Breakthrough Performance in the New Work Environment.* CLC Research.

Deloitte (2017). *Rewriting the Rules for the Digital Age: 2017 Deloitte Global Human Capital Trends.* https://www2.deloitte.com/content/dam/Deloitte/global/Documents/About-Deloitte/central-europe/ce-global-human-capital-trends.pdf.

Deloitte (2015). *The Coming Revolution in Global Human Capital Trends 2015: Leading in the New World of Work.* Westlake, Texas: Deloitte University Press, 90–91. https://documents.deloitte.com/insights/HCTrends2015.

Dorsey, D. and Mueller-Hanson, R. (2018). *Performance Management that Makes a Difference: An Evidence-based Approach*, SHRM. https://www.shrm.org/hr-today/trends-and-forecasting/special-reports-and-expert views/documents/performance%20management.pdf.

Friedman, Z. (2018). Student Loan Repayment is the Hottest Benefit of 2018, *Forbes*, Oct 18. https://www.inkl.com/news/student-loan-repayment-is-the-hottest-employee-benefit-of-2018.

Glassdoor (2015). *Employment Confidence Survey* (Q1, 15). https://www.glassdoor.co.uk/blog/uk-job-seeker-confidence-peaks/.

Glassdoor (Chamberlain, A. 2016). Friday's jobs report: Which jobs are seeing wage growth? Aug. 29. https://www.glassdoor.com/research/wage-growth-jobs-report-august-2016/#.

Gratton, L. (2020). Four principles to ensure hybrid work is productive work. *Sloan MIT Review*, Nov 9, https://sloanreview.mit.edu/article/four-principles-to-ensure-hybrid-work-is-productive-work/?og=Home+Editors+Picks

Hackman, J.R. and Oldham, G.R. (1975). Development of the job diagnostic survey. *Journal of Applied Psychology*, 60(2), 159–170.

Heneman, R.L. (2002). *Strategic Reward Management: Design, Implementation, and Evaluation.* Charlotte, NC: Information Age Publishing.

Herzberg, F. (1966). *Work and the Nature of Man.* New York: World Publishing Co.

Jesuthasan, R., Jilek, L. and Poonja, J. (2018). Agile rewards in a modern work ecosystem. *Workspan*, November/December. https://www.worldatwork.org/workspan/issues/november-december-2018

Jesuthasan, R. and Boudreau, J. (2021). Work without jobs. *MIT Sloan management Review*, Spring 2021. https://sloanreview.mit.edu/article/work-without-jobs/.

Jesuthasan, R. and Boudreau, J. (2018). *Reinventing Jobs: A 4-Step Approach for Applying Automation to Work*. Boston: Harvard Business Review Press.

Johnson et al. (2019). *Peak Performance: When Agile Meets Reward,* Mercer, May 9. https://www.mercer.com/our-thinking/career/voice-on-talent/peak-performance-when-agile-meets-reward.html

Jones, K. (2017, February 15). The most desirable employee benefits. *Harvard Business Review.* https:// hbr.org/2017/02/the-most-desirable-employee-benefits

Leach, D.J., Wall, T.D., Rogelberg, S.G. and Jackson, P.R. (2005). Team autonomy, performance, and member job strain: uncovering the teamwork KSA link. *Applied Psychology,* 54(1), 1–24.

Mercer (2016). *Performance management: Time to stop the process outshining the purpose,* Mercer. https://www.uk.mercer.com/content/dam/mercer/attachments/europe/uk/uk-2019-mercer-performance-management.pdf

Mercer (2015). *Snapshot survey: Total remuneration.* https://www.imercer.com/products/total-remuneration-surveys

Mercer (2013). *2013 Global performance management survey report,* Society for Human Resource Management, Corporate Executive Board. https://www.mercer.com/content/dam/mercer/attachments/global/Talent/Assess-BrochurePerfMgmt.pdf

O'Dwyer, M. (2021). Black staff at PWC paid 41pc less than White employees. *The Telegraph*, Jan 27.

OECD (2018). Rising employment overshadowed by unprecedented wage stagnation. OECD, http://www.oecd.org/economy/oecd-employment-outlook-19991266.htm.

O'Malley, M. (2019). What makes a company culture great? What the "Best Companies to Work For" do differently. *Harvard Business Review,* December 16. https://hbr.org/2019/12/what-the-best-companies-to-work-for-do-differently.

Pfeffer, J. (1998). Rethinking reward practices: Myth and reality. *Reward,* July.

Rigby, D.K., Sutherland, J. and Takeuchi, H. (2016). Embracing agile. *HBR,* May. https://hbr.org/2016/05/embracing-agile.

Rock, D. (2008). SCARF: A brain-based model for collaborating with and influencing others. *NeuroLeadership Journal,* 1, 1–9.

Scholtes, P.R. (1995). Do reward and recognition systems work? *Quality Magazine,* December, 27–29.

Schwartz, J., Stockton, H., Wagner, D. and Walsh, B. (2017). *The future of work: The augmented workforce2017 Global Human Capital Trends.* Deloitte Insights, https://www2.deloitte.com/us/en/insights/focus/human-capital-trends/2017/future-workforce-changing-nature-of-work.html/?id=dup-us-en:2sm:3li:4dup_gl:5eng:6dup.

Semper, J. (2017). GE's cultural transformation in the global workplace. *Money Control.* Feb.7. https://www.moneycontrol.com/gestepahead/innovation-and-leadership/video/ges-cultural-transformation-in-the-global-workplace-8073921-99.html.

Sheppard, B.H. and Sherman D.A. (1998). The grammars of trust: A model and general implications. *Academy of Management Review,* 23(3), 422–437.

SHRM (2018). *Employee job satisfaction and engagement: Revitalizing a changing workforce.* Society for Human Resource Management, https://www.shrm.org/hr-today/trends-and-forecasting/research-and-surveys/Documents/2016-Employee-Job-Satisfaction-and-Engagement-Report.pdf.

Tyson, S. (1995). *Human Resource Strategy.* London: Pitman.

Wall, T.D. and Wood, S.J. (2005). The romance of human resource management and business performance and the case for big science. *Human Relations,* 58(4), 429–462.

Warren, T. (2013, November 11). Microsoft axes its controversial employee- ranking system. *The Verge.* http://www.theverge.com/2013/11/12/5094864/microsoft-kills-stack-ranking-internal-structure.

Zingheim, P.K. and Schuster, J.R. (2007). *High Performance Pay Fast Forward to Business Success.* Scotsdale, AZ: WorldatWork.

10
Strategies for developing people

As we have previously discussed, higher level skills are in short supply in industries as diverse as construction, health, pharmaceuticals, defence and high technology, with even greater shortages predicted given demographic trends. Demand is high for the talent and the skills needed for jobs that will remain in human hands – those involving managing people, applying expertise or creativity, and social interactions. In PwC's 20th CEO survey (2017), 77% of the CEOs interviewed saw the lack of availability of key skills as the biggest threat to their business. With 'the war for talent' back with us, offering opportunities for development is key to attracting talent. With growing talent shortages, it's no longer a question of simply finding talent; we also need to build it.

CHAPTER OVERVIEW

In this chapter we consider some of the contemporary trends in learning and development. We shall consider the role of employers with respect to reskilling and upskilling the workforce in the new skills required for work. We shall cover:

- New skills for a changing work world
- The challenge of building a flexible, agile workforce

DOI: 10.4324/9781003219996-12

- Lifelong learning and development
- Towards a strategic approach to development
- Changing learning design

LEARNING OBJECTIVES

- To consider key trends and changing work demands in terms of skills
- To explore a range of approaches to development, including technology-based
- To consider the changing role of the L&D professional

INTRODUCTION: NEW SKILLS FOR A CHANGING WORK WORLD

Against today's fast-changing backdrop the need to develop people has never been more acute. When, where and how work is carried out are being totally transformed. Technology and AI increasingly incorporated into routine tasks, with 50% of current work activities technically automatable by adapting currently demonstrated technologies. Seventy-five per cent of jobs are predicted to have a third of their tasks automated in the near future. McKinsey Global Institute estimates that 14% of the global workforce will need to switch occupational categories by 2030 as the world of work is disrupted (Manyika et al. 2018).

As many old jobs disappear or are deconstructed, and as new jobs emerge at an ever-increasing rate, employees who retain their jobs will require constant adaptation to keep pace with the new format of work and future jobs. Many will face working alongside robots and AI (Gartner 2018) and will need new skills to do this. The protracted lockdowns during the global pandemic have accelerated the trend towards home working, or hybrid forms of working, enabled by technology.

So whether it is to build skills that provide competitive advantage, or to embrace the potential and normalisation of technology, or as part of a process or cultural shift, everybody who works is going to need to carry on learning new skills, and in different ways. Since technology is continually evolving, the life cycle of employees' competencies is shrinking, and the skills learned in traditional training environments often have a short shelf life. However, according to McKinsey (2020), despite the changing needs of organisations and their employees, most companies still rely on the same methods to deliver learning as they did four years previously.

Training is still the commonest form of off-the-job development. Typical criticisms of conventional training include a lack of tailoring to individual needs if a 'sheep dip' approach to training is still taken. Many staff surveys highlight the same issue with monotonous regularity: line managers do not know how to help other people to develop. They are often perceived to be too busy, unsupportive, have inappropriate management styles or simply do not see developing others as part of their role. Indeed, some managers will resort to training as a remedial solution to a 'people problem'. Few organisations as yet are using experiential environments or digital interventions such as mobile learning exercises or group-based online courses. Indeed, Deloitte's 2019 Human Capital Trends suggests that 86% of leaders recognise that changing the way people learn at work is their biggest organisational development challenge.

THE CHALLENGE OF BUILDING A FLEXIBLE AND AGILE WORKFORCE

HR and L&D need to be leading the discussion with executives about what the firm and its people will look like in 10 years' time. Bryan Hancock (McKinsey, January 2020) urges CEOs to look ahead: 'Develop a perspective now on the realities of your workforce. Where will those human beings be in five to ten years, and how can you help them take the next step forward? I'd encourage leaders to think about those people now and help them advance'.

As we discussed in earlier chapters, workforce planning should provide answers to questions such as what are the critical capabilities our organisation needs to be successful over the next five to ten years? What does that demand in tasks and in skills? And what do we have now? Workforce planning presents choices: should you train your existing employees to acquire the new skills, or hire a new generation? If you decide on the former, options include redeployment, or moving people elsewhere in the company; upskilling people to become more advanced at what they do in current roles, keeping their skills in synch with fast-changing markets; or reskilling people to take on something different or for entirely new roles, keeping them employable through an internal career marketplace. Every option requires skill gaps to be identified and investment in employees' continuous learning.

Traditional L&D approaches take time. However, in today's context, with the pace of change accelerating, workforce development strategies must swiftly ensure that an organisation's employees are ready to face new challenges and opportunities. This may mean adapting people's existing skills to meet the needs, being creative at low cost, using TedTalks, podcasts and expert sessions to get people thinking differently.

However, the KPMG 2018 Global CEO Outlook reports that only 46% of respondent companies feel that they're ready to take on the development challenge even though the cost of reskilling is lower than firing and hiring. Few organisations are looking ahead at closing future skills gaps when they design their training programmes. Short-termism is reported to lie at the heart of the problem. Moreover, CEOs are failing to invest in experts in organisation development (OD) and learning and development (L&D) who can enable culture change, or if they are, their efforts are not bearing fruit as reflected in this quotation from an NHS report:

> All health services will need a flexible, agile workforce in the future. Whilst many have made recent investments in workforce reform, change is needed to develop a workforce that is sufficiently flexible, specialised and self-renewing to be properly responsive to changing stakeholder expectations
>
> (HEE 2019)

When skill gaps are ignored, or training programs are out-of-date, the only way to fill those skill gaps is through expensive recruitment. What is really needed, 'is a deep-seated conviction, among business unit heads and line leaders, that people really matter – that leaders must develop the capabilities of employees, nurture their careers, and manage the performance of individuals and teams' (Guthridge et al. 2008).

Lifelong learning and development

For most organisations the greatest opportunity to fill skill gaps is by developing the skills of the current workforce and building a culture of lifelong learning. People who will be successful in the digital age are those who can learn on a continuous basis.

If organisations are to successfully attract and retain the best new talent, they must provide growth opportunities. Young people entering the jobs market recognise the need for ongoing learning in the workplace - and will expect an employer to provide them with serious development opportunities. Skilled workers too recognise that lifelong learning is a necessity, and many are consciously developing new skills as career currency, to make themselves employable should they wish, or be required, to move on from their current employer. Now and in the future, most learning will take place within organisations and the ecosystems surrounding them. The days of learning ending as the school gate closes appear long gone.

It is in an organisation's interest to reskill and upskill people to sustain desired business outcomes in a digital world. With the advent of digital talent marketplaces turnover is likely since in-demand skills will rotate more frequently, as individuals interact with more companies than ever before. To retain talent, organisations must offer training, mentoring and other opportunities that prepare employees for future jobs they will perform – inside or outside the company. With sufficient advance notice, employees whose jobs will be automated or changed can be trained in key areas of competency to become an internal talent supply pool that is future-proofed.

So how do we achieve the great leap forward in life-long learning to equip people with the digital and other relevant skills they will need for the new workplace?

As organisations transition to new work models, they must support a model of lifelong learning. HR/L&D practitioners should start by adopting the principle that employees can grow and learn within the company. They must identify workers who score highly for learning agility. A self-development culture should be encouraged, with development seen as primarily the individual's responsibility but supported by the organisation. Individuals should be encouraged to set themselves upskilling goals – just one or two, such as learning about AI.

Towards a strategic approach to development

As businesses adapt to take advantage of new technologies, they need a dynamic skills and talent strategy to create a workforce for the future by continuously reskilling and upskilling people for the digital future. This both helps avoid skills shortages and also keeps employees engaged and satisfied by offering them opportunities for professional development. Gallup research suggests that changes in employee engagement are reflective of changes in development opportunities. PwC (2020) report that the benefits to companies with advanced upskilling programmes include:

- A strong company culture and engagement (60%)
- Increased innovation and digital transformation (50%)
- Improved ability to attract and retain talent (45%)
- Enhanced employee experience.

It is important to take a systemic approach to development. For while high quality training is valuable, translating improved skills into performance requires high quality people management. Reward systems should reflect the achievement by managers of people development targets and individuals should be financially compensated if their improved skills enhance their contribution. A CIPD focus group of HR Directors confirmed that talent management, learning and career growth, employee engagement, leadership and management development, reward, are inextricably interlinked with retention and business success. Adopting a systemic approach will require investment: in the team, not just the role; in developing a dynamic training capability; in building sustainability for new and extended roles, while also emphasising human strengths in the collaborative relationship between people and between people and machines.

Creating a workforce development strategy involves looking ahead, understanding your workforce's current and future needs, identifying new skill sets including 'learning how to learn', supporting the workforce with technology, and a mix of upskilling, reskilling, unlearning and talent mobility (CIPD 2020). The strategy should be guided by a vision, philosophy and set of values. What is the philosophy which will underpin development – do you want people to be self-sufficient or do you see development as a partnership between the individual and the organisation? Will development be demand-led or provider-led? Should development be offered to all workers, or just future leaders? Will contingent workers be offered the same opportunities as those on permanent contracts?

In the early years of the current century, in raising the flag of the 'War for Talent', McKinsey emphasised the recruitment, development and retention of the 'A' players – the top 20% or so of managers. More recently there has been a growing recognition that the 'B' players – the capable performers who make up the bulk of the workforce –also matter. As Guthridge et al. (2008) put it:

> *To manage talent successfully, executives must recognize that their talent strategies cannot focus solely on their top performers.*

Often people in quite junior roles, such as front-line staff and technical specialists, are as vital to overall success as the 'A' players. Some companies, like Walmart, are investing in their frontline employees – giving them options to learn. Learning new skills can lead to improvements in capability, performance and productivity. Aviva, the insurance company, has a strategy of managing the 'vital many' rather than risk alienating the bulk of the workforce by focusing exclusively on high-flyers.

The question more inclusive development strategies need to answer is 'how do we ensure that all employees are developed to their full potential and maximum effectiveness'?

Identifying skills gaps

A talent development strategy should ensure that employees' skills are kept up to date as jobs continue to evolve with technology. As ever it is important to start with business goals, and the skills needed to achieve them. Identifying gaps in skills and knowledge to deliver future business plans involves three distinct phases - Supply Analysis, Demand (or Needs) Analysis and Gap Analysis across the workforce – to create a baseline to measure progress. In any development strategy there are likely to be three areas of focus:

- Organisational level, where corporate requirements such as Induction, Quality Improvement, Leadership, Customer Care and Culture Change Programmes are addressed
- Departmental/Business Unit level, where job-related training and development is likely to take place
- Individual level, where people are usually motivated to close the gap between their current and desired capabilities

Certain development activities, such as the identification of talent, high-flyer schemes and succession planning, usually involve all three levels. There is also increasing recognition that new ways of working may require behaviour change as much as a skill change and some behaviours are likely to become more valued than they were historically.

Some organisations are very clear about where their gaps are, at any point in time. Amazon for instance is looking for people with knowledge of robotics and Cloud technology but also user-experience design, HR, marketing. Even if the way ahead is not always crystal clear, for many organisations, since future roles will often involve a greater use of technology, digital skills are a key development priority. For example, JPMorgan Chase has introduced several schemes to develop the digital skills of current and future workers as part of its five-year, $350 million commitment to skill building. They include a 10- to 14-week immersive coding academy for high-performing technology staff and a degree apprenticeship that allows people to earn a degree while working within the company's technology business.

Deciding who should be developed for what can be tricky and having a guiding framework and criteria for decision-making can be helpful. Organisational priorities usually take precedence though a development strategy should ideally be sufficiently flexible that it can adapt to individual needs and take account of the reality of most people's working lives. The pace of change and demanding workloads of most employees may act as deterrents to time-consuming formal development or educational programmes. Employees will often claim that they are too busy to attend conventional training courses or too exhausted to undertake part-time education out of work hours. Since development solutions can take many forms, not least using technology, the options available should ideally be as innovative as employees are now required to be.

Relevance to individuals and the organisation

To ensure an optimum return on the time and other resources invested in development, those activities should be learner-centred and well targeted to address real needs in areas that are relevant to both the individual and the organisation, for instance 'essential' transferable skills such as problem-solving, teamworking and communication. For people with highly sought-after skillsets, individualised pathways can be created that identify and develop their capabilities to the next level. One employee, for instance, might need a rapid injection of job-related skills due to a new role or a change in technology. Another person may have reached the stage in his or her career when a development stretch is required, such as by taking on a major new responsibility or studying an MBA programme.

In industries where there are specific skills shortages and where professional qualifications are necessary for certain job functions, such as accountancy, giving staff the opportunity to study is particularly critical. At PricewaterhouseCoopers (PwC) employees typically spend more than 50 days in off-the-job training during their first three years. PwC trains more than 20% of the chartered accountants in the United Kingdom and its business diploma – a four-year development programme – is run in association with the London Business School.

People may need guidance from the company to understand which kinds of jobs within the company could help them grow and the critical skills they need. They may need help figuring out where improvement is needed, aligning their learning to opportunities, filling skills gaps, trying new experiences, building their careers. At EY (Ernst and

Young), the international financial consultancy, staff receive detailed industry training as well as coaching in people skills. Everyone is allocated a counsellor and is also informally mentored. People take responsibility for their careers, with programmes in place to ensure they can achieve success quickly.

Gaining clarity about career goals – and guidance – can emerge in career conversations with managers who can help individuals build skills by matching skills gaps to a variety of blended learning opportunities such as virtual, online content, team-based programmes, peer-to-peer learning. Technology tools can also help people understand their strengths and critical skills gaps. Having discovered their career goals and purpose, people tend to be more engaged in work and motivated to build transferable skills, creating value by applying new skills to solving real work problems.

WHAT TO DEVELOP?

Competencies

Over the past two decades competencies have been commonly used to provide a common language within organisations to describe the skills, knowledge and behaviours required to achieve desired organisational outcomes. They are used as a means to assess the skilled elements of individual performance, to identify skills, behavioural and knowledge gaps and to ensure that development opportunities are well targeted to meet specific objectives. They can be used to develop learning tools, self-assessment questionnaires and other feedback processes to ensure that individual needs are understood, and also to aid job mobility. Some organisations offer managers 360-degree (or multi-rater) feedback based on a range of competencies. One software company, for instance, provides feedback from skilled facilitators followed by a range of optional competency-based workshops which managers can choose according to the needs identified through the feedback.

However, competencies are increasingly thought of as too complicated; defining exactly how to deal with a thousand possible scenarios is seen as too instrumentalist and, in extreme cases, as bureaucratic hindrances to performance if they lie at the heart of over-engineered HR processes. Increasingly, competencies are being described as 'capabilities', or 'characteristics' since they reflect what at individual and team level contributes in aggregate to the building of organisational capabilities such as customer focus.

Transferable enduring capabilities

The coronavirus pandemic has accelerated an existing demand for transferable skills to enable rapid shifts in business models, as organisations try to redeploy people at warp speed. For instance, during lockdowns, restaurants had to close their in-house service and operate a take-away/delivery service, requiring different skills and procedures. So the focal point of learning is switching to developing enduring transferable capabilities such as resilience. For PwC the most in-demand skill set includes adaptability, problem-solving, creativity and leadership. For Deloitte (*Skills change but Capabilities endure*) these include:

- Emotional intelligence: how to understand and react to the emotions and experience of others
- Teaming: how to collaborate effectively with people who don't share our physical space, language or organisational context

- Sense-making: how to create meaning out of shared experience
- Critical thinking: how to analyse, synthesise and reconstruct information
- Adaptive thinking: how to recognise and apply new patterns.

Given that the future workforce must respond to the increasing pace of change and likely external disruption, people need to be adaptable or 'change-able' in the face of uncertainty, tolerant of complexity and ambiguity, resilient, capable of sense-making. The most desirable employees are the active learners – those with curiosity and the ability to innovate. People need to embrace continuous learning and be multi-skilled, able to absorb and optimise technology and also make the most of knowledge and innovation to improve customer outcomes. People will also need a broad business understanding and a strong grasp of strategic priorities. They will need to be goal focused and operationally effective, with sound programme management and continuous improvement skills.

Given the need for rapid, skilled decision-making at all levels, demand for analytic skills will increase. Many higher-skilled jobs involve dealing with complex theoretical phenomena that require logical reasoning and also social and organisational skills like facilitation and prioritisation. A Workday study of CFOs (2018) argues that cognitive flexibility is the most important skill needed while Stahl et al. (2012) suggest that in the future the ability to quickly adopt and apply new information will become more important than any number of hard skills.

There is likely to be a premium on the creative skills needed to balance mechanised processes. People working across organisational boundaries need good 'soft' or 'human' skills such as social and emotional intelligence to engage with customers, other staff and with partner organisations. They will need to be collaborative, working towards common goals; open to new opportunities; resourceful and entrepreneurial; able to communicate authentically and build relationships and trust; demonstrate cultural agility and the ability to manage differences, negotiate, resolve conflict, adjusting own style if necessary.

Inclusive leadership

These 'human' skills are especially important in leaders. The Workday study found that the leadership qualities required to run an Agile enterprise include being humble, adaptable, visionary, engaged – somewhat different from the traditional business competencies required of leaders. In the highly pressurised UK National Health Service, there has long been a call for compassionate, inclusive and effective leaders at all levels:

> Inclusive leadership means progressing equality, valuing diversity and challenging power imbalances. This means paying close attention to all the people you lead, understanding the situations they face, responding empathetically and taking thoughtful and appropriate action to help. In other words, the most effective leaders demonstrate empathy, an essential element of emotional intelligence. This ability to identify and manage one's own emotions and be mindful of the emotions of others is vital as employees are unlikely otherwise to feel truly respected and empowered. Empathy must start at the top.

It is thought that 'These leadership behaviours create just, learning cultures where improvement methods can engage colleagues, patients and carers, deliver cumulative performance improvements, and make health and care organisations great places to work' (NHS Point of Care Foundation 2014).

HR/L&D can help by

- Developing engaging, compassionate leaders at every level – including new and emerging leaders. Workshops and coaching can help leaders reflect on their early experiences, find their own beliefs and purpose, and make engaging behaviours more habitual.
- Extending boundaries to create new leadership development opportunities. Work with business partners, universities, nongovernmental organisations, and other third-party organisations to create a range of new leadership experiences, including pro bono and community service projects.
- When the number of engaging leaders amounts to a critical mass, their energy and mutual support can change the engagement culture of the organisation.
- Measuring and rewarding the achievement of staff engagement. Recognise leaders who are engaging and hold to account those who are not.

Changing learning design

Given that many workforces now operate remotely, and that learning design, perceptions and expectations have been changing, the traditional training and development path is arguably not as effective as before. As the learning landscape is being transformed, L&D professionals are expected to adopt entirely new learning paradigms, methods and learning technologies. In today's virtual environments the shift is away from traditional in-person 'classroom' learning methods, now driven online largely by digital availability and accessibility of knowledge, toward facilitation and practical application.

The volumes of information available online is a double-edged sword. How can the learner be certain that the information they are consuming is valuable, or even accurate? Content curation has become important - the ability to find high-quality content and deliver it to learners. As a result, progressive L&D functions are focusing on really improving the learning capability of the workforce, in essence by 'teaching them how to learn' and making learning a value at the heart of the organisation. Such functions foster and support a mobile, on-demand learning and social learning culture, align performance needs with business needs, and prepare employees and leaders for future responsibilities.

The role of the learning professional has become far more wide-ranging, spanning multiple disciplines and new areas of expertise, as reflected in new job titles such as:

- Content curator
- Asset creator
- Instructional Design/Content Developer
- Programmer
- Learning Data Analyst
- Talent Development Partner
- L&D/OD/Change Managers

L&D professionals must ensure their programmes are learner-centred, using forms of digital learning that increase people's technology skills and also motivate and engage a multigenerational workforce within a modern learning ecosystem. The focus should be not only on learning and skill development, but also on achieving behavioural change across broad segments of the workforce as they apply new learning and skills to day-to-day work. Designing an effective learning programme requires L&D professionals to bridge the gap between fulfilling the needs of the learners and satisfying the learning requirements of the organisation (Eoyang 2013). Accordingly, there is a growing emphasis on clear objective-setting, contracting between participant and line manager before programmes, flexible programme design and rigorous evaluation, including attempts to establish return on investment (ROI).

Learning design may need to be modified or adapted to better fit the learner-centred rather than the instructor-centred emphasis that has developed in learning design, particularly for technology-based learning methods. The design process involves first identifying the client's goals then putting together a design team that consists of a diverse group of perhaps half a dozen learners who actively contribute to the content and structure of the programme, including deciding the time commitment required. Resources in a variety of formats such as pre-reading, reference materials, and/or different kinds of exercises can be customised according to the goals and format of the learning programme. Ideally, any training should lead to practical application and help people to come up with solutions themselves, rather than simply forcing them through hoops.

A growing trend among L&D professionals is using micro-learning as a device for reflection and group work. Virtual briefings and networks can be helpful in raising managers' awareness of the strategic issues for their organisation. As a facilitator, you can insist that everyone should participate with video and use smaller, intimate breakouts. As facilitator you make contact, ask questions, send out small group assignments in advance, or simply ask the learning programme participants to comment on an article you've shared. Such daily interactions with complex topics are designed to deepen the participants' engagement with not only the content but also the learning community around them. Following the learning event, by sending the learners frequent reminders about some of the concepts you're currently working on, they'll be able to keep these important topics in mind during busy days and will be able to connect them to their everyday work. Reinforcing learning to sustain behavioural changes has never been easy but directly linking desired behaviours to actual business outcomes relevant to employees can keep behavioural change on track.

Technology-based learning

In a remote working environment, in-person training is non-existent and during the pandemic there has been an explosion of interest in the use of technology to stimulate learning. Remote-learning experiences must deliver the skills and behaviours employees need, while also inspiring the consistent application of those new skills and behaviours so that performance ultimately improves. Technology makes learning and support easy to scale yet personalised to suit the needs of people with different roles in the change process, providing skills and accessible resources so that people can help themselves, rather than L&D doing it for them. While initially e-learning failed to take off in any substantial way, many pundits predict a huge growth of more effective online learning as the new technologies offer just-in-time accessible learning materials that are stimulating real interest. For instance, Chatbots, also known as digital learning assistants in corporate environments, help employees learn at their own pace, at any hour of the day, and provide a highly personalised learning experience.

Compared to traditional reskilling programs, a modern learning experience platform combined with high value learning content can make training efficient and help people develop new skills through their day job and create their own learning journey, for roles which may not yet exist. A variety of new forms of technology-based learning include:

- Virtual/Augmented/Mixed reality
- Artificial intelligence
- Gaming
- Internet of things
- Unbundling
- Adaptive learning
- Digital literacy

Increasingly people choose to learn through a blend of learning solutions that combine face-to-face with for instance e-learning, podcasting, attending professional meetings, live classes, conferences or seminars, certificate programmes, social networking and project work.

In the era of social networking people can gain access to a wide range of learning resources. Social learning platforms enable learners to transcend organisational boundaries between departments, time zones, and geographically dispersed offices to build and cultivate organic communities-of-practice around the concepts and topics they're interested in developing. This changes the role of L&D from primarily delivering face to face development and increasingly involves sourcing and curating materials, resources or experiences that people will learn from.

At multinational broadcaster SKY, Tracy Waters, director of people experience, wanted to adopt a more agile approach to learning. One of the first targets was manager development and an active move away from instructor-led training. The team researched manager needs and tested various tools including an app with digital resources and checklists. This was complemented by group workshops, nudge campaigns, videos and larger group experiences. Each time they had the data to tell them what was working, which led to further iterations. Now almost all products emerging from Waters' team are developed in this user-focused, data-driven way (Faragher 2019).

Reflective activity

- What is the role of context (e.g. job demands, work–life balance, social network) in the use and effectiveness of technology-based learner-driven methods?

Other off-the-job learning and development processes

- *Action learning*: Group sessions to problem-solve on real life issues. These can enable individual needs to be met in the work context. Helps develop self-reliance for solving future problems. Learning groups are increasingly being used in a number of organisations such as Pfizer and Fujitsu.
- *Attachments (or shadowing)*: Becoming a temporary assistant to another person in order to gain an understanding of their job. Employers should not underestimate

the value of encouraging workers to shadow one another in order to gain transferable skills and to develop a deeper understanding of different functions within the business. In addition to providing a solid foundation for staff looking to take on more formal qualifications this knowledge sharing strategy is a low-cost way to achieve greater cohesion within the business and well as possibly the most effective way to upskill people.

- *Brainstorming or 'mind-showering':* Having an ideas communication system – like a suggestion box and rewarding the best idea(s) on a regular basis.
- *Case studies/Case histories:* Examples of the experiences of other industries or managers that might be examined. Broadens horizons, gives ideas for different ways of doing things.
- *Contact developing (networking):* Encouraging membership of/attendance at professional or local business groups. Builds a network with other managers' industries to gain new insights and create ideas.
- *Counselling:* Recognising where an individual's behaviour indicates a personal or work-related problem or giving guidance on how to solve a problem. 'Unblocks' people who are in difficulty, builds good communication.
- *Conferences:* To help people see the 'big picture' or buy in to corporate objectives. To share the experience of other people and organisations. Increases sense of belonging, heightens commercial awareness.
- *Distance learning:* Encouraging further study or education which can be done at the person's own pace. Need not be directly related to current role. Broadens knowledge and increases skill base.
- *Exposure to senior management:* Observes and perhaps becomes involved in more strategic issues and decisions. Strengthens natural ability in this area and builds confidence.
- *Learning resources – films/videos/DVDs/podcasts:* Wide selection available for a variety of techniques and skills. Aids learning by presenting information in a memorable way.
- *Modelling:* Having team members observe another individual who displays outstanding performance. Illustrates best practice in a practical way.
- *Networking:* A powerful way of expanding relationships, knowledge, business and career opportunities.
- *Non-executive director/trustee appointments:* Supporting high potential managers to take up non-executive director appointments. Assigning an individual to a committee, along with managers from other departments or externally. Broadens horizons and increases confidence.
- *Outdoor team development:* Outdoor team building and training events. Not directly related to current job but can be enjoyable and build team spirit.
- *Presentations:* Short presentations (10–15 minutes) using visual aids or simulations (see Simulations) to impart skill or knowledge.
- *Role playing:* Trying out difficult situations in relative safety. Offers opportunity for feedback and coaching.
- *Secondments:* Individuals spend a period of time working in a different part of the organisation. Widens their viewpoint and experience.
- *Self-development and self-analysis:* A variety of techniques exist to aid this process including keeping a personal journal, creating a learning log recording new experiences, doing value exercises, personal skills and management style audits.

- *Seminars/team briefings:* Conducted by internal or external facilitators for specific groups. To distribute knowledge or brainstorm (pool ideas) on problems. Encourages team spirit, opens up creativity and communication, increases learning.
- *Simulations:* Can be done in seminars or team briefings. Recreations of the job environment or a specific job situation. Enhances problem-solving and skill in real situations.
- *Volunteering:* Growing in usage as both a development opportunity for individuals and teams and also for carrying out an employer's corporate social responsibility commitments. Timberland is amongst a number of companies who commit company time and money to collective effort to assist community projects.

At Google, giving staff time not only to learn but to innovate in their jobs is enshrined in Google's working practices. The most notable manifestation of this is the company '70–20–10' policy for engineers, which prescribes that each programmer should spend only around 70% of their time doing their core job. Twenty per cent should be spent on related activity or a project that will help them do their core job better while the remaining 10% can be spent on less focused 'blue sky' thinking, such as dreaming up new products. The fruits of this policy are evident in the ongoing streams of new and innovative products.

Employees (known as 'Googlers') are given a chance for both personal development and a taste of the wider business. Examples include a job shadowing programme and an 'ambassadors' programme, where European staff can undertake a job swap with a Googler from the Asia–Pacific region. Personal and skills development are also reflected in the GTG (Googler to Googler) learning initiative, a series of training sessions given by Google staff for their colleagues. Sessions can cover skills as diverse as coding, mathematics or salsa dancing.

On-the-job development

Since most adults appear to learn best by experience, on-the-job learning is therefore likely to be the primary source of development. When skills are built through work, not just in addition to work, building capabilities becomes everyone's job, especially managers'. Structural support for this could involve rethinking the annual performance review process to provide more regular feedback, periodic check-ins, opportunities to take part in projects, setting goals and creating plans to develop skills. At Unilever responsibilities for learning are clear: individuals are responsible for managing their own learning; line managers are responsible for supporting them: L&D and HR for building a learning culture. Rather than work getting in the way of development, development is part of work.

One of the key sources of development on-the-job is having some *challenge,* without being 'stretched' to breaking point. Job enrichment is achieved by making job content more challenging, either technically or managerially. It could be thought of as *deepening* the job and develops ability in a current role. Challenges come in various forms and have greater or lesser motivational effect depending on the individual. Typically, a rewarding form of development occurs when someone is given responsibility for a venture whose outcome is not guaranteed, where the outcome is important and noted by others. It is important that achievements should be recognised by others, especially managers, and appropriate rewards (even if only a show of esteem) be given.

Another key source of learning is *variety.* This can also take many forms, including the chance to try new things, meet new people, develop new work interests. Again, imaginative problem-solving between manager and direct report can assist in identifying opportunities for variety in any job, however mundane. Having the opportunity to represent your employer at a conference, for instance, can be useful. Ironically, *hardships* are apparently a major source of development, providing that people are able to recover some learning from the experience. Some people may find the ongoing cost-cutting approach represents a form of hardship. Focusing on how to overcome difficulties can generate positive and creative solutions. Having a (peer) mentor can help in this process. *Other people*, especially bosses, are a major source of development. The role-modelling effect is strong – with both good and bad bosses – and emphasises the importance of training senior managers to act consistently with organisational values.

Other on-the-job methods of development include:

- *Career counselling.* Some major corporations have trained directors to act as career counsellors for other people. This is an organisation-wide responsibility, rather than being restricted to direct reporting relationships. Each director takes on a small 'caseload' of people who are regarded as key to the future, but for whom there may be no immediate prospect of promotion. The benefits in the form of improved morale and retention of key people can be great.
- *Delegating:* Either temporarily or permanently. Giving a person part of your job to do as a development exercise. Stretches the person and develops management ability.
- *Feedback:* Gaining regular performance feedback from colleagues (peer assessment), managers and subordinates. Gives more rounded information to person, builds internal communication.
- *Research assignments:* Short-term study with report back. Keeps people informed of developments in their field; is a good refresher for the person.
- *Reading/reviewing:* Circulating links to journal articles or snippets from newspapers and publications. Keeps people up to date with the latest techniques and issues.
- *Self-assessment tools:* In many organisations, tools are now provided to encourage self-development, including the use of development centres and learning resource centres. These can often include skills inventories, behavioural instruments and provide routes to relevant learning resources.
- *'Sitting by Nellie' or pairing:* A traditional method of learning involving one individual partnering a more experienced person and having them explain what they are doing. Trains the person in the detail of the job – can be part of coaching.
- *Task forces:* Groups of people from different parts of the organisation asked to examine a specific issue, as a team, from a variety of perspectives. Improves inter-department communication, helps solve real work problems.
- *Team building:* Events run with small specific team to promote understanding of individual roles and contribution. Helps to play to people's particular strengths.
- *Visits:* Arranging a tour for small groups or individuals to other organisations or parts of the group to observe processes. Broadens knowledge, creates exchange of ideas.

Coaching and mentoring

Coaching and mentoring are two of the more powerful ways to support other people's development. Knowledge workers in agile organisations want managers who are less directive and who have more of a coaching style. Coaching involves managers having regular conversations with individuals and the team about tasks they could take on, which would stretch them to improve their skills and knowledge. Coaching managers give support and guidance rather than instructions, ask questions rather than provide answers and also give direct feedback to the learner, helping workers reach decisions themselves. The emphasis should be on building to strengths, rather than on overcoming weaknesses, and on opportunities, rather than problems. This increases the skills base and strengthens communication.

Many line managers, especially those with a technical background, may need training to develop a coaching style of management. Organisations such as British-American Tobacco and Microsoft train managers in coaching skills. Often training is offered to managers in tandem with new appraisal schemes which generally separate out job review processes from development discussions and review how well managers develop others in their own performance management and reward processes. With honest appraisal and support for team-working (including a reward strategy that reinforces team development), human and organisational needs can converge and lead to an energizing new working environment.

Mentoring typically takes a longer term, much less task-focused perspective, and generally focuses on issues relating to career development. Mentors are not usually in a line reporting relationship with the mentee and are generally at a more senior level in the hierarchy than the learner and will often involve role modelling. This can increase the learner's understanding of how the organisation operates and is useful for exploring career development issues as well as gaining sponsorship. Many mentors do not work in the same organization as the learner, and increasingly relationships formed through networking are a primary source of contacts and development advice. The mix will depend on the needs of both the business and of individuals, but a planned investment in developing coaches and mentors throughout an organisation will pay dividends in providing a supportive culture for talent management.

Peer mentoring

Many organisations encourage peer mentoring to address both individual needs for access to information and support and organisational needs for teamwork and greater collaboration across silos. Peer mentoring involves two, three or more individuals agreeing to have a development relationship with one another with the clear purpose of supporting individuals to achieve their job objectives. HR can create mechanisms whereby peers can identify likely peer 'resources' and establish such relationships. Often this is through the use of a database of people who have specific expertise and who are willing to act as peer mentors. These can be matched against people who express specific needs. HR can help people to think through their objectives and give guidance on how to approach peers with a view to forming a formal mentoring relationship. Sometimes organising a café-style kick-off event helps to get peer mentoring underway.

At Prudential Portfolio Managers an online system described informally as a global virtual university allows for just-in-time training. This covers 11 technical areas such as portfolio management, and generic skills such as delegation and performance management. Knowledge management is built into the system. This gives people the resources they need to manage their own learning following an assessment of their skill needs. Sometimes people are looking for a mentoring relationship with someone who can help them increase their understanding of how another part of the business operates. Other people wish to link up with individuals who have developed their careers in particular ways within organisations. When an employee enters a particular learning area, the first page supplies the names and contact details of other employees with expertise in the area who are willing to provide support.

Ideally, a peer coaching relationship should offer participants reciprocal benefits. One example is a training manager and a human resources manager from the same organisation who were called on to work on the same major project for a period of several months. There was a history of some hostility between the two departments which they represented, and, as individuals, they did not warm to each other's styles. However, they took the decision to go through a formal contracting process to see if they could help each other. The project proved to have benefits for both individuals and for their departments. The individuals concerned now have a much greater understanding of one another's needs and what they can offer.

Participation

Skills development can occur in other ways too. Participation in workplace decisions can improve the capabilities of employees, enabling them to perform better. It can improve communication and coordination among employees and organisational departments and help integrate the different jobs or departments that contribute to an overall task. Employee Involvement (EI) interventions can improve employee motivation, particularly when they satisfy important individual needs. Motivation is translated into improved performance when people have the necessary skills and knowledge to perform well and when the technology and work situation allow people to affect productivity. Skill training in group problem solving and communication can increase employee participation in decision making (Cummings and Worley 2014; Dignan 2019; Cheung-Judge and Holbeche 2021).

Evaluation

Learning and development is often considered a cost rather than an investment and L&D professionals are expected to prove the value of their learning programmes. Evaluation frameworks – such as the Organisational Elements Model (OEM): Kaufman, Keller and Watkins (1995); Responsive evaluation: Pulley (1994); The Success Case Method: Brinkerhoff (2005) – have mainly been designed for the purpose of assessing the value of training rather than other learning interventions. Thalheimer's Learning-Transfer Evaluation Model (LTEM), which assesses learning at eight levels, states that training has only been successful when the participant applies the learned material in their behaviour. Many frameworks derive from Donald Kirkpatrick's (1996) original evaluation framework which four levels of assessment:

1 Reaction – what do participants think about the activity at the time?
2 Learning – how have skills, knowledge or attitudes improved as a result of the activity?
3 Behaviour – how does participants' changed behaviour affect their constituents, e.g. their workgroup?
4 Results – how do these improved behaviours, skills and knowledge translate into bottom-line impact?

This last point is perhaps the most critical from the business perspective. A metrics dashboard can assess skill development progress but increasingly 'hard' measures of the impact of development activities are required. These are always very difficult to distinguish from a host of other variables. IES (Tamkin et al. 2002) reminds us that that not everything has to be measured in financial terms but can also be measured in behavioural impacts, i.e. how well a learning initiative has been able to influence employees' behaviour. For example, you might also want to measure whether your employees have started using new platforms, whether teams are functioning more effectively, whether people are taking part in discussions more actively, or whether leaders have started having 1:1s with their team members more often.

To effectively measure the impact of learning, it's important to combine qualitative data like employee feedback, behavioural patterns, and other observations with quantitative data from various sources, including your learning platforms and quantitative surveys. Moreover, while social media, simulations, games, and Massive Open Online Course (MOOC) are increasingly being used, we need a better understanding of their effectiveness. Brinkerhoff (in Tamkin et al. 2002) suggests focusing on three questions:

- How well is our organisation using learning to drive needed performance improvement?
- What is our organisation doing that facilitates performance improvement from learning? What needs to be maintained and strengthened?
- What is our organisation doing, or not doing, that impedes performance improvement from learning? What needs to change?

To measure the direct impact of individual learning on business performance (Level Four evaluation) the link between the objectives of the individual, the development activity and the individual's performance must be strong and credible. Kirkpatrick suggests the following guidelines to implementation when trying to assess the impact of training on business results:

- Use a control group, if possible
- Allow enough time for results to be achieved
- Measure both before and after training, if feasible
- Repeat the measurement at appropriate times
- Consider the cost of evaluation versus the potential benefits
- Be satisfied with the evidence if absolute proof isn't possible to attain.

In one financial services organisation, poor business results led to a freeze on promotions and a squeeze on management development with any spend needing to be fully justified. The HRD team, in partnership with some of the business heads, argued that the company would lose some of its 'star' employees unless some form of development was offered. The question was, where should limited investment be focused?

The HRD team had been engaged in the identification of leadership competencies and it was decided that these could be used as the basis of a development centre for an identified group of 'at-risk' high-flyers. In addition to aiding retention, the outputs of the centre were to be information, which individuals could use to drive their personal development plans with their managers. To ensure that these plans could be relevant, managers were involved before and after the event in identifying individual objectives and in providing on-the-job coaching. Managers clearly needed, and received, careful briefing about their role.

Individuals and managers needed to discuss and agree, prior to the event, what the individual's main development needs were relative to the competencies. Various tools were provided, including 360-degree feedback, to help them to prioritize objectives. They had to be quite specific about how addressing that need would help. So they had to answer questions such as:

- If you were to learn to deal better with that situation, what difference would that make to you, to other people and the business?
- How will you know that you are making progress on that objective? How will you deal differently with the situation?
- How will people respond differently to you? What difference will that make to you, to others and to the business?

Participants therefore came with very clear objectives and measures of success in mind. They were active partners with the HRD and Management team who were delivering the activities to ensure that the centre met their needs.

Immediately following the centre, individuals met with their manager and agreed a practical action plan to build on the outputs of the centre. The participants were followed up over the next 18 months at three- and six-monthly intervals. The results were impressive. In addition to the 'soft' targets of the centre, such as making people feel valued, boosting morale etc., there were many examples of the impact on the bottom line of improved performance as a result of people taking part in the centre. One participant was able to pinpoint how, by changing his own leadership style as a result of the feedback and coaching he had received, he was managing his own team more effectively (and the team agreed). Nothing else had changed – it was the same team, and the market conditions were just as tough. However, within a year of the centre, that team had outperformed all other comparable teams, producing millions of pounds' worth of extra sales revenue.

Pressure to prove that development activities add value is usually at its highest when business results mean that every item of expenditure needs to be justified. However, carrying out evaluations on this scale can be time consuming and costly too, except that the costs are likely to be hidden. This is partly because salaries of trainers and trainees are usually excluded when costs are calculated. Marilyn McDougall and Angela Mulvie (1997) carried out a study of how companies measure the impact of HRM to the bottom line. They found that many organisations make access to management knowledge and skills available to employees on a general basis as part of a philosophy of continuous learning. Participants are therefore not expected to prove how the training has helped them produce improved bottom-line results, though the researchers predicted that this situation might change.

And indeed, the advent of technology-based training provides valuable data about the real impact of an intervention. It makes training accessible on demand, can reach a wider audience and can achieve real impact. In-person conference organisers who may previously have reached 2000 attendees at most can now reach tens of thousands of fee-paying attendees since geography is no barrier.

In future, choices about where to focus development, and evaluation of outcomes are likely to involve use of predictive analytics, instead of trusting intuition or a hunch. Learning analytics can help you identify where your investments are paying off and where the learning materials need to be improved to optimise the production value of your training. More efficient learning approaches can shorten the time to competence, increase retention, and decrease the average cost per learner. As the number of learners grows, even greater economies of scale can be achieved. Analytics can be used to assess the impact of upskilling on the business through stronger culture and engagement, faster innovation and digital transformation; the percentage of people growing their careers with new projects and opportunities.

Reflective activity

- How can training and development activities, learning, and the organisation of the learning function best support an organisation's business strategy?

CONCLUSION

It is truism that organisations that wish to attract and retain talent must provide people with opportunities for growth. Businesses that invest in reskilling and upskilling their workforce will build greater agility, responsiveness to sudden market changes and remain competitive. We have considered learning from a broader, more strategic perspective that includes formal training and development; self-directed, technology-based, informal learning; continuous learning; coaching and capability development.

Building a responsive, agile twenty-first-century workforce is not just about the skills of the workforce; it's about creating productive, empowered and dynamic workplaces where continuous improvement, learning and innovation are the norm. Senior leaders should build a culture of lifelong learning and encourage people to prioritise development. HR/L&D can work towards creating a growth culture in which learning is valued and supported, and where the enhanced skills of the individual are put to good use. In such a development culture, the pressure to measure a return on every development activity may be less strong than in a culture that believes any offline activity is a cost. It is in the interest of individuals to take responsibility for managing their development, but the organisation can help 'kick-start' the process by providing people with the opportunity to understand what to develop and how. This will be enhanced in organisations where personal development planning is a core element of a performance review process. Even though returns to the business may not be immediate, investing in developing people will produce bigger returns in the long run.

REFERENCES

Brinkerhoff, R.O. (2005). Training the success case method: A strategic evaluation approach to increasing the value and effect of training. *Advances in Developing Human Resources*, February. https://www.researchgate.net/profile/Robert-Brinkerhoff-3/publication/237773207_Training_The_Success_Case_Method_A_Strategic_Evaluation_Approach_to_Increasing_the_Value_and_Effect_of/links/544114170cf2a76a3cc75b6a/Training-The-Success-Case-Method-A-Strate

Cheung-Judge, M-Y and Holbeche, L.S. (2021). *Organization Development: A practitioner's guide for OD and HR*, 3rd Edition, London: Kogan Page.

CIPD. (2020). *Learning and Skills at Work 2020*. London: Chartered Institute of Personnel and Development.

Cummings, T.G. and Worley, C.G. (2014). *Organization Development and Change*. Chicago: Cengage Learning.

Deloitte (2019). *Leading the social enterprise: Reinvent with a human focus, 2019 Deloitte Global Human Capital Trends*. https://www2.deloitte.com/ro/en/pages/human-capital/articles/2019-deloitte-global-human-capital-trends.html

Deloitte Insights (2019). Skills change but capabilities endure. *Deloitte Center for the Edge*. https://www2.deloitte.com/content/dam/insights/us/articles/6332_From-skills-to-capabilities/6332_Skills-change-capabilites-endure.pdf

Dignan, A. (2019). *Brave New Work: Are You Ready to Reinvent Your Organization?* London: Penguin.

Eoyang, G. and Holladay, R. (2013). *Adaptive Action: Leveraging Uncertainty in Your Organization*. Stanford, CA: Stanford University Press.

Faragher, J. (2019). Should HR embrace agile methodology? *People Management*, 24 Oct.

Gartner (2018). Future of work scenarios 2035: 'I'd Rather Have a Bot Do It'. https://gtnr.it/2OSt622

Hancock, B. (2020). How will your team fare in the future of work? *McKinsey*. https://www.mckinsey.com/business-functions/organization/our-insights/todays-skills-tomorrows-jobs-how-will-your-team-fare-in-the-future-of-work?cid=other-eml-alt-mip-mck&hdpid=-8047f6a6-c693-4786-bc58-4cbceb97474d&hctky=2592654&hlkid=99ee2d94e87642b08210d

HEE (2019). *NHS Interim People Plan*. https://www.longtermplan.nhs.uk/wp-content/uploads/2019/05/Interim-NHS-People-Plan_June2019.pdf

Kaufman, R., Keller, J. and Watkins, R. (1995). What works and what doesn't: Evaluation beyond Kirkpatrick. *Performance and Instruction* 35(2), 8–12.

Kirkpatrick, D. L. (1996). Revisiting Kirkpatrick's four-level model. *Training and Development*, 50(1), 45–49.

KPMG (2018). *Growing pains. 2018 Global CEO Outlook*. KPMG Insights. https://home.kpmg/xx/en/home/insights/2018/05/ceo-outlook.html

Manyika, J., Lund, S., Chui, M., Bughin, J., Woetzel, J., Batra, P., Ko, R. and Sanghvi, S. (2017). *Jobs lost, jobs gained: What the future of work will mean for jobs, skills, and wages*. McKinsey Global Institute. http://bit.ly/mck-future-of-jobs. https://www.mckinsey.com/featured-insights/future-of-work/jobs-lost-jobs-gained-what-the-future-of-work-will-mean-for-jobs-skills-and-wages.

McDougall, M. and Mulvie, A. (1997). HRM's contribution to strategic change: Measuring impact on the bottom line. *Strategic Change*, 6(8), 451–458.

Pulley, M. L. (1994). Navigating the evaluation rapids. *Training and Development*, 48(9), September, 19–24.

PwC (2020). *Talent Trends 2020, upskilling: Building confidence in an uncertain world*. https://www.pwc.com/gx/en/ceo-agenda/ceosurvey/2020/trends/talent.html

PwC (2017). *20th CEO survey - global talent. The talent challenge: Harnessing the power of human skills in the machine age*. PwC. http://bit.ly/pwc-ceo-survey.

Stahl, G., Bjorkman, I., Farndale, E., Morris, S.S., Paauwe, J., Stiles, P., Trevor, J. and Wright, P. (2012). Six principles of effective global talent management. *MIT Sloan Management Review*, Winter.

Tamkin, P., Yarnall, J. and Kerrin, M. (2002). *Kirkpatrick and Beyond: A review of models of training evaluation, Report 392*. Brighton: Institute for Employment Studies.

Workday (Dunne, S.). *Global Finance Leader Study: Why CFOs must find common ground with their HR and IT peers*. https://www.workday.com/en-gb/pages/stories/cfos-common-ground-hr-and-it.html

11
Supporting flexible career development

CHAPTER OVERVIEW

In previous editions of this book and earlier chapters of this edition I have looked at the changing nature of the psychological contract and its implications for ('white-collar') careers and for HR. In this chapter we return to the topic, looking at changing career expectations, in particular considering the issue of how employees can achieve work-life balance, a career conundrum which has grown in significance in recent years. We shall cover:

- The changing psychological contract
- Enabling mobility
- Career pathing
- Flexible working

LEARNING OBJECTIVES

- To explore how the psychological contract may be shifting
- To discuss practical options HR can take to meet employee needs

DOI: 10.4324/9781003219996-13

INTRODUCTION: THE CHANGING PSYCHOLOGICAL CAREER CONTRACT

The old career paradigm used to go something like this: as long as employees were doing a good job, they might expect continuing employment and be able to contemplate promotion up a vertical career ladder. In return, the employer expected high levels of performance and loyalty from employees.

However, ongoing organisational change and uncertainty since the 1990s seriously undermined key aspects of this 'psychological contract' between employers and employees. 'Jobs for life' became a thing of the past and flatter organisational structures challenged the expectation about career development being 'onwards and upwards'. Employers shed jobs and abandoned previous career management practices based on the myth that careers could be planned by organisations. 'Employability' and 'manage your own career' were supposed to have replaced job security as part of the 'new deal'.

In the early years of the millennium, during the so-called 'War for Talent', the balance of power in the employment relationship swung in favour of skilled employees. During a prolonged period of growth and full employment that followed, the discussion moved on to less of a focus on 'careers' and more on 'talent management' (from the employer perspective) and 'lifestyle' (from the employee perspective). Yet in his 2005 book *Happiness: Lessons from a New Science* Lord Layard argued that that there is a paradox at the heart of our lives. While most people want more income, the evidence suggested that in general people had grown no happier in the previous 50 years, even as average incomes have more than doubled. This paradox is true of Britain, the United States, continental Europe and Japan. The search for a better lifestyle, and for greater balance between work and the rest of life, is becoming the dominant issue for most employees regardless of age.

Fast forward to 2018 and Gallup's State of the Workplace report shows that the primary reason people leave their jobs is for career growth opportunities. After all, with the prospect of longer working lives, people will naturally think more strategically about their jobs. For many employees, as 'jobs' are deconstructed by technology to be replaced by 'tasks', the career way ahead is unclear. And in the early stages of a potential recession following the pandemic crisis, with job losses and retrenchment, the power balance in the employment relationship appears to have swung back in favour of the employer. In such a scenario, the psychological contract of 'mutual development' is in danger of being breached and may cause people to 'hunker down' to hold on to their current roles at the very time when they should be actively developing new capabilities. This creates the risk of damage to employee well-being, loss of trust and a stressed and conforming rather than committed workforce.

Towards a new psychological contract – helping people to help themselves

To maintain healthy psychological contracts, career management and development should not simply be a question of leaving people to it. It should be a partnership between the organisation and individuals, since it is in both parties' interests to collaborate. Employers should respond to employee desires for career development and employees need to adopt an enterprising approach to their own career development. Many employees would value insight and advice on how to develop their careers in the digital age, and on what skills and experiences they should amass to ensure their employability and job satisfaction in years to come. They want career conversations and coaching to help them set goals, manage their development and control their career.

Of course, not everyone needs help. Many employees accept responsibility for managing their own career. They tend to be self-aware architects of change, constantly looking for new ways to improve their practice and challenge the status quo. These self-empowered individuals usually have a clear sense of what is important to them, and indeed this is a common characteristic of individuals identified as key contributors by their employers. Such new-style employees are often motivated by teamwork and want to develop a range of broader skills rather than simply achieving the highest possible rank in the shortest time possible. Typically, they actively negotiate development opportunities as part of their recruitment package and take responsibility for their own learning.

Guidance

Companies in the fast-moving technology sector seem to be among the first to offer support for new forms of career development. Some organisations are providing self-development processes such as development centres to help people to manage their own careers. People can learn what skills they have and exactly what they need to work on in order to get to where they want to be. Various learning platforms built on next-gen AI can help people understand what their career drivers are, and take stock of their talents, skills, job experience, motivators, aspirations and life-factors. Artificial Intelligence will increasingly enable an 'outside-in', more rounded picture of people's skills and capabilities, capturing both the skills that people develop and use in-house and other capabilities evident in their social media profiles.

PricewaterhouseCoopers (PwC) offers employees an independent career counselling service to help people recognise their development needs and work out what they must do to meet them. In one-to-one sessions people can talk through their career preferences and the options, both within the company and outside. The service is self-referred and confidential. Individuals are helped to set objectives to enhance their performance and match their needs to those of the business and also create a more satisfying working life. The career management service also helps employees to write their own job description.

A key feature is the emphasis on helping individuals to clarify their personal values and to use this enhanced awareness to help them find ways of increasing their job satisfaction in the here and now. This twin emphasis on the needs of the organisation and those of the individual, on the present and the future, allows people to develop a pragmatic approach to development planning.

Organisations can also provide resources and a variety of growth opportunities to assist employees to progress. For example, work shadowing, secondments and project teams give junior employees the chance to work more closely with others at a more senior level, while for more senior staff, taking on a community role, such as sitting on charitable or educational governing bodies, can provide an outlet for an individual's skills as well as communicating positive messages about the organisation.

In response to low career satisfaction ratings in a staff survey, and after extensive consultation with employees, one science-based organisation designed a range of self-help career tools for individuals to use. Initially, take-up of some of the tools was low. It was only when line managers were trained to take on a coaching role and employees were trained in how to apply the tools that the self-development tools became more widely used. The firm drew up possible elements of a career framework as shown in Figure 11.1.

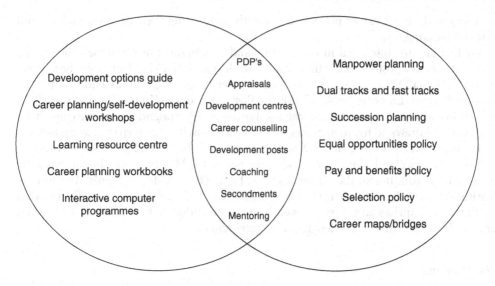

Figure 11.1 Possible elements of a career framework.

The aim is to create a self-development culture and currently the organisation is focusing on 'overlap' areas such as personal development planning processes and appraisals. Plans are in place to develop complementary organisational processes such as succession planning and pay and benefits which will add 'muscle' to the policies. So providing organisational support for careers can help people to help themselves.

Case: Imperial College – Postdoc and Fellows Development Centre

Research and innovation play a critical role in delivering competitive advantage in the UK's ambitious economic and industrial strategies. The UK Concordat to Support the Career Development of Researchers recognises this and aims to set the gold standard in researcher development. However, becoming a full-time academic at a research university is not an easy path to travel and in most universities, researchers are left to fend for themselves with respect to career development.

An independent review led by Professor David Bogle recognised that there is still much to do to create the healthy and supportive culture needed to ensure researchers are given every opportunity to thrive and realise their potential in the increasingly diverse, mobile and global environment. Indeed, a study by research funder Wellcome (2019) points out that university researchers in the United Kingdom generally suffer from a toxic work culture. 78% of researchers report high levels of competition even within teams and lack of support, resulting in highly pressurised working environments. Only 19% of early career researchers feel secure in pursuing their career.

Imperial College London, a global leading research-intensive university, is tackling these challenges head-on. Imperial is sector-leading with regards to its specific support for researchers and is the only university so far with its own dedicated centre for Postdocs and Fellows. For over a decade, Dr Liz Elvidge, founder and Head of the award-winning Postdoc and Fellows Development Centre (PFDC) at Imperial College, has been helping postdoctoral researchers achieve their career goals – and also advising them about a variety of different career paths and generally supporting their decision-making and skill-set building.

Liz first became interested in the training and development of researchers during her own first stint as a postdoc. Since then, she has worked at Heriot Watt University, been Head of Academic Staff Development at Cambridge University and has led the Centre at Imperial for over 10 years. Liz's own book What Every Postdoc Needs to Know (Elvidge et al. 2017), written in collaboration with two colleagues, illustrates Liz's straightforward and empathetic approach and draws on her many years of experience as well as her own stint as a postdoc.

Liz launched the Centre in 2009, with Sir Gareth Robert's 'SET for Success' funding and set it up as a stand-alone unit loosely attached to the HR function. She subsequently obtained core funding for the Centre, its value having been widely recognised within the institution where 16% of staff are in academic roles and 35% are researchers. The Centre's small team comprises administrators and adviser/consultants, four of whom have PhDs and are familiar with the challenges facing researchers.

The challenge

A postdoctoral research position comes after a PhD doctorate degree. It is a fixed-term contract, typically funded through a grant awarded to a Principal Investigator of a research project. Currently Imperial has 2,500 postdocs and fellows on its books. After completing a postdoctoral position, researchers can apply for a fellowship which provides funding directly to them and their research. Imperial has its own fellowship scheme, while there are similar schemes run by the Royal Society, Research Councils UK, and charities such as Wellcome. A successful fellowship will put a researcher in a good position to apply for long-term faculty positions, such as a lectureship.

However, only 10% of postdocs nationally go on to permanent academic positions (the figure is slightly higher for Imperial postdocs). What's more, research conducted by the PFDC shows that the longer people stay in postdoctoral positions, the more they want to become academics – yet the less likely that becomes as time goes by. In fact, four years seems to be a 'breakpoint' for postdocs, after which time the academic door effectively closes, as others come through with fellowships.

'There's a real challenge in dealing with a population where 90% will ultimately be disappointed and in some cases believe that they are a failure at something they have been doing for so long', Liz says. The Centre helps its users understand that being a postdoc is not a long-term career and encourages them to be realistic about the fact that they are not likely to get an academic job at Imperial at the end of their contract. Therefore, managing their career is their own responsibility. Equally, Liz is clear that she does not want anyone to leave Imperial without a career, and the support on offer via the Centre aims to ensure that postdocs are well placed to achieve this. This also means helping postdocs understand that careers outside of academia – such as in industry, publishing and research administration – should not be viewed as 'alternative' or lesser, but rather that they are all equally valid paths.

Practical support

The PFDC aims to support postdocs' career preparation whatever path they ultimately choose with a variety of initiatives, including pop-up briefings following a new announcement or funding stream; leadership courses; away days and much more. When postdocs arrive at Imperial, they are given a welcome booklet full of useful, practical information and are invited to a welcome lunch to introduce them to key contacts. The Centre has a monthly online newsletter and a very active Twitter feed.

The PFDC offers a programme of professional skills and career development training, support and opportunities, to enable all Imperial College London postdocs and Fellows to succeed in their current position while planning their next step. The support on offer includes:

- Training sessions - such as preparing successful fellowship applications, persuasive communication and various funder showcases
- Residential writing retreats –providing dedicated time and space to write
- Individual support – one-to-one advisory sessions on issues that individuals would like to discuss, e.g. discuss their CV, job searching, fellowship applications (including review of draft applications), lectureship positions, moving out of academia, issues related to working in their lab/team.

One of the most successful initiatives is the mock interview scheme comprising realistic simulations for specific posts. Any postdoc can ask for an interview for any prospective job. Liz's team analyses the application and puts together a set of tailored interview questions – chaired by a member of PFDC staff, with postdocs making up the two or three panellists. These are drawn from a pool of postdoc volunteers – who also benefit themselves by seeing the required standard to be shortlisted and the interview process.

'We give them a hard time – there's no point otherwise – but also lots of constructive feedback', Liz says. 'Around 50% of postdocs land the job following a mock interview. That's substantially higher success rate than without one. Candidates often come back surprised and say, "the questions were virtually the same as the mock interview – how can that be?" Well, the answer is that we've been doing this a long time and we've got a database of questions'.

In particular the Centre provides very tailored support to postdocs applying for fellowships. One extraordinary success story concerns the UKRI Future Leaders Fellowship scheme (FLF) which aims to develop, retain, attract and sustain research and innovation talent in the United Kingdom and provides up to seven years of funding for at least 550 early career researchers and innovators, tackling difficult and novel challenges. For round 2, the college had nine shortlisted candidates and were awarded eight. Liz and her team went through all the draft applications and provided mock interviews and detailed feedback. The successful candidates achieved £12 million in research funding, providing the successful Fellows with a solid springboard for their careers.

Next steps

Liz and her team are not complacent however, believing that 'We're only as good as the last thing we've done'. Going forward, the PFDC is spearheading some new schemes, such as Pathways for Postdocs – an online resource portal that collates existing material that postdocs find useful in easy to digest skill-based tip sheets. The Centre is careful in its use of language, so as not to appear to devalue jobs in industry relative to academic pathways. The PFDC will also be launching a new shadowing scheme, allowing postdocs to shadow staff who have studied for a PhD or postdoc, but gone into a different professional role. Initially, that will involve shadowing Imperial staff for example in the research office or other administrative roles, but it could be rolled out to external companies, perhaps drawing on the pool of former Imperial postdocs now working in industry.

For several years the PFDC has administered a network of postdoc reps – regular postdocs who represent their department, campus or larger group and raise the concerns of their peers and also inform them about future opportunities. Now the PFDC is seeding a network of academic champions in each department, often full Professors, all of whom are known to Liz, who can make sure that the issues of postdocs are well represented at a more senior level, for example regarding training. Every postdoc at Imperial is contractually permitted to undertake up to ten days training allowance per year – something quite unique in the sector.

Liz believes strongly that the key to credibility in a hot-house university environment is a reputation for successful delivery. Liz regularly meets with all Heads of Department to update them and exchange information about postdoc progress and opportunities. She is able to use her influence, straight talking and relationship network at senior levels to ensure that postdocs have access to training; 'If the Principal Investigators protest and say: "I really don't think my postdoc can be doing that," we can say: "actually, you don't make that choice"'.

The PFDC also commissioned research looking at the barriers faced by female postdocs as well as black, Asian and minority ethnic postdocs, when applying for fellowships. After reviewing the results with the Vice Provost (Research), a course of action is planned. Liz is a member of many departmental committees and an Athena SWAN Assessor. In 2015, she was awarded the Dame Julia Higgins Medal for 'outstanding support for female early career researchers and academics'.

Looking ahead, Liz also notes that, while fellowship recipients, probationary lecturers and lecturers are all on a more solid footing than postdocs, they are still shaping the future direction of their careers and deciding what sort of academic they want to become. Her thoughts are now turning to providing the practical advice and support required by new academics and teaching fellows.

By any measure of impact, the type of support provided by the Centre is proving highly successful, not only in providing these junior, temporary staff with support in the vital issue of careers, but also in enhancing Imperial's reputation as an employer. Imperial has held the HR Excellence in Research Award since 2012 for its 'concrete steps to enhance working conditions for researchers'. Furthermore, the Centre's work around the Future Leaders' Fellows has been included in Imperial's Research Excellence Framework (REF) statement (the measure by which universities' research success is judged), which helps Imperial distinguish itself further in the highly competitive global higher education sector.

Reflective activity

- Postdocs usually do not end up working for the University long-term. Why should they be offered career services if they are not part of the long-term staff?
- What kind of careers advice is available in your organisation?

ENABLING MOBILITY

Gartner (2020) suggests that only 27% of workers feel that their employers make it easy to find and switch into attractive internal opportunities. Rigid hierarchies limit internal mobility, and companies can make it quite difficult for employees to move internally. Mobility is not always about moving upwards – it can also entail a sideways move such as temporary job swaps, and involving employees in part-time projects, that can help people gain valuable new skills and experiences. Often there is considerable stigma attached to the idea of a sideways move. Fear of failure can be a deterrent and many people who have experienced such moves commonly report a lack of support to help them get up to speed and function effectively in their new role as quickly as possible.

In contrast, agile organisations appear to have built-in clarity about where support for employee mobility sits. As Aghina et al. (2015) point out:

> Agile organizations, by contrast, deliberately choose which dimension of their organizational structure will be what we call their "primary" one. This choice will dictate where individual employees work—in other words, where they are likely to receive coaching and training and where the infrastructure around their jobs is located. Day-to-day work, performance measurement, and the determination of rewards, on the other hand, are more likely to happen in teams that cut across formal structures. The primary home of employees remains an anchor along their career paths, while the crosscutting teams form, dissolve, and reform as resources shift in response to market demands.

Human resource and training professionals can help managers to enrich jobs and keep people motivated and learning on the job. For example, during the pandemic, Nationwide, a UK building society, committed to making all 18,000 employees feel safe and offered reassurance to staff that their roles would be secure for the year ahead. This led to new thinking about redeploying staff differently. HR and L&D professionals can also encourage employees to take a positive view of lateral career development. Some organisations deliberately position sideways moves as developmental. They feature strongly in company newsletters individuals working on lateral transfers and pay one-off bonuses in recognition of the effort and learning curve involved. Since lateral moves often release bottlenecks and create opportunities for others, care has to be taken to ensure that the benefits of sideways moves do not seem biased in the organisation's favour.

Setting up a formal internal mobility programme

A strategy is needed to equip diverse people to drive their own career moves by gaining experience, building networks and growing their reputation. To make internal mobility achievable across an entire company requires some programming. This is where a well-thought-out policy on lateral moves and the provision of help where necessary can make it possible for individuals to step out comfort zones and embrace new experiences. Companies should communicate with their employees about the organisation's career development philosophy and drive an ongoing discussion around internal mobility. Important questions may include: What is the role of the employee versus the role of the manager? Are employees empowered to drive their own career movement, or are managers responsible for orchestrating career moves? Furthermore, what is the company's perspective on, and management of, critical career success factors such as depth versus breadth of expertise, international assignments, and level of mobility? Factors such as these can help inform employees' career decisions.

Setting up an internal mobility programme requires deliberate effort to identify the pathways to mobility, so that you can communicate where the opportunities are. Job requirements can be defined in ways which enable people to undertake a realistic self-assessment and competencies can help ensure a good match between opportunity and the potential candidate. This way, a data bank of people requiring specific forms of development can be matched against available options that may include job swaps and secondments. Corporate structures that block internal mobility and talent hoarding managers must be put in their place – team members must feel free to consider internal moves without the risk of penalty.

A good talent mobility platform can help match people to opportunities and enable these nimbler forms of mobility. Bersin (2020) provides an overview of various Talent Marketplace platforms but also points out that this is not a solution that can be 'solved' simply by buying a software tool or platform. 'Creating a culture of internal mobility is a top to bottom effort. It changes the way careers work; it changes the way you reward and pay people; and it changes the nature of management, leadership, and learning'.

The increased mobility of staff can also be assisted by greater awareness of the roles of different business groups, often gained from briefings hosted by different business groups at the place of work. Where this is combined with an open job posting scheme, 'surprising' moves can prove very successful for all concerned. Technology can dynamically provide insights into what people are learning – so people can be matched with jobs and stretch opportunities. GE for example has an online portal where employees can post their skills and desired opportunities and managers with vacancies and projects can be signposted to staff with requisite skills. Training and coaching can help, especially in providing employees in new roles with the 'new tools of their trade'. Again, Human Resource professionals can facilitate this process to ensure that human capital is being maximised.

CAREER PATHING

As the road to internal career progress is rarely clear, companies must be more creative when thinking about the nature of the road and the destination. Career pathing and internal mobility software can help systematise the process, increase the visibility of opportunities and make it easier to identify and grow internal talent. Mobilising internal talent is beneficial; Glassdoor research suggests that articulating a prosperous career path and maintaining a positive culture are the most important ways to ensure worker satisfaction.

Career pathing is about finding the sweet spot between worker aspirations and capabilities and the goals of the firm. To be most effective career pathing should be integrated into a company's overall talent management strategy. By aligning talent management processes and providing linkage between job roles, desired competencies and key experiences, career paths can lead to a well-rounded, highly trained workforce that is agile and equipped to deal with future challenges.

One British local authority had difficulties recruiting and retaining junior staff working in its customer call centres. The work was not well paid and there were few opportunities for progression. Many employees wanted to stay working locally and, when they became frustrated at the lack of opportunity to move on to a higher paying job within the council, they tended to move to higher paying jobs in the local area instead, usually having completed their lengthy and expensive training programme. To try and stem this outflow of now well qualified staff, HR&OD, working with an external consultant, led a process to identify with stakeholders a number of career paths to other parts of the local authority. Career centre staff were involved in the process and their needs and motivations were taken into account. Former call centre staff who had 'made it' to new positions within the council were also involved. This provided a rich seam of information and experience for ambitious employees to draw on.

Proposed career paths were considered and refined by all parties and supervisors were trained to hold career conversations with staff. Many former call centre staff have subsequently made lateral moves or gained promotions in other parts of the council. The call centre is now seen as a desirable place to work and has also become a recognised talent pool for the whole organisation. Locally, the council's reputation has become that of employer of choice and there is no shortage of new candidates eager to work in the call centre.

Process of developing career paths

To create career paths, it is vital to consult subject-matter experts, interview functional leaders, job holders and carry out external industry benchmarking. As developing career paths can be complex, software that has career pathing and internal mobility capabilities can help. This will help you systematise your efforts and make internal mobility more accessible and achievable across your entire company.

I have adapted the process suggested by Cao and Thomas (2013) as follows:

Create a career roadmap

These show what a prototypical career looks like in terms of sequential positions, roles, and stages that are typically presented in a diagram. They outline common avenues for moving within and across jobs in ways that facilitate growth and career advancement. Typical questions to explore when defining career paths include:

- What are the target jobs? Given the purposes for which you are developing career paths, what set of jobs, occupations, roles/or levels does it make sense to target?
- What are the positions or roles that comprise a typical career path of a person in this job/occupation?
- What series of positions or roles should a person hold if his or her goal is to make it to a more senior level in this job/occupation?
- How does the typical career path of today differ from the career path of the future, given the organisation's strategic direction?
- What positions or roles will comprise a successful career path in the future?
- What positions/roles/jobs allow one to gain the experience and competencies important at higher levels, and how do they fit together to form a career path?
- What positions/roles/jobs tend to lead to promotions, and how do they fit together to form a career path?
- Are there realistic or typical paths that cut across units or departments within the organisation? If so, what are those paths?

Draft career paths

Organisations may use existing competency grades or job bands to define vertical and horizontal hierarchies at each career stage and they can also do so by compiling organisational knowledge to create a general framework. Some companies choose to provide additional information such as common moves and critical development experiences when changing careers, the number of employees in a particular job role and the growth across those populations, and different job categories in particular business units. This information is particularly useful as employees become more versatile and move across job roles in different parts of the business to increase their capability.

- Are any typical career paths missing from the initial draft model?
- Are any of the draft paths inaccurate or uncommon?
- How should the initial draft career paths be changed to reflect the organisation's strategic direction?
- Do the initial draft paths capture both realistic paths within this occupation, and realistic cross-occupation paths? If not, what paths are missing?

Build position profiles

These create distinctions between job roles in career paths by outlining their core responsibilities, skills and requirements. It is also important to determine the qualifications and expertise associated with different career positions, roles and stages. This might include the recommended or required qualifications, skills, technical training, licenses and certifications for successful job holders.

- Review the required qualifications at each level. What additional education or training (if any) would you recommend that a person have to perform well at a higher level?
- What general types of experience would you recommend that a person have to perform well at this level?
- Are there certifications for this job that are not required, but that you would recommend obtaining?
- What are the key developmental experiences that a person must obtain at this point in his or her career that will prepare him or her for the next career step?
- Are there specific stretch assignments that a person should seek at this point in his or her career?
- *Expertise*. Within a given career path, what is the relative value of breadth versus depth of expertise for (a) individual success and (b) organisational success?
- *Connectivity*. To what extent are various career or occupational paths interconnected, and how might such connections be used for individual, organisational or industry growth?

Identify core competencies and expected behaviours

Competencies should specify the differentiating behaviour of outstanding performers, and also serve as performance standards that define expected results in different functions. Some companies have introduced the concept of 'vertically integrated' competencies in order to vertically align career path design with the strategic talent management process. These tend to be the same competencies from one career stage to the next but differ in their expected scope (e.g. basic understanding, basic proficiency, expert level) and impact at each level.

- Review the overall list of competencies associated with the job. Which, if any, of those competencies are accrued or strengthened at the first point in the career path?
- Does the relative importance of this competency increase or decrease at successive levels or roles in the organisation? If so, how?
- Are there patterns or combinations of competencies that are valuable and should be identified in the path?

Incorporate training and development

Organisations can link career paths to employee development by prioritising position profile characteristics and identifying key experiences that employees should acquire (depth and/or breadth) as they move along the career path. What specific competencies would be strengthened through critical developmental experience X? What skills or capabilities does a person gain through that experience? Training can help upskill employees so they can more easily switch to a new internal role and contribute faster once they switch. Developmental opportunities may include, for example, leadership training courses, stretch assignments, cross-functional teams, profit and loss responsibility or international assignments. These experiences provide the opportunity to develop competencies that are important for the next career stage. Outlining critical development experiences allows managers and employees to have more meaningful career conversations.

Establish accountability

Organisations should build accountability for the process by defining the roles and responsibilities of individuals who support it. An internal hiring target will encourage HR to hire internally at least some of the time and hiring managers to consider the internal wealth of talent. Success stories will motivate hiring managers to consider internal talent and encourage your existing employees to keep an eye on internal opportunities, while making your company more attractive to external recruits.

To empower managers to become career champions, HR should provide managers and employees with the necessary tools, guidelines, templates, and training to ensure that both parties are committed to their role in the career development process and understand its importance. Potential career management resources could include physical or virtual career development Centres of Excellence, career advisors, training to help managers become better career coaches, employee self-assessments, and career discussion guides. The British Council offers sessions for staff on 'my career and aspirations conversations' and one for managers on how to lead these in an open, honest and balanced way: setting it up, preparation, rapport, listening, questioning, coaching, action planning, etc.

Measure internal hiring success

There are many benefits to building workforce mobility. Comprehensively measuring and monitoring the outcomes of internal talent mobility will prove that hiring internally is simply cheaper and less risky than hiring externally. In a learning culture people become more mobile, learn faster and stay longer since in organisations that actively plan for careers and provide ongoing training and a clear career path people may feel there is a future for them in the organisation. By developing people's skills companies effectively build talent pools for succession purposes.

Case: developing innovative career tracks in a scientific environment

In recent years, especially in organisations with flatter structures, the trend for career development to take place through a generalist route has become well established, even within scientific/technical environments. 'Core' employees have by implication been encouraged to become multi-skilled, business-oriented individuals and often the only way to make vertical career progress is by taking on management or customer facing roles. Reverting to traditional technical ladders can help employers retain the specialist staff they need. For instance, Schlumberger, the oil services group, introduced a career path for the technical community which has proved to be a strong motivator. Recruits were promised promotions, status and compensation comparable to those of senior managers, as well as opportunities to shape research and product-development agendas. Schlumberger has also become one of the exploration and production industry's leading recruiters of women engineers by introducing flexible working practices (Guthridge et al. 2008).

One UK organisation operating as part of a government agency directly employs large numbers of scientific and engineering staff, almost all of whom are highly qualified. On the whole, the workforce has a relatively young age profile with 44% of employees being between the ages of 20 and 30. The organisation is attractive to many potential recruits because of the high-powered scientific nature of the work carried out. However, many recruits join with high expectations about rapid pay progression. Given the constraints on public sector pay awards, shrinking incomes and the ongoing uncertainty of the sector within which the organisation operates, these expectations are somewhat doomed to disappointment.

The organisation operates a matrix structure, with pressure to reduce bureaucracy and fixed overheads. The business requires that customer requirements are captured quickly and that a more flexible service is offered to a wider range of clients. The majority of the work carried out is project based. To achieve these objectives, the organisation needs to continue to attract but also retain high-calibre staff. On the plus side, the work is challenging and rewarding but on its own this is not enough to retain high-calibre staff who can earn more in commercial companies. Technical training is widely available and there is some management training although some of this is unfocused. The organisation has a 'sink or swim' environment, which appeals to some of the high-flyers, although some people quickly 'go stale'. On the whole, staff are highly educated and articulate, with high expectations. Retention is becoming an issue since many employees can see no obvious career progression.

Career issues

Prior to UK central government reforms, most of the civil service operated a similar pay and grading system which allowed for a degree of mobility for employees through a well-established system of promotion boards. Individuals could ask for and receive career counselling from senior civil servants. Promotion was often achieved by migrating between government departments and smaller entities, such as the organisation in question. Career ladders for both management and scientific grades co-existed up to certain senior levels. Despite the many limitations of the previous system, it did have the benefit of offering clarity.

In the current set-up, obvious technical career ladders have disappeared. Formal progression systems such as through gradings, job titles and pay have also been disaggregated. In theory, this separation should make progression on merit easier. However, in real terms the system offers drawbacks as far as employees are concerned and also in meeting the needs of the internal job market. Where once a person's job grade was used as a proxy for likely competence by project managers who were choosing staff for new projects, the complexity of the new system means that resourcing projects is very much a matter for the resource manager (who knows the population's skills) and project managers. This means that employees need to maintain good relations with resource managers if they wish to have their interests promoted for interesting projects.

In terms of career progression, while technical and managerial careers do exist, most employees soon learn that what amounts to career advancement is through customer-facing roles such as project management. The current structure offers limited scope for other forms of advancement. A few posts exist for technical leaders who are role models and quality monitors. Similarly, a few resource managers are responsible for allocating individuals to projects. Apart from these roles, progression to business area manager is what most employees are likely to aspire to and qualifications for these roles are largely based on having taken responsibility for managing projects of increasing size and complexity.

This leads to the problem that employees perceive that the only way to progress is through management and that the organisation does not value technical work. Whereas in the past, employees would have been encouraged, and expected, to spend several years in purely scientific roles, now it is not uncommon for employees to be managing customer projects within their first year of employment. For people who join the organisation with a strong desire to carry out scientific work, the current options are disappointing since they are obliged to leave behind the detailed scientific work if they want to be promoted. Some leave the organisation after a few years to carry out more highly paid project management roles in industry. They reason that since they are not doing what they wanted to do, namely scientific work, they might as well be more highly paid for managerial work elsewhere. Another problem is that early access to project management roles, and the relatively quick progression this makes possible for some, means that promotion opportunities tend to dwindle by the time people are in their early thirties. Again, this is a critical age for turnover.

Career tracks, not ladders

To address the problem the HR team, in partnership with management, adopted a five-phase strategy for career development. The aims of the proposed system were as follows:

- To meet individual needs and aspirations
- To create a system which is manageable and affordable
- To provide public recognition of status
- To ensure that the new system is fully integrated with HR
- To be flexible and enable individuals to switch between career tracks
- To be consistent with the parent organisation's systems and processes

The phases were as follows:

1. Research into staff aspirations and gaining ownership
2. Competency profiling
3. Developing a training framework
4. Developing a coaching culture
5. Defining career stages and developing a range of career tracks which are clear, feasible and desirable to employees

The research process involved a wide range of staff and senior management as well as some former staff. In response to the findings, a Career Levels framework was introduced to offer people clear insight into a wider range of choices and the kinds of development needed to support those choices. Each level is defined in terms of inputs, i.e. the knowledge, skills, understanding of the individual, as well as outputs, or how they apply these and the criteria they need to meet to deliver at that level.

Levels are primarily a reflection of the individual's personal contribution rather than a definition of a job or role. The framework uses clear technical and managerial competencies to define the kinds of roles people can engage in to match their own levels of development. While there are two primary career routes – technical and managerial – each route contains a number of common features and things which must be achieved in order for careers to progress, including zigzagging between these routes.

Employees will not be required to move jobs in order to move up the levels, but people will be expected to grow their own jobs, taking on new responsibilities and developing their contribution. It is also intended that people will be able to progress upward through the career levels, with the gaps growing larger between the 'higher' levels, or sideways to develop additional competencies or expertise.

Since the concept of levels applies to the person rather than the post, people hoping to move up a level follow the same system as people not changing jobs, i.e. they have to demonstrate evidence at their annual review that they are operating at a higher level. Open job posting was introduced and opportunities are advertised with an indication of the skills and competencies required for the post. Anyone with the required competencies can apply for job opportunities, and could be accepted, for any level. Professional development alone will be not be sufficient to ensure level adjustment but will be considered alongside other evidence of relevant experience. It is how the development is used that matters.

An important element of this framework is enabling line managers, including project managers, to become better coaches and developers of people who can provide real support for development. Levels provide much needed clarity about technical careers and enable staff to measure their progress. They provide a mechanism for matching capability to customer need now and in the future. They are also a planning tool for assessing needs for recruitment, development and succession purposes. They can also be used to create team profiles.

Reflective activity

- What do you consider to be the pros and cons of the career approach described in this case study?

CAREERS AND WORK-LIFE BALANCE

For many employees 'career' now means having the chance to also pay attention to other parts of their lives. Arguably, this is an area where responsible employers can provide clear and unequivocal support for better balance, rather than appearing to endorse the principle of work–life balance but doing nothing to make reality match the aspiration. Employers can offer flexible work schedules and ensure employees to take their holiday entitlement. Senior managers must act as role models with respect to balance and encourage others to work flexibly.

In the United Kingdom, organisations such as Watford Borough Council have developed clear family-friendly policies such as providing childcare vouchers and are supportive of flexible working. Littlewoods recognises that employees have a life (and dependants) outside work. Company policies allow people to change their work patterns as their circumstances change, for instance with elder care arrangements. Job-shares are encouraged and time off for emergencies is considered normal so that people do not have to resort to subterfuge to deal with a family crisis. Business Express, which is part of the Littlewoods group, offers employees five days' paid leave for family reasons each year. Fathers have ten days' paternity leave as a right. Having this as a right means that employees are more likely to be open about their needs rather than simply taking 'sick' leave. This means that the organisation can plan for the leave and avoid unexpected downtime.

US casual-lifestyle retailer Eddie Bauer uses its work–life programmes to help employees lead more productive and balanced lives. The firm has won many accolades for its approaches to employee support, including being named as one of the 'Best Companies to Work For' by Washington CEO magazine. A flexible work environment and an exceptional benefits package that covers routine and non-routine challenges of work and home make Eddie Bauer an employer of choice. The Employee Assistance programme offers a Child and Elder Care consulting and referral service; this gives employees and their family members access to personal counselling and legal and financial assistance.

Among other initiatives introduced are:

- Balance Day, a free day once a year when employees can 'call in well'. This is in addition to normal time off
- As well as the usual array of benefits, extras include a casual dress code and alternative transport options such as preferred parking for carpools
- Its Customized Work Environment programme offers options such as job-sharing, a compressed workweek and telecommuting
- A plan that allows employees to enjoy group buying power for mortgage loan discounts
- Emergency child-care.

Employers with employee-friendly policies argue that these policies are helping the business, as well as employees. In the case of Eddie Bauer, the work–life programmes have led to fewer sick days, less absenteeism and lower health-care costs. Lloyds TSB's policies are based on the belief that by offering employees peace of mind they are more likely to see greater productivity. By encouraging an overt and planned approach to leave for family issues, the company can also plan and arrange appropriate cover. Retention has also improved since people appreciate working for a supportive employer. At the UK City of Bradford Council, staff value the council's efforts to promote a good work–life balance, including its investment in services such as life coaching, cognitive behavioural therapy and alternative therapies. Staff can carry out voluntary work during council time if they match it with the same amount of their own time.

Flexible working

Flexibility has been a buzzword for decades. It applies to both the need for organisations to structure themselves so that they are highly responsive to the changing environment and also the effect this has on the nature of employment. Successive UK governments have introduced legislation to make flexible working more widely available and it has been strongly supported by employer organisations, trade unions and campaigning bodies. Flexible working is seen as helping families and individuals reconcile caring responsibilities and work, as an important means of increasing the quality of work and also delivering economic benefits such as better retention and recruitment and better productivity (Beatson 2019). So great are employee desires for flexibility that some are opting to become Charles Handy's 'portfolio' workers, who create their own career profiles by juggling several roles. The term 'sunlighting' is used to describe people who take time off from their regular work to do paid work elsewhere.

While prior to the pandemic most employees still worked traditional hours, often with a commute at either end of the day, in the United Kingdom, the number of part-time jobs increased faster than full-time equivalents rising from 6 million in 1992 to 8.59 million by 2019. Part-time and shift working are well established in the manufacturing, retail and leisure industries. People working part-time (mainly women at the time of writing) can arrange their schedule in a variety of ways (working mornings only for example). However such jobs tend to be more vulnerable to lay-offs during difficult periods and in periods of high unemployment, people prefer full-time jobs rather than part-time. In 2017, over 60% of people working part-time in Spain and Italy wanted a full-time job and 40% in France. This compares with 13% in the United Kingdom, 11% in Germany and 6% in the United States (OECD database. All figures include self-employed).

Despite the professed desire of employees for flexible working the underlying trend for all other forms of flexible working covered in the CIPD's Megatrends survey (Beatson 2019) is flat and much of any modest rise is driven by the increase in zero-hours contracts, which in large part reflects better reporting rather than increased use. Even though the pandemic has led to many workforces being based at home, research suggests that many younger people, mainly men, aim to return to office working. And while the range of flexible working options has increased in recent years, it appears that concerns over career progression are still preventing certain groups, especially fathers, senior and middle managers, from requesting a flexible working pattern.

So if flexible working may be the answer to meeting both organisational needs for flexibility and employee needs for better balance, managing a flexible workforce will require corresponding changes in HR systems and thinking as well as more accurate planning. Flexible working must not jeopardise career opportunities. As we have discussed, it often appears easier for some companies to use contractors, consultants and freelance workers rather than enabling their own staff to work flexibly. Using contractors allows organisations to call upon a body of experts when they are needed rather than keeping them on the payroll all the time. Contractors can juggle other jobs while maintaining a relationship with a company.

Firms may be reluctant to let staff go part-time but may be more willing to accommodate job-sharing. The Internet means that jobs can be shared across the globe. Flexi-workers tend to have a range of options: they can work annualised hours where an employee's workload is calculated over a whole year, or compressed hours, where work is condensed into fewer days. Extended leave arrangements are common as is study leave, demonstrating that employers are keen to support the needs and aspirations of their staff while also keeping the business operationally efficient. Less common are term-time-only working, 'key-time' working, voluntary reduced hours, associate schemes, etc.

Flexible working can be requested by anyone at Nationwide where more than 5000 staff work reduced hours while a number job-share, work from home or have term-time-only contracts. Staff can take a career break of up to six months during which they continue to receive all benefits, except pay. Other benefits include private health-care, concessionary mortgages, quarterly rewards and a long holiday entitlement. Employees can choose to retire at any time between 50 and 75, with a decent pension to look forward to, as the company pays 23.8% of salary into a scheme, with staff contributing 5%.

Even before the pandemic the idea was gaining ground that a much wider range of jobs can be based away from an office environment, thanks to technology. Working from home is increasing in many sectors and the pandemic has proved that remote working is both possible and flexible. Positive experiences of remote working during lockdowns may have persuaded many employers and workers to continue virtual working, or to engage in a hybrid form of working, with some time spent back in the workplace. Laptops, fast Internet speeds, mobile phones and other devices enable people to work from home, avoiding long commutes and heavy transport costs. People in sales roles are also able to stay out on the road spending time with customers, rather than having to come into the office to file reports.

Telecommuting produces a number of benefits for organisations. It allows office buildings to be disposed of and their capital released. In theory, it also means that people are more likely to be able to better focus on their job since there are fewer 'social' workplace distractions. However, there is some evidence that, despite the benefits to many telecommuting employees, such as being spared the costly physical commute to the office, many people miss the community aspect of organisations. And for managers, to the challenge of managing a more flexible workforce which includes greater numbers of contractors, temporary staff and remote workers, will be added the need to manage knowledge when staff have no strong loyalty to the organisation.

Realising the benefits of flexible working

Some pointers about how HR can realise some of the benefits of flexible working can be found in research on flexible working in small firms by the CIPD for the British Chambers of Commerce (2007):

Understand your business

Flexible working arrangements that work well for another business won't necessarily work in yours. Some jobs can be done from home, while in others, being there all the time is essential. Consider both what is right for your organisation and where your employees' needs lie. How can flexible working improve the service to your customers?

Communicate effectively

Making your people aware of the opportunities for flexible working can be built into induction programmes and reinforced by training. Having a clear set of organisational values can also help in selling the benefits of flexible working.

Define roles and responsibilities

It's important that managers and individuals understand their responsibilities for making flexibility work. People need to see it from the organisation's point of view as well as their own. It's about give and take – not just individuals getting what they want. When there is a well-understood culture, teams can often sort out their own issues.

Try it out

You don't have to do it all at once. If there are concerns about whether flexible working is feasible, it can be helpful to have a trial period of the proposed working arrangement. But think in the longer term about the effect on others whose jobs may be more difficult to do on a flexible basis. Ask people to come up with their own ideas.

Make flexible working acceptable

You may have comprehensive written policies but bringing these to life can be challenging. If you and your managers are not seen to 'walk the talk', flexible working won't be taken seriously. Explaining how flexible working benefits the business as well as employees is crucial. And senior staff need to lead by example.

Measure and evaluate

Remember: if you can't measure it, you can't manage it. And be open to ideas for improvement. Large organisations are not always good at evaluating the effectiveness of their flexible working practices. Research (Beatson 2019) shows that small firms are perfectly capable of monitoring the impact of flexible working on business outcomes. Covid-19 has acted as a springboard to gathering health and well-being data – through staff surveys, focus groups and so on, and developing dashboards than can demonstrate progress, as well as ROI.

CONCLUSION

Careers remain a number-one agenda item for many employees. In today's diverse, global and technologically charged work environment, careers are no longer perceived as strictly vertical movements up the rungs of a ladder but more as series of paths which could represent a particular role, development experience, or job competency along an individual's career journey. Looking ahead, people with valuable specialist skills may have new career routes opening up to them.

Increasingly, the challenge for employers will be to retain those employees who are highly employable – and helping people develop themselves and their careers has been proved to do this. Well-crafted career paths with contextualised success factors can play a pivotal role in retention, driving organisational change and building workforce capability.

The responsibility for talent development extends beyond managers and HR. Employees too must play an active part themselves by seeking out challenging assignments, cross-functional projects and new positions. The idea of managing your own career has caught on, but many employees lack the time and know-how to do this. The skills of career self-management can be learnt, and the wise employer makes resources available for this. Helping people to come to terms with what careers look like in the new economy involves helping them recognise that jobs as we knew them may cease to exist.

REFERENCES

Aghina, W., De Smet, A. and Weerda, K. (2015). *Agility: it rhymes with stability*, McKinsey & Company. https://www.mckinsey.com/business-functions/organization/our-insights/agility-it-rhymes-with-stability

Beatson, M. (2019). *Flexible Working in the UK*. London: CIPD. https://www.cipd.co.uk/Images/flexible-working_tcm18-58746.pdf

Bersin, J. (2020). *Talent marketplace platforms explode into view*, Published July 3, updated July 18. https://joshbersin.com/2020/07/talent-marketplace-platforms-explode-into-view/

Cao, J. and Thomas, D. (2013). *When developing a career path, what are the key elements to include?* http://digitalcommons.ilr.cornell.edu/student/43/

Elvidge, E., Spencely, C. and Williams, E. (2017). *What Every Postdoc Needs to Know*. London: World Scientific Europe.

Gartner. (2020). Gartner says HR leaders must build a robust strategy to improve talent mobility, February 27, 2020. https://www.gartner.com/en/newsroom/press-releases/2020-02-27-gartner-says-hr-leaders-must-build-a-robust-strategy-

Guthridge, M., Komm, A.B. and Lawson, E. (2008). *Making talent a strategic priority*. www.mckinseyquarterly.com, pp. 49–50.

Wellcome (2020). *What Researchers Think About the Culture They Work In*. London: Wellcome. https://wellcome.org/sites/default/files/what-researchers-think-about-the-culture-they-work-in.pdf

12
High flyers and succession planning

DOI: 10.4324/9781003219996-14

In Chapter 10, we considered inclusive approaches to talent management. In this chapter, we consider high-flyer schemes and succession planning, part of the panoply of organisation-owned 'exclusive' talent management approaches that focus on so-called 'critical talent'.

CHAPTER OVERVIEW

In this chapter, we shall look at how some of these exclusive approaches – such as senior management development programmes, graduate entry, accelerated development, MBA recruitment – may be changing to reflect emerging organisational needs for agility in a turbulent context. We shall cover:

- 'Our people are our greatest asset'
- Conventional fast-track schemes and succession planning
- Drivers for new approaches
- Alternative approaches
- Retaining leadership talent
- Case study and recommendations

LEARNING OBJECTIVES

- Explore conventional approaches to succession planning and fast-track schemes, their purposes and limitations
- Consider possible alternative approaches more suited to agile contexts

INTRODUCTION: 'OUR PEOPLE ARE OUR GREATEST ASSET'

The employment landscape is changing in a number of ways. Retention and engagement remain major issues around the world, the demand for leadership skills is higher than ever and yet the supply is not there. In the wake of the Covid-19 pandemic, many companies are in survival mode and thoughts of succession planning, a subset of workforce planning, have been put on the back burner. Succession plans look to the future, but not truly knowing what the future looks like due to the Covid-19 crisis can make the process more challenging. Both fast-tracking and succession planning are projected to become more pressing issues once growth returns. Yet Deloitte research (2018) found while that 86% of leaders believe leadership succession planning is an 'urgent' or 'important' priority, only 14% believe they do it well.

The increasingly international or global nature of many organisations' operations has cross-cultural implications for resourcing strategies for key positions. The nature of many roles is changing thanks to technology, as we discussed in earlier chapters. Another trend – the emphasis on lifelong learning and continuing professional development – is becoming well established. This reflects the increasing recognition that the competitive advantage of organisations depends on the calibre and motivation of their 'knowledge workers' and their ability to stay at the leading edge of their field. This is particularly clear in the IT sector where business success relies on the product development skills of a few key individuals.

The truth of corporate value-speak such as 'Our people are our greatest asset' has been painfully evident when talented individuals move on. In the increasingly fragmented job landscape, loyalty to the employer is becoming a thing of the past and many organisations are urgently reviewing ways of securing the commitment of people whom they do not want to lose. This is forcing organisations to develop new definitions of who is a 'key' employee, rather than limiting the definition to those who have high potential, and the ability to reach the top jobs. Companies that use this time to focus on the growth and development of their future leaders and critical contributors will have a strong advantage when regular business returns. The time to act is now. In the face of increasing competition for the best talent, strategic talent management and succession planning are key to building effective future leaders and a resiliently agile workforce.

CONVENTIONAL TALENT MANAGEMENT

Note that although I shall sometimes refer to 'conventional' fast-track and succession planning schemes in the past tense, I am conscious that such approaches are still very much with us.

Succession planning

Succession plans are conventionally developed to ensure that key senior positions have appropriate successors to the current post-holder, identified and groomed as potential replacements. The aim is, of course, to ensure that the organisation has a small pool of potential successors for key roles, especially the top jobs, in the future. Many large organisations are still structured hierarchically, with as many as 12 management levels between first-line supervisors and top management. Future leaders are helped to progress swiftly through these levels, acquiring relevant experience and skills as they go.

Typically, succession planning for top executive positions features:

- Contingency (emergency replacement)
- Replacement (of one person by another at a certain time)
- Succession (employees who may be groomed for a post over a number of years)
- Development (of employees with high potential)

The implicit assumption is that most senior management roles can be filled from within, and that growing internal talent is preferable to the riskier option of external recruitment.

Some organisations however insist that potential can only exist outside and hence rely heavily on external recruitment to source key management positions. This may be because of a widespread ignorance of the current skills of the existing workforce or assumptions that external is 'better'. However, such policies usually have a largely negative effect on the morale of existing employees.

If organisations want to be prepared for the future, they must be able to link long-term business strategy to the talent landscape and identify the components of job roles critical to the organisation's success – and that includes leadership roles. Organisations must make informed, evidence-based decisions around executive selection, high-potential identification, and succession planning. An important question to answer when taking stock of current employees is what and who is key now and in the short- to medium-term future? The answer to that question may be different now from what it might have been several years ago. HR must bring this information together to formulate a talent management strategy that maps out goals and priorities and creates a plan to fill future positions.

Succession planning process

Many companies have a central HR team responsible for overseeing the succession planning process. In decentralised succession planning systems, central functions typically attempt to collect information on key employees and a series of management committees provide input to the processes of development and succession planning within an international business group or location. These committees review the succession plans of each business unit within the international business.

A typical succession planning process involves three stages:

1. *Define the organisation's future leadership requirements and create 'success profiles'* – the required experience, skills and desired leadership competencies. Leadership requirements are defined by looking to the future, assessing strategic high-level goals, taking into account any upcoming changes or new initiatives for the organisation and deducing the implications for leadership. Then, the key drivers and internal and external challenges are considered, such as regulatory or job market change that could impact the organisation's ability to achieve these goals. The next step is to conduct a gap analysis, comparing where your organisation is today with where it wants to be and identifying any gaps that need to be filled in order to achieve its goals.
2. *Assess potential successors for each role*
   This assessment should be against the success profile versus the individuals perceived potential and readiness. Certain competencies, such as strategic vision and the ability to manage change, are usually regarded as differentiators for top jobs. Senior post vacancies should be checked against the succession plan first.
3. *Close leadership gaps through individual (or cohort-based) development*
   This might include planned experiential opportunities, real-time mentoring and coaching, a series of 'broadening' moves to positions of real influence. A slightly broader group, perhaps up to 10% of the population, would be developed for senior management roles. For most other employees, advancement up the career ladder is more gradual.

HR and L&D set talent goals for the coming year to support the organisation in achieving its objectives. These should be SMART (specific, measurable, achievable, realistic and relevant, time-bound) and linked to corporate goals. These steps should pave the way for the creation of a sustainable succession plan, and for top talent to succeed.

'Fast-Tracking'

Fast-track programmes, described by Altman (1997) as 'the conscious, purposeful process of grooming that individuals go through on their way to the top', have long been a common feature of corporate career management. Fast-track schemes are designed to accelerate the development of people considered to have high potential, enabling them to acquire relevant skills and experience on their way up the corporate ladder in the shortest time possible. Indeed, the term 'fast-track' is attractive to many potential recruits and is designed to appeal to 'the best' candidates in the job market.

> One expects achievement (performance) to be directly translated into climbing the organizational ladder: upward mobility is not only an achievement in its own right, but doubly so, since it is a negation of the alternative options: immobility (getting 'stuck' on the career ladder) or even demotion, if not dismobility (sacking) altogether.
> Altman (1997)

Conventional 'fast-tracks' are available to a very small minority of employees, perhaps no more than 2–3% of the workforce, who are deemed to have potential for taking on general management or other executive roles. McKinsey research (2017) found that some employees disproportionately create or protect value, and high performers are 800% more productive than average ones. The assumption is that 'high-potential' people will carry on moving up the organisation when those who are less able cease to progress.

Most 'high-flyers' are identified as such early in their careers, often at graduate entry. Other high-potential employees join organisations having obtained an MBA or professional qualification or having begun a fast-track career elsewhere. Sometimes individuals are told about their perceived potential, though such assessments are often far from transparent and remain confidential to the Human Resources professionals and senior line managers responsible for making such career judgements.

Of course, every organisation must attempt to secure its future leaders but whether conventional fast-tracking should be seen as the main means of achieving this remains open to question. After all, conventional fast track programmes generally work best when an organisation's environment, market conditions and structures are relatively stable and predictable – conditions very unlike those of recent years. HR and L&D professionals need to be able to answer the following questions:

- Are we retaining top talent?
- Is our existing talent base ready to become our next generation of leaders?
- And is our investment in learning and development helping us achieve strategic business goals?

Drivers for new approaches?

Though still widely prevalent, conventional 'exclusive' talent approaches are not without drawbacks. In the past many organisations defined high potential and recruited and developed high-flyers in the image of existing senior managers, rather than identifying the skills and behaviours required of future leaders in line with the general business direction. In one financial services organisation, the process of identifying potential through management development reviews was known as 'cloning'! When hiring managers secure talent from the same pool over and over, they inevitably build up homogeneous teams that are far from diverse, have similar perceptions and blind spots.

Then there is the issue of whether the actual performance of 'high-flyers' is seriously monitored. Such judgements are often made early in a person's career, often at entry. Early assessment is no guarantee that people can really cope with more serious responsibilities over time. More often than not, once an individual is labelled a 'high-flyer' it is unlikely that such opinions will be reviewed unless he or she seriously fails at some important activity. Similarly, people who are not classed as fast-track material early in their careers are often denied the opportunity for real advancement even if their talents later prove to be highly relevant to a significant role. If you missed the early opportunity for rapid advancement, you do not usually have a second chance.

A common challenge is about who is accountable for succession planning. This was often seen as a 'stand-alone' activity and generally considered the responsibility of a specialist Human Resource unit. Indeed, People professionals have a critical role in supporting and facilitating the process. They have access to confidential information, offer career advice, and have expertise in assessing and advising on individual and corporate development needs. They must develop and maintain relevant databases, design and manage assessment processes and compile information on potential succession candidates. Many organisations could make more effective use of their HR technology investments to support their talent programmes and succession planning practices.

However, succession planning needs to be owned by line managers and actively championed by the leadership team. After all, CEOs are now required to demonstrate, particularly to boards and regulators in some sectors, that their succession planning and talent strategy clearly links to their business strategy and is equipping the business with the future talent it needs ahead of the increasing pace of disruption.

Another common issue is the unworkability of succession plans in practice. Even posts with several designated internal 'successors' are frequently filled by people from outside the organisation or the successors themselves are not available when the post becomes vacant or the post itself is subsequently reengineered out of existence. During mergers many roles simply cease to exist, or individuals from the acquired company who had previously been judged to have potential are not given opportunities for political reasons.

With the trend toward flatter, leaner structures in recent decades, many organisations gave up the attempt to plan for succession or manage fast-track processes (Larsen et al. 1998). After all, in a 'flat' structure, where was a 'high-flyer' to 'fast-track' to? (Holbeche 1997). At the same time, employers became more demanding and upped the entry-level stakes for most 'career' roles to a first degree at least and usually a professional qualification as well. This has potential consequences for new recruits whose expectations were raised by the recruitment process but were not met. One government department hired a number of people with PhDs for relatively junior executive officer jobs. Not surprisingly, several of these expensively hired new recruits left months later when the reality of their employment conditions and limited prospects hit home.

Understandably, in times of change, the basic parameters of planning, such as knowing where the organisation is going, the skills needed for the future and the resources the organisation currently has, are difficult to establish. Planning exclusively around roles seems short-sighted in such circumstances. This is particularly marked in some of the oil companies where overseas assignments as part of a broad career route for high-calibre employees became increasingly difficult to fill. This is partly explained by the rise in the number of dual-career families but also by the increasing unwillingness of employees to make sacrifices if they are not guaranteed promotion on return from the assignment. Moreover, processes that aim for a win-win for organisations and employees are still elusive, according to Deloitte (2018): 'We found few organisations that were combining a disciplined, data-driven process with a user-friendly, people-centric approach that adequately engages stakeholders'.

Reflective activity

- How do we define 'potential'?
- How can we ensure that people with potential have a real development challenge and appropriate recognition?
- How can we ensure that the organisational needs and those of the individual are met?

IDENTIFYING POTENTIAL – RETHINKING WHAT 'KEY' LOOKS LIKE

Organisations need to think through what they mean by potential and how to assess it.

Formal methods

Participants for succession planning programmes can be identified using formal techniques, such as performance appraisals and talent review processes. Many organisations routinely use assessment centres to select candidates for fast-track development. Competency models, simulations, psychometric profiles and 360-degree feedback processes are increasingly used not only for individual development but also for talent identification. Nationsbank use competencies as the means of developing executive success profiles for spotting potential and development purposes. Competency-based methods may be too limiting and mechanistic to assess skills such as leadership. Competencies should be based on a good understanding of future strategy, link to the organisation's values and its strategic goals, and define the likely capabilities needed in business-critical positions. This is particularly the case in organisations that consider leadership development and succession planning as key tools in changing the organisation's culture, as in the BP Amoco case in this chapter.

Informal methods

Alongside formal methods to identify potential, informal methods, such as conversations with managers, can be enlightening. According to CEB (in Deloitte 2015), high potential employees have three key common characteristics: aspiration, ability, and engagement. High potential employees like what they do, want to do more, and show potential to lead larger numbers of people and perform increasingly complex tasks. Some organisations invite employees to propose themselves as potential talent pool members. These often include employees who might have missed the fast-track first time round but who now appear to have the skills and attitudes that the organisation needs as it moves forward. This is not a purely philanthropic approach. Both the cost of external recruitment, especially if the new recruit does not 'fit' and soon leaves, and the failure to maximise the potential of existing employees suggest that fast-tracking and succession should be a continuous, wide-based process rather than a scheme.

Whichever assessment method is used, organisations should be very clear and consistent about how they define 'potential'. It is important to distinguish between an employee who performs better than their peers in his/her current role – and a high potential employee who can grow typically as many as two levels beyond his/her current rank. Exceptional performers may be the best at their current jobs but may not have the ability to transition to more senior positions.

Developing and updating success profiles

Leadership competencies are used to create 'success' profiles for executives. Leadership is highlighted as an area of competence in itself because business leaders need to be able to provide focus and bring people with them in times of change. Some of the skills considered critical in would-be leaders include:

- Business function knowledge – how well the candidate understands the various business functions (sales, marketing, software development, manufacturing, operations etc.) and the sub functions within each function, e.g. for manufacturing, this includes production, quality control, manufacturing engineering, inventory control etc.
- Business Interaction acumen – the candidate's knowledge of and ability to effectively interact with the upper/middle and top management executives from other business functions.
- Financial acumen – the candidate's understanding of the key financial numbers on the company and division's income and cash flow statements, how the profitability of its current products relates to them, budget planning and performance, and the company's strategic plan goals.
- Business Strategy skills – product/market research, product/market development and planning, strategic thinking and planning, and financial and product contingency planning.
- Executive skills – championing innovation, leadership, consistently achieving profitable financial results, successful strategic growth, establishing an appropriate work culture, outside audit and market analyst interaction, Board and top management interaction etc.
- Management skills – planning (including MBO), controlling, organising, coaching and leading (Stevenson 2019).

The type of succession planning model used depends on the number of roles that share a common profile. As ever, a warning note needs to be sounded: if leaders are to be capable of performing in today's and tomorrow's constantly changing environment, beware the limited shelf life of success profiles when business requirements change. Competencies must be integrated into the business planning process and updated.

One model of succession planning concentrates on identifying a discrete list of candidates who are 'ready now' to step into open positions, those who will 'probably' succeed and those who will 'possibly' succeed. The more well defined the performance criteria, the better the data, the more accurate the review. Assessments should be grounded in actual examples of behaviours and outcomes, demonstrated consistently over time. With remote working during the Covid-19 pandemic, examples of good leadership became easier to see in teams who remained productive while working virtually.

The trend currently is to develop potential leaders with a broad range of leadership competence in addition to any specific business experience they may have. Organisations as diverse as Texaco, Unilever, GSK and Philips, use success profiles built on generic 'leadership' competencies as a focus for executive development and as a means of bringing about culture change. Unilever uses competencies for the assessment of potential, for graduate recruitment, executive recruitment, leadership training, appraisal (performance development planning) and rewards. Texaco's Core Leadership Competencies emphasise behaviour-based leadership in addition to specifically business-related skills.

Development should give fast-track and succession candidates more exposure to the parts of the company's business that they are unfamiliar with, such as a particular function, or involvement in the strategic, financial and budget planning for key divisions, cross functional assignments, interaction with higher level management and/or the Board on particular subjects. Fast-tracking then becomes almost a state of mind as well as a development route. The 'fast' element should include opportunities to acquire the skills and experience needed by the organisation in the short and medium term.

Building talent pools

A talent planning process should be underpinned by a learning-focused culture that is nimble and responsive to changes. If the way ahead is very unclear, building talent pools for succession planning purposes at different levels in the organisation allows people with real talent to shine through and helps manage risk. The talent pools you create will vary depending on the organisation and its strategic goals. Some organisations nurture pools of generic leadership talent and create emerging leader programmes and 360-leadership assessments to base leadership development plans on. One UK financial services organisation introduced a three-year structured development programme for a large group of existing and new employees of different levels and ages. The short-term payback to the organisation was high morale among programme participants and widely applied learning. Other organisations aiming to develop successors for specific mission and operation critical roles identify the required competencies for each job-specific talent pool and use their 'professional community' approaches to create the talent pools in key areas where the organisation lacks bench strength.

Increasingly, succession planning activities are both/and – they are being extended beyond a small, privileged group of 'key employees' to include a much wider group in recognition of the fact that knowledge workers and intellectual capital are the real assets of an organisation. At a major insurance company, for instance, all director-level jobs are backed up with possible successors. Below director level, the pool of candidates being developed to fill positions at a given level in the organisation includes a wider population and allows for changes in roles. Campbell's Soups identify talent at departmental, country and global levels. This is based on an assessment of potential, not just performance. Assignments help people develop skills and leverage strengths. United Airlines broadened the management levels included in succession planning by lowering the administrative burden through the use of client/server technology. This has enabled individual career planning and organisational succession planning to be better integrated.

One IT company focused on building up a broad cadre of individuals alongside providing accelerated high-flyer development for a few. So all employees have the opportunity to carry out career self-assessments and access a range of development opportunities. These include a career development workshop which helps people to gain a realistic view of their strengths and development needs, an understanding of the career options within the company and, most importantly, a greater insight into their own values and motivations. The success of this approach in retaining employees in a highly competitive job market is evident in much-reduced staff turnover rates. This range of integrated activities and processes make it practically possible for employees to manage their own career, including making internal moves. The UK's Post Office has developed a succession planning system which breaks away from the conventional elitist mould which it replaces and aims to develop a broad group of people with senior management potential.

Developing the talent pipeline in Nestlé

Nestlé is a large global food and beverage manufacturer. Its aim is to manufacture and market products in such a way as to create value that can be sustained over the long term for shareholders, employees, consumers and business partners. The business focus is very much on nutrition, health and wellness and coming up with new products to meet international trends, while at the same time driving down costs.

Nestlé's multi-channel talent pipeline aims to feed two broad capability requirements of the organisation. First, the core capability pool is populated with employees who make up the larger portion of the workforce and have the technical skills and capabilities that are essential to keep the organisation running. The second group of people, a smaller portion of the workforce, is the high potential pool. This comprises employees who are considered to have sufficient potential to become their high performers and senior managers of the future. Each category is filled with a combination of existing employees and new recruits.

In addition, Nestlé has taken a more radical approach to managing talent by creating 'talent puddles'. Whilst these are similar to talent pools, they are more targeted, creating a talent bank in specific areas of the business where there is a shortage of skilled applicants for specific jobs and difficult-to fill roles. The initiative began with the supply chain function but has since been extended to other areas of the business. These small puddles of talent can be readily brought into the business, thus reducing the costs and speeding up the recruitment process.

Global talent pools

Standard Chartered PLC has a structured approach to building talent pools at different levels and across many locations. There are regular business reviews on talent from Board level down to country management team level and a global leadership pipeline is developed through a range of simple and effective processes. Outcome-based, rather than process measures are tracked. For Country Management Trainees, locally tailored programmes are available. International graduates are provided with two-year development through rotations and global programmes. Junior High Potentials are locally managed and reviewed in 56 countries. Mid-career MBAs are a strategic form of hiring which supplements the leadership pipeline. Middle management high potentials are reviewed by ten global leadership teams. Senior Management High Potentials are reviewed by the Group Management Committee. For more detail of Standard Chartered PLC's talent management processes, see Chapter 13.

When soft-drinks giant Coca-Cola was forced to look outside the organisation to recruit senior marketing professionals, it decided it was time to establish a programme to identify the talent it had internally. Although the company already had a reputation for growing talent from within, in 2005 only 67% of senior roles were filled internally – a figure that rose to 93% by 2007, thanks to building an internal talent pipeline through the use of a development centre process.

In 2005 a meeting of the global marketing people development forum, a quarterly meeting of marketing leaders from each of Coca-Cola's eight geographical regions, identified a particular senior role – division marketing manager – as central to the company's succession planning in each region. The challenge was to make sure that the talent going into these roles could work anywhere.

The first step was creating a joint job description so that each region had the same understanding of what the role required. A global senior marketing leadership development centre was designed using a combination of Coca-Cola's marketing competencies and the company's core leadership competencies. Testing for this critical combination was based on reality, rather than a series of hypothetical situations. For example, there is a marketing expense exercise in which the general manager is asking the marketing manager to make choices regarding resources and budget allocation. There is also feedback based on personality preferences and 360-degree review. When participants leave the centre, they are given detailed feedback from a marketing leader and a coach.

Each event is held in a different country and brings together eight top people from across the globe in one place. As a result, marketing leaders from each area are able to see the calibre of international talent and there has been an increase in 'poaching' talent from one region to another, which is a positive development (*People Management*, 7 August 2008).

DEVELOPING FUTURE LEADERS

How can future leaders learn to practise leadership effectively in the short term and also develop their strategic capability? Simply moving high potential individuals around the organisation at speed may not be the best way of developing them or assessing whether they really do have the ability to build sustained performance. Indeed, most companies do this in a very ad-hoc way, which may or may not result in the best business outcome. In fact, it may actually prevent candidates from developing and applying their skills in ways which put them to the test and improve business results.

GE, a company previously known for moving its people around every two years or so found that their rapid mobility strategy had become one of their biggest problems, because people could 'run away' from their mistakes and never got enough depth in a business area to really perform well. So they created a new mobility strategy they called 'More Electric, Less General' (Bersin 2020). Keeping high potential employees longer in development posts so that they can deliver meaningful performance before progressing on to the next experience may not only increase future leaders' credibility with staff, it can also help to close the common gap in understanding between those at the top of organisations and those lower down the hierarchy about how to make things happen.

With respect to the development of multinational leaders a DDI/CIPD (2008) study found that UK high-potentials are much less likely than those in other cultures to get clear communications about the importance of their development or sufficient feedback about their performance. Providing deepening and broadening experiences such as participation in special projects and opportunities, linking up with international counterparts, should be part of the development mix. Even hardship can be developmental, according to previous research by the Centre for Creative Leadership. But if future leaders are to consciously learn from mistakes about what not to do next time, a 'sink or swim' approach may be unhelpful. Development opportunities appear to be most enriching if they provide access to new, varied challenges, where there is a degree of difficulty in the task and where outcomes are important and highly visible, especially if success is by no means guaranteed.

When decisions about filling senior posts are being made, HR must be knowledgeable about each management position and what it really requires in terms of experience, technical/job knowledge, management/executive skills, financial skills, interpersonal and leadership skills. HR should have information on each succession candidate and his/

her skill sets and past performance results against key specific business objectives. So HR should consider collecting and tracking data about how well individuals are developing as well as how inclined they are to stay, such as high performer average engagement scores, high-to-low performance ratios, critical competency scores and percentage of goals met and exceeded. Having this information allows the HR leader to effectively interact with line executives and to potentially offer challenge if a succession candidate is recommended for a particular position but may not be really suitable due to some performance and/or skill deficiencies.

I have retained the following case study from the original version of this book as I think the business-ownership and coherence of the talent process described is impressive. Information is from 2001 and based on research carried out in BP shortly before the merger between BP and Amoco. I am particularly grateful to Dr Candy Anderson whose role at the time was BP's Manager High Potential Development, where she provided the managing director with strategic support on a variety of issues, including a review of BP's leadership talent pool, supply and demand for the top 25 succession and the supporting infrastructure to develop world-class leadership. Candy now runs her own company.

The assessment and development of high potential at BP Amoco

In a company with the size and reputation for development of BP Amoco, it is hardly surprising that the assessment and development of people perceived to have high potential should be taken seriously.

Within BP Amoco, 'high potential' refers to the perceived ability to reach one of the top 100 jobs out of a workforce of 94,000. The majority of people who are thought likely to reach such roles are among the 25,000 professional and middle management employees. Previously, high-potential employees were principally the responsibility of a group-level committee with representatives from the three businesses (i.e. Oil, Exploration and Chemicals), the Regions and Corporate and focused primarily on deployment. Career development often took the form of a series of moves around the main businesses, acquiring different levels of responsibility and experience.

The limitations of this relatively basic way of developing future leaders were recognised but attempts to improve the process were not without challenge. One initiative was the introduction of Personal Development Planning to supplement the company-driven deployment approach to development. This introduced more of a partnership between individuals and the organisation. People were given the opportunity to reflect on their career aspirations and short-, medium- and long-term goals. In some cases, people aspired to strategic, rather than operational roles and there was a 'reality check' against performance feedback to suggest whether an individual's aspirations were realistic.

The identification of high-potential employees needed special attention. Though graduate recruitment was, and remains, the main entry point for high-flying employees, formal assessment of high potential tends to take place at a relatively junior level, some four to ten years after joining the company. While talent can be spotted at this stage in a person's career, lack of line management or cross-functional experience may make it difficult to recognise undeveloped management talent. However, for employees who were not perceived at this early career stage to have high potential, the route to the top jobs was much more difficult. Candy Albertsson felt that only a junior level programme for identifying potential was wasteful of late-blooming talent. She introduced the idea and gained support for developing a senior-level assessment that would enable the identification of potential later in one's career.

Improving the processes

Candy's objective was to ensure that the group as a whole would benefit from the effective identification and development of high-potential talent. Clearly, the challenges of winning the support of the top 20 business heads for changing processes which appear to be working well from a local business perspective required high-level influencing skills and credibility. Working with a small team of management development specialists, Candy set about creating the infrastructure for improved processes, including winning senior-level support. Key moves included the globalisation of the junior-level Assessment of Leadership Potential (ALP) assessment programme to create one standard Group programme. This replaced four established regional junior-level assessment programmes. Other key moves were the introduction of a senior-level assessment programme – the Leadership Enhancement through Assessment and Development (i.e. LEAD) – and the introduction of a cohort review process for high potentials at Group level.

An 18-month study generated a set of nine leadership competencies, which were used as a means of providing a consistent approach to high-flyer development at group level. These competencies were measured in a 360-degree feedback process. However, while 360 provided good individual development data, it could not be used to compare between different people. Further data from the 360-degree process cannot be aggregated and therefore it is not possible to assess the aggregate strengths and development needs of the organisation. It was important to build on the early success of the new tools by building a standardised process and means of measurement across the group.

Candy believed in making these processes as transparent as possible, and the competencies were a good start in showing people what successful performance looks like:

> It is important to communicate to people what skills are required, and what the expectations of performance are in the organization. You need to provide a user-friendly way for people to measure. 360 is a powerful development tool, but it has its limitations.

A limitation of the use of 360 was that while each leadership competency can be examined through a questionnaire, different raters, such as the individual's line manager, peers or direct reports, may not have had the opportunity to observe a particular competency. Similarly, certain jobs may not provide the opportunity for the job-holder to demonstrate that particular competency. When views about development are being made based on incomplete or potentially unrepresentative information, the drawbacks of the process need to be recognised. The LEAD programme addressed these limitations.

The LEAD programme

Candy Albertsson set about introducing the concept for a new process for the later identification of talent to supplement the junior-level assessment process and to provide the standardised objective yardstick needed across the group. She led the project team which started developing the LEAD Programme. A key strategic objective of the programme was to gain quality data on the main organisational training and development needs as well as an overview of the talent pool within BP Amoco. Candy worked in partnership with a consultant, Joel Moses, in the design phase and the first programme was piloted. It was managed in-house and was once per quarter. The programme was championed by the Deputy Chief Executive and high-potential committee. Participants in this process included employees of long standing, often with 20 years' experience, many of whom may not have aspired to a senior level role earlier in their career. The participant pool of about 1,000 managers was drawn from the top 1,500 managers.

The LEAD programme was essentially an assessment centre in which all nine leadership competencies were assessed. It was intended to complement existing performance data rather than being seen as a pass/fail or ranking exercise rendering all other data redundant. However, the data which came from the centre in the form of a LEAD report were widely used and important. Development Groups including a line manager, a mentor and HR specialist carried out a 'reality check' on the assessment report. The report addressed each of the nine leadership competencies, plus feedback on style and approach. An important element was the in-depth feedback to individuals which went beyond the feedback typically covered in a performance review. LEAD provided participants with one and a half hours of development feedback from a line manager and there was a process in place to link feedback to action plans – the Development Group, which is described later in this chapter.

An important benefit of the LEAD programme was the development opportunity it provided for observers. It was critical that observers were able to assess behaviours as objectively as possible and to translate their observations into feedback. The observers, who were very senior line managers (i.e. the top 300), were trained in coaching and feedback skills and were required to fully understand the leadership competencies which they would be observing and evaluating. Key benefits of senior managers taking part in this skilled process were the positive impact on their own approaches to management and the further bedding down of the competencies from the top of the organisation. Observers generally valued taking part in the process and this strengthened the base of support for the programme. This common approach to understanding what was required of future leaders provided a powerful tool which generated 'developmental blueprints' used by individuals, line managers and development committees.

How the LEAD programme worked

Each LEAD programme was run over four and a half days in two parallel teams of six participants and three observers. Delegates took part in a business simulation which reflected the environment BP Amoco leaders face in complex global markets. However, to ensure that there was a level playing field and that the simulation did not favour people with specific forms of knowledge or experience, the exercise was set outside the oil industry. The simulation contained a number of written and verbal exercises, including an in-tray. Actors were used for a situation in which participants were required to coach their 'direct report'. The simulation also contained a number of team problem-solving challenges on business, regional and group issues.

The programme was designed to measure leadership at strategic and operational levels by examining an individual's approach to decisions and problems, rather than using psychometric tests. Observers were trained for one day before the start of the simulation and then had a day's integration meeting in which they aggregated and reviewed their observations on each individual. The output of these discussions was an agreement of whether each of the nine competencies demonstrated by a participant was a strength, development need or weakness. Strengths are defined as where the individual demonstrates 'real power' in the competency; the 'development zone' is where the level of competence is 'probably sufficient for the individual's current level of responsibility but will need to be strengthened for higher levels of responsibility'; potential weaknesses are areas of limitation which could have 'significant impact' on their performance at higher level and are a priority for development. Participants received on-site feedback on Friday morning from one of the managers who had observed the process.

The written report which followed the programme consisted of a leadership competency profile and three to four written pages elaborating on each of the nine competencies, on development priorities and options. An individual's leadership competency profile could be compared against a number of development profiles identified for critical business situations such as start-ups, business expansions and alliance building. These profiles were developed from interviews with 40 senior line managers and could be used to determine 'development moves' or 'ideal fits'.

Validating the findings

One of the common criticisms of assessment or development centres is that there is a lack of follow-through when participants are back at work. Does anyone care or notice if someone has started to improve on an area of weakness? Is the information from the programme valid in the work context? Will information about strengths and weaknesses be taken into account when decisions are made about jobs? The LEAD programme attempted to provide a comprehensive follow-through from the centre, integrating with other existing processes and performance information to ensure that the data were used.

Following LEAD, all participants were strongly encouraged to establish a Development Group consisting of their line manager, an HR development specialist and a mentor. A minimum of two meetings was recommended and the aim was to enable participants to link their feedback to a written action plan back in the workplace. It is very easy for findings from a development process to be discredited or ignored if participants can say 'well, I'm not like that at work'. The development group's function was to provide the reality check for the data emerging from the LEAD programme. Ninety per cent of the Development Groups validated LEAD reports in this way, which was very powerful in strengthening the metric.

Once the findings had been validated, the reality check and action plan were permanently attached to all copies of the individual's LEAD report. The report was then available to Group and business development committees and was used for selection and development moves. The action plan was incorporated into performance appraisal objectives and personal development plans. Multiple comments could be added over time as development needs were addressed. As such, it was a living report (see Figure 12.1).

Identifying organisational strengths and development needs

Data on individual strengths, development needs and weaknesses were aggregated to provide a composite picture of the competency areas which needed special attention. This allowed trends to be identified and information which could be used to determine organisational training and development needs. It also highlighted areas within the talent pool where there might be issues or gaps. Candy Albertsson believes that no other tool can provide an organisation with data of this quality and strategic significance, particularly since the top 300 generated the data in the first place. This information can then be used to proactively identify appropriate training and development solutions.

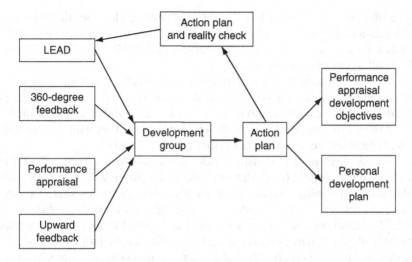

Figure 12.1 Linking competency assessment to development.

Reflective activity

- What were the major challenges faced by BP Amoco that the LEAD programme was meant to address?
- How was executive support for the process gained and applied?
- How relevant would these approaches be to a company in a fast-moving sector, such as IT?

The future leaders' programme

Updating the story to 2020, BP now runs a Future Leaders programme (FLP), a successor to the LEAD programme for new high-potential entrants. The programme is designed to bring in the collaboration, learning and forward thinking that the business needs in a digitally fluent and networked world. Indicators of potential for BP include learning agility: how you cope and thrive when faced with new situations. This requires openness, curiosity and humility in equal measure which are also characteristics that mark out BP's best leaders. Flexibility and resilience are two other traits to highlight at this stage in an FLP's career. The more stretch and challenge that people can experience early on the greater the benefit. This requires being adaptable and happy to cope with the uncertainty of often fast-changing environments or circumstances.

All fast-track processes need managing and individuals on such tracks need ongoing monitoring and support to ensure that they are delivering what was intended and able to make the progress implied. To help people settle into BP, participants have a FLP buddy who helps them navigate BP operating systems, connect them with friends and provide a community inside and outside of BP. Participants are given opportunities to work in different parts of the business, to start to build and lead teams. As one participant put it, 'Being a member of the FLP community gives participants immediate credibility. People trust you and give you meaningful projects to demonstrate your ability to add value in a particular area within BP. Also many people want to meet and get to know you. Initially, balancing time between your team, the FLP community and various other BP related groups that you may be a part of can prove to be challenging. However the chance to make a broader impact early on and to leverage your learnings to other areas within BP are key highlights. Lastly, the value of your immediate global BP community through your fellow FLP colleagues cannot be overlooked'.

Throughout the FLP programme each participant has a mentor and a business sponsor, while first line managers also act as a coach and a mentor as well. Their advice helps hone participants' technical expertise and soft skills, grow in confidence while simultaneously showing them how the additional skills and experiences they gain can increase the number and type of future career opportunities presented to them.

Networking is a key feature of FLP, with various communities of practice (COP) or continuous improvement forums (CIF) that provide an employee access to colleagues in similar roles and/or disciplines across the globe and senior advisors share valuable information on relevant work issues, incidents, technologies and learnings within and external to BP. This group periodically has regional and global face-to-face meetings, where even more in-depth sharing and learning occurs. These development opportunities including industry related conferences that allow participants to form networks with discipline experts at peer companies and help BP to stay ahead of legislative changes and new technologies. The FLP Global Event is a major networking opportunity, giving FLP employees training and access to executive leaders within the Downstream business.

The opportunity that FLP affords participants to get diverse experiences and an early test of leadership potential is a real strength of the programme. The FLP's that make the most of this as well as those that show a good balance of IQ and EQ and go beyond labels and hierarchy are those that are perceived as most successful.

Changing approaches to mobility

Bersin (2020) suggests **Facilitated Mobility** as an alternative to the conventional planned but ad hoc career model. People get a stretch assignment or are 'assigned' to take on an important new role or move – whether horizontal or vertical. This is a more dynamic process and to be effective requires managers to play a big role in development coaching.

Conversely, another model proposed by Bersin (2020) is what he calls **Agile Talent Mobility**, where people move around all the time, work on multiple projects, join various teams or initiatives, on-demand or need-based, and work on more than one project (or 'gig') at a time. This requires the company to operate more like a professional services firm and less like a hierarchy of jobs and functions. Such mobility can only work when there is a transparent workforce plan, self-assessment tools and the culture and systems align to enable agility. Performance management is based on 'results' not 'reputation', making the company more accountable, dynamic, and agile as a result. People may have 'career managers' who help them with their career or functional skills, but they also have project managers, team leaders and other leaders that they work for as well. Over time many companies are moving in this direction, but for most this is a new idea.

Many HR leaders study patterns of mobility to figure out which moves have the highest potential for success. McKinsey research (2020) suggests that reallocation of high performers to the most critical strategic priorities is the talent factor most likely to lead to outperforming the competition. However, these newer types of mobility scenarios cannot be planned or programmed into conventional career models. They happen in real-time (Bersin 2020). They require a learning-focused culture that is responsive to all these changes and that identifies and nurtures its top performers.

We now turn our attention to succession planning.

A partnership – balancing organisational and individual needs

Succession planning has long been seen as an organisationally owned process aimed at securing the organisation's future. Planning processes are often held in 'secret' with the organisation's judgement on employees' potential, readiness for a move and current abilities withheld from the individual. Development moves have been offered to the individual who has been expected to fall in with these plans. However, high-flyers are becoming more discriminating about what they require from their employer and less compliant with organisational 'offers' unless these meet the individual's needs.

If the 'empowered' employee has his or her own plans, can succession planning hope to incorporate these? AlliedSignal Aerospace aims to meet both the needs of individual employees, teams of employees and also the organisation through its integrated approach to performance management, development processes and succession planning. The NHS in Scotland aims to develop a coherent architecture of learning, experience and personal development at all stages of a manager's career, up to and including the boardroom. The framework includes learning support in the forms of action learning sets, mentoring and 'critical companionship', which is a helping relationship, in which an experienced facilitator (often, but not always a colleague) accompanies another on an experiential learning journey, using methods of 'high challenge' and 'high support' in a trusting relationship. The overall purpose of critical companionship is to enable others to practise in ways that are person-centred and evidence-based. Some organisations are developing 'maps' of managerial careers to enable people to spot opportunities for themselves as well as gear their development to areas of interest to them.

In the Springfield ReManufacturing Corporation, employees are provided with a list of all jobs available in the organisation and are asked to identify the next position they would like to hold. Training and development programmes are then built around qualification for the next position. Supervisors and managers track employees' progress and feedback results through individual annual reports. Similarly, managers are asked to provide a list of people whom they believe could fill their position. The management team then assesses whether potential candidates require further training before they are 'ready' for their specified jobs. This approach has led to the development of a pool of committed potential successors at every level in the organisation.

The question of how open an organisation should be about how a person's potential is perceived is often asked. There are fears that people may have expectations raised which may not be fulfilled, or that 'high potentials' will become more demanding if they know how they are perceived. These fears may be justified. On the other hand, if people are also made aware that while opportunities for promotion may be limited, other opportunities can be made available, the expected exodus may not be as large as anticipated. One FMCG company, for instance, trains its executive group in career counselling techniques. Each executive has a number of high-flying 'clients'. The objective here is not to promise rapid progression up the hierarchy but to convey the message that the organisation values these individuals and is interested in their development. Being open with these individuals has not proved a problem, quite the reverse.

Case: succession planning for the top jobs in BP Amoco – a strategic approach

Succession planning for the top jobs in BP Amoco is based on a structured, long-term assessment and development format. The 200 high-potential candidates viewed to have the capability to reach the top 100 jobs in the company are mainly drawn from the top

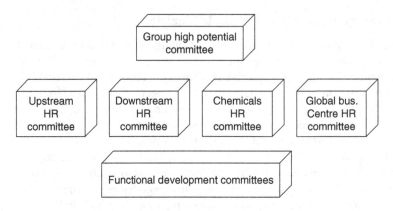

Figure 12.2 The supporting committee infrastructure in BP Amoco.

2500. A broader group of achievers are expected to reach the top 500 roles (i.e. Group Leadership), but development of these people takes place largely within their own businesses, i.e. Oil, Exploration, Chemicals or Global Business Centre. The supporting infrastructure for succession planning consists of a set of functional development committees within each of the businesses. These link into HR committees within each business which in turn link to the group-level HR committee (Figure 12.2).

Draft plans are initially generated by a combination of current incumbents' knowledge of direct reports and others and the HR secretariat for each committee. The committees then work to finalise the plans based on personal knowledge of potential successors and high potentials. This personal knowledge is developed through an ongoing annual review of all high-potential individuals. Each committee focuses on a different group of high potentials. Succession planning is taken very seriously by the business.

The high-potential population is divided into four groupings or 'cohorts' and these are based on their:

- Stage of their development, e.g. their grade at the time
- Historical rate of progression, e.g. moving through the grades every 18 months as opposed to the norm of two years
- Longer-term potential, i.e. perceived ability to reach the top 100 or even top 20 jobs.

The four cohorts are grouped according to the approximate number of years required for individuals to reach the top jobs. Progress within cohorts is reviewed using a Development Checklist which summarises whether a person has acquired all the key experiences for their stage of development. The checklist, prepared by the Group HR Executive support team, is easy for senior managers to understand and helps the review process to work smoothly (Figure 12.3).

The cohort analysis is done annually, with one cohort being reviewed per quarter. Only half a cohort will be reviewed at a time, with special attention being paid to those who will move in the next 12 months. Cohort membership is not static. Feedback about individuals is provided by committee members or by Dr Candy Albertsson using a structured process. Nor is the information concerning the review kept secret. Feedback on development and gaps has an impact on personal development plans and individual performance objectives. Typically, 20% move up in a cohort annually. There is not

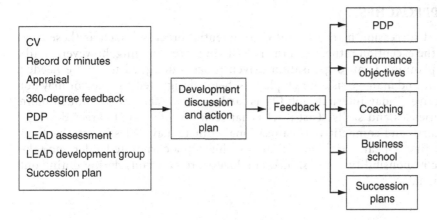

Figure 12.3 The cohort review process in BP Amoco.

necessarily an even distribution between the cohorts. On a few occasions, a relative short-age of identified junior talent prompted the high-potential committees to actively seek out potential lower down the organisation. It is also recognised that telling people that they are part of the high-potential programme tends to encourage and motivate them.

However, the primary purpose behind grouping individuals into cohorts is that it enables more closely targeted development opportunities to be made available accord-ing to the individuals' stage of development. To reach the top 100 jobs it is essential that individuals are able to work across boundaries. They must have some international experience and have built up international exposure to reach the most senior roles. So for people in cohort four, i.e. 15–20 years away from a top job, it is considered important that they acquire some cross-functional experience. During their tenure in this cohort, individuals will be likely to attend a junior version of the LEAD programme, known as ALP and take part in the 'Stage 1' management development programme.

Stage I offers a strategic overview of the business – the issues and deliverables within the regions. Participants meet with members of the most senior management tiers and gain a better understanding of their region. People in cohort three, 10–15 years away from the top jobs, have the opportunity to acquire international experience and cross-business exposure. They are likely to have people management and bottom-line respon-sibilities. They will also be invited to take part in the Stage II management development programme which has a clear group focus on business strategy and people management. For people in cohort two, five to ten years away from a top job, there are opportunities to attend an international business school and the LEAD programme.

In cohort one, with only five years before individuals are considered ready for a top 100 job, development is very individually focused. It is also expected that these senior managers will take a lead role in the development of others – by acting as mentor or an observer on the LEAD or ALP programmes. They will be invited to Group Leadership meetings and contribute to group-level initiatives. They are able to state their aspirations through the personal development planning process and their names start to appear on candidate lists. There is an internal job/people broker who networks their names with line managers and committee members, coaches high potentials on their development and builds momentum for a role change. The top 500 roles each have a candidate list of potential successors, categorised as 'possible', 'emergency' and 'preferred'.

NEWER APPROACHES

Sophisticated succession planning and high potential processes such as these continue to be the exception rather than the rule. Things are changing, however. While succession planning is an organisation-driven process designed to secure needed future leaders and manage risk, for employees, being designated a successor may not be so attractive. Today internal mobility is far less about 'careers' and much more about 'experiences and skills'. Fast-tracks that seem to offer rapid career development in a harsh and competitive organisational climate may be less attractive than they may at first appear. Far from seeking to whizz up a corporate ladder and take on yet more responsibility, some skilled employees are now considering opting out of employment.

Aligning expectations

Newer approaches recognise the importance of aligning high potential employee and senior leader expectations about development programmes and career paths. The emphasis on individuals' values and choices is very much in line with the current climate in which employees are becoming more selective about who they want to work for. Career development is an obvious arena for negotiation between organisations and employees. Increasingly some knowledge workers are looking for more congenial working arrangements in organisations whose ethos they can espouse. As one 'high-flyer' said as she joined her new employer, 'at last I'm working for a company whose product I believe in'. Some companies now offer senior employees various forms of flexible working arrangement including flexible retirement, in order to retain them.

Possible new approaches appear less organisation-driven and more based on an adult–adult employment relationship that recognises the increasing power of the knowledge worker to make demands of the organisation that go beyond pay and rations. High performing professionals want to try new things, learn adjacent skills, take international assignments and get a chance to work with different leaders. There is already a good deal of anecdotal evidence that employees with transferable skills and experience are more confident of being employable and less tolerant of the frustrations of poor management, inappropriate reward and few growth opportunities. Ironically, the very skills which many employers crave – such as the ability to get things done, be innovative, customer oriented etc. – are precisely the skills that will help people get jobs elsewhere.

Deloitte (2018) recommends a 'centred' approach to succession planning that is designed to put the people involved – both the leaders managing the process and the successors who are being considered – at the centre, supported by processes that help decision-makers maintain objectivity. People-centred design tools channel emotions productively into the succession planning process and allow organisations to consider objective talent assessment criteria without the process being perceived as threatening to the current leader community. All incumbents and succession candidates, especially those at the middle/upper and top management levels, establish a Personal Development Plan for the upcoming year. The aim is to create a succession programme that leaders want to participate in, which can only happen when all participants appreciate its value and feel that it is fair and easy to navigate – and that it ultimately creates more opportunity for all involved.

Shorter timeframes

Succession planning is a long-term discipline in a short-term world (Deloitte 2018). PepsiCo is shortening the time frame of the conventional long-term succession planning model. Instead of the usual annual updates on the development of possible successors, brief quarterly updates are provided – and appointments are delayed so that they happen closer to when successors are likely to step into their roles (Cappelli and Tavis 2018). In Deloitte (2018) research, an associate vice president of leadership development explained how his organisation's succession planning had been broken into nine executive talent review sessions per year - to create more focus and depth. Seeing leadership succession planning as part of their day-to-day job helps keep leaders proactively engaged in the shorter term while also pursuing long-term success. Cappelli and Tavis (2018) point out that newer approaches use data analysis to identify the skills required for particular jobs and for advancement, enable managers to suggest to individual employees what kinds of training and future jobs make sense for them, given their experience and interests. By putting high potentials into a succession planning process and communicating clearly how they can attain these goals, HR can reassure them of their place in the organisation and help them identify their best career options to advance in their careers as they wish.

Retaining leadership talent

If the primary objective of succession planning is the identification and growth of leadership talent, related objectives include the retention of talent and continuity of leadership. Identifying high potential employees is one thing; retaining them is another. CEB (2015) suggests offering high potential employees a 'talent deal' that provides them with a variety of special opportunities, benefits and commitments, while also defining commitments or responsibilities expected from them in return. Managers must understand the importance of assessing and developing their people through 1-on-1 development discussions and informal feedback throughout the year. They should be encouraged to conduct regular 'stay interviews' with high performers to uncover what motivates them and to identify and address the risks of losing them. Such employees are often at high risk of burnout and being overworked. Supportive managers will attempt to remove any unnecessary forms of stress, including concerns over job security, and can help keep people on track.

MAXIMISING SUCCESSION PLANNING

In this section we consider some recommendations on how organisations can maximise their investment in succession planning and high potential development.

Recommendation one: integrate succession planning with other initiatives

Link succession planning and corporate strategy

Among the limitations of conventional succession planning is the tendency for the planning process to be divorced from the corporate strategy and from what the organisation is trying to achieve longer term. If succession planning takes place in isolation from the way the organisation is going, 'successors' are unlikely to have the relevant skills and behaviours for leadership roles in the future. In devising new approaches to succession planning, it is important to have a clear business imperative and be able to identify how the process must impact on the business.

Workforce planning (see Chapter 7) should highlight gaps in the organisation's capability to deliver its longer-term strategies. Typically, these gaps should be filled by judicious recruitment, both for specific roles and to build up the supply of new talent within the organisation. Gaps in the organisation's current capability can also be filled through management development. The danger in a rapidly changing environment is to assume that gaps can only be filled by recruitment rather than development, because development takes too long. This contingency approach to planning can backfire in several ways. Not only do new people usually need time to become effective in their roles, but if their 'fit' with the organisation does not work, expensive mistakes can be made. Similarly, a policy of external appointments for key roles can demotivate internal candidates, especially if they have developed the relevant skills for a key role.

The challenge is to strike a balance between organisational and individual needs by filling gaps through both development and recruitment. A happy compromise between external and internal recruitment to high-flyer schemes appears to have been struck in a UK retail bank. Their leadership development programme lasts for two years and the programme's aim is to develop the perceived potential of internal and external high-flyers by exposing them to a range of learning and business opportunities. Recruits to this programme include a number of individuals in their forties, who have been with the company for a number of years and whose potential for senior roles has only recently been recognised.

Of course, in times of change, developing a longer-term corporate strategy with clearly defined goals and management requirements is not always possible. Even a well-defined corporate strategy will need to flex with changing circumstances and succession planning processes will need to do the same. To ensure successful execution, succession planning requires the development and fostering of a learning-focused culture that is responsive to all these changes and that identifies and nurtures top performers. To achieve that, it is vital to align the organisation's talent strategy to its business strategy and to get executive buy-in to create a learning-focused culture that will support succession planning. The Corestates Financial Corporation addressed this issue by focusing on its corporate vision, principles and core values rather than detailed corporate and business plans and so provided a focus for the development of leaders during a period of rapid change in the banking industry.

Link succession planning with management development, leadership performance and assessment

Talent management activities should be developed in an integrated way with other HR policies and practice. So if what is required in changing industries are innovative, proactive succession strategies aimed at strengthening business success, it is important to tie together succession planning, employee development and the use of assessment instruments to enhance leadership performance. In Hershey Foods Corporation, assessment instruments can be used to assist in the candidate/job matching process. In the Post Office, career planning, talent review and succession planning are linked. AlliedSignal Aerospace integrates performance management, development, succession planning and reward processes. Texaco combines the use of competencies, the development of the 'talent pool', culture change and succession planning. For senior management positions in Texaco, the key to differentiating candidate readiness for advancement is through the demonstration of Texaco's Core Leadership Competencies. In Philips, leadership competencies are at the heart of an integrated set of processes which include selection, performance appraisal, development, education and training and succession planning.

Schering-Plough Pharmaceuticals review successor and high-potential talent within a three-year framework for management and organisation development. Of course, in a short-term results-oriented organisation, the benefits of an integrated approach to succession planning may need selling to the senior management team. Senior management attention is usually focused on matters financial, technological or concerned with market share. In a decentralised organisation this task can be even more difficult, especially if the regional operations see no reason to 'share' information about high-potential individuals with the centre. In BP Amoco, the most senior levels of management are directly involved in the management of high-potential programmes, with the High Potential Committee chaired by the Deputy Chief Executive.

Recommendation two: be clear about what else you want to achieve through succession planning

It is therefore important to be clear what objectives are being served by the succession planning process and to set measures to ensure that those objectives are being achieved.

A key objective of succession planning is the identification of candidate 'pools' from among existing employees who are ready for advancement. For this to happen systematically, a meaningful and effective system for talent pool review and development needs to be created. This will involve management development assessment and planning against agreed criteria which are clearly understood and stem from business requirements. Data will need to be collected, analysed; decisions taken and plans made. The process will need to be monitored to ensure that the 'talent' identified is being developed and demonstrated in practice.

For the data-gathering to be effective, line managers across the organisation will need to be involved, trained and take responsibility for identifying and nurturing the organisation's potential. Of course, this is easier said than achieved, especially in a decentralised organisation where the benefits of business unit autonomy have to be weighed against the longer-term benefits to the organisation as a whole of developing people potential as a corporate rather than local resource. As has already been stated, any planning system of this sort needs to be reviewed to ensure that it is meeting needs and moving in line with the business. It also needs to be as simple and transparent as possible. This does of course suggest an automated process to some extent but the decisions about the process should in every case precede automation considerations.

Create a lever for critical cultural change

Of course, if businesses are going through change, they are likely to require different skills and behaviours of employees in general and of leaders in particular. Given the generally recognised importance of leaders 'walking the talk', succession planning can develop leaders whose skills and values are in tune with the changing culture of the organisation.

One financial services organisation highlighted the problems caused by senior managers failing to practise the teamworking values which they advocated for others. The company in question attempted to bring about behaviour change by training senior management in leadership skills and using upward feedback processes. When that failed to produce significant changes in behaviour, feedback results were fed into decision-making about bonuses. Management behaviour soon shifted in the desired direction.

In Rhône–Poulenc Canada succession planning is linked to management development, organisational strategy and culture. In making these connections, it is important to identify both starting points – by carrying out an audit of the current culture – and 'destination' points in the targeted culture. These should be described in terms of competencies or behaviours. The leadership competency models should be built around the targeted culture and assessment and development tools developed for 'high-potential' candidates in the succession planning pool. In Rhône–Poulenc, 360-degree models and psychometric tests are used, together with performance measurement data. The information gathered is fed into the succession planning system.

In a major pharmaceutical company, leadership planning is considered as important as succession planning. Through the Leadership and Development Review, managers are judged not simply on what they produce but on how they perform against the values of the organisation. As such, the leadership planning process becomes transformational in supporting the business, not just a transactional exercise. Leadership development takes place mainly on the job and feedback from managers is an important part of fine-tuning leadership ability.

For leadership development to become a process, not an event, Federal Express has created a Leadership Institute which conducts week-long courses where attendance is required as managers move into the various levels. A special emphasis is placed on developing the 'soft' skills of leadership. A parallel process known as the Leadership Evaluation and Awareness Process (LEAP) is used to assess and prepare individuals for their roles as managers. The process allows people who are interested in formal leadership roles to put themselves forward and receive self-development tools and personalised coaching. FedEx leaders and employees are directly involved in helping other people to develop. This has produced twin benefits by increasing the readiness of managers for leadership responsibilities as well as reducing the turnover of front-line management.

Recommendation three: create the processes, then assess and monitor performance

Processes must be developed to track the performance and progress of those identified in the talent pool as well as systems for reviewing, refining and making changes to talent management initiatives in line with changing organisational priorities. The basic questions to ask when developing succession plans are relatively straightforward and stem from the Human Resource planning cycle as follows:

- *Selection.* Who are the right people to meet our business needs?
- *Performance appraisal.* How have they performed against their objectives?
- *Development planning.* What is their potential? What steps do they need to take to realise that potential?
- *Education, training and learning.* What learning opportunities are required to support their development?
- *Succession planning.* Who will fill our key positions now and in the future?

The core processes are also relatively simple in theory, but more difficult to implement in practice for a variety of reasons. Typically, these include succession planning being seen as a 'stand-alone' activity or as a responsibility of Personnel alone, processes becoming outdated or inappropriate and inadequate data flow. At the very least, succession planning processes should include:

- Ongoing planning activity which assesses how well the organisation is placed to meet replacement requirements etc.
- Individual performance and potential assessment
- Individual development planning

Interconnected processes include:

Selection
- College recruiting – the 'milk round'
- Experienced new hire selection, including MBA recruitment
- Internal job movement

Performance appraisal
- Appraisal of job responsibilities and accomplishments
- Reviewing personal and team effectiveness
- Assessing the balance between what has been achieved and how

Development planning
- Talent reviews
- Assessment of potential
- Identification of development needs
- Career development planning
- Development action planning and review

Education, learning and training
- On-the-job development
- Educational and training programmes
- Learning groups
- Peer coaching
- Learning 'logs' and development portfolios
- Programmes to support organisational and individual development needs

Succession planning
- Identification of successors and potential successors for key roles
- Creation of development opportunities for potential successors

Effective collation of information

It is important to create a process and IT infrastructure which allow for the integration of information from a range of sources including different forms of feedback and enable succession planning to work effectively. There need to be simple and direct methods of assessing employee potential, for spotting opportunities to help individuals to develop. Information needs to be tracked and data kept up to date. Individual and job profiles must also be kept up to date so that effective opportunity matching can occur. A coherent set of processes is evident in Wendy's International. A suite of activities includes ongoing disciplined job analysis, screening tools for success, assessment centres, Human Resource planning, individual development planning and outcome-based evaluation.

In United Airlines, the process of pushing succession planning down the management ranks is assisted by automated processes which overcome the limitations of paper flow logistics. This has enabled individual career planning and organisational succession planning needs to be married up more efficiently. Internal resumés are used to ensure that relevant skills are captured, together with candidates' internal/external history, future assignment and relocation interests. These can then be matched against selected management positions. Having access to the information online has resulted in streamlined reporting and improved staffing for vacancies.

The usefulness of any review process depends to a large extent on the quality of information provided by line management. Often, divisions are asked to supply the following:

- the strategic plan
- a review of the previous year
- information about each individual, their performance, promotion potential and functions to which they are perceived to be best suited
- details of past job and training history including current performance ratings
- future career development plans, especially of high-flyers
- individual career ambitions
- information on individual's cross-functional moves, including international experience
- information on an individual's training and skill levels

In BOC (now part of the Linde Group) additional data gathered includes what new jobs may be created in the future and who might fill them. The process is regulated by standard forms. Each business is also required to report on the strengths and weaknesses of its management, professional and technical workforce and produce an action plan to address problem areas. Companies such as Xerox use a computerised succession planning system for storing information on both staff and positions.

Succession planning systems should be incorporated into human resource planning systems so that detailed planning exercises can be undertaken for any part of an organisation. Employee information such as:

- Skills and performance profiles linked to overall business criteria
- Training and development profiles
- Individual succession plans with alternative career/succession plans can be supplemented by data modelling to facilitate:
- Resourcing and job/skills matching
- Tracking of expertise and experience in key project areas
- Successor identification
- Identification of 'what if?' scenarios.

Recommendation four: use development planning and interventions to achieve organisational success

Assignments and project work arising from education and training are being taken seriously by senior management as a means of both developing high-flyers and addressing real business problems.

In decentralised organisations people responsible for management development and succession planning face a number of challenges. One of these is how to identify and develop 'high-potential' employees in different regions without harming the autonomy of regional management. The aim should be to balance the short-term needs of individual businesses with the long-term needs of the organisation. In some organisations, generic competencies are used for the identification of potential while the development opportunities are made relevant to the local business in which the individual is operating. When the benefits to the region's business become apparent, regional managers usually develop a cooperative approach towards taking part in 'central' succession planning.

Manage assignments as well as development in place

In the case of international assignments, support may be required prior to, during and after the assignment to reintegrate the individual and their learning. A number of organisations are now using mentors for setting people up for success, even when there is no overseas element to the assignment.

For most high-flyers, development in place is likely to be the norm. Providing challenges and assignments to develop skills and leverage strengths should lead to retention. Some organisations are collaborating in providing shared development opportunities for their high-flyers. Such opportunities include secondments to other organisations in the network and joint working groups on industry-related issues.

Create key management ownership of the process

Of course, relying on Human Resource processes alone for the identification of potential is not necessarily the best policy. It is important that line managers consider that they have a responsibility to spot and nurture talent as an organisational resource. Line managers are also ideally placed to assess actual performance and are a key partner in the objective-setting process. Engaging line managers from an early stage is critical to ensure that they are committed to organisational approaches to talent management.

Some organisations such as Schering-Plough Pharmaceuticals are now measuring and rewarding managers for their part in developing others. Training and feedback processes can be helpful in enabling senior managers to take on this role. Involving senior managers in assessing potential through assessment centres, for instance, can be helpful in building up awareness and ownership of the process.

It is also important that there is line ownership and senior management support for succession planning. Without this ownership, the day-to-day identification, development and management of high-flyers may be confined to the occasional training or assessment intervention. It may be necessary to sell the importance of this to senior management and to garner support from critical constituencies.

CONCLUSION

The purpose of conventional succession planning is to supply successors for key posts in the organisation in the future. In the current climate of ongoing economic and organisational change, there are opportunities to learn from the past as well as to examine how to maximise the diversity and potential of fast-track and succession planning processes.

Succession planning should sit within a coherent, flexible and integrated set of organisational development processes.

While a holistic approach to succession planning is helpful, it can be easy to 'take one's eye off the ball' and lose sight of whether the processes are meeting requirements. Choosing and using the right metrics is essential, as well as ensuring that all stakeholders in the process are playing their part. So with that warning note, an integrated approach, focused on building organisational capability to meet current and future business objectives, is the starting point for succession planning.

We have discussed how a proactive, strategic approach to talent management jointly owned by the line and HR offers considerable organisational benefits in terms of developing a flexible pool of high calibre talent to meet future needs. Adopting a 'partnership' approach with individuals turns succession planning into a validated process rather than a fortune-telling exercise. Involving employees in the succession planning process in an open and honest way should allow for more detailed, realistic career planning and lead to improved motivation, commitment and better retention.

Succession planning needs to be a continuous process, rather than an annual event. It should be focused on longer-term development and retention, rather than short-term replacements or emergencies, but also be flexible. It should centre on what is needed, rather than on who is in place. It should facilitate the removal of blockages to diversity and enable healthy mobility towards key positions. It should create a pool of available talent at all levels in the organisation to meet both individual and organisational needs.

Any organisation which 'puts all its eggs in one basket' is potentially leaving itself exposed longer term. Fast-tracks can happily co-exist alongside other development routes. As we have seen (Chapter 10) more inclusive approaches to talent development can enhance an organisation's talent pool and support employer branding in the labour market. They provide a means of maximising internal employee potential, increasing employee engagement and improving retention.

To be effective, succession planning requires the fostering of a learning-focused culture that is responsive to change and that identifies and nurtures top performers. To be seen as credible suppliers of excellent future leaders, HR departments must model leadership behaviour. And the good news is, developing good leaders pays dividends. Not only does field study evidence (Barling et al. 1996) suggest that leadership behaviours and effectiveness increase following training, the DDI/CIPD study (2008) found also that the companies that develop leaders well have high RoEs and profit margins. And – who knows? – by developing leaders at all levels, HR will be building corporate agility, reinforcing employer brand, creating better employee engagement and potentially winning the war for talent!

REFERENCES

Altman, Y. (1997). The high-potential fast-flying achiever: Themes from the English language literature 1976–1995. *Career Development International, MCB*, July 2, 324–330.

Barling, J., Weber, T. and Kelloway, E.K. (1996). Effects of transformational leadership training on attitudinal and financial outcomes: A field experiment. *Journal of Applied Psychology*, 81(6), 827–832.

Bersin, J. (2020). *Talent marketplace platforms explode into view*, Published July 3, updated July 18. https://joshbersin.com/2020/07/talent-marketplace-platforms-explode-into-view/

Cappelli, P. and Tavis, A. (2018). HR Goes Agile, *Harvard Business Review*, March–April. hbr.org › 2018/03 › hr-goes-agile

CEB study cited on fairness and goal setting in *Deloitte, Global Human Capital Trends 2015.*

DDI/CIPD. (2008). *Global Leadership Forecast 2008–09: The Typical, the Elite and the Forgotten.* London: CIPD.

Deloitte. (2018). The holy grail of effective leadership succession planning: How to overcome the succession planning paradox, *Deloitte Insights*, September 27. https://www2.deloitte.com/us/en/insights/topics/leadership/effective-leadership-succession-planning.html

Deloitte. (2015). *The coming revolution in Global Human Capital Trends 2015: Leading in the new world of work*, Deloitte University Press, pp. 90–91. https://documents.deloitte.com/insights/HCTrends2015

Holbeche, L.S. (1997). *Career Development in Flatter Structures*, Horsham: Roffey Park.

Larsen, H.H., London, M., Weinstein, M. and Raghuram, S. (1998). High-Flyer management-development programs: Organizational rhetoric or self-fulfilling prophecy? *International Studies of Management & Organization*, 28(1), Human-Resource Development for the Future (Spring, 1998), pp. 64–90 (27 pages).

McKinsey. (2020). *Beyond hiring: How companies are reskilling to address talent gaps*, McKinsey & Company, February 12. https://www.mckinsey.com/business-functions/organization/our-insights/beyond-hiring-how-companies-are-reskilling-to-address-talent-gaps

McKinsey. (2017). *Attracting and retaining the right talent*, McKinsey & Company, November 24. https://www.mckinsey.com/business-functions/organization/our-insights/attracting-and-retaining-the-right-talent

Stevenson, M. (2019). *Succession planning in 2020*, HR Exchange Network, December 26.https://www.hrexchangenetwork.com/shared-services/articles/succession-planning-in-2020

13
Global HRM

Today many organisations – large or small – have gone global. Yet in today's 'VUCA' business environment, Western companies developing a global presence face a host of complex issues unimagined just 25 years ago, including fierce competition from companies with lower labour costs in nations such as India and China. These challenges are compounded by the complexities of compliance with an ever-growing array of international labour laws and growing employee expectations in many developing economies.

DOI: 10.4324/9781003219996-15

CHAPTER OVERVIEW

In this chapter, we consider what global HRM addresses and look at some of the challenges of 'glocal' – thinking global, acting local' with respect to HR strategies. We shall cover:

- International and global HRM theory
- Challenges facing global businesses
- Global HR leadership, teams and structures
- Global vs local
- Global talent management
- Supporting transnational teams

LEARNING OBJECTIVES

- Discuss approaches to international and global HRM
- Analyse some theoretical and practical perspectives on the challenges of implementing global HRM

INTRODUCTION: INTERNATIONAL AND GLOBAL HRM THEORY

As we discussed in Chapter 1, International HRM (IHRM) is a growing field that concerns the management of human resources in different contexts in which international firms operate. It includes comparisons of how HRM and Industrial Relations practices operate in various countries (comparative IHRM) and also how HRM is conducted across countries and cultures in multi-national and international companies (tending towards the global HRM concept) (Dowling and Welch 2004; Iles and Zhang 2013).

As organisations globalise, they typically seek to standardise organisational design, systems, processes and procedures. Global HRM means supporting, managing and engaging employees around the world, deploying common policies and building structures which can support business operations and a corporate culture which connects employees, as well as facilitating learning and innovation worldwide. At the same time, they need to adapt to the local market and culture (Scullion et al 2007).

Alongside deploying common policies, HR must also take into account local legislation, customs and culture to create an offer that is consistent across the world, but which can flex to meet local requirements. Global organisations therefore must operate according to the old dictum 'think global, act local' (or 'glocal'). In practice, few global HR teams appear able to achieve a high level of global integration or resolve 'global' versus 'local' dilemmas. Corporate approaches which generally come unstuck at local level are in areas such as management by objectives, pay for performance, terms and conditions.

For Brewster et al. (2002, 2016), the role HRM plays in contributing to global business success is little understood. They point out that 'although HR forms a very substantial part of their operating costs, so far there has been very little serious attention paid to thinking strategically about it'. For Fons Trompenaars (1997), even the notion of HR management is an Anglo-Saxon concept which is difficult to translate to other cultures: 'It borrows from economics the idea that human beings are "resources" like physical and monetary resources. It tends to assume almost unlimited capacities for individual development. In countries without these beliefs, this concept is hard to grasp and unpopular once it is understood'. Equally, the lack of an effective multi-cultural HR strategy can potentially undermine the organisation's ability to grow its capabilities and optimise its international business opportunities.

An aligned global HR agenda must equip the organisation to deal with its strategic objectives and capitalise on the opportunities of scale, scope and diversity. Convergence is the adoption by a global organisation of similar HR practices across the world (standardisation). Convergence involves centralising operational decision making and implies a high need for cultural control. The parenting style of the parent company tends to be reflected in the level of control and in the choice of areas in which complete standardisation is required. For Stroh and Caligiuri (1998), the three aspects of people management critical to the success of global companies are as follows:

- The adoption of flexible management policies and practices worldwide
- The inclusion of the HR function as a strategic business partner in global business
- The development of global leaders

The global HR agenda will also include a focus on facilitating international mobility, skills requirements, skills transfer, management development and organisation development. This will involve hiring staff across geographic boundaries, and also training managers about the cultures and sensitivities of the host country. Sparrow (2008) suggests that global HR standardisation and coordination should apply to:

- Performance management processes
- Capability/competency systems
- Talent management processes
- Employment brand (Sparrow 2008)

I would also add optimising the benefits of diversity, facilitating organisational learning, and enabling cross-boundary or transnational teamworking.

Undoubtedly, the task of global HR at the centre today is more complex and demanding than in the days when multinationals (MNEs) simply issued edicts from HQ which had to be implemented locally. In the global organisation, however, such centrist approaches may not be effective. The danger of too much centralisation is that culturally inappropriate policies are imposed and fail to be implemented. Divergence, or decentralised decision-making, is the approach taken by a global organisation when it adapts its HR practices across the world to suit local conditions. Too much localisation can mean decision-making becomes bogged down, delivery gets fragmented, and resources are wasted with endless reinvention of wheels.

There is some coalescence of view about the more challenging aspects of global HRM:

- Culture, alignment (of strategy and practice, and of HR practice with business strategy)
- Integrating global processes and policies with local practices
- The question of standardisation vs localisation (i.e. a global policy as in the geocentric vs the local adaptation of the polycentric)
- Managing paradoxes and multi-dimensioned issues

With respect to brand, the challenge is to create a local appeal without compromising upon the global identity. Divergence is necessary because, while an organisation may use a single brand and deliver similar products and services all over the world, workforces in different operating countries may have very different needs. Salary benchmarks and typical working hours may be different. Cultural differences may affect workplace facilities, communication protocols and management frameworks. This can be a complex set of variables to manage under a single employer brand.

So while the activities and functions involved in managing people globally are similar to those in domestic organisations, the nature of HRM in global companies may differ according to multiple factors – geography, parent company culture, life cycle stage and so on. These influence the global HR agenda in any given company. Factors affecting the choice between convergence and divergence (Harris and Brewster 1999) are the:

- extent to which there are well-defined local norms
- degree to which an operating unit is embedded in the local environment
- strength of the flow of resources between the parent and the subsidiary
- orientation of the parent to control
- nature of the industry
- specific organisational competencies, including HRM, that are critical for achieving competitive advantage in a global environment.

Before discussing global HR strategy in more detail, let us consider some of the stages of evolution of international business and also some of the challenges facing global organisations and their leaders.

The development of international organisations

Companies typically evolve through four stages of internationalisation – domestic/export, international, multinational and global (Adler and Ghadar 1990). The domestic stage is where the company focuses on the home market and exports out; cultural issues typically play little part at this stage. Cultural differences in foreign markets play a greater part at the international phase which is where production, marketing and manufacturing of products is moved to the relevant market to facilitate local responsiveness, lower costs, secure external relationships and transfer learning (Scullion 2005).

In the next phase, multinational companies focus on achieving competitive advantage by globalising the product and keeping costs low. Many multinationals operate a regional approach with mini-HQs which standardise suitable approaches within regions. Others operate as multi-country/multi-domestic by establishing subsidiary countries – often operating independently – with full support functions like HR. Transnational companies such as Standard Chartered act local while drawing on global resources. Finally, global companies gain global advantage by focusing on quality and adapting products to individual markets. With a global approach and global customers information sharing is encouraged. Cultural sensitivity is paramount. These different life cycle phases arguably require different business strategies, different types of management approach and each stage has different implications for people management and for international careers (Adler 1995).

1. Domestic	2. International	3. Multi-National	4. Global	Adler & Ghadar 1990
Product/Service focused (Export)	Market focused Multi-domestic approach	Market focused Multinational approach	Focus on Strategic advantage	
Allow foreign clients to buy	Increased customer base	Produce & market internationally	Gain global advantage	
No expatriates	Many expatriates	Some expatriates	Many expatriates	
Foreign trips: junket/reward	Foreign trips: Control/solve/ punish/develop	Foreign trips: solve/ develop	Foreign trips: career + org. development	
Money motivates	Money & adventure	Challenge & Opportunity	Challenge & advancement	
Career fast track = domestic	Career fast track = mainly domestic	Career fast track = Token International	Career fast track = Global	
Technical / functional skills required	Technical / functional skills required plus cultural adaptation	Technical / functional skills required plus cultural sensitivity	Technical / functional skills required + cross cultural influence & synergy	

Figure 13.1 The 'international manager'.

Scale, scope and complexity

While increased scale presents opportunities, it also creates difficulties and requires sensitivity to local differences (Sinclair and Agyeman 2004). Global leaders face challenges of scope and complexity and must leverage the benefits of scale, build an integrated consistent global culture or brand and facilitate learning and innovation. To maximise the benefits of operating globally, organisations must be able to mobilise resources according to requirements. To ensure this happens effectively, leaders need to motivate people to work for global as well as local goals (Brake 1997). Operationalising this sensitivity at local level remains a challenge, since typically the benefits of scale and maximise efficiency are leveraged through standardisation and eliminating what is considered unnecessary duplication.

Dealing with constant change

On their way to becoming global, organisations usually reengineer, redesign and re-evaluate their processes, procedures and products, as well as their workforce, services and public relations (Harris 2002). Change is therefore a constant feature of global organisations as leaders manage increasing numbers of cross-border acquisitions, mergers, partnerships and alliances (Kets De Vries and Florent-Treacy 1999). This requires change management capability and adaptive strategies for gaining 'buy in', yet achieving 'buy-in' to change across a global workforce can be difficult. Global leaders, themselves in short supply, need to manage employees with a diverse range of cultural backgrounds and values, languages, different employment experiences and expectations. Moreover, what is considered to constitute effective leadership behaviour will differ across cultures (Dickson et al. 2003).

Challenges facing global businesses

Global businesses operate in an interconnected, dynamic and uncertain global environment. Business leaders face intense and shifting global competition, technological revolution, constant change, increased exposure and cost pressures. Thanks to technology, borders of time, distance, language and markets are being eroded. Cost drivers and talent supply affect the location of value-adding activities. Dealing with different national and business cultures, employment market conditions, legal requirements, time-zones and languages creates significant challenges for leaders. Managers are also under pressure to adapt their organisation to the local characteristics of the market, the legislation, the fiscal regime, the socio-political system and the cultural system.

The interconnected nature of global business creates a complex and unpredictable environment that leaves major international businesses more vulnerable than before to new threats and risks. What happens in one part of the world has repercussions elsewhere and global organisations are keenly exposed to geo-socio-political and economic shifts, as events of the past few years have illustrated. Wars in Afghanistan and Iraq, terrorist attacks in various parts of the world, computer viruses, and ongoing political uncertainty and instability in many countries have not only had tragic and terrible human consequences but also created new levels of uncertainty and risk that have had a powerful economic effect, as has the global banking crisis and ensuing economic volatility. Deregulation, changing security arrangements and slower growth in declining markets add to the complexity (Collings et al. 2007).

Corporate ethics and reputations

Ethics are high on global organisations' agendas, if only for self-protection. Global brands are under particular pressure to improve their environmental and social responsibility credentials, with concerns about climate change, the environment and the growing gap between rich and poor (within and between nations) fuelling demand from consumers and investors alike for ethical, responsible and sustainable business practice. Thanks to social media consumer pressure groups can broadcast their campaigns and boycotts to international audiences. They now talk of their ability to 'swarm', to rally activist allies for 'direct action' against the various worldwide bases of a single corporation on a single day. Because of their pervasiveness they are seen as particularly powerful, 'capable of doing great good and causing considerable harm' (Holt et al. 2004: 70). Leaders need to be proactive in managing their organisational reputations in the face of worldwide demands for higher standards of business practice, accountability and responsibility.

Managing a global workforce

Working in international business involves collaborating with colleagues in a culturally diverse workplace. The diversity of a global organisation's workforce can be one of its greatest strengths. Studies show that workforce diversity leads to superior business performance, an improved bottom line, competitive advantage, creativity, employee satisfaction and loyalty, lower absenteeism, strengthened relationships with multicultural communities and attraction of the best and the brightest candidates (Caligiuri and Stroh, 2006; McCuiston et al., 2004; Ng and Tung, 1998; Schneider Ross, 2002). Understanding how to communicate across cultures, motivate and unify the workforce to strive for organisational success, is of paramount importance (Towers Perrin, 2006).

Moreover, leading at a distance presents additional challenges to global leaders (Smith and Sinclair 2003; Smith and Bond, 2006), adding an extra layer of complexity to communications. When managing at a distance, achieving coordination and control through direct supervision is not easy and new ways of cooperating to achieve tasks and meet organisational goals must be found. Reduced physical contact also reduces the information available for making judgements. Coaching and communicating can be more difficult particularly as managers can't pick up physical cues that reveal problems or learn about what's going on from a casual conversation. It's harder to ensure individuals fully understand their goals and are working effectively to meet them when there are distance and language barriers between team members.

Managers must learn the art of accommodating cultural differences, motivating, engaging, collaborating, networking and communicating with employees through virtual methods as well as face-to-face. Teleconferencing and web conferencing are useful tools to enable teams to meet remotely and interact with each other, even asynchronously. HR can offer training and development to ensure that leaders are culturally aware and able to utilise all these tools effectively.

GLOBAL HR LEADERSHIP, TEAMS AND STRUCTURES

Global HR structures typically comprise a headquarters' function while field operations are delivered by local HR professionals. Global HR teams typically have to juggle a range of operational issues such as staffing foreign subsidiaries and establishing compensation rates. Both HR at the centre and in different country locations need to operate as a worldwide team, take into account the cultures of different countries and decide which aspects of policies and systems should be addressed locally and which are truly global. HR strategy implementation is managed through relationships between the team in the centre and the field. They need to be able to share information and power with one another which requires a degree of flexibility in both behaviour and policies. In many global companies the real challenge is raising the standards of the overall global HR team. Tact and compromise are likely to be hallmarks of HR teams who find effective ways of collaborating on global and local issues.

Global HR also need a strategic perspective and must be able to anticipate the HR needs of their organisations. Getting the right operational-strategic balance should ensure that the HR contribution is proactive rather than reactive. According to Stroh and Caligiuri (1998), 'the biggest barrier to HR units becoming strategic is their own lack of expertise of international business-related issues'. Paul Sparrow (2008) also argues that global HR must avoid getting trapped in the operational. For Larson (2008), successful global HR leadership involves knowing your business – especially in the global context; she suggests going out and visiting customers. Helping to create the global HR agenda is one way of both building the HR team and of developing a shared understanding of the overall business goals and direction, as well as figuring out ways to deliver what is required.

Getting the HR structure right is crucial. Sparrow (2008) suggests dividing regional time between the largest or small-but-important strategic units and getting sites that are off the 'radar map' to self-manage. Sparrow (2008) describes how one global organisation applied the 'Ulrich model', with shared services concentrating on administrative and transactional personnel activities separately from the main HR group. HR business partners worked to an 'embedded HR' model in which HR personnel provided dedicated support as generalists, business partners and account managers aligned to a business unit of the holding company. Specialist centres of excellence or expertise were responsible for capability management. This involved clarifying organisational capabilities and crafting necessary policies and HR investments to maintain the critical fields of knowledge.

GLOBAL VS LOCAL HR APPROACHES

While global companies may strive to establish consistent approaches, cultural differences can make standardised approaches very unacceptable locally and a global model of HRM may not be appropriate. Decision logics need to be developed for when to parachute in HR support or not. It is clear that the so-called Ulrich model does not work everywhere. Emerging markets for instance have a range of politico/economic/environmental influences that place different demands on HR.

Culturist researchers study the effects of culture on the design and implementation of HRM policies and practices. Though some HRM policies may contain universal elements, others vary since they are culture-bound. Budhwar and Khatri (2002) found that, with respect to recruitment strategies, collectivist cultures in Asian settings seem to prefer the use of internal labour markets in order to promote loyalty to the firm. Culturalist scholars argue that it would be very difficult for a multinational company to successfully apply common HRM practices in different national cultures, for example implementing an individualistic HRM system (e.g. merit-based pay and promotion) in a collectivist culture (Ramamoorthy and Carroll 1998; Aycan 2005). In such cultures, simply imposing western-style appraisal schemes and training programmes that encourage frank face-to-face dialogue would be very inappropriate and undermine employee motivation.

Getting the best out of convergence and divergence requires coordination and integration with particular attention to cross-cultural sensitivities. Evans et al. (2002) propose the following coordination tools:

- Knowledge management
- Capability management
- Know-how and best practice sharing
- Cross-boundary teams
- Cross-boundary steering groups
- Global process management

Enabling integrating mechanisms include:

- Global mindset
- Transnational leadership development
- Normative integration
- Face to face relationships

HRM itself is an integration tool. Subsidiaries are held together by global HRM; different subsidiaries can operate coherently only when they are enabled by efficient structures and controls. Striking the right balance between the corporate and the local and designing the right kinds of structures and controls is essential.

What should be local?

Employment law and labour relations

Labour law and employee relations clearly differ according to location. Trades unions and Works Councils may have specific negotiating protocols and labour relations histories. Laws in each country may mean a different approach is needed for taxation, employment contracts, statutory benefits or performance management. HR therefore must understand international regulations that apply to the labour and employee relations of enterprises that operate in more than one country, especially analysing the common labour and employment issues in each of the countries within which the MNE operates to determine:

- What are the risks?
- What potential liabilities are there at various levels?
- How do international bodies influence and shape employment legislation?

HR may need access to advice on comparative employment law in global legal systems, for instance as it applies to:

- Terminations and reductions in workforce
- Non-compete agreements
- Discrimination, harassment and victimisation
- Privacy protection – notice, choice, onward transfer, security, data integrity, access, enforcement
- Immigration laws

HR at the centre (Global HR) must decide whether to work with global colleagues in a 'hands off' way on such matters – to monitor, guide and advise, provide strategic planning, set limits and approve exceptions – or whether to manage totally from headquarters, integrating central headquarters directly with line management in the field. Factors to consider in determining who does what will include the calibre of the local HR teams, efficiency orientation, global service provision, information exchange, localisation of decision-making.

What should be in the centre?

With respect to talent, three core processes constitute global HRM (Brewster et al. 2005):

1. Talent management/employee branding
2. International assignments management
3. Managing the international workforce

While some core-managed processes, such as global leadership development, top team recruitment and high-flyer development remain centralised, others can emerge 'bottom up' from local markets and regions. Additional core HR processes will typically include:

- Global workforce planning
- Global leadership through international assignments

- Compensation, benefits and taxes
- Health, safety and crisis management
- Evaluation of HR contribution

A synergistic approach is where new HRM practices emerge from integrating approaches from the individual cultures involved (Jansenns and Brett 2006). While many companies consider that sourcing company talent from around the world is a key responsibility of global HR, in decentralised and federated organisations this can be difficult to achieve. The BP Amoco approach described in Chapter 11 shows one company's approach to integrating the regional and global sourcing and development of talent.

Global HR should be responsible for determining how learning can best take place in different locations and enabling the process. A number of multinationals, such as Coca-Cola, have created the position of Chief Learning Officer who is responsible for ensuring that the company's human capital is put to good use on a global scale. Similar approaches have been taken on issues concerning employee rights. American Express and many other companies have designated 'Company Ombudsmen/women' who are responsible for ensuring that company and employee interests are fairly and appropriately served.

Corporate values, especially with regard to diversity, when rigidly imposed may run counter to local norms. One American company takes an inflexible approach to maintaining core values, such as insisting that discrimination will not be tolerated. They have, however, allowed some flexibility in the manner in which this value is imparted in different locations. Consistency of intention is balanced by flexible pragmatism in delivery.

With respect to vision/mission/values/strategy, Paula Larson, previously Executive Vice President – HR Office of CEO, Invensys plc (2008), argued that employees everywhere need to have a clear line of sight to purpose and values. HR and management teams should not necessarily adjust the message but recognise differences ... making clear what are the big 'rules' or non-negotiables. Global leadership teams in particular need to talk with employees everywhere about what the values mean to them and model the behaviours implied by the values. The key message is to be clear about the 'what' and the 'why' to be delivered but leave room for local discretion about the 'how'.

Larson argues that while it may be difficult to gain deep insight into every national culture within a global operation, nevertheless it is important to use a cultural 'lens' to develop understanding – being careful not to typecast but cultural 'factoids' are probably a 'safe' place to start to deepen that understanding. Larson also counsels against assuming that every local cultural approach should be given precedence over the corporate. Having strong academic underpinnings for statements, beliefs and suggestions, for instance on global leadership competencies, offsets 'this is the way it's done around here' cultural challenges between organisational and national cultures. Similarly with respect to change management – it is important to know the difference between 'I'd rather not change, thank you very much' and relevant cultural differences.

HR services at the 'centre' should bring design skills, for instance, to corporate change processes. So if an organisation is contemplating a joint venture with another company in another culture, HR should use its diagnostic and OD skills to identify and ameliorate as far as possible potential 'hotspots' that can emerge from different working practices, leadership styles, organisational cultures etc and are likely to cause problems. Acting on this information can be vital to ensuring that the joint entity stands the best chance of succeeding. Similarly, if an organisation plans to open a facility in a 'new' country, HR needs to carry out a comprehensive and early analysis of the HR system in that country, including the education level of potential workers, employment laws and national cultural norms relating to work practices. Recommendations can be made which reflect the realities of the political, economic and labour context.

In delivering its agenda, Global HR should:

- Be an integral partner in forming global strategy and strategic management
- Develop international expertise
- Lead in developing people processes and concepts that feed into global strategy
- Lead in scanning global HR issues that impact on decision making and organisational responsiveness to global requirements
- Help top management and teams understand the structural, cultural and people implications of globalisation
- Assess, identify, and develop the global competencies required to deliver the global strategy
- Distribute and share the responsibilities for IHR through dynamic relationships with the business
- Play a key role to play in offshoring by building up centres, hiring in and developing managers, knowledge sharing and knowledge transfer

GLOBAL TALENT MANAGEMENT

While in principle the staffing task for Global HRM is no different from in a home (domestic) setting, i.e. hiring individuals with the requisite skills for a particular job, several key factors make the task different. These include different labour markets; the types of staff involved; mobility problems: legal, economic, cultural barriers; different management styles; varied compensation practices; labour laws. A key enabler of global sourcing of talent is having an effective international Human Resource Information System (HRIS) or international talent platform which can make the strategic deployment of staff possible globally. Staffing is also a means to promote a corporate culture with local appeal without compromising the global identity.

Staffing policies

For top management or key positions in particular, choosing a local candidate from the host country or deploying someone from the headquarters assumes cultural significance. Perlmutter and Heenan (1979) identified three typical types of staffing policies used in global companies:

- Ethnocentric: key management positions are filled by the parent country individuals (such as in Procter & Gamble, Toyota and Matushita). Here the assumption is that one's own culture is superior and/or that the host country lacks qualified professionals. This approach overlooks important cultural factors and limits advancement opportunities for host country nationals which can lead to resentment, lower productivity, and high turnover in employees. To maintain a unified corporate culture, value must be created by transferring core competencies.
- Polycentric: the host country nationals manage subsidiaries whereas the headquarter positions are held by the parent company nationals. This decentralised control

approach often lacks standard forms or procedures. Host country nationals have limited opportunities to gain experience outside their own countries. There may be gaps due to language barriers; cultural differences may isolate corporate HQ from foreign subsidiaries. On the other hand, the firm is less likely to suffer from cultural myopia and the staffing model is less expensive to implement.

• Geocentric: the best and the most competent individuals hold key positions irrespective of the nationalities. This hybrid of Ethnocentric and Polycentric approaches is based on informed knowledge of home and host countries. It enables firms to make best use of its HR and to build a cadre of international executives, who feel at home working in several countries. It also helps build a strong unifying corporate culture and informal management network, reduces cultural myopia and enhances local responsiveness. The downside is that hiring on a geocentric basis is relatively expensive and national immigration policies may limit implementation.

To these global strategies Stroh and Calgiuri (2006) added Regiocentric. These authors examined variations in the extent of global integration and local responsiveness in 46 companies. They found that HR practices (recruitment, selection, socialisation) varied according to global business strategy. They also found that companies with ethnocentric strategies were less successful in terms of return on capital, sales growth, return on equity and profit margin than companies operating under any of the other three strategies. It appears that geocentric staffing policy works best in global HRM since it helps build a strong cultural and informal management network that aids the productive deployment of staff.

The role of the international manager

The role of the international manager is changing and with it the skills required to be effective are changing too. No longer is it sufficient for an international high-flyer to have technical skills and to act as a trouble-shooter, flitting from country to country. With organisations trying out new forms of coordination and integration, the international manager now is someone who can exercise leadership across a number of countries and cultures simultaneously, perhaps on a global or regional basis.

While international managers plan, direct, organise and control just like any other manager, the context in which they carry out their duties is much more complex than in purely domestic settings. For this reason, international managers must be culturally sensitive in their business practices and should learn to bridge the cultural gap that exists between their methods of doing business and those of the host country. Increasingly, personality factors and emotional intelligence are seen as critical to effectively managing local operations. In particular, managers must be aware of how cultures vary and that these variations influence behaviour and expectations.

Selecting international managers

Identifying and developing global leaders is a key concern for international companies. In their research into Global Leadership, Sinclair and Ageyman (2004) found that when selecting people for international roles, few organisations appear to use a specific list of international competencies. In many organisations, only functional expertise appears to count. They also found that leaders at the highest level played an active ongoing role in identifying what leadership capabilities were required, reviewing performance and development plans and supporting high potential talent, for example through mentoring.

Given the growing shortage of international managers, a number of companies are seeking to recruit employees, especially graduates, who are willing to manage abroad, rather than trying to persuade reluctant existing employees. They market the international nature of their activities and emphasise the prospects of early international experience to attract graduates who are specifically seeking an international career. The recruitment of foreign students is becoming easier and cheaper through the use of technology. Accessing CVs of overseas university students on-line is a common feature of sourcing for graduate entry. Mobility and the willingness to move across borders are seen as prerequisites to future success. Many Chinese and Indian firms in particular expect their high-flyers to be mobile and gain international experience.

International assignments are often used to address a particular business problem or opportunity and their potential use as an excellent training ground for refining the core skills of future organisational leaders is often missed. Arguably, the skills and competencies required to perform effectively in an international context are of a high order and should not be left to chance. Research (Tung 1988) found that the greater the consideration paid during the selection process to adaptability and the ability to communicate, the higher the success rate in the assignment.

Capabilities required for effective global leadership

Clearly the scope of the organisation's international activities will have a bearing on the skills required of international high-flyers. According to Michel de Zeeuw, previously General Manager of Unisys, graduate recruits ideally should have specific skills such as computing ability, as well as good communication and teamworking skills since they will be required to work with people from different countries. This is in addition to specific technical skills such as accountancy if they are moving, for instance, into a finance function.

Research by Tubbs and Schulz (2006) indicates that the skill sets of a competent manager within a localised environment differ from those of competent global managers. However, there are certain skills and characteristics which most international careers have in common. According to Professor Peter Smith (1992):

> Working effectively across cultures is not therefore simply a matter of applying skills found to be effective within the culture of one's own country or organization. It requires also that one can understand and cope with the processes of communication and decision-making in settings where these are achieved in a different manner.

International leaders need to change their frame of reference from a local or national orientation to a truly international perspective. This involves understanding the global business environment, influences, trends, practices, political and cultural influences and international economics. They need to develop competitive strategies, plans and tactics which operate outside the confines of a domestic marketplace orientation, manage crises, improvise and be open to continuous learning as they deal with new and unfamiliar issues. They need to be open-minded, willing to try new things, innovative and responsive to stay ahead of the competition. Adaptive thinking and the ability to anticipate, prepare for changes and make good decisions quickly is invaluable.

Language skills are an essential gateway into understanding, communicating and working effectively within the culture of the host country. A leader or manager with limited language ability runs the risk of missing out on the subtleties which can make the difference between business success or failure. Maury Peiperl of the Centre for Organizational Research at London Business School carried out research in 15 countries looking at the skills of international managers. The Peiperl study (1998) found that when it comes to language skills, British managers compare unfavourably, speaking on average 1.7 languages in contrast to their counterparts in 14 other countries who speak an average of 2.8 languages each.

Peiperl states that:

'The skills needed and the ones where chief executives see a gap are adaptability in new situations, international strategic awareness, ability to motivate cross-border teams, sensitivity to different cultures and international experience. They have less to do with the traditional talents of achieving targets (though that's always important); vision and change management are the needs of today'. Peiperl's survey found that British and German managers had the same two gaps in their skills portfolio: being able to motivate cross-border teams and to integrate people from other countries.

Having an emotionally intelligent leadership style and social orientation is vital to successfully leading multi-national teams and having the political astuteness and interpersonal skills to develop relationships with key stakeholders. Good cross-cultural awareness is essential but merely recognising that cultural differences exist is not enough. International managers need to be able to manage those differences if the team is to operate successfully. This requires tact and diplomacy and the flexibility to navigate different views and manage conflict. Personal character and ethics are critical for motivating and inspiring teams, projecting credibility and building relationships. Conversely, at the US semiconductor company Intel, the company does not try to impose a company culture on the national culture; rather, it takes for granted that these differences exist. The preferred approach to team meetings at Intel, wherever they are run, is to ensure that the meetings are structured and run in a particular way. This approach is based on the belief that having a common framework and routine provides stability, which helps overcome potential difficulties which may arise from cross-cultural differences.

The complexity and distances involved in operating globally means effective managers must empower others to work effectively without frequent face-to-face contact. They need to develop processes for coaching, mentoring and assessing performance across a variety of attitudes, beliefs and standards and also using various channels.

Since most organisations promote from within, a major question for some organisations is whether local managers can make a successful transition into international leadership roles. Tubbs and Schulz in a 2005 study used the 'Big Five' personality dimensions (extraversion, agreeableness, conscientiousness, emotional stability and openness to experience) along with locus of control to describe successful global leaders. People exhibiting an internal locus of control felt they had greater control over events than did those with an external locus of control. Those people with an internal locus of control, Tubbs and Schulz argued, would make the better international leaders since they are likely to be more resilient and better able to cope with stress.

Some leading industrialists suggest that even these skills are not enough to ensure that future international leaders are able to lead effectively over time. The traditional role of making order out of chaos will shift to one of continually managing change and complexity in ways which are responsive to customers and competitive conditions. International leaders will need to understand different – and sometimes conflicting – social forces without prejudice. They also need to be able to manage their personal effectiveness and achieve a satisfactory balance between work and home.

DEVELOPING GLOBAL LEADERS

The challenges for organisations operating in a global environment highlight the need for effective leadership and having senior managers with an international orientation. Developing global leaders is an essential part of a strategic HR agenda. This may require sending managers on overseas assignments as developmental experiences, not simply because there is a technical need for their skills. Operating internationally, global leaders can be presented with widely diverging socio-economic and environmental conditions. Countries vary in terms of time-zones, languages, infrastructure, regulations and laws, levels of bureaucracy and business culture. These differences create additional challenges for leaders in managing their business identity, maximising efficiency and implementing required standards.

Stroh and Caligiuri (1998) suggest that 'successful multinational corporations recognize the value in having global managers with the expertise to anticipate the organization's markets and to respond proactively. These organizations have learned that leaders who are flexible and open to the demands of the global market have made possible the organization's international business success'.

Global HR should also be involved in developing a global orientation in 'local' or host country managers. Typically, 'local' managers can be introduced to global leadership through visits to the corporate headquarters and other company centres around the world.

Many global companies want a leadership talent management process which is able to respond to the unique needs of a given market yet also able to produce the benefits of consistency and fairness (Cabrera, 2004). Sinclair and Agyeman (2004) investigated a variety of innovative methods used by organisations to support and encourage effective global leadership practices. In particular they focused on developing leaders in processes for consensual decision-making; managing and developing performance throughout the organisation; maximising responsiveness to survive in a dynamic, competitive environment; facilitating knowledge sharing and the flow of resources through the company; encouraging a global focus rather than local allegiances; managing global change processes; supporting diversity; and deliberate focused efforts to manage the company's reputation.

Leaders' own reported strategies to enhance their effectiveness included keeping up-to-date and broadening their perspectives though reading, building relationships and networking; seeking new experiences to build their capabilities; developing and reviewing processes for effective and regular communications; developing strategies for motivating and facilitating high performance across diverse teams and distances; taking a proactive approach to managing potential dilemmas arising from cultural difference; creating learning opportunities and developing self-awareness; and processes for effective change management.

Facilitating international mobility

HR has a key role to play in facilitating international mobility. There are many forms of mobility, such as frequent commuters, employees on short-term business trips, tax-equalised or reduced package expatriates, permanent transferees, reverse or acculturation moves, virtual international employees in cross-border project teams as well as globally outsourced or insourced sites. In many global organisations HR teams share responsibilities for facilitating international mobility across the life cycle of the international assignment (GMAC 2008).

Managing expatriates

Modern expatriation is driven by the need to source and develop scarce skills for immediate tasks and also for the development of global leadership especially in an organisations' top talent (Minbaeva and Michailova 2004; Hocking et al. 2007; McNulty and Inkson 2013). In addition, recent increases in demand for expatriates ('expats') have led to different expat arrangements such as recruiting self-initiated expats as home or third country local hires. Organisations may also use expat assignments to raise global awareness and improve relations between local offices and the 'Centre'. For example, Roffey Park research has found an increasing demand for leaders to be able to work effectively in matrix structures (Wellbelove 2015). Organisations expect their expats to improve their ability to communicate across cultures, lead informally across boundaries and better manage in complexity and ambiguity, all skills much in demand (Bonache and Brewster 2001; Stahl et al. 2009).

Research suggests that people who have international experience (excluding holidays abroad) tend to be better problem solvers and display more creativity. They are also more likely to create new businesses and products and be promoted. Increased duration of time abroad increases the chance of solving problems that require creative thinking. This effect was even more pronounced when subjects had made an effort to adapt to their host countries (Maddux et al. 2010, p. 24).

Supporting expats

Special policies are required for expatriate staff, covering:

- How they should be remunerated – pay and allowances (home-based or host-based pay).
- Training
- Review
- Career management
- Re-entry

Expatriates can be difficult to manage because of:

- Problems associated with adapting to and working in unfamiliar environments.
- Concerns about their development and careers.
- Concerns about family matters.
- Difficulties encountered when they re-enter their parent company after an overseas assignment.

Providing support to expats before and during their expat experience can improve their ability to lead in a global environment and help overcome these difficulties to some extent. Before the assignment, alongside providing language and training on the cultures and sensitivities of the host country, HR can ensure that practical arrangements – accommodation etc – work well in the host country. Potential expats can be helped to understand their own motives and the influence their motives could have on their learning (Geerts 2014). Effective training can help expats to acquire the right skill set to perform their jobs effectively and to demonstrate behaviour congruent with the host country organisational culture.

Modern expatriation has a stronger focus on expats learning from the experience. During the assignment, expats should be encouraged to create opportunities for regular reflective practice for example by setting up peer to peer coaching, or expat action-reflection learning groups. They could work with a personal coach to deepen their learning from the experience and increase their ability to practise critical self-reflection as a life skill. Formal and informal feedback mechanisms are fundamental to leaders' development. Formal training programmes can be useful, not just for improving and solidifying skills and increasing understanding of the organisation, but also for providing networking and mentoring opportunities and exposure to diverse views.

Reward implications

With the COVID-19 vaccine's uneven roll-out across the globe, many companies are thinking about the future of their workforces – where they will work and how to compensate people in different locations. An increasingly mobile workforce is going to require at least parity in pay and benefits wherever they are working geographically. Typical reward options include:

- Home-based pay – The provision of remuneration (pay, benefits and allowances) to expatriates that is the same as in their home country.
- Host-based pay – The provision to expatriates of salaries and benefits such as company cars and holidays that are in line with those given to nationals of the host country in similar jobs.

While some companies like Facebook have opted for location-based salaries to cut operational costs, others are sticking to value-based salaries to attract competitive talent. Given that most European countries are likely to continue to have different approaches to reward, the use of total compensation packages is set to increase. Expatriate conditions that guarantee a level of secured income are becoming less frequent. A number of organisations are beginning to consider paying the difference between the total compensation in two locations by way of a cash supplement.

Employees in years to come will no doubt become skilled at comparing the overall value of such packages. Competitiveness in the global labour market may well depend on employers thinking ahead about how their compensation package can be used to attract and retain the best talent and create incentives in line with the strategy and the context. Ultimately business leaders should choose an option that enables them to take care of their people, so their people can take care of the business.

SUPPORTING TRANSNATIONAL TEAMS

Another vital area for HR activity is supporting transnational teams to achieve business success. Transnational teams, as defined by Bartlett and Ghoshal (1989), bring together individuals of different cultures working on activities which cross-national borders. Team development involves the full range of HR activities such as selecting staff for teams, clarifying roles, developing appropriate appraisal mechanisms, enabling performance, building reward processes and career planning. Research carried out by Snell et al. (1998) for the International Consortium for Executive Development Research (ICEDR), indicates that transnational teams need to balance three drivers relating to worldwide competition: local responsiveness, global efficiency and organisational learning.

In successful international organisations, HR strategies and policies support these drivers. More flexible approaches to team development, aligned to the business needs, are needed if transnational teams are to be appropriately supported. However, ICEDR research suggested that HR teams in many multinationals were not in a position to fully support transnational teams. In many cases HR policies perpetuated traditional organisation structures rather than the more 'web-like' structures of transnational operations.

Local responsiveness is critical as teams must make allowances for the specific demands of different cultures and market conditions. Variety and diversity are key features of transnational teams since members are often dispersed geographically and need to be able to deal with local issues appropriately. Some companies take a polycentric approach to staffing, with new members added only if they add value.

Typically, transnational teams work as virtual teams, so they not only need all the training and development usually made available to co-located teams but also have the added dimension of communicating and forming relationships mainly through technology rather than in person and in different time-zones. Cross-cultural awareness training can be helpful as can deliberate team building activities when a team is first formed. Teams can be trained in conflict resolution and in how to establish ground rules which can lead to integrated teamwork.

The demand for global efficiency means that a high degree of coordination and integration is required. In some companies this is achieved by deliberately understaffing teams so that team members must collaborate in order to make up for the shortfall. Teams need updating in the company's strategies and processes so that team members understand the big picture within which they are operating. Emphasising the corporate values is a means of blending together teams in a way that transcends national and functional boundaries. To aid integration further, team leaders can be trained to achieve decisions by consensus and individuals can be given responsibility for carrying out tasks on behalf of the whole team. In one company, the business planning process involves team members in researching and reporting back to the rest of the team on the needs of a range of external constituents.

If the HR function is to support transnational teams it is important that the HR group itself operates as a transnational team, for example with team members in different regions leading on themes of corporate importance, such as succession planning. This may require the HR team to undergo its own team development process before supporting other teams.

Teams also need to leverage knowledge continuously around the world and be able to institutionalise the learning within the organisation as a whole. Formalised communications can be a helpful spur to organisational learning. IBM's International Airlines Solutions Centre has developed an intelligence network which enables the knowledge generated by transnational teams to be shared. Improved use of international HR talent platforms and information systems should mean that teams can source talent elsewhere in the organisation which might otherwise be 'hidden' in the hierarchy. To enable opportunity matching, such systems should include data on individuals' preferences about where they would like to work.

Formal reward systems are often problematic with respect to international teamwork. In the early days of establishing its international business, an international software provider found that each 'local' business fought for its own business and supplied customer service locally. Rewards were heavily geared to business winning. When the business had achieved a critical mass, the sales operation was restructured so that sales were carried out by the UK team only, leaving all the 'local' operations to supply customer service only. Since rewards continued to be based on sales, rather than customer service, this change was understandably unpopular with the local teams.

The ICEDR team found that where individual goals and incentives were used, they appeared to encourage local responsiveness. Surprisingly few companies in their survey used formal team-based incentives. Similarly, few appraisal and reward schemes appeared to recognise learning even though executives acknowledged the value of organisational learning through transnational teamwork.

Case: talent management at Standard Chartered plc

In the following case study, developed for the CIPD by Tansley et al. (2007) and that featured in the last edition of this book, we consider how Standard Chartered Bank (SCB) set out to revamp its talent management approach. In particular, we look at how to develop global managers and how to evaluate their performance, especially the behaviour the firm wishes to encourage. A key tenet of this approach is 'that people perform best when they play to their strengths'.

Standard Chartered plc is listed on both the London Stock Exchange and the Hong Kong Stock Exchange and is consistently ranked in the top 25 among FTSE-100 companies by market capitalisation. Standard Chartered has a history of over 150 years in banking and operates in many of the world's fastest-growing markets with an extensive global network of over 1400 branches (including subsidiaries, associates and joint ventures) in over 50 countries in the Asia-Pacific Region, South Asia, the Middle East, Africa, the United Kingdom and the Americas.

As one of the world's most international banks, almost 60 000 people are employed, representing over 90 nationalities, worldwide. With strong organic growth supported by strategic alliances and acquisitions and driven by its strengths in the balance and diversity of its business, products, geography and people, SCB is well positioned in the emerging trade corridors of Asia, Africa and the Middle East. The bank derives over 90% of profits from Asia, Africa and the Middle East.

Key drivers for talent management

SCB seeks to develop the capability to respond to market changes, evolve business strategies and achieve its ambitious growth aspirations, and these are the key drivers for its talent management initiatives. The HR function (see Figure 13.2) provides employee self-service and extensive data analysis across the bank's 56 operating countries to allow all global HR processes to be consistently adopted and monitored across the bank's markets.

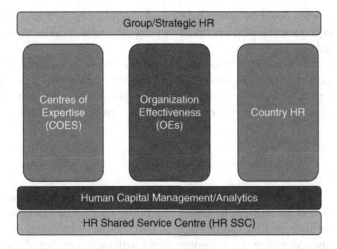

Figure 13.2 Standard Chartered Bank HR structure.

The issues and challenges of talent management in Standard Chartered

SCB is experiencing fast growth in the international domain, and it has a particular interest in ensuring that the talents of its diverse workforce are maximised through employee engagement and inclusivity. One way in which it is attempting to do this is through human capital management and the use of robust technologies. Data for all SCB's direct employees across 56 markets are held on one HR management information system, Peoplewise, which is powered by Peoplesoft technology. Using comparable, standardised and robust data provided through the global Peoplesoft system and the Human Resources Shared Service Centre in Chennai, India, the bank is able to provide extensive data reporting capability. This strategy enables most of its global processes to be consistently tracked across the Bank's markets, including data on core demographics, performance, reward, training, talent management, diversity and development.

Global processes

The global talent management processes are enabled by HR but owned by line management. At their heart these processes are strengths based as well as data and research driven. Talent classification leads to quarterly Talent Reviews and succession planning. The staff engagement survey data feeds into performance review and reward, and then into individual objectives and development plans.

Appraisal is a key part of talent management at SCB, not only in its own right, but also because it is used to classify employees into five categories, ranging from high potentials (HIPs) to underperformers. This system allows the bank to manage its talent by revealing the skills and potential inside its workforce – and showing where there are gaps. 'High-potentials (HIPs) are people with significant headroom, who would be expected to rise at least two further levels in the foreseeable future', Geraldine Haley (previously Group Head of talent management and leadership development) explains. Second are *critical resources*: people who have the potential to improve and whom the bank certainly wants to keep, but who are not real high-flyers. Third are *core contributors*. 'They are valuable resources who are probably doing what they do best now', Geraldine Haley says.

Fourth are *under-achievers*, who could be doing better and should be helped to do so. Bottom of the pile are *underperformers*, who are 'in the wrong job and should be moved into another role or managed out'.

All employees, from juniors to one level below the board, are assessed annually according to this system in conjunction with their interim reviews. Combining classification with appraisal has kept the burden for managers to a minimum because they see it as part of the same process. It also helps to ensure management accountability and therefore accuracy of data.

'Conversations that Count'

Alignment of different aspects of talent management is another challenge, and SCB have a number of initiatives that seek to address it. One particularly successful example is through the use of five briefings entitled 'Conversations that Count', which are short guides to quickly enable managers to have vital conversations with each member of their teams. Conversations on performance and on development have a set schedule that involves planning in January, reviewing in July, and assessing in December. These five main 'conversations' take place on a flexible basis on engagement, strengths and career, and are related to the needs of the individual team member. It is felt that when a conversation between manager and employee is the 'right' conversation undertaken in the 'right' way, it can help increase engagement, enable people to develop and use their strengths, enable the bank to keep its best talent, encourage energy, innovation and fun, satisfy customers, and deliver better business and financial results.

Managers are advised that their HR regional manager can then help them access further sources of support if needed, including training programmes and extra information on their HR information system. These conversations are:

- *Perform* – at the start of January employees are asked to draft business and financial objectives for the year ahead and consider how they will deliver the values of the business during the year. A meeting is then arranged to discuss this, and managers will also share information that provides context – e.g. their own objectives. SMART objectives are then agreed, and consideration given to what the objectives mean for the employee's learning.
- *Learn and develop* – at the start of January the employee is asked to draft a document that will set out: what he or she needs to learn – bearing in mind objectives and future career goals, and how he or she needs to learn – drawing on a wide range of learning options. A meeting is held with the manager to discuss the learning the employee needs in order to achieve excellence in the role and deliver this year's objectives. Resource constraints such as time and budget have to be considered and how to work imaginatively within those constraints. The year's learning and development priorities are then agreed, written down and signed off.
- *Build careers* – the time may be right for a career conversation when the employee has mastered the core aspects of his or her job and is ready for additional or fresh challenges and it has been 12–18 months since the last career conversation. A meeting takes place where the employee discusses his or her career goals. Tools are provided beforehand to assist with the employee's reflections.
- *Engagement review* – a 'lite' engagement review takes place once a year with existing team members already known well by the manager. Ahead of the meeting

the individual is briefed, open questions are asked during the meeting, and agreed actions recorded and commitment made to follow up. A 'full' engagement review is for team members who are new to the manager. During the meeting, the manager is required to ask open, focused questions under the headings: 'Know me', 'Care about me' and 'Focus on me'.

• *Build strengths* – in order to have the 'great conversation', when the manager and the HR manager believe the time is right, the employee is asked to complete an online questionnaire called StrengthsFinder™ which is designed to identify talents and strengths. It need only be completed once because the talents it reveals are enduring; it is used to support the development of a person who performs well and has high potential.

One of the bank's Strengths coaches helps the employee to understand the talents it reveals, and how he or she can be developed towards strengths. The conversation with the manager takes place after this to explore what the employee has learned, to discuss the actions he or she will take to develop talents into strengths, to consider opportunities to use his or her talents and strengths more often, and to record agreed actions and sign off. The employee is encouraged to have a follow-up session with the Strengths coach every six months. So 'Conversations that Count' are an essential way in which different elements of talent management are aligned.

Standard Chartered plc's approach is a highly structured and integrated one involving steps that make the process clear to the managers undertaking the reviews by focusing on the dialogue that is required to take place in various conversations. This notion of 'conversation' also appears in other areas of HR practices that relate to talent management. For example, Hirsh (2003: 237) suggests that the succession planning process also involves dialogue between key parties, and she coins the useful term 'succession dialogues'.

Global talent pools

There are regular business reviews on talent from board level down to country management team. Outcome, rather than process, measures are tracked. At the level of Country Management Trainees, locally tailored programmes are made available. International graduates are provided with two-year development through rotations and global programmes. Junior High Potentials are locally managed and reviewed in 56 countries. Mid-career MBAs are strategic hirings which supplement the leadership pipeline. Middle management high potentials are reviewed by ten global leadership teams. Senior Management High Potentials are reviewed by the Group Management Committee.

Creating an inclusive culture

As well as developing leaders, SCB aims to build a high-performing and inclusive culture. SCB is a very diverse organisation, with more than 100 nationalities represented throughout the bank and more than fifty nationalities within the most senior 500 employees. The gender balance at SCB is broadly equal, with 47% of employees being female. However, only 16% of senior managers are female and one of the bank's priorities for 2008 is to raise that percentage.

Competition for talent across many markets is intense. The bank believes its inclusive approach known as Diversity and Inclusion, or D & I, gives it a distinct advantage over its competitors, creating a much larger pool of talent for recruitment. It also provides engaging opportunities for employees to develop, both as individuals and as part of a team.

Diversity through inclusion

SCB focuses on three strands of diversity – nationality, gender and disability (with a particular focus on visual impairment). Over 300 people across SCB now have a D & I role, and a D & I Ambassador role was created for a number of senior employees to raise awareness of D & I across the business. Many D & I issues are market-specific. To address this, SCB appointed 50 D & I Champions across 48 markets and territories, as well as 28 Country Councils to support the Champions. In 2006 D & I Champions and Councils took part in a review and action planning process, listening to employees in order to determine local D & I issues. Examples of the issues raised include:

- Employees would welcome the opportunity to work more flexibly
- Greater opportunities to gain international experience without relocation
- Unintentional exclusionary behaviour often goes unnoticed

In 2006 SCB piloted a D & I awareness programme in various countries to make staff aware of, and understand, the role that D & I can play in helping create an inclusive culture. Awareness-raising sessions were also held with the global leadership team meetings to help deliver the message in each business area. Key priorities include:

- *Valuing employees* – employee retention is a key management priority and an integrated approach to managing employee retention is being developed.
- *Engaging employees* – effective employee engagement leads to increased productivity and revenue and lower employee turnover. SCB has measured employee engagement globally since 2001 and continues to see an increase in engagement each year. In 2006, 97% of employees completed the survey (Gallup Q12).
- *Empowering women* – the increasing size of Standard Chartered, along with the success of various global initiatives and the value these have demonstrated, have led to a programme focused on helping women to reach their full potential. The programme, known as GOAL, was launched in India in 2006. GOAL uses the principles of sports-based social inclusion to build women's self-esteem, strengthen their leadership skills and provide access to education opportunities. Participants attend coached netball sessions and undertake a modular leadership course. Best performers will be rewarded with scholarships, micro-finance opportunities and potentially, internships at SCB's branches.
- *Health and safety* – SCB is committed to creating a healthy, safe and fulfilling environment in which people can work. During 2006 SCB introduced a zero-tolerance safety process for identifying risks. All the bank's offices were inspected, and ongoing health and safety training aims to ensure an embedded health and safety awareness culture.
- *Employee well-being* – in 2006 SCB introduced employee volunteering on a global basis to support individuals' commitment to community initiatives. The scheme

gives each employee an additional two days' leave each year for voluntary work they fund themselves. So far over 1000 employees have chosen to take this opportunity. SCB also launched a pilot of the reward level programme in five countries. This rewards employees who demonstrate outstanding business performance with an additional five days' leave, sponsored by Standard Chartered, to spend on a project that ties in with SCB's community strategy.

• There is also a global approach to flexible working and continued annual family days across the bank. In November 2006, a global Employee Well-being week was introduced for all employees. A variety of events were held across the bank with record levels of employees involved in talks on different topics, such as physical activities, family days, health checks, healthy food, quizzes, competitions, comedy and even massages. In Singapore, for example, more than 500 people had health screenings, while in Korea, more than 300 employees and customers received finger pressure therapy from visually impaired therapists.

Reflective activity

1. What are the advantages/disadvantages of these initiatives, and for whom?
2. Is this a case of HRM convergence, divergence or a hybrid?

SENSITIVITY TO CULTURE

Even in mature international companies, many well-intended 'universal' applications of management theory have turned out badly because they have failed to take account of local culture.

Culture presents itself on different levels. At the highest level is the culture of a national or regional society. The way in which attitudes are expressed within a specific organisation is described as a corporate or organisational culture. Finally, there is the culture of particular functions within organisations: marketing, research and development, personnel. People within certain functions will tend to share certain professional and ethical orientations.

According to Trompenaars and Hampden-Turner (1997), 'culture is like gravity: you do not experience it until you jump six feet into the air. Local managers may not openly criticise a centrally developed appraisal system or reject the matrix organisation, especially if confrontation or defiance is not culturally acceptable to them. In practice, though, beneath the surface, the silent forces of culture operate a destructive process, biting at the roots of centrally developed methods which do not "fit" locally'.

The following case study is about an OD specialist navigating a hierarchical culture to diagnose the root cause of low performance, and motivating a talented team unfamiliar with underperformance to change their ways of working. I am grateful to Jaimini Lakhani, formerly Organisation Design director at Burberry for this account.

Case: local cultures and root causes

When Jaimini Lakhani joined Burberry in 2010 as Director of Organisation Design, based in London, she was charged with bringing the digital strategy and new operating model to life.

Burberry, under the leadership of Angela Ahrends, enjoyed considerable success throughout the first decade of this century. For years within the Asia region, the South Korea market for Burberry, the upmarket fashion brand, was the reliable top performer. Then the track record of success started to wobble. The one-year income and margin slipped for three consecutive quarters – a red flag in the retail sector. While the overall luxury fashion market in South Korea showed mild slow down, competitors were not impacted to the same degree. That led to a belief that there must be internal operations that were impeding performance.

During the period that the Asian markets, had been growing fast, the Regional team had sought limited input from the Global team as there were no perceived problems in the way they were operating. Within the Asia Region Burberry had just bought back the huge franchise network in China which was now growing incredibly fast; the Japan market had a two-year float date ahead and the CEO was keen to explore sub-regions as a way to create capacity for the leadership to manage that huge shift. As South Korea – the regional star performer – started to perform less well, particularly against competitors, the immediate reaction was to restructure. Given the declining performance of the operation in South Korea, and the challenges afoot, the Regional President became open to getting some help from the Global team. As Jaimini reflects, when it comes to being able to make a useful OD intervention, 'timing is everything'.

A sensitive diagnostic process

Jaimini, accompanied by the Regional Head of HR, went on a fact-finding diagnostic tour of four Asian markets, including South Korea, to see if she could help get to the root cause of the problem. In Asian cultures generally but particularly in South Korean culture there is typically great respect and deference shown towards managers by staff. Therefore it was important that Jaimini and her colleague were introduced to staff by the country director – in effect giving staff permission to cooperate with the enquiry.

From her preparations and from the data available on sales, staff profile and so on, Jaimini was well aware of the business challenges. Jaimini wanted to hear about the operations on the ground; listen to staff views, ideas and offers of help. For all concerned, this diagnostic process was a big deal – after all they had had no visits from the Global team before on team and operational matters. It was crucial for Jaimini to start by building trust. Recognising that for most staff English was not their first language, the diagnosis was carried out quite formally through a series of one-to-one meetings in Seoul with a cross-section of staff as well as store visits. Given the hierarchical nature of the local culture, Jaimini was keen to avoid misinterpreting signals she was picking up from these conversations.

What started to become clear was there were a few structural issues that needed fixing. For instance, the South Korea operation was organised by channel like premium brands such as Ralph Lauren, but this was not a strategic choice for Burberry as a luxury brand. More importantly, the major issues appeared to revolve around leadership dynamics both within country and also the relationship between country and region. South Korea had the largest number of long serving employees in the Asia region. Many of the most senior leaders in the team including the Country Director had led success for this market with practices that were now changing given the shift in brand strategy. New talent was eager to subscribe to these new practices. There was an over-reliance on the Country Head of Operations and untapped potential in new talent. Regional leadership had been more focused on stabilising the China market after buying back the franchise network and had not spent time with the team in South Korea. Yet given that senior leaders were revered – personally and culturally – addressing the leadership dynamics issue was going to be a sensitive matter that could not be handled by the Regional Head of HR alone.

From this initial diagnosis of the root cause a less dramatic yet much more sensitive intervention seemed appropriate. This is where the skill, judgement and courage of the OD practitioner came to the fore. As the fact-finding trip came to an end, Jaimini met with the Regional President and Regional HR lead in Hong Kong to share her observations and tentative conclusions. Given the sensitive nature of the messages she was about to give, this was a tough call, but the company values required that she deliver them, nonetheless. The OD role was to ensure that those who needed to act were pointed to the right area. So Jaimini fed back what she perceived about the leadership dynamics, though added the caveat that her observations may not have factored in other personal circumstances and she might have missed some cultural cues. She also talked about the organisation design issues but pointed out that the leadership issues should be addressed first since any redesign would be unlikely to succeed without the right leadership dynamics.

The Regional President was unlikely to have heard these sensitive messages from his own HR team if Jaimini had not delivered them and therefore he was reflective of these observations. In a different culture, the task might have fallen to local HR to deliver the message and help find solutions to the problems identified. The Regional President soon recognised that Jaimini had provided him with a service based on trust and a mutual interest in the brand and was keen to know what could be done. The Regional Head of HR took over responsibility for implementing the recommendations. This included eventually delivering a detailed organisation design with Jaimini's help.

Back in South Korea, the Country Director was increasingly uncomfortable with the strengthening of the regional layer in the redesign as he felt he was losing his autonomy to operate. Honest, humane conversations took place with him to help him find a role that was more suited to his style and where he could succeed. Jaimini continued to have conversations with regional and local HR leaders to provide them with a process to support individuals there. Once they had the right leadership in place, the South Korea team engaged in a detailed organisation design process, soon regained energy and sales got back on track.

As Jaimini reflects, OD is very contextual and, as an OD practitioner, your role must flex to meet the situation and cultures within which one is operating. In this case, by making this critical intervention at the right time, Jaimini acted as bridge between the organisation's needs both globally and regionally and also as a conduit to skilled support for those implementing change and for those affected by change.

Trust your intuition

Jaimini observes that, from an HR/OD standpoint you are bringing different strengths and values, looking at a situation with a fresh set of eyes. To be effective in helping clients it's important to do your homework and read up beforehand. You need a robust enough methodology, and to know your own skillset, but trusting your own intuition is the best guide; 'the more I've done that, the more things work well'. After all, OD is very human based practice. You need to be able to empathise with the people and ask yourself what you would do in that situation.

The way Jaimini and her team practise OD is very collaborative, all working towards a common goal, sense-checking their instincts, especially before delivering tough messages. You need the experience and confidence to make that leap. To build that confidence it's useful to watch and learn from role models – Jaimini for instance learned how to trust her intuition by working with Angela Ahrendts. Then you can look for alternatives if something does not feel right.

CONCLUSION

We have discussed how the internationalisation of business life requires cultural sensitivity and greater awareness of cultural patterns. In developing an integrated global business, an HR strategy that is fully integrated with the business strategy is essential. The environmental demands on global businesses have placed leadership development, talent sourcing and management, corporate reputation and leading for diversity centre-stage. It is important to identify and focus on a few critical HR practices rather than attempt a large number of initiatives that do not deliver. At the same time, local responsiveness should be incorporated into the global strategy of multinational companies, without undermining the corporate culture and standards – a delicate balancing act. Finally, it is worth recognising that global network cultures are more complex than those in 'conventional' single country organisations and require much greater coordination and persistence.

Reflective activity

- What are the main issues in international and global HRM?
- What are the factors that affect the degree of convergence or divergence?
- What are the main global HR policies?
- What are the main considerations in managing expatriates?

REFERENCES

Adler, N.J. (1995). Competitive frontiers: Cross-cultural management and the 21st century. *International Journal of Intercultural Relations*, 19(4), 523–537.

Adler, N. and Ghadar, F. (1990). Strategic human resource management: A global perspective, in R. Pieper (ed.), *Human Resource Management in International Comparison*. Berlin: de Gruyter, pp. 235–260.

Aycan, Z. (2005). The interplay between cultural and institutional/structural contingencies in human resource management practices. *The International Journal of Human Resource Management*, 16(7), 1083–1119.

Dowling, P.J. and Welch, D.E. (2004). *International Human Resource Management: Managing People in a Multinational Context*, 4th Edition. Cincinnati, Ohio: South-Western Pub.

Bartlett, C.A. and Ghoshal, S. (1989). *Managing Across Borders: The Transnational Solution*. Cambridge, MA: Harvard Business School Press.

Bonache, J., Brewster, C. and Suutari, V. (2001). Expatriation: A developing research agenda. *Thunderbird International Business Review*, 43(1).

Brake, T. (1997). *The Global Leader: Critical Factors for Creating World Class Organization*. Chicago, IL: Irwin Professional Publishing.

Brewster, C., Houldsworth, E., Sparrow, P. and Vernon, G. (2016). *International Human Resource Management*, 4th Edition. London: CIPD - Kogan Page.

Brewster, C., Sparrow, P. and Harris, H. (2005). Towards a new model of globalizing HRM. *International Journal of Human Resource Management*, 16(6), 949–970.

Brewster, C., Harris, H. and Sparrow, P. (2002). *Globalizing HR.* London: CIPD.

Budhwar, P. and Khatri, K. (2002). A study of strategic HR issues in an Asian context. *Personnel Review* 31(1), 166–188, April.

Cabrera, L. (2004). *Political Theory of Global Justice: A Cosmopolitan Case for the World State.* New York: Routledge.

Caligiuri, P.M. and Stroh, L.K. (2006). Multinational corporation management strategies and international human resources practices: Bringing IHRM to the bottom line, *The International Journal of Human Resource Management*, First published in 1995, 6(3), 495–507.

Collings, D.G., Scullion, H. and Morley, M.J. (2007). Changing patterns of global staffing in the multinational enterprise: Challenges to the conventional expatriate assignment and emerging alternatives. *Journal of World Business* 42(2), 198–213, June.

Dickson, M.W., Den Hartog, D.N. and Mitchelson, J.K. (2003). Research on leadership in a cross-cultural context: Making new progress and raising new questions. *Leadership Quarterly*, 14, (6), 729–768.

Evans, P., Pucik, V. and Barsoux, J-L. (2002). *The Global Challenge: Frameworks for International Human Resource Management.* Boston, Mass: McGraw-Hill.

Geerts, A. (2014). *Global Nomads; Learning from Expatriated Experiences.* Horsham, UK: Roffey Park.

GMAC. (2008). *Global Relocation Trends Survey.* OAK BROOK, Illinois: Global Relocations Services.

Hampden-Turner, C. and Trompenaars, F. (2020). *Riding the Waves of Culture: Understanding Diversity in Global Business*, 4th Edition. New York: McGraw-Hill.

Harris, P.R. (2002). European challenge: Developing global organizations. *European Business Review*, 14(6), 416–425.

Harris, H. and Brewster, C. (1999). International human resource management: The European contribution, in C. Brewster and H. Harris (ed.), *International HRM: Contemporary Issues in Europe.* London: Routledge.

Hirsh, W. (2003). Positive career development for leaders and managers, in J. Storey (ed.), *Leadership in Organizations: Current Issues and Key Trends.* London: Routledge.

Hocking, J.B., Brown, M. and Harzing, A. (2007). Balancing global and local strategic contexts: Expatriate knowledge transfer, applications, and learning within a transnational organisation. *Human Resource Management*, 46(4), 513–533.

Holt, D.B., Quelch, J.A. and Taylor, E.L. (2004). How global brands compete. *Harvard Business Review*, 82(9), 68–75.

Kets de Vries, M.F.R. and Florent-Treacy, E. (1999). *The New Global Leaders: Richard Branson, Percy Barnevik, David Simon and the Remaking of International Business.* San Francisco, CA: Jossey-Bass.

Larson, P. (2008). Presentation: HR Partnering in a Global World, National Conference, Harrogate, CIPD.

Iles, P. and Zhang, C. L. (2013). *International Human Resource Management: A Cross-cultural and Comparative Approach.* London: CIPD.

Janssens, M. and Brett, J. M. (2006). Cultural intelligence in global teams: A fusion model of collaboration. *Group & Organization Management*, 31(1), 124–153.

Maddux, W.V., Galinsky, A.D. and Tadmor, C.T. (2010). Be a better manager: Live abroad. *Harvard Business Review*, 24, September.

McCuiston, V.E., Wooldridge, R.R. and Pierce, C.K. (2004). Leading the diverse workforce: Profit, prospects and progress. *Leadership and Organization Development Journal*, 25(1), 73–92.

McNulty, Y. and Inkson, K. (2013). *Managing Expatriates: A Return on Investment Approach* (Kindle). New York: Business Expert Press.

Minbaeva, D.B. and Michailova, S. (2004). Knowledge transfer and expatriation in multinational corporations: The role of disseminative capacity. *Employee Relations*, 26(6), 663–679.

Ng, E.S.W. and Tung, R.L. (1998). Ethno-cultural diversity and organizational effectiveness: A field study. *International Journal of Human Resource Management*, 9(6), 980–995.

Perlmutter, H. and Heenan, D. (1979). *Multinational Organization Development*. Reading, MA: Addison-Wesley.

Ramamoorthy, N. and Carroll, S. J. (1998). Individualism/collectivism orientations and reactions toward alternative human resource management practices. *Human Relations*, 51, 571–588.

Peiperl, M. and Coles, M. (1998). Global managers despair at heirs. *Sunday Times*, November 8.

Schneider-Ross. (2002). *The Business of Diversity*. Andover: Schneider-Ross.

Scullion, H. (2005). International HRM: An introduction, in H. Scullion and M. Linehan (eds.), *International HRM: A Critical Text*. London: Palgrave.

Scullion, H., Collings, D.G. and Gunnigle, P. (2007). International human resource management in the 21st century: Emerging themes and contemporary debates. *Human Resource Management Journal*, 17(4), 309–319.

Sinclair, A. and Agyeman, B. (2004). *Building Global Leadership: Strategies for Success*. Horsham: Roffey Park.

Smith, P.B. (1992). Organizational behaviour and national cultures. *British Journal of Management*, 3, 39–51.

Smith, A. and Sinclair, A. (2003). *What Makes an Excellent Virtual Manager?* Horsham: Roffey Park Institute

Smith, P. and Bond, M. (2006). *Understanding Social Psychology Across Cultures: Living and Working in a Changing World*. London: Sage.

Snell, S.A., Snow, C.C., Canney Davison, S. and Hambrick, D.C. (1998). Designing and supporting transnational teams: The Human Resource agenda. *Human Resources Management*, 37(2) (Summer), 147–158.

Sparrow, P. (2008). Global HR presentation, Annual Conference, Harrogate, CIPD.

Sparrow, P., Brewster, C. and Harris, H. (2004). *Globalizing Human Resource Management: Tracking the Business Role of International Human Resources Specialists*. London: Routledge.

Stroh, L.K. and Caligiuri, P.M. (1998). Increasing global competitiveness through effective people management. *Journal of World Business*, 33(1), 1–16.

Tansley, C., Turner, P., Foster, C., Harris, L., Sempik, A., Stewart, J. and Williams, H. (2007). *Talent: Strategy, Management, Measurement*. London: CIPD.

Towers Perrin. (2006). *Winning Strategies for a Global Workforce*. Towers Perrin Global Workforce Study.

Tubbs, S.L. and Schulz, E. (2006). Exploring a taxonomy of global leadership competencies and meta-competencies. *Journal of American Academy of Business*, 8(2), 29–34.

Tung, R. (1998). *Selection and Training of Personnel for Overseas Assignments*. Cambridge, MA: Ballinger.

Wellbelove, J. (2015). *Living in a Matrix*. Horsham, UK: Roffey Park Institute.

Part III
Building strategic change capability

Part III

Building strategic change capability

14

Transforming organisations by design

DOI: 10.4324/9781003219996-17

CHAPTER OVERVIEW

In this chapter we consider the challenges of bringing about major change using organisation design. Innumerable articles refer to the high failure rate of change initiatives and here we consider some of the possible risk factors and what HR can do about them. We start by looking at conventional organisation design, which itself is undergoing transformation as we shall discuss in the next few chapters. We shall also look as mergers and acquisitions (M & As), a key area where change management is needed. M&As are typically embarked upon to save costs and acquire valuable assets yet a study of the financial benefits of mergers and acquisitions by Hall and Norburn (1987) found that returns to shareholders are at best 'slight' and at worst 'significantly negative'. To be successful in their aims M&As must be managed in a way that gets the 'people bits' right. We shall cover:

- What is Organisation Design?
- Designing organisations
- Mergers and acquisitions: getting the 'people bits' right

LEARNING OBJECTIVES

- Provide an overview of Organisation Design (ODS)
- Explore organisation design process in the context of mergers and acquisitions.

INTRODUCTION: WHAT IS ORGANISATION DESIGN (ODS)?

'Organization design is a cornerstone of a firm's competitive advantage and performance. Research is clear that even the most cunning strategy will not reach its potential if an organization's structures, processes, and systems do not support it' (Worley and Lawler 2010).

Although in the literature the two fields of Organisation Development (ODV) and Organisation Design (ODS) are often considered as separate, in the main practitioners don't make a distinction between them (Varney and Garrow, 2013). Cheung-Judge and Holbeche (2021) describe them as 'two traditions that are historically distinct but are strongly related'. Since change affects all elements of any systems model, neglecting any element contributes to the reputed 70% failure rate of change initiatives. It is not surprising then that practitioners see the two (OD&D) as part of the same thing – a change process.

Distinctions can however be drawn. ODS has its roots in classical organisation theory and tends to be associated with the 'technical' planned and project managed top-down aspects of organisational strategy, structure and systems change transformation. With reference to the McKinsey 7S model (see Figure 14.1), Francis et al. (2012) put forward the distinction between Organisation Design (ODS), as dealing with the 'hard' elements of change i.e. strategy, structure and systems and ODV, the 'soft' elements of change i.e. staff, skills, shared values and style.

Conventionally the fundamental premises of ODS are about economic rationalisation. ODS is underpinned by such concepts as scientific management, economies of scale, standardisation of work and the workforce, financial capital being seen as the scarce resource, corporate headquarters exercising operational control. It involves making strategic choices, identifying intended benefits, designing structures, networks, processes and

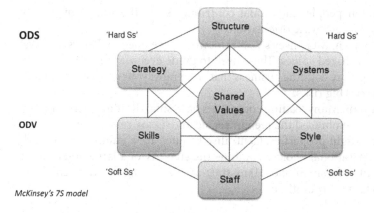

ODS

ODV

McKinsey's 7S model

Figure 14.1 Theoretical distinction between ODV and ODS.

roles to align the organisation around strategy and business imperatives. Typically, ODS drives structural change and will impact on cultural change. The success factor of ODS is the extent to which organisation-wide alignment is achieved with business strategy (Divakaran et al. 2013).

As previously discussed, Organization Development is about building healthy and effective organisations. The success factor for ODV is the extent to which organisational effectiveness is achieved and sustained. It does this by focusing on group dynamics and improving the ways people work together. It uses techniques based on behavioural science, psychological theory and process facilitation. ODV takes the organisation design forward to implementation by delivering the internal changes required by the strategy. While not all change processes require organisation design, all organisation design processes require organisational development if they are to succeed.

'Excellent' organisation designs

Many organisations over the last few decades have been influenced by management theories based on consultancy research into successful organisations – such as Jim Collins' *Good to Great* (2001) – and have attempted to adopt design principles based on them. For instance, Peters and Waterman's research into leading US companies of the 1980s, published in their 1982 book *In Search of Excellence* offers eight lessons:

- A bias for action. 'Getting on with doing the job'. Rapid decision-making unhampered by bureaucracy. This has since been absorbed into the concept of 'Agility'.
- Close to the customer. Trying to serve each customer as an individual. This has since become the notion of customer-centricity, another core element of agility. This means that managers should listen to the customers and frontline staff, as often managers are too remote to know what customers think, feel or want.
- Autonomy and entrepreneurship. Each part of the business acts as an entrepreneurial centre, rather than as a part of a machine, thus creating greater innovation. Today, entrepreneurialism is necessary to achieve transient advantages.

- Productivity through people. Individual contributors are the source of quality, bring an early employee-centric orientation.
- Hands-on, value-driven. McKinsey's 7-S framework developed by Peters and Waterman started with shared values. These need to guide everyday practice.
- Stick to the knitting. Stay with the business that you know; your core competencies. Diversification carries big risks.
- Simple form, lean staff. Many leading companies have small headquarters and simple processes, having embraced the reengineering and 'Lean' revolution.
- Simultaneous loose-tight properties. Centralised values are a guiding framework, but autonomous operational choices combine the stability of a large organisation with the adaptability of a small one. Many start-ups are seeing the same challenge as they grow into large corporations.

'Visionary' companies

Other influential design theories included the principles of long-lasting so-called 'visionary' companies researched by Collins and Porras which had successfully been in business for over 50 years. These principles described in their influential book *Built to Last* included:

- Clock Building, Not Time Telling – go beyond a great leader to building a great institution
- No Tyranny of the 'Or' - embrace the genius of 'And'
- More Than Profits – find your organisation's purpose and build the 'core ideology'
- Preserve the Core/Stimulate Progress – change everything readily, except the core beliefs and values
- Big Hairy Audacious Goals (BHAGs) – think big, aim high
- Cult-Like cultures – cult-like adherence to the culture
- Try a Lot of Stuff and Keep What works – try a lot of experiments and keep what works
- Home-Grown Management – hire leaders from within
- Good Enough Never Is – strive to do better tomorrow than you did today

Reflective activity

- Which of these principles is pertinent today?
- How does the way your organisation operates differ from the principles defined by Peters and Waterman or Collins and Porras?

DESIGNING ORGANISATIONS

There is no single correct way to do organisation design but using a model and following a sequenced process should provide a sound framework for diagnosis of what needs to change or be strengthened in the design. Most systems models hail from an era of more stable, 'mechanistic' thinking. There are many systems models available, such as Galbraith's Star Model™, the Burke-Litwin Framework, Nadler and Tushman's Congruence Model, McKinsey 7-S Model, Weisbord's 6-Box Model, and Leavitt's Diamond Model. Each represents a set of organisational elements and depicts the relationship between them but only some show any relationship to their operating environment (as an open system). These do not all list the same elements, nor show the same linkages between them.

Conventional hierarchical organisations are typically designed as closed systems for stability and efficiency. Systems models such as the Nadler-Tushman Congruence model (1989, Figure 14.2) suggest a cause-effect linkage between the organisation's input – (its environment, history, resources and strategy) – and its throughput (work, people, formal and informal structure) – to deliver relevant output at system, group and individual levels. It looks at how these elements interrelate. For example, do the organisational structure and culture complement each other, or do they compete? The challenge is to balance the processing elements in both the formal and informal aspects of organisation - including structures and technology, information flow and people's roles and skills – to respond to the inputs and achieve desired outputs.

Given the escalating demands coming from the business environment, organisations should be viewed through an open and whole systems lens, where context is critical. More recent systems theory views organisations as open systems. Any change in any part of the system will produce different effects. Since the environment changes constantly, interactions within a system are inherently complex.

Structures

A typical design strategy involves aligning corporate strategy, core competencies and an appropriate structural archetype (functional, matrix and so on). Traditional success factors for ODS include size, role clarity, specialisation and control. However, traditional strategies rely on stable task environments and industry structures as well as sustainable competitive advantages to drive both short- and long-term performance, conditions far

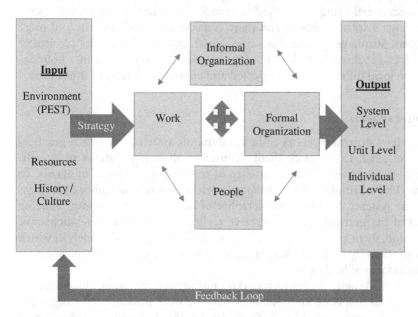

Figure 14.2 Nadler and Tushman's Organizational Congruence Model.
Source: Nadler, D. A., & Tushman, M. L. (1989). Organizational Frame Bending: Principles for Managing Reorientation. Academy of Management Executive, III(3), 194–204.

from widespread today. Moreover, for Bolman and Deal (1997), structural theory puts an over-emphasis on the following assumptions:

- Organisational control and coordination are essential for maintaining rationality
- There is a 'best' structure for any organisation
- Specialisation and division of labour increase the quality and quantity of production
- Changing the structure is the best way of dealing with structural flaws

New success factors for organisation design include speed, flexibility, integration and innovation. While traditional structures were initially mostly functional, today there are many variations on more flexible structural archetypes such as process, product, market, geographic, matrix, project, modular, virtual, reconfigurable (Galbraith) and boundary-less structures.

Boundaryless structures

For Ashkenas (1998) all such design archetypes should acknowledge that organisations must operate fluidly across four boundaries – vertical, horizontal, external and geographic (which also encompasses cultural and time zone differences). Whereas a vertical structure differentiates through status, and authority and decision-making power passes up through levels, boundaryless organisations focus attention on whoever has useful ideas so committed individuals making faster, better decisions. Whereas horizontal organisations operate between functions, product lines and units, with units maximising their own goals, boundaryless organisations operate via processes that permeate horizontal boundaries, together with quality, continuous improvement, and high performing team initiatives. With respect to external boundaries, typically clear boundaries exist between insiders and outsiders reflecting a 'we-they' approach. In boundaryless organisations, customers help firms resolve problems and there is a confluence of interests and more efficient operations. Strong geographic boundaries with cultural differences can isolate innovative practices, resulting in lack of leverage of good ideas, whereas in a boundaryless organisation local differences are respected and valued as a source of innovation.

Complex adaptive systems

Newer thinking views organisations as complex, dynamic systems, for which practical models do not yet exist. Complexity theory considers all living systems to be self-organising, complex adaptive systems, made up of interacting networks of agents. In 'The Web of Life' (1997), Fritjof Capra calls the network 'the central metaphor of ecology' (p. 10). 'In the new systems thinking, the metaphor of knowledge as a building is being replaced by that of the network. As we perceive reality as a network of relationships, our descriptions, too, form an interconnected network of concepts and models in which there are no foundations' (p. 39). This, Capra argues, becomes a source of inspiration for a more empowered form of leadership.

So while one set of design success factors does not replace the other, the emphasis, indeed the whole paradigm, is shifting. Reflecting the network notion, cluster organisations are perhaps at the extreme fluid end of a dimension that has traditional functional hierarchy at the other. Here people work in groups from 30 to 50, in sub-clusters of 5–7, undifferentiated by job title. There are no direct reporting relationships; decision-making is delegated to those who do the work; leadership rotates according to task competence; members of the group are accountable and groups are linked by contacts among members.

Design metaphors

Design assumptions are also shifting (Morgan 1986):

- From machine metaphor of organisation (control, predict, re-engineer) to living system (self-organised, experience based, a strong life force to be reckoned with);
- From directive to self-responsibility (assumptions: you can never direct a living system – you can only disturb it);
- From traditional hierarchy to culture-focused organisational change (from focus on structure and system to paradigm and behaviour).

So for adaptability and agility, the more relevant metaphor is organisation as living system (self-organised, self-responsibility, experience-based, a strong life force to be reckoned with) that leaders must nurture. The living system metaphor works well because as humans and as organisations, we are complex and the usual human reaction to complexity is to try and simplify things in order to be able to understand and change them. However, if you try to fix one thing without understanding how all of the pieces fit together, and if you don't work simultaneously on the whole, the bits that you neglect almost always cause failure.

Hindering or helpful bureaucracy?

While all organisations need some elements of bureaucracy to control and manage integration, too much complexity can lead to rigidity and slow decision-making. So is bureaucracy inevitably damaging to the pursuit of agility? Adler and Borys (1996) draw a distinction between those bureaucratic structures that inhibit effective performance ('hindering bureaucracy') – typically rigid and with high levels of centralisation – and those that lead to better organisational performance ('enabling bureaucracy'). Hindering bureaucracies are formulated to enable a higher level of control over employees; obeying rigid rules and regulations is mandatory; creativity, risk-taking and changes are not welcomed. Organisational members working under highly centralised circumstances may experience feelings of powerlessness as they attempt to meet customer needs; they are less likely to demonstrate extra-role behaviours (Raub 2008). These may result in decreased employee commitment and performance.

In contrast, in an enabling bureaucracy, the focus is on using formalised rules, procedures and regulations in a way that results in problem-solving (rather than punishing failure) and a higher level of efficiency. Formal rules and regulations contribute to enhanced organisational performance; standards are used to improve workers' capabilities and serve to transfer the best way of performing tasks, provide alignment between different jobs, and facilitate work process redesign.

Centralisation, another design concept, refers to the extent to which employees are involved and participate in organisational decision-making processes (Anderson and Kochan 2012). The key requirements of customer-centric design are to understand, and be responsive to, the customer experience; to act on data, and embed change quickly. As discussed above, employees therefore need high levels of discretion and authority to act

364 • BUILDING STRATEGIC CHANGE CAPABILITY

to serve the customer's needs. Flexible bureaucracies are characterised by a shared leadership style as well as a higher level of accountability among followers that can contribute to the proliferation of creative ideas as well as extra-role behaviours (Adler and Borys 1996; Saparito and Coombs 2013).

Follow a design process

In the same way that there are different systems models, there are also different processes you can adopt for organisation design. These processes all have phases of one type or another. They include 'Design Thinking', Appreciative Inquiry, Consultancy Cycle, Agile, Self-Design (University of Southern California) and 6-phase design. The latter involves using change management to move from today to tomorrow through 6 phases - preparing for change, scoping, macro-design, micro design, transition and implementation. The self-design method involves preparation, contracting, assessment, planned learning, design success criteria, organisation design and change implementation. Each phase involves a host of activities and potentially different groups of people who must be coordinated.

Each process begins with an assessment or exploration of the design issues and context. It may seem odd that a consulting cycle or appreciative inquiry process can also be used for organisation design work – but why not? The commonality of phases means that it is relatively straightforward to use them in combination(s). So, for example, the phases of process consulting can proceed at the same pace as the phases of the OD process.

In an ideal world, design work would begin at the beginning and move steadily through the phases – starting, designing, planning to transition, transitioning, optimising, while leading the process and communicating and engaging with stakeholders throughout. In reality, this sequence of steps rarely happens. Projects can start at more or less any point in any of the phases. Nevertheless, design work fails if some of the phases are missed out altogether. Wherever the work actually starts you must work 'backwards and forwards', ensuring all phases are covered.

Starting the consulting/design process

In any process model, the starting phase typically involves:

1. Identify the client
   The challenge for the organisation designer is to work out who is the real client of the design work, what are the vested interests in the work that may not be obvious, and how easy it will be to work with the client(s)
2. Meet the client
   When a practitioner and someone in an organisation meet to discuss potential design work, in consulting speak, this is called 'gaining entry'.
3. Agree the work (also known as 'contracting')
   In the first or any follow up meeting, agree the design work, including:
   - What the situation, issue or concern is
   - Who the client is (it may not be the person you, the consultant, are speaking with)
   - The purpose and outcome of any work
   - How this work links to the mission/purpose of the organisation

- What timescales the client is working to
- What level of resources the client has to bring to the project (personnel, expertise, money, time, equipment, etc.)
- How client and consultant will work with each other – their roles and approaches
- What access to information and personnel is required
- The next steps (Block 2011)

4. Assess the context (diagnosis)

Once the actions from the initial meeting have been agreed, start the internal and external environmental scan. Gather other data – financial, customer, employee – from a variety of sources. Failure to invest in the assessment and scanning can lead to more expensive mistakes that need to be rectified later.

5. Begin the leadership alignment activity

Leaders who spend time thinking through the rationales for a redesign – focusing on its contribution to organisational performance and impact on the work and the workforce – tend to commit themselves to the solution. This makes a big difference to the speed at which work can progress. However this is often problematic since leadership team members are not always 'on the same page'. Navigating organisational politics and the political dynamics often means that you face compromises, tensions or ethical dilemmas that force you to ask yourself whose interests you are serving and to manage the consequences of your answers.

6. Communicate with stakeholders

The way an OD project is shaped and implemented is interwoven with stakeholder needs and responses. Stakeholders are those individuals and groups of people who you need to 'get on side' as you do the design work. They have to understand the 'why, what and how' to become supporters of the work (or at a minimum not saboteurs). Often stakeholders have conflicting interests, which makes your skill in sense-making – intuiting who is for/against/neutral – critical.

This work involves categorising, classifying and mapping stakeholders. 'Categorising' means clustering them according to their type. 'Classifying' means determining their 'political' orientation to the design work. 'Mapping' means recognising their relative level of ability to influence or impact the success of the design. Working with stakeholders means more than communicating with them. It means involving them, listening to them and being responsive to what they say; in other words, engaging with them throughout. Doing this from the start of the design work is in the long-term best interests of the project – even if it may seem a heavy investment of resources to begin with.

7. Check leadership commitment. Leading OD work involves both bringing technical expertise to the design work– a role often fulfilled by HR/OD or an external consultant – and leading people into the new design – a role typically taken by the business 'owner', i.e. the person taking the design work from inception into 'business as usual' (Ashkenas and Francis 2000). These two leaders must work in a close and collaborative partnership to ensure the design succeeds. Additionally, there are other organisational leaders who must be committed to the design work.

8. Present work so far and propose next steps

The end of the starting phase – data collection, leadership alignment work and presentation of findings – is marked by documenting findings and proposing next steps. Depending on the size, scale and complexity of the piece of work, the document could be a formal business case, project charter, plan on a page, contract, agreed proposal, or a simple e-mail. Regardless of size of project a document in writing should specify the rationale behind doing the work and the next steps. This document enables a decision to be made on whether or not to go ahead with the next phase of the piece of work. If the go-ahead is given, the document guides the project planning and life cycle and aids in monitoring the progress of the project.

Case: terminal five, Heathrow

Jaimini Lakhani, now an independent OD consultant, joined BAA as organisational change lead following eight years with Accenture. At the time (2003–2006) Mike Clasper was BAA's CEO and Margaret Ewing was Group finance director from 2002 to 2006. During that time and under their combined leadership, BAA's performance improved dramatically. The year 2005/06 saw an increase in revenue of 7.4% to £2.23bn, operating profit increased by 8.1% to £710m during the same period and capital expenditure increased 8.1% to £1.5bn. At the same time, Clasper and Ewing also led BAA's defence against a fierce takeover battle with Ferrovial which eventually saw the airport authority sell for £10.3bn in 2006, a much higher price than the acquirer had originally offered.

At the time Jaimini joined the company, the vast construction project to build Terminal Five (T5) at Heathrow was underway. BAA's strategy was expansion and innovation, especially with respect to running retail operations in other international terminals, a strategy Jaimini strongly bought into and was excited to support. After all, BAA was known as a savvy retailer having founded World Duty Free and was already operating an effective international retail footprint.

Jaimini joined a newly formed business unit that combined BAA's infrastructure development (Capital) with its Supply Chain activities. Money was being invested in both groups to prepare them to support the future growth strategy. Jaimini's role was to design an operating model for the combined unit. Early on in Jaimini's initial assessment, however, it became clear that because of leadership challenges the two departments would struggle to work in a complementary way. To her surprise, one of her early recommendations was to decouple the two units, effectively making her own job redundant.

However the six-year, £4.2 billion programme to build Terminal Five (T5) was underway and needed to get better traction if it was to hit the company's audacious deadlines. BAA had never before undertaken a programme on this scale or integrated assets at this level. The HR team had made bold moves to change leadership and influence the decision for T5 to be operated as a separate entity. Jaimini joined the T5 leadership team as Head of Organisational Effectiveness (OE), with responsibility for HR, OD, Learning and Communications. Also integrated into the team was industrial relations which were managed centrally at group level given the complicated union environment that included BAA, contractor and airline employees. Jaimini herself worked closely with Andrew Wolstenholme, T5 Project Director, directly involved in day-to-day programme management and instilling HR processes for the 800 BAA staff on the project team.

The programme was organised into four main teams – Airside, Buildings, Systems and Rail. The T5 programme needed to shift focus year on year as the programme moved through different phases. The early years were spent on the various physical stages such as diverting two rivers, clearing the land (moving enough earth to fill Wembley stadium one and a half times), boring the tunnels that would support the extension of the Piccadilly underground line, the installation of a monorail system to connect the terminals, etc. In the later stages of the construction programme three satellite buildings needed to be built, leaving enough time to integrate the complex sets of systems including 11 miles of baggage conveyer belt. The T5 site required over 8,000 workers across 30 nationalities to work daily as 'one team' including executing its award-winning safety programme which recorded over 2 million worker hours without a reported incident. There also needed to be a smooth handover to British Airways the client and Heathrow Airport the operator.

When Jaimini first took on her role, the OE team was fragmented, under-resourced and OD was often called upon just to facilitate team workshops. From Jaimini's perspective, the T5 programme was an opportunity to deliberately create a different culture both within her team and also across the programme. The ambitious demands of the programme required a high performing, unified team that could operate strategically and operationally over the course of the final three years. She established an OD team on the ground with four expert practitioners embedded in each of the main teams, e.g. Airside, Buildings, Rail, Systems. These were multi-functional roles to partner with the different teams over their people and organisational needs. At one time the Buildings team were not hitting the milestones, so an OD specialist was commissioned to help the team. He used an open space breakthrough exercise to achieve a mindset shift and enhance people's confidence. One member of the OE team specialised in industrial relations as each of the 60 contracting companies had its own unions.

Jaimini was also responsible for physical context change. This meant looking ahead, building trust, ensuring that the right capabilities would be in place as the construction side of the programme ramped down in the final year and the balance of work transitioned to operating the new terminal. To keep the transition on track, Jaimini measured progress to assess if the right people were in place at the right time. As Jaimini reflects, even when you are trying to create behaviour change, it is important to set standard default measures so that you know whether you are achieving your aspirations and base changes in strategy on evidence.

One particular concern was about how to retain key talent right to the very end of the programme and beyond, especially as BAA were in discussions to construct the new Terminal two building. The aim was to achieve 80% retention of key talent. Some of the personnel on T5 were integrated into operations but as teams merged, jobs became smaller and limited. Employees who relished large scale, complex programmes were feeling less challenged. To avoid uncontrolled turnover, Jaimini and her team looked six to eight months ahead of every phase so that they could focus on integrating back key talent into new roles in a timely way. Those whose skills were most needed wanted to know that there was a future for them and were incentivised to stay, which they mostly did to the end. These people received friendly chats about the future over coffee so they understood that they were valued.

There was also a common focus on how best to hand over from the Programme team to the operational team as T5 went 'live'. Jaimini facilitated a session with the leadership team early in the final year to learn from terminal openings elsewhere and to identify the principles that would matter to BAA. People brainstormed the many things that can go wrong at such openings, such as security, problems with baggage systems and passenger flow and worked out what to do to mitigate these. The discussion on baggage systems resulted in the Head of Baggage Systems being promoted to the top table so these risks were always visible and addressed swiftly. Jaimini kept such issues front of mind at the top table by reminding the team of how well they were following their own guiding principles.

As an HR/OD practitioner, Jaimini was free to focus on building capabilities and leading reviews of what was working well, and what needed to be improved. It was clear that the transition would require new capabilities within the leadership team every year as the programme changed shape. Jaimini reflects that, to add value as Head of Organisational Effectiveness you must have an equal voice at the top table. As she points out, people dynamics are crucial. You have to act as an off-the-record sounding board especially for the Project Director who is essentially the CEO and you must sustain the right chemistry to do that.

As Jaimini reflects, organisation development is so contextual that you need to be able to adapt to the unexpected, as well as anticipate change. Before the launch of T5, there were several dramatic events which could have blown the programme off course but did not. There was the 2006 transatlantic bomb scare that forever changed airport security regulations and required extraordinary crisis management measures for two weeks. Heathrow Airports Operations Ltd won the pre-award for the construction of Terminal 2. British Airways, who were to be the primary users of Terminal Five, were frequently on strike, causing disruption and anger to the public. So as Jaimini suggests, 'If the factors you are dealing with, including the politics, have never come together in that combination before, you have to be able roll with the punches, reflect and learn from events, helping others to do the same'.

Reflective activity

- Who were the key stakeholder groups in this case study?
- What ways have you used/found successful in getting leadership alignment? How do you know when you have it? How do you maintain it? What are the pros and cons of seeking leadership alignment?

MANAGING MERGERS AND ACQUISITIONS

Mergers are amongst the strategic options available to executives seeking to increase market share, geographic reach and so on. They hold out the attractive prospect of increasing earnings per share (EPS) to shareholders. However, the risks attached to mergers are mainly linked to the Human Resource arena. It is the range of issues relating to people within merging organisations which can determine whether the merger is as successful as it might be, or indeed whether it succeeds at all. While there is increasing awareness that human factors have an influence over the success of the merger, executives are often at a loss to know how to address the different issues. Frequently, they are so absorbed with the nature of the business deal and in securing their own interests that the organisational implications of the deal are only considered once the deal has been struck.

Bungling the handling of a merger can result in losing key people – who often constitute the market value which attracts the acquiring organisation in the first place. People are a vulnerable asset – and the benefit of this asset can be destroyed if senior managers do not anticipate and prepare for the emotional response of employees at the outset. Meridian Consulting suggest that failure to create additional value through the combination and deployment of the intellectual property gained from M&As represents a new type of risk, known as knowledge risk. They calculate this as follows:

> The knowledge value at risk – that is the amount of shareholder value the firm stands to destroy if they fail to successfully integrate and leverage acquired intellectual

property – equals the premium paid multiplied by the acquiring company's price-to-earnings ratio, i.e.

Value at risk = premium $ P/E ratio

Mergers and acquisitions, when two organisations are brought together, or are required to collaborate as in a strategic alliance, are organisation design projects writ large. They highlight the need for very effective change management and should really be thought of as large and complex change projects. The integration decision should involve diagnostics, assessing the degree of cultural and functional integration required to help the combined company achieve its strategic ambitions. Meridian Consulting argue that if the combining organisations are to become capable of achieving shared business goals, three abilities must be grown, i.e.

- The ability to talk with one another
- The ability to work with one another
- The ability to learn from one another.

Yet culture clashes between the merging organisations are the most common cause of merger failure. While their strategies and structures, including systems and processes, are usually different, the main factors which can undermine successful integration are differences in the two organisations' politics, decision-making, cultures, values and leadership styles. Employees are sensitive to those differences which affect them most, especially if they perceive the acquisition to be hostile.

Similarly, employees are often hit by multiple waves of anxiety and need to be supported through the transition. The roles, behaviours and attitudes of managers make a big difference to how well employees adjust to a merger. In many mergers, the roles of one group of directors simply disappear. Where directors survive the merger, the relative positions which directors occupy in the new organisation seem to affect whether other employees consider their organisation to be a 'winner' or 'loser' in the merger process. When senior managers of the acquired company lose their jobs, employees of that company can feel especially vulnerable.

HR has potentially a key role to play in anticipating and reducing the impact of culture clashes, in supporting people in integrating working practices and in bringing about successful new organisations. Key employees need to be retained and ways of transferring knowledge across the organisation found. Major issues and risks need be addressed as early as possible. Yet HR professionals are often not involved until late into the merger process when many decisions have been taken (and sometimes damage caused).

Whatever the rationale for the merger, it seems that the way the merger process is handled will have a major impact on whether the organisation is able to achieve its business aims. When the acquiring company seeks to impose its procedures onto the acquired company (Devine et al. 1998), this often results in the acquirer unwittingly snuffing out the vital spark which made the acquired company seem such an interesting proposition. Organisational change can seem threatening to employees because when the change is imposed top-down, such as in the decision to acquire another company or to sell off part of the organisation, employees feel that they have no control over what is likely to happen. This is when the consequences of change can appear profoundly negative to employees.

Transformation can threaten people's mental models of how their organisation should act, what work should be like and what their own prospects look like. For instance, when one pharmaceutical company acquired another, partly in order to absorb the other company's research capability, there was some surprise among managers of the acquiring company when exciting research projects they were expecting from the acquired research workforce failed to materialise because the acquired scientists did not trust the acquiring company's management. The phenomenon became known in the organisation as 'burying the babies', i.e. employees kept their best projects safe in case they needed to jump ship. The critical thing seems to be not so much whether there are job losses or whether organisations are renamed but how these processes are carried out. Open and honest communication and fair principles are very important in maintaining employee commitment.

Mergers need managing

Planning and managing mergers require a skilled team of merger planning experts. Some companies are clearly focused on people issues right from the start of the merger process. These tend to be adept acquirers who have learned from past experience and who use taskforces of specialists with merger process experience. With the full backing of the board, these taskforces are highly adept at creating communications appropriate to the situation and in making sure that the relevant relationships are established early on. The role of an influential and skilled Human Resources professional can be critical here.

Each phase of a merger has implications for leadership and for HR. These phases are:

- the 'run-up' or pre-merger
- the immediate transition (the first 100 days or 6 months)
- the integration (the longer-term coming together of the two parties)

The 'run-up' period should be used to carry out an effective HR due diligence and develop an awareness of the likely challenges and pressure points. Key employees need to be identified and encouraged to stay in both the acquired and acquiring organisations. The 'run-up' team should make a realistic assessment of the probable management workload and find ways of easing the burden somewhat.

Experienced companies often use a different team to manage the transition, and an effective handover is essential between teams. Typically, there is a clear 100-day plan which addresses most of the integration issues at the level of human resource matters, systems and processes. The process of recruiting into positions needs to be handled in such a way as to minimise the potential for 'winners and losers'. Of course, personnel issues, including policies and procedures, are not the only things which need managing. Other critical integration issues include:

- IT
- Product ranges
- Supply chains
- Head offices

Senior managers and directors have a key role in leading the change process. Ideally, at least one or two senior managers from the acquired company should be retained to provide other employees with reassurance. If the takeover is not hostile, willing collaboration between management teams before and after the merger appears to make a positive difference to the way the change is handled.

During the transition period, the pace of change is usually so fierce that keeping an eye on normal business is not easy. Research highlights the importance of managing the integration of the organisations as a critical project alongside keeping the business-as-usual going and customers satisfied. This conscious management of the integration should carry on for as long a period as is necessary. Managing the longer-term integration usually involves training line managers and making them responsible for the real bedding in of the new organisation. In the most successful cases, at least one board member takes responsibility for overseeing the integration for the period of time required for the 'new' organisation to have fully emerged.

Even when handled 'professionally', mergers can still backfire. One company closed down its customer support site – when a merger made it obsolete – only to find that a competitor was opening a new facility nearby the very next week. The people whose jobs were made redundant and who had received generous pay-offs went straight into similar jobs with the rival company, taking their expertise and competitor knowledge with them.

John Kotter's (1996) well-known study of why change efforts often fail identified the need for 'change accelerators' as follows:

- Creating a sense of urgency and 'readiness' for change
- Creating powerful guiding coalitions who are willing to bring about change and letting a clear vision emerge
- Communicating the change continuously and in many different ways
- Coordinating efforts, measuring and communicating progress
- Keeping morale and energy levels around the change project high by celebrating progress so far, and using that energy to tackle the more important obstacles to change
- Consolidating improvements while eliminating remaining obstacles to change

In all of these steps, leaders, managers and HR have vital roles to play.

While Kotter's (1996) original thinking was well suited to traditional hierarchies, he has since revised his recommendations to suit a more agile, networked approach. In his 2014 book *Accelerate: Building Strategic Agility for a Faster-Moving World*, Kotter argues that the change accelerators still apply but should be applied concurrently rather than sequentially. The new change delivery system envisages an organisation-wide army of volunteers to drive change. Increasing urgency is about overcoming inertia. Leaders need to take risks and be more transparent, be willing to engage early to discuss concepts and unformed ideas. They should take a decentralised approach with less emphasis on centrally managed communications and engagement opportunities and make more use of formal and informal networks. We shall consider these points in more detail in the next chapter.

Communication

Though often spoken of together, communication and engagement are not the same. A simple way of illustrating the difference is to say that effective communication is structural (via channel choice, e.g. newsletter, email, chatbot) and effective engagement is social (via participation and networking).

The importance of communication cannot be over-emphasised, particularly in the pre-merger phase and between the merging companies. For example, a UK manufacturing company agreed to be acquired by a Swiss company. The management team were pleased and excited as the firm had been 'on the market' for some time. However, contact between the two companies dwindled, leaving the UK company's management team unclear about the Swiss company's plans and expectations. In a state of limbo, the UK firm was effectively 'off the market'. Some senior managers jumped ship because they had no guarantees for the future. There was no new product development, no investment and customer orders dropped off. Lack of communication led to suspicion, demoralisation, and loss of key personnel and business, even before the contract was signed.

Internal communications are critical throughout, as many management teams learn the hard way that it is better to communicate even when you have nothing to say. HR needs to work alongside or as part of management teams, ensuring that formal communications are effective, and that staff are being kept informed. A PwC study (2011), however, suggests the HR department typically does not focus on communication or motivation issues during major organisational change such as a merger or demerger, precisely at the very time when they are most needed. The starting point for communication is usually the merger announcement, which is nearly always highly sensitive. Holbeche and Garrow (2000) found that employees sometimes only found out about the merger when listening to the radio on their way to work. If HR is not involved in the run-up phase, there is usually no clear communication plan for employees – all the attention has been paid to other stakeholders.

When a merger is under way, communication mechanisms need to be in place that encourage an upwards flow of information in addition to top-down announcements. Communications should be as open and two-way as possible, with staff being given opportunities to discuss the latest news. Employees really need to know why the merger is happening so that they can work out the options for themselves. Issues such as the rationale for the merger, whether it is a proactive or reactive response, how the merger partner was selected, whether this is a merger or a takeover – all need addressing. Key messages may need to be repeated in many different formats. Staff response to the messages about change should be anticipated and questions-and-answer sessions built into presentations.

What can help is an early statement about the vision for the merged organisation. When the Halifax and Leeds Building Societies merged, they decided that their merger would create 'a Yorkshire-based world-class alternative to the clearing banks'. When the Environment Agency was formed out of up to 80 separate bodies, the aim was to provide 'a better environment in England and Wales for present and future generations'.

Early contacts set the tone and arrogance is common. 'Them and us' attitudes can easily result from inappropriate first contacts. The reaction of employees on both sides of the merger/acquisition will be conditioned by factors such as the clarity and credibility of the messages given publicly and internally – and by their general perception of the 'other party': is it a business they want to work with/for? Managers may need to be adept at managing rumours and should pay attention to the first impressions formed by staff in the acquired organisation based on their first encounter with employees from the acquiring company.

In one case, employees in both the acquired and acquiring companies were told on day one why the merger was happening, and it was made clear to employees that 'good' people were in no danger of losing their jobs. People were asked to commit to the new company on the basis that 'we'll see you are alright'. None of the senior management from the acquired company survived the merger. On day two a presentation by the new chairman and chief executive conveyed an unfortunate impression to employees in the acquired company. The chairman insisted that the previous management had 'got it all wrong' and that his vision would lead to a successful company. While the message was no doubt meant to be motivational, and many 'acquired' employees agreed that they had been constrained by the previous management, the impression of arrogance created by the chairman's speech was confirmed by early attempts to impose one set of working practices on to another. What made matters worse was that there was in fact no strategic plan to support the chairman's claim and personnel matters such as appointments were left in abeyance. Many employees lost patience and left.

Gaining buy-in

Gaining emotional and intellectual engagement from staff is no mean feat. Typically, mergers are both mechanical/structural and psychological/cultural. All aspects of the merger need managing. In drawing up a checklist of the mechanical aspects of the merger, which tends to be the focus of director attention, care must also be given to being able to provide answers to employee questions which will set the scene for the psychological/cultural merger.

Merger mechanics	Psychological impact
Communication – road shows, etc.	What's happening? When will I know if I have a job? Will there be redundancies and if so, when will they be announced?
Business strategy – loose/tight coupling	Why is it happening? Does it make sense? What changes are planned and when will they be announced?
Organisational structure	Where will I be in 6 months? Will there be changes in reporting structure? Who will I be reporting to in future?
Appointments and exits	Will I have a job?
Terms and conditions	Will our terms and conditions change?
Managing performance	Will I lose out? What is expected of me? Will there be Performance Appraisals?
Training and development	Do I have a future?

Fear of the unknown is a major contributor to employee uncertainty. While not all of these questions lend themselves to easy answers, people at least need to know when solutions to some of the problems will be worked upon. In managing communications around the different phases of a merger, HR should bear in mind the psychological impact on employees of these changes and aim to offer answers to these core questions. Devine (1999) suggests that formal communications should aim to:

- *Inform* – about the organisational/personal implications
- *Clarify* – the reason for the change, the strategy and benefits

- *Provide direction* – about the emerging vision, values and desired behaviours
- *Focus* – on immediate work priorities and actions, together with medium-term goals and dignity
- *Reassure* – that the organisation will treat them with respect

Some HR processes, such as rationalising pay and conditions may take time to achieve. While there is no blueprint as to which issues must be tackled in what order, it is important to communicate a broad architecture of the merger process, together with targeted HR and management actions at each stage so that employees and senior managers can be reassured.

Reflective activity

- Think of an organisational project that you are a stakeholder in/of. How do you like to be communicated with about it? What level of engagement do you have in it?
- What would make you feel the communications and engagement addressed to you are at a minimum 'good enough'?

Waves of change

Mergers and acquisitions set off 'waves of change' within the organisations concerned. Unless these are managed, business performance can nosedive as a result of employee uncertainty and because senior managers concentrate their time on the merger, to the detriment of the existing business.

In the pre-merger phase, it is essential to explain to employees the strategic business reasons for the merger. Whatever approach is adopted, many organisational cases point to the importance of recognising and understanding the differences between the organisational cultures as early as possible so that sensitive issues can be carefully handled. Similarly, employee loyalties to their colleagues, ways of working, company brand should not be underestimated. Employees may need to be allowed to 'grieve' the loss brought about by the merger as well as celebrate the new opportunities.

Typically, anxiety is highest at the time of the merger announcement and when the first job losses are announced. The rumour mill is very active at this stage. People wonder how they will be affected, if at all and what their own prospects will look like in the new organisation. They are on the alert to signs, such as which company gets the lion's share of the best appointments, which indicate their likely fortune. Employees are hungry for information and this is typically when formal communications are at a standstill (Figure 14.3).

Organisation Design work comprises both leading the structural change work and also leading people into the new design. Research suggests that over 40% of the changes take place in the first two months. In the immediate transition, major events include the appointment of a new board of directors and key appointments/redundancies. As the new structure emerges, different groups are affected at different times.

Often senior managers have been through their own anxiety and emerged the other end. They must state and explain the 'why' of design or redesign, supporting people in making sense of the context of the design/redesign work, telling the stories of how it is going. Their focus may be on the next key business issue and it may be hard for them to appreciate the anxieties of people working in a front-line role who are being affected by restructuring in some cases up to two years after the merger. Head-office staff are often

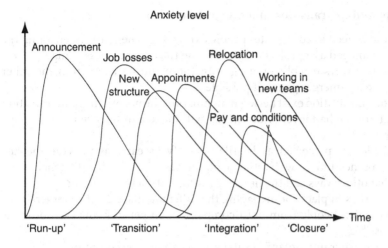

Figure 14.3 Typical emotional waves following a merger.

the first to be affected by an early decision to close down an office. Field staff may wait for some time before the merging companies rationalise their outlets. Failure to pay attention to what people need leads to increased workforce anxiety and multiple individual interpretations of the situation. Other key questions that heighten employee anxiety are about which head office will be used, especially where relocation is involved, and when/ how terms and conditions will be integrated. Leaders should aim not to 'sell' the design/ redesign but to acknowledge anxieties, and help people make sense, for themselves, of what is going on so that they may make informed choices.

HOW HR CAN HELP AN ORGANISATION THROUGH A MERGER

Communication alone is not enough – as previously stated, mergers need managing, especially the personnel issues. It is clear that the HR function has a potentially key role to play in a merger. The way difficult personnel issues such as redundancies are handled will have a long-term effect on the morale of survivors and be a telling indication of the values of the new organisation. New appointments must be seen to be fair and employees treated with dignity. Personnel processes should be documented, and decisions should be open to scrutiny. The longer-term integration phase is often the period during which sites are closed or merged and staff are informed about relocations. New terms and conditions may be announced. Often a more fundamental revision of working practices and structures takes place.

Involvement should begin in the run-up phase. Early identification of sensitive issues can reduce their impact over time. Time must be set aside to work with directors and individuals on the critical HR issues. Pay and conditions can become a huge issue and should be dealt with early in the transition period but are often deferred. If HR lacks a strategic perspective, the HR team risks being overtaken by the host of operational and mechanical issues which must be dealt with. This is a time when a new organisation is being forged and decisions should be taken with this in mind. Help from consultants can enable HR teams to focus their energies strategically during an important period. Research suggests that some of the critical contributions which HR can make are as follows.

Get involved in planning, transition and integration teams

- HR professionals need to contribute specific expertise to these teams, enabling the merger to be managed as a project, while keeping the core business going
- Develop effective ways of collaborating with the planning team from the other company in the pre-merger phase, if possible
- Does clear communication exist between members of the negotiating and transition teams? What are the handover issues which will make a difference to the success of the integration?
- If the acquisition is perceived as hostile, identify as early as possible the key information you need to know if a thorough human resource due diligence is not possible. What other ways can the necessary information be obtained?
- What framework is in place for managing the different phases of the merger?
- Find ways in which people from both companies can get to know each other as quickly as possible
- Identify how the emerging organisational vision can best be communicated
- Take a 'best of both' rather than 'equal shares' or 'acquirer dominates' approach to deciding who has which roles, which working practices etc. are adopted
- Adopt fair principles on the handling of redundancies.

Identify the HR issues and carry out an effective human resource due diligence by

- Comparing terms and conditions of employment and salary scales including the structure of share options and to whom they are available, severance terms in contracts, incentive and bonus schemes in terms of immediate and future commitments
- Gathering information about the management team – how critical are they and will they all remain post-acquisition?
- Gaining perspectives of the management team – their view of the company, employees' view of the senior team
- Understanding the existing skills of the present HR team – are they adequate to coordinate proposed changes to the business?
- Understanding the organisation structure
- Identifying what is required in terms of workforce plan to achieve the business strategy
- Identifying key personnel and having initial plans for securing ongoing commitment. To what extent is the necessary knowledge and skill critical to running the business vested in a few staff?
- Identifying the likely level of redundancies involved and prospects for early retirements
- Identifying which job descriptions and/or profiles will need to be changed
- Finding out how communication of the sale has been dealt with so far including the processes used for communication
- Comparing ways of working and identifying major differences that will need to be addressed
- Agreeing the management culture of the combined organisation and what will need to be done to achieve it

- Considering the size and location of existing offices. Deciding whether office closures will be necessary and whether the provision of new office accommodation will be appropriate or possible
- Finding out details of any industrial disputes and the number of appeals on job evaluations by the Hay Committee within the last 12 months
- Is the organisation unionised or does the staff council or similar employee representation group have any negotiation rights and if so, what do these rights include?
- Being realistic about timescales. Does everything have to be done at once? Many companies attempt to integrate terms and benefits as quickly as possible. If delay is required, there should be a clearly communicated plan so that employees know when key issues will be addressed. Merging cultures may take two years or longer
- Agreeing a clear communication plan for the first 100 days. What clear central message will be sent to all employees?

Carry out effective HR integration of the following

- Remuneration
- Benefits
- Terms and conditions
- Culture and management style
- Career and other development issues
- Communication and climate
- Employee relations.

Ensure that management teams have the skills they need to manage the merger well

Line managers usually play a key role in central project teams. Management teams need to be quickly welded together, with at least a common approach on key Human Resource issues. Some team building may be needed. Management teams need the following:

- Strategic management skills, especially understanding how to add value to the new business
- Integration skills – being able to make decisions about structure, roles and dealing with sensitive situations
- Change management skills – being able to bring people with them through change
- Cultural skills – being able to understand the dynamics of organisational culture, deal with culture clashes and the emergence of a new culture
- People skills – being able to understand the reactions and concerns of employees and support them through change.

Help line managers to communicate effectively during the transition phase

Managers also have a key role in sustaining communications about the merger process to all employees even when there is 'no news'. Given the symbolic importance of senior management behaviour, managers may need practical help in understanding how to communicate with employees from both companies in the early days. Managers may need to be made aware of the symbolic power of language to help or hinder the merger process. They may need to recognise that a merger is likely always to be an emotional issue for employees and that employees need to be communicated with, and convinced of, the benefits at an emotional not simply rational level.

In the first month of a merger between two professional service firms, line managers were given the chance to reflect on how they were going to help implement the organisational changes. For some the main challenge was 'getting staff into confidence mode – our task is to raise staff morale'. Many managers also felt the need to ask questions of their own directors, rather than assuming that they were being kept in the dark. Some managers recognised the importance of sitting down with their team and personalising the messages which were largely being conveyed via corporate videos. The managers were mainly concerned about the apathy resulting from apparent lack of change following the merger announcement. They recognised that they would need to prepare their colleagues for the ongoing waves of change which would eventually arise from the merger.

Since managers are in the front line for communication, it is essential that they have the ability to develop two-way communications. HR can provide practical help with team briefings and feedback processes. Managers need to communicate why the merger has taken place, what the organisation is trying to achieve and how each person's role contributes to achieving this. They need to have a wide range of management styles appropriate to different circumstances and may need help in developing their coaching ability and flexibility.

Manage individuals with dignity

Chief executives, often very action-oriented, are keen to get through the difficult business of reorganisation and job loss as quickly as possible. Speed is helpful as long as it does not compromise dealing with staff fairly and treating them with dignity. The handling of key changes for individuals – such as job changes, appointments and relocations as well as exits – sets the tone for how staff view the new organisation. Handling redundancies inappropriately usually results in a morale backlash among 'survivors' (Marks and Mirvis 2001).

Develop and implement actions to retain key employees

Good people have to stay if the two organisations are to learn from each other's strengths. Line managers need to identify and keep close to key staff at all levels and actively involve them in the merger process. If such people are neglected in the early months, they often jump ship. Some organisations develop retention strategies which involve some sort of inducements such as 'golden handcuffs' to encourage people to stay. There appears to be some evidence that, even without financial incentives and firm guarantees, letting people know that they are valued and quickly finding ways of using their talent in the new organisation can be sufficient encouragement for some.

Keep the top in touch with the bottom

HR is uniquely placed to build in upward feedback to keep the boardroom in touch with what is really going on in an organisation. In the Roffey Park research senior people described being sucked into the detail of the operational issues and the mechanics of the merger. It was only with the benefit of hindsight that they realised that understanding and managing people's perceptions and expectations were equally vital to promoting a healthy emergent organisation. The culture of the new organisation begins from day one, not when vision and values statements start to appear (Miller 2000).

Individual transitions need to be handled well and employees should be allowed to deal with their bereavement about departing colleagues – and the changing organisation. This does not mean holding formal 'wakes' but celebrating the end of one set of working practices formally can help people integrate the new.

Real communication, and for an extended period, may be necessary if employees are to feel committed to the new organisation. HR may need to act as the line management 'conscience' on communication once there is a semblance of 'business as usual' returning. This is where the special skills of trainers can come into their own. Typically, trainers have good communication skills and are in touch with the 'mood' of employees who are attending courses. Trainers who understand the business dynamics and the sensitivities involved in creating a new culture can provide a useful steer to line managers who are charged with communications in the early days post-merger.

Help to clarify roles

Once the shape of the new organisation becomes clearer, people may need help in clarifying their roles, knowing where they fit in the organisation's purpose and how to be successful in the new set-up. This may require them to learn new skills or adjust their working practices. Briefings for line managers and some training for individuals may be necessary. Typically, in the early days of a merger a number of temporary policies and short-term priorities are identified. Line managers often need a basic set of 'tool kit' training sessions which are short and focused. These can help build up managers' confidence where responsibility, reporting lines and roles are still ill-defined.

David Waters, a senior manager with significant experience of managing mergers points out:

- Be aware that there are some things you can plan for, and you should make every effort to put plans in place for these. However, some things such as predicting the emotional reaction to the news and dealing appropriately with it are easier to plan for than to cope with. Those on the receiving end of other people's reactions may themselves need support, whether this is from other senior managers, members of the planning team, external mentors or others.
- Senior management teams must stay close to the merger during the period of transition and not become shut off – that is when energy gets dispersed.
- While it is important to use appropriate resources and skills during mergers, make sure that, as far as possible, internal staff lead the integration effort, rather than relying on external consultants. According to David Waters, 'the whole thing is about confidence, not over-confidence, that you can carry people with you'.
- When attempting to integrate cultures, start with the people with the right attitude to people – high energy, prepared to confront things.
- Never make promises you cannot keep.

CONCLUSION

In this chapter we have discussed how major organisation design challenges, such as mergers and acquisitions, can be tricky territory and are most successful when the 'people' issues are well handled. While HR practitioners do not have to be experts in organisation design, they are uniquely placed to help the organisation realise its strategic ambitions – by getting their 'people' strategies right. HR needs to be represented on planning and transition teams and use the opportunity to challenge management thinking about what – and who – is required in the new organisation.

If handled well, trust can be built, and successful integrations can act as a springboard for further major change which brings significant business benefits. As Deal and Kennedy (2000) point out, they are an opportunity to develop a new management style and culture, as well as to manage and improve costs. They are also an ideal opportunity to put the right people in the right jobs and reenergise the organisation. They provide the rationale for putting performance on the map and for measuring the performance of the business and the success of the integration process following the merger. And of course, in an ideal world, they provide the opportunity to do things differently, while adding value to the business; to deliver excellent service to the client while providing a rewarding experience for all employees. Bear in mind that in many organisations sustaining a fit-for-purpose design now requires continuous redesign. To achieve all this, a strategic HR contribution can be pivotal and the HR practitioner who helps his or her organisation achieve these benefits can truly be said to have added value.

REFERENCES

Adler, P.S. and Borys, B. (1996) Two types of bureaucracy: Enabling and coercive. *Administrative Science Quarterly*, 41(1), 61–89.

Anderson, K., and Kochan, F. (2012). Examining Relationships between enabling structures, academic optimism and student achievement. Thesis for the degree of Doctor of Philosophy (PhD), Graduate Faculty of Auburn University.

Ashkenas, R.N. (1998). *The Boundaryless Organization: Breaking the Chains of Organizational Structure*. San Francisco, CA: Jossey-Bass.

Ashkenas, R.N. and Francis, S.C. (2000). Integration managers: Special leaders for special times. *Harvard Business Review*, 78(6), 108–116.

Block P. (2011). *Flawless Consulting: A Guide To Getting Your Expertise Used*. Hoboken: Wiley.

Bolman, L.G. and Deal, T.E. (1997). *Reframing Organisations: Artistry, Choice and Leadership*, 2nd Edition. San Francisco: Jossey-Bass.

Capra, F. (1997). *Web of Life: A New Synthesis of Mind and Matter*. Flamingo: Publisher.

Cheung-Judge, M-Y. and Holbeche, L.S. (2021). *Organization Development: A Practitioner's Guide for OD and HR*. London: Kogan Page.

Collins, J.C. (2001). *Good to Great: Why Some Companies Make the Leap... and Others Don't*. New York: HarperCollins.

Deal, T.E. and Kennedy, A.A. (2000). *The New Corporate Cultures: Revitalizing the Workplace after Downsizing, Mergers and Reengineering*. London, UK: TEXERE Publishing Limited.

Devine, M. et al. (1998). *Mergers and Acquisitions: Getting the People Bit Right*. Horsham, UK: Roffey Park Management Institute.

Divakaran, A., Neilson, G.L. and Pandrangi, J. (2013). How to design a winning company, *Strategy + Business*, Issue 72, Autumn, 153–178.

Francis, H., Holbeche, L.S. and Reddington, M. (2011). *People and Organisational Development: a new agenda for Organisational Effectiveness*. London: CIPD/Kogan Page.

Galbraith, J. The Star model™. https://www.jaygalbraith.com/images/pdfs/StarModel.pdf

Hall, P. and Norburn, D. (1987). The management factor in acquisition performance. *Leadership and Organization Development Journal*, 8, 23–30.

Holbeche, L. and Garrow, V. (2000). *Effective Mergers and Acquisition*. Horsham: Roffey Park Management Institute.

Kotter, J. (2014). *Accelerate: Building Strategic Agility for a Faster-Moving World*. Boston, MA: Harvard Business School Press.

Kotter, J. (1996). *Leading Change*. Boston, MA: Harvard Business School Press.

Marks, M.L. and Mirvis, P.H. (2001). Making mergers and acquisitions work: Strategic and psychological preparation. *Academy of Management Executive*, 15(2), 80–95.

Miller, R. (2000). How culture affects mergers and acquisitions. *Industrial Management*, 42(5), 22–27.

Morgan, G. (1986). *Images of Organization*. Beverly Hills: Sage.

Nadler, D.A. and Tushman, M.L. (1988). A model for diagnosing organizational behavior, in M.L. Tushman and W.L. Moore (eds), *Readings in the Management of Innovation*, 2nd Edition, pp. 148–163

PWC. (2011). *Talking about the people side of M&A*. PwC. https://www.pwc.co.uk/assets/pdf/talking-about-the-people-side-of-m-and-a.pdf

Raub, S. (2008). Does bureaucracy kill individual initiative? The impact of structure on organizational citizenship behavior in the hospitality industry. *International Journal of Hospitality Management*, 27(2), 179–186, June.

Saparito, P. A. and Coombs, J. E. (2013). Bureaucratic systems' facilitating and hindering influence on social capital. *Entrepreneurship: Theory and Practice*, 37(3), 625–639.

Varney, S. and Garrow, V. (2013). *The Palace: Perspectives on Organisation Design*. Brighton: Institute of Employment Studies.

Worley, C.G. and Lawler, E.E. (2010). *Built to Change Organizations and Responsible Progress: Twin Pillars of Sustainable Success*. Research in Organizational Change and Development 18:1–49.

15

Bringing about culture change

Companies around the world are coming to the realization that the right strategy is crucial but not always sufficient. And when great strategies fail, leaders often instinctively know the reason. Their next question is, how do we fix our culture?

(Couto et al. 2007)

DOI: 10.4324/9781003219996-18

In today's fast-changing environment, if the external demands on an organisation are greater than its capacity to respond, its fortunes and those of its stakeholders are likely to decline. This means that an organisation's culture should be conducive to change rather than being forced to react by circumstance. In practice, many of the 'brakes' on implementing strategy lie in the way the organisation's culture (or the 'way we do things around here') operates and the lack of 'buy-in' to change by employees. The forces of inertia and resistance common to many organisations can be substantial. It is therefore not surprising that, as Couto et al. suggest, leaders seek to change the culture. However, while changing strategy and structure can be difficult enough, what is much harder to achieve, and takes longer to happen, is changing the organisation's culture.

CHAPTER OVERVIEW

In this chapter, we look at the nature of culture and culture change and consider the role HR/OD can play in this. We will explore various aspects of Organisation Development theory and look at how an organisation development mindset can enhance HR's contribution to successful culture change. We shall cover:

- SHRM and culture change
- What is meant by culture?
- Cross-cultural models
- Is it possible to change culture?
- Paradigms of change and OD
- Role of OD/HR in culture change

LEARNING OBJECTIVES

- To consider aspects of culture and culture change
- To explore what an OD mindset might entail
- To look at how HR/OD can stimulate and embed culture change

INTRODUCTION: THE CHALLENGE OF CULTURE CHANGE

It has long been assumed that HR systems influence organisational cultures. As the stewards and keepers of the culture, HR leaders are responsible for reinforcing desired employee behaviours and beliefs – and in turn, realising the performance gains of a thriving culture. HR therefore has a key role to play in helping build the healthy, change-able organisational cultures their organisations aspire to have. A change-able culture is characterised by a positive work climate; work practices and employee mindsets that are flexible and adaptable to changing needs; employees who are energised, aligned and committed to the change and able to play their part in achieving it.

However, managing the process of culture change can be daunting since culture permeates all aspects of the organisation's system. Obstacles that prevent the system from operating in its preferred way need to be identified and eliminated. New practices and processes need to be introduced. Changes can come so thick and fast that in many organisations it may be hard to isolate just one change process that needs to be managed. A systemic approach to culture change is needed.

In addressing culture an Organisation Development (ODV) mindset is required since it brings a focus on human dynamics, is systemic and strategic but can also get into the practical detail of change. After all, 'OD is about adapting. It is probably something we have all seen over the last few years as change has changed itself to be more convulsive, rapid and even seismic. We have had to adapt to this and the more successful companies who have weathered the more recent storms may well have been OD-oriented companies deliberately or unknowingly. They may have called it change or agile thinking, but they were probably "being" OD practitioners' (Perry Timms – *The Time Is Now*). We shall return to the theme of OD later in this chapter.

WHAT IS MEANT BY 'CULTURE'?

Organisational culture is a vast topic that has many strands – defining culture, working cross-culturally, developing high performance cultures, changing culture, managing integrations of different cultures – to name but a few. Culture is variously described as:

> ...the sum total of all the shared, taken-for-granted assumptions that a group has learned in coping with external tasks and dealing with internal relationships.
> Edgar Schein (2004)

> ...the set of values of an organization that helps its members understand what the organization stands for, how it does things and what it considers important.
> (Ricky W. Griffin, Management, Houghton Mifflin Company, Boston 1990)

> ...a system of beliefs, values, and assumptions shared among an organization's inhabitants
> (Davis 1984; Sergiovanni and Corbally 1984; Kuh 1991; Denison 1996)

> ...a system of shared meaning held by members, distinguishing the organisation from other organisations
> (Martins and Martins 2003: 380)

> ...patterns of behaviour based on shared values and beliefs within a particular firm
> (Holt 1990)

> ...the collective mental programming of the human mind which distinguishes one group of people from another
> (Hofstede 1991)

Culture is a living changing system that embraces our personal and social life as well as our work life – the way different people think and behave is not accidental. Indeed, Naomi Stanford (2010) asks the question, *is* an organisation a culture or does an organisation *have* a culture? For Gareth Morgan, culture is one of nine organisational metaphors, or ways of understanding organisations. So all-pervasive is organisational culture that it is often likened to a fishpond where the fish swimming around never notice the water – they take it completely for granted.

Organisational culture is reflected in the way organisational members behave and in the beliefs, values and assumptions which they share. Some of these assumptions may be so taken for granted that they only become visible when change threatens them. The assumptions may be reflected in the formal systems, such as the reward scheme, or may be more active in the informal or 'shadow' system in which the grapevine, political behaviour and networks flourish (Rodgers 2007).

Typically, culture is most visible in manifestations such as the way employees treat one another, how they dress, the size and layout of office space, the appearance of the reception area and how customers are treated. Less visible, but good indicators of culture are the organisation's rituals and routines, the amount and nature of political activity and the symbolism of certain aspects of an organisation's history which affects how people feel about the company.

Prominence of culture theories

Organisational culture theory came to prominence in the 1980s following a period where national culture differences were much studied. In the turbulent business context of the time, no organisation could remain the same for long and survive. Cameron and Quinn (2011) argue that the challenge, therefore, was not to determine *whether* to change but *how* to change to increase organisational effectiveness. As a result theorists' attention shifted away from researching national cultures and focused more on organisational culture.

The origin of much research into organisational culture is based, among others, on the work of Deal and Kennedy (1982). According to this view, organisational culture is more central to organisational success than factors such as structure, strategy or politics. Peter Drucker argued was that organisational culture trumps strategy because behavioural and attitudinal forces are too strong to change quickly enough to execute strategy. Jeffrey Pfeffer (2005) saw culture as so important because: 'What remains as a source of competitive advantage, in part because it is difficult to imitate and in part because other sources of success have been eroded by competition, is organisational culture and capability, embodied in the workforce'.

Culture became recognised as a powerful means to hold organisations together, and provide market differentiation, 'against a tidal wave of pressures for disintegration, such as decentralization, de-layering, and downsizing. At the same time, traditional mechanisms for integration—hierarchies and control systems, among other devices—were proving costly and ineffective' (Goffee and Jones 1996). Building the organisation as a community that people wanted to belong to featured prominently in many management texts. Consequently, from the 1980s onwards, organisational culture became such a common theme in management literature; it was described by Pascale and others as a 'fad'.

Theories of high-performance cultures proliferated. As discussed in the last chapter, popular management writers such as Peters and Waterman (1982) linked strong organisational culture and firm success in top Fortune 500 companies. Organisational cultures that were not conducive to performance were described as 'toxic'. Strong culture came to be seen as a desirable force that can shape the firm's overall effectiveness and long-term success. Cameron and Quinn (2011: 21) argue that 'the sustained success of these firms has had less to do with market forces than with company values; less to do with competitive positioning than with personal beliefs, and less to do with resource advantages than with vision. In fact, it is difficult to name even a single highly successful company, one that is a recognized leader in its industry, that does not have a distinctive, readily identifiable organizational culture'.

Yet the fortunes of many of the organisational culture role model firms described by Peters and Waterman (1982) later declined. What was going on? Cameron and Quinn (2011) argue that the demise of some of the Fortune 500 companies undoubtedly resulted from slow, laggardly or wrongheaded change efforts. As T. S. Eliot pointed out: 'The overwhelming pressure of mediocrity, sluggish and indomitable as a glacier, will mitigate the most violent, and depress the most exalted revolution'.

Reflective activity

- What do you consider the pros and cons of a strong culture?
- Which organisations do you consider have a strong culture today?

Organisations as political systems

Organisations as political systems can be rife with power struggles, defensive behaviour and anxiety and conflict, explicit or covert. Behind the formal organisation reflected in an organisation chart, there lies the informal or 'shadow system' in which culture is more truly reflected than in formal mechanisms such as structures. This is where the real power lies. Networks, gossiping, politics, actual work standards versus espoused standards, for example over customer response times; who gets promoted and why; who gets car parking spaces, are all powerful political and cultural messages. A classic work by Mintzberg and Waters (1985) identifies four political arenas:

- the complete political arena (characterised by conflict that is intensive and pervasive)
- confrontation (conflict that is intensive but contained)
- the shaky alliance (conflict that is moderate and contained)
- the politicised organisation (conflict that is moderate but pervasive)

The informal system is often enduring and may or may not represent the chaos organisations often dread because it is hard to control.

Culture as a control mechanism

All organisations require a certain degree of order and consistency. Every system has a drive for coherence and a drive for differentiation. To achieve this, organisations either utilise explicit procedures and formal controls or implicit social controls through the culture. For instance, each organisation has behavioural norms for getting things done – by identifying principal goals; work methods; how members should interact and address each other; and how to conduct personal relationships (Harrison 1993). Each organisation evolves a unique profile reflecting the values and beliefs of the collective membership (Sims 1994). Through culture – transmitted overtly and covertly – organisational members develop a shared mental order, a common understanding that unites them, helps them to understand how they fit in, what is valued, appropriate and inappropriate (Davis 1984; Sathe 1985; Schein 1992; Whitt 1993; Allen and Cherry 2000).

Reflective activity

- How would a newcomer start to recognise and understand your organisation's culture?
- Would she/he be likely to describe this as a strong culture?
- In your organisation, which influence day to day performance most strongly – the formal or the informal aspects of organisation? How do you know?

How culture is transmitted

In order to keep the culture alive, the organisation has to ensure that its culture is transmitted to organisational members (Martins and Martins 2003). New employees are quickly socialised into the culture, a process known as 'acculturation', for instance through induction and onboarding. Acculturation encompasses the process of being made a member of a group, learning the ropes, and being taught how one must communicate and interact to get things done. The aim of socialisation is to establish a base of attitudes, habits and values that foster cooperation, integrity and communication. For new employees this requires adaptive behaviour within the organisation that leads to new belief systems. This new and adaptive behaviour is instilled through organisational values and beliefs associated with rituals, myths and symbols to reinforce the core assumptions of organisational culture (Hofstede 1991).

The cultural web (Johnson and Scholes 1993, Figure 15.1) suggests that culture is dynamic and changing slightly all the time. As an organisation grows, its culture (paradigm, or shared system of beliefs about the organisation) is modified, shaped and refined by symbols, stories, heroes, slogans and ceremonies. All firms have their stories. OD can seek to influence how culture emerges, for instance by shifting the nature of stories being told. In firms that socialise well the morals of the stories all tend to 'point north'. For example, Proctor and Gamble fires one of their best brand managers for overstating the features of a product. The moral: ethical claims come ahead of making money.

As Table 15.1 illustrates, simple deliberate changes to different cultural elements can start to shift a culture towards teamwork.

Johnson and Scholes (1993)

Figure 15.1 How culture is transmitted – The cultural web.

Table 15.1 Shifts towards a culture of teamwork

Physical structures	Create an open-plan layout Place posters to remind employees about teamwork
Language	• Encourage employees to adopt positive language and to greet with a smile • Senior leaders to role model the approach
Rituals and ceremonies	• Organise staff meetings, team building sessions and off-site 'bonding' activities like adventure or sports
Stories and legends	• Create strong messages with teamwork as emphasis
Shared values	• Place teamwork at the workplace and its definition above other values • Remind people that other values are important as well.

You may wish to complete the cultural web analysis tool to assess what aspects of culture change may be needed in your organisation.

Table 15.2 Cultural web analysis

(a) Stories
1. What core beliefs do stories reflect?
2. How pervasive are these beliefs (through levels)?
3. Do stories relate to:
4. Strengths or weaknesses?
5. Successes or failures?
6. Conformity or mavericks?
7. Who are the heroes and villain?
8. What norms do the mavericks deviate from?

(b) Routines and rituals
1. Which routines are emphasised?
2. Which would look odd if changed?
3. What behaviour do routines encourage?
4. What are the key rituals?
5. What core beliefs do they reflect?
6. What do training programmes emphasise?
7. How easy are rituals/routines to change?

(c) Symbols
1. What language and jargon are used?
2. How internal or accessible is it?
3. What aspects of strategy are highlighted in publicity?
4. What status symbols are there?
5. Are there particular symbols which denote the organisation?

(d) Organisational structure
1. How mechanistic/organic are the structures?
2. How flat/hierarchical are the structures?
3. How formal/informal are the structures?
4. Do structures encourage collaboration or competition?
5. What type of power structures do they support?

(e) Control systems
1. What is most closely monitored/controlled?
2. Is emphasis on reward or punishment?
3. Are controls related to history or current strategies?
4. Are there many/few controls?

(f) Power structures
1. What are the core beliefs of the leadership?
2. How strongly held are these beliefs (idealists or pragmatists?)
3. How is power distributed in the organisation?
4. Where are the main blockages to change?

Culture models

Schein argues that before any attempt is made to change organisational culture, it is imperative to carry out a culture diagnosis to understand the existing culture and how it is sustained. There are many models to understand culture. Some suggest that organisational culture exists at different levels (Whitt 1993; Schein 2016a).

Artefacts — e.g. visible organizational structures and processes; office space, behaviours

Espoused values — e.g. strategies, goals, philosophies, vision and mission statements

Underlying assumptions — e.g. unconscious, taken-for-granted beliefs, values, feelings, thoughts, perceptions

After Edgar Schein

Figure 15.2 Cultural levels.

Standard elements of culture (as per this depiction after Edgar Schein) include:

Level 1- Artefacts

The ways in which system presents itself, both to itself and to the outside world (e.g. traditions, rituals, myths, stories, ceremonies, customs, language, physical and social environment). Think branding, colour schemes and logos. Artefacts are easy to spot and they give the mood and feel of a place. The question is; why do these things happen?

Level 2- Espoused values

The official ways in which a system explains the reasons why things are done in a certain way. Values, beliefs, policy. Ask 'why'? and these are the answers you'll get.

Level 3- Shared tacit assumptions (e.g. thoughts, unconscious perceptions)

These are the hidden beliefs behind what's going on that a system might not even be aware of itself. These hidden beliefs give the ambience, the undertone to everything.

And this is where OD/change makers really need to look. These shared tacit assumptions influence absolutely everything that happens, but they're not easy to uncover. If you don't understand these assumptions, then any change imposed is unlikely to succeed. Changes need to be made at all levels for lasting shifts to occur.

Defining organisational culture types

Every organisation is different and has its own unique culture based on a complex combination of people's shared attitudes, beliefs, assumptions and behaviours. There can also be many sub-cultures in any organisation of size. These may reflect factors such as the nature of the work people do, age, gender, national culture, shared habits such as smoking. For instance, marketing teams may have a different sub-culture from that of engineering teams though they are likely to have at least some elements in common deriving from the overall company culture. Trompenaars argues that the culture of a company includes the models and standards that influence how employees act, and the organisation's cultural setting is affected by the corporate culture that a company adopts (Trompenaars & Hampden-Turner 2003:158). Indeed, company culture can sometimes be so strong it transcends national culture differences. So, IKEA stores throughout the world for example adopt the same Swedish work practices.

A variety of models can be used to determine the overall nature of an organisation's culture, often depicted as a series of culture types. These types suggest the different kinds of interactions that are present between employees and their organisation. Examples include the Harrison/Stokes role, power, support and achievement culture types, the Denison Organisational Culture Model, Charles Handy's 'Gods of Management', Goffee and Jones Sociability vs Solidarity, OCI (constructive, aggressive/defensive/passive/defensive), Trompenaars (paternalistic, bureaucratic, egalitarian, unstructured), Hofstede (power distance, individualism-collectivism, uncertainty avoidance, masculine-feminine, long-term orientation).

In the Harrison and Stokes model, each culture type has its characteristics, strengths, dark sides and limitations. These authors argue that strengthening and balancing a culture can mitigate its negative aspects. While this model is critiqued as simplistic, at least a cultural assessment should lead to a better-informed conversation about how to make the culture function more productively.

One of the best-known models for assessing culture - the Cameron and Quinn Competing Values framework – suggests that every organisation combines a mix of four different types of organisational culture that compete with one another under one leading cultural style. The four parameters of the framework include internal focus and integration vs external focus and differentiation, and stability and control vs flexibility and discretion (as shown in Figure 15.3 below).

Based on these parameters, the framework breaks organisational cultures into four distinct quadrants or cultural types: The Clan Culture, the Adhocracy Culture, the Market Culture, and the Hierarchy Culture. Elements of different culture types can co-exist to serve different organisational purposes.

Here is a broad summary of the four types and their specific qualities:

The Clan Culture: This culture is rooted in collaboration. Members share common-alities and see themselves as part of one big family who are active and involved. Leadership takes the form of mentorship, and the organisation is bound by commitments and traditions. The main values are rooted in teamwork, communication and consensus. The John Lewis Partnership is a prominent clan culture where the culture is focused

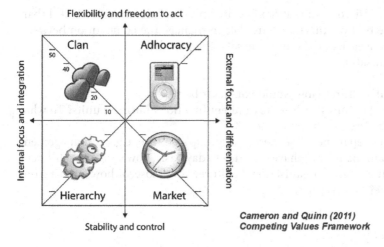

Figure 15.3 Competing values framework.

on building respectful relationships with employees, customers, suppliers and the environment itself.

The Adhocracy Culture: This culture is based on energy and creativity. Employees are encouraged to take risks, and leaders are seen as innovators or entrepreneurs. The organisation is held together by experimentation, with an emphasis on individual ingenuity and freedom. The core values are based on change and agility.

The Market Culture: This culture is built upon the dynamics of competition and achieving concrete results. The focus is goal-oriented, with leaders who are tough and demanding. The organisation is united by a common goal to succeed and beat all rivals. The main value drivers are market share and profitability. General Electric under ex-CEO Jack Welch was a good example of this culture. Welch vowed that every G.E. business unit must rank first or second in its respective market or face being sold off.

The Hierarchy Culture: This culture is founded on structure and control. The work environment is formal, with strict institutional procedures in place for guidance. Leadership is based on organised coordination and monitoring, with a culture emphasising efficiency and predictability. The values include consistency and uniformity. Think of stereotypical large, bureaucratic organisations such as McDonald's or the emergency services.

Quinn and Cameron developed the Organizational Culture Assessment Instrument (OCAI), a validated survey method based on their framework. Leaders and OD/HR can use surveys such as the OCAI to gain insights into the dominant culture of their organisation, and to assess the gaps between their current culture and the preferred culture, for instance to make empirical comparisons of an organisational culture before and after any major change initiative, reorganisation or merger.

The OCAI research suggests that it is rare for companies to share equal traits from all four cultural types, with no single dominant type. However, it is likely that departments within an organisation may exhibit subdominant traits, such as the accounting department having a mainly Hierarchy/Control culture, while the development team is shaped by more of an Adhocracy/Creativity culture.

Quinn and Cameron discovered that flexible organisations are more successful than rigid ones because the best organisations are able to manage the competition between cultures while activating each of the four value sets when needed.

Think of your organisation:

- Is there an overall culture? How would you describe it?
- Are there different cultures within the different functions/business units? To what extent do these differences create tensions?
- Thinking of your department/business unit/group's culture, e.g. its management style, the way team members behave on a day to day basis, how similar or different is it from the actual overall organisational culture? How close, or how far is it from the 'ideal' culture? Why is this?

Defining ideal culture

Many 'top-down' culture change efforts are driven by the need to better align culture with strategy. Culture can be a source of sustainable advantage if it enables, for example, improved:

- Organisational performance
- Organisational agility
- Employee well-being
- Community/client relationships

The desired culture is often described in terms of an ideal set of practices such as high-performance work systems (HPWS). Such systems recognise committed employees as valued partners of the business who make it possible to create and maintain competitive advantage. HPWS attempt to create a work environment that allows employees greater involvement and responsibility. Employees have good access to information, are well trained, feel more secure in their roles and are well rewarded.

Characteristics of such systems include:

- Appropriate management and leadership
- Flexibility built in
- A fair employee value proposition
- Empowerment, involvement and accountability

What does your organisation's 'ideal' or 'desired' culture look like? It may be defined in terms of the desired working practices or according to the values and characteristics required to deliver the strategy – such as innovation and risk-taking; attention to detail; outcome orientation; people orientation; team orientation; competitiveness and stability (Robbins and Judge 2010).

Comparisons with cultural stereotypes can help identify desired cultural elements. Chitkara, P. and Davidson (2013) compare 'analogue' with 'digital' organisational cultures. With respect to customers and demands, analogue cultures are driven primarily by policies whereas digital cultures respond to changing economic and citizen needs. Digital cultures have rapid decision-making, a results-focus and empowered employees with an orientation towards innovation, improvement and overcoming constraints. People work in mixed teams in cross-functional and integrated communities. There is strong collaboration, a focus on rapid launch and learn and a culture that encourages, measures and rewards innovation.

Many businesses describe their desired cultures in broad terms; others are more specific, with culture defined in more micro-terms that describe the characteristics and behaviours that express core organisational values. For example, the Sony Corporation aims to be a very customer-centric organisation and believes its corporate culture is a way to retain customers in the electronics, gaming, entertainment and financial services markets. The firm believes its culture is manifest through employee behaviour that is:

- Reliable – increases customer satisfaction by ensuring that employees are capable of addressing customers' needs and inquiries about the company's product
- Credible – its staff have the skills and knowledge required to satisfy customers, so training to improve standards and development to reinforce the corporate culture is a strong feature
- Cordial – where the culture facilitates warm and friendly relations between employees and customers, leading to high customer satisfaction

Different business strategies may require, or themselves be the product of, different cultures. In companies with a strategy that requires a culture of opportunity, you may see an emphasis on preparing for the future – so staff will be ready for next position; there will be a broad view of professional development and plenty of support for it. For a culture of professionalism, you might see empowerment, significant autonomy and responsibility, respect for choice and work-life balance. For a culture of engagement, you might see an emphasis on mutual fit and support. There might be an emotionally warm, friendly atmosphere, high involvement and a sense of 'We'll take care of you'.

More generally, given the fast-changing business environment, as living human systems organisations need to be able to learn from continuous waves of change so that change becomes seen as a natural and inevitable part of organisational life and not an isolated and threatening incident. They need continually to develop new capabilities and improve upon those that already exist. For organisations on the path towards agility, the culture must be conducive to the development or enhancement of the organisation's change/learning capabilities. Not only does the organisation need a change capability to orchestrate the transition from traditional to agile, it will also need to have an established ability to re-purpose resources, assets, people, budgets, systems and processes to approach the norm of change as usual (Cummings and Worley 2014). So the culture as a whole must become change-able.

CROSS-CULTURAL MODELS

National cultures differ in many ways and these differences will be reflected in varying preferences, values and work behaviours. Navigating cultural differences requires cultural intelligence, i.e. knowledge, mindfulness and adaptive behaviour (Henson 2002; Francesco and Gold 2005).

Table 15.3 National cultural dimensions

Communication	Verbal and non-verbal
Concepts of time	Adherence to schedule
Group dependence	Importance of group over the individual
Hierarchy/authority	Perception of rank in relationship to others
Openness to diversity	Gender, race, religion, language, country of origin
Physical space	Space and privacy needed for personal comfort
Relationships	Importance for business interactions
Status attainment	Perceived level of 'success'
Tolerance of change	Perception of control over one's destiny

Cultural value dimensions compared

Various authors have distinguished between national cultures on the basis of how their values differ. Edward Hall (1966) explored how different national cultures viewed the concept of time – linear assumptions of time, i.e. yesterday, today, tomorrow are sequential vs circular – (i.e. the past and the future are present today). Hofstede's (1991) cultural dimensions theory, updated by Hofstede and Minkov (2010), is a framework for cross-cultural communication. It describes the effects of a society's culture on the values of its members, and how these values relate to behaviour such as timekeeping and decision-making. National differences along these six dimensions can be compared:

- power distance index
- individualism vs collectivism
- masculinity vs femininity
- uncertainty avoidance index
- long-term versus short-term orientation
- indulgence/restraint

For instance, in cultures with high power distance (such as France) organisations are likely to have autocratic management and a strong hierarchy, whereas those with small power distance (such as the United Kingdom) are likely to operate with greater equality. If managers whose preference is for low power distance find themselves working in high power distance, notions of 'empowerment' for instance may be difficult to implement.

Trompenaar's dimensions (based on data collected from over 46,000 managers from more than 40 nationalities) are:

- Universalism vs Particularism (truth and goodness apply to every situation/circumstance and relationships matter a lot)
- Individualism vs Collectivism
- Neutral vs Emotional
- Specific vs Diffuse
- Success = Ascription vs Achievement
- Passage of time
- Relationship to the environment

Trompenaar's dimensions also include:

- Performance orientation: The degree to which a collective encourages and rewards group members for improvement
- Future orientation: The extent to which individuals engage in future oriented behaviours such as planning and investing for the future, e.g. the Swiss preference is risk averse and planful; Russia is at the opposite end of this dimension
- Gender egalitarianism: The degree to which a collective minimises gender inequality
- Assertiveness: The degree to which individuals are assertive, confrontational and aggressive in their relationships – can do attitude
- Humane orientation: The degree to which collective encourages and rewards individuals for being fair and caring, e.g. Egypt & Malaysia are high; France and Germany are low
- Power distance: The degree to which members of a collective expect power to be distributed equally
- Uncertainty avoidance: The extent to which a society relies on social norms, rules and procedures to alleviate unpredictable future events

Another leading study of cross-cultural values applied to leadership and management is the GLOBE project. The GLOBE six Leadership dimensions are:

- Charismatic/Value-based: Reflects the ability to inspire, motivate and to expect high performance outcomes from others on the basis of firmly held core beliefs. Highest score=Anglo cluster (6.05), lowest = Middle East (5.35/7)
- Team-orientated: Emphasises team building and implementation of a common goal among team members. Highest = Latin America (5.96); lowest = Middle East (5.47)
- Participative: Reflects the degree to which managers involve others in making and implementing decisions. Highest = Germanic Europe cluster (5.86); lowest = Middle East (4.97)
- Humane orientated: Reflects supportive leadership but includes compassion and generosity. Highest = South Asia (5.38); Lowest = Nordic Eu (4.42)
- Autonomous: Independent and individualistic leadership. Highest = Eastern Eu (4.20); Lowest = Latin America (3.51)
- Self-Protective: Ensuring the safety and security of the individual. Highest = Southern Asia (3.83); lowest = Nordic EU (2.72)

These different dimensions, and where national cultures stereotypically sit along them, tend to play out when people of different national culture backgrounds work together. People may have different attitudes for instance towards time-keeping, where and how decisions get made, what 'success' looks like, what the purpose of meetings is. The notion of 'face' may be defined differently and be very much to the fore in some cultures and not in others. These differences are not 'right' or 'wrong' but they may jar with the practices and national culture of the company or parent organisation.

Cultural contingencies in decision-making

Cultures also differ with respect to attitudes to decision-making (Adler 2008). When a problem is recognised, some cultures prefer problem-solving and changing the situation, while others prefer to accept the situation as it is. Searching for information is interpreted differently – from this being about gathering 'facts' to being about gathering ideas and possibilities. Some cultures prefer decision making to be delegated and decisions are made quickly while other cultures prefer team decision-making, with decisions made slowly. With regard to implementation, some cultures see this as the responsibility of one person, managed from the top and a slow process while others see this as the responsibility of the team, involves participation of all levels and a fast process. Current business preoccupations that involve the pursuit of innovation, experimentation and organisational agility will be easier to implement in some cultures than in others. For a practical look at how national differences can play out in various cross-cultural organisational contexts, check out *Mind your manners: managing business cultures in the new global Europe* (3rd Revised Edn, 2011) by John Mole, Nicholas Brealey International.

Ethical dilemmas

These differences in cultural values are also likely to give rise to ethical dilemmas, situations where there is more than one right answer. These can be complex to reconcile when companies do business across borders. For example in some countries it is respectful for businesspeople to exchange gifts (such as traditionally in Japan), while in other countries generous gifts are considered bribery. Indeed, managers in some countries may have a higher tolerance for bribery than those in other parts of the world. Very low wages may be considered unethical in wealthy developed countries. So Western companies manufacturing their product in factories in some developing countries where pay is typically very low are increasingly being censored in the court of public opinion. But developing countries may accept those wages if they encourage investment and improve living standards. Such differences can make it difficult for managers to know how to behave.

Hampden-Turner and Trompenaars (1993) highlight the dilemmas that can arise when people from different national cultures work together across geographical or other boundaries. These become very prominent for instance in merger situations, or working in global teams, or when there is a new manager from a different cultural background. OD can help managers develop cultural intelligence – become more aware, look for the whole and surface the underlying values. In the example above, they can help managers find a balanced approach – neither sticking rigidly to what's done at home nor condoning bribery – by:

- Honouring human values that suggest what is fair and right.
- Respecting human dignity by valuing employees, providing safe and humane working conditions
- Respecting basic rights – to health, education and equal opportunities in the workplace; paying a living wage
- Good citizenship – protecting the environment; when possible, sharing a portion of the company's gains with others

HR/OD and cultural dilemmas

Hampden-Turner and Trompenaars also explored dilemma theory and looked at processes for reconciling (not resolving) these dilemmas.

When confronted by an ethical dilemma:

- Describe the ethical dilemma you are facing.
- List the actions you're considering in order to reconcile this dilemma, and any concerns you have about each possible choice.
- Are any core human values being violated (such as respect for human dignity, respect for basic civil rights and good citizenship)? If so, list your specific concerns. Are there any local traditions or customs that are important to respect in this situation? – if so, write them down.
- Document your thoughts about how ethical your company's or your current practices are if you take into account the context of the situation.
- List some ideas for resolving the dilemma. As you draw up your list, aim for creative solutions that benefit everyone involved.

DEFINING ORGANISATION DEVELOPMENT (ODV)

Working with culture is the heartland of organisation development. It is particularly when attempting to shift any aspect of culture that HR requires an understanding of the principles of organisational development.

ODV is variously defined as:

- A systematic application of behavioural science principles and practices to understand how people and organisations function and how to get them to function better within a clear value base (Cheung-Judge and Holbeche 2021)
- A system-wide process of data collection, diagnosis, action planning, intervention, and evaluation aimed at (1) enhancing congruence among organisational structure, process, strategy, people, and culture; (2) developing new and creative organisational solutions; and (3) developing the organisation's self- renewing capacity. It occurs through the collaboration of organisational members working with a change agent using behavioural science theory, research and technology (Beer and Huse 1980)
- About helping each other to release the human spirit and human capability in the workplace (French and Bell 1978)
- All the activities engaged in by managers, employees and helpers that are directed toward building and maintaining the health of the organisation as a total system. Schein (1978) argues that OD should *not* be associated with what consultants and helpers do. A healthy organisation can develop itself; its managers are the primary practitioners of OD.
- A process (and its associated technology) directed at organisational improvement (Margulies 1972).

All change begins with a disturbance of the status quo. Cultural issues often present themselves as operational problems to be solved or fixed – such as poor productivity – or the pursuit of opportunities for growth, such as how to innovate more. Typical objectives of OD activity might include:

- to increase the level of inter-personal trust among employees
- to increase employees' level of satisfaction and commitment/engagement

- to confront problems instead of neglecting them
- to effectively manage conflict
- to increase cooperation and collaboration among employees
- to increase organisational problem-solving
- to put in place processes that will help improve the ongoing operation of an organsation on a continuous basis
- to unite people around a common purpose

These are all indicative of a need for cultural renewal to improve organisational health and may require First or Second Order Change (Bartunek 1987). Indeed, Cameron and Quinn (2011) argue that, against a fast-changing backdrop, the frightening uncertainty that traditionally accompanied major organisational change has been superseded by the frightening uncertainty now associated with staying the same.

IS IT POSSIBLE TO CHANGE CULTURE?

Can you change culture, or does it just emerge? This is a subject of great debate among theorists. On the one hand, some theorists argue that changing culture is a doomed exercise: 'Many managers have found from bitter experience that attempts to manage culture can result in frustration and confusion' (Baron and Walters 1994). 'Not only are attempts to script culture change doomed to failure, the attempt to manage culture tends to be seen as unethical, a threat to individual liberty' (Barratt 1992). 'By changing their cultures without changing their reward system, companies run the risk of sending their employees terribly mixed signals' (Hawk 1995).

On the other hand, O'Reilly (1989) believes that it is possible to change or manage organisational culture by choosing the attitudes and behaviours that are required, identifying the norms that promote or impede them, and then taking action to create the desired effect. Change appears possible if leaders lead the change: 'Such change is complex, takes time, and requires leadership, which is something quite different from even excellent management. That leadership must be guided by a realistic vision of what kinds of cultures enhance performance' (Kotter 1995).

Arnold (2005: 579) states that 'culture can be seen as something that can be managed or changed when the existing culture is inappropriate or even detrimental to the organisation's competitive needs'. In other words, there must be a 'burning platform'. Similarly, Martins and Martins (2003: 395) argue that organisational culture change can only take place when most or all of the following conditions exist:

- Turnover in leadership. New top leadership which can provide an alternative set of key values may be perceived as more capable of responding to the crisis.
- Young and small organisation. The younger the organisation, the less entrenched its culture will be and it is easier for management to communicate its new values when the organisation is small.
- Weak culture. The more widely held a culture is, and the more members agree with its values, the more difficult it will be to change; thus, weak cultures are more amenable to change than strong ones.
- A dramatic crisis. This is the shock that undermines the status quo and calls into question the relevance of the current culture.

With respect to dramatic crisis, many organisations have found that aspects of their culture have either helped or hindered their ability to thrive during the pandemic. The UK's

NHS Confederation, for instance, representing different component elements of the national health service, reflected on the amazing practice demonstrated by staff in all parts of the institution during the pandemic. The Confederation concluded that, 'we need to hold on to this different way of doing things and strip away the unnecessary bureaucracy, reporting and regulation that for too long has stifled the service. We need everyone to embrace a culture that empowers local leaders and clinicians to lead, giving them the ability to make good decisions for the communities and partnerships they serve'. The challenge now will be to build on these breakthroughs before new more effective practice gets washed away by ongoing demands.

Schein (2016) argues that because deliberate culture change is difficult to achieve, it should be attempted only when certain conditions are present:

- Good reasons for changing the culture
- Strongly shared principles and values
- Capability to align organisational elements
- Obvious leadership commitment
- Recognising what degree of change is possible
- Accepting that planned culture change takes time

If any of these conditions is missing, achieving lasting culture change will be harder.

Harrison (1993: 21) suggests that, although it is possible to change organisational culture, changing the fundamental cultural orientation of an organisation has the following drawbacks:

- It is difficult to achieve, requiring deep changes in values and management style and in organisation systems, structures and rewards systems.
- It takes a long time, three to five years or much more.
- It creates turmoil and stress within the organisation.

The effort usually results in the organisation suffering a decrement in performance at first, which often causes the leadership to abandon the effort before it bears fruit. Therefore, organisations should undertake conscious culture change only because it is necessary to do so. Harrison also counsels that, given the difficulty of producing culture change, it is important to focus more on building to the strengths of the culture, using these to balance out less-effective cultural elements and only changing those few things that are real impediments to success. Denison (1996) argues that organisational climate (i.e. the local work unit atmosphere or 'mood') can more easily be changed than culture. For Schein (2017) too, 'A climate can be locally created by what leaders do, what circumstances apply, and what environments afford. A culture can evolve only out of mutual experience and shared learning'.

American theorist Richard Pascale (2001: 29) questions the ethics of cultural programmes such as induction, or culture change. 'Most high performing organisations have an awesome internal consistency which powerfully shapes behavior. 'Creating a strong culture' is a nice way of saying that an organisation's members have to be more comprehensively socialised. Trendy campaigns 'to become a strong culture' encounter resistance when an organisation's members are asked to give up their idiosyncrasies and some of their individuality for the common good. The end result is usually the status quo.

(Conversely) The absence of cultural rules makes organisational life capricious. When social roles are unclear, no one is speaking the same language; communication, and trust break down. In effect, the power to implement change and execute effectively relies heavily on one's social currency, something a person accumulates over time. Strong culture firms empower employees helping them build this social currency by providing continuity and clarity. Organisations which do not facilitate this process incur a cost.

The crux of the dilemma is this: We are intellectually and culturally opposed to the manipulation of individuals for organisational purposes. At the same time, a certain degree of social uniformity enables organisations to work better. The less we rely on informal social controls, the more we must inevitably turn to formal financial controls and bureaucratic procedures'.

- Where do you stand on this dilemma highlighted by Pascale?

Critical success factor for culture change: values and purpose

Since culture is changing all the time anyway, the question is perhaps not whether you want culture to change but whether you want to manage it. How can HR/OD play into that? Posner et al. (1985) were among the first to recognise the importance of shared values in creating a unified culture. According to Devine (2005), 'Perhaps the most important task is to build an organisation with a set of values and an identity that is sufficiently compelling for talented people to buy into'.

Why should values and organisational purpose be so important in culture change? Pascale et al. (2001) argue that values serve as the primary safeguard against our great fear that corporations are fundamentally amoral and that their members, once socialised, will pursue inappropriate goals. Identification with common values and the firm's transcendent purpose resolves a key paradox since it enables employees to reconcile personal sacrifices 'necessitated by their membership in the organisation'. Placing oneself 'at the mercy' of an organisation imposes real costs. There are long hours of work, missed weekends, bosses one has to endure, criticism that seems unfair, job assignments and rotations that are inconvenient or undesirable. The countervailing force for commitment under these circumstances is the organisation's set of transcendent values which connect its purpose with significant higher-order human values – such as serving mankind, providing a first-class product for society, or developing people. This is the foundation of trust between organisation and individual. However, attempts to change culture top-down, for instance through formulating new values, often lead to situations where what is practised is at odds with what is espoused, leading to loss of trust. (Trice and Beyer 1993; Schuh and Miller 2006; Khandelwal and Mohendra 2010).

Most firms that have avoided the pitfalls of strong cultures consciously minimise the downside of socialisation by cultivating not just any obsessions but those that serve to continually draw attention away from internal matters to the world outside. The four most common 'obsessions' are (1) quality, (2) competition, (3) customer service and (4) productivity. Each demands an external focus and serves as a built-in way of maintaining vigilance. Positive examples are McDonald's obsessive concern for quality control, Toyota's for productivity and Morgan Stanley's with competition.

- How clear and uplifting are your organisation's purpose and values? To what extent do your organisation's mission and vision statements inspire people's commitment?

ROLE OF OD/HR IN STIMULATING CULTURE CHANGE

For leaders and HR/OD consultants aiming to stimulate cultural change the task is to:

- Align culture, process/systems, values and organisational arrangements to create an environment that people will thrive in
- Link changes in the culture with organisational goals and effectiveness
- Build robust and effective leadership and management practices
- Provide a range of communication vehicles through which employees can become involved in decision-making
- Work to ensure that people-oriented values drive practice and help individuals, groups and the organisation to thrive.

Culture change is usually a highly emotional experience and the likely first reaction from employees will be resistance. To instil trust between employees and management, honest and open communication between all members during this process is crucial. Clearly leadership development, clear communications about vision and purpose, ensuring people have the chance to be involved in change, revising HR practices such as reward are just part of the culture change HR 'kit-bag'. As one UK local government HR director put it, 'HR/OD is part of our strategic business. We help to articulate and deliver the vision. What does OD do? We are the change agents. We should be open to change ourselves. We held workshops to get people's ideas. They all had to be assimilated so that HR knew the emotional side of change. There is an HR/OD presence on all departmental teams. What is the added ingredient of OD? It's vision, articulation and being a change agent. The mechanisms of internal communications and employee engagement are used to develop the organisation. We help to focus outcomes. OD for us means hearts and minds and values'.

An OD consultant faces many paradoxes in managing culture change – for instance the challenge of communicating the complexity of the change situation but in a clear enough way as to create meaning; between following a detailed top-down plan and responding opportunistically to unforeseen circumstances and emergent opportunities. Schein offers the following advice with regard to HR/OD's role:

- Don't over-simplify culture. It's far more than 'how we do things around here'.
- Focus on a problem and how culture is influencing it instead of trying to change culture directly.
- Culture is always helping and hindering problem solving. It's important to understand both.
- Be very specific about behaviour, how it's impacting your problem and the future state of the behaviour you want to see.
- Culture change may evolve from a small but effective change in behaviour.
- Think about culture systematically.

Schein (2016b) argues that helping leaders to gain insights into how to address cultural issues requires 'humble' consulting. *If it is successful, and people like it, and it becomes a norm, then you can say it has become a culture change.*

Making culture change happen: two paradigms of change and OD

Choosing culture change methods is often presented as polarities between different paradigms: traditional OD and expert change management and more emergent OD approaches. These reflect the development of the field of OD over time.

Traditional expert change management

The heritage of the formula-led 'engineering of organisations' approach, in which cultural change is approached programmatically, derives from rational bureaucratic frameworks where the machine metaphor is dominant – and by deduction human beings are passive. Brown (1998: 189–192) for instance presents managing organisational culture change as a series of steps:

1. Analyse the existing culture – establishing a norm gap
2. Experience the desired culture – systems, introduction and involvement
3. Modify the existing culture – making change happen; getting from where we are to where we want to be
4. Sustain the desired culture – ongoing monitoring and evaluation of the degree of success of our change journey toward renewal

Table 15.4 Programmatic vs dialogic OD approaches

Programmatic, diagnostic, pre-planned; the 'clinical system' or 'mechanical' metaphor of improvement	*Dialogic, emergent, co-created; the 'social mobilisation' or 'living system' metaphor of improvement*
• Linear thinking • Top-down • Change driven • 'Closing gaps' • Task-centric • Initiatives, toolkits • Advocacy • Tell, sell, achieve 'buy-in', roll-outs • Dealing with 'resistance' • Deliverables • Project organisation, detailed plans, milestones, etc. • Controlling, audits and data • Learning from experience • Consultant as expert	• Systemic thinking • Can start anywhere • Transition driven • 'Unleashing potential' • People-centric • 'I can only create the conditions for change to emerge' • Inquiry • Self-organised, co-create, embody the new • Different energies emerge in the system • Inspired action, prototypes • Networks, communities, big picture, story-telling • Change in mindsets and behaviour • Learning from the emerging picture • Consultant as facilitator and reflection partner

Sources: Michael Roehrig, 2012 and others.

Dialogic approaches

More recent OD theory and practice has moved beyond conventional diagnostic and planned change approaches towards a view of organisations as dialogic networks and reality as socially constructed (Bushe and Marshak 2014: 86). The human dynamics focus recognises that human diversity exists in any social system. In contrast to linear, planned change approaches, emergent change is continuous and iterative, more transformational. Rather than change starting at the top, change can start anywhere and spread out. If diversity is surfaced during change, multiple gains are possible, so common ground needs to be sought and engagement is critical to sustain change momentum.

Indeed, from a complexity perspective, Stacey (2015) and Shaw (2002) argue that organisational reality is enacted through conversation. Shaw suggests that organisations are created, sustained and changed through complex, interconnected conversational network-based processes. Shaw argues that the role of what has been traditionally termed 'the change agent', is to enter into and, with awareness, what John Heron and Peter Reason (2006) call 'critical subjectivity' and to fully participate in these conversational networks. This is with a view to both showing how patterns of meaning-making are perpetually being constructed through the normal everyday conversational activities within organisations and also enabling alternative forms of conversational sense-making to emerge. Therefore, if different conversations can be facilitated, different realities can be enacted.

Bushe and Marshak (2015) identify three elements in an emergent change process:

1. A disruption in the ongoing social construction of reality is stimulated or engaged in a way that leads to a more complex organisation.
2. A change to one or more core narratives takes place.
3. A generative image is introduced or surfaces that provides new and compelling alternatives for thinking and acting.

Newer OD methods include strengths-based approaches such as Appreciative Inquiry (Cooperrider and Whitney 2005) and large-group interventions such as Real-Time Strategic Change (Jacobs 1997) through which such disruption can take place. These draw on social constructionist theories as ways of engaging more people through dialogue and conversation in the changes facing their organisations.

Dynamic OD

Varney (2019) draws on complexity theory in her formulation of 'Dynamic OD'. This involves actively involving multiple perspectives to gain insight into the dynamic complexity of organisational life. This focus on multiple, diverse voices has much in common with Dialogic OD. However, while Dialogic OD works to reveal multiple realities, Dynamic OD is concerned with learning from the multiple perspectives embedded in a complex reality. Its tools and approaches include dynamic patterning social movements, viral change and informal coalitions (Varney 2015). It's about helping people become aware of the need for change and generating a social movement. Axelrod (2010) argues that people need their voices to be heard in change and he too proposes that OD methods should be used to widen the circle of involvement, connect people to each other, create communities for action and promote fairness.

Varney advocates her 'C' methodology that is about HR/OD supporting people to increase Cross-functional interaction, become a much more Connected workforce, design processes to enable them to engage in regular Co-construction and Co-creation, help the system to surface Collective intelligence and make Cross-boundary work the norm. HR/OD should support L&D colleagues to reshape the learning process to make Collaborative learning a requirement rather than an exception, making growth strategy an occasion for Co-venturing, and using Co-Creativity as a tool for innovation.

So, having to choose between planned and emergent methods may be a false dichotomy. While the diagnostic, planned approaches can raise awareness of the need for change, to create cultural shifts and more sustainable implementation it is better to focus on the human dynamics of emergent change.

Reflective activity

- In your experience of culture change, which approaches have you found most effective to inspire, model, nurture and embed culture change?

The role of leaders

Whichever approach is adopted, senior leaders play a critical role in culture change. According to Bushe and Marshak (2016), 'OD thrives when it works with leaders who want to create great organisations and are willing to lead an emergent process that engages stakeholders in proposing and acting on solutions to adaptive challenges. To be successful, leaders must be just as interested in improving the organisation's adaptive capacity as they are in any specific change. This, however, violates a widely held but problematic belief – that leaders must have a 'vision'. We need a new narrative of leadership that acknowledges the courage required of leaders who say, 'I don't know the answer, but I know what the problem is, and I will engage those who will have to solve the problem in an adaptive, emergent process of change'.

Leaders have many cultural tools at their disposal. They can stimulate change and embed the new cultural norms through primary and secondary embedding mechanisms (Schein 2016a). Primary mechanisms include what leaders pay attention to, measure and control; how they react to critical incidents and organisational crises; criteria for allocation of rewards and status, recruitment, selection and onboarding, promotion and excommunication. Leaders also control the secondary mechanisms – organisation design, structure, systems, procedures, design of physical space. They are at the hub of stories, legends and myths as well as formal statements of organisational philosophy.

Leaders need to use these mechanisms judiciously to move towards the desired culture, using themselves as instruments to role model those behaviours. If the 'walk' and the 'talk' do not align, people will not follow. How leaders engage in dialogue with stakeholders, especially the workforce, will send a clear signal about whether leaders' preference is to maintain the status quo or whether they really want a positive change, are open to possibilities, welcome people's ideas and do not claim to have all the answers.

The UK's Co-Op, a long-standing trusted brand that has been in business since the 1840s nearly failed when a crisis erupted following losses in its banking operation which exposed fundamental governance and leadership issues across the business. While HR was initially involved in firefighting in the aftermath of the crisis, the team then turned its attention to rebuilding the organisation, exemplified by the mission 'rescue, rebuild, renew'. HR set about restoring employee pride, reconnecting staff to the original mission of an ethical business that returns profits to individual members and fixing a broken leadership model.

The firm brought together 5,600 leaders in 'Being a Co-op leader' discussions to consider a new community-led business proposition. This planted the idea of a more consensual form of leadership and collective responsibility. HR then launched a programme 'Back to being Co-op'. More than 54,000 staff members came together in events across the country. These events, fronted by senior leaders, used actors to explore the company's rich history and to surface the behaviours and values that would serve the organisation in the future. This opportunity to work together with people from across the organisation to share common goals was a revelation for all concerned and emphasised the value of working collaboratively.

Since these events, employee engagement scores have risen to 80% and business results have improved significantly. HR plans to build on these successes by offering a potential MBA in co-operative businesses to help develop the next generation of ethical leaders. As the HR Director points out, 'We have stimulated colleagues to feel proud again, but we're just at the beginning. We need to sustain it' (*People Management*, June 2017).

Planning for emergence

Effective change leaders tolerate uncertainty, welcome upheaval and energise organisations to gain active involvement rather than passive buy-in. They can build powerful human networks connecting people, ideas and processes in collaborative engagement. They can amplify the natural cultural change process by planning for emergence:

- Instituting strategic dialogue, actively informing employees about the business
- Ensuring strategic alignment (agreement among leadership team members regarding key strategies)
- Actively working to create alignment of behaviour and core values
- Focusing on the future, as much as the present
- Reminding employees what the vision is and how it links to their current activities
- Signposting the future: establishing a strategic agenda and guiding questions
- Creating a frame and spirit of enquiry
- Giving permission and encouragement to explore
- Setting up cross—functional task forces
- Encouraging participation in industry groups so that people are aware of trends
- Encouraging small scale initiatives and experimentation
- Rewarding risk-taking, even if it means tolerating some failures
- Requiring 'bottom-up' involvement in decisions, including customers
- Investing in development and capability-building
- Promoting from within
- Amplifying what works
- Engaging different energies in the system
- Adapting structures and processes to support the new, building the organisation around teams, not individuals
- Creating forums for learning that are visible and useful
- Identifying lessons learned to support ongoing change
- Creating own positive stories by publicly appreciating and valuing successes; rewarding and promoting people who build organisational capability

Change leaders can promote rapid iteration as the change network tests ideas and learns from experience. They can maintain effective and flexible communications with stakeholders to resolve any conflicts between change networks and the hierarchy. Moreover, culture change need not be a formal program but can be stimulated by encouraging provocateurs and mavericks, developing supportive infrastructure, changing the context to change the habits, shaping group norms through new incentives, relaxing or removing 'old' rules and controls, ensuring leaders and managers demonstrate relevant cultural attributes and encourage employees to care intensely about executing strategic objectives. This can help lift the barriers that are holding back innovation.

Embedding cultural shifts

As stated earlier, Stokes and Harrison (1992) argue that since culture change is difficult to achieve it is better to think in terms of 'strengthening' what works and 'balancing' out what does not work rather than 'changing' organisational culture, which tends to provoke defensiveness. A balancing approach allows a culture's benefits to be preserved while adding countervailing elements. It's about bringing consistency and strengthening what works while everything around that can change. The focus should be on the change process, not just the desired change outcomes. In particular, attention should be paid to the emotional and covert aspects of change (Marshak 2006). All conscious efforts to change culture should celebrate what is good about the past and present but reinforce the new ways of working. Culture change can reinforced/sustained through:

- Reward
- Policies
- Symbols
- Feedback
- Communication
- Education and development
- Recruitment and induction/acculturation

Shifting behaviours should be reinforced by formal messaging. For instance, to stimulate learning practice and create and sustain an openness to change, there should clear and consistent messages from the top about the big issues; people should be encouraged to read broadly and explore new ideas together. Embedding change involves carrying this logic throughout the system. A knowledge management process should be created that connects networks. Managers should be trained in the new management approaches. Performance management systems should be revised to reinforce learning and collaboration with real accountability. Financial rewards and career incentives should reinforce innovation and continuous improvement (McCann et al. 2009).

During the pandemic, many management teams became acutely aware of the importance of employee well-being, as many people suffered a worsening of their mental health. The challenge is how to maintain this focus on well-being beyond the pandemic so that it becomes core to the culture and part of the management agenda, not bundled into the People Plan, so that leaders talk about it, check, respond and resource keeping people well. One company used various vehicles for managers to hear the voices of people, to find out how they were feeling. Then a high-engagement ideation session exploring people's ideas about going back to work led to a range of suggestions which were incorporated into what was described as a 'weird social experiment' that is owned by management. The successful delivery of this experiment is being reflected in the changing the accountabilities of managers.

Case: building a customer-focused culture in Ford Retail UK

Ford Retail comprises a collection of car dealerships which, when the group first came together, had strong local identities but little in common with others. The CEO had plans to use Ford Retail's size and geographical coverage to break new ground. At the same time the group had a strategy for improvement, which put building a customer focused culture centre-stage. There was desire to do things differently, but people did not know how. A strongly led HR strategy was developed to bring the company together, with leadership development helping create a cultural transformation to focus on customer service rather than simply using traditional car sales tactics.

The HR director started by taking the group's board members off-site for two days to think about leadership – the values of the organisation they wanted to create and the behaviours that were acceptable. Twenty-five top managers in key roles below the board then took these and refined them into 30 leadership behaviours, which were in turn cascaded down to all 300 Ford Retail managers in a two-day programme. In each case, the managers and directors attending these off-site events first took part in a 360 degrees assessment. This was intended to give them some understanding of their own management styles, something that had not happened before in Ford Retail. Management styles in car industry are traditionally directive and for some this process appeared threatening initially. However, the process helped people see for the first time a blueprint for change, a vision.

Further work on leadership followed, including coaching training for all managers, and a programme aimed at developing greater accountability, by challenging any behaviour that did not meet expectations. A joint programme with managers from the John Lewis Partnership involved managers from the two firms learning from each other and acting as mentors to each other.

Alongside the leadership work, a cultural shift got underway to give greater focus on the customer. A strategy called 'Moments of Truth' (MoT) used the Sears' employee-customer profit chain to instil the idea that if the company treats its people well, they will get things right for the customer more often. Every employee attended a workshop, preceded by a half-day briefing. 45% of the workforce took up the additional opportunity of working toward an occupational qualification in customer service.

The HR team used good HR management information to track key performance indicators and improved benchmarking by setting up a forum for HR practitioners in the car industry which meets to share information and experience. All these initiatives have led to significantly improved employee engagement, together with reduced staff turnover and a strong customer-centric culture has developed with the firm winning multiple awards for customer service (Syedain 2012).

Reflective activity

- If you were in the HR director's shoes, what would be your next focus to ensure the culture shift was fully embedded?

CONCLUSION

Organisational culture is increasingly acknowledged as a key component of strategic effectiveness. We have discussed how getting to grips with culture can be difficult. Schein defined culture as an entity which is nearly impossible to measure, study or change. Organisational culture is not completely 'homogeneous' but is quite specific to a given organisation. Moreover no organisation adopts a single type of culture; complex organisations might have multiple sub-cultures that overlap and disagree with each other (Williams et al. 1993: 23). Handy illustrated the fact that employees who are successful in an organisation with a particular culture, may not be so in another.

Changing the organisation's culture can be an emotional process for employees and trust between employees and management is crucial to implementing the change successfully. The culture change process should be communicated to employees openly and they should become involved and must be kept up to date with the progress. The important role senior management plays in the management of organisational culture change cannot be overstated. Managers must lead by example and should accept that some resistance to change is a normal part of the change process and manage it accordingly. To embed culture change, reward systems in particular should be revised to encourage behaviour that is in line with the desired culture and penalise behaviour that which is not. Changing the culture of an organisation is a complex process and will not happen overnight but is necessary to ensure a thriving future for the organisation in a volatile context.

In the next chapter, we shall look at both organisation design and development in the context of organisational agility.

Reflective activity: addressing common culture challenges

How would you address the following two scenarios that are common challenges facing HR/OD teams?

A. How might OD/HR help create a culture of alignment and engagement?
B. How might HR/OD help create a culture of innovation, entrepreneurship and resource fluidity?

Suggestions:

A. How might OD/HR help create a culture of alignment and engagement?
   - Build a better alignment between strategy and culture by developing clear purpose, strategy and priorities and mapping these against both current and desired cultures
   - Coach leaders on how to communicate consistently and personally with the workforce
   - Engage the whole organisation in strategic thinking and planning
   - Build a more high-performing cross-organisational interface (based upon pursuit of excellence)
   - Deliberately build a richly diverse culture by seeking, hiring and developing employees from personally and professionally diverse backgrounds
   - Sharpen the clarity around performance and accountability (team and individual)

- Consistently check culture metrics such as employee engagement, customer outlines and performance indicators. In this way, HR leaders can make sure the culture strategy stays on track
- Ensure opportunity for voice, equity and co-creation as well as growth and learning
- Focus on both the customer and the staff experience; use feedback from both to target improvement
- Support line managers in building worthwhile tasks and jobs and the skills to coach their teams
- Develop leaders who can energise, motivate and deliver the values
- Adjust reward systems to reflect customer focus and the new strategic direction

B. How might HR/OD help create a culture of innovation, entrepreneurship and resource fluidity?

A company culture must always look to the future. This means embracing innovation. Employees at all levels need to feel the freedom to posit ideas for consideration. And those ideas need to be thoroughly discussed and evaluated.

- Foster entrepreneurship and innovation through bounded (strategically aligned) autonomy at department/business unit/team level
- Look at ways to encourage collaboration between teams of employees. This reinforces the idea that everyone is part of a much larger team
- Encourage transparency; that way everyone knows the important information and can take ownership of what's happening. Employees who are proud to work for their employers ultimately take more ownership in the company's destiny. They will be more engaged and will pour more energy into ensuring success than the average employee.
- Help to develop and embed a sense of a 'one organisation' (joined up) approach to problems and opportunities
- Influence the top team to develop behaviours and processes that can shift resources quickly to new strategic priorities (an antidote to silos) and that also lead quickly to stopping things that are not working
- Influence and develop an approach and process that can simultaneously focus upon cost reduction, process and service improvement and revenue enhancement
- Identify the blocks to innovation and entrepreneurship and obtain top team commitment to act upon these
- Provide freedom to fail by protecting groups that are experimenting to find a way to the future
- Ensure employees receive regular feedback on performance and recognition
- Align reward systems to ensure individual, team and organisational performance are rewarded.
- Develop line managers to support and coach their teams.

REFERENCES

Adler. (2008). *International Dimensions of Organizational Behaviour*, 5th Edition. Mason, Ohio: South Western Cengage.

Allen, K.E. and Cherrey, C. (2000). *Systematic Leadership: Enriching Meaning in Our Work*. Lanham, MD: University Press of America.

Arnold, J. (2005). *Work Psychology: Understanding Human Behaviour in the Workplace*, 4th Edition. London: Prentice Hall Financial Times.

Axelrod, R.H. (2010). *Terms of Engagement: Changing the Way We Change Organizations.* New York: Penguin, Random House.

Barrett, R. (1992). *Building a Values-Driven Organization.* New York: The Free Press, pp. 44–45.

Bartunek, J.M. (1987). First-order, second-order, and third-order change and organization development interventions: A cognitive approach. *The Journal of Applied Behavioral Science,* 23(4), 483–500.

Beer, M. and Huse, E.F. (1972). A systems approach to organization development. *Journal of Applied Behavioral Science,* 8(1), 79–101, January.

Chitkara, P. and Davidson, V. (2013). *Shifting to a digital culture.* Booz and Company. https://www2.cio.com.au/author/2147447231/pankaj-chitkara-and-varyadavidson/articles

Brown, A.D. (1998). *Organizational Culture,* 2nd Edition. London: Pitman.

Bushe, G.R. and Marshak, R.J. (2016). The dialogic mindset: Leading emergent change in a complex world. *Organization Development Journal,* 34(1), 37–65.

Bushe, G.R. and Marshak, R.J. (2014). The dialogic mindset in organization development. *Research in Organizational Change and Development,* 22, 86.

Bushe, G.R. and Marshak, R.J. (2009). Revisioning organization development: Diagnostic and dialogic premises and patterns of practice. *The Journal of Applied Behavioral Science,* 45, 348–368.

Burke, W.W. (2011). A perspective on the field of organization development and change: The Zeigarnik effect. *Journal of Applied Behavioral Science,* 47, 143–167.

Cameron, K.S and Quinn, R.E. (2011). *Diagnosing and Changing Organizational Culture Based on the Competing Values Framework,* 3rd Edition. San Francisco: Jossey Bass.

Cheung-Judge, M.Y. and Holbeche, L. (2021). *Organization Development: A Practitioner's Guide for OD and HR,* 3rd Edition. London: Kogan Page.

Cooperrider, D.L. and Whitney, D. (2005). *Appreciative Inquiry: A Positive Revolution in Change.* San Francisco: Berrett-Koehler Publishers.

Couto, V., Mourkogiannis, N. and Neilson, G. (2007). Culture change: Calling on philosophers and engineers. *Strategy + Business Magazine* (Booz Allan), June.

Cummings, T.G. and Worley, C.G. (2014). *Organization Development and Change,* 10th Edition. Cincinnati, Ohio: South-Western College Pub.

Davis, S. (1984). *Managing Corporate Culture.* Cambridge, MA: Ballinger.

Deal, T.E. and Kennedy, A.A. (2000). *Corporate Cultures: The Rites and Rituals of Corporate Life.* New York: Basic Books.

Denison, D.R. (1996). What is the difference between organizational culture and organizational climate? A native's point of view on a decade of paradigm wars. *Academy of Management Review,* 21, 619–654.

Devine, M. (1999). *A Mergers Checklist.* Horsham: Roffey Park Management Institute.

Francesco, A.M. and Gold, B.A. (2005). *Organizational Behavior,* 2nd Edition. New York: Pearson.

French, W.L. and Bell, C.H. (1999). *Organization Development: Behavioral Science Interventions for Organization Improvement,* 6th Edition. New York: Pearson.

Goffee, R. and Jones, G. (1996). What holds the modern company together. *Harvard Business Review,* 74, 133–148.

Hall, E. (1966). *The Hidden Dimension.* Garden City, NY: Doubleday.

Hampden-Turner, C. and Trompenaars, A. (1993). *The Seven Cultures of Capitalism.* London: Doubleday Currency.

Hampden-Turner, C. and Trompenaars, A. (1997). *Riding the Waves of Culture: Understanding Diversity in Global Business,* 2nd Edition. London: Nicolas Brealey Publishing.

Handy, C. (1993). *Understanding Organizations,* 4th Edition. London: Penguin Books Ltd.

Harrison, R. (1993). *Diagnosing Organizational Culture: Trainer's Manual.* Amsterdam: Pfeiffer.

Harrison, R. (1972). Understanding your organisations character. *Harvard Business Review,* 50(3), 119–128.

Harrison, R. and Stokes, H. (1992). *Diagnosing Organization Culture.* Amsterdam: Pfeiffer.

Hawk, E.J. 1995. Culture and rewards. *Personnel Journal,* 74(23), 30–31.

Henson, R. (2002). Culture and the workforce, in K. Beaman (ed.), *Boundaryless HR: Human Capital Management in the Global Economy*. Austin, TX: Rector Duncan Associates, pp. 121–141.

Heron, J. and Reason, P. (2006). The practice of co-operative inquiry: Research 'with' rather than 'on' people', in P. Reason and H. Bradbury (eds.), *Handbook of Action Research*. London: Sage Publications, pp. 144–154.

Hofstede, G. (1991). *Cultures and Organizations: Software of the Mind*. London: McGraw-Hill.

Hofstede, G. and Minkov, M. (2010). Long-/short-term orientation: New perspectives. *Asia Pacific Business Review*, 16(4), 493–504.

Holbeche, L.S. (2006). *Understanding Change; Theory, Implementation and Success*. Oxford, UK: Butterworth-Heinemann.

Holt, D.H. (1990). *Management*. Englewood Cliffs, NJ: Prentice Hall.

Jacobs, R.W. (1997). *Real Time Strategic Change: How to Involve an Entire Organization in Fast and Far-Reaching Change*. San Francisco: Berrett-Koehler Publishers.

Johnson, G. and Scholes, K. (1993). *Exploring Corporate Strategy - Text and Cases*. Hemel Hempstead: Prentice-Hall.

Khandelwal, K. and Mohendra, N. (2010). Espoused organizational values, vision, and corporate social responsibility: Does it matter to organizational members? *Vikalpa: The Journal for Decision Makers*, 35(3), 19–36.

Kotter, J.P. (1995). Leading change: Why transformation efforts fail. *Harvard Business Review*, 73(2), 59–67.

Margulies, N. (1972). Myth & magic in OD. *Business Horizons*, 15(4): 77–82.

Marshak, R.J. (2006). *Covert Processes at Work: Managing the Five Hidden Dimensions of Organizational Change*. Berrett-Koehler Publishers.

Martins, N. and Martins, E. (2003). Organisational culture, in S.P. Robbins, A. Odendaal and G. Roodt (eds.), *Organisational Behaviour: Global and South African Perspectives*. Cape Town: Pearson Education South Africa, pp. 379–400.

McCann, J., Selskey, J. and Lee, J. (2009). Building agility, resilience and performance in turbulent environments. *People & Strategy*, 32(3), 44.

Mintzberg, H. and Waters, J.A. (1985). Of strategies deliberate and emergent. *Strategic Management Journal*, 6, 257–272.

Morgan, G. (1997). *Images of Organization*. California: Sage

O'Reilly, C. (1989). Corporations, culture, and commitment: Motivation and social control in organisations. *California Management Review*, 31(4), 9–25.

Pascale, R., Milleman, M. and Gioja, L. (2001). *Surfing the Edge of Chaos*. New York: Crown Business.

Peters, T.J. and Waterman, R.H. (1982). *In Search of Excellence: Lessons from America's Best-Run Companies*. New York: Warner Books, pp. 223–24, 286.

Pfeffer, J. (2005). Producing sustainable competitive advantage through the effective management of people. *Academy of Management Perspectives*, 19(4), 65–106.

Posner, B.Z., Kouzes, J. M. and Schmidt, W. H. (1985). Shared values make a difference. *Human Resource Management*, 24, 293–309.

Robbins, S.P. and Judge, T.A. (2010). *Essentials of Organizational Behaviour*, 10th Edition. Boston, MA: Pearson.

Rodgers, C. (2007). *Informal Coalitions: Mastering the Hidden Dynamics of Organizational Change*. Basingstoke: Palgrave Macmillan.

Roehrig, M., Schwendenwein, J. and Bushe, G.R. (2015). Amplifying change: A 3-phase approach to model, nurture and embed ideas for change, in G.R. Bushe and R.J. Marshak (eds.), *Dialogic Organization Development*. Oakland, CA: Berrett-Koehler, pp. 325–348.

Sathe, V. (1985). *Culture and Related Corporate Realities*. Homewood, IL: Richard D. Irwin.

Schein, E. and Schein, P. (2017). *Organizational Culture and Climate*, 5th Edition. New Jersey: Wiley.

Schein, E.H. (2016a). *Organizational Culture and Leadership*, 5th Edition. San Francisco, CA: Jossey-Bass.

Schein, E.H. (2016b). *Humble Consulting: How to Provide Real Help Faster*. Berrett-Koehler Publishers.

Schein, E.H. (1978). The role of the consultant: Content expert or process facilitator? *The Personnel and Guidance Journal*, 56(6), 339–343.

Schuh, A.M. and Miller, G. (2006). Maybe Wilson was right: Espoused values and their relationship to enacted values. *International Journal of Public Administration*, 29(9), 719–741.

Sergiovanni, J.E. and Corbally, T.J. (1984). *Leadership and Organizational Culture: New Perspectives on Administrative Theory and Practice*. Champaign, IL: University of Illinois Press.

Shaw, P. (2002). *Changing Conversations in Organizations: A Complexity Approach to Change*. London: Routledge.

Stacey, R. (2015). Understanding organizations as complex responsive processes of relating, in G.R. Bushe and R.J. Marshak (eds), *Dialogic Organization Development*. Oakland, CA: Berrett-Koehler, pp. 151–175.

Stanford, N. (2010). *Organisation Culture: Getting It Right*. London: Economist.

Syedain, H. (2012). New Focus, peoplemanagement.co.uk, July.

Trice, H.M. and Beyer, J.M. (1993). *The Cultures of Work Organizations*. Englewood Cliffs, NJ: Prentice Hall.

Varney, S. (2019). An OD-based framework for advancing change practice. *e-Organisations & People*, 26(1), 63–69.

Whitt, E.J. (1993). Making the familiar strange: Discovering culture, in G.D. Kuh (ed.), *Cultural Perspectives in Student Affairs Work*. Washington, DC: American College Personnel Association.

Williamson, A. et al. (1993). *Changing Culture: New Organisational Approaches*, 2nd Edition. London, UK: Institute of Personnel Management.

16

Designing sustainably agile and resilient organisations

> *In its scale, scope and complexity the transformation of the Fourth Industrial Revolution will be unlike anything humankind has experienced before.*
>
> Klaus Schwab, founder of the World Economic Forum (2016)

So powerful are the various forces for change in the business environment, in particular instability and technological advances, that for business leaders the main challenge is to manage at the rapid speed of business the context dictates. Executives are struggling to design firms that can drive performance efficiently in the short term and be flexible enough to sustain performance over the long term. Traditional organisation design concepts and approaches appear out of date. The 'new normal' requires organisations to develop their

DOI: 10.4324/9781003219996-19

adaptive capability – or agility – if they are to survive and thrive. An agile organisation is one that can intelligently and proactively seize opportunities and react to threats and make timely, effective, sustainable changes that generate competitive advantage and give them leverage in their marketplace or ecosystem (Holbeche 2018). To create an agile organisational culture that enables agility, mindsets and routines may need to shift.

CHAPTER OVERVIEW

In this chapter we shall bring together concepts of organisation design and development that we have discussed in the last two chapters and apply them in the context of organisational agility. We shall explore some of the challenges of scaling up agility, especially in traditional organisations, and the typical cultural, behavioural and 'mindset' shifts required for agility. We shall consider an adaptive approach to organisation design and development that may offer a way forward for organisations wishing to become more agile. We shall cover:

- A new era: challenging paradigms
- Resilience
- Scaling up agility
- Developing agile leadership
- Agile approaches to change

LEARNING OBJECTIVES

- Explore how organisational agility and resilience can be designed and developed
- Consider how HR/OD can help overcome some of the barriers to organisational agility and resilience

INTRODUCTION: THE NEED FOR AGILITY

Organisations across a broad spectrum must respond to a constant array of change mandates - new business strategy development and deployment, merger and acquisition integration, work re-design, community organising and more. Organisational change is becoming broad-based, system-wide, fast-paced and with unpredictable outcomes because of constant turbulence. To remain successful organisations must be able to change in a way that creates a new alignment when the environment changes. As Professor Ed Lawler III (2014) puts it, superior performance is only possible when there is a high degree of fit between the requirements of the environment and the capabilities of the firm. In today's increasingly turbulent environments, this fit is temporary at best.

Not surprisingly, many leaders aspire for their organisation to become agile – able to adapt what they do, the strategy they pursue, the structures they put in place, how they work and the tools they use, the products they sell, the channels they use – just to keep abreast of the way the marketplace is developing. Adaptability implies ability to change; however, as is still commonly reported, around 70% of organisational change initiatives are thought to fail, perhaps because conventional change management tends to work in a linear, planned way, as we discussed in the last few chapters, and many organisations have not yet learned how to change at whole system level.

Various studies suggest that organisations typically struggle to become more agile (Economist Intelligence Unit 2009; CIPD 2014). Scaling up for agility remains difficult, not least because the quest for agility calls into question organisational paradigms of various kinds – strategy, change management, the nature of leadership and organisational design. Poor change implementation and inappropriate operating models can be major barriers to agility. However, some of the main factors inhibiting organisational agility are cultural, and the behaviour of senior leaders in particular has a strong influence on how agile their organisations can become.

Talking of organisational agility ...

Words such as 'agile', 'adaptive' and 'flexible' are used almost interchangeably to describe the aspired-for organisational agility. Agile was originally an approach devised by software development teams to help them systematically achieve both disciplined execution and continuous innovation, something that was previously difficult to accomplish in twentieth-century hierarchical bureaucracy (Denning 2013). Since the Agile Manifesto of 2001, the concept of 'agility' has become a management breakthrough, systematised into a set of management practices and values that involve a radically different kind of management with a different goal (delighting the customer), a different role for managers (enabling self-organising teams), a different way of coordinating work (dynamic linking), different values (customer-centricity, experimentation, innovation, continuous improvement) and different communications (radical transparency and lateral conversations).

Widening the concept further, an agile organisation is both adaptive and proactive – it can intelligently and proactively seize opportunities and react to threats and make timely, effective, sustainable changes that generate competitive advantage and give them some leverage in the marketplace or in their ecosystem (Holbeche 2018). This goes beyond simply having an agile IT or R&D department – a whole system capability is required if organisations are to rapidly adapt, interact effectively with the client environment and thrive in such a fast-changing context.

McKinsey (De Smet et al. 2015) defines six building blocks for creating a high-performing agile digital enterprise as follows:

- Strategy and innovation – focus on future value and drive, fuelled by experimentation
- The customer decision journey – deep analysis and ethnographic research to understand how and why customers make decisions
- Process automation – reinvented processes and customer journeys through automation and process innovation
- Organisation – agile, flexible and collaborative processes and capabilities that follow strategy
- Technology – two-speed IT that enables rapid development of customer-facing programs while evolving core systems designed for stability and high-quality data management more slowly
- Data and analytics – usable and relevant customer analytics tied to goals and strategies

Since agility is strategic, operational, behavioural and dynamic, to create an agile organisation, a single fix is not enough. If we attempt to change behaviours within the human system simply by adopting Agile tools and techniques, but without the underlying philosophy and principles of Agile, we are doomed to disappointment. Change works then only at superficial level – the underlying 'informal' human system may continue to operate much as before. So companies need systemic change capability and a humanistic perspective to design to develop an organisation that is continuously adaptive, able to change its ways of working in order to deliver optimum value to customers and to do so at a moment's notice.

A NEW ERA – CHALLENGING PARADIGMS

The quest for organisational agility significantly challenges accepted paradigms of what it means to be, and to run, an organisation.

Notions of strategy

In a seemingly stable, linear world, companies believed they could predict what might happen in the environment based on previous trends, develop a strategy, mobilise resources and cost-effectively deliver what the market wanted. In her book *The End of Competitive Advantage*, Rita Gunther McGrath (2012) argues that today no firm can maintain competitive advantage; instead, a firm must embrace customer-based innovation and look to develop multiple value propositions (or 'transient advantages') that continuously evolve with changing customer needs. Leaders must simultaneously seek opportunities for growth at the edge and redesign their offers while also ensuring they are not squandering value within the core. This requires strategic ambidexterity (O'Reilly and Tushman 2004) to both exploit existing value propositions and explore new opportunities. This also means balancing dynamism with the need for the stability that comes from hierarchies. For Unilever this balance is achieved by putting the customer at the heart of strategy.

Customer centricity and organisational agility

Agility also challenges assumptions about in whose name value is created. 'The digital revolution has given birth to an interconnected world that binds customers, employees, managers, and systems together in a network of unprecedented complexity and opportunity. Making sense of those connections and building value requires a new interdisciplinary model of work that is redefining how companies succeed today'.

Indeed, for agility, the challenge is to re-think the goal of the entire organisation in terms of adding value to customers faster and generating the innovations required to meet changing customer needs and achieve customer loyalty. 'The shift necessitates a fundamental change in our prevailing theory of the firm... The current theory holds that the singular goal of the corporation should be shareholder value maximization. Instead, companies should place customers at the center of the firm and focus on delighting them, while earning an acceptable return for shareholders' (Martin 2011).

Customer-centricity begins with the belief that there is only one customer: the person who buys or uses your organisation's services or products. However, the 'one-customer' message can be controversial and confronting in top-down 'internal-customer' cultures that reinforce structural divides, creating an unhelpful dynamic which distracts attention from the cross-business alignment required for collaboration in service of the end-customer needs, drawing workers into inward-facing roles. As Galbraith (2005, p. 6) notes, 'The product–centric mind-set is an entrenched one and does not relinquish dominance easily'.

Customer-centricity requires at least an enabling form of bureaucracy since it focuses the whole organisation 'outside-in' on meeting the needs of the users or purchasers of its products or services. Galbraith (2005) describes this as a fundamental paradigm shift – away from the bias of the organisation and its agents to operate on the side of the seller (i.e. itself) in any transaction, and towards operating on the side of the buyer. At the core of customer-centricity are four key principles:

- deep insight into the customer experience
- a focus on building relationships with customers to improve this experience and enhance loyalty (and thus retention)
- the gathering, interpretation and active use of customer data
- organisational agility to respond to insights from data and embed change.

Technology is a critical enabler of these principles, and itself acts as a stimulus for change. Agile organisations are obsessed with the purpose of providing customer value through knowledge and innovation; they are prepared to put in significant effort to establish exactly what their customers want, and then put those things first. This puts organisational culture and people – their talents, values and behaviours, ability to continuously deliver customer value – at the centre of a value creation system (Rebours and Pauly 2016).

To deliver customer value businesses must be organised in new ways. Agile organisations are dynamically networked – to enable them to proactively gather knowledge and use expertise as fast and as well as possible to produce customer value. Agile businesses are ruthlessly decisive – and must be prepared to dispose of parts of organisation that do not contribute to the goal of providing optimum value. They embrace experimentation and generate new learning, often co-creating new products with customers. This approach to organising people and work embeds many HR and OD best practices – including self-management, transparency, direct and frank communication, individual change agency, and team-based decision-making – and places these qualities firmly in service of better outcomes for the end-user, for business and for employee engagement.

During the pandemic customer-centricity was a major feature of successful business responses, according to McKinsey (Callaghan et al. 2021). Consumer companies adopted a common set of agile practices – such as focusing intently on understanding their customers' shifting and evolving needs and providing positive customer experiences during and after points of sale. Top teams focused on a handful of clear objectives tied to enterprise strategy according to what drives the most value to consumers. Working teams came up with key initiatives to accomplish these objectives. To enable faster decision making, many teams deployed daily (often virtual) 'stand-up' meetings with clear goals to enable rapid issue resolution. Consumer companies also made headway in adopting more agile mindsets and behaviours. Many leaders adopted a mindset in which they strived to serve their employees, instead of the other way around; they focused on setting the vision for the organisation while also empowering and enabling teams to succeed. As they look toward the new normal, companies should look for ways to make these benefits last and build on them.

The empowered employee

The customer experience is defined by what marketeers call 'moments of truth': those interactions where customer loyalty is earned or trust is lost, moments which are defined by the customer and are judged by an emotional, rather than rational response. This places an emphasis on the skills of frontline employees to deliver the experience customers want. Some organisations attempt to control the service environment through closely defined roles, with employees following prescribed scripts and protocols. However this does not usually deliver the flexibility and authenticity customers have come to expect, often results in delays and obstacles to problem-solving when the customer agent has to act beyond their authority and is also demotivating for employees. When the managerial culture tends to overcontrol, or protocols require multiple authority levels, or where there is an overarching backdrop narrative which talks about risk over trust – then individual employee belief in empowerment is undermined.

Recognising this, many organisations now look for ways to 'empower' staff, particularly those in customer-facing roles. The implicit working assumption is that empowerment means sharing knowledge, skills and decision-making authority with employees so that they can benefit customers by solving service problems without having to escalate to senior decision makers and using their own best judgment to exceed customer expectations. On the one hand, empowerment is an employee mindset or perception which combines three core factors (Peccei and Rosenthal 2001, p. 839):

- A **motivating belief** in the intrinsic value and importance of the organisation's customer-service ethos
- A sense of **competence** in their role and ability to deal with problems
- A feeling of **autonomy** to exercise control and take self-determined decisions

On the other hand, empowerment is possible when organisations ensure that people have the skills, information and authority they need to make their own decisions. Examples of initiatives to encourage employee autonomy and support frontline empowerment are plentiful, for example giving contact centre employees budgetary freedom to offer discounts or surprise customers with loyalty gifts, or to offer compensation.

Need for a systemic approach

Creating the conditions for an empowered mindset requires a systemic approach towards a more enabling form of bureaucracy, combining a number of HR practices such as individual training and development to communicate the *what* and *why* of customer-centric values, and related positive behaviours and practices. The cultural shift to Agile means embracing not just a range of methodologies and work practices but also the values that were described in the Agile Manifesto. In an agile organisational culture, experimentation is considered the norm and integrated learning is valued. This enables people to see and solve key problems real-time in adaptive and coherent ways, through incorporating lean and agile principles, within a systemic framework. Thus empowerment, continuous improvement, radical transparency, knowledge-sharing and different communications (horizontal conversations) become key cultural features of agility and customer-centricity.

Redesign of structures, jobs and processes (see ING's example below) may be necessary to allow for the use of discretion and decision-making, and to minimise the handoffs or escalations required. Leadership development should teach the importance of modelling customer-centric values in action, the practice of trusting, non-directive management, and coaching to build and embed competence. Goal-setting, reward and recognition initiatives need to reinforce and incentivise pro-customer practices, and communicate values.

Given this context, it can be useful to move towards empowerment one step at a time – again using a test-and-learn approach. One company provided mobile phones to frontline contact centre employees, way beneath the job grade normally allowed, so they could call customers directly to take feedback and improve service problems. Against the resistance of other staff and managers who saw this as a risk, the HR leader positioned this as an experiment, established trackable success measures, and engaged resistant leaders in steering the project. Sure enough the metrics proved a positive impact on customers and business outcomes, and there were unexpected improvements in employee engagement (Moody 2017).

Dynamic capabilities

Fast-changing markets require the ability to reconfigure the firm's asset structure and accomplish the necessary internal and external transformation. For agility, the key capability is change-ability. To keep pace with, or outpace, their environment, adaptive organisations require dynamic capabilities, or '...*the ability to sense and seize new opportunities, and to reconfigure and protect knowledge assets to achieve sustained competitive advantage*' (Teece 2009). The capability to change depends on the ability to scan the environment, evaluate markets, and quickly accomplish reconfiguration and transformation ahead of the competition.

This means that a firm must 'sense' the *external* opportunity, collect and filter available information, build a 'paradigm' of industry/market evolution and then *internally* seize the opportunity. So the firm must recognise the need for change and reorganise if necessary to achieve new combinations. Organisations and their employees need the capability to learn quickly and to build strategic assets. For Worley and Lawler (2010)

> Agility is a dynamic organization design capability that can sense the need for change from both internal and external sources, carry out those changes routinely, and sustain above-average performance. The final characteristic – sustained above-average performance – is the sine qua non of agility.

To develop dynamic capabilities certain routines must be practised:

- *Anticipating* – rigorous review of changing customer needs and industry forces, and an evaluation of likely scenarios
- *Sensing* – looking for trends and monitoring the environment to sense changes, especially anomalies in customer behaviour, competitor moves, supply chain shifts; then rapidly communicating these perceptions to decision makers who formulate responses
- *Responding* – experimenting and testing new products or services respond to market shifts faster than competitors do
- *Adapting* – building capacity to implement changes, reworking and testing some business processes and structures to fit the new environment

Leaders in particular need to be able to anticipate, sense what's going on, analyse trends and strategise to synchronise three systems: the market, the organisation and the human (Heifetz et al. 2009). According to Snowden and Boone's Cynefin framework (2007), when faced with a normal or complicated environment, leaders must first sense, analyse, categorise and then respond. But when the world moves to complex and chaotic environments, companies must instead first probe or act, then analyse and adjust. Leaders must help their organisations become more comfortable looking out at an uncertain horizon and learning how to sense and act in real time. They must encourage testing, prototyping and then enable the organisation to implement in a way that helps it move faster than the system in which it operates. This also means that:

- Everyone needs to be externally aware and 'savvy' – willing to voice views and possible solutions and allowed to act on such knowledge
- Products and services need to be innovated continuously – to meet the demands of the marketplace and customers
- Costs must be kept low on all fronts – tapping into the goodwill of local staff to implement cost cutting initiatives while also innovating
- Organisations need to be flexible and adaptable – in structures, roles and responsibilities
- Key staff need to be able and willing to continuously develop themselves – flexible sourcing and multi-skilling
- Organisations should aim for high engagement with staff – to tap into the discretionary effort of all their knowledge workers
- Organisational culture needs to be highly adaptable, agile, organic, with everyone, regardless of rank, acting like they are the owner of the business with commitment to invest and contribute to its success

However, as we have previously discussed, shifting from one way of operating to another is not easy. Many companies set up incubators or centres of excellence during the early stages of a digital transformation to cultivate capabilities. To be successful, however, these capabilities need to be integrated into the main business. This is where HR/OD must play a leading role because agility stalls when the human aspects of change are neglected or misunderstood; when the real motivation for change is cost-cutting rather than innovation; when the practices of Agile are introduced without the underlying philosophy and principles, such as empowerment, experimentation and iteration. This is compounded when there is an unbalanced employment relationship in which the employee takes all the risk. When such factors are in play, the informal or 'shadow' system will usually seek to actively undermine new approaches. While emphasising agility-building interventions such as systems thinking or creative problem-solving workshops at an individual or team level may be helpful, if efforts to build agility across the organisation are weak, then individual and team-level efforts ultimately may fail.

RESILIENCE

Agile methodologies and values alone are no panacea. While agility implies speed and flexibility of response, not all external context variables can be foreseen or easily responded to, nor are they within the full control of organisations. The corollary to agility from an organisational point of view is resilience, which is the capacity for anticipating and responding, when faced with fast/and or disruptive change that cannot be avoided. This is the ability to bounce back from difficulty, absorb, learn and even re-invent if required. Resilience at organisational level is about those factors that render an organisation robust – anticipation, shared purpose, involvement, renewal, learning, leveraging knowledge, networks, employee engagement and well-being, the appropriate balance of risk-taking and risk management and the ability to cope with ambiguity. People want to share their ideas because their work is meaningful, and they feel valued. Without resilience and the learning cushion it provides, organisations' adaptive capacity can become overburdened and agility risks becoming 'fragility'. So, both agility and resilience need to be developed in tandem.

Resiliently agile organisations have a learning mindset in the mainstream business and underlying customer-centric, lean and agile processes and routines that drive innovation. The organisation usually sets the boundaries within which ideas are needed. In such a culture employee voice is valued; there is respect for everybody's contribution and intelligence is regarded as a collective asset. There are mechanisms whereby people can feed in their ideas and learning from mistakes is encouraged. After all, if you are experimenting, and trying to implement fast, you are bound to make some mistakes. Agile firms regard innovative initiatives as learning opportunities where people can learn fast and adapt without fear of blame or punishment (McGrath and Gourlay 2013). This is what Edmondson (2008) referred to as 'execution as learning', for instance, when people learn from redesigning work processes and feel psychologically 'safe' to do so.

To reinforce psychological safety and deliberately create a solution-focused culture of innovation one organisation encourages staff to 'fail fast' and 'fix it quick'. At Google offices a wall sign reads 'Fail Well', reinforcing the importance of learning and experimentation; 'failure' is reframed as 'just not there yet'. Google encourages managers to cultivate their own growth mindset by helping them understand how skills, characteristics and abilities are not pre-set but can be developed.

Resiliently agile organisations are paradoxical. They require a degree of stability – provided for instance by shared routines, processes and standards – for change to occur. These paradoxes are evident in tensions between bureaucratic requirements and agility; between collaboration and control; between economic and social pressures. From a complexity perspective, competing value sets can co-exist. It is possible (and desirable) to have simple and complex things simultaneously, such as repeated patterns which provide familiarity versus ideas from the edge which result in innovation.

Reconciling paradox requires dialogue and leaders who embrace ambidexterity. Pisano (2019) points out that leaders can encourage empowerment and accountability by publicly holding themselves accountable, even when that creates personal risks. Shared purpose provides the 'glue' which holds the organisation together as it changes (Springett 2005) and a holding structure for such conversations to take place. So, it's important that people feel they have a stake in the organisation, that they align to the purpose of the organisation; that they genuinely find their work meaningful and want to deliver. Thus, a resiliently agile organisational culture is change-able and facilitates change within the context the situation the organisation faces.

AGILITY AND ORGANISATION DESIGN

Organisational agility is now filtering into mainstream organisation design, challenging every accepted design paradigm. Attempting to scale up agility in a conventional bureaucratic organisation has implications for all aspects of Galbraith's Star model™ – including culture, structures, processes and related people attitudes and behaviours that allow for the delivery of its products and services. Since for agility an organisation's design must be adaptive, traditional command and control structures and processes no longer mobilise people flexibly enough.

As we have discussed, organisation design is about far more than structures. Galbraith's STAR™ model highlights the dynamic design system interlinkages between the organisation's environment, strategy, structure, processes, technology and its people that in turn produce the culture, behaviour and performance required. So a resiliently agile organisation has a change-able culture and structure and an outside-in orientation that maximises customer value. This requires a reinvention of management roles, practices, values and communications (Denning 2013). It also requires a strong employment relationship so that people are willing and able to give of their best in a sustainable way and they feel that both they, and the organisation, win through their efforts.

The need to scale up

Digital start-ups are able to work at the pace required from the outset; they have a flexible culture and mindset; there is empowerment and distributed accountability, access to relevant technology, greater connectivity and democratisation of information that results in high productivity. Digital organisations work with other organisational partners in their ecosystems. However, truly agile businesses, beyond their start-up phase, are the exception rather than the rule. There is a growing consensus amongst major consultancies such as McKinsey and Accenture (Timmermans and Schulman 2017; De Smet et al. 2018), that for maximum value and to achieve innovation and increased customer satisfaction, agility in traditional organisations needs to be scaled up beyond R+D units or specialist technology functions to become a whole organisation capability.

The biggest challenge is experimentation. How can established organisations achieve innovation while not changing the core business? Agile is a poor fit with the hierarchical bureaucracy common in large US organisations. Many organisations aiming to deliver agile customer-centric strategies are constrained by structures whose boundaries keep separate the skills, information, insights and authority which together combine in new products and services. Siloed thinking and action slow down responsiveness and create obstacles to change. Particularly in large, traditional, product-focused organisations, the challenge of becoming 'customer-centric' and innovative can feel unwieldy and complex.

Change-able organisational forms

Worley and Lawler (2010) suggest that organisations must break away from traditional design assumptions, proposing instead a built-to-change model, which means that each design element or feature must be constructed with flexibility in mind, and then aligned dynamically to enable both adaptability and sustained high levels of performance. The basic features of this framework are a robust strategy, an adaptable organisation design, shared leadership and identity, and value-creating capabilities. Adaptable designs have structures, processes, people, and rewards that capture value from a flexible intent and support the idea that the implementation and re-implementation of a robust strategy is a continuous and normal process. So bureaucratic structures and processes should be redesigned and simplified to provide a clear line of sight to purpose, coordination and employee empowerment. This way, organisations can become 'ambidextrous'.

Agile organisation designs are defined by their features – maximum surface area structures, a collection of high-performing teams, each with a clear purpose and the skills it needs, transparent information and decision-making processes, and flexible talent and reward systems. If you have a growth mindset you can make moves towards agility a multi-step process. By introducing cross-function teaming, people can start to figure out what works. This makes adopting the experimental practices of more agile firms – work where you can, test and learn, fail fast and move forward – easier and all the more effective to apply.

New organisational forms are emerging, often in tech-led environments, which offer frameworks to learn from and adapt for use. Increasing numbers of organisations attempt to scale up agility by embracing innovative organisation types (e.g. 'ambidextrous' organisations like Microsoft that is set up to both explore new developments and exploit existing products and markets); 'collaborative' organisations such as P&G; 'self-organised' firms with distributed structures and emergent behaviour such as Wikipedia, Google; 'learning' organisations such as Toyota. Worley and Lawler (2010) cite American Express Co. and Nike Inc. as organisations that have increased their surface area by adopting front-back, process-based or network structures that increase the centrality of customer demands or make a variety of stakeholder demands more salient.

What such organisational archetypes have in common is less structure and hierarchy – those things that inhibit flexibility – than traditional organisations. That does not mean they don't have any, it's just that they are more organic. Flexibility is built in – to structures, teams, systems, processes, roles and people's mindsets. They are typified by flattish structures, teamwork, lateral integrator roles and managers who coach and facilitate performance more than 'manage' it. There is a whole process focus with clear customer value and the 'right' levels of authority, accountability and empowerment. With strong cross-organisational collaboration, teams can leverage knowledge and resource across units.

In the early days of agility, these teams – often called squads, combining developers, testers, data analysts, customer-journey specialists and user-interface designers – played their biggest roles in the digital corners of companies. But similar models have now been launched across the whole spectrum of business. For instance, Dutch-based ING Bank, once a traditional banking structure, with a conventional hierarchy, has transformed the way it works in recent years and is now regarded not just as a case study for change, but as a learning destination for other businesses wishing to find out about agility in action. They chose this route because changing customer expectations driven by the digital revolution meant that a radically new approach to organisation was needed to make speed, innovation and excellent customer outcomes possible.

ING has embraced agile principles to create new structures, roles and team formations (*tribes, squads* and *chapters*), which formalise customer-centricity and shared learning and minimise hindering bureaucracy (Mahadevan 2017). ING learned from pioneering organisations in other industries, such as Spotify, that have found that better business results occur when people are entrusted, enabled and empowered to deliver customer results without constant checks and balances within the hierarchy. Becoming agile by adopting iterative approaches to change, high levels of training, self-managing teams and empowerment appears more suited to ING's business environment and its new business model. As the COO, one of the change architects, describes it, '*We gave up traditional hierarchy, formal meetings, over-engineering, detailed planning, and excessive "input steering" in exchange for empowered teams, informal networks, and "output steering"'* (Mahadevan 2017).

Adopting such post-bureaucratic designs may require work to shift leadership and employee perspectives, behaviours, attitudes and skills; role descriptions and that broader area of *culture*, in four important areas: organisation and work design; employee empowerment; leadership development and performance management.

Of course, governance too needs to evolve, shifting from Taylorist notions of authority and decision-making. In agile organisations, individuals and teams at all levels have high-stakes work, clear responsibilities and goals and are held accountable for results. A change-able organisation balances innovation and risk management; keeps bureaucracy to the minimum; has appropriate checks and balances (Adler and Borys 1996; Saparito and Coombs 2013). As one commentator [1] put it, 'On the one hand it's about the role of rules. There are some rules which enable people to be on the same page – for instance playing a sport. Then there are those rules which inhibit people's ability to be adaptive. Any group of people is inherently adaptive, but the moment that rules replace principles, you inhibit agility. So organisations aiming for agility should operate less by rules and be more principles-based. Then when people understand what's happening in the moment, they know what to do to translate principles into actions'.

Paradigm shift: from structure to culture

Besides changing the structure, agile organisations must change their processes and people models. So Agility requires a shift away from the traditional paradigm of organisational change being about structure (i.e. a top-down focus on hierarchy and systems) to culture-focused change (i.e. a focus on networks and behaviour). Agile organisations operate as multi-faceted networks with permeable boundaries that can flex to adapt to the situation the firm finds itself in. So as companies reorganise workflow and teams around customer-driven process and measures, organisation charts shift away from traditional hierarchies to become network and relationship maps. Within a networked system, these interconnections become ever more complex and lack the clarity often superficially provided by conventional linear or cause-effect approaches to strategic management. And the more complex the environment, the more difficult it can become for traditional hierarchical organisations to adapt and become 'agile'.

Success in shifting towards agility, customer-centricity and innovation depends upon building (or acquiring) new capabilities, redesigning roles and organisation, simplifying unnecessary 'red tape' and embedding new cultural norms to create a workforce which recognises the importance of the customer and feels both capable and empowered to support them and to innovate. Collaboration and the ability to work across boundaries, including the customer interface, are essential means of getting work done.

The question is, can you move from being a conventional organisation to an adaptive one? If so, how? Can you design in agility or is becoming agile a more 'organic' process? So strong are the drivers of agility that it's tempting to reach for off the shelf solutions. However, your approach should depend on your situation: for instance, according to whether you are in slower or faster markets. If you are in an industry where things are relatively stable but complex, your response would be different from if your situation is unstable and complex, what Stacey (1996) refers to as the 'zone of complexity'.

The challenges of scaling up

Research (EIU 2009; PMI 2012) suggests that many firms struggle to scale up agility beyond a few discrete departments that may have adopted agile methodologies. As a result, they fail to even keep abreast of developments, let alone lead in their fields. Each company will have its own unique set of barriers to agility and organisational behaviours are predetermined by patterns of basic assumption.

In established firms the existing organisational culture will typically exert pressure for maintaining the status quo. So, in organisations with top-down command and control leadership, rigid, bureaucratic structures, inflexible cultural routines and complicated governance, there is little scope for experimentation and learning. Such organisations are usually rife with politics and leaders of 'siloed' structures usually resist notions of cross-boundary collaboration or the sharing of ideas and resources. Rational problem-solving and decision-making are undercut by ambiguity.

Other barriers to agility include lack of capacity to act – arising from poor decision-making, implementation and investment; lack of synchronisation that leads to frustration, gaps and/or duplication; narrow jobs and worker disempowerment. Attempting to develop agility in such contexts is likely to lead to conflicts over the development process, business process and between people.

Mindset shifts required

A more significant barrier to agility is fixed mindsets at any level. For leaders schooled in conventional management practices, dealing with ambiguity and complexity in today's business environment is not easy. Many leaders struggle to deal with the inevitable paradoxes and ambiguities of complexity, such as how to balance the long and short term; whether it is possible to be both business-driven and people-driven; how to achieve both innovation/enterprise and compliance. These are often false dichotomies since both are necessary. In any case, there are limits to how much senior managers realistically can be in tune with what's happening across the organisation or at the front-line of the customer experience. Corporate leaders can accelerate agile transformation by adopting new learning and leadership models. They need to be open to learning from the front-line.

Since agility requires experimentation and the short term to be informed by the longer-term view, a significant shift in leadership thinking and approach may be needed (Snowden and Boone 2007). Executives trained in the linear thinking typical of strategic management and focused mostly on short-term share value, may be risk-averse and resistant to experiments or investment without 'proof' that agility will pay-off. Attempts to maximise short-term shareholder value – for instance through aggressive cost-cutting that leads to the loss of valuable talent or reduces the quality of the customer experience – risk undermining agility and significantly reducing shareholder value in the medium term. Leaders must learn how to lead by influence rather than dictate and take the longer-term view.

Agile shifts the traditional role of line managers from being controllers of the work process to that of enablers and coaches of individuals and self-organising teams. For the people doing the work the shift is from reporting to managers to deliver a set of objectives to having the responsibility and accountability for working iteratively as part of a self-organising team without direct intervention from any manager. Suddenly, everyone is accountable. For many managers and workers, these are very significant changes for which they are often ill-prepared. Failing to provide relevant development can leave people floundering and relying on practices that may have worked in a previous era but are ill-suited to Agile.

Paradigm shift: bureaucratic versus agile values

Agile values can seem counter-cultural in a functionally siloed hierarchical organisation with short-termist attitudes, 'blame cultures', entrenched and inflexible governance, bureaucratic processes that leave little space for new routines that support experimentation and innovation. In Agile, the customer is the primary focus of the work; cross-functional work is constantly adapting, with teams and roles switching as needed and processes adjusted continuously to reflect the current situation. Bureaucratic requirements are therefore secondary. In a strong bureaucracy the requirements of the work and the customer are secondary to those of bureaucracy.

Agile thrives on transparency, whereas hierarchical bureaucracy is notoriously political and non-transparent as a means of control; finding out what's really going depends on access to informal networks. Agile works on the principle of empowerment and trust in the competence of workers since its iterative ways of working provide a transparent framework for workers to show what they can do. Hierarchical bureaucracy typically assumes worker incompetence and expects mediocre performance that must be managed to be acceptable. When Agile is introduced into such a context, miscommunication and misunderstandings are likely, leading to lack of trust and risk-aversion.

Moreover if Agile is introduced as merely another business process and firms continue to operate according to big plans and heavy processes, there is a risk of mixed messages and the potential gains of Agile, with its incremental and iterative ways of working, are limited. Unless the various practices associated with Agile are underpinned by Agile values and the mindset that they represent, they quickly become just another set of mechanistic operational measures designed to save costs.

Stress and 'resistance'

As people and machines increasingly work together to achieve more sophisticated, accurate and cost-effective delivery, the consequences for workers may be mixed, for some resulting in augmented, more interesting and value-adding work while others experience greater demands, threats of obsolescence, hollowed out jobs and insecurity. In such circumstances, employee resistance is both understandable and to be expected. If the human aspects of change are neglected when Agile is introduced, or if there is an unbalanced employment relationship in which employees carry all the risk, engagement and trust are unlikely.

Many people find coping with ongoing change and the challenges of uncertainty, insecurity, and constant hard work debilitating and in some contexts levels of employee stress are high. The cost of workplace stress can be significant, with just some of the consequences including disengagement, (Robertson and Cooper 2010; HSE 2016), job burnout (Maslach et al. 2001), presenteeism (Johns 2010) and sickness absence. Personal resilience and well-being can be built or fortified when people feel a strong sense of connection with their organisation through shared purpose, are involved in the changes that affect them, are engaged and connected through networks, and when there is a genuine management focus on employee engagement and well-being.

SCALING UP AGILITY

So is it possible to build a more agile, resilient culture in a conventional organisation? This is more of an art than a science. Organisations aiming for agility must reinvent themselves around customer journeys, products, and other axes of value creation. Senior leaders in particular need to lead the way by modelling more agile thinking and practice.

In my model of resiliently agile ways of working (Figure 16.1), adaptive organisations are able to manage complexity by developing new routines (strategising, implementing, linking and providing the context for people to thrive) that require people to look at things with new eyes and to think, act and work in new ways. It's important to see these routines as ongoing processes rather than one-offs.

Strategising

A key Agile design principle is that people should understand and be involved in the success of the business. In times of exponential change, in organisations of any size, conventional strategy works only up to a point before it hits a brick wall – of silos, anxiety and so on – that slows down the implementation stage. In a resiliently agile organisation, the strategy-making process shifts – from being decided by a few and handed down to those who must implement – to *strategising* which involves people from across the organisation who are going to implement and who are in tune with what's happening on the ground so that they understand and own the direction of travel. Staff may not necessarily be involved in deciding *why* we are doing what we are doing, nor the *what* – more likely the *how*. Strategising allows organisations to stay on course against a changing backdrop in successfully delivering the innovative outcomes they want to achieve. Strategising allows

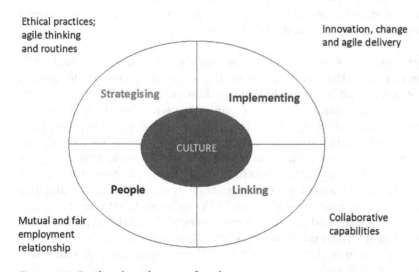

Figure 16.1 Resiliently agile ways of working.

organisations to deliver short-term objectives against longer-term aims. It also readies the organisation for change.

The most effective leaders are good at perceiving what needs to happen – by drawing accurate and incisive conclusions from trends and data from the external environment and using these in their decision-making. They proactively scan and monitor the business environment, anticipate changes, encourage participation, provide relevant resources and learn from what happens. This involves continuously looking outside, anticipating changes, feeding customer and employee intelligence into decision-making. It's about asking, 'what needs to be different? What will it take to unleash the power we have?'

Top management still needs to set a broad direction, be clear and consistent about purpose and ambition – what the organisation is looking to achieve and why – and should also engage others in finding solutions. The task of senior leaders is to establish an aspirational purpose, develop a widely shared strategy and manage the climate and commitment to execution (Worley et al. 2014) for instance by encouraging a number of 'quick wins', bringing together a variety of different people.

To develop new ways of looking at things and enhance their judgement against the broader business context, senior leaders should find opportunities to expose themselves and others to new thinking and practice – for instance through visits to other organisations, or through scenario planning ('...an exploration of alternative futures which opens up our thinking to current drivers and trends which may have an impact on the future', Sayers 2010). Such methods can help teams avoid becoming trapped by outdated mental models, or emotional biases, and make better sense of the external world. Some of the major challenges identified may be about creating and implementing new business models, designing new organisational and management approaches, innovating, continually improving organisational capabilities, remedying weaknesses, addressing risks, accelerating and sustaining culture change. Typically, this means prioritising just a few key areas of focus, such as:

- What are the key capabilities we need to build for the future?
- What are the opportunities for growth in the changing scenario?
- What's our vision and direction for the whole organisation and how can everyone understand the role they play in delivering these?

There are many interventions coming from the field of organisation development (OD), group and team dynamics that can help the strategy-making process. Senior leaders should regularly take at least half a day (off-site) to do some long-term planning, challenge their assumptions, consider what the organisation will need to do differently and think about the scope of change necessary. They must engage the right people – the executive team and others who influence groups and the culture. They should use focus groups to hear the views of the workforce. They should broaden the scope of strategy making to involve exploratory thinking across industries, marketplaces, time zones and so on. They must accept the messy parts of strategy formulation and give the process time to become more refined so that links can be made between the organisational plan, business goals and measurable objectives, and individual performance plans. They should ensure there is a clear course of action and communicate the strategy across the organisation so that everyone knows their part in delivery, with measurement in alignment with goals.

Viewing changing organisational systems through the lens of complexity, emerging principles for strategising include:

- build a 'good enough' vision;
- tune your place to the 'edge of chaos';
- when life is far from certain, lead from the edge with clockware and swarmware in tandem; uncover and work with paradox and tension;
- listen to the shadow system;
- go for multiple actions at the fringes: let direction arise.

Involving the people who will implement strategy in developing it should avoid the usual 'strategic implementation gap'. It's about creating strategy and new sources of value through generative relations; growing complex systems through 'chunking'; building a space, a community to concentrate, co-create and learn together. Paul Tolchinsky uses the jazz band analogy to illustrate the notion of empowerment. Different individual jazz players, skilled in their own right, willingly use their skills to best effect to create wonderful music together, often extemporising, often featuring solo slots, spontaneously going with where the energy is to produce wonderful music for, and with, their audience.

For many senior leaders, strategising involves a significant shift in their preferred way of operating. It requires top leaders to move away from command-and-control styles to broad direction-setting and capability-building. They must manage the tension between the urgency of financial stress and the pace of innovation while deliberately encouraging organisational learning. Leaders must become digitally literate and gain an understanding of how AI, analytics, blockchain and so on work, so that they can have intelligent conversations with data scientists. They must think critically about the impact of technology on the business and develop a vision based on an understanding of how technology and customer needs will change. They may find that making the organisation competitive in the digital age may or may not involve technology.

Moreover, for speed and customer responsiveness, leadership and accountability should be exercised at all levels, with empowered decision-making and continuous feedback. A strong customer focus provides parameters within which employees can proactively and productively use their ideas. Top leaders must establish the principle and practice of taking decisions as close to the action as possible and create the context for others to make good decisions. Part of this is about democratising data by making it available to everyone. This is not so much 'knowledge is power' as 'knowledge shared is power'. Employees need to know the importance of using the right procedures to ensure that data is accurate and reliable and kept up to date. Both management and the workforce need to become externally focused with an outside-in mindset that starts with the customer, works backwards to meet their needs, feeds in market intelligence and ideas and delivers creatively on market opportunities. When information is transparently shared, people are better able to make effective decisions. This increases the pace and quality of decision-making, as well as more widely encouraging the willingness to experiment, learn and adapt as part of the process. The traditional strategy process is thus upended: instead of sense, analyse, categorise and then respond, complexity requires leaders to probe or act, then analyse and adjust (Snowden and Boone 2007).

On the other hand, Kelly (1995), in his 'informed approach to complexity', argues that context should determine the approach taken. He uses the machine metaphor of 'clockware' to describe the conventional management operations whose function is rational, planned, standardised, repeatable, controlled and measured. The living system metaphor of 'swarmware' refers to those management processes that explore new possibilities through experimentation, trials, autonomy, freedom, intuition and working at the edge of knowledge and experience. Sometimes the mechanical, planful approaches are most appropriate – for instance where there are high levels of certainty and agreement among agents. Conversely, when the world is far from certain and there is little agreement (edge of chaos), swarmware, with its adaptability and openness to new learning, is more appropriate. The art is to balance data and intuition, planning and action, according to the situation.

Implementing

More agile ways of working are transforming the way businesses work. Agility involves a range of operational methodologies that capitalise on advances in technology together with leading-edge practices and work processes focused on customer loyalty and underpinned by principles of innovation management. However agile implementation is not simply about the use of Agile manufacturing techniques such as SCRUM, Lean and Just-in-Time, two-week Sprints, team-based iterative project working. Without the underpinning Agile values, the practices soon become discredited and ineffective.

To take advantage of the technology you have to build the organisational capability to respond to what it can do. It's as much about culture and behavioural change as it is about process change. Toyota for instance has long had a culture of continuous change and improvement that is inculcated into every worker through principles such as kaizen, team work and respect for others. It is easy for workflows to operate, communication around tasks is fluid and silos are minimal. These principles lead to efficient and fluid execution of daily work.

During periods of turbulence, change-able companies perform significantly better than their counterparts. Agile teams have proved particularly resilient during the pandemic crisis since by using agile techniques, such as re-examining their priorities reflected in objectives and key results (OKRs), they have speeded up their work and adapted to new industry challenges. Their methodologies lend themselves well to a virtual environment.

To scale up agility, companies need systemic change capability, flexible models, processes and routines supportive of ongoing innovation, new ways of managing teams and measuring value in terms of innovation and customer loyalty. These include incentives for implementation, information transparency, six sigma and knowledge management initiatives, formal after-action reviews, change skills embedded in line managers and flexible resource allocation. As in the case of ING, scaling up to hundreds of teams, these teams must all have the same direction, or confusion will reign. At an enterprise level, the connective tissue – the stable backbone – consists, for example, of a 90-day priority-setting and resourcing cycle, a common culture, 'chapters' (that is, groupings of employees with similar functional backgrounds) responsible for consistency, a longer-term vision for specific functional areas, and agile leadership. In scaling up agility, these enterprise-level elements of unity become extremely important.

Agile implementation is essentially about innovation as well as production. Disciplined innovation is a key feature, as described by Collins and Mortenson (2011) when considering the breakthroughs achieved by Apple, such as the iPod: '...the great task, rarely achieved, is to blend creative intensity with relentless discipline so as to amplify the creativity rather than destroy it. When you marry operating excellence with innovation, you multiply the value of your creativity'. These authors also observe that, rather than the development of the iPod being a single step breakthrough story, it was instead 'a multi-step iterative process based more upon empirical validation than visionary genius'. This requires testing and exploration, a knowledge-rich context for innovation where information is shared, learning and diversity are encouraged, creativity and knowledge-sharing are rewarded. To encourage innovation, it is vital to build some 'slack' into the system. Though from an efficiency perspective slack is sometimes considered wasteful, in practice it provides vital breathing space for ideas to flourish.

As we discussed in Chapter 9, in line with today's increasingly VUCA environment, GE, a company that has long been admired for the way its approach to strategy, portfolio and talent interconnect in a strong HR culture, aims to become an agile organisation. GE is strategically restructuring to focus on its high tech and industrial businesses, emphasising things like power and water infrastructure, advanced jet turbines and imaging equipment. With respect to operations, GE had previously proselytised and practised Six Sigma, a manufacturing quality protocol that aims to systematically boost quality control and eliminate mistakes. However GE found that Six Sigma made experimentation difficult, so developed instead its FastWorks platform for creating products and bringing them to market. This encourages an entrepreneurial mindset and borrows from Agile techniques to a large extent. There's a focus on rapid and frequent experimentation, learning from the market, only funding projects that prove themselves, and requires an acceptance and willingness to move on from failures.

For a strategy of growth through innovation, GE needs employees to collaborate, make quick and effective business decisions, and provide customers with superior products and services. GE routinely benchmarks itself against other organisations that are also involved with real-time project management. Learning from this resulted in a change to one of the primary operating processes, along with changes to operating principles – from growth to simplification. This has meant reducing bureaucracy and 'siloes', introducing new ways of working, getting close to the customer, producing better, faster outcomes for customers. Managers need to cultivate empowered, collaborative, cross-functional teams, in which accountability is collective.

Linking

No organisation is an island since it delivers its services along a value chain across organisational boundaries to its customers. In Agile, those boundaries are transcended more fluidly, with customers themselves increasingly involved in co-creating the services they require. This requires linking capability – high degrees of collaboration and new attitudes towards the nature of risk, including how to build meaningfully trusting relationships across organisational and other boundaries. For instance, one international engineering company found that many of its clients' needs were changing due to technical advance and political uncertainty. Its engineers learned to work in partnership with clients to co-create breakthrough technical and scientific solutions to client problems in a way that overcame barriers and inherently created mutual learning, loyalty and trust – and repeat business.

The convergence of computer networking and telecommunications technologies is making it possible for groups of companies to achieve powerful competitive advantages by coordinating geographically and institutionally distributed capabilities into a single virtual company or process. Hagel et al. (2010) argue that, whereas the twentieth century had been about scalable efficiency, the new economy is about scalable collaboration. For instance P&G is constantly scouting the world for new ideas. Its 'Connect and Develop' website connects technology entrepreneurs throughout the world. The company's aim is to take an 'outside-in' approach to research and development, with 50% of ideas coming from outside of P&G. While lean manufacturing worked well amongst a narrow set of business partners which are tightly aligned, scalable collaboration can embrace many thousands of participants. Thus linking capability – the ability to build and maintain collaborative and productive working relationships – across boundaries of time, geography, organisation – is an essential element of agile working. At the same time, human strengths should be emphasised in the collaborative relationship between people and between people and machines.

People practices

In knowledge and service-intensive types of work, people are still the main means of production. Agile workers are multi-skilled, flexible people with 'change-able' mindsets, skills and behaviours. Useful attributes include adaptability, resilience, tolerance for complexity, resourcefulness, entrepreneurial mindset, but more important is learning agility and continuous learning, including a willingness to unlearn unhelpful old habits. People need to be aware of their strengths and weaknesses so dynamic feedback loops for the individual, groups and the organisation as a whole are essential.

What will digital do to company staffing strategies – will they need new or fewer people? What skills and specialist knowledge will be needed, what processes and systems, ways of working? Agility in how you think, behave and network is needed to bridge the gaps. Once you have worked out what development is required, experiential on-the-job learning is needed since by testing and trying, feedback and iterations, people learn how to work in new ways. One company helped employees along this transition journey towards agile ways of working by offering learning (e.g. self-paced learning on a digital platform as well as full-day virtual boot camps) and applying it in practice by together defining the purposes and objectives of the new teams. High-quality videos and all-company virtual meetings conveyed some of the key messages in an effective way and built a sense of community. Exposing people to diversity of thought is important. Another company encourages regular 'Learning out loud' one-hour sessions where networks from across the organisation's boundaries focus on a specific topic. One such topic was 'how can the workforce become future-ready?'

Of course, people's willingness to adapt is not just about what they think or know; it's also about how they feel. Their knowledge of their organisations, their aspirations, fears and views about how they are treated all influence how well they adjust to new ways of working. So change leaders must maintain disciplined attention and attempt to regulate employee distress. Protecting leadership voices from below (Heifetz and Laurie 2001) may require conflict to be surfaced. To build employee resilience it is also important to focus on energy – a key component of 'work engagement' (Salanova et al. 2005; Scott 2019). Energy practices relate to beliefs, meaning and purpose, commitment, self-confidence and visions and are highly correlated to job satisfaction.

High commitment SHRM plays its part in the quest for greater agility. One people practice that has been under sustained pressure for reform is the performance management process. While many software companies have led the way in sweeping away traditional performance management practices that appear to constrain agility, innovation and employee engagement, many large and well-established organisations have struggled to re-imagine this aspect of what is often a hindering form of bureaucracy.

A key plank of the emerging agile culture in GE is its new performance development approach described in Chapter 9. Previously, under the leadership of Jack Welch in 1980s and 1990s GE promoted the 'rank and yank' style of performance management which linked development opportunities and high rewards for those amongst the top 10% of performers while those in the bottom 10% left the organisation. Today the focus is on building the workforce the organisation needs to be competitive both today and in the future. The shift in how GE employees think about and track their performance mirrors these broader transitions at the company to substantially simplify its business and mirrors a broader business strategy shift towards innovation. Accordingly, GE has adopted a more experimental, feedback-rich approach to developing strategy, culture, ways of working and approach to talent – reviewing and adopting what works and learning from what does not.

Agile organisations embrace nimble talent management systems. A growth mindset is needed so agile organisations recruit individuals who are quick learners and like change. They use rigorous onboarding processes to make sure people understand the culture and are willing to work with the culture to drive experimentation through to innovation. For instance all new entrants to Harley Davidson understand that digital permeates all aspects of organisation – it is team-based, empowered, decision-making is pushed down the levels and continuous learning is expected of all employees.

Research suggests that people tend to be engaged and perform at their best when they experience a positive psychological contract (or 'deal') (Guest 2007; Holbeche and Matthews 2012). Human resource practices that emphasise the genuine mutuality and fairness of that 'deal' – a win-win for employee and organisation – are key aspects of a positive working environment. Agile organisations use a variety of reward practices, including bonuses, stock, team and individualised pay, and opportunities for growth, that encourage both current performance and change.

HR can help deliver these and other key elements of a fair deal – such as empowerment, supportive management; shared purpose around which communities can align; policies to enhance work-life balance and staff well-being; ensuring that 'front-line' staff have the relevant professional and skills development to prepare them for a digital future; providing career opportunities; advancing the equality and diversity agendas and developing engaging leaders and managers. These all go a long way towards creating agile, high engagement cultures.

Developing agile leadership

The role of leaders – in setting the tone and providing sponsorship, moving from command and control to direction-setting and capability-building – is crucial to agility. If leaders espouse agility and customer-centric strategies, yet what they actually pay to attention to sends quite a different message, that will be picked up by both customers and employees. And although one visionary leader may promote a customer-centric strategy, if this is undermined by resistance or a lack of energy from their peers who prefer to cling on to their hierarchical domains and bureaucratic controls, not only will this delay and disrupt progress, but it may destroy it entirely. How financial results are reported and the extent to which customers are mentioned are good indicators of what is really valued. ING Bank now presents its results in the context of its customer strategy.

Building a connected and aligned leadership cadre is always critical to organisational goal success, but arguably even more so when the agile transformation requires a mindset shift away from an internally focused product-orientation to an externally focused customer-centric perspective; away from leadership styles reflective of a bureaucratic 'golden cage' to leadership for agility and empowerment. As Peccei and Rosenthal (2001) point out, management attention and role-modelling are among the most important influencers of pro-customer employee empowerment. Organisations committed to customer-centricity, such as ING, recognise this and give it conscious focus: '*We have spent an enormous amount of energy and leadership time trying to role model the sort of behavior—ownership, empowerment, customer centricity—that is appropriate in an agile culture*' (ING leader, Mahadevan 2017).

For Bushe (2017), leaders need open minds. Management teams need to review their own behavioural preferences, how these translate into visible behaviour and attitudes, and how well this aligns with leading the change. Given their visibility and influence, senior leaders in particular need to fearlessly role model agile behaviours, such as real collaboration, which for some may be counter their natural dispositions. Leaders need to embrace disruption, build shared value, dare to be open, especially towards risk (IBM Institute for Business Value 2013). Leaders must be transparent – sharing results from failed experiments as well as from successes so that the organisation can continue to learn.

But to be trusted, leaders must be values-based. Increasingly the models of leadership applied to agility are those that place people and transparency centre-stage while acknowledging complexity - variations on authentic, values-based leadership such as servant leadership (Greenleaf 1998; Hall 2007) with its critical capabilities of listening, empathy, healing, awareness, persuasion, conceptualisation, foresight, stewardship, commitment to the growth of people, building community. While the journey to agility has to start with themselves, some leaders may need support, for instance from coaches or mentors, in developing the qualities attributed to agile leaders.

Agility requires high degrees of interdependence, openness and collaboration. In many cultures, speaking up to a person of higher status is taboo. Schein (2016a) argues that, to enable openness, it is the duty of senior leaders to use the art of 'humble inquiry' to create a climate in which lower-level employees feel safe to bring up issues. Radjou and Kaipa (2013) suggest that leaders must leave their comfort zones and have the humility and capacity for introspection that is indispensable to learning agility and to building the organisation's change capability.

Google endorses the idea that vulnerability is a strong leadership quality. Google encourages its managers to recognise and understand their personal values then use them to advantage to create a stronger sense of purpose and meaning in their work. Part of the Google experience includes encouraging new managers to acknowledge and share their transition stories and struggles with one another. This is based on the belief that being open and honest about their challenges paves the way for benefiting from the advice and experiences of others, as well as from the reassurance of knowing they are not alone.

Leaders must learn to strike the right balance between loose and tight control (Weick 1976) according to the situation. They may need help in doing this, so HR among others can work with leaders to help them transition from traditional to agile management. They can ensure top team sign-up and clarity about purpose and ambition, increase leaders' sense-making skills and ability to deal with complexity by exposing them to new thinking and practice, for instance through scenario planning or visits to other organisations who are trying new approaches. They can emphasise the importance of leaders acting as role models of values, provide feedback and use story-telling to reach leaders at a deeper emotional level to persuade them to stop acting like a traditional boss and embrace agile leadership. They can help shape a leadership culture by recruiting and developing future leaders who already demonstrate agility and accountability. They can build shared leadership by getting people involved in redesigning values, cultural practices and HR policies.

CHANGE APPROACHES

To be congruent, agility requires a transformation process that recognises complexity and resembles the desired end-state. As we discussed in Chapter 14, a conventional design process is usually top-down, working to a plan, often almost secretive in nature. These programmatic, diagnostic, pre-planned change processes that reflect the 'clinical system' or 'mechanical' metaphor of improvement can become potential obstacles to agility. Tell-tale signs of linear thinking - such as 'closing gaps', task-centric deliverables, initiatives, toolkits, tell, sell, achieving 'buy-in', roll-outs, dealing with 'resistance', project organisation, detailed plans, milestones, controlling, audits and data – fit poorly with Agile aspirations for empowerment, engagement, iteration, collaboration and customer focus.

So today, rather than working to a fixed, 'best practice' design idea, it's more about empowering the organisation to evolve its own structures in a timely way. So, if a formal redesign is necessary, for instance when incorporating new technologies and methodologies, agile approaches to change should be adopted that are more suited to complexity and the exponential pace. These tend to be people-centric, transition-driven and about 'emergence', 'unleashing potential', reflecting the 'social mobilisation' or 'living system' metaphor of improvement.

Similarly, as discussed in the last chapter, more recent approaches to organisational development place an emphasis on change occurring through conversations (Wheatley 2017). These dialogic group and whole system methods are inquiry-based, self-organised and underpinned by systemic thinking. They enable people to notice the dynamic patterns of which they are part, with agility residing in the small changes. These methods encourage the various parts of the system to connect with itself, bring people together from across organisational boundaries engaging multiple perspectives to address issues, co-create solutions and build meaningful communication, creativity and engagement. In virtual asynchronous settings flexible software tools can capture conversational pieces between teams around a particular theme or project. 'Fishbowl' conversations between two experts can be recorded and made available. Galbraith's 4D's framework – Dialogue, Decisions, Design and Development – offers a useful sequence to apply.

The short-term must be informed by a long-term perspective starting with purpose and customer value as the desired (measurable) outcome of the transformation. Change can start anywhere; thus 'bottom-up' or 'pull' approaches to change are often more effective than 'top-down' or 'push' approaches. Thus change is not done 'to' but 'with' people to build ownership of the change. Rather than change projects being rigidly controlled, and information held by only a few on a 'need to know' basis, the emphasis should be on transparency and openness – a 'need to share'; there should be dialogue, active involvement and stakeholder participation.

Change becomes 'business as usual' and involves organising work around motivated individuals, valuing interactions over process and tools, balancing trade-offs between quantity, quality and pace in achieving results. 'Good enough' and 'what works' supplants the goal of perfection. Change ripples through networks and communities, with big picture story-telling, inspired action and prototypes embodying the new, producing changes in mindsets and behaviour as learning from the emerging picture takes place. As a result, different energies emerge in the system. Sources: Cheung-Judge and Holbeche, 2021, Roehrig, 2015 and others.

Whole scale change, one of many large-scale interventions, provides a method for engaging people through dialogue in a way that builds critical mass, ownership and commitment for what the organisation needs to do. It combines systems theory and practical methodology and involves bringing the complexity of the whole system into the same room, whether the scale is large or small, working on multiple things at the same time. It's about embracing all the various elements – strategies, processes, technologies and staff – in a way that allows for simultaneity and allows people to work out how all these things fit together. When people are engaged in an exploration and discovery process, they can better shift their own paradigm. As with action research and action learning, the assumption is that 'if I know what you know, and you know what I know, together we're smarter, and together we can find a common solution'. It's about connecting people, creating communities for action and also forming fast-response teams around issues. Thus whole system change is a method to rapidly engage the whole system in meeting organisational agility and flexibility demands and shatters the old paradigm about how long it takes organisations to change.

Such approaches can co-exist alongside formal, structured approaches to organisation design. For instance, various parts of the workforce can be involved in establishing criteria for what a new design must achieve, process mapping to establish the strengths and weaknesses of the current set-up and building an informal lateral foundation. Lateral linking mechanisms (such as disciplines collaborating with each other to act as knowledge hubs) can also be informed by staff stakeholders, not only top management. Staff can identify mechanisms to learn and improve performance over time; for instance exploring which core elements of work process can be standardised to free up space for needed innovation. Decisions about management positions, formal overlay teams and whether the organisation is going to operate as a matrix, or a line organisation, are usually made by senior management.

Holistic scorecards of the right performance metrics that link to the vision should be developed to ensure that high standards are embedded and lived as an institutional value.

On the one hand, Agile values and a special focus on the customer should become the critical measures by which change is conceived, implemented and evaluated. On the other, Lawler (2014) argues that for sustainable high performance, the way value is measured should accord with 'quadruple bottom line' performance standards – how organisations perform financially, environmentally, socially and in how they treat their employees. This is achieved by constant concern for the common good, balancing the needs of different stakeholders including employees, aiming for sustainable and global value creation. A number of firms such as Wholefoods Market and Johnson and Johnson now measure their success in this way (Mackey and Sisodia 2013).

CULTURAL SHIFTS REQUIRED FOR AGILITY

As we discussed in the last chapter, culture change takes time, is not linear or 'programmable'; there needs to be collective acceptance of uncertainty, ambiguity, risk and setback. General principles suggest that while leaders set the climate and model the behaviours for individuals, teams and business units to follow, real change is rooted in performance and the job to be done. Culture change involves intellect and emotions, so opportunities should be found for people to try out new things and behave in new ways. It's about practising new behaviours, building confidence, not changing attitudes.

So how can leaders build a context conducive to agility?

Arguably by creating the conditions for change to emerge; where people can better connect and decide to work, learn and change together to produce outstanding customer outcomes; where people feel empowered to create the desired changes that deliver the outcomes the organisation wants. This means building a shared leadership culture, supported by genuinely two-way communications and agile values.

For example, one leading cereals manufacturer recognised the need to become more agile and innovative in product development and reaching new markets. It put together some cross-functional 'power teams' to explore possible new product and market solutions. The teams adopted a simple iterative process with a common vocabulary, with prioritised work programmes for each iteration. The results included a more focused range of new products and higher sales. One power team worked on the challenge of cultural transformation for agility and started by delivering an impactful leadership conference at which leaders at all levels had the chance to work through the implications of agile for their ways of operating. The result was an energised leadership cadre actively engaged in leading culture change.

All conscious efforts to change culture should celebrate what is good about the past and present but also reinforce the new ways of working. It's about communicating often and sincerely about the organisation's vision and values, making certain these are understood and truly hold meaning and value. And of course, culture change towards agility should be reinforced/sustained through new symbols as well as HR policies. Agility should permeate processes such as feedback, communication, education, coaching and development, recruitment and induction/acculturation. Performance management, reward and recognition systems and promotion opportunities should be revised to reinforce learning, engagement, feedback, teamwork, improvement, innovation and collaboration (with real accountability). Contracts and incentive structures must reflect this understanding as well (McCann et al. 2009). Managers should be trained in the new management approaches.

Bringing about a 'controlled' approach to 'emergent' culture change requires top-level commitment to agility and visibility – in setting the tone, active sponsorship and role modelling of the Agile values. If senior leaders are hopeful and hope-inspiring, this has a contagious effect on employee resilience (Norman et al. 2005). Deliberate role modelling and teaching of values by leaders and effective two-way communication are the essential ingredients. Future top leaders should be assessed for their learning agility – their tolerance of complexity, resourcefulness and resilience. If leaders have the learning agility and support needed to make that journey, they will influence others to do the same and will reap the rewards of an energised, agile and sustainably effective organisation. As Schein (2016a) points out: 'The bottom line for leaders is that if they do not become conscious of the cultures in which they are embedded, those cultures will manage them. Cultural understanding is desirable for all of us, but it is essential to leaders if they are to lead'.

Gaining true commitment to agility is not always easy. For instance, when the CEO of an international engineering company decided that his firm must aim for organisational agility, it was because he could see that technology would soon make many of the company's services obsolete. However his management team initially were not persuaded of the merits of becoming more agile – after all, the company was still successful at that point. Agile was not just a new business process, but rather would involve a fundamental transformation of the way work was managed, and power distributed, in the company. This was a very traditional, hierarchically structured business and the agile principles were counter-cultural.

To challenge their thinking the CEO organised a week-long 'Lock Down' for the management team during which the senior leaders met with external strategists and representatives of various innovative businesses. Most executives, but not all, were convinced of the need to go agile. One influential director refused to adopt the new, more inclusive methods of communicating. After a short while the CEO challenged this director to either adopt the practices or leave the organisation. The director chose to stay and as he started to see the benefits of agile, he became an enthusiastic advocate. Without strong executive commitment and drive the Agility imperative might have failed.

As stated earlier, an agile design principle is that everybody should be involved, understand and know clearly what their part in the success of the business is. The challenge then was to bring the wider organisation on board. The CEO was concerned that, despite the turbulent business context, intelligence was reaching engineers working on projects too slowly via the conventional top-down cascades of information. Consequently, the engineers saw no reason to change what they were doing. The CEO adapted the 'team of teams' approach pioneered by General Stanley McChrystal in Afghanistan in the mid-2000s. General Stanley McCrystal (2015) took the risk of making HQ information available to troops wherever they were behind enemy lines via mass phone conversations. In weekly 'cadence calls' people were able to feed back field intelligence live to the centre as well. At the time there was a fear that having these weekly calls could lead to the enemy getting access to this intelligence. General McCrystal took the view that 'hey, the enemy has the information anyway. We might as well let our troops have the information too'.

The CEO adapted this cadence call method as part of a suite of two-way methods of communication. This includes Yammer feeds to share customer and marketplace intelligence information, and solutions to problems, real-time, as widely as possible, bottom-up as well as top-down. The calls (and Yammer feed) helped everybody to be involved, hearing and sharing ideas, problem solving in real time. This ensures that people are empowered to act and puts a modern twist on the old adage that 'knowledge is power', becoming instead 'sharing knowledge is power'. The CEO recognised that total openness is a vital ingredient of Agile communication. While it's true that co-location is obviously ideal for Agile teams, when this is not possible, teams can use technology to maintain open and continuous communication.

Following the top team offsite 'Lock Down' to address some of the issues they needed to face, there was a series of 'sprints' of 100 days involving teams drawn from across the organisation to address the problems identified, come up with feasible solutions, try them out and start to implement them. The CEO set clear priorities and deadlines and held people responsible for meeting them. To avoid paralysis in decision making, work was carried out on streamlining and clarifying roles/responsibilities in the decision-making process. This helped create an action bias throughout the organisation, together with the ability to quickly deploy and then redeploy resources, talent and skills.

The CEO also recognised that new behaviours were needed to support the new objectives and that to 'unlearn' existing behavioural patterns there must be both a demand for new behaviour that builds on the desired values and an opportunity to practise it. The CEO put together a cross-organisational team to define eight high-level 'operating principles' (or values) that would introduce a new way of thinking, speaking and acting in the workplace for both managers and workers. The principles would act as behavioural 'guard rails' by which the organisation would hold itself accountable. To bring these principles to life a short series of 'sprints' (initially of 100 days) took place that led to a new behavioural social system and more dynamic structure.

Of course, embedding new practices takes time and the engineering company continues to build on what they have learned from other contexts and from their own experiments. It is recognised that, for sustainable agility, agile values are even more important than agile practices, and that an integrated approach is required rather than a series of ad hoc initiatives.

Reflective activity

- What were the mechanisms used by the CEO to embed new ways of working?
- How would you attempt to build alignment around agility within a management team?

CONCLUSION

So can you transform a conventional organisation into an adaptive one?

We have discussed how by putting together strategising, decision-making, culture and people who are committed to the direction you are heading towards, you start to build agility. If you engage people in the formal process of organisational redesign, you are more likely to create structures and processes that work, with people building capability as they learn new approaches. If you work assiduously to unblock barriers to agility, such as by simplifying previously overly complicated policies, more flexibility will be possible. If you use every opportunity to reinforce the new, and the reason why this is needed, and you learn from experiments, you can start to flexibly 'institutionalise' the new, which itself should be seen as a provisional prototype to be reviewed for effectiveness.

There are many legitimate areas for HR to use its expertise add value, and so the time is right for practitioners to embrace agility and customer-centricity, collaborate with colleagues from marketing, sales or other external facing functions which lead customer experience projects. To build workforce resilience and agility in a sustainable way, existing workers should be actively equipped for the digital future through continuous reskilling. And at the same time emphasising human strengths in the collaborative relationship between people and between people and machines.

Purpose around the customer provides the 'glue', which holds the organisation together as it transforms itself and is the core of an agile organisational culture. Perhaps the next stage is that proposed by Lawler (2014) who argues that the most effective organisations are enterprises that are sustained by solid financial performance, while improving the lives of people, the health of communities in which they live and the condition of the planet. These have the greatest capability of all to flexibly reconfigure both their organisation and work system designs.

Once you start to spread this understanding about who you are as an organisation, why you exist, how you want to be, that message spreads far beyond the boundaries of an organisation. You start improving things, not blindly following rules but asking deeper and more important questions. Indeed, lessons from system-wide change suggest that the organisation itself is the best laboratory for learning; that structural and interpersonal changes must complement and reinforce each other; that adult learning starts with behavioural change rather than cognitive change (Beer and Huse 1972).

By taking an integrated approach to implementing agility, there is less risk of agility becoming simply the latest management fad and more chance of delivering high value outcomes for delighted customers and other stakeholders. At the same time, HR will be equipping the organisation with the keys to sustainable success – resilience, motivation and adaptive capability fit for the twenty-first century. In the process, HR gets closer to the customer itself, improves its own practices, and increases its relevance and credibility.

REFERENCES

Adler, P.S. and Borys, B. (1996). Two types of bureaucracy: Enabling and coercive. *Administrative Science Quarterly*, 41(1), 61–89.

Anderson, K. and Kochan, F. (2012). *Examining relationships between enabling structures, academic optimism and student achievement.* Thesis for the degree of Doctor of Philosophy (PhD), Graduate Faculty of Auburn University.

Beer, M. and Huse, E.F. (1972). A systems approach to organization development. *Journal of Applied Behavioral Science*, January.

Bushe, G. (2017). Where organizational development thrives, *HR Magazine*, September 27. http://www.hrmagazine.co.uk/article-details/where-organizational-development-thrives

Callaghan, S. et al. (2021). *How consumer companies are adopting agility during the COVID-19 pandemic,* McKinsey & Company, February 12. https://www.mckinsey.com/industries/consumer-packaged-goods/our-insights/how-consumer-companies-are-adopting-agility-during-the-covid-19-pandemic?cid=other-eml-alt-mip-mck&hdpid=9a15c957-25d9-4a07-894c-c768793fb1bd&hctky=2592654&hlkid=102f200f390e4d698620c18e6b1912a5

Cheung-Judge, M-Y. and Holbeche, L.S. (2021). *Organization Development: A Practitioner's Guide for OD and HR*, 3rd Edition. London: Kogan Page.

CIPD. (2014). *HR getting smart about Agile Working,* London: CIPD. https://www.cipd.co.uk/knowledge/strategy/change/agile-working-report

Collins and Hansen, M.T. (2011). *Great by Choice: Uncertainty, Chaos, and Luck—Why Some Thrive Despite Them All.* New York: Random House Business.

Denning, S. (2013). Why Agile can be a game changer for managing continuous innovation in many industries. *Strategy & Leadership*, 41(2), 5–11. https://doi.org/10.1108/10878571311318187

De Smet, D., Duncan, E., Scanlan, J. and Singer, M. (2015). *Six building blocks for creating a high-performing digital enterprise,* McKinsey & Co., September 2015.

Greenleaf, R. (1998). *The Power of Servant Leadership: Essays by Robert K. Greenleaf;* Edited by Larry C. Spears. San Francisco, CA: Berrett-Koehler Publishers, Inc.

Guest, D. (2007). HRM: Towards a new psychological contract, in P. Boxall, J. Purcell and P. Wright (eds.), *Oxford Handbook of Human Resource Management.* Oxford: Oxford University Press.

Hagel, J., Seely Brown, J. and Davison, L. (2010). *The Power of Pull: How Small Moves, Smartly Made, Can Set Big Things in Motion,* 1st Edition. New York: Basic Books.

Hall, T.M. (2007). (Ed.) *Becoming Authentic: The Search for Wholeness and Calling as a Servant-leader.* South Bend, IN: Cloverdale Books.

Heifetz, R.A., Grashow, A. and Linsky, M. (2009). *The Practice of Adaptive Leadership: Tools and Tactics for Changing Your Organization and the World.* Boston, MA: Harvard Business Press.

Heifetz, R.A. and Laurie, D. L. (2001). The work of leadership. *Harvard Business Review*, 79(11), December, 131–140.

Holbeche, L. (2018). *The Agile Organization*, 2nd Edition. London: Kogan Page.

Holbeche, L.S. and Matthews, G. (2012). *Engaged: Unleashing the Potential of Your Organisation through Employee Engagement.* Chichester, UK: Jossey Bass.

Health and Safety Executive (HSE). (2016). *Work related stress, anxiety and depression statistics in Great Britain 2016.* http://www.hse.gov.uk/statistics/causdis/ stress/stress.pdf?pdf=stress.

IBM Institute for Business Value. (2013). *Reinventing the rules of engagement, CEO insights from the Global C-suite Study.* https://www.ibm.com/downloads/cas/EAWNJWR3

Johns, G. (2010). Presenteeism in the workplace: A review and research agenda. *Journal of Organizational Behavior,* 31(4), 519–542.

Kelly, K. (1995). *Out of Control - The New Biology of Machines, Social Systems, and the Economic World.* New York: Basic Books; Reprint edition.

Lawler, E.E. III. (2014). The quadruple bottom line: Its time has come, *Forbes,* May 7, 06:03pm. https://www.forbes.com/sites/edwardlawler/2014/05/07/the-quadruple-bottom-line-its-time-has-come/#f58db960123a

Mackey, J. and Sisodia, R. (2013). *Conscious Capitalism: Liberating the Heroic Spirit of Business.* Boston: Harvard Business Review Press.

Mahadevan, D. (2017). ING's agile transformation. *McKinsey Quarterly,* January. https://www.mckinsey.com/industries/financial-services/our-insights/ings-agile-transformation, accessed on 09/12/2017

Marshak, R.J. (2006). *Covert Processes at Work: Managing the Five Hidden Dimensions of Organizational Change.* San Francisco: Berrett-Koehler Publishers.

Martin, R.L. (2011). *Fixing the Game: Bubbles, Crashes, and What Capitalism Can Learn from the NFL.* Boston: Harvard Business Review Press.

Maslach, C., Schaufeli, W. and Leiter, M.P. (2001). Job burnout. *Annual Review of Psychology,* 52, 397–422.

McCann, J., Selskey, J. and Lee, J. (2009). Building agility, resilience and performance in turbulent environments. *People & Strategy,* 32(3), 44. http://rhesilience.com/blog/wp-content/uploads/2012/01/Building-Agility-Resilience-and-Performance-in-Turbulent-Environments.pdf

McCrystal, S.A. (2015). *Team of Teams: New Rules of Engagement for a Complex World.* London: Penguin Books.

McGrath, R.G. (2012). *The End of Competitive Advantage: How to Keep Your Strategy Moving as Fast as Your Business.* Boston: Harvard Business Review Press.

McGrath, R.G. and Gourlay, A. (2013). *The End of Competitive Advantage: How to Keep Your Strategy Moving as Fast as Your Business.* Boston: Harvard Business Review Press.

McKinsey (De Smet, A.). (2018). *Scaling up Agility,* McKinsey & Company, February 23. https://www.mckinsey.com/business-functions/organization/our-insights/the-organization-blog/scaling-up-organizational-agility

Moody, D. (2017). Customer-centric HR, *Croner-I,* December.

Morgan, G. (1986). *Images of Organization.* Newbury Park, CA: Sage Publications Inc.

Nadler, D.A. and Tushman, M.L. (1988). A model for diagnosing organizational behavior, in M.L. Tushman and W.L. Moore (eds.), *Readings in the Management of Innovation,* 2nd Edition, New York: Ballinger, pp. 148–163.

Norman, S., Luthans, B. and Luthans, K. (2005). The proposed contagion effect of hopeful leaders on the resiliency of employees and organizations. *Journal of Leadership and Organizational Studies,* 12(2), 55–64.

O'Reilly, C.A. III and Tushman, M.L. (2004). The ambidextrous organization. *Harvard Business Review,* April. https://hbr.org/2004/04/the-ambidextrous-organization

Peccei, R. and Rosenthal, P. (2001). Delivering customer-oriented behaviour through empowerment: An empirical test of HRM assumptions. *Journal of Management Studies,* 38, 6.

Pisano, G.P. (2019). The hard truth about innovative cultures. *Harvard Business Review,* January–February issue.

PMI. (2012). *Pulse of the profession in-depth report: Organizational agility.* https://www.pmi.org/-/media/pmi/documents/public/pdf/white-papers/org-agility-

Radjou, P. and Kaipa, N. (2013). *From Smart to Wise.* San Francisco, CA: Jossey-Bass.

Raub, S. (2008). Does bureaucracy kill individual initiative? The impact of structure on organizational citizenship behavior in the hospitality industry. *Journal of Hospitality Management,* 27(2), 179–186.

Robertson, I. and Cooper, C. (2010). Full Engagement: The integration of employee engagement and psychological wellbeing. *Leadership and Organization Development Journal,* 32(4), 324–336.

Roehrig, M., Schwendenwein, J. and Bushe, G.R. (2015). Amplifying change: A 3-phase approach to model, nurture and embed ideas for change, in G.R. Bushe and R.J. Marshak, (eds.), *Dialogic Organization Development*. Oakland, CA: Berrett-Koehler, pp. 325–348.

Salanova, M., Agut, S. and Peiro, J.M. (2005). Linking organizational resources and work engagement to employee performance and customer loyalty: The mediation of service climate. *Journal of Applied Psychology*, 90(6), 1217–1227, December.

Saparito, P.A. and Coombs, J.E. (2013). Bureaucratic systems' facilitating and hindering influence on social capital. *Entrepreneurship: Theory and Practice*, 37(3), 625–639.

Sayers, N. (2010). *A Guide to Scenario Planning in Higher Education*. London: The Leadership Foundation for Higher Education.

Schein, E. (2016a). *Organizational Culture and Leadership*, 5th Edition. San Francisco: Jossey-Bass.

Schein, E.H. (2016b). *Humble Inquiry: The Gentle Art of Asking Instead of Telling*. San Francisco: Berrett-Koehler.

Schwab, K. (2016). The Fourth Industrial Revolution: What it means and how to respond, weforum.org, January 14.

Scott, S. (2019). Optimise your energy to maximise your personal productivity. *Croner-i* (November).

Snowden, D.J. and Boone, M.E. (2007). A leader's framework for decision making. *Harvard Business Review*, 85(11), 68–76, 149 December.

Stacey, R. (1996). *Strategic Management and Organizational Dynamics*. London: Pitman Publishing.

Teece, D.J. (2009). Dynamic capabilities and strategic management: Organizing for innovation and growth. *Organization Science*, 20(2), 410–421, January.

Timmermans, K. and Schulman, D. (2017). *Increasing agility to fuel growth and competitiveness*, Accenture Strategy. https://www.accenture.com/t20170331T025702Z__w__/us-en/_acnmedia/ PDF-4/Accenture-Strategy-Increasing-Agility-to-Fuel-Growth-and-Competitiveness-Research-v2.pdf

Wheatley, M. (2017). *Who Do We Choose to Be? Facing Reality | Claiming Leadership Restoring Sanity*. San Francisco: Berrett-Koehler.

Worley, C.G., Williams, T.D. and Lawler, E.E. III. (2014). *The Agility Factor: Building Adaptable Organizations for Superior Performance*. San Francisco, CA: Jossey-Bass.

Worley, C.G. and Lawler, E.E. III. (2010). Agility and organization design a diagnostic framework. *Organizational Dynamics*, 39, 194–204.

Worley, C.G. and Lawler, E.E. III. (2006). *Built to Change*. San Francisco, CA: Jossey-Bass.

NOTE

1 Verzera, S. Adaptive Organization Design, https://www.youtube.com/watch?v=skHM-weutBHg

17

Learning across boundaries

There is nothing new under the sun; but there are new suns.

Octavia E. Butler 1998

The Fourth Industrial and Information Revolution is irrevocably changing today's work world. The need for organisations to innovate and adapt to a rapidly changing marketplace and economic landscape, especially now as technology races forward, is a given.

DOI: 10.4324/9781003219996-20

Understanding where and how to innovate is more of a challenge. As Butler (1998) points out, we need to broaden our horizons since our current understanding of what will generate future value in a fast-changing world is limited. What is clear is that organisations need to be good at knowledge generation, appropriation and exploitation. As Leadbetter (2000, p. 70) argues, companies need to invest not just in new machinery to make production more efficient, but in the flow of know-how that will sustain their business.

Many of the capabilities associated with 'agile' organisations – such as the ability to sense and respond to changes in their environment, to move information freely between customers and decision makers, and to improve organisation capability through learning from experiments – are consistent with the characteristics of learning organisations. Since intangible organisational value is largely held by the workforce, developing the abilities and potential of those who work on behalf on the organisation is now a strategic necessity. To transform an organisation, it is necessary to look beyond training and attend to structures and the organisation of work as well as the culture and processes (Finger and Brand 1999).

CHAPTER OVERVIEW

In this chapter we shall consider the importance of building a learning culture. We shall look at the roles of leaders and HR in building this culture. We shall also consider how learning can take place formally and informally across boundaries through teams and networks. We shall cover:

- Defining learning organisations
- Knowledge management
- Building a learning culture
- Team working across boundaries

LEARNING OBJECTIVES

- To explore the importance and elements of learning cultures
- To consider how barriers to shared learning can be overcome

INTRODUCTION: DEFINING LEARNING ORGANISATIONS

The notion of 'the Learning Organisation' became popular in the 1990s, then appeared to fade away in the noughties. Definitions of what is meant by the term vary. Peter Senge, author of *The Fifth Discipline* (1990, p. 1) and one of the leading proponents, states that a learning organisation is one 'where people continually expand their capacity to create the results they truly desire, where new and expansive patterns of thinking are nurtured, where collective aspiration is set free, and where people are continually learning how to learn together'. Such organisations foster inquiry and dialogue, making it safe to share openly and take risks. For David Garvin (1993) a learning organisation is: 'an organisation skilled at creating, acquiring and transferring knowledge, and at modifying its behaviour to reflect new knowledge and insights'.

These authors concur that learning organisations are skilled at five main activities: systematic problem solving, experimentation with new approaches, learning from their own experience and past history, learning from the experiences and best practices of others, and transferring knowledge quickly and efficiently throughout the organisation. Each is accompanied by a distinctive mind-set, tool kit, and pattern of behaviour. Senge (1990) identified five disciplines that are essential to creating an organisation which can learn. These are:

- Systems thinking – which considers the interrelatedness of forces and sees them as part of a common process. 'System dynamics' involves looking for the complex feedback processes which can generate problematic patterns of behaviour within organisations.
- Personal mastery – which acknowledges that we are all a significant part of the systems we work within and 'the most significant leverage may come from changing our own orientation and self-image'. Concepts include personal visioning, treating emotions respectfully and the leader as coach.
- Mental models – which involve the ability to reflect and the theories which make up our current reality. Having the ability to develop and test new mental models will be essential for future-oriented learning and development.
- Shared vision – which involves gaining the commitment and focus which comes when a vision is genuinely shared. The vision should provide clues as to the organisation's deep purpose and ways must be found of involving people at every level of the organisation to speak and be heard about things that matter to them.
- Team learning – in which collective aspiration gives team members a compelling reason to begin to learn how to learn together. Team learning is vital because teams, not individuals, are the fundamental learning unit in modern organisations. Team learning is built around 'dialogue' – the capacity of team members to suspend assumptions and enter into free-flowing discussion that allows the team to 'think together'. Thus, a team can uncover insights that would not be attainable individually.

WHY LEARNING ORGANISATIONS?

Various studies (De Geus 1997; Collins and Porras 2002; Peters and Waterman 2004) suggest that becoming a learning organisation provides a competitive advantage. As Ghoshal and Bartlett (1998) suggested, 'The age of strategic planning is fast evolving into the era of organisational learning'. Learning organisations are built to last, are superior competitors whose brand equity their competitors cannot match, and they attract and retain the best talent. Arie de Geus, who headed up Royal Dutch Shell's Strategic Planning Group in the 1980s, with colleagues conducted research into 'long-lived' organisations that had been trading successfully for more than 100 years, as Shell nearly had at that time. They were curious to know what accounted for these 'living' companies' longevity. They found these organisations shared some common features:

- Sensitive to their environment: able to learn and adapt
- Comprised of a community with a shared identity
- Able to build constructive relationships inside and outside of the business
- Able to govern their growth and evolution effectively

With respect to strategy, such organisations have a diverse, adaptable portfolio. They are tolerant of activity at the margins, including by mavericks. They are future focused and use scenarios, imagining many versions of the future to guide decision-making. They survey the environment often and plan long-term. They learn as they go along: 'You do not navigate a company to a predefined destination. You take steps, one at a time, into an unknowable future' (De Geus 1997, p. 186).

Similarly, Ghoshal and Bartlett (1998) found that what they called the 'individualised' organisation had the following characteristics:

- Its ability to inspire creativity and initiatives in all its people
- Its ability to link and gain leverage from pockets of entrepreneurial activity and individual expertise via organisational learning
- Its ability to renew itself continuously.

Their argument also spans individual action, structures, capabilities, concepts and processes as a portfolio. 3M for instance was good at encouraging creativity; McKinsey and Skandia were good at gaining leverage through organisational learning; ABB was good at corporate renewal.

Conversely, many of the so-called 'Excellent' companies in the Peters and Waterman study later failed to maintain their leading edge when market conditions became more turbulent. These previously successful organisations may perhaps have become complacent and over-confident (Kahneman 2011). Previous mental frameworks or paradigms for success (i.e. internal representations of the external worlds in which we operate) may have been stuck in the past, becoming a 'blind spot' that caused executives to ignore what was hidden in plain sight. Seeing no reason to continue to learn, their lack of market sensitivity effectively screened out the arrival new challengers. By the time they became alert to the danger, it was usually too late to respond effectively. Typical symptoms of failing to learn include:

- Duplication of effort
- Wasted time (which managers do not even notice because they are too busy)
- Repeated learning curves
- Slower rate of innovation
- Higher threats to the speed and quality of service

Too often companies get in the way of their own attempts to innovate when they miss out the vital enabling factor -equipping individuals in the organisation with the broader mindsets and skillsets they need to do this. Many also fail to adopt the kinds of learning practices required for innovation. As De Jong et al. (2015) point out: 'a surprising number of impressive innovations from companies were actually the fruit of their mavericks who succeeded in bypassing their early approval processes. Clearly, there is a balance to be maintained: bureaucracy must be held in check, yet the rush to market should not undermine the cross-functional collaboration, continuous learning cycles and clear decision pathways that help enable innovation'.

So lower levels of learning in the post-industrial society reduce a company's life expectancy in a world in which success depends on the ability to maximise the use of the available brainpower. Particularly when facing new situations, leaders and managers must establish routines that bring limiting paradigms to light and then enable them to be changed so that individuals and organisations can adapt more effectively to the new environments which surround them. It is important to be systematic, to go through the usual routines, check the facts versus assumptions and open up the issue for other people's ideas. Leaders and managers can shape the dynamics of their own teams by surrounding themselves with a diversity of people who are unlikely to see things automatically from the same point of view. Such groups could be tasked to question upcoming decisions and the thinking on which they are based.

New measures of value

In today's knowledge and service economies, factors of production are no longer land, labour or capital, as in the industrial era, but talent, skills and knowledge. The trend towards greater use of mental-based skills and talents rather than the application of human physical power will accelerate. At the heart of the Information Revolution is low-cost computing and connectivity which is transforming work, services and products and enabling people to communicate externally and internally on a more extensive basis than ever before. This speeding up of communication brings new opportunities for creating value and the need for new measures to protect existing value. Apple for instance succeeds by perceiving unrecognised marketplace needs and creates new products to fill them.

Zuboff (1988) argued that 'The 21st century company has to promote and nurture the capacity to improve and innovate. That idea has radical implications. It means learning becomes the axial principle of organisations. It replaces control as the fundamental job of management'. This transition is still ongoing. Learning involves innovating or creating new knowledge, retaining that knowledge, and transferring the knowledge throughout the firm. Increasingly, firms are organised in a distributed fashion to take advantage of differences in expertise, labour costs, and access to markets that exist around the world. Managing these distributed organisations effectively requires that knowledge be retained and transferred from one organisational unit to another. Ray Stata was famously quoted in a 1995 edition of *The International Journal of Organisational Analysis*: 'The rate at which individuals and organizations learn may become the only sustainable competitive advantage left'.

New measures of value suggest that the market value of a company is based on both financial capital and intellectual capital. Intellectual capital represents the intangible assets of an organisation. One element of this is 'structural' capital, in which some of the organisation's knowledge, processes and procedures can be captured and retained as intellectual property. Developing and exploiting knowledge capability within an organisation may be one of the few relatively untapped sources of competitive advantage. The other two forms of capital – 'customer', such as the brand, reputation, relationships and 'human', such as people deploying their talents – represent the real competitive advantage since it is the ongoing development of ideas, products and services that meet customer needs which ensures that the organisation is sustainable.

Some companies – such as GE and Johnson and Johnson – are leading examples of business success being enriched by learning practice. GE's Crotonville learning centre drives continuous learning by managers and other leaders, as they return to Crotonville to learn and teach at critical transitions in their careers. Johnson & Johnson, inspired by its famous credo, constantly improves products and invents new ones, always with the user at the centre of its focus. Toyota Motor Co. uses lean manufacturing and continuous improvement to make small but never-ending improvements in products and processes. Such companies operate from a foundation of solid basic principles and values, as well as their continuous learning to keep them thinking and acting ahead of their competition. They constantly create markets, market approaches, products and greater customer value, and they never let slip the market advantage they have worked so hard to acquire by letting their competition out-think or act ahead of them or faster than they can.

Since few organisations have a blueprint for the future or can confidently predict the precise talents and skills needed for future success, growing flexible and high-calibre talent with the skills to survive and thrive in conditions of low agreement and low certainty makes sense. A well-educated workforce will anticipate, accept and eagerly support change. If an organisation focuses on building good intellectual capital, it will become an employer of choice for talented new entrants interested in rapid development. The challenge of managing intellectual capital is ensuring that it does not walk out of the door. This requires a long-term view, a willingness to learn from the situations you find yourself in and a strategic approach to talent planning which not only creates tight links between the organisation's strategies and a broad range of learning activities but also has an underpinning culture in which learning is valued and encouraged. In other words, to prepare for an unknown future, you need good people who feel connected to the organisation and are willing to contribute to the shared endeavour over time:

> If a company has not organized its personnel in a way that allows fast learning and the conditions of 'flocking' (learning in groups), or if it doesn't do, intensively, things like career development, it will be hurt.
>
> (De Geus, 1997)

To create the conditions for mobility, the space for innovation, and an effective system for sharing knowledge, a strong win–win relationship is needed between employees and employers. This means recruiting with cohesion and continuity in mind and developing the potential of the community's members. This becomes the foundation for faster institutional learning on which success in the New Economy depends.

Knowledge management

Knowledge, especially access to knowledge, will increasingly play an important role with regard to power. Knowledge reduces uncertainty and supports flexibility in attitude and behaviour. Knowledge management is about harnessing the knowledge and experience that people have. Knowledge of all forms exists in different parts of an organisation, but very few organisations have a 'map' of the knowledge available. Consequently, latent knowledge is vastly under-utilised. The amount and pace of change within businesses today makes it difficult to keep abreast of existing knowledge, let alone identify the knowledge needed for the future. A Chief Executive of Hewlett–Packard, for example, has been quoted as saying 'If HP knew what HP knows, we would be three times as profitable'. Managers may therefore be unaware of the vast potential on offer.

Traditional accounting systems for valuing organisations typically fail to register the value of that knowledge since it is notoriously difficult to measure and, by its nature is 'implicit', 'tacit', inside people's heads. The real value of a company is what acquirers are willing to pay to gain access to staff and their skills and knowledge. In sectors such as advertising, fund management and consultancies, many organisations on the acquisition trail have found that they have bought nothing if key staff in the acquired company walk away.

In some sectors, in quest of leanness, staff turnover has been so great that there are often few people left within the business who really know how to get things done. Arnold Kransdorff (1995) studied organisations that previously had low rates of staff turnover and now experienced a wholesale turnover of staff every four or five years. He coined the term 'corporate amnesia' to describe the loss of learning to the company when staff left. He found that in some cases, expensive mistakes were repeated while in others, high-cost systems could no longer be used since all the staff were new and there was no one left with the relevant experience who could teach them. Particularly costly was the loss of customer information acquired over years by employees who were invited to retire early.

'Explicit' information, as detailed in databases, staff manuals and process maps, shows only a small part of the real knowledge assets of a company. The intangibles, such as know-how, information on stakeholder relationships, experiences and ideas, represent the critical knowledge. Such information tends to stay in the informal system of the organisation where it is shared by only a few people. Information alone is not the real asset; it is what people do, or are prepared to do, with that information which turns it into valuable, shared knowledge. It is how people convert information into knowledge and the way they use that information to shape decisions which represents the real knowledge asset.

Knowledge tends to generate other knowledge when people work collaboratively and share ideas with each other. This reinforces the idea that knowledge management is not the exclusive domain of IT specialists but is of direct relevance to line managers and HR professionals. It's about connecting people and creating a culture where senior people think that knowledge sharing is worth investing in. Flatter, agile structures, with their emphasis on teamwork and smart ways of working, should be ideally suited to the generation and sharing of knowledge. Performance management and incentive systems should enable and reward the building and sharing of knowledge and skills.

Develop a knowledge management framework

If knowledge underpins every value-added activity that an organisation carries out, learning and the generation of new knowledge should be encouraged and managed as a strategic asset and the processes of creating and sharing knowledge identified. The first step is to determine what knowledge really is important for delivering strategic objectives and who has that knowledge. This may involve brainstorming to find out what knowledge is critical to the organisation and prioritising the strategic knowledge assets. This body of knowledge must be managed and developed for its full potential to be realised. Assign someone to manage these, making people accountable for managing that critical knowledge.

Decide on a knowledge 'architecture' including guidelines which gives people guidance on what kind of data are valuable enough to retain and make available. These will include not simply product information but also useful practical knowledge such as lessons learnt from experience with customers, projects, etc. It's important to map how this knowledge integrates with other key processes, spotting when knowledge assets are being under-utilised and finding ways of getting knowledge onto people's agenda.

Identify ways in which knowledge can be captured, shared, communicated and organised for easy retrieval and for existing knowledge to be built upon. Start with existing projects and involve people in figuring out how knowledge sharing can work so that that they understand the benefits to them and take ownership of the knowledge process. Provide appropriate infrastructure in the form of communications technology, systems design and applications tools. Typical mechanisms for information transmittal and diffusion include brief reports, stand-up meetings, daily e-mails and town meetings, rewarding people for using these mechanisms, and disciplining people who do not, and creating central repositories of relevant knowledge.

However, some general enabling conditions must be in place for knowledge management to be effective. Top leaders must own the learning and knowledge management agenda. They must work to create a culture of trust and teamwork in which collaboration is the norm and also build an appropriate infrastructure, together with supportive technology, to facilitate learning. As Morgan (1993) suggests:

> You can't create a learning organization ... But you can enhance people's capacities to learn and align their activities in creative ways.

Reflective activity

- Why do some organisations learn and others fail to learn?
- How can you increase the rate of learning at your firm?
- What is stopping you from implementing more ideas more quickly?

Barriers to sharing knowledge

While people at the top of organisations generally want innovation and people on the front line are usually keen to innovate, there are a number of important barriers to organisational learning embedded in business-as-usual that prevent organisations from making the most of their intellectual capital. One challenge is the pace of change which often prevents people from pausing to reflect. Another challenge is the increasingly flexible nature of the workforce. Capitalising on the skills, knowledge and experience of the workforce is challenging enough, but capturing the knowledge of a flexible, mobile workforce, including consultants, contractors and others whose affiliation to the company might be temporary, is even more difficult.

A more fundamental barrier may have its roots in the ongoing uncertainty of the employment market, concerns about job security for many people and a lack of career progression routes. Traditionally people have progressed their careers through hierarchies by becoming knowledgeable – about issues, technical and professional bodies of knowledge and about how the organisation works – and being able to use that knowledge to get things done. The axiom 'knowledge is power' is evident when skills and knowledge are in short supply, as are certain types of IT skills currently.

In the information age, there is a potential clash between employee and employer needs with respect to how information is developed and distributed. The dictum 'knowledge is power' is in conflict with 'knowledge is to be shared'. From the organisational perspective there are clear benefits in the pooling of information, about clients for example, and the generation of shared knowledge, thus preventing the organisation from becoming dependent on any single employee's knowledge. From the individual point of view, however, there can be little incentive to share information if by so doing you render yourself dispensable or lose bonuses by doing so.

Although flatter structures should facilitate knowledge sharing, they can also reinforce people's desire to hoard information since they intensify competition for scarce promotion opportunities. The internal market value of certain types of knowledge can lead to political battles being waged in many organisations. In these uncertain times, valuable experience and expertise are seen to be a means of keeping your job when those about you are losing theirs. For some people, career uncertainty is not the issue. They may simply not want to share their expertise beyond their own boundaries if it means reducing their power base as 'the expert'. While Charles Handy (1997) identified knowledge as only one of seven forms of power, knowledge can give individuals internal and external career trading power which few would wish to give up, given the ongoing uncertainty of the jobs market.

Clearly there has to be a shared platform of trust and mutual benefits, such as the opportunity for employees to develop valuable new skills through the team process if people are to see benefits in collaboration. For while there is plenty of anecdotal evidence that people who develop effective knowledge management processes derive development and personal satisfaction from their new forms of learning, yet the barriers to knowledge collaboration can be strong.

HR and other systems such as reward can sometimes undermine people's willingness to share information which might be useful to others. For example one major UK broking firm became concerned that they were failing to serve clients well because the relevant client information was usually in the head of one 'client manager' individual. If that individual was sick or left the firm, their knowledge was no longer available. For fear of disrupting powerful client managers a new policy was quietly introduced that led to the redistribution of responsibility for client management to a wider group. Clients soon became increasingly irritated by the numerous new contacts they were receiving from the same firm, while previous client managers were unaware that other employees were in touch with the same client.

The firm installed expensive hardware and software to ensure information about clients was kept up to date. They were puzzled when employees did not update records or use the new resource. This was not a case of 'technophobia' – another common barrier to knowledge management processes, as previously client managers had managed their own client database. They came to recognise that because people continued to be individually rewarded for the 'deals' struck, there was no incentive for people to share information about the client. It was not until rewards were attached to the quality of the client relationship, and teams were able to share some of the bonuses attached, that people's behaviour and use of the system began to change. Some of the previous main critics of the new system became its champions when they could see advantages to them in ensuring that the client information was kept fresh and updated.

Another common barrier to the sharing of organisational learning is that people often focus rather narrowly on their jobs, rather than on the purpose of the organisation as a whole. In organisations with a heavy emphasis on short term delivery, making time for reviewing what they have learned and sharing knowledge for longer-term gains can seem an unwarranted extra, an impediment to getting the job done now. Some teams demonstrate 'us and them' mentalities which cause defensive and political behaviour over turf issues. Perhaps the biggest obstacle to shared learning is if people get blamed when things go wrong.

One reason why some leaders may fail to recognise the importance of organisational learning may be embedded in the dominant culture of rationalism reflected in many Western management theories of recent years. These only tend to value explicit knowledge. Nonaka and Takeuchi (1995) suggest that Japan is fundamentally more innovative because the Japanese emphasis on the holistic nature of mind and body, values tacit knowledge, which is both elusive and abstract. Indeed, the growing interest in recent years in emotional and other forms of intelligence, has finally percolated into Western management vocabulary. It is increasingly recognised that developing the emotional intelligence of senior managers is key to helping them to champion knowledge management in their capacity as leaders. It provides insights into how to support a culture change from a relatively hierarchical and inflexible system to a more flexible, innovative, customer-focused learning culture.

When the new CEO of a major electronics company visited all its decentralised business units, he was amazed to find that there were many initiatives under way in separate units which could be useful to the work of other units – but no one apart from the CEO had the full picture. The CEO insisted that interchanges between units were established so that the organisation could benefit more widely from these new approaches.

So the tone set by senior management is absolutely critical to the successful implementation of learning and knowledge management strategies. Leaders must recognise the importance of learning and maximising knowledge for innovation and should actively promote research and development across the organisation to create and market new products, services and ways of working. They should develop success criteria for knowledge management projects and invest in a standard, flexible knowledge infrastructure using multiple channels for knowledge transfer.

Leaders must recognise the impact of their own behaviour, such as how they react to critical incidents, which teaches people what leaders really care about. They should work to create a safe and respectful climate where individuals and teams learn to speak up, trust each other, feel comfortable experimenting, take risks and learn together. It's about stimulating a growth and innovation mindset where people work at the intersection between disciplines, ask themselves 'what if' questions, seek out diverse perspectives and want to test ideas. To create a psychologically safe climate requires leaders to be humble, willing to accept that they do not have all the answers, and genuinely curious about other people's perspectives. This is not about compromising on work standards. As Pisano (2019) points out, a tolerance for failure (to enable experimentation) must be matched by an intolerance for incompetence (to strengthen accountability and delivery). Building a culture of competence means that leaders at all levels should deliberately encourage employee development and raise standards of performance, including in the recruitment of new talent.

Overcoming barriers to the sharing of knowledge

Overcoming all these barriers is a tall order yet is essential. Any organisation seeking to introduce knowledge management systems needs to be clear about potential obstacles to the sharing of knowledge and address those obstacles so that people can identify the 'what's in it for me?' factor.

Key to this is individuals being able to identify sharing of knowledge as being in their interest. In broad terms, knowledge management has to address three key activities:

- Motivating people to share information
- Developing a system for managing and storing information
- Motivating people to use the knowledge available to them

Successful learning organisations avoid corporate amnesia and perpetuate their advantage by encouraging people at all levels to collect and capture information across all boundaries, making sure that information is shared – not forgotten or hoarded. (Advances in electronic media over the past decade or so have made this much easier). Sharing existing knowledge makes it more productive and helps to create new knowledge. The more information is used, the more it develops and grows. So if casual information sharing becomes a way of organisational life, when key talent leaves the organisation, at least some of their knowledge will remain with colleagues. Linking individual growth and progression to knowledge acquisition will assist this process.

Reflective activity

In your organisation:

- What can managers do to increase the likelihood that their firms learn from success as well as failure?
- How can innovation be fostered in organisations? When is an open innovation policy likely to be successful?
- What qualities do we value when recruiting or designing learning programmes?
- To what extent are people empowered to try out new ideas?
- Do we recognise and reward risk-taking?
- Are people blamed for failure when initiatives do not succeed?
- What are the main knowledge assets and how is knowledge shared?
- What are the most effective methods of learning and developing new ways of thinking?
- Do teams and business units actively collaborate on projects?

REQUISITES FOR A LEARNING CULTURE

For knowledge management, or the development of intellectual capital, an open, collaborative culture is needed in which learning is valued (Mueller 2011). Though teams are the central learning unit, learning organisations with a supportive context tend to work at scale.

Supportive leadership

Supportive leadership is vital to the creation of a learning culture. CEOs must set the style, creating a clear shared vision and values about the effective creation and dissemination of knowledge. Yet conventional leadership theories may not be enough to equip leaders for this task. In line with the living system metaphor, Richard Hale and Dave Ulrich (2021) suggest that post-pandemic leadership in 'an unknowable normal' may be more about anthropology and curiosity than analytics and solutions. They suggest that the ability to lead from a position of not knowing will be the leadership differentiator for the future and requires 'leadership curiosity or the ability to explore options and ask good questions may be more important than total clarity. Exploring options or mysteries may be the path to wisdom and insight rather than intellectual cleverness, problem-solving, or question answering'.

Similarly, leaders may need to adopt the practices of elite teams described as 'superforecasters' by Tetlock and Gardner (2015). These improve their predictive ability by accepting that nothing is certain or predetermined. Therefore, it is important to be open-minded, curious, self-critical and honest. It's about being willing to change one's mind and frequently checking one's own and others' cognitive biases. The emphasis should be on growth, quality improvements, resilience and empathy.

HR can determine with senior managers what the learning culture should look like, set clear expectations about how the organisation should operate, then agree actions and responsibilities to move the culture in the desired direction. Trust is a vital enabling component in the human aspects of knowledge management. Leaders need to encourage this by communicating at the right level – senior managers often talk down to employees, or at too senior a level to make sense lower down the organisation – so they must express clearly both in language and through their own behaviour the value the organisation places on learning. Getting the communication right is all the more important when connecting with staff in remote working contexts. Some of the ways leaders and managers can do this include:

- Giving everyone in the team enough air time, for instance agreeing a 'right to speak' during Zoom calls.
- Holding 'lockdowns' to ensure key issues get the time and attention they need from the right people.
- Talking freely about what they are learning from outside the organisation's boundaries.
- Using experts to impart information and involving contractors and flexible workers in communications strategies.
- Showing interest and publicly questioning others about what they are learning.
- Personally conducting after-action reviews.
- Reviewing projects at key junctures.
- Working to eliminate any resistance to learning that might appear.
- Encouraging cooperation by focusing on key moments of truth and identifying the interdependencies, making sure people are getting the help they need from others, including from managers.
- Actively eradicating 'blame culture' behaviours.
- Making sure that people are recognised and rewarded for learning and the sharing of best practice with growth, jobs, promotions and even financial compensation; and people who don't learn are managed out of the organisation.

Leaders must demonstrate how they themselves continuously learn and force themselves to stay open to learning, even when business conditions make it difficult. During the pandemic there were many examples of managers changing their ways of interacting to engage staff working virtually. Some are regularly spending a few minutes on Zoom in one-to-one conversations with each of their team members asking, 'what are your current priorities?' 'what are you worried about?' 'is there anything you need to know?' By focusing on what really matters and connecting with what people really care about, leaders have been able to help their teams to successfully navigate a host of problems and priorities. Daily collective check-out meetings via video conference at the end of the working day can include both a task and a mood review, as well as sharing new learning. To sustain this innovative approach to managing people going forward, especially as more hybrid working patterns are likely to emerge, will mean deliberately ensuring that people working in different ways feel included and valued.

Learning for self-development

Creating a win–win employment relationship involves offering people development opportunities. Whether in the context of personal development, leadership development and organisational development, we know that learning has the capacity to transform people and organisations. Increasingly, firms are creating the infrastructure for self-development through online or virtual training, providing a mix of learning and development methods ranging from digital learning to team-based collaborative learning that provide opportunities for accelerated self-development. While decades ago, some large companies set up corporate universities, many now establish learning resource centres. One such centre is designed to support five operational objectives:

- The development of key role and core organisational competencies
- Training by alternative media
- Corporate initiatives such as the executive learning programme
- Professional studies in line with the company policy
- Enabling vocational qualifications.

Key to the centre's success is actively encouraging employees to take responsibility for their own development, internalising lessons as they go along, asking themselves questions such as 'what are we learning? What is this teaching us'? Employees create development plans and negotiate their needs with their managers. If development is directly linked to a person's role, it is considered legitimate that they spend work time acquiring the new skill or knowledge. Employees have access to a wide range of resources at the learning centre whose staff are available to provide help and advice. If employees are unable to visit the centre in person, materials are sent out to them physically or accessed virtually. Materials on similar topics are provided in a variety of formats to suit different learning styles and remote learning. Copies of management development materials from training programmes are also available so that people can catch up on development they may have missed. The centre also provides development resources for different kinds of teams. The centre is proving an attractive feature for recruits and also shows existing employees they are valued.

Underpinning learning cultures are notions of organisations as living communities with a shared identity and a common set of values. Training is provided to support individuals to reach their maximum potential. There is job mobility, promoting from within, networking and knowledge sharing is encouraged. Firing people is a last resort. Astra Zeneca (AZ) shows commitment to its workforce through investing in development. AZ recognises that to drive growth through innovation they must empower their workforce to renew and refresh the skills and capabilities they need to thrive in an ever-changing world. They are creating a learning ecosystem based on the 3 Es – *Experience*, such as stretch assignments, learning reviews, shadowing, job rotations; *Exposure* – coaching, mentoring, feedback, teamwork, networks, communities of practice; *Education* – e-learning, webinars, seminars, structured programmes and accreditations. The aim is to equip all employees with future-ready capabilities fit for an unpredictable environment. For instance, in the Digital Awareness Hub (Part of AZ's Digital and Data Academy) people can learn about What is Digital? Digital Leadership; Digital Lexicon; Organisational Responsiveness; Change Readiness; Data; Data Science and AI; Agile; Design Thinking; Lean. Learning methods encourage collective sense-making.

Training

Training plays an important part in building an agile learning culture. L&D can ensure that training and educational activities are both short- and long-term oriented and build the skills people really need. These include the ability to confidently seek knowledge from other people, inside and outside the organisation, as well as team skills and the willingness to collaborate with others to create new solutions. For some employees, technophobia prevents them from keeping up in today's workplace. A few years ago, recognising that some employees needed help, Marks & Spencer declared an IT amnesty for staff so that all employees could get up to speed with computers. Providing training in IT systems, digital and information skills can help employees develop key skills for the workplace of tomorrow, which will enhance their employability. These include basics such as time management, learning techniques and networking skills. Other useful skills include resource investigation, communication and diagnostic skills, and team-based problem-solving.

Unipart, a company intensely focused on operational excellence and lean management has developed learning routines which target operational performance and continuous improvement. It has an in-house learning and development operation, the Unipart U (or university) that acts as a one-stop shop for all the organisation's learning. Staff use the U's database to work out what they need to know and then take responsibility for learning it. They go to the 'Faculty on the Floor' for short, focused training and problem-solving sessions in the work area of each business unit, rather than traditional classrooms and they apply it immediately: 'learn at 10 – do at 11'. The Unipart U provides programmes that lead to national vocational qualifications, and also offer assistance to more senior staff including access to a body of knowledge on strategy. This reflects the 'Unipart Way' that brings together a philosophy of empowerment and devolved accountability, an alignment of objectives from top to bottom of the organisation, a core process improvement methodology (deployed consistently throughout the organisation), and continuous learning and progression (every employee has a development plan and a coach).

It is important to remember, however, that learning is not just another word for training. According to Sharon Varney (2008), many established practices around learning (e.g. analysing learning needs and articulating desired learning outcomes) are firmly rooted in the training world and may not serve us so well when our goal is to unlock the transformational nature of learning in pursuit of organisational change and transformation.

To foster a learning culture in the virtual world, the learning experience should be re-imagined. There must be a shift away from conventional e-learning towards co-creating virtual experiences with employees so that people can apply the learning directly, and also experiment. The design principle should be that one-size-fits-one, not all. A learning experience might include for instance short videos, including executives talking about their own learning, bringing a range of learning resources to bear on so-called 'moments of truth' where problems need to be addressed and embedding learning through facilitation in team meetings. Pre- and post-learning activities can keep the dialogue going in a helpful, reinforcing way.

Feedback

Building a learning culture is not simply a question of increasing spend on training but is also about developing learning routines. For WL Gore and Associates, innovation is key. So learning routines, which occur at both the individual and team levels, focus on generating, nurturing and commercialising new ideas. The organisational design and culture are based on mutual accountability, support for learning and trust.

Learning organisations and the people in them use their own experience and that of others to improve their performance. In WL Gore and Associates, all employees or 'members' are involved in ongoing feedback loops. This means they routinely seek feedback from their colleagues on ideas they have or actions they've taken and give feedback to others, including offering forward focused ideas and suggestions, on a regular basis. They learn from past experience, review and systematically assess both their successes and also their failures, recording lessons learnt in a form that employees find open and accessible. This dynamic activity ensures that everyone is learning from everyone else all the time. Since continuous learning is systemically built into the organisation's DNA and infrastructure, communication is open and widespread, and it is assumed everyone 'needs to know'.

Risk-taking

Ongoing programs need managers and employees who are trained in the skills required to perform and evaluate experiments. As they do so they need to feel the psychological safety which is so vital for experimenting and learning. In a learning culture, unlike in a 'blame culture', some risk-taking and a few mistakes are tolerated in line with the 'fail fast, learn well' philosophy. As De Geus 1997 (p. 183) points out, 'Space must be created for people to experiment and take risks. At the same time, people cannot simply do what they like at the expense of the organisation's common purpose. Clearly, one needs both: empowered people and effective control'.

To create a learning culture, leaders need to understand that their actions influence and shape the system. Managers should also be sensitive to the ways they handle crisis, conflict and tension within the organisation. Many leaders find that accepting emergence, learning and the uncertain future that it implies can make them feel anxious. They may need support or training from HR/L&D to learn new ways of engaging. Managers need to understand their own tolerance of risk and ambiguity, develop ways of openly examining their individual and collective responses to anxiety, for instance when they avoid taking decisions when they do not feel they have enough data and so miss the moment to act. As Peter Cheese (2021) states: 'You can't steer a ship by looking at the wake – we have to learn to work in agile ways, innovate and try things, accept failure as part of learning and learn as we go, while maintaining a strong guiding focus on vision and purpose'.

When the five-star Mandarin Oriental Hotel in London was preparing to relaunch itself after a lengthy and expensive renovation, a devastating fire broke out that meant the hotel had to be immediately closed again. The new general manager and her team took the decision to retain all 750 staff while the work was carried out. Some were given the opportunity to be seconded to one of the other Mandarin Oriental sites abroad while the majority chose volunteering at major charities. These experiences gave staff a new perspective on their own roles. People were better able to empathise with colleagues and guests. Staff shared pictures of their experiences and a MOve Back training programme allowed each employee to put their knowledge into practice and also experience the hotel as a guest. The result has been high levels of staff engagement and collaboration. The fact that the leadership and HR already had strong processes and communication channels in place meant they could be agile when they had to change strategy. Having a plan allowed them to be flexible (People Management April, 2019).

Specific knowledge roles

Various Western companies have acknowledged the importance of the management of knowledge by appointing a 'chief knowledge officer'. Though these are currently few in number in the UK, many have grouped together in networks to share learning on a pan-organisation basis. This is not considered to be a breach of confidentiality. What works for one organisation does not necessarily work for others, but knowledge officers are honing their insights as to how to shape their own companies' cultures to be supportive of the management of intellectual capital. HR can also help set up networks that bring together communities with a common interest in developing and sharing knowledge.

Other new roles and responsibilities are being created. In some companies, there is a senior-level 'knowledge sponsor' who ensures board-level attention for knowledge issues. Then there are knowledge managers/facilitators who offer support to client teams. Knowledge owners provide the expert input, and their responsibility is to keep up to date with the information flow. On the technical side there are information service providers and webmaster roles.

DEVELOPING LEARNING ACROSS BOUNDARIES

While creative thinking is coming up with something new, and invention is the creation of something that has never been made before, innovation is the implementation of something that has not been made before and typically involves prototyping. In periods of incremental change, when innovation results in improved service or products, customers should be heavily involved in co-creation as they are the route to market. In times of crisis when normal business is disrupted, such as during the COVID-19 pandemic, innovation is recognised as key to providing breakthrough solutions. Teams are getting together virtually to ask themselves:

1. What problem do we solve for our customers?
2. In what new ways could the problem be solved?
3. What new problems will our customers have?
4. What big assumptions are we making about our business which might no longer be true?
5. What entirely new product or service could we sell?
6. How would a dynamic new start-up solve our customers' problems with new techniques?

Teams

Teams are the primary innovation vehicles in agile organisations. So learning design must incorporate a development focus on team, as well as individual. Teams can become active learning units if L& D:

- Teach people skills such as problem solving, appreciative inquiry, and setting up and evaluating experiments. Create some space for people to engage in reflection and analysis.
- Help people build their understanding of how adults learn, so they can develop their own learning strategies. Support them with practical tools such as questionnaires,

checklists or journaling (keeping a diary) that help them reflect on what they are learning.
- Open up organisation boundaries to stimulate the flow of ideas, through for example, cross-functional projects, action learning teams focused on real business problems, or social learning groups. At an individual level, adopting augmented reality for learning thanks to increasingly sophisticated portable hardware such as headsets and glasses, allows individuals to move around a room between tasks, learning as they go.

L&D can help teams establish learning organisation practice. For instance, following a learning activity, people can be encouraged to consider 'who also would benefit from this?' and transfer relevant and helpful learning to others. The UK's HMRC recognised that the HR team needed to continue to develop its own expertise if HR was to be able to play its part in building a learning organisation. Groups of HR professionals took part in day-long masterclasses for instance to understand macro-economic trends and the lessons to be learned from neuroscience. A key plank of the learning involves asking the HR community to share what they've been learning with others, helping the team face the future with confidence and revitalise and empower staff (People Management May 2016).

Case: cross-boundary team working

Effective teamworking across time or geographical boundaries can be difficult. A major international engineering company, whose UK base has a number of sites throughout the south and west of England, introduced some aspects of cross-boundary working in recent years through various quality initiatives. The company wanted to increase the amount of project working which brings together the talents of key individuals from different sites for extended periods.

Two teams were required to work together across two sites, 40 miles apart. Team A was longer-established and had essentially been working on a single major project with a very long-term deadline, while Team B had a range of projects with shorter deadlines. While team A, consisting of a central team of 30 people, was based at one site, team B was split between two sites. Both teams were considered by managers and the teams themselves to be highly successful, though team A was felt to have greater potential than had yet been realised, and the two sub-teams within team B operated almost independently of each other. Team members reported a sense of pride at being part of their team and were clearly motivated by being able to contribute to their team's success.

Research into how the potential of this team collaboration could be realised led to certain conclusions. It was found that having an effective leader becomes perhaps more critical for a cross-boundary team than for a conventional functional team. The two team leaders took it in turns to be the overall team leader. The leader has to manage the political interface and act as a shield for the team from the rest of the organisation. In finding its own 'third way', the team needs the freedom to experiment and be genuinely 'empowered' to discover the best ways of working. This is usually not a problem as long as the team is seen to be successful. In the early stages, though, the team leader may find his or her credibility under strain as the team learns from its mistakes. The leader needs to be prepared to create an environment where experimentation is encouraged, and team members are supported for doing so.

Given the diverse backgrounds of team members, and that there may initially not be a lot of common ground between them, the role of the leader in providing a tangible focus and direction for the team becomes all the more important. They perform the important role of providing drive and determination in the face of difficulties. The leader must be both strategic and operational, seen as someone who 'leads from the front', setting a strong vision and objectives for the team. Within the two teams this was an aspect of leadership that was going well at the level of broad objectives, in that everybody was aware of the longer-term goals and quality/cost objectives. What was going less well was the setting of shorter-term objectives which gave people real focus in the context of a lengthy project.

The overall leader's role was both internal and external to the team. Both leaders were reported to be 'sold on teamworking' and were effectively acting as coach and mentor to different team members. It was widely recognised that they needed to have excellent interpersonal skills not just for communicating with the team but also for helping the team communicate effectively with each other. In terms of style, both teams felt that decision-making should be the ultimate responsibility of the leader, to avoid functional experts pulling rank, but that decision-making should be carried out in a participative way. The team leader was also seen as being responsible for communicating the team's successes to the wider organisation and building up a strong profile for the team throughout the business. The team leader therefore needs to be visible, both to the team itself and within the organisation as a whole.

Team builder

It was recognised by both groups that there was a need for someone within the team who could act as the 'spur to team excellence'. On some occasions this was carried out by the team leader, but not always. In both teams, an individual was identified as a model for good team behaviour, proving that the team can change for the better. They were seen as natural leaders who are self-motivated, confident and charismatic. They were also seen as supportive of failure and willing to try new things. As such, even without formal authority, the team builders were seen as the internal motivator of the team to improve things, providing continuity, whereas the overall leader had to manage both the internal and external interfaces.

More so than in a conventional team, the Belbin team role of team builder is called for. This aspect of the role is managing conflict within the team. This is an area where problems are more likely, given the complexities within a cross-boundary team. Interviewees noted that the team builder acts as the oil on troubled waters, diffusing conflict through clarifying roles and creating a 'union of individuals around common objectives'.

Facilitators

The combined team used facilitators from the outset to help establish effective functioning of the team, especially in the early stages. The key functions of facilitators were described as enabling open communication, mediation and breaking down hostilities within the team. Opinions were divided as to whether facilitators would be needed over the long term and therefore whether the facilitator should be internal to the team or an external person. There was strong agreement, however, that in the early stages it was important for the facilitator to be external. It was felt that internal facilitators would not be considered impartial and would be likely to suffer from role conflict. It was also felt that an external facilitator would be more professional and expert in this role.

Team members

Team members noted that there were a number of characteristics which were essential to working successfully within a cross-boundary team. Individuals must be committed to the team, with a real desire to achieve team goals. This means that team members must be able to balance their focus on team goals alongside functional goals. Individuals must also be willing to share success and failure with the rest of the team. Accepting their share of responsibility for both means that team members must be also prepared to confront others who fail to deliver things for which they are accountable.

Team members must be willing to help each other but they should also be able to learn from others and explore new areas outside their own environment. Simply relying on one's own functional knowledge is not enough. After all, a cross-boundary team is likely to consist of a number of people who are expert in their own field but may not know much about other areas. It is important that members understand the broader business context within which the project is being conducted and appreciate the different elements of the project being carried out by others.

This does not entail having a detailed understanding of other people's technical specialisms, but enough of a sense of their priorities and requirements to ensure that the project plan can work smoothly, without people making unnecessary demands on others through ignorance. Members therefore have to be able to liaise across boundaries within their team and between the team and the rest of the organisation, including their boss.

Adjusting to cross-boundary working involves being able to work effectively without hierarchical structures, since cross-boundary working often cuts across hierarchical levels, with senior people reporting to a more junior project leader. It was also seen as important that team members were experienced within their functional field and were not in the position of having everything to learn before they could contribute. As such, people in this case study felt that a cross-boundary team was inappropriate for someone who needed coaching or training on their functional specialism. However many teams embarking on Agile working benefit from the support of Agile coaches.

For both teams, interpersonal relationships within the team were felt to be a strong feature of team success. In team B, strong relationships were built up within each of the sub-teams but working relationships between the two sites were not built up due to the geographical divide. There was a clear sense that team members respected each other and that the environment was one of trust and confidence. These relationships were aided to some extent by social activities outside the work environment. Although these social events were considered beneficial for team-working, the relationships within the team seemed to be developed mainly at work.

Role clarity

Team members need to be clear not only about their own role, but also about the roles of other team members. Role boundaries and team responsibilities need to be understood to minimise the potential for conflict through role overlap, or gaps in provision which will threaten the success of the team. This is an area which is ideally addressed by the team leader in the 'forming' stage of team development when group members begin the shift from independence to interdependence. Time must be spent communicating the vision for the team and clarifying individual and team responsibilities and objectives. The research has highlighted the importance of setting a clear focus for cross-boundary teams, uniting activity around a common purpose. This is particularly important given the individual's functional ties outside the team and the danger that, without clarity of cross-boundary team objectives, individuals will fall back on functional links.

Communication and co-location

The key difference between the two teams was about communication, which seemed to be largely due to the fact that one team (A) was co-located, while the other was not. Members of team A were very positive about the level of communication within the team. They were able to hold frequent informal discussions as well as regular review meetings. The dissemination of information was felt to happen on a regular basis which meant that information received was timely and relevant.

This was in contrast to team B, who felt that there were clear divisions between the two sites. They were united in blaming the poor communication between the two halves of the team on the geographical divide. Members in each of the sub-teams felt that they were well informed about their part of the team but had very little knowledge of what was happening at the other site. The fact that there were very few face-to-face encounters between the two sub-teams seemed to lead to conflict which then took time to resolve.

Clearly, co-location, though ideal, may not be practicable, especially in global organisations in which virtual teams become the norm. However, this case highlights the importance of at least an occasional opportunity to 'personalise' the relationship through meetings, visits, video conferencing, the use of electronic 'team rooms' and other means of helping people to establish a relationship with one another. This is in addition to the need for regular briefings and updates so that people can feel part of the larger whole.

Measures

Within the teams there was agreement that measures were important, but that what was currently measured were the 'hard' measures relating to project targets, resource usage, etc. These measures were set on an individual basis. There was no conscious monitoring of 'soft' measures relating to team processes and learning; consequently, there was a sense that the effectiveness of the team was judged entirely on results rather than taking into account how those results had been achieved. In a cross-boundary team where there is potential for teamworking to be seen as peripheral to individuals' main role, the use of soft measures may help keep the team focused on learning and gaining more transferable skills.

Team learning

Although there was general agreement that team learning did occur within both teams, it was also apparent that this was very much at an informal, unconscious level than through any formal learning process. One of the problems with the informal learning was that there was no retrieval system so that the team as a whole could learn from its mistakes and successes. Eventually a more formal approach to reviewing learning was adopted following an off-site facilitated team review. These included regular debriefing of learning events, general learning reviews of team processes as well as technical learning reviews and harnessing the expertise of more experienced team members. When these processes were introduced, team members commented on the way in which trust had been built through the open approach to learning and that this is an important element of team 'bonding'. They also remarked on the increase in job satisfaction they felt when time has been allocated to understanding how an effective end result has been achieved.

Benefits of cross-boundary team working

Clearly, when cross-boundary teams work well, they bring benefits to both the organisation and to individuals. One of the key characteristics of both cross-boundary teams studied was that the people in the teams were very enthusiastic about this form of teamwork and proud to be part of teams which they recognised as successful. This success was a powerful motivating factor itself, but interviewees also valued the personal growth gained from the experience. They felt stretched within the team, commented favourably on the new insights they had gained into other aspects of the business, and appreciated their relative freedom from organisational constraints.

The only real demotivators were linked with recognition; in particular, team members resented the lack of recognition of success outside the team. They recognised that working across boundaries involves a great deal of complexity, whereas they had the sense that 'the organisation does not accord enough importance to the concept of cross-boundary teamworking'.

As cross-boundary working becomes the norm, rather than the exception, the challenge for organisations will be to ensure that these sophisticated team skills are nurtured, developed widely and rewarded. If not, people with these eminently transferable skills are likely to find a ready market for them elsewhere.

In this organisation, these 'building blocks' of cross-boundary teamworking have now been applied to other teams beyond the original two. In a real sense, enabling these teams to work effectively was a joint responsibility between the line and HR. Line managers were responsible for the performance and outputs of the teams, while HR were able to help find ways of getting the teams working even more effectively. HR provided the teams with a mechanism for monitoring some of the important 'soft' issues which were affecting performance. With the minimum of training or other conventional interventions, HR were able to help the teams to continue to help themselves.

Reflective activity

- Why is cross-boundary team working important?
- How can such teams more actively learn from one another?
- How can people working remotely come to feel part of a learning community?
- In what other ways can organisations encourage cross-boundary learning?

External collaborations

Just as the massive growth of AI, robotics and cognitive computing has produced a tidal wave of data, so the global economy has enabled the flows of talent, products and money across borders. Innovations often emerge from external partnerships. Some companies have established inter-organisational networks to explore knowledge management issues and to develop strategies for maximising the value of knowledge. One such network is the Knowledge Exchange which aims to put a financial measure on an organisation's intellectual capital.

Another group of companies formed a consortium – Strategic Management of Knowledge and Organisational Learning – which acknowledges the need for organisations to collaborate in order to develop and share know-how on knowledge management. This consortium recognises that these issues must form part of the top management agenda, if more value and sustainable advantage are to be created through knowledge processes. Consortium members understand that the strategic management of knowledge and organisational learning are inextricably interlinked.

The Consortium recognises that there are key elements and relationships which shape how knowledge priorities are selected and focused upon. They note that without the aligning force of business strategy, knowledge initiatives remain disparate and uncoordinated. However, with strong business drivers, knowledge can take on a purpose and direction. Consortium members also recognise while that the main driver for leveraging of knowledge is the value to be created and should therefore be guided by business strategies/strategic imperatives, they also recognise that people and relationships are key to success. The management challenge is to implement the processes that will support and liberate people's capabilities.

There are opportunities for sharing and developing knowledge inside the company and with external stakeholders, such as customers. Companies need to learn about their customers and their needs, and learning can become reciprocal if there is trust and a sense of partnership. NCR in the UK has developed a Learning Centre which has developed a reputation for thought leadership within the high-technology sector. The facilities are available to clients. Leading thinkers address industry gatherings on a range of business and strategic topics. Du Pont supplies customers with a Gold Card which gives them access to Du Pont research.

Increasingly professionals are collaborating with peers in other companies to share ideas and learning. The UK's National Health Service has several national and regional special interest networks that bring staff together from many institutions to explore issues and develop their practice in particular fields. Such networks can be self-organising or gently supported with encouragement from the Centre. Such voluntary arrangements often migrate to become a more formal kind of alliance. For instance open-source innovation is increasingly pursued by large and small companies in pharmaceutical, scientific or engineering sectors working together to develop complex innovations. These are good examples of how healthcare can be improved through conversations and connections (Donaldson et al. 2011).

These forms of collaboration provide all concerned with 'Collaborative Advantage' (Lank 2005). McKinsey predicts that the next cycle of innovation, that of institutional innovation, will be driven largely by the harnessing of knowledge flows across partnerships within ecosystems, as is already happening in industries such as pharmaceuticals. Companies will then move from a focus on scalable efficiency to scalable learning that will speed up the rate of innovation as more ecosystem partners join forces and discover new ways to create value for their customers and ecosystem partners (McKinsey 2019).

Support for peer learning

Learning organisations have cultures that encourage people at all levels to teach each other.

Within companies, networking often happens accidentally or as part of the informal system. Smokers' rooms, in-house gyms and other facilities attract people with similar interests who create networks that cut across hierarchical levels and enable new information circuits to be formed. Networks can also be established through formal means for specific or 'agenda-free' purposes. When experimenting with building learning networks, disseminate information in a timely and extensive way and share 'best practice' via the intranet, etc. Ensure that usable information is catalogued and stored with the relevant technology and that all staff have open access.

3M, a company well known for encouraging innovation, deliberately encourages and enables networking as a means of getting people to share ideas. In 3M, there is a strong culture in which risk-taking is good, innovations can be made by everyone, individual responsibilities are clear and there is a tolerance of honest mistakes. Informal working, including working at home, and teamworking are encouraged.

Create a physical work environment which facilitates shared learning

Physical infrastructure can aid learning. Nowadays, the ergonomics of many companies' large offices are designed to facilitate different kinds of work – with quiet spaces for focus, café-type arrangements for networking, colourful zones with unusual furniture to stimulate creativity, etc. In the corporate headquarters of British Airways, the physical environment was specifically designed to facilitate employee networking. A 'street' complete with coffee bars is intended to create a community environment in which collaboration will naturally take place. This has enabled 'structured' networking in which people with specific forms of knowledge can help one another. Similarly, an office space provider whose various building complexes are occupied by multiple small business tenants organises monthly coffee mornings for all tenants to be able to meet informally in the shared space and potentially spark new business opportunities together.

A number of companies support informal peer mentoring and shadowing through online systems which allow individuals to log their strengths and areas where they would like help to build their capability. The systems match people looking for help with those who are willing to provide support in specific areas. An early example is that of Café VIK, developed by Elizabeth Lank, previously programme director, knowledge management at ICL (now Fujitsu). Café VIK (Valuing ICL Knowledge) was both a physical and virtual 'global coffee room' (in Kippenberger 1997). This acted both as an information exchange service and also as a physical location in the UK where employees could meet informally to share knowledge. Café VIK was developed following extensive staff consultation. So that the knowledge on offer could be made as relevant as possible to the different professional communities within the company, staff were asked 'what kind of information will help you to do your jobs?' A database of people's skills/expertise and project experience facilitated networking. Data warehousing ensured that information was kept up to date. The new service was introduced via roadshows and take-up was substantial. Information sheets were available on the company intranet which featured both issues sheets and attachments offering solutions based on people's experience.

Supportive people systems

Over and above such initiatives, the organisation needs to apply systems thinking to work out how the people systems and processes can underpin the learning organisation. HR can use its processes to motivate and equip employees for learning. For instance, HR can hire and promote people who have strong intellectual curiosity and learning agility and are motivated by learning and experimentation. They can work with managers to design jobs with this in mind, allowing people some 'slack' – i.e. space to reflect and work together to develop ideas. Slack might take the form of giving people embarking on innovation greater access to technology, increasing staff knowledge by investing more in L&D, providing support personnel to ensure that normal work gets done while the innovation process is under way. Slack might also take the form of recruiting for scarce skills, e.g. data-driven mindset to bring in the right capabilities. These actions all provide a cushion of time and resource and reduce the pressure to create sub-optimally in haste.

Google's famous workforce rules require employees to spend 10% of their time on innovation projects that are not part of their current job. Having time to innovate can be a reward in itself: Intuit gives its best business innovators three months of 'unstructured' time that can be used in one big chunk or spread out over six months for part-time exploration of new opportunities. This is about deliberately making the connections between the company's explicit strategies and the ways people actually relate to one another and to the organisation. Innovation can be part of everyone's work routine if they incorporate it into accomplishing their team's goals. When employees cease to be overloaded with unnecessary data and start to perceive the benefits to their own effectiveness of sharing information, they are more likely to willingly collaborate in the generation of useful knowledge. HR can help managers develop the skills of non-judgemental listening and brainstorming. 'Whacky' ideas should be encouraged.

HR and L&D can help provide answers to the employee 'what's in it for me' question. L&D can help people to develop valuable information skills and find synergies between the individual's need for growth and personal development and the company's needs. The philosophy should be about supporting people to reach their full potential. Job mobility, networking, knowledge sharing and promoting from within should be encouraged. HR can work with managers to create effective career development practices that are conducive to the sharing of knowledge since people will see that they do not need to hold on to knowledge in order to progress their career. They can ensure that staff are equipped with the appropriate technology – Statoil supplies its employees with laptops and advanced communications equipment at home.

HR can make sure that people are rewarded appropriately for developing and sharing knowledge. When employees know that their knowledge and experience are an asset that can add value to the business – and they are rewarded for sharing that knowledge – they do not fear doing so. Team-based reward and recognition can be used to reward good learning behaviour. In one company, bonus awards are determined by team performance. Each person is awarded a bonus based on their individual contribution, but the organisation then applies a multiplier based on team performance.

CONCLUSION

We have discussed how the accelerating pace of change in the competitive environment now requires organisations not only to move fast to meet market needs but also to leverage their human resources to the maximum if they are to gain and retain competitive advantage. Crisis perhaps provides managers with the opportunity to fundamentally rethink how they manage knowledge in future. There needs to be a clear strategy with regards to the types of knowledge the organisation wishes to develop, capture, integrate into the main business processes and be able to rapidly retrieve. IT and HR systems need to complement each other but the real challenge is human. Developing and sharing knowledge should not rely solely on people's goodwill but it should be in employees' interests to do so since they become equipped with the skills required for the Information Age, that will help them become more employable and develop their career. A win-win employment relationship is vital to ensuring that knowledge management is effective for all stakeholders. After all,

> If it hasn't got the right underlying contract with its people that means, 'I'm interested in your potential, rather than in your immediate output over the next three months', then I think the bell is tolling.
>
> (De Geus 1997)

To build trust that leads to knowledge sharing and the development of exciting new products and services, leaders and managers must take the lead in developing a culture that is conducive to learning and knowledge-creation, especially in a virtual working environment. Managers must encourage others to learn continuously from one another and be prepared to do so themselves. They must build collaborative capabilities and ensure employees are provided with the appropriate environment and infrastructure, including time and connectedness, to work together on the shared task.

For their part, HR and L&D professionals can create a focus on continuous corporate and personal renewal by implementing policies, which value diversity, inclusion and employee well-being. They can help individuals and teams to address skill gaps, play to their strengths, release their potential for innovation and ensure they are rewarded for doing so. Given the centrality of their role, HR and L&D can act as knowledge hub, build social capital inside and outside the organisation, connect people with each other and ensure that the organisation can operate as a cohesive whole, able to maximise its collective knowledge assets.

If the pandemic teaches us anything, it is that a learning culture can be a game changer when it comes to navigating today's turbulent and disruptive context. In a true learning organisation, continuous learning becomes a way of life and helps the organisation become more resilient. Translating learning about the effectiveness of the more relational ways of managing people demonstrated during the crisis into management practice going forward is likely to become a key source of sustainable innovation.

REFERENCES

Butler, O.E. (1998). *Parable of the Talents*. New York: Seven Stories Press.

Cheese, P. (2021). Managing during uncertainty, *People Management*, April/May.

Collins, J. and Porras, J.I. (2002). *Built to Last: Successful Habits of Visionary Companies*. New York: HarperCollins.

De Geus, A.P. (1997). *The Living Company*. Boston, MA: Harvard Business School Press.

De Jong, M., Marston, N. and Roth, E. (2015). *The Eight Essentials of Innovation Excellence*, McKinsey & Co. https://www.mckinsey.com/business-functions/strategy-and-corporate-finance/our-insights/the-eight-essentials-of-innovation

Donaldson, A., Lank, E. and Maher, J. (2011). *Communities of Influence: Improving Healthcare through Conversations and Connections*. Boca Raton: CRC Press.

Finger, M. and Brand, S.B. (1999). The concept of the 'learning organisation' applied to transformation in the public sector, in M. Easterby-Smith, L. Araujo, and J. Burgoyne (eds.), *Organizational Learning and the Learning Organization*. Sage.

Garvin, D.A. (1993). Building the learning organization. *Harvard Business Review*, 78, 80.

Ghoshal, S. and Bartlett, C. (1998). *The Individualized Corporation*. Heinemann.

Hale, R. and Ulrich, D. (2021). How leaders lead post-pandemic: Explore mysteries more than solve puzzles. *Mayvin,* March 26. https://mayvin.co.uk/how-leaders-lead-post-pandemic-richard-hale-dave-ulrich/

Handy, C. (1997). *The Hungry Spirit.* London: Hutchinson.

Kahneman, D. (2011). *Thinking, Fast and Slow.* London: Penguin Books.

Kippenberger, T. (1997). Searching for the 'Holy Grail' at ICL. *The Antidote,* 2(2), 34–36. https://doi.org/10.1108/EUM0000000006336

Kransdorff, A. (1995). Succession planning in a fast-changing world. *Training Officer,* 31(2), 52–53.

Lank, E. (2005). *Collaborative Advantage: How Organisations Win by Working Together.* London: Palgrave McMillan.

Leadbetter, C. (2000). *Living on Thin Air.* London: Penguin.

McKinsey & Company. (2019). *How the best companies create value from their ecosystems,* 19 November [online] https://www.mckinsey.com/industries/ financial-services/our-insights/how-the-best-companies-create-value-from-their-ecosystems (archived at https://perma.cc/J9JE-PFC2) [accessed 13 February 2021]

Morgan, G. (1993). *Imaginization: The Art of Creative Management.* London: Sage.

Mueller, J. (2011). The interactive relationship of corporate culture and knowledge management: A review. *Review of Management Sciences,* 10, 1–19.

Nonaka, I. (1991). The knowledge-creating company. *Harvard Business Review,* November–December, p. 97.

Nonaka, I. and Takeuchi, H. (1995). *The Knowledge-Creating Company.* Oxford: Oxford University Press.

Peters and Waterman. (2004). *In Search of Excellence: Lessons from America's Best-run Companies,* 2nd Edition. London: Profile Books.

Pisano, G.P. (2019). The hard truth about innovative cultures. *Harvard Business Review,* January–February issue.

Senge, P. (1990). *The Fifth Discipline.* New York: Doubleday Currency.

Stewart, T.A. (1997). *Intellectual Capital: The New Wealth of Organizations.* London: Nicholas Brealey.

Tetlock, P.E. and Gardner, D. (2015). *The Art and Science of Prediction.* New York: Crown Publishers.

Varney, S. (2008). Learning – key to organizational transformation in a complex world. *Developing HR Strategy (March).* London: Croner.

Zuboff, S. (1988). *In the Age of the Smart Machine: The Future of Work and Power.* Oxford: Butterworth-Heinemann.

18
Conclusion

The best way to predict your future is to create it.

Abraham Lincoln

These are very challenging times for organisations and we're all operating with greater uncertainty than ever before. Since this book was first published in 1999, HRM theory and HR practice have moved on significantly. The changing business environment has raised awareness of the critical importance to business success of 'human capital'; the search for 'talent' has become a holy grail; 'employee engagement' is treated as key to high performance; people management and development are seen as vital levers of competitive advantage in organisations worldwide. So HR – the people function – should be at the forefront of leading exciting and indisputably value-adding developments.

DOI: 10.4324/9781003219996-21

CHAPTER OVERVIEW

In this chapter, we shall review HR's journey towards this nirvana. We will look back at some of the key themes in the book and look ahead at some possible future directions HR might take. We shall cover:

- Attracting and mobilising talent
- Building performance capability
- Building effective leadership
- Creating healthy and successful organisations
- Ensuring good governance
- Developing HR leadership

LEARNING OBJECTIVES

- To review key messages from the book
- To explore possible future HR contributions

INTRODUCTION: LOOKING BACK TO LOOK TO FORWARD

In the past couple of decades, the field of SHRM theory has moved on and the HR function has made great strides in many areas. However Kaye (1999) raised an important concern about SHRM. Does SHRM benefit employees as well as their organisations? Kaye (1999) suggests that SHRM may be improving the bottom line of companies but may be hurting employees – especially when workers are viewed as commodities. As Kaye explains, a broadening of SHRM will be required.

I agree with Kaye on this but suspect that things may already be changing to produce a more balanced set of outcomes for SHRM. We have discussed how changing social and political environment and technological advances are challenging the role of business, the nature of business models and driving new ways of working. Technology in particular is disrupting the workforce, transforming both the job content and the skills required for the digital age. The days of permanent, full-time employment are perhaps on the wane and instead we increasingly see various forms of contingent working, new management approaches and flatter, team-based organisational structures where people expect to have more say. Jobs are more mobile; more flexible, hybrid working patterns are emerging. As people will be working for longer, career models are being transformed; work in future will be more about self, rather than your current employer. Providing opportunities to work flexibly, prioritising employee health and well-being, must become the norm.

Other major drivers of change – including climate change, 'black swan' events such as the health crisis and the pandemic, growing national isolationism and populism, protests against gender and racial inequalities – challenge many deep-rooted aspects of society and ways of doing business. Businesses and HR, the people profession, must step up to confront discrimination and make inclusion in all its forms a reality, creating opportunities for all. Trust-building will become a major challenge since various reports into corporate scandals in recent years have resulted in generally low levels of trust in leaders in many business, political and public settings.

Yet trust oils the wheels of agility and the ability to change course – a vital necessity since organisations will almost certainly continue to change in ways as yet unknowable. This puts a particular onus on leaders to lead in ways that are ethical, transparent and build trust, especially given the uncertain backdrop which increases people's sense of unease. Amongst many ethical issues that must be addressed is data privacy. With the wide range of apps and AI now available, the GDPR is requiring HR to look at what information is held about people and how this is used.

To tackle some of these major challenges it has become apparent that action is needed at societal level as well as across the business community. Businesses and governments must look beyond the neo-liberal shareholder value model of globalisation, with its short-termist focus. If not, they can expect pressure from all angles to respond, to show that they can act responsibly and fairly, including towards the environment, communities and society as a whole. We are perhaps at an inflection point, moving from a business world entirely defined by growth and wealth-generation for shareholders to something broader and more multi-faceted that places stakeholders, including people, at the centre. Indeed, embracing quadruple bottom line thinking – people, planet, profit and purpose – provides perhaps a more appropriate and clearer steer on how to navigate today's complexities and produce outputs that matter to all stakeholders not only in the short-term but also over time.

HR rising to the challenge

The scope of HR has expanded in recent years and roles are being created in new HR specialisms, many with a technical or analytical flavour. Indeed, Deloitte argue that this line of travel will continue since 'The future of HR must be one of expanded focus and extended influence: expanding its focus to encompass the entirety of work and the workforce, and extending its sphere of influence to the enterprise and business ecosystem as a whole' (Volini et al. 2020).

Many HR teams continue to gradually evolve their operating models to help them address the tactical, operational and strategic needs of their organisation in the most efficient and effective ways possible. Indeed a few HR teams, as featured in this book, are in the vanguard of digital HR transformation. Others have become so skilled at what they do that they can operate as an external profit centre.

Yet, more generally, the HR function still struggles to be seen as a credible player, especially with respect to the degree to which HR is aligned to business strategy. While no one doubts the importance of Finance as a function, HR still seems to be under the sceptical spotlight, having to prove that it adds value.

So what does the future hold for HR? Will HR remain largely a pragmatic, transactional functional whose value is ever in doubt? Or will HR's role be to provide value-adding leadership, geared to building organisational capacity and capability? The jury is still out. Some practitioners will say that their organisation is not ready for a strategic HR approach, that what really counts is delivering the 'pieces' well in the here and now. Other practitioners argue that it is precisely because the function contents itself with administration, hiring and firing, that HR is not valued.

I would argue that this is a false dilemma which can be partly reconciled through the ways in which HR organises its delivery. While in some organisations HR continues to be organised along generalist lines, especially in SMEs, the dominant HR architecture, particularly in large organisations, tends to be along the lines of the 'Ulrich' functional role model, whether HR operations are outsourced or insourced using call centres or shared services. While this may be a sensible way of sharing responsibilities, and should allow for both operational and strategic excellence, many HR teams have struggled to make the HR structure work. It has in some cases created unhelpful role divisions which may make it difficult for the HR team as a whole to develop a strategic approach and may cause problems when it comes to implementation.

However, early adopters of the model continue to develop and modify the structure as they learn what works, often slimming down the number of business partners to create genuinely strategic roles, while more generally business partnering becomes synonymous with internal consultancy. Increasingly centres of excellence offering specialist expertise are being recognised as adding value. There is growing demand for expertise in strategic areas such as organisation design, succession planning, designing talent recruitment and retention strategies. The ongoing modification of the application of this conceptual framework for HR roles reflects practical experience and feedback about how to address both short-term and longer-term needs at the same time. In other organisations, strategic delivery is through a more hybrid architecture involving consultants, where the right team deals with the day-to-day operational issues and HR leaders provide not only oversight but also exert influence at executive committee level.

We have discussed the views of various pundits who have argued that HR structures should be separated out to enable a better focus on strategic matters. Other pundits suggest that having a separate 'HR' strategy group would be a mistake; that HR plans should be seen as so integral to the business strategy that they do not need a separate unit to address them. In recent times much has been written about employee-centricity as the frame within which HR should operate. Perhaps this is the surest way of aligning HR and business strategies – making them one with people at the centre!

The real challenge, according to a CIPD-convened focus group of senior HR managers and directors, is to 'keep the eye on the ball', having worked out what the 'ball' is in the first place. Several comments reveal common views of what HR needs to focus on:

- 'anything from not doing 'day-to-day' work to looking ahead three years'
- 'influencing the board and the direction of the company'
- 'making a difference to the bottom line'
- 'developing the frameworks, policies and initiatives to move the business forward'
- 'integrating future business goals/needs with people issues/needs in a plan'
- 'clear thinking/policies/right direction/motivation of staff'.

Whichever structural model is adopted for HR matters less than the delivery focus it enables. As well as supporting the way work is done today, HR should be focusing on the way people will be working tomorrow. This means taking a strategic and systemic view of how jobs, ways of working, teams, leadership and management practices will evolve, together with their skills implications, and focusing energy on preparing the path for a smooth transition. Deloitte (Volini et al. 2020) argue that HR broadening its focus from employees to organisation and work and the workforce represents what they call 'exponential' HR.

What is important is to gauge the actual needs and readiness of your organisation for what it intends to do strategically. Does it have the core capabilities, culture, systems and processes, working practices and human skills to accomplish what it wants to do? If not, what will be required to ensure that strategic aims can be accomplished? This means defining the implications of business strategy for organisational capability, such as the firm's ability to learn, and developing measurable actions to build that capability. If, for example, managing costs is a strategic aim, does the organisation have the capability to create high productivity, use resources efficiently and become a low-cost provider in its marketplace?

An inflection point

The pandemic of 2020–2021 perhaps marks an inflection point in HR's journey, with a rapid acceleration of various underlying trends. The crisis has shone a spotlight on the amazing agility organisations can display when under great pressure and working to a clear, shared objective. Business leaders have learned the power of collaboration and innovation. Firms such as Unilever and Siemens have pivoted their business models in a matter of days to produce much needed goods such as hand sanitisers and ventilators. The pandemic experience has been a great leveller. When communicating with their newly remote workforce, business leaders have learned the value of being human and empathetic. HR teams too have demonstrated great employee-centricity. Having to move fast has meant that many HR teams have focused laser-like on creating a digital work-force seemingly overnight. They have paid attention to amplifying communications, providing explicit support to the workforce from managers, leaders and specialist HR resources to help build employee resilience.

However, it would be a mistake to assume that alignment with business strategy in a crisis means focusing HR delivery exclusively on short-term requirements, important though these are. The challenge will be to integrate learning from what organisations have done well during the protracted lockdown periods, into new ways of working going forward. Since the HR function is always likely to be thinly resourced, there is a risk that time pressures may push strategic matters down the 'to do' list and cause a 'snap back' to previous ways of working, with the potential for functional irrelevance.

So while HR can and must get the operational basics right and apply agile disciplines to its ways of working, this should also allow HR to make a really strategic contribution to business success. As I have emphasised throughout this book, the focus of short-term activity should always be informed by a view of what the organisation will need longer-term. That is because as organisations change, what they need from HR, and therefore the scope of the HR role will also change.

Post-pandemic is the critical time to put in place the strategic changes you want to see for the long-term. HR should also be the key interpreter, problem-solver and strategic cat-alyst with regard to people issues. A strategic and systemic approach within an OD frame of reference is needed. To develop longer-term strategic goals which can inform activity in the here-and-now and create value-adding 'deliverables' that contribute to sustaina-ble performance HR professionals must demonstrate real business acumen and have a thorough understanding of their business and what it is trying to achieve. They must think through the implications of context for their organisation's intended strategy – such as changing demographics, the more competitive landscape, the changing nature of customer preference – and consider how the labour market and the nature of work will affect the kind of future workforce required.

For a CIPD focus group of senior HR managers and directors, translating executive priorities into the people and organisation strategies that will deliver the people out-comes required for business success was about:

- Looking at what the organisation needs to deliver (medium and long term)
- Identifying the support needed to implement business decisions across countries and business units
- Supporting the business objectives of the firm by timely, intelligent and common-sensical HR activities and planning.

These outcomes should be measurable so that the relevant value logic for the organisation can be tracked through. HR must ensure that wherever work takes place, it is carried out ethically. Embracing technology and analytics should free up HR to better target HR activities to improve employee engagement and clarify the engagement – performance link. Indeed, this should enable improvement along the whole employee experience journey and help put the 'human' at the forefront of the HR agenda. Indeed, 'HR' strategies are probably better called 'People' strategies if they are named at all.

Partnership with the line

Responsibility for the design and implementation of effective people strategies should be shared between the line and HR. For this to happen, there needs to be give and take on both sides as well as mutual understanding and respect. A common language helps! The same HRD focus group highlighted the importance of communicating in business language rather than professional jargon:

- Simple rather than sophisticated
- Business focused
- Human!

HR must understand the practical implications of delivering people-related business strategies and ensure that all aspects of HR delivery are professional, accurate and effective. Line managers may need skills training or updating to effectively carry out their people management responsibilities in today's changing workplace.

Of course, strategic business partnership is not a one-way street. If line managers genuinely believe that HR issues have a critical impact on achieving business success, they should insist on involving HR professionals in the business strategy-making process. That way, expensive mistakes can be avoided, and potential opportunities can be identified at the optimum time.

For CIPD's CEO Peter Cheese (2012): 'If HR doesn't have a seat at the boardroom table, we should have the confidence to challenge the CEO and say: these issues about skills, talent, innovation, engagement, diversity are crucially important; this is what we need to be doing; this is why you need me at the table. Just as companies need financial and marketing strategies, so they need a human capital strategy to support the business strategy'.

The key thing is to focus on what matters and be clear about priorities. Let us now recap some of the key areas where HR might contribute value, now and in the future, looking through a slightly longer-term lens. By 2030, will HR teams be leading employee-centric practice and will management teams be demonstrating human-centred leadership? If so, how will we get there?

ATTRACTING AND MOBILISING TALENT

In today's fast-changing business environment talent is the key source of competitive advantage and the need to develop organisational capability is at the heart of HR's remit. For most organisations today, the big challenge is to get the right people with the right skills in the right place at the right time – and retain them. Business leaders are more likely than ever before to seek help from HR in addressing key questions:

- Do I have enough of the right people to deliver success today and tomorrow?
- How can the people-technology interface be optimised?
- What's the right kind of workforce model for us?
- How can we make diversity and employee well-being real?
- How do I ensure I have the capability and the skills to innovate and grow?

HR can and should lead thinking and practice about how to secure and retain the talent needed for success, about what drives outcomes through people, about how to motivate and mobilise talent working in new ways to produce high-quality outputs. This means asking – and finding answers to – questions such as these:

- What forms of talent will be needed and where will these be obtained?
- How will the current workforce factor into the future landscape?
- What kinds of leadership and management capabilities, structures and technologies will be required in the years ahead?
- How can we create an excellent employee experience at all stages of the employee lifecycle?
- How can we support both employee well-being and performance?
- How do we equip people with the digital and other skills they will need to be successful?
- How do we support people working remotely or on hybrid work arrangements?
- How do we build a sense of community for the whole workforce?
- How can we help managers and the workforce transition to a digital work world?

Essentially the answers to many of these questions requires rethinking how we use HR talent micro-practices to build a healthy and effective workforce. As we have discussed, these include workforce planning, building diverse talent pipelines, strategic recruitment, improving the capability of managers and leaders, enhancing employee engagement, continuously developing skills and providing opportunities for growth and careers, developing more holistic rewards and building a culture conducive to learning, creativity and knowledge sharing.

Understanding and developing the experience of employees in all phases of their working lives should be top of every HR team's agenda. The real challenge is to adopt a 'best-fit' approach to talent management and the employee experience, understanding different demographics and tailoring different propositions for different talent segments. At the same time, this should be about understanding people as individuals, not just as members of a demographic group.

Post-pandemic we can envisage staff working according to different working patterns and locations. We can use digital tools and portals to give people access to support on health, well-being and other important issues. Yet while technology increasingly enables work to be carried out remotely and at any time, in a world that is more connected than ever before, individuals are increasingly feeling isolated and desire human interaction. Not surprisingly mental health issues in the workplace have risen to the forefront of media attention, echoing the growing focus on mental health issues particularly affecting young people due to the social media pressures to achieve and look and be perfect.

To build a sense of community, communication must be different, reaching out to the workforce more regularly. We have to create workplaces and working arrangements that are healthy, people-led and values-focused.

We have talked about redefining 'talent' and the need for inclusive as well as exclusive talent development approaches, ensuring we have both high potential future leaders and also a workforce equipped with the digital and other skills they will need to succeed. We have talked of the importance of HR embracing the benign power of technology, for instance in automating operations and recruitment, in monitoring employee mood, and of using analytics to understand what the key employee engagement issues are, to clarify concerns, spot health trends and to be able to pinpoint the human capital contribution to business success.

In many sectors machines are not replacing humans but enabling work to be done that human beings cannot do as well as computers. For instance in the nuclear, oil and gas industries aerial, land and underwater robots are being used to perform complex and important tasks that no human being could safely carry out in such hostile environments. Medicine, the law and many other traditional professions are using technology to improve efficiency and accuracy and to swiftly draw together intelligence from various data sources that previously would have taken months to analyse (*The Economist* 2016).

Whether this benign enhancement of human capabilities will continue longer term is questionable, even if PwC's (2017a) predictions that autonomous intelligence – the next stage of technological development when adaptive intelligent systems will no longer need humans to make decisions but themselves can take over the decision-making process – seem like science fiction fantasy. And yet they may not be so far away in reality.

At the same time HR must avoid the potentially malign use of technology, such as for intrusive surveillance purposes. Despite its business advantages, for the pessimists, a future work world dominated by technology also presents a mass of threats, not least of potentially widespread unemployment and loss of personal privacy. For while technology and data can help businesses to create evidence-based and more personalised recommendations for customers, social media usage has enabled data centres to capture information about job candidates and potentially use it against them in recruitment contexts.

We have considered the potential risk of built-in biases in AI and other technologies that we must guard against in building a diverse and productive workforce. In many contexts there are shrinking offerings for employees, with limited resources for continuous development, ongoing reorganisations in the quest for flexibility and growing demands – for more speed, efficiency, accountability and value for money (Aon 2018). Mobile technology has enabled greater flexibility – and people can work from anywhere – but they are also expected to do so in 'always on' cultures.

The media are abuzz with stories of the human consequences of poor management and unfair practice, such as work intensification, changing employment contracts, insecurity, perceptions of loss of autonomy, in-work poverty and non-disclosure agreements to silence criticism. This narrative is driven by the assumption that all employers care about is productivity and in some cases, such reports are well-founded (Graeber 2018). These demands create pressurised work environments where only the successful 'swim' rather than 'sink'. Far from meaningful work, many employees experience only the negative aspects of work as described by Studs Terkel, (*Working* 1974):

'a search... for daily meaning as well as daily bread, for recognition as well as cash, for astonishment rather than torpor; in short, for a sort of life rather than a Monday through Friday sort of dying'.

HR must lead the way in valuing people and creating the conditions where people can both earn a living and 'have a life'. This will mean engaging the workforce in continuously reimagining work to ensure meaning and purpose – personal, societal and organisational. HR must develop an end-to-end employee experience that integrates both employees and contingent workers and keeps a firm lens on equality, diversity and inclusion practice throughout all aspects of the employee experience. Workplaces should be designed to accommodate and engage with all employees with diversity and inclusion in mind to ensure no one feels at a disadvantage (CIPD 2015). Employee well-being should be seen as a strategic business outcome.

BUILDING PERFORMANCE CAPABILITY

If organisations are to be successful, they need high performance from their workforces. The other main challenge relates to innovation. In order to innovate, organisations need to be bold and prepared to take some risks. They need a culture conducive to innovation, risk-taking and learning that is built on trust. Business leaders need to know:

- Am I creating the right environment for success? How can we organise ourselves and work with agility to deliver outstanding customer outcomes?
- Do the business culture and leadership enable people to give of their best?

These are now being recognised for the strategic issues they are. While HR may have been trying to get these issues on the strategic agenda for years, the irony is that they are usually only treated as serious business issues when line managers too see their importance. So will HR seize the opportunity to bring about culture change conducive to high performance? Will developing leaders at all levels become a central plank of HR strategy?

While HR's primary role is ensure that the organisation has the right people (skills, knowledge, motivations) to deliver, HR must also reimagine the organisation to ensure it can delivery. This is about working with the company culture to create the conditions for expanded levels of creativity, exploration and problem-solving. This requires the systemic thinking so typical of organisation development and design. How will HR support the development of a high-performance culture? How will work processes need to be managed to achieve high-quality deliverables? How will the core competencies be activated? What aspects of the organisation's culture will need to be strengthened, balanced out or changed? HR teams must develop their own answers with their stakeholders to fit their current and future organisational context.

Arguably, by 2030, many workforces will comprise people and machines working together to rapidly create high value innovative products and services for an ever more demanding customer base. HR will be creating on-demand access to capabilities, whether human or machine, across the organisation. We're not there yet and currently some roles are being enhanced by technology while others are being 'hollowed out' or are disappearing altogether. HR has to lead in ensuring that human work can be augmented, rather than eliminated, by technology.

HR's contribution therefore needs to go beyond revising policies and simplifying performance management approaches. They need a vision of a high-performance organisation to act as longer-term focus. Such a vision is typically underpinned by humanistic values and is geared to enabling both high performance and also employee well-being.

Components of such a vision include developing the behaviours, systems and processes geared to increasing customer value such as shared leadership throughout the organisation to create momentum; decentralised and devolved decision-making; development of people capacities through learning at all levels; and performance, operational and people management processes aligned to organisational objectives; encouraging a wellness culture that helps reduce absenteeism. It's about building inclusive organisations that treat people fairly and respond to diverse voices.

HR needs to understand what types of performance are needed in their organisation and must support teams and managers in making the transition to new ways of working. As advanced technologies disrupt the nature of many jobs and employment relationships, many managers now have responsibility for teams comprising employees and contractors, working to various patterns. HR can help line managers to manage for performance, create clear accountabilities and set performance standards which help employees raise the bar on their own performance. HR should advocate performance management practice that is regular and offers feedback that motivates the workforce, helps them improve and holds them to account.

As jobs are disaggregated, for many people in future, work will consist of a series of tasks through which they have to navigate their employment and career prospects. HR can help line managers recreate work to design 'jobs' in such a way that people can still have meaningful work experiences. HR can help line managers create a highly productive work climate in which people are clear about their roles, have challenging objectives, access to the information and other resources they need to do their jobs, receive effective coaching, appropriate rewards and recognition of achievement as well as career paths through which they can grow.

Organisations pursuing agility and customer-centricity will operate mainly through teams, some of which will be self-organising. HR can support collaborative ways of working across the organisation and its ecosystem, making teams the main focus for action and performance management. Managers may need help figuring out their own role with respect to supporting teams. Working with line managers, HR can ensure that work is allocated fairly within teams, with team members having equal opportunity to be involved in stretching projects.

Great results come from highly motivated and engaged people. HR/L&D can provide upskilling and reskilling opportunities - both personalised and team-based – in the fundamental transferable skills that build the cultural capabilities, such as speed and customer focus, on which future business success in the digital world will depend. At the same time today's volatile context makes the task of understanding the drivers for engagement – such as career development, well-being and flexible working – more complex. Data analytics can help pinpoint where to focus engagement effort for greatest effect. These ingredients should not only produce high performance that is sustainable but also higher employee commitment which in turn leads to greater customer satisfaction and better results for investors and other stakeholders.

BUILDING EFFECTIVE LEADERSHIP

HR must ensure that the leadership of the organisation has the capabilities required for the future, including the ability to lead through ambiguity and operate not only as business leaders but also leaders of human systems. This involves critically evaluating the quality of current leadership and consciously developing succession for the medium term, incorporating fresh ways of thinking. Again, the changing business requirements should drive the assessment agenda:

- Are leaders scanning the environment for new opportunities for their organisation?
- To what extent is the current leadership able to create an adaptable, change-oriented organisation in which accountabilities are clear, employees are highly motivated and committed and where the culture is supportive of learning and innovation?
- Are leaders able to provide clarity of direction in ambiguous circumstances so that employees are clear what needs to be done and what is no longer relevant?
- Do leaders develop and manage effective relationships with internal and external stakeholders?

HR should challenge the C-Suite to avoid taking people for granted and coach executives to develop their emotional intelligence and social skills so that they can supply the empathetic approach needed when communicating and leading remotely.

Shared leadership

In many settings the belief that a single person is the leader or manager is at odds with reality. As a result of the technology-driven, fast-moving context that characterises the twenty-first century, successful organisations will increasingly rely on highly independent, knowledgeable individuals working as part of multi-disciplinary teams who can make good decisions fast. So HR should encourage the development of shared leadership at every level. This is when leadership is distributed amongst a set of individuals instead of being centralised in the hands of a single individual who acts in the role of leader (Pearce and Conger 2002, pp. 1–3). Shared leadership is variously defined as:

- an activity that is shared or distributed among members of the team that will underpin this way of working
- a dynamic interactive influencing process among individuals in groups for which the objective is to lead one another to the achievement of group or organisational goals or both.

A key distinction between shared and traditional models of leadership is that the influence process involves more than just downward influence of subordinates by a positional leader. It is a social process between people through which people working together can solve problems in an increasingly complex world, where individuals have specific experience, knowledge and competencies but are dependent on complementary experience, knowledge and skills in others. Shared leadership is about the quality of the interaction rather than people's formal positions and is evaluated by how well people work together to enhance the process. Shared leadership is where everyone is involved in acts of leadership, where communication and making sense of conflict require that the process is democratic, honest and ethical and where the common goal is improved customer outcomes.

As such, the shared leadership model is well suited for enabling continuous and inclusive organisational change. The formal leader's role is to create the climate in which the team can flourish through team building, resolving conflicts and being clear about the vision. The best results often come when employees are involved in goal-setting and decision-making from the outset. By shifting the perspective from viewing leadership purely as a single-person activity to also viewing it as a collective construction process, opens up space for all participants to express their agency at every stage of the change process, from ideation to implementation (Tams 2018). When individuals feel that they have an impact on the organisation and that they have some power and responsibility, they have a greater desire for success. Evidence suggests that shared leadership can increase risk-taking, innovation and commitment which should result in improved customer outcomes and an organisation that is responsive, flexible and successful.

CREATING HEALTHY AND SUCCESSFUL ORGANISATIONS

Learning, agility and renewal are hallmarks of healthy organisational cultures. HR can play a key role in spurring the sharing of knowledge and learning through its role as corporate integrator and spreader of good practice across the organisation. Acting as change agent, HR should lead on building a more collaborative, agile, learning culture and structure. Organisational design and development are relatively neglected areas in many HR teams. Yet with an OD mindset and the help of analytics, HR can help break down hindering bureaucracy and support more integrated and empowered team-based working.

By acting as organisational 'glue' HR can ensure that the organisation is greater than the sum of its parts. This is about ensuring that there is enough enabling consistency – so that people understand what the company stands for, and how their role contributes to organisational success and what standards are expected – and also creating enough flexibility in structures, roles, skills and mindsets to ensure that the organisation can remain agile and innovative. For members of the HRD focus group this was about:

- Creating a cohesive framework/common company language
- Developing flexible, broad-minded and multi-skilled businesspeople
- Communicating clearly to people about the things that affect them

As well as developing a deep understanding of how to bring about change within complex systems, HR needs to develop a culture change agenda which is strategic and future-focused, rather than reactive and simply 'picking up the pieces'. HR therefore must:

- Think big picture
- Act as internal change agent – with an eye on strategic business plans and organisational effectiveness
- Make uncertainty manageable

HR must be able to anticipate where change will be needed, and act as a proactive enabler and implementer of change, in a way that puts the organisation on the 'front foot', builds organisational resilience and adaptability before problems occur and creates new opportunities for the organisation.

HR should develop expertise in internal communications and ensure that every medium is used to best effect to create effective information flows, participation and learning. Organisations must ensure fair practice for all, wherever they are based; for instance ensuring that people who are working at home and therefore not visible in the office do not miss out on opportunities. There will be growing mental health issues to actively address via policies and support services. HR must lead the way in providing a safe and healthy working environment, devising structures and ways of working which not only optimise employee well-being but also are hard to imitate working conditions, especially around knowledge work. Bringing about change will require collaborating with other change agents, working in integrated teams with other functions and guiding senior management in the roles they must play to bring about effective change.

Ensuring good governance

Many organisations will not survive into the post-pandemic world. Organisations may stumble as they face increasing uncertainty, financial difficulties, moral dilemmas, possible risks to their corporate reputation. Arguably by 2030, those organisations that do survive and thrive will have attractive reputations – for their products and services, the way they operate and also as an employer. They are likely to be pursuing a higher-level purpose. After all, if a business interacts positively with the society in which it works, people are more likely to say that 'this is a good business' whose products and services they want to buy, or that they want to work for. These will also be organisations which can learn and change tack quickly when needed.

As the experience of many HR teams during the pandemic suggests, HR can play a key role in ensuring that teams can make decisions really quickly, within a framework of good governance, allowing organisations to flex as faster, more radical shifts are re-quired. HR also has a growing role to play in developing good governance, especially the implementation of values-based practices, such as CSR, diversity and environmental policies, and ensuring that the behaviour of leaders at all levels is fair and appropriate. HR must challenge unethical workplace behaviour which can range from minor trans-gressions to illegal activity but are essentially actions that harm the legitimate interests of the organisation, its workforce, customers and wider society. After all, as we have seen in recent years, organisational reputations, once undermined by poor or dishonest practice, tend to be permanently damaged. Firms can only rely on goodwill for so long. They must prioritise creating a fair culture.

The term 'business ethics' exposes an unavoidable inherent tension: managers must continuously balance the needs of the organisation and its stockholders with the needs of other stakeholders. Moreover ethics is a moving target. Social values shift over time, influenced by a complex web of factors. Employers must champion diversity and inclu-sion, keep a close eye on those values and aim to proactively address ethical dilemmas emerging in their companies. Yet, as the Institute for Business Ethics (2021) points out, the ethical risks that business faced in the pre-Covid-19 world have not gone away. 'In some cases, they might have been sharpened by the current climate of uncertainty, the concrete risks of being made redundant for some, and the changed interpersonal interac-tion due to working from home arrangements for others. This means that organisations need to be more alert to some ethical risks that might affect the most vulnerable groups in particular'.

Few ethical issues are more contentious than executive pay, with pay packages re-ceiving scrutiny and substantial backlash for appearing vastly excessive in comparison with the average worker's pay package. 'Fairness' is a morally and politically loaded term that means different things to different people. Yet fairness matters and is an important part of rebuilding trust in business. PwC (2017b) raise the questions, 'Can companies therefore ignore inequality and just get on with the business of generating wealth, leaving governments to deal with redistribution? Can they adopt the Milton Friedman stance that 'the primary social responsibility of companies is to make profit'? Or should they consider themselves as social entities in their own right, where concerns of fairness and justice hold sway?'

In principle, HR as the guardian of reward and recognition, concerned with motivation and engagement, should be seeking to influence executive pay decisions and curb pay excess, as tends to happen in small companies. Yet in large companies, the best Reward professionals can usually hope for is to advise Remuneration committees. Parkes and Davis (2013) question whether HR professionals have the 'courage to challenge' or are set to be permanent 'bystanders'. They argue that although there is a clear understanding of the expectations of ethical stewardship, HR professionals often struggle to fulfil this role because of competing tensions and perceptions of their role within their organisations. But this is not about HR acting merely as company compliance officer, imposing the dead hand of complicated and over-burdensome policy and scrutiny which produces a risk-averse and slow-moving culture. It is much more about leading discussions at all levels which create a shared focus on ethical practice, develop authentic leaders and ensure that what is promised by the employer brand promise is delivered in reality. It's about arguing for transparency in reward structures and taking into account the average employee when determining executive pay. And as investors step up demands for companies to link executive pay to environment, social and governance (ESG) targets and bonus plans, there is an opportunity for remuneration committees to be influenced by HR as they reshape executive packages.

Despite the tensions, Parkes and Davis suggest that the involvement and active modelling of ethical behaviour by today's business leaders can create a corporate culture that supports ethical business practices and socially responsible action even while making their firms more competitive in the marketplace. An open approach is needed to surface organisational values and build HR procedures which build socially responsible organisations and narrow the growing gap between the super-rich and the rest of the business world.

The CIPD (2019) suggests the following:

- Consider how leadership, management and HR practices shape the ethical climate.
- Use internal communications to encourage high ethical standards and ensure that the values and/or code of ethics are not in contrast to the climate.
- Cascade regular 'moral reminders' in newsletters and business updates confirming not only the ethical expectations, but also reaffirming the leadership support to uphold those values.
- Ensure there is a triangulation of available evidence to support workforce-based recommendations. Regularly extrapolate important insights from all stakeholders and agree critical indicators.
- Monitoring behaviour has been found to reduce unethical behaviour and draws attention to the individual's moral standards and awareness. Balance this with engendering trust.
- Commit to – and deliver – inclusion across the organisation in order to achieve either a benevolent or principled climate.
- Strive towards positive outcomes for the workforce (like well-being) as well as for the business (like profit and loss) in equal balance.
- Don't let short-term business outcomes lead to decision-making that could be deemed unfair and be detrimental to the business in the long run.

- Review policies and practices to ensure they are fair and unbiased. Consider the fairness lens for everyone in the workforce: if it could cause a detriment to an under-represented group, it is unfair.
- Keep political behaviour (such as ambiguous decisions or promoting favoured employees) in check, challenging it when it becomes unhealthy.

CSR should become fully embedded in all aspects of business strategy and the way this is delivered. It is also about building sustainability into HR practice, for instance by making sustainability key to recruitment and onboarding, developing ethical employer brands and strong incentives for staff, including opportunities for volunteering. It's about providing good quality training and conveying the right message to staff with creativity and passion. While ensuring ethical practice may always be more of an art than a science, effective HR practitioners relish the challenge.

DEMONSTRATING HR LEADERSHIP

Earlier in the book I suggested that HR exercising real leadership is about more than leading the HR team – it is also about making a full leadership contribution to the development of the organisation as business professionals with value-adding people and culture expertise. This is about HR using itself as instrument to bring into being the organisation that will thrive in 2030.

The credibility of HR professionals is based partly on their track record of delivering accurate results in a business-like way but also on their ability to build trust and influence at all levels, especially at senior levels. If you have a history of honesty and of following through on what you say you will do, people will be more easily influenced, because they can take what you say at face value. This is the platform for strategically positioning HR as 'credible activist' and 'paradox navigator', working in dialogue with executive teams to figure out what will drive results through people and organisation, or as Dave Ulrich puts it, 'not just the workforce but the workplace'.

Influencing people is an ongoing event that involves mapping the political terrain, working out who you need to influence about what and building relationships with these people. If you are trying to influence others to your way of thinking, be open to people's suggestions and make a point of listening to people's ideas and thoughts and consider what they have to say. By so doing, you'll become a better communicator, because you'll be able to make connections and specific points, and be able to persuade the people you're talking with by building on things that they have said. You may get some very good new ideas out of the bargain.

Building an image of professionalism through knowing your business allows HR to usefully introduce best practice thinking – but critically and pragmatically rather than falling into the 'initiative of the month' trap. This requires HR to network with other members of the HR profession and line managers from other organisations, picking up ideas and developing a global idea of what externally judged good practice looks like. This will enable HR to more confidently assert what needs to be done with regard to the people implications of business strategies in their own organisation and potentially also recommend potential business opportunities.

And in common with members of other professions, in preparing for the future, HR professionals must develop their capacity and capability through professional development. Practitioners must be willing to learn and may need to both broaden and deepen their skills for their expanded roles and in order to keep at the leading edge of their professional expertise and competence. While the skills required will vary according to role, the CIPD (2020) suggests that HR's innovation value will come in future from being a fluid broker of people, able to secure the people with the right skills at the right time and on the right employment contract. They will be employee experience creators adding value at every stage of the employee life cycle. They will focus on the digital enablement of human potential, understanding how and when digital can enhance human potential and partners with digital experts to help achieve this.

They will also role model the way the organisation should be working in relation to digital and technology. They will become expert at de-constructing and re-constructing work, as well as reconstructing the people model to achieve best outcomes. They will be facilitators and relationship builders, working effectively with multiple partners and stakeholders across and beyond organisational boundaries to achieve objectives and integrated change. They will protect time for horizon scanning around the needs of their organisation and the future world of work. Above all they will be a humanising influence in a virtual world, providing a strong voice internally and externally on ethics and values.

Generic skills prerequisites include strategic thinking and action, business understanding, interpersonal and consultancy skills, planning and implementation skills, coaching, organisation development and design. To these should be added empathy, compassion, emotional intelligence, knowledge of diversity and inclusion issues. HR must embrace technology and use it strategically, not just reactively for tracking purposes. They should borrow relevant approaches from other disciplines such as marketing, finance, IT. People analytics can be used to extract key messages about the workforce and the organisation's capability requirements. There is a great deal that can be done by HR teams themselves to develop the skills needed to deliver new types of people strategies. This involves assessing how well the HR team is equipped to manage change and upskilling the team as appropriate.

HR leaders should actively develop a cadre of the most senior HR staff to become a high performing team and potential successors.

The importance of having a growth mindset is most obvious in managing change, which requires a proactive rather than risk-averse reactive stance. Organisations are already feeling the disruptive forces which will affect their future income streams. HR can facilitate discussions about what pre-emptive or proactive actions can be taken in order to mitigate the challenges. Today OD is central to an organisation's agenda. Getting a handle on the principles and skills of organisation design and development, especially working in partnership with an OD specialist, will help clarify how to deliver what the organisation needs. This involves understanding how the organisation works as a system, identifying where change needs to occur to enable the organisation to achieve its goals, applying project management disciplines and integrating separate initiatives into a change framework.

To create coherent change execution also means working in partnership with line managers and other specialist functions such as Finance and IT.

The ability of HR to facilitate and drive workplace change has been vividly illustrated during the pandemic. HR teams have provided support around remote working, digital skills development and changed the rules of engagement to put the 'human' back into HR, making HR leaders the guardians of employee well-being. One company has already brought together HR and sustainability teams under a single remit to ensure environmental values are embedded into its culture and reflected in its employer brand. This ability to integrate people responsibilities with other areas of the business is likely to grow in importance.

Managing culture – which is the identity of the firm in the minds of its best customers and its best employees – involves being willing to look 'outside-in' and challenge the status quo. It involves being able to diagnose the kind of culture required to deliver the business strategy and encouraging leaders to 'walk the talk' with regard to the desired culture and values. This is what Ulrich now refers to as providing a guidance system for the organisation, focusing on talent, leadership and capability and the pathway to get there.

Challenging senior leaders can be a risky thing to do and will require confidence or 'attitude', as Dave Ulrich once described it, on the part of HR. Leaders may have blind spots, so you need to have the courage of your convictions as well as using the political influencing skills described above to help people 'unlearn' old assumptions. According to Jeffrey Pfeffer (1996), this is an area that HR needs to develop: 'the comparatively low power of human resources is often further reduced by the reluctance of its executives to engage in organizational politics'.

On the other hand, it's about knowing how to use data insights and analysis effectively to plan, exert influence over senior executive decision-making and make appropriate business cases for action in key people areas. It's also about getting leaders thinking about what information and data analysis might be needed in order to manage the consequences of decisions that will inevitably have to be made.

Developing HR careers

Developing HR careers may mean moving around the various structural roles available – shared services, centres of excellence and business partnering – working on joint projects with others, ensuring cross-fertilisation and development. Business partners will be senior people, who know how to operate P&Ls and are most likely to have a mixture of backgrounds. Increasingly, organisational strategists will be from a range of backgrounds, of which the HR route may be only one: 'The top HR slot is no longer reserved for the career HR professional. Increasingly business experience, coupled with highly developed consulting skills, is the prerequisite for senior HR roles' (SHRM 2002). More recent studies suggest a similar trajectory, with the addition of tech-savviness. A Harvard Business Review article suggested that of 60 new roles that are likely to be created in the HR field over the next ten years, 21 will have high levels of organisational impact and half will include a mid-to-high tech component.

This may indeed result in the clearest alignment yet between HR and business strategies, when the people leaders have a wide range of experiences and deep understanding of what needs to be done with respect to people and organisation, and where professional expertise is a value-add. And while being tech-savvy and business acumen are core requirements, the cornerstone of HR roles should be empathy, so that HR leaders can support employees in a more humane way. While in future the operational side of HR may shrink, for instance being outsourced, the need to enable diversity and inclusion, drive ethical practice and enhance the employee experience will grow. Successful HR leaders of the future will be those who can rise to these complex challenges to bring undoubted value to their organisations.

CONCLUSION

Extreme critics might argue that by aligning HR strategies to a shareholder value business agenda, HR is colluding with furthering the misery of workers. I believe that, even in organisations that have not yet embraced a triple or quadruple bottom-line philosophy, ensuring a fair balance between the needs of the business and those of people is HR's job.

So in summary, HR leaders who embrace a change agenda can help shape the future by 'future proofing' their organisation. As we have discussed they have many ways to do this, for instance by developing employer brands which are meaningful to current and future employees. They can build employee-centric value propositions which marry up employee needs for work–life balance and well-being with employer needs for flexibility. They can create processes through which people development happens both on and off the job. They can support managers in creating meaningful jobs with line of sight to the organisation's purpose and the customer. They can help managers manage change effectively and get the most from talent by upskilling managers with the skills they need to be effective people managers, such as coaching. They can build employee engagement as the basis of great employee relations by identifying the key drivers of employee engagement in their context and focusing initiatives on these.

It's about creating a strong, unique workplace culture that puts people at its centre. To do this HR leaders must embrace the disciplines of HRM, HRD and OD+D, adopt technology and evidence-based practice. HR can design structures, roles and processes which facilitate cross-organisational teamworking and shared learning. They can develop policies that ensure the organisation practices what it preaches – on CSR, diversity and inclusion, environment, healthy working. They can improve the quality of leadership by driving forward leadership selection, succession planning and development processes which result in leadership at all levels. And most of all they can role-model the changes they want to see, becoming capable and authentic deliverers of real value to their organisations. As Peter Cheese (2017) reflects: 'After all, the HR profession has its hands on so many of the levers of change. And by ensuring that we are more engaged with the governance of business, we can help build the agile and responsible organisations we will need in the future'.

HR's agenda becomes ever more strategic and vital to future success. HR must lead on ensuring that the future of the workplace is human by balancing people and costs, transforming the organisation to ensure it meets its full potential and has the right people in the right place at the right time, including the right forms of leadership capable of enabling and empowering employees. If workers are clear about what they want in terms of growth and development opportunities, employers must find a way to deliver.

No HR practitioner would claim that delivering a strategic and value-added contribution is easy. However, I suggest that many of the practitioners featured in this book demonstrate that success is possible, each responding in their own way to addressing the challenges of their organisation's changing needs. They are developing and implementing aligned and integrated HR agendas which help their organisations to reinvent themselves and equip them for the future. By being confident and courageous, and maintaining humanity at work, HR can make a real difference to working lives and livelihoods, improve organisational effectiveness and business results. If HR delivers on its mandate – to build healthy and successful organisations that can thrive in a world where the old rules are changing – then HR will be fulfilling a true leadership function.

REFERENCES

Aon. (2018). *Trends in global employee engagement.* https://insights.humancapital.aon.com/talent-rewards-and-performance/engagement-2018?utm_source=Ceros

Cheese, P. (2017). Pulling the levers of change, *People Management*, June.

Cheese, P. (2012). Raising the bar for HR leadership, *People Management*, July.

CIPD. (2020). *People Profession 2030: A Collective View of Future Trends.* London: CIPD. https://www.cipd.co.uk/knowledge/strategy/hr/people-profession-2030-future-trends

CIPD. (2019). *People and Machines: From Hype to Reality.* London: Chartered Institute of Personnel and Development.

CIPD. (2015). *Best to Good Practice Report.* London: CIPD. www.cipd.co.uk/knowledge/strategy/hr/good-practice-report

The Economist. (2016). *Automation and anxiety: Will smarter machines cause mass unemployment?* Retrieved from: http://www.economist.com/news/special-report/21700758-will-smarter-machines-cause-mass-unemployment-automation-and-anxiety

Graeber, D. (2018). *Bullshit Jobs: A Theory.* Simon and Schuster.

Institute for Business Ethics (2021). https://www.ibe.org.uk/knowledge-hub/pay/remuneration.html

Kaye, L. (1999). Strategic human resources management in Australia: The human cost. *International Journal of Manpower*, 20(8), 577–587.

Parkes, C. and Davis, A.J. (2013). Ethics and social responsibility – Do HR professionals have the 'courage to challenge' or are set to be permanent 'bystanders'? *International Journal of Human Resource Management*, 24(12), 2411–2434.

Pearce, C.L. and Conger, J.A. (2002). All those years ago: The historical underpinnings of shared leadership, in C.L. Pearce and J.A. Conger (ed.), *Shared Leadership: Reframing the Hows and Whys of Leadership.* Thousand Oaks, CA: SAGE Publications, pp. 1–18.

Pfeffer, J. (1996). When it comes to 'Best Practices' why do smart organizations occasionally do dumb things? *Organizational Dynamics*, Summer.

PwC. (2017a). *The Economic Impact of Artificial Intelligence on the UK Economy.* PwC. https://www.pwc.co.uk/economic-services/assets/ai-uk-report-v2.pdf

PwC. (2017b). The ethics of pay in a fair society, https://www.pwc.com/gx/en/people-organisation/pdf/pwc-fair-pay.pdf

SHRM. (2002). *The Future of the HR Profession.* Society for Human Resource Management.

Tams, C. (2018). Bye-Bye, heroic leadership. Here comes shared leadership, *Forbes,* March 9. https://www.forbes.com/sites/carstentams/2018/03/09/bye-bye-heroic-leadership-here-comes-shared-leadership/

Ulrich, D. (1997). *Human Resource Champions: The Next Agenda for Adding Value and Delivering Results.* Cambridge, MA: Harvard Business School Press.

Volini, E., Schwartz, J. and Denny, B. (2020). *2021 Global Human Capital Trends*, Deloitte. http://response.deloitte.com/HCTrends 2021

Index

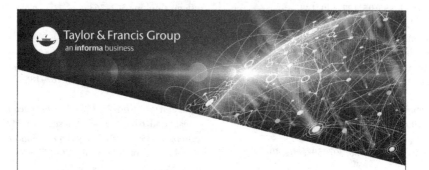

Printed in the United States
by Baker & Taylor Publisher Services